◎Harden's

London
Restaurants

2018

Survey driven reviews of 1,800 restaurants

RATINGS & PRICES

Ratings

Our rating system does not tell you – as most guides do – that expensive restaurants are often better than cheap ones! What we do is compare each restaurant's performance – as judged by the average ratings awarded by reporters in the survey – with other similarly-priced restaurants. This approach has the advantage that it helps you find – whatever your budget for any particular meal – where you will get the best 'bang for your buck'.

The following qualities are assessed:

F — Food
S — Service
A — Ambience

The rating indicates that, *in comparison with other restaurants in the same price-bracket*, performance is…

5 — Exceptional
4 — Very good
3 — Good
2 — Average
1 — Poor

> ## NEW SINCE 2015!
> Remember we turned our old marking system on its head.
> **5** is the new **0**!

Prices

The price shown for each restaurant is the cost for one (1) person of an average three-course dinner with half a bottle of house wine and coffee, any cover charge, service and VAT. Lunch is often cheaper. With BYO restaurants, we have assumed that two people share a £7 bottle of off-licence wine.

Telephone number – *all numbers are '020' numbers.*

Map reference – *shown immediately after the telephone number.*

Full postcodes – *for non-group restaurants, the first entry in the 'small print' at the end of each listing, so you can set your sat-nav.*

Website and Twitter – *shown in the small print, where applicable.*

Last orders time – *listed after the website (if applicable); Sunday may be up to 90 minutes earlier.*

Opening hours – *unless otherwise stated, restaurants are open for lunch and dinner seven days a week.*

Credit and debit cards – *unless otherwise stated, Mastercard, Visa, Amex and Maestro are accepted.*

Dress – *where appropriate, the management's preferences concerning patrons' dress are given.*

Special menus – *if we know of a particularly good-value set menu we note this (e.g. "set weekday L"), together with its formula price (FP), calculated exactly as in 'Prices' above. Details change, so always check ahead.*

Food Made Good Star Rating – *the sustainability index, as calculated by the Sustainable Restaurant Association – see page 8 for more information.*

HOW THIS GUIDE IS WRITTEN

A quarter century of the Harden's survey

This guide is based on our 27th annual survey of what 'ordinary' diners-out think of London's restaurants.

In 1998, we extended the survey to cover restaurants across the rest of the UK; it is by far the most detailed annual survey of its type. Out-of-town results are published in our UK guide.

This year, the total number of reporters in our combined London/UK survey, conducted mainly online, numbered 8,500, and, between them, they contributed 50,000 individual reports.

How we determine the ratings

In the great majority of cases, ratings are arrived at statistically.

This essentially involves 'ranking' the average survey rating each restaurant achieves in the survey – for food, service and ambience – against the average ratings of the other establishments which fall in the same price-bracket.

(This is essentially like football leagues, with the most expensive restaurants going in the top league and the cheaper ones in lower leagues. The restaurant's ranking *within its own particular league* determines its ratings.)

How we write the reviews

The tone of each review and the ratings are largely determined by the ranking of the establishment concerned, which we derive as described above.

At the margin, we may also pay some regard to the proportion of positive nominations (such as for 'favourite restaurant') compared to negative nominations (such as for 'most overpriced').

To explain why a restaurant has been rated as it has, we extract snippets from survey comments ("enclosed in double quotes"). On well-known restaurants, we receive several hundred reports, and a short summary cannot possibly do individual justice to all of them.

What we seek to do – *without any regard to our own personal opinions* – is to illustrate the key themes which have emerged in our analysis of the collective view.

Restaurants are helping change the way we eat.

North Sea cod is back on the menu, thanks in part to the many restaurants who gave the popular fish a break by taking it off their menus. Tonnes less plastic will be clogging up our oceans after a growing number of restaurants and pubs stopped automatically sticking straws in every drink they served. And, in response to the public's increasing appetite for more vegetable based dishes, chefs are shaking up their menus and offering platefuls of plant-based deliciousness.

These are just three of the myriad of ways in which restaurants are changing, responding positively to the urgent environmental and health demands we all face, by using food as a force for good.

That's why we are proud to partner with the Sustainable Restaurant Association again this year – to include their Food Made Good sustainability stars awarded to restaurants that have demonstrated they are serving food that not only tastes good, but does good too.

At the beginning of the decade food waste was seen in the sector as a dirty, difficult problem, best swept into a dark corner of the kitchen. Now, it's starting to be viewed as a business opportunity with restaurants like Spring creating scratch menus using ingredients otherwise deemed surplus to requirements.

As the issues that affect our food system evolve, so the SRA has moved on, introducing a new means of assessing restaurants.

Now it defines a Good Restaurant as one that will do these ten things:

Support Global Farmers	Source Fish Responsibly
Value Natural Resources	Serve More Veg & Better Meat
Treat People Fairly	Reduce Reuse Recycle
Feed Children Well	Waste no Food
Celebrate Local	Support the Community

Winners at the 2016 Food Made Good Awards included:

Lussmanns Fish and Grill – *People's Favourite Restaurant*

Poco – *Food Made Good Restaurant of the Year*

Captain's Galley – *Food Made Good Scottish Restaurant of the Year*

The Gallery, Barry – *Food Made Good, Welsh Restaurant of the Year*

Arbor Restaurant – *Food Made Good Environment Award*

www.foodmadegood.org · **www.thesra.org**
@the_sra.org · **@foodmadegood.org**

SURVEY FAQs

Q. How do you find your reporters?
A. Anyone can take part. Simply register at
www.hardens.com. Actually, we find that many people who
complete our survey each year have taken part before.
So it's really more a question of a very large and ever-
evolving panel, or jury, than a random 'poll'.

Q. Wouldn't a random sample be better?
A. That's really a theoretical question, as there is no
obvious way, still less a cost-efficient one, by which one
could identify a random sample of the guests at each of, say,
5,000 establishments across the UK, and get them to take
part in any sort of survey. And anyway, which is likely to be
more useful: a sample of the views of everyone who's been
to a particular place, or the views of people who are
interested enough in eating-out to have volunteered their
feedback?

Q. What sort of people take part?
A. A roughly 60/40 male/female split, from all adult age-
groups. As you might expect – as eating out is not the
cheapest activity – reporters tend to have white collar jobs
(some at very senior levels). By no means, however, is that
always the case.

Q. Do people ever try to stuff the ballot?
A. Of course they do! A rising number of efforts are
weeded out every year. But stuffing the ballot is not as
trivial a task as some people seem to think: the survey
results throw up clear natural voting patterns against which
'campaigns' tend to stand out.

Q. Aren't inspections the best way to run a guide?
A. It is often assumed – even by commentators who ought
to know better – that inspections are some sort of 'gold
standard'. There is no doubt that the inspection model
clearly has potential strengths, but one of its prime
weaknesses is that it is incredibly expensive. Take the most
famous practitioner of the 'inspection model', Michelin. It
doesn't claim to visit each and every entry listed in its guide
annually. Even once! And who are the inspectors? Often
they are catering professionals, whose likes and dislikes may
be very different from the establishment's natural customer
base. On any restaurant of note, however, Harden's typically
has somewhere between dozens and hundreds of reports
each and every year from exactly the type of people the
restaurant relies upon to stay in business. We believe that
such feedback, carefully analysed, is far more revealing and
accurate than an occasional 'professional' inspection.

SURVEY MOST MENTIONED

These are the restaurants which were most frequently mentioned by reporters. (Last year's position is given in brackets.) An asterisk* indicates the first appearance in the list of a recently opened restaurant.

1	J Sheekey (1)
2	Clos Maggiore (2)
3	Chez Bruce (4)
4	Scott's (6)
5	Le Gavroche (3)
6	The Ledbury (5)
7	The Wolseley (8)
8	Gymkhana (7)
9	Gauthier Soho (14)
10	Brasserie Zédel (9)

11	The Delaunay (11)
12	La Trompette (13)
13	Andrew Edmunds (16)
14	Fera at Claridge's, Claridge's Hotel (12)
15	The River Café (15)
16	The Cinnamon Club (10)
17	Bocca Di Lupo (21)
18	Dinner, Mandarin Oriental (31)
19	Galvin La Chapelle (19)
20	Pollen Street Social (17)

21	Benares (23)
22	La Poule au Pot (19)
23	Trinity (-)
24	Gordon Ramsay (24)
25	Sexy Fish (36)
26	Le Caprice (30)
27	Medlar (22)
28	Galvin Bistrot de Luxe (27)
29	Noble Rot (-)
30	The Goring Hotel (-)

31	Bleeding Heart Restaurant (27)
32	The Five Fields (-)
33	Bentley's (-)
34	A Wong (40)
35	Chutney Mary (-)
36	Fischer's (-)
37	Pied à Terre (26)
38	Moro (32)
39	Hoppers (-)
40	Enoteca Turi (-)

SURVEY NOMINATIONS

Best breakfast/brunch

1 The Wolseley (1)
2 The Delaunay (2)
3 The Ivy Chelsea Garden (-)
4 Riding House Café (9)
5 Caravan King's Cross*
5= Granger & Co*
7 Cecconi's (3)
8 The Ivy Kensington Brasserie (-)
9 Milk (-)
10 Breakfast Club*

Best bar/pub food

1 The Anchor & Hope (1)
2 Harwood Arms (2)
3 Bull & Last (4)
4 The Anglesea Arms (-)
5 The Eagle (-)
6 The Camberwell Arms (5)
6= Pig & Butcher (6)
8 Earl Spencer (-)
9 The Marksman (-)
10 The Ladbroke Arms (3)

Most disappointing cooking

1 Oxo Tower (Restaurant) (1)
2 The Chiltern Firehouse (2)
3 Alain Ducasse at The Dorchester (-)
4 Dinner, Mandarin Oriental (9)
5 The Ivy Café*
6 Le Gavroche (-)
7 The River Café (-)
8 Pollen Street Social (4)
9 Tredwell's (-)
10 Chez Bruce (-)

Most overpriced restaurant

1 The River Café (2)
2 Sexy Fish (1)
3 Gordon Ramsay (4)
4 Oxo Tower (Rest?) (3)
5 Dinner, Mandarin Oriental (-)
6 The Chiltern Firehouse (6)
7 Alain Ducasse at The Dorchester (9)
8 Le Gavroche (8)
9 Aqua Shard (-)
10 Hutong, The Shard (10)

SURVEY HIGHEST RATINGS

FOOD

SERVICE

£100+

	FOOD		SERVICE
1	The Araki	1	The Araki
2	The Ledbury	2	The Ledbury
3	Marianne	3	Le Gavroche
4	The Clove Club	4	Hélène Darroze
5	Ormer Mayfair	5	Marianne

£75–99

1	Sushi Tetsu	1	Sushi Tetsu
2	The Five Fields	2	The Five Fields
3	Roux at Parliament Sq	3	Club Gascon
4	Chez Bruce	4	Chez Bruce
5	Jamavar	5	L'Autre Pied

£60–£74

1	108 Garage	1	108 Garage
2	HKK	2	Oslo Court
3	Dinings	3	Cabotte
4	Anglo	4	Otto's
5	Tamarind	5	HKK

£45–£59

1	José	1	The Anglesea Arms
2	A Wong	2	Margot
3	Babur	3	The Barbary
4	The Barbary	4	José
5	Jin Kichi	5	Pig & Butcher

£44 or less

1	Santa Maria	1	Paradise Hampstead
2	Barrafina	2	Barrafina x 3
3	Bleecker Burger	3	Brady's
4	Silk Road	4	Kricket
5	Padella	5	Kiln

SURVEY HIGHEST RATINGS

AMBIENCE	OVERALL
1 Sketch (Lecture Rm)	1 The Ledbury
2 The Ritz	2 Marianne
3 Céleste	3 The Araki
4 Marianne	4 The Ritz
5 Galvin at Windows	5 Le Gavroche
1 Clos Maggiore	1 Sushi Tetsu
2 The Berners Tavern	2 The Five Fields
3 Bob Bob Ricard	3 Clos Maggiore
4 Duck & Waffle	4 Chez Bruce
5 Sushisamba	5 Gauthier Soho
1 La Poule au Pot	1 108 Garage
2 108 Garage	2 HKK
3 Smith's Wapping	3 Oslo Court
4 Oslo Court	4 Clarke's
5 The Wolseley	5 Smith's Wapping
1 José	1 José
2 The Anglesea Arms	2 The Anglesea Arms
3 The Barbary	3 The Barbary
4 Andrew Edmunds	4 Margot
5 Margot	5 Pig & Butcher
1 Barrafina	1 Barrafina
2 Brasserie Zédel	2 Kricket
3 Dishoom	3 Brady's
4 temper Soho	4 Paradise Hampstead
5 Blacklock	5 Kiln

SURVEY BEST BY CUISINE

These are the restaurants which received the best average food ratings (excluding establishments with a small or notably local following).

Where the most common types of cuisine are concerned, we present the results in two price-brackets. For less common cuisines, we list the top three, regardless of price.

For further information about restaurants which are particularly notable for their food, see the cuisine lists starting on page 244. These indicate, using an asterisk*, restaurants which offer exceptional or very good food.

British, Modern

£60 and over
1 The Ledbury
2 The Five Fields
3 Marianne
4 The Clove Club
5 Ormer Mayfair

Under £60
1 The Frog
2 Pig & Butcher
3 10 Greek Street
4 The Anglesea Arms
5 The Camberwell Arms

French

£60 and over
1 The Greenhouse
2 Le Gavroche
3 Pied à Terre
4 La Trompette
5 Gauthier Soho

Under £60
1 Cabotte
2 Blanchette
3 Casse-Croute
4 Café du Marché
5 Gazette

Italian/Mediterranean

£60 and over
1 Murano
2 Locanda Locatelli
3 Assaggi
4 Bocca Di Lupo
5 L'Anima

Under £60
1 Padella
2 Palatino
3 Margot
4 Ottolenghi
5 L'Amorosa

Indian & Pakistani

£60 and over
1 Jamavar
2 Trishna
3 Tamarind
4 Gymkhana
5 Amaya

Under £60
1 Babur
2 Kricket
3 Paradise Hampstead
4 The Painted Heron
5 Café Spice Namaste

Chinese

£60 and over
1 HKK
2 Hakkasan Mayfair
3 Hunan
4 Min Jiang
5 Yauatcha

Under £60
1 A Wong
2 Silk Road
3 Shikumen
4 Yming
5 Singapore Garden

Japanese

£60 and over
1 The Araki
2 Sushi Tetsu
3 Dinings
4 Roka
5 Umu

Under £60
1 Takahashi
2 Jin Kichi
3 Bone Daddies
4 Pham Sushi
5 Yoshino

British, Traditional
1 Scott's
2 The Ritz
3 St John

Vegetarian
1 Mildreds W1
2 Gate SW6
3 Ganapati

Burgers, etc
1 Bleecker Burger
2 Patty and Bun
3 Honest Burgers

Pizza
1 Santa Maria
2 Pizza Pilgrims
3 Pizza East

Fish & Chips
1 Brady's
2 Toff's
3 North Sea Fish

Thai
1 Som Saa
2 Kiln
3 Sukho Fine Thai Cuisine

Steaks & Grills
1 Zelman Meats
2 Goodman City
3 Blacklock

Fish & Seafood
1 Scott's
2 Outlaw's
3 One-O-One

Fusion
1 108 Garage
2 Bubbledogs (KT)
3 Providores

Spanish
1 José
2 Barrafina Drury Lane
3 Moro

Turkish
1 Mangal 1
2 Fez Mangal
3 Best Mangal

Lebanese
1 Cedar
2 Maroush
3 Arabica

THE RESTAURANT SCENE

Turning point?

There are 193 newcomers in this year's guide. This is the second largest figure recorded in its 27-year history, but a tad lower than last year's record-breaking 200.

Closings are up a little on last year's 76 to 84: a figure at the upper end of that typically recorded (the third highest), but still well below the record (of 113 in 2004).

Net openings (openings minus closings) slipped to 110: just below the low 120s in the two preceding years. A further sense that the market is no longer 'screaming along' comes from the ratio of openings to closings – at 2.3:1, this is a second year of decline from 2016's high peak.

Is this the dreaded Brexit-effect many fear? It may be in part (see 'So stupid, so short-sighted, so xenophobic' below), but another significant factor is a slight decline in the fully independent restaurant sector in London as chains – and in particular small chains – proliferate.

Indies give way to small chains

Harden's has historically favoured listing indies over multiples, and the declines noted above partly reflect this methodology. We have never sought to track bigger groups, excluding openings from our statistics after a chain becomes more numerous than a couple of spin-offs.

But the proliferation of small groups is one of the big stories of the current restaurant market. Familiar one-offs are all of a sudden 'rolling out'. The Ivy is the most obvious example, but there are other smaller ones (such as Mildreds). Meanwhile, it is taken as read that newer brands will seek to clone themselves at the earliest opportunity.

If branches we have historically excluded are added into our statistics, this would imply another pretty hot year, with the number of previously excluded spin-offs more than doubling from 25 to 53, to give an 'aggregate' newcomers total of 246 this year vs 225 a year earlier.

So, in the 'quality-ish' restaurant sector, this would imply the growth rate is still strong after all. And while there is some shift from indies to small groups, this growth in the small chain market is still good news for restaurant-goers, and undercuts the worst of the Brexit-doom scenarios.

"So stupid, so short-sighted, so xenophobic…"

In accepting his Lifetime Achievement Award at this year's Harden's London Restaurant Awards, Jeremy King chose the above words to describe Brexit. It shows how little things have moved on in the year since Bruce Poole – in accepting the same award twelve months earlier – addressed the same issue more pithily: "Without Europeans, we're f##ked".

Why are top restaurateurs not more sanguine about Brexit?

Could it be anything to do with the fact that according to the British Hospitality Association, 75% of London's waiting staff come from Europe? And also a very high proportion of its chefs, sous-chefs, kitchen porters…

With the post-Brexit uncertainty and the hit to the pound, it has seldom been so hard to recruit staff. Chef Alexis Gauthier recently made catering press headlines describing the current situation as 'toxic' and saying that in 20 years in London restaurants he has never seen such pressures on recruiting people.

London's restaurants nowadays are a superb advertisement for the capital. They are also a fine advertisement for the pluspoints of immigration. When Britons speak proudly of having the greatest restaurant city on earth, it is the diversity of the capital's offering – with restaurants from all points of the globe – which is usually touted as its world-beating feature. Of really traditional British restaurants, there are vanishingly few. It's not why people want to come!

Where and what's hot

After Central London, East London remains London's prime area for restaurant openings, although almost as popular was South London this year (East had 39 debuts vs South's 36). A particularly weak performance from West London made it the least interesting point on the compass: a distinction traditionally reserved for North London.

Modern British and Italian cuisines remain the most popular for new openings. But meat-based cuisines were less to the fore than last year, with Indian openings pipping them to the post as the third most popular category. Japanese openings, in fourth place, continue to lead other more 'traditional' categories such as French.

The hottest of the hot

Every year, we choose what to us seem to be the most significant openings of the year. This year our selection is as follows:

Core	Lorne
La Dame de Pic	Luca
Honey & Smoke	108 Garage
Ikoyi	Plaquemine Lock
Jamavar	Western's Laundry

Prices

The average price of dinner for one at establishments listed in this guide is £53.20 (compared to £51.37 last year). Prices have risen by 3.6% in the past 12 months (up on 2.1% in the preceding 12 months). This rate compares with a general annual inflation rate of 2.9% for the 12 months to August 2017, accelerating the trend seen last year of restaurant price rises running somewhat higher than inflation generally.

OPENINGS AND CLOSURES

Mare Street Market
Mayfair Garden
Megan's by the Green *(SW6)*
Mei Ume
Meraki
Messapica
Minnow
Monty's Deli
Mother
Nanashi
The Ned
Neo Bistro
Nobu Shoreditch *(EC2)*
Noizé
Nutbourne
Oak N4
108 Garage
Oree *(W8, SW3)*
The Other Naughty Piglet
Over Under
The Oystermen Seafood
Kitchen & Bar
Palatino
Pamban
Il Pampero
The Pantechnicon
Parlez
Passione e Tradizione
Pastaio
The Petersham
PF Chang's Asian Table
Piebury Corner *(N1)*
Pisqu
Pizzastorm
Plaquemine Lock
Plot
Pomaio
Pomona's
Popolo
Quartieri
Radici
Rambla
Red Rooster
Rick Stein
Rigo'
Rola Wala
Sabor
Saiphin's Thai Kitchen
Santo Remedio
Sibarita
Skewd Kitchen

Smoking Goat *(E1)*
Sophie's Steakhouse *(W1)*
Southam Street
Sparrow
Spinach
Stagolee's
Stecca
Sticky Mango at RSJ
The Stoke House
Strangers Dining Room,
House of Commons
Street XO
Summers
Sumosan Twiga
Table Du Marche
TAKA
Tamarind Kitchen
Tandoor Chop House
temper City *(EC2)*
Temple & Sons
Test Kitchen
tibits *(SE1)*
Timmy Green
Tom Simmons
Tratra
Trawler Trash
Treves & Hyde
The Truscott Arms
Tuyo
The Vincent
VIVI
Waka
Walnut
Westerns Laundry
The Wigmore, The Langham
Winemakers Deptford
XU
Yolk
Zheng

Closures (84)

Almeida
Alquimia
Antico
Atari-Ya *(NW4)*
L'Autre Pied
Barnyard
Bibo
La Brasserie
Brasserie Gustave
Buoni Amici
Café Pistou
Canvas
The Chancery
Chapters
Chor Bizarre
Le Coq
Cornish Tiger
CURIO + TA TA
Dabbous
The Depot
Les Deux Salons
Dickie Fitz
Emile's
Escocesa
Fields
Fish Club
Foxlow
Grain Store *(N1)*
Habanera
Hibiscus
Hill & Szrok Pub *(N1)*
Ho *(W1)*
Hush *(EC4)*
Ichiryu
Imli Street
Inaho
Indian Zilla
K10 *(EC2)*
Kerbisher & Malt *(EC1)*
Koffmann's, The Berkeley
KOJAWAN, Hilton Metropole
Kricket, Pop Brixton *(SW9)*

Kurobuta Harvey Nics *(SW1)*
The Lady Ottoline
Leong's Legends *(W1)*
Lobster Pot
Lotus
Magdalen
Market
Masala Grill
Matsuri
Murakami
New Mayflower
The Newman Arms
160 Smokehouse *(NW6)*
Orso
Osteria 60
Ottolenghi *(W8)*
Patio
Poco *(E2)*
Polpo, Harvey Nichols *(SW1)*
Princess Victoria
The Richmond
Rivington Grill *(EC2)*
RSJ
Salmontini
Samarkand
San Daniele del Friuli
Shotgun
Smoke and Salt (Residency)
Sophie's Steakhouse *(WC2)*
Spring Workshop
Sumosan
Tartufo
Toto's
Tsunami *(W1)*
Vico *(WC2)*
Vintage Salt *(EC2)*
Vintage Salt *(N1)*
Wazen
West Thirty Six
The Woodford
Wormwood
Yumi Izakaya

DIRECTORY

Comments in "double quotation marks" were made by reporters.

Establishments which we judge to be particularly notable have their NAME IN CAPITALS.

A Cena TW1   £50   3 4 4
418 Richmond Rd   020 8288 0108   1–4A
This favourite, rather smart St Margaret's Italian as ever earns consistent praise from satisfied locals: "a terrific restaurant, with lovely food and attentive service". It's handy before or after a game at nearby Twickenham, too. / TW1 2EB; www.acena.co.uk; @acenarestaurant; 10 pm; closed Mon L & Sun D; booking max 6 may apply; set weekday L £33 (FP).

A Wong SW1   £46   5 5 3
70 Wilton Rd   020 7828 8931   2–4B
"Andrew Wong is a magician!" – and his "new-school Chinese" in Pimlico provides not only some of "the most exhilarating food in London", but also, contrary to cultural stereotypes, the service here is "exceptionally graceful and helpful". The setting is "lively" (if "crowded") too, and in the evening, there's also the option of a small Chef's Table, or eating in the "decadent" 'Forbidden City' basement bar. There's a wide range of eating options too, from "incredibly inventive dim sum", to a "fabulous 10-course tasting menu". / SW1V IDE; www.awong.co.uk; @awongSW1; 10.15 pm; closed Mon L & Sun; credit card required to book.

The Abingdon W8   £65   3 3 4
54 Abingdon Rd   020 7937 3339   6–2A
In a "quiet backstreet south of High Street Ken", this posh gastropub stalwart remains "a tremendous local" for a loyal well-heeled crowd ("it's full of regulars, so must be doing something right!"). Top Tip – the best seats are in the booths. / W8 6AP; www.theabingdon.co.uk; @TheAbingdonW8; 10.30 pm, Fri & Sat 11 pm, Sun 10 pm.

About Thyme SW1   £53   2 3 3
82 Wilton Rd   020 7821 7504   2–4B
Long-serving manager Issy is a popular host at this "reliable" Pimlico stalwart, serving "good, Spanish-orientated" dishes. / SW1V IDL; www.aboutthyme.co.uk; 10 pm; closed Sun.

L'Absinthe NW1   £49   2 4 3
40 Chalcot Rd   020 7483 4848   9–3B
Burgundian patron, Jean-Christophe Slowik always makes this "lively" corner bistro in Primrose Hill "a fun place to be". There's some question as to whether its "limited" and "distinctly French" menu "needs re-inventing", but "it does now offer brunch and Sunday lunch". / NW1 8LS; www.labsinthe.co.uk; @absinthe07jc; 10 pm, Sun 9 pm; closed Mon, Tue L, Wed L & Thu L.

Abu Zaad W12   £23   3 3 2
29 Uxbridge Rd   020 8749 5107   8–1C
"Excellent fresh food prepared to order and in very generous portions" underpins the appeal of this "lively" Syrian café at the top of Shepherd's Bush market, serving a wide array of mezze, wraps, and juices plus more substantial fare. / W12 8LH; www.abuzaad.co.uk; 11 pm, Sat & Sun midnight; No Amex.

Adams Café W12   £33   3 5 3
77 Askew Rd   020 8743 0572   8–1B
"Thoughtful, charming service" and "hearty, uncomplicated dishes" ("delicious tagines and other Tunisian/Moroccan specialities" like brik à l'oeuf) mean the folk of 'Askew Village' are lucky to have this sweet café, which "has maintained excellent quality for over 25 years", and where "the BYO policy (£3 corkage) leads to a very modest bill" (although it is also licensed). By day, it's a British greasy spoon. / W12 9AH; www.adamscafe.co.uk; @adamscafe; 10 pm; closed Sun.

Addie's Thai Café SW5   £33   **3** **2** **2**

121 Earl's Court Rd   020 7259 2620   6–2A

"The bill's so modest, you wonder if they forgot something!", at this "wonderful, small and compact" street food café in Earl's Court. / SW5 9RL; www.addiesthai.co.uk; 11 pm, Sun 10.30 pm; No Amex.

Addomme SW2   £41   **4** **3** **2**

17-21 Sternhold Avenue   020 8678 8496   11–2C

Next to Streatham Hill station, this "small and modestly furnished" café and take-away (overseen by Stefano and Nadia from Capri) is "top of the pile locally" serving "terrific pizzas from the wood burning oven, together with a range of specials changed weekly at very reasonable prices!" / SW2 4PA; www.addomme.co.uk; @PizzAddomme; 11 pm.

The Admiral Codrington SW3   £58   **2** **3** **4**

17 Mossop St   020 7581 0005   6–2C

An age-old favourite backstreet boozer – albeit with a touch of "Chelsea elegance" – the 'Cod' is still "all in all a great place" when it comes to atmosphere, although its food offer has received a more mixed billing in recent times. / SW3 2LY; www.theadmiralcodrington.co.uk; @TheAdCod; 10 pm, Thu-Sat 11 pm, Sun 9 pm; No trainers.

Afghan Kitchen N1   £26   **4** **3** **2**

35 Islington Grn   020 7359 8019   9–3D

"A great little local standby" for a "quick bite" – this Afghan canteen by Islington Green scores well for consistency and value with its "small selection" of simple dishes. The only quibble is that "the menu is static" – "but you know what you're getting every time". / N1 8DU; 11 pm; closed Mon & Sun; Cash only; no booking.

Aglio e Olio SW10   £48   **3** **3** **3**

194 Fulham Rd   020 7351 0070   6–3B

"No frills good food" – in particular "perfect pasta" – fuels the "loud and buzzy" atmosphere ("manic on Chelsea match days") at this "fun", little café, near Chelsea & Westminster Hospital. "Still my firm favourite after over 10 years; the menu is reassuringly unchanged and the quality is excellent". / SW10 9PN; www.aglioeolio.co.uk; 11.00 pm.

Al Duca SW1   £53   **3** **3** **2**

4-5 Duke of York St   020 7839 3090   3–3D

"No more expensive than some chains, but with better and varied Italian staples" – this "slightly tucked-away", low-key St James's fixture is boosted by its "attentive and friendly staff", and has for many years now provided a consistently "pleasant" and "reasonably priced" experience. / SW1Y 6LA; www.alduca-restaurant.co.uk; 11 pm; closed Sun.

Al Forno   £47   **2** **4** **4**

349 Upper Richmond Rd, SW15   020 8878 7522   11–2A

2a King's Rd, SW19   020 8540 5710   11–2B

"Service is attentive to just the right level" at this "friendly" small chain of slightly old-fashioned local Italians across southwest London. The pizza and pasta dishes are at "good value" prices, and there's a "really pleasant atmosphere, be it for dinner with friends or Sunday lunch with the littlies". / 10 pm-11 pm.

Alain Ducasse at The Dorchester W1   £134   2 2 2
53 Park Ln   020 7629 8866   3–3A
"It seriously makes me doubt the Michelin rating system" – the world-famous Gallic chef's Mayfair venture is *"not in the same league as the Waterside Inn or Fat Duck"* yet inexplicably retains its 3-star top billing. Admittedly, many reports do advocate this hotel dining room's *"discreetly opulent surroundings"*, its *"courteous"* staff and its *"awesome"* cuisine, but far too many sceptics say it's *"waaaayyyyyyy overpriced"* for *"muted"* food that's *"nice but not a wow"*, and find the luxurious interior rather *"soulless"*. / W1K 1QA; www.alainducasse-dorchester.com; 9.30 pm; closed Mon, Sat L & Sun; Jacket required; booking essential; set weekday L £95 (FP).

Albertine W12   £56   3 3 4
1 Wood Ln   020 8743 9593   8–1C
"Enhanced rather than revolutionised, so it continues to feel like an old local favourite" – this veteran Shepherds Bush wine bar (once the haunt of BBC types from the former TV Centre nearby) has been taken over and spruced up by Allegra McEvedy (whose mother opened it in 1978) leaving it *"less scruffy, while maintaining its informality"*. There's *"not a huge menu"* but the food is *"vastly improved"* and there's *"interesting wine"* too. / W12 7DP; www.albertinewinebar.co.uk; @AlbertineWine; 11 pm, Thu-Sat midnight; closed Sat L & Sun; No Amex.

Albion   £54   2 2 2
NEO Bankside, Holland St, SE1   020 3764 5550   10–3B
2-4 Boundary St, E2   020 7729 1051   13–1B
63 Clerkenwell Rd, EC1   020 3862 0750   10–1A
"Possibly a bit bland" sums up the lukewarm reactions to Sir Terence Conran's trio of *"un-memorable"* all-day pit stops in Bankside, Clerkenwell and Shoreditch. They are *"light, clean and smart"*, so make *"a good alternative for business meetings"*, but it's *"difficult to be fantastically enthusiastic"* about the *"reasonably average and slightly expensive"* food and *"sometimes erratic"* service. / 10 pm-11 pm, Sun-Sat E2 Fri & Sat 1 am, EC1, Fri & Sat midnight, Sun 6 pm-11 pm.

Alcedo N7 NEW   £43   3 4 3
237 Holloway Rd   020 7998 7672   9–2D
"A new arrival bringing a touch of class and much needed good bistro food to Holloway". *"The menu is limited, but all carefully prepared, and the proprietor is very friendly"*. / N7 8HG.

The Alfred Tennyson SW1   £61   3 3 4
10 Motcomb St   020 7730 6074   6–1D
"There's a good buzz about this place" – a comfortably converted Belgravia Pub (part of the Cubitt House Group), formerly known as The Pantechnicon Dining Rooms (and re-named to avoid confusion with their forthcoming venture in the nearby building of the same name). *"The food is simple, but well-cooked"* and fair value for such a prime address. / SW1X 8LA; thealfredtennyson.co.uk; @TheTennysonSW1; 10 pm, Sun 9.30 pm.

Ali Baba NW1   £25   3 2 2
32 Ivor Pl   020 7723 5805   2–1A
This *"unique family-run Egyptian café"* behind a Marylebone takeaway owes its *"engaging personality"* to its location in the owners' living room. There's an *"interesting"* choice, so *"order a variety of starters with one or two main courses"*, and remember to BYO. / NW1 6DA; alibabarestaurant.co.uk; @alibabalondon; midnight; Cash only.

Alounak   £27   3 2 3
10 Russell Gdns, W14   020 7603 1130   8–1D
44 Westbourne Grove, W2   020 7229 0416   7–1B
These *"reliable BYO Persian cafés"* have provided *"authentic and cheap"* Middle Eastern food for 20 years at two atmospheric venues in Bayswater and Olympia. / 11.30 pm; no Amex.

Alyn Williams,
Westbury Hotel W1
£96   **3 3 2**

37 Conduit St   020 7183 6426   3–2C

"Top notch cuisine and super service" still secure many plaudits for Alyn Williams's (windowless) Mayfair dining room, in the bowels of a hotel off Bond Street, but it put in a more uneven performance this year. *"As quite often happens with hotel restaurants, its atmosphere can lack"* however, and it took significant flak from critics this year for a number of *"disappointing"* and *"unjustifiably expensive"* meals. / W1S 2YF; www.alynwilliams.com; @Alyn_Williams; 10.30 pm; closed Mon & Sun; Jacket required; set weekday L £56 (FP).

Amaya SW1
£80   **4 2 3**

Halkin Arc, 19 Motcomb St   020 7823 1166   6–1D

"Amaya-zing!". *"Your taste-buds go pop with delightfully subtle tapas"* capturing the *"distinctive flavours of Indian grills"* at this *"chic"* modern Belgravia operation, arranged around an open kitchen – perennially one of London's top nouvelle Indians. / SW1X 8JT; www.amaya.biz; @theamaya_; 11.30 pm, Sun 10.30 pm; set weekday L £44 (FP).

The American Bar SW1
£58

16 - 18 Saint James's Place   020 7493 0111   3–4C

"Benoit is the perfect host" at this preppy St James's hideaway, at the end of a cute mews (splendid outside tables in summer), festooned with the ties and hats donated by patrons in decades past. Best known as a drinking den (*"the 'White Mouse' is a must"*), it also nowadays has a fairly substantial 'club-brasserie-style' menu, served from breakfast on, but – especially if you are having a dram – *"bring lots of money"*. / SW1A 1NJ; thestaffordlondon.com/the-american-bar; @StaffordLondon; 10 pm; booking L only.

Ametsa with Arzak Instruction,
Halkin Hotel SW1
£91   **3 3 2**

5 Halkin St   020 7333 1234   2–3A

"It was like having a magician as a waiter", say fans of the Arzac family's Belgravia outpost, extolling *"course after course of treats, from mouthfuls to more substantial dishes, all exploring new tastes"*. The room itself can seem *"as dull as ditchwater"* however, and critics are disappointed by food they find *"more startling to the eye than agreeable to the palette"*. / SW1X 7DJ; www.comohotels.com/thehalkin/dining/ametsa; @AmetsaArzak; 10 pm; closed Mon L & Sun; set weekday L £68 (FP).

L'Amorosa W6
£47   **4 4 3**

278 King St   020 8563 0300   8–2B

"High end cuisine at local prices" has won renown for Andy Needham's *"unassuming looking"*, venture near Ravenscourt Park, whose *"smart, but down-to-earth style"* gives no hint that it serves *"some of the best and best value Italian food in town"* (*"the pasta is very good, with lots of flavour"*). *"Thoughtful staff"* are *"charming"* too, and although *"it's a neighbourhood place, people travel from miles around to eat here"*. / W6 0SP; www.lamorosa.co.uk; @LamorosaLondon; 9.30 pm, Fri & Sat 10 pm; closed Mon & Sun D.

Anarkali W6
£36

303-305 King St   020 8748 1760   8–2B

"A cut above the after-pub curry house", this *"high-quality"* Hammersmith Indian of decades standing has been able to thrive *"in an area of high competition (Zing, Potli)"*. In summer 2017 it closed for a total reformat under long-term owner Rafique – when it re-opens we expect it to be good, but we've removed the (very solid) ratings as a sharp break with the past seems to be on the cards. / W6 9NH; www.anarkalifinedining.com; @anarkalidining; midnight; closed Mon L & Sun L; No Amex.

The Anchor & Hope SE1 £52 **4**2**2**
36 The Cut   020 7928 9898   10–4A
"Sometimes you have to bare-knuckle it for a table" at this "bursting-at-the-seams" boozer, a short walk from the Old Vic – still hanging on to its crown as the survey's No. I pub. "It's worth the crush though" for the "simple", yet "sophisticated" pub grub "done oh-so-well", which still "trumps the stretched staff, the slightly chaotic ambience and tired fixtures". "I really wish you could book" ("unfortunately you can only reserve for Sunday lunch"). / SE1 8LP; www.anchorandhopepub.co.uk; @AnchorHopeCut; 10.30 pm, Sun 3.15 pm; closed Mon L & Sun D; No Amex; no booking; set weekday L £32 (FP).

Andi's N16 £43 **3**4**4**
176 Stoke Newington Church St   020 7241 6919   1–1C
"Amazing brunch and a gorgeous little garden!" are highlights of this "very good addition to Stokey", where La Patronne, 'Great British Menu' judge Andi Oliver, is "exceptionally friendly and jolly", and provides an imaginative, modern British menu. / N16 0JL; www.andis.london; @andisrestaurant; 10.30 pm; closed weekday L.

Andina E2 £51 **4**3**3**
1 Redchurch St   020 7920 6499   13–1B
"Great ceviche" along with the "authentic cocktails (I know, I have Peruvian friends)" are the star turns at this "noisy and full, but not expensive" South American hotspot in Shoreditch: "raw fish seemed adventurous at first, but it was so well flavoured you just wanted to eat more!". / E2 7DJ; www.andinalondon.com; @AndinaLondon; 10.30 pm; booking max 6 may apply.

The Andover Arms W6 £51 **3**5**4**
57 Aldensey Rd   020 8748 2155   8–1B
With its "roaring fire in winter" and "good service" this "traditional small pub" in a cute corner of Brackenbury Village is one of London's jollier hostelries. No fireworks on the food front, but its hearty gastropub scoff is very dependable. / W6 0DL; www.theandoverarms.com; @theandoverarms; 10 pm, Sun 9 pm; No Amex.

ANDREW EDMUNDS W1 £56 **3**4**5**
46 Lexington St   020 7437 5708   4–2C
"THE place for a date in Soho" – "time stands still" at this "intriguing" townhouse that wins the hearts of legions of Londoners with its "dark and Gothic" Bohemian, candle-lit charm, its "casual yet engaged staff", and its "splendiferous wine list (without hefty mark-ups too)". Don't expect great comfort (although the "cramped quarters do make for romantic closeness") and while "the no-frills cooking is very flavoursome it's not haute cuisine". / W1F 0LP; www.andrewedmunds.com; 10.45 pm, Sun 10.30 pm; No Amex; booking max 6 may apply.

Angelus W2 £72 **3**5**3**
4 Bathurst St   020 7402 0083   7–2D
"You get looked after like an old friend even if you've never been before", if you visit Thierry Tomasin's prettified pub near Lancaster Gate – a "small and intimate venue" ("you eat in close quarters") whose star turn is the "fab wine list you'd expect from Le Gavroche's former head sommelier". Most (if not quite all) reports are of "reliably good French cuisine" to match. / W2 2SD; www.angelusrestaurant.co.uk; @AngelusLondon; 11 pm, Sun 10 pm.

Angie's Little Food Shop W4 £32 **3**3**3**
114 Chiswick High Rd   020 8994 3931   8–2A
Angie Steele's cute café is becoming quite the Chiswick favourite – her super-healthy salads, cakes and juices are "great for brunch, a quick snack or coffee". / W4 1PU; www.angieslittlefoodshop.com; 7 pm, Sun 6 pm; L only.

Angler,
South Place Hotel EC2 £93 **3** 2 2
3 South Pl   020 3215 1260   13–2A

"*Ultra fresh seafood and superb views*" are undisputed attractions of this rooftop venture near Moorgate. But while the terrace (heated in winter) is undoubtedly "*lovely*", the overall impression of the venue as a whole can be "*pretty soulless*", and fans concede that it's "*so expensive*" too ("*the bill's only fine if you're a banker*"). / EC2M 2AF; www.anglerrestaurant.com; @southplacehotel; 10 pm; closed Sat L; May need 8+ to book; set weekday L £66 (FP).

The Anglesea Arms W6 £56 **4** 4 4
35 Wingate Rd   020 8749 1291   8–1B

"*Back to its former glory. Hurrah!*" – This "*well-established pub*" in a side street near Ravenscourt Park is "*just what a gastropub should be with a cosy pubby bit at the front with a roaring fire (offering some quality ales) and a restaurant bit at the back*" serving "*exceptionally well thought-through dishes at very reasonable prices*". / W6 0UR; www.angleseaarmspub.co.uk; @_AngleseaArmsW6; 10 pm, Fri 11 pm, Sat & Sun 10 pm; closed weekday L; no booking.

Anglo EC1 £69 **5** 4 2
30 St Cross St   020 7430 1503   10–1A

"*Light years ahead of some famous names in terms of quality*" – Mark Jarvis and Jack Cashmore's Hatton Garden yearling has "*an unlikely location*" ("*you squeeze into a little shop*") and its "*slightly dull and muted*") but "*don't let the room put you off*" – "*the quality is arguably unbeaten for the price in Central London*" and "*to change the menu so regularly, but with such imagination and high quality every time takes some serious talent*". Top Tip – "*the lunchtime menu with accompanying wines is a real bargain*". / EC1N 8UH; www.anglorestaurant.com; 9.30 pm; closed Sun; booking max 4 may apply.

L'Anima EC2 £71 **4** 4 3
1 Snowden St   020 7422 7000   13–2B

"*Benissimo!*" – "*the food is consistently good, even after Francesco Mazzei's departure*" at this well-known Italian near Liverpool Street. "*The price is quite hefty*", but as a business venue it's "*perfect (or would be if it was a little less noisy)*", thanks to its "*well-organised*" service and "*cool, modern, white interior*". / EC2A 2DQ; www.lanima.co.uk; @lanimalondon; 11 pm, Sat 11.30 pm; closed Sat L & Sun.

L'Anima Café EC2 £56 **3** 3 2
10 Appold St   020 7422 7080   13–2B

"*Sustained high levels of Italian fare, and reasonably strong service*" make it worth remembering this "*busy, if slightly cavernous room*" near Liverpool Street – ideal for an informal business bite – majoring in "*excellent pizza*", plus pasta. "*It's not cheap though*" (although there is a deli section where you can grab & go, or perch at a shared table). / EC2A 2AP; www.lanimacafe.co.uk; @LAnimacafe; 10 pm; closed Sun.

Anima e Cuore NW1 £40 **5** 4 1
129 Kentish Town Rd   020 7267 2410   9–2B

"*Don't judge a book by its cover – some of the best Italian food in London hides behind the rundown exterior*" of this tiny Kentish Town BYO, serving a "*long and interesting menu*". "'*Heart and Soul*' is the absolute truth: the venue is a dump, but the honest graft put in by the team wins through every time*". Top Tips: "*cucumber ice cream is a standout*", and "*when there are truffles on the menu, portions are generous and prices low*". / NW1 8PB; @animaecuoreuk; 9 pm, Sun 2.30 pm.

Annie's £44 2 3 4
162 Thames Rd, W4   020 8994 9080   1–3A
36-38 White Hart Ln, SW13   020 8878 2020   11–1A
"Happy and relaxed" hangouts in Barnes and Strand-on-the-Green, Chiswick, drawing a busy mix of locals meeting up for a bite and a drink. "The food, though mostly enjoyable, is not the main event – it's the quaint, charming ambience and friendly waiting staff that make them so appealing". / www.anniesrestaurant.co.uk; 10 pm, Sun 9.30 pm.

The Anthologist EC2 £54 2 2 3
58 Gresham St   0845 468 0101   10–2C
"Deservedly busy", attractive bar/restaurant near the Guildhall whose "spacious tables work for meetings, brunch, lunch, dinner…". "It's a lazy option as the food's good not great, but it's close to work and easy to book". / EC2V 7BB; www.theanthologistbar.co.uk; @theanthologist; 11 pm, Thu & Fri 1 am; closed Sat & Sun.

L' Antica Pizzeria NW3 £40 4 4 3
66 Heath St   020 7431 8516   9–1A
"Tiny, buzzy and cosy Neapolitan pizzeria" on Hampstead High Street, loved by locals for its "excellent pizza from the wood-fired oven". / NW3 1DN; www.anticapizzeria.co.uk; @AnticaHamp; 10.30 pm; Mon-Thu D only, Fri-Sun open L & D.

L'Antica Pizzeria da Michele N16 NEW £20 3 4 3
125 Stoke Newington Church St   020 7687 0009   1–1C
"You can have any pizza you want, provided it's either a margarita or marinara" at this first UK outpost, in Stokey, of the Naples original (est 1870). The occasional report says it "doesn't live up to the hype", but on most accounts "it's everything you could want, with speedy, no-nonsense service and exceptional pizzas straight outta Napoli". / N16 0UH; www.damichele.net; @damichelelondon; May need 6+ to book.

Antidote Wine Bar W1 £59 2 2 3
12a Newburgh St   020 7287 8488   4–1B
"Perplexingly refreshing" – the view of one fan of this quirky, Gallic-run wine bar and restaurant, seconds from bustling Carnaby Street, which has an elegant, small upstairs dining room. Its profile is tiny nowadays though, despite its heart-of-Soho location, and critics say "the food's pretty average, at a price that merits better". / W1F 7RR; www.antidotewinebar.com; @AntidoteWineBar; 10.30 pm; closed Mon & Sun.

Anzu SW1 £43
Saint James's Market, 1 Norris St   020 7930 8414   4–4D
Press reviews have not been kind to this Japanese brasserie in the luxe but unengaging St James's Market development, and – though it did inspire the odd positive report – the low level of feedback it inspired from reporters gave insufficient confidence for a rating as yet. / SW1Y 4SB; www.anzulondon.com; @anzurestaurant.

Applebee's Fish SE1 £62 4 3 2
5 Stoney St   020 7407 5777   10–4C
"Superb!"… "a proper fish restaurant" is how all reporters view this "lovely café", where "sensitive cooking" does real justice to the "simply prepared" dishes. "Prices are a bit high, but that's normal for somewhere on the edge of Borough Market". / SE1 9AA; www.applebeesfish.com; @applebeesfish; 10 pm, Thu-Sat 11 pm; closed Sun; No Amex.

Apulia EC1 £50 **3 3 3**
50 Long Ln 020 7600 8107 10–2B
"Fabulously hearty, rustic Puglian dishes, served with a smile" and at "good-value prices" win numerous very enthusiastic reviews for this "far-from-standard" Italian, beside Smithfield Market; but "it's a great place for supper, rather than 'a destination". / EC1A 9EJ; www.apuliarestaurant.co.uk; 10 pm; closed Sun D.

Aqua Nueva W1 £68 **2 2 3**
240 Regent Street (entrance 30 Argyll St) 020 7478 0540 4–1A
Part of a ritzy, roof-top complex with terraces above Oxford Circus, this glossy Spanish venue adjoins Aqua Kyoto (its Japanese sibling) and Aqua Spirit (a bar), and is a more low-rise, less famous alternative to its well-known Shard-based siblings, Aqua Shard and Hutong. On limited feedback, its scores aren't bad at all, but it attracts few reports nowadays, and there's a slight feeling that it's (perhaps unjustifiably) been abandoned to out-of-towners. / W1B 3BR; www.aqua-london.com; @aqualondon; 11 pm, Sun 8 pm; set pre theatre £36 (FP).

Aqua Shard SE1 £104 **1 1 2**
Level 31, 31 St Thomas St 020 3011 1256 10–4C
"An utterly disgraceful fleecing of out-of-towners looking for a glamorous 'occasion' meal but getting ripped off!" – that's the gist of too many reports on this 31st-floor chamber which is "so completely disappointing" it "risks giving the Capital a bad name". "You do get a remarkable view of London" and romantics say it's "the perfect place to watch the sunset and the lights coming up over the City"… "but that's it!". Top Tip – "breakfast is the still-not-cheap-but-cheapest way to sample this otherwise extortionate experience: book the earliest slot to ensure a window table and the chance to watch the city awake!!" / SE1 9RY; www.aquashard.co.uk; @aquashard; 10.45 pm; set weekday L £64 (FP), set brunch £78 (FP).

Aquavit SW1 £77 **3 3 3**
St James's Market, 1 Carlton St 020 7024 9848 4–4D
With its "classy and spacious" Manhattan-esque decor, this spin-off from the Big Apple's acclaimed Nordic fine dining stalwart, in the new St James's Market development, is "ideal for people-watching", and – with its "clean-tasting Scandi fare from exceptional ingredients" – both "a great addition" to the capital, and one that's "perfect for a business lunch". On the downside, the "cavernous space is slightly sterile", and muted ratings overall mean this is "not yet a chip off the NYC block". / SW1Y 4QQ; www.aquavitrestaurants.com; @aquavitlondon; set weekday L £52 (FP), set pre-theatre £53 (FP).

Arabica Bar and Kitchen SE1 £52 **3 2 3**
3 Rochester Walk 020 3011 5151 10–4C
"Delicious Middle Eastern-North African food" keeps a "lively and hipsterish crowd" well fed and happy under the arches by Borough Market. "If you want somewhere with character and food with oodles of flavour, this is the place" – "I left with a warm glow and a spring in my step". / SE1 9AF; www.arabicabarandkitchen.com; @ArabicaLondon; 10.30 pm, Sat 11 pm, Sun 8.30 pm; closed Sun D.

The Araki W1 £380 5 5 3
Unit 4 12 New Burlington St   020 7287 2481   4–3A
"Can heaven be far away?" – "If you can afford it, Mitsuhiro Araki's Mayfair restaurant is a unique experience" and a "world class" one that for a second year won the highest food-rating of any restaurant in the UK. "Be one of nine diners enjoying a specially prepared meal from one of Tokyo's top chefs" that's "as close to Japan as you can get in London". "You feel like you are at a theatrical performance, sat in line watching the numerous chefs, and Mr Araki himself, and there are too many amazing dishes to mention". "The price is world class too" of course but "worth every penny for what you get" (in the view of all reporters, including those who are themselves Japanese). "Clients can't fail to be impressed… and at that price so they should be!" STOP PRESS. On October 2, Michelin finally woke up, and awarded the Araki the three stars it should have granted last year. / W1S 3BH; www.the-araki.com; seatings only at 6 pm and 8.30 pm; D only, closed Mon; booking essential.

Ariana II NW6 £29 3 2 2
241 Kilburn High Rd   020 3490 6709   1–2B
Family-run Afghani in Kilburn, handily close to the Tricycle Theatre, serving grilled meat or veg with rice and salad – "for the money, it's really, really good… and it's BYO!". / NW6 7JN; www.ariana2restaurant.co.uk; @Ariana2kilburn; midnight.

Ark Fish E18 £39 3 3 2
142 Hermon Hill   020 8989 5345   1–1D
"You can rely on good quality fish" at this popular chippy in South Woodford, run by the Faulkner family (who have in their time managed Lisson Grove's famous Seashell, and Dalston's Faulkners). / E18 1QH; www.arkfishrestaurant.co.uk; 9.45 pm, Fri & Sat 10.15 pm, Sun 8.45 pm; closed Mon; No Amex; no booking.

Arlo's SW12 £49 2 3 2
1 Ramsden Rd   020 3019 6590   11–2C
"It ain't the only restaurant in town offering quality steak at an affordable price" but fans say this Balham yearling "stands out for its simple, limited menu of unusual British-sourced cuts, plus nine or ten sides cooked exactly to order". One or two incidents of poor preparation are also reported however, hence the middling grades. / SW12 8QX; www.arlos.co.uk.

Arthur Hooper's SE1 NEW £63
8 Stoney St   awaiting tel   10–4C
This stylishly monochrome spot overlooking Borough Market is named after the fruit salesman who once occupied the building. Chef Lale Oztek presents a modern European menu of seasonal fare, much of it sourced from the market and surrounding shops. / SE1 9AA; www.arthurhoopers.co.uk; @arthurhoopers; 10.30 pm, Fri & Sat 11.30 pm; booking max 6 may apply; set weekday L £40 (FP).

Artigiano NW3 £56 3 2 2
12a Belsize Ter   020 7794 4288   9–2A
"A good standard has been maintained" over the years at this "very pleasant" (if "rather squashed") Italian in Belsize Park – no-one hails it as London's best, but it's "dependable". / NW3 4AX; www.etruscarestaurants.com; @artigianoesp; 10 pm; closed Mon L.

L'Artista NW11 £40 3 4 4
917 Finchley Rd   020 8731 7501   1–1B
"Service with a smile" helps ensure this age-old pizza and pasta favourite in the Golders Green railway arches is "always full-to-bursting". "If you have kids, what you want is a big, noisy place full of Italians who love small children" – "what more could you ask for?". / NW11 7PE; www.lartistapizzeria.com; 11.30 pm.

L'Artiste Musclé W1   £48   ② ② **5**
I Shepherd Mkt   020 7493 6150   3–4B
This wonderfully named Gallic bistro in quaint Shepherd Market is a "favourite cheap place" that "has not changed" for 40 years or more. "An amazing wine list, too!" / W1J 7PA; @lartistemuscle; 10 pm.

Artusi SE15   £44   **4 4 3**
161 Bellenden Rd   020 3302 8200   1–4D
This three-year-old, "heart-of-Peckham gem" offers "consistently good Italian cooking with vivid flavours in even the simplest dishes"; and its "good value" makes it "very popular with local hipsters". (There's now also a Deptford spin-off too called Marcella.) / SE15 4DH; www.artusi.co.uk; @artusipeckham; 10.30 pm, Sun 8 pm; closed Mon L.

Asakusa NW1   £36   **5** ② ②
265 Eversholt St   020 7388 8533   9–3C
"Incongruously, a really good Japanese set in a rather shabby faux-Tudor setting" – this surprising outfit near Mornington Crescent impresses with its "exceptional prices for the quality". / NW1 1BA; 11.30 pm, Sat 11 pm; D only, closed Sun.

Asia de Cuba, St Martin's Lane Hotel WC2   £82   ② ② **3**
45 St Martin's Ln   020 7300 5588   5–4C
"Brilliant decor" and "lovely mojitos" have always been highpoints at this "sexy as…" West End boutique hotel, near the Coliseum. The Cuban-inspired fusion cuisine is "expensive", and even fans are "not sure it's authentic", but "the menu always offers something unusual", and won better ratings this year. / WC2N 4HX; www.morganshotelgroup.com; @asiadecuba; 11 pm, Fri & Sat midnight, Sun 10.30 pm; set pre-theatre & Sun L £51 (FP).

Assaggi W2   £76   **4 5** ②
39 Chepstow Pl   020 7792 5501   7–1B
"Thank goodness it's back!" – This resurrected, first-floor pub dining room in Bayswater (long renowned as London's top Italian) reopened a couple of years ago under one of its original owners to the ecstatic delight of its long-term fanclub and has "now expanded downstairs" (see Assaggi Bar). As ever, "Nino and his team are superb" in terms of charm, and although the consensus is that the "rather expensive" rustic fare is perhaps "not the best in town" any more, it remains "eternally high achieving". As ever the acoustics of this simple room can be "challenging". / W2 4TS; www.assaggi.co.uk; 11 pm; closed Sun; No Amex.

Assaggi Bar & Pizzeria W2 NEW   £57   **4 3** ②
39 Chepstow Place   020 7792 5501   7–1B
"A great addition to Notting Hill/Bayswater" – the Assaggi team have taken over the ground floor of the pub they have occupied for so many years to create this "superb", more achievably priced, all-day pizza/pastaria, with tapas "catering to the discerning and top pizza". / W2 4TS; www.assaggi.co.uk; No bookings.

Assunta Madre W1   £106   **3 3 3**
8-10 Blenheim St   020 3230 3032   3–2B
"Fantastic fresh fish", flown in daily, is the boast of this Mayfair 'Pescheria' – offshoot of a famous seafood restaurant in Rome – which generated consistent (if slightly limited) support this year and escaped the brickbats of former years for its hefty prices (although arguably "Estaitorio Milos is better value for a similar formula"). / W1S 1LJ; www.assuntamadre.com; @assuntamadre; 10 pm.

Aster Restaurant SW1 NEW   £58   3 3 3
150 Victoria St   020 3875 5555   2–4B
*"A genuinely Nordic addition to Victoria's new concrete canyons!" –
D&D London have 'gone for it', with Helena Puolakka's
"French/Scandinavian hybrid cuisine" at this Nova-development newcomer,
comprising a ground floor café, and more "comfortable" (and business
friendly) upstairs space ("with views of the surrounding glass and steel
buildings"). On the downside, despite "lovely" design the very urban milieu
can seem "sterile" and – given some "bland" dishes – the overall effect can
seem "just a bit meh". Most reports though are of "interesting" cooking,
and undoubtedly this is "a great plus in what has hitherto been a bit of a
desert". / SW1E 5LB; www.aster-restaurant.com; @AsterVictoria; 9.30 pm.*

Atari-Ya   £31   4 2 1
20 James St, W1   020 7491 1178   3–1A
7 Station Pde, W3   020 8896 1552   1–2A
1 Station Pde, W5   020 8896 3175   1–3A
595 High Rd, N12   020 8446 6669   9–1B
75 Fairfax Rd, NW6   020 7328 5338   9–2A
*"Always packed and rightly so" was the worst report this year on this group
of Japanese caffs, run by a food import business, where the dishes ("mostly
excellent sushi") can be "divine". The decor, though, is "very simple" and
the resulting atmosphere "pretty rubbish". / www.sushibaratariya.co.uk;
W1 8 pm, NW6 & W5 9.30 pm, W9 9 pm, N12 & W3 6.30 pm, Sat & Sun 7 pm;
NW6 closed Mon, W5 closed Mon & Tue.*

L'Atelier de Joel Robuchon WC2   £117   2 1 2
13-15 West St   020 7010 8600   5–2B
*"Astronomical" prices have always been a feature of this star French chef's
opulent Covent Garden outpost, where you kick off in the glam, rooftop
cocktail bar, and then descend to one of two luxurious dining floors (be it
the dark, ground floor, where you perch on high stools near the open
kitchen, or the more conventional first floor). But while many fans do find its
"theatrical" succession of exquisite ("miniscule") dishes to be "unbelievably
enjoyable", others feel its level of achievement nowadays is "a far cry from
the heady times when it first opened": "sky high prices are totally justifiable
in my book, but only if performance warrants them… but the food was
really flat and service careless and terribly slow". / WC2H 9NE;
www.joelrobuchon.co.uk; @latelierlondon; 11.30 pm, Sun 10 pm; No trainers;
set weekday L £57 (FP).*

The Atlas SW6   £50   4 4 4
16 Seagrave Rd   020 7385 9129   6–3A
*"A standard-bearer for the gastropub category" – this "beautiful, traditional
pub" is hidden-away near West Brompton tube and offers "gourmet food"
with "a nice Italian slant", delivered by "cheery and charming staff". There's
also "a cracking, huge, new terrace garden" (expanding the old one), which
is "a real gem". / SW6 1RX; www.theatlaspub.co.uk; @theatlasfulham; 10 pm.*

Augustine Kitchen SW11   £51   3 4 2
63 Battersea Bridge Rd   020 7978 7085   6–4C
*This little Savoyard bistro is "now well established in Battersea after a slow
start" and is overseen by "a chef who cares and staff who want to look
after you". There were a couple of 'off' reports this year ("don't know
what's happened"… "I don't get this place"), but mosts feedback says it's
"a really worthwhile local", with "good food" and "great price/performance
ratio". / SW11 3AU; www.augustine-kitchen.co.uk; @augustinekitchen; closed
Mon & Sun D; set weekday L £28 (FP).*

Aurora W1 £58 3 4 4
49 Lexington St   020 7494 0514   4–2C
This "really friendly" and supremely "cosy" stalwart (opposite Andrew Edmunds) is little known, but has long been a good option for a "romantic" bite in Soho. It earns consistently solid praise for its modern European cooking, with some "excellent dishes" on the small menu. Top Tip – "sit in the great secret garden" out back. / W1F 9AP; www.aurorasoho.co.uk; 10 pm, Wed-Sat 10.30 pm, Sun 9 pm.

The Avalon SW12 £49 2 2 3
16 Balham Hill   020 8675 8613   11–2C
"Big, busy (noisy) Balham gastropub" with an "attractive, large back room" and lovely garden. Fans applaud its "good no-nonsense cooking" but ratings are under-cut by those who find it "too un-memorable". / SW12 9EB; www.theavalonlondon.com; @threecheerspubs; 10.30 pm, Sun 9 pm.

L'Aventure NW8 £67 3 4 4
3 Blenheim Terrace   020 7624 6232   9–3A
Catherine Parisot's "charmant" Gallic classic in St John's Wood "provides a thoroughly enjoyable evening" combining a "lovely" superbly "romantic" setting with a "small, expertly executed menu" of archetypal cuisine bourgeoise. La Patronne's occasional stormy outbreaks were not in evidence this year. / NW8 0EH; www.laventure.co.uk; 11 pm; closed Sat L & Sun.

The Avenue SW1 £68 2 4 3
7-9 St James's St   020 7321 2111   3–4D
A "lovely, light room", "excellent value set menus" and "impeccable service" all help make D&D London's "vast" Manhattan-style brasserie a useful choice, especially for business diners, aided by its "prestigious" St James's location. The food? – "reliable without ever hitting the heights". / SW1A 1EE; www.avenue-restaurant.co.uk; @avenuestjames; 10.30 pm; closed Sat L & Sun.

Aviary EC2 NEW £53
10th Floor, 22-25 Finsbury Square   020 3873 4060   13–2A
Overlooking Finsbury Square from the 10th floor, this new ETM-group venture is long on glam' with its big rooftop terrace and marvellous views of the City skyline, and serves a modern British brasserie menu. / EC2A 1DX; aviarylondon.com; @AviaryLDN:

Awesome Thai SW13 £29 3 4 3
68 Church Rd   020 8563 7027   11–1A
Opposite the Olympic Studios cinema in Barnes, this very popular family-run local is "permanently packed" due to its "really well-realised, traditional Thai dishes", "service-with-a-smile" and "good value". "It gives more upmarket places a run for their money!" / SW13 0DQ; www.awesomethai.co.uk; 10.30 pm, Sun 10 pm; Mon-Thu D only, Fri-Sun open L & D.

Le Bab W1 £45 5 4 3
2nd Floor, Kingly Ct   020 7439 9222   4–2B
A superb gourmet take on the kebab, off Carnaby Street – everything is made from scratch in-house and there's "good cocktails, too". / W1B 5PW; www.eatlebab.com; @EatLeBab; 10 pm, Sun 7 pm; booking max 6 may apply.

Babaji Pide W1 £45 3 2 2
73 Shaftesbury Ave   020 3327 3888   5–3A
Two-year-old Turkish concept on Shaftesbury Avenue that's "finally found its stride", with improving food scores this year. Created by Hakkasan founder Alan Yau, it majors on 'pide' – a bit like pizza – and the "freshly made food is better than expected". / W1D 6EX; www.babaji.com.tr; @babajipidesalon; 11 pm, Fri & Sat 11.30 pm, Sun 10 pm.

Babette SE15 NEW £39 3 3 4
57 Nunhead Lane   020 3172 2450   1–4D
*Positive initial reports on this revivified Old Truman Pub in Nunhead, where
the blackboards on its brick walls mostly offer sharing boards, as well as a
few main dishes. / SE15 3TR; www.babettenunhead.com; @babettenunhead;
11 pm, Fri & Sat midnight, Sun 5 pm; closed Mon & Tue, Wed & Thu D only,
Fri & Sat L & D, Sun L only.*

Babur SE23 £56 5 5 4
119 Brockley Rise   020 8291 2400   1–4D
*"A stalwart of the Forest Hill dining scene that's worth a trip into
SE London!". For over 20 years, this surprisingly "exotic" modern Indian has
"had people beating a path to its door" on account of its "delightful service"
and some of London's best Indian cooking – "eye-catching", "subtly-spiced
and aromatic" dishes "with intense and unique flavours". / SE23 1JP;
www.babur.info; @BaburRestaurant; 11.30 pm.*

Babylon,
Kensington Roof Gardens W8 £75 2 2 4
99 Kensington High St   020 7368 3993   6–1A
*"Stunning views from high up in Kensington", "on a rooftop with lovely
gardens and its own lake", make this "moody, night-clubby" venue "unlike
any other in London". "The food may not live up to everything else –
it's solid if unspectacular – but it's a great choice for a date or Sunday
lunch". / W8 5SA; www.virginlimitededition.com/en/the-roof-gardens/b; 10.30 pm;
closed Sun D; SRA-Food Made Good – 2 stars.*

Bacco TW9 £58 3 2 2
39-41 Kew Rd   020 8332 0348   1–4A
*A "classic Italian menu" consistently well realised ("when it's good it's very
good") help make this "an excellent local", and it's particularly "convenient
for Richmond theatre-goers". / TW9 2NQ; www.bacco-restaurant.co.uk;
@BaccoRichmond; 11 pm; closed Sun D; set pre theatre £39 (FP).*

Bageriet WC2 £12 4 4 3
24 Rose St   020 7240 0000   5–3C
*"A little piece of Swedish heaven", "tucked away" down an alleyway
in Covent Garden – this "tiny café" serves "excellent coffee" and "fabulous
Nordic treats". "The cinnamon buns are the way better than any I've
tasted in Sweden (and I've tasted a lot by the way!)". / WC2E 9EA;
www.bageriet.co.uk; @BagerietLondon; 7 pm; L & early evening only, closed Sun;
no booking.*

Bala Baya SE1 NEW £67 3 2 3
Old Union Yard Arches, 229 Union St   020 8001 7015   10–4B
*"A bright spark sorely needed in Southwark" – this "Tel Aviv inspired"
newcomer from Israeli-born chef Eran Tibi (formerly of Ottolenghi et al)
provides "imaginative Middle Eastern fusion" dishes "in an unusual setting
under the Waterloo arches". "It could be a tad less expensive", though,
"the music could be a bit less loud", and service is "smiley" but not always
on the case. / SE1 0LR; balabaya.co.uk; @bala_baya; 11.30 pm, Sun 5 pm; closed
Sun D.*

The Balcon,
Sofitel St James SW1 £67 2 2 2
8 Pall Mall   020 7968 2900   2–3C
*The "pleasingly light and airy dining room" at this former bank off Trafalgar
Square, with its bistro-style cooking, perhaps fails to thrill. But it does get
a thumbs-up as a business rendezvous, and for a "very good value prix fixe
pre-theatre menu". / SW1Y 5NG; www.thebalconlondon.com; @TheBalcon;
10.45 pm, Sat & Sun 9.45 pm.*

Balthazar WC2 £70 2 2 **4**

4 - 6 Russell St   020 3301 1155   5–3D

"Transport yourself from touristy Covent Garden to an altogether chic and classy world", say fans of Keith McNally's "absolutely heaving" Grand Café, liked particularly for its "enjoyable brunch" and suitability for business entertaining. "For standard brasserie fare, it's very expensive" however – "presumably you're paying for the very stylish interior". / WC2B 5HZ; www.balthazarlondon.com; @balthazarlondon; midnight, Sun 11 pm; set pre theatre £47 (FP).

Baltic SE1 £57 **4 4 4**

74 Blackfriars Rd   020 7928 1111   10–4A

"Lovely, gutsy Polish home cooking" washed down with lashings of homemade vodka helps induce good vibes at this "friendly" fixture in an "airy" Georgian factory-conversion near the Cut. "It's good to see east European food being given the gourmet treatment", and the bar "is a good pit stop for drinks" too. / SE1 8HA; www.balticrestaurant.co.uk; @balticlondon; 11.15 pm, Sun 10.30 pm; closed Mon L.

Baluchi,
Lalit Hotel London SE1 NEW £77

181 Tooley St   020 3765 0000   10–4D

A former school hall (St Olave's) decorated with a striking midnight blue ceiling houses this new dining room, in a five-star hotel near Tower Bridge (part of a luxury hotel group spanning the subcontinent). Initial feedback is limited, but such as we've had is ecstatic about its stunning cuisine and setting. / SE1 2JR; www.thelalit.com/the-lalit-london/eat-and-drink/baluchi/; @TheLalitLondon; 9.30 pm.

Bandol SW10 £65 **3 3 3**

6 Hollywood Road, Kensington   020 7351 1322   6–3B

"Excellent" sharing plates of summery Provençal and Niçoise cuisine shine at this two-year-old, a sibling to nearby Margaux. The location is part of the appeal for Chelsea types – "you can't beat the Hollywood Road scene!" / SW10 9HY; www.barbandol.co.uk; @Margaux_Bandol; 11 pm, Sun 10 pm; set weekday L £39 (FP).

Bang Bang Oriental NW9 NEW £36

399 Edgware Rd   no tel   1–1A

Successor to the food court at the former Yaohan Shopping Plaza – also known as Oriental City – which was demolished in 2014, this gargantuan (30,000 sq ft) Asian food hall in Colindale boasts a restaurant, supermarket and community space with room for 450 diners. / NW9 0AS; www.bangbangoriental.com; @bangbangofh.

Bangalore Express EC3 £39 **3 3 3**

1 Corbet Ct   020 7220 9195   10–2C

"Always good tastes and good value" win fans for this "reliable" contemporary-style Indian, right in the heart of the Square Mile. / EC3V 0AT; www.bangaloreuk.com; @bangaloreuk; 11pm.

Bánh Bánh SE15 £36 **3 4 3**

46 Peckham Rye   020 7207 2935   1–4D

The Nguyen family achieves positive (if not quite unanimous) support for the "tasty and cheap Vietnamese fare" at their bare-brick-walled Peckham Rye yearling. / SE15; www.banhbanh.com; @BanhBanhHQ; 9.30 pm, Fri & Sat 10 pm; closed Mon.

Banners N8 £46 **3 4 5**
21 Park Rd 020 8348 2930 9–1C
This all-day haven of "hearty, generous, seriously tasty scoff" is a Crouch
End legend, with its epic brunch being the favoured (some would say only)
time to visit. With its Caribbean flavours and "ramshackle world music
vibe", it's "not at all refined, but that's why we love it!". / N8 8TE;
www.bannersrestaurant.com; 11 pm, Fri 11.30 pm, Sat midnight, Sun 10.30 pm;
No Amex.

Bao £28 **4 3 2**
31 Windmill St, W1 020 3011 1632 5–1A
53 Lexington St, W1 07769 627811 4–2C
13 - 23 Westgate St, E8 no tel 14–2B
"Heaven in a bun"; "very special steamed bao, with great fillings",
plus other "incredible" street food dishes – "as good as in Taiwan" – all at
"realistic prices" have made this Soho café (and its more recent Fitzrovia
spin-off) one of the biggest hits of recent years. You can book in WC1 for
the basement, but in Soho "you have to queue behind a bus-stop-type sign
on the other side of the road" – "the bao are to die for... so you long
as you didn't die of the wait to get them..." / W1F Mon-Wed 10 pm, Thu-Sat
10.30 pm, W1T Mon-Sat 10 pm, E8 Sat 4 pm; W1F & W1T closed Sun, E8 open
Sat L only; W1 no bookings, E8 takeout only.

Baozi Inn WC2 £24
26 Newport Ct 020 7287 6877 5–3B
Just off the main Chinatown drag, this Sichuan canteen won a name with its
bold, street-food-inspired dishes ("very garlicky and not shy with the chilli
spice") and kitsch Maoist memorabilia. Mid-survey in May 2017 it emerged
with a toned down look and reduced but pricier menu – we've removed the
ratings for now as change seems to be afoot. / WC2H 7JS;
www.baoziinnlondon.com; 9.30 pm; Cash only; no booking.

Le Bar EC1
59 West Smithfield 020 7600 7561 10–2B
What was 'Cellar Gascon' next to Club Gascon has recently rebranded and
re-launched with a more modish new look, serving Gascon 'Frapas' (French
tapas) alongside 'hand-crafted' cocktails. / EC1A 9DS; www.lebarlondon.co.uk;
@lebarlondon; midnight.

Bar Boulud,
Mandarin Oriental SW1 £69 **3 4 4**
66 Knightsbridge 020 7201 3899 6–1D
"Conveniently below street level opposite Harvey Nick's" this "Knightsbridge-
crowd, but friendly" spin-off from the NYC original is "a den worth the
descent" and particularly popular for a "thoroughly reliable" business bite
thanks to its "smooth service" and "famous burgers" hailed by many
as "London's best" (although the the menu is primarily "a good choice
of American-influenced French bistro fare"). / SW1X 7LA; www.barboulud.com;
@barbouludlondon; 10.45 pm, Sun 9.45 pm; No trainers; set weekday L &
pre-theatre £41 (FP).

Bar Douro SE1 NEW £53 **4 3 3**
Arch 25b Flat Iron Square, Union St 020 7378 0524 10–4B
"A wonderful additional to London" in Bankside's new Flat Iron Square,
whose pretty blue-and-white tiled interior with "all bar seating" ("the stools
are a bit uncomfortable") help make it akin to a Portuguese Barrafina –
from your perch you get "a theatrical view of the immaculate assembly
of brilliant small dishes, served with broad smiles". / SE1 1TD;
www.bardouro.co.uk; @BarDouro; 11.30 pm; booking max 4 may apply.

Bar Esteban N8 £43 ④④④
29 Park Rd 020 8340 3090 1–1C
"Wonderful, every single time" – so say local fans of this "favourite" Crouch End bar, with its yummy tapas and fun vibe. / N8 8TE; www.baresteban.com; @barestebanN8; 9.30 pm, Fri & Sat 10.30 pm, Sun 9 pm; closed weekday L; booking max 8 may apply.

Bar Italia W1 £32 ②③⑤
22 Frith St 020 7437 4520 5–2A
"Legendary", "open-all-hours" haunt redolent of post-War Soho, whose basic interior is "pleasantly untouched" by the passage of years. "You don't go for the food, but for the coffee and the buzz" and for "an institution that's a one-off. May it never, ever go!" / W1D 4RF; www.baritaliasoho.co.uk; @TheBaristas; open 24 hours, Sun 4 am; No Amex; no booking.

Bar Termini W1 £35 ③③⑤
7 Old Compton St 07860 945018 5–2B
"Simply the best coffee you'll find anywhere" is part of the resolutely and genuinely Italian approach at Tony Conigliaro's tiny (expect no great encouragement to linger) but characterful Soho bar, known also for its definitive Negronis and authentic bites. In early summer 2017, a much larger 'Centrale' branch opened near Selfridges, with an expanded food offering including salads and panzerotti (akin to a fried mini-calzone). / W1D 5JE; www.bar-termini.com; @Bar_Termini; 11.30 pm, Fri & Sat 1 am, Sun 10.30 pm.

The Barbary WC2 £49 ⑤⑤④
16 Neal's Yard awaiting tel 5–2C
"Bringing the fun and fizz of the best places in Jerusalem and Tel Aviv to London" – the debut of Palomar's little brother in Neal's Yard fully lives up to its stablemate's trailblazing performance, with "a brilliant selection of totally delicious and vibrant Mediterranean dishes", eaten "in a small plate, counter eating-style format", complete with "loud banging music and chefs dancing along". "Perfect for a drop in and quick bite, but beware of the queues!!" STOP PRESS: The Barbary now takes bookings for lunch and early dinner. / WC2H 9DP; www.thebarbary.co.uk; @barbarylondon; 10 pm, Sun 9 pm; no booking.

Barbecoa £73 ②②②
Nova, Victoria St, SW1 no tel 2–4C
194-196 Piccadilly, W1 020 3005 9666 4–4C
20 New Change Pas, EC4 020 3005 8555 10–2B
"Good quality meat but SOOOO overpriced" – that's the trade off at Jamie Oliver's good-looking chain of luxury grills, which added a new, swish-looking branch right by Piccadilly this year. So long as you are packing the company's plastic, the City original (in a big mall), which has "great views of St Paul's", can be "perfect for business". / EC4M Mon-Sat 11 pm, Sun 10 pm, W1J Mon-Thu 11 pm, Fri & Sat midnight, Sun 10.30 pm.

Il Baretto W1 £76 ②②②
43 Blandford St 020 7486 7340 2–1A
"Rather straightforward Italian fare" is on the menu at this "buzzy (or noisy?) basement" venue in Marylebone. As ever, it fails to whip up huge enthusiasm, but does have a dedicated fan club: "it's not everyone's favourite, but I have yet to have a bad meal here". / W1U 7HF; www.ilbaretto.co.uk; @IlBarettoLondon; 10.15 pm, Sun 9.45 pm.

Barrafina £43 5 5 5

26-27 Dean St, W1   020 7813 8016   4–1D
10 Adelaide St, WC2   020 7440 1456   5–4C
43 Drury Ln, WC2   020 7440 1456   5–2D

"The wait can sometimes be twice the time spent at the counter", but no-one seems to mind at the Hart Bros kick-ass small group of Barcelona-inspired tapas haunts in Soho (now relocated to the ground floor of Quo Vadis) and Covent Garden. "The buzz is amazing" and, having nabbed a perch (fewer than 30 in each branch), everyone "loves the open kitchen and watching the keen staff at work", while the dishes themselves are genius – "fresh seafood is amongst the highlights" but "even something as simple as tomato bruschetta is transformed here". (So far, the February 2017 departure of founding group exec head chef, Nieves Barragán Mohacho, to found Sabor, has had zero effect on ratings – the new incumbent is Angel Zapata Martin.) / www.barrafina.co.uk; 11 pm, Sun 10 pm; no booking, max group 4.

Barrica W1 £55 3 2 2

62 Goodge St   020 7436 9448   2–1B

"A truly wonderful tapas place" near Goodge Street station, where "standards remain really high". "You get a genuinely Spanish experience, with a superb selection of wines that you won't easily find elsewhere". / W1T 4NE; www.barrica.co.uk; @barricatapas; 10.30 pm; closed Sun.

Barshu W1 £58 4 2 2

28 Frith St   020 7287 6688   5–3A

"Less a meal than a dare!" – the "seriously spicy cooking gives way to rich depths of flavour for the strong-hearted and willed" at this "excellent" Soho café. "If you want a Sichuan fix, go!" – there are "some real lip-smackers in there, including some wonderful unusual dishes (smacked cucumber, gung bao chicken, ants climbing trees...)", but "you still suffer Chinatown-style woes – sometimes indifferent service, and poor ambience". / W1D 5LF; www.barshurestaurant.co.uk; @BarshuLondon; 10.30 pm, Fri & Sat 11 pm.

Bbar SW1 £58 3 4 3

43 Buckingham Palace Rd   020 7958 7000   2–4B

A "good pit stop near Victoria" serving "great burgers and steak" and other fare, plus Saffa wines, all "under the South African banner". / SW1W 0PP; www.bbarlondon.com; @bbarlondon; 10 pm; No shorts.

Bea's Cake Boutique WC1 £39 3 3 3

44 Theobalds Rd   020 7242 8330   2–1D

"Delicious cupcakes" have helped this cosy café near Holborn Library blossom into a spin-off chain. It's an "unexpectedly feminine tea room serving wonderful cakes, proper teas and lunchtime sandwiches". / WC1X 8NW; www.beasofbloomsbury.com; @beas_bloomsbury; 7 pm; L & early evening only.

Bean & Hop SW18 £11 3 3 2

424-426 Garratt Lane   020 7998 6584   11–2B

All the key bases are covered at this "good neighbourhood spot" in Earlsfield, serving "varied brunches", "excellent coffee and tempting cakes by day", and "great homemade pizza with a selection of craft beers in the evening". / SW18 4HN; www.beanandhop.co.uk; @beanandhop.

Bears Ice Cream W12 £6 3 3 3

244 Goldhawk Rd   020 3441 4982   8–1B

Just one "wonderful" flavour of Icelandic ice cream blended with a myriad of "tempting toppings" is the winning recipe of this simple parlour (with small garden) on the busy gyratory at the foot of Askew Road – "guaranteed smiles all round!" / W12 9PE; www.bearsicecream.co.uk; @bears_icecream; 8.30 pm; L & early evening only.

Beast W1 £115 1️⃣2️⃣2️⃣
3 Chapel Pl 020 7495 1816 3–1B
"Ludicrous pricing" ("so crazy I struggle to find the adjectives") is the
unanimous verdict on this dramatic-looking, candle-lit, Goodman-owned,
steak-and-crab experience off Oxford Street – even from reporters who
applaud the "great fun and good food". "I've never been so outraged
as when I found out our Norwegian king crab starter for six was £470!!
Bonkers!… Daylight robbery!…". / W1G 0BG; www.beastrestaurant.co.uk;
@beastrestaurant; 10.30 pm; closed Mon & Sun; May need 7+ to book.

The Begging Bowl SE15 £45 4️⃣3️⃣2️⃣
168 Bellenden Rd 020 7635 2627 1–4D
"Wonderful" if tightly packed Thai street-food café in Peckham that's
an "outpost of real excellence in SE London" thanks to its "short choice
of genuinely spiced dishes". / SE15 4BW; www.thebeggingbowl.co.uk;
@thebeggingbowl; 9.45 pm, Sun 9.15 pm; no booking.

Beijing Dumpling WC2 £33 4️⃣2️⃣2️⃣
23 Lisle St 020 7287 6888 5–3A
"Watching the chefs making the dumplings in the window is an incredibly
comforting experience" at this "very busy", "tightly packed" little Chinatown
pit stop, where "there are regular queues outside" (although "you can book
and walk straight in!"). / WC2H 7BA; 11.30 pm, Sun 10.30 pm.

Bel Canto,
Corus Hotel Hyde Park W2 £68 2️⃣3️⃣3️⃣
1 Lancaster Gate 020 7262 1678 7–2C
Opera singers appear on the quarter hour at this long-established Bayswater
basement dining room, where the traditional dishes often feature luxury
ingredients. / W2 3LG; www.belcantolondon.co.uk; @london@lebelcanto.co.uk;
10.30 pm; D only, closed Mon & Sun.

Bellamy's W1 £61 3️⃣4️⃣3️⃣
18-18a Bruton Pl 020 7491 2727 3–2B
Owner Gavin Rankin (ex MD of Annabel's) "keeps a strict eye" on this art-
lined brasserie, whose "classic", "unchallenging" French cuisine and
"competent and well-oiled" service make it "the very definition
of civilisation" to its "tidily dressed and mostly besuited" Mayfair clientele.
(It's one of a handful of restaurants ever visited by The Queen). / W1J 6LY;
www.bellamysrestaurant.co.uk; 10.30 pm; closed Sat L & Sun.

Bellanger N1 £59 2️⃣3️⃣3️⃣
9 Islington Grn 020 7226 2555 9–3D
"It's the best thing that's happened to Islington for years", say fans of Corbin
& King's "elegant", all-day brasserie on Islington Green, who say its "clubby,
wood-lined" interior "feels like it's always been there", and that it's
"interesting take on Alsatian brasserie cooking (with brilliant tartes
flambées)" makes "an excellent choice for breakfast, lunch or dinner".
A sceptical minority however are left cold by the experience: "it's all too
faux, the food's only passable, service is drilled but charmless, and all-in-all
it's a pretty set, with no actual drama". / N1 2XH; www.bellanger.co.uk;
@BellangerN1; 11 pm, Sun 10.30 pm; set dinner £36 (FP).

Belpassi Bros SW17 £40 3️⃣3️⃣3️⃣
70 Tooting High St 020 8767 6399 11–2C
For a "fantastic, simple dinner of Italian meatballs and sides", fans tip this
"casual and relaxed", brick-lined newcomer in Tooting: the work of brothers
Livio and Lorenzo (who used to sell similar fare from a truck). There are
numerous options when it comes to the balls, sauces and bases.
/ SW17 0RN; www.belpassibros.com; @BelpassiBros; 9.30 pm, Thu-Sat 10 pm,
Sun 8.30 pm; booking max 4 may apply.

Belvedere Restaurant W8 £69 2 3 4
off Abbotsbury Rd in Holland Park 020 7602 1238 8–1D
"A wonderful location, actually in Holland Park itself" – and set in a grand
17th-century ballroom – provides unbeatably *"romantic surroundings"* for
this well-known destination. The food struggles to match the setting,
but there are nevertheless reports of *"superb celebratory meals"* and
"excellent-value Sunday lunches". Top Tip – *"best upstairs, or by the
balcony on summer evenings"*. / W8 6LU; www.belvedererestaurant.co.uk; 11 pm,
Sun 3.30 pm; closed Sun D; set weekday L £43 (FP).

Benares W1 £108 2 2 2
12a Berkeley Square House, 020 7629 8886 3–3B
Opinions again divide on Atul Kochar's acclaimed contemporary Indian,
which occupies a sprawling and first-floor site on Berkeley Square. Critics –
who accuse it of *"going through the motions"* – drag down its overall ratings,
but the majority lavish praise on his *"innovative"* cuisine's *"delicate spicing"*,
and say a meal is a *"wow, how-did-they-make-it-taste-so-good experience"*.
/ W1J 6BS; www.benaresrestaurant.co.uk; @benaresofficial; 10.45 pm, Sun 9.45 pm;
closed Sun L; booking max 10 may apply; set weekday L & pre-theatre £66 (FP).

Bentley's W1 £84 3 4 4
11-15 Swallow St 020 7734 4756 4–4B
*"Celebrating over 100 years of serving some of the best fish and seafood
in London"* – Richard Corrigan's *"British classic"* near Piccadilly Circus
is *"expensive"*, but *"utterly reliable"* – *"it's easy to forget that this is one
of the best restaurants in the West End"*. Downstairs *"the booths in the
busy oyster bar are best"*: the *"old-fashioned, silver service"* upstairs is more
comfortable but *"not as involving"* as below. Top Menu Tips – *"exceptional
oysters and lobster"*. / W1B 4DG; www.bentleys.org; @bentleys_london; 10.30 pm,
Sun 10 pm; No shorts; booking max 8 may apply; set weekday L £57 (FP).

Berber & Q E8 £48 5 2 5
Arch 338 Acton Mews 020 7923 0829 14–2A
"The best beef short ribs in town... and the chargrilled cauliflower rocks!" –
be it meat or vegetarian, all dishes dazzle at this *"pretty damn cool"* and
"very reasonably priced" North African-inspired grill in a Haggerston railway
arch – they even have their own collaboration beer with a great local
brewery. / E8 4EA; www.berberandq.com; @berberandq; 10.30 pm, Sun 9.30 pm;
D only, closed Mon; May need 6+ to book.

Berber & Q Shawarma Bar EC1 £47 4 3 3
Exmouth Market 020 79230 0829 10–1A
"Perfectly formed Middle Eastern cuisine", revolving around spit-roasted
chicken and lamb, is the focus at this new Exmouth Market venue from
Hackney's Berber & Q, which *"punches well above its weight"*. *"Although
it caters to carnivores, it's also a vegetarian paradise"*. *"Shame you can't
reserve a table"*. / EC1R 4QL; www.berberandq.com; @berberandq; 10.30 pm,
Sun 9.30 pm; closed Mon; no booking.

Bernardi's W1 £58 3 3 4
62 Seymour St 020 3826 7940 2–2A
*"The beautifully designed room looks like an amazing space from the pages
of Elle Decor"* and helps instil a *"buzzy atmosphere"* at this *"fun Italian"*,
on the border between Marylebone and Bayswater. *"These guys can cook"*
too... *"but you certainly pay for the pleasure"*. / W1H 5BN;
www.bernardis.co.uk; @BernardisLondon; 11 pm, Mon & Sat 10.30 pm, Sun 9.30 pm.

The Berners Tavern W1 £75

10 Berners St 020 7908 7979 3–1D

"The magnificent room" – "not an intimate affair, but a breathtaking and fun showpiece" that "makes you feel glamorous and special" – underpins the appeal of this "impressively grand" chamber, north of Oxford Street. The modern British cuisine (overseen by Jason Atherton) is "OK", but "unduly expensive" – "you're there for the ambience". Top Tip – "brunch here makes for a perfect Sunday morning". / W1T 3NP; www.bernerstavern.com; @bernersTavern; 11.45 pm, Sun 10.15 pm; set weekday L £53 (FP).

Best Mangal £42

619 Fulham Rd, SW6 020 7610 0009 6–4A
104 North End Rd, W14 020 7610 1050 8–2D
66 North End Rd, W14 020 7602 0212 8–2D

"Very good charcoal-grilled meat", "super-fresh salads" and "generous portions" have made a name for this Turkish operation that has expanded to three branches in its 21 years in Fulham. / www.bestmangal.com; midnight, Sat 1 am; no Amex.

Bibendum SW3 £104

81 Fulham Rd 020 7581 5817 6–2C

"You could never tire of the feeling of decadence and class", say fans of this "lovely and refined" dining space within the iconic Michelin Building on Brompton Cross (converted by Sir Terence Conran in the late 1980s), where "a visit is best when the sun is shining and streaming in through the beautiful windows". Claude Bosi took over in early 2017, with a view to restoring it to its former glory, but initial reports are deeply divided. To advocates, "this classic venue has been re-imagined" and "is now better than Hibiscus" (his previous highly regarded venture). Critics though "miss the old Bibendum with its wholesome fare" and feel the new more ambitious culinary régime comes at "ridiculous prices". / SW3 6RD; www.bibendum.co.uk; @bibendumltd; 11 pm, Sun 10.30 pm; booking max 12 may apply; set Sun L £58 (FP), set weekday L £59 (FP).

Bibendum Oyster Bar SW3 £52

Michelin House, 81 Fulham Rd 020 7581 5817 6–2C

"New menu, new chef, new decor: all very good" – that's the upbeat view on this long-established Chelsea rendezvous, off the foyer of the Michelin Building, where Claude Bosi's new régime has added luxurious hot staples to the bill of fare alongside its traditional cold seafood platters. It still hasn't re-established itself as the local magnet it once was however, and critical reporters say "it's an old favourite that has gone completely downhill". / SW3 6RD; www.bibendum.co.uk; @bibendumrestaurant; 10 pm; closed Sun D; no booking.

Bibimbap Soho £28

10 Charlotte St, W1 020 7287 3434 2–1C
11 Greek St, W1 020 7287 3434 5–2A
39 Leadenhall Mkt, EC3 020 72839165 10–2D

Fans say these Korean canteens in Soho and Fitzrovia (with a take-away in the City) are "hard to beat compared with other fast-food places". "They do one thing" – the signature mixed rice dish they're named after – "and do it well". / 11pm, EC3 3 pm; W1 Sun, EC3 Sat & Sun; no bookings.

Big Easy £57   2 2 **3**
12 Maiden Ln, WC2   020 3728 4888   5–3D
332-334 King's Rd, SW3   020 7352 4071   6–3C
Crossrail Pl, E14   020 3841 8844   12–1C
"The closest you can feel to America in London" conveys much of what need
to know – pro or con – about these US-style BBQs in Chelsea, Covent
Garden and Canary Wharf. "What's not to like – bottomless beer
or margaritas, a constant supply of chicken and ribs with sides of coleslaw,
fries and beans, chirpy and attentive staff and great music!", is the friendly
view. "Just awful" is the riposte. / www.bigeasy.co.uk; Mon-Thu 11 pm, Fri & Sat
11.30 pm, Sun 10.30 pm.

The Bingham TW10 £64   **4 5 4**
61-63 Petersham Rd   020 8940 0902   1–4A
"Smart and sophisticated, without being snobby" – the "really comfortable"
dining room of this boutique hotel in Richmond on Thames, which boasts
"a beautiful setting on the river". Staff ensure you are "well looked after"
and its "slickly prepared" food helps make it a logical choice for a special
occasion. Top Tip – "the market menu lunch is exceptional value"; eat it
on the balcony overlooking the garden. / TW10 6UT; www.thebingham.co.uk;
10 pm; closed Sun D; No trainers.

The Bird in Hand W14 £49   **3 3 4**
88 Masbro Rd   020 7371 2721   8–1C
"Excellent pizzas" top the bill at this converted pub in the backstreets
of Olympia. "Prices are a little high", and "with the rest of the menu they're
sometimes trying to be too clever", but overall it's a "great local". Sibling
to the Oaks in W2 and W12. / W14 0LR; www.thebirdinhandlondon.com;
@TBIHLondon; 10 pm, Sun 9.15 pm; booking weekdays only.

Bird of Smithfield EC1 £59   2 2 2
26 Smithfield St   020 7559 5100   10–2B
Limited but upbeat feedback on this "buzzy" five-storey Georgian
townhouse in Smithfield – it's most worth knowing about for its summer roof
terrace. / EC1A 9LB; www.birdofsmithfield.com; @BirdoSmithfield; 10 pm; closed Sun.

Bistro Aix N8 £56   **4 3 4**
54 Topsfield Pde, Tottenham Ln   020 8340 6346   9–1C
The "fine, traditional French cuisine" at chef-proprietor Lynne Sanders's
small and smartly turned-out bistro is "worth a trip to Crouch End". "It's a
lovely venue with a good vibe", and has become a local fixture after
15 years on the site. / N8 8PT; www.bistroaix.co.uk; @bistroaixlondon; 10 pm, Fri &
Sat 11 pm; Mon-Thu D only, Fri-Sun open L & D; No Amex.

Bistro Union SW4 £57   **3 3 3**
40 Abbeville Rd   020 7042 6400   11–2D
Adam Byatt's "friendly", bistro spin-off from Trinity in Clapham is a
"neighbourhood winner", and even if not as accomplished as its sibling
provides "plenty of choice" and scores "mostly hits" on the food front. Top
Tip – "Sunday supper club with the children – they eat free and you can
take your own wine with no corkage -£26 for set 3 courses". / SW4 9NG;
www.bistrounion.co.uk; @BistroUnion; 10 pm, Sun 8 pm; booking max 8 may apply.

Bistro Vadouvan SW15 NEW £55
30 Brewhouse Lane   020 3475 3776   11–2B
Chef-patron Durga Misra (Brasserie Chavot) and co-founder Uttam Tripathy
(Potli) both hail from the same town in India (although they only met years
later at college). They have realised a long-held dream with this Thames-
view Putney Wharf newcomer, which offers French cooking with Asian
spicing. / SW15 2JX; bistrovadouvan.co.uk; @BistroVadouvan; 10.30 pm.

Bistrotheque E2 £58 **3** 2 4
23-27 Wadeson St   020 8983 7900   14–2B
"Its hip heyday is a decade in the past, and it's now a tourist trap for those in search of cool east London" – that's the cynical view on this light and airy warehouse-conversion, but more numerous are fans who still tip it as a fun brunch haunt. / E2 9DR; www.bistrotheque.com; @Bistrotheque; 10.30 pm, Fri & Sat 11 pm; closed weekday L.

Black Axe Mangal N1 £48 **5** 4 2
156 Canonbury Rd   no tel   9–2D
"If you don't mind the noise" ("not everyone's into heavy metal!"), Lee Tiernan's head-banging Highbury Corner yearling is "certainly more than a few notches up from your average kebab house" and practically all reporters "love, love, LOVE" the "varied and meat-heavy" dishes ("lamb offal flatbread was one of the culinary highlights of the year!)". "He's gonna need a bigger restaurant…" / N1; www.blackaxemangal.com; @blackaxemangal; 10.30 pm, Sun 3 pm; D only Mon-Fri, Sat L & D, Sun L only; no booking.

Black Prince SE11 £38 **3** 3 3
6 Black Prince Rd   020 7582 2818   2–4D
Though it's consistently well-rated, there's nothing overly gastro' about this classic Kennington boozer, serving classic pub grub with the odd bit of gentle 21st-century updating (eg corn & beetroot slaw with your chicken 'n' chips). / SE11 6HS; www.theblackprincepub.co.uk; 11 pm.

Black Roe W1 £68 **3** 2 2
4 Mill St   020 3794 8448   3–2C
High-fashion, Hawaiian-inspired two-year-old in Mayfair that showcases 'poke' – marinated raw fish – and hot dishes cooked on a kiawe (mesquite wood) grill. The result is "delicious, fresh, healthy food" presented in a "sexy ambience (although the music's a bit loud)" – but it's also "very expensive". / W1S 2AX; www.blackroe.com; @blackroe; 10.45 pm; closed Sun.

Blacklock £39 **4** 4 4
24 Great Windmill St, W1   020 3441 6996.   4–2D
13 Philpot Lane, EC3   020 7998 7676   10–3D **NEW**
"My inner caveman loves this place!" – "Chops, crispy on the outside and juicy in the middle" provide "amazing meat and amazing value" at this "laid back and very cool", "no frills" Soho basement, which is "a case study of picking something you're good at and sticking with it". In Spring 2017 it opened its second branch – a larger City outlet off Eastcheap. Top Tip – "the amount of food on the 'All In' has to be seen to be believed!"

Blanchette £50 **4** 3 4
9 D'Arblay St, W1   020 7439 8100   4–1C
204 Brick Lane, E1   020 7729 7939   13–1C
"You can imagine you have been whisked away to France", particularly at the "noisy and boisterous" Soho original of this Gallic duo (which "looks like it's been there for years, but is actually only three years old"), whose year-old East End sibling is also providing "a great addition to Brick Lane". Founded on a traditional mix of "cheeses, cut meats and small plates", the arrival of ex Bibendum chef Tam Storrar as chef/director seems to have taken the menu in a "more complicated and increasingly Mediterranean" direction. / 11 pm, Sun 9 pm.

Blandford Comptoir W1 £60 333
1 Blandford St 020 7935 4626 2–1A
"The justly-renowned wine-list" is the key feature of Xavier Rousset's "crowded" yearling, but its "friendly" style and "simple, effective" Italian dishes, all contribute to its very high popularity as "a good addition to Marylebone". / W1U 3DA; blandford-comptoir.co.uk; @BlandfordCompt; 10 pm; No Amex.

Bleecker Burger £22 522
205 Victoria St, SW1 no tel 2–4B NEW
Unit B Pavilion Building, Spitalfields Mkt, E1 07712 540501 13–2B
Bloomberg Arcade, Qn Victoria St, EC4 awaiting tel 10–2C NEW
"The juiciest, most flavourful burgers blow the socks off competitors". Former NYC corporate lawyer Zan Kaufman launched his burger biz from the back of a truck five years ago. A permanent site in Spitalfields opened two years ago, followed by venues in Victoria and the City's new Bloomberg Arcade. The "street" has been dropped from the branding, but not the quality: fans feel that "If you don't think Bleecker is the best burger in London, you need your taste buds examined".

Bleeding Heart Restaurant EC1 £66 335
Bleeding Heart Yd, Greville St 020 7242 8238 10–2A
"The convivial atmosphere never fails to be stunning, and the Gallic cooking seldom fails to please" at this "unique Dickensian-style" warren, on the fringe of the City: "a perfect place to impress that special someone in your life", be it romantically or on business! The "gorgeous and imaginative wine list" is key to its appeal, as are staff who are "friendly but, hard to understand given the strong French accents!" (It's a big operation, comprising a restaurant, wine bar and tavern, all interlinked, and all with somewhat different price points.) / EC1N 8SJ; bleedingheart.co.uk/restaurants/the-restaurant; @bleedingheartyd; 10.30 pm; closed Sat & Sun.

Blixen E1 £47 333
65a Brushfield St 020 7101 0093 13–2C
"Relaxed, casual and cool" all-day brasserie, right by Spitalfields Market, whose handsomely decorated, "bustling" quarters "get especially busy for weekend brunch". / E1 6AA; www.blixen.co.uk; @BlixenLondon; 11 pm, Sun 8 pm.

Blue Boat W6 £50 223
Distillery Wharf 020 3092 2090 8–2C
"A very enterprising newcomer on the riverfront in a new development in Hammersmith". The main attraction is its big sun-trap terrace, but "the quality of the modern pub grub is a welcome surprise". / W6 9GD; www.theblueboat.co.uk; @BlueBoatW6; 10 pm, Sun 9 pm.

Bluebird SW3 £74 333
350 King's Rd 020 7559 1000 6–3C
"Like the new look!" – This D&D landmark has just had "lots of work done refurbishing it" and, with its "very spacious and pleasant" interior and contemporary cuisine that's "not cheap but value for money", it seems to be emerging as the "lovely" venue it's always had the potential to be. Can it be that after 20 years, they've finally sorted the place out? / SW3 5UU; www.bluebird-restaurant.co.uk; @bluebirdchelsea; 10.30 pm, Sun 9.30 pm; set weekday L £46 (FP).

Blueprint Café SE1 £48 224
28 Shad Thames, Butler's Wharf 020 7378 7031 10–4D
A "wonderful location" with "great views over the Thames" is reason enough to visit what is now a stand-alone D&D group restaurant since the Design Museum headed west to Kensington. The food here has always tended to be "a bit hit and miss" and "unexciting", and this year is no exception… / SE1 2YD; www.blueprintcafe.co.uk; @BlueprintCafe; 10.30 pm; closed Mon & Sun; no booking.

Bó Drake W1 £52 2️⃣2️⃣3️⃣
6 Greek St   020 7439 9989   5–2A
Korean and US influences seem most apparent in the spicy tapas of this vibey, small Soho two-year-old, although its performance varies from "exceptional" to "amateurish". / W1D 4DE; www.bodrake.co.uk; @bodrakesoho; 10.30 pm, Sun 8.30 pm; closed Sun; booking max 6 may apply.

Bob Bob Cité EC3
122 Leadenhall St   awaiting tel   10–2D
Tomorrow and tomorrow and tomorrow... – we've been billing the arrival of BBC – sibling to Soho's glam Bob Bob Ricard – for over a year now as its opening is pushed back and back, but it is finally slated to appear in January 2018. Set to occupy the entire third floor of 'The Cheesegrater' – more 'press for champagne' buttons are promised, alongside cooking provided by well-known chef, Eric Chavot. When it finally arrives, one thing is certain: it won't be subtle... / EC3V 4PE; www.bobbobricard.com.

Bob Bob Ricard W1 £85 3️⃣4️⃣5️⃣
1 Upper James St   020 3145 1000   4–2C
"Everyone is dazzled by the exotic boothed interior and the press-for-champagne buttons", when visiting this lavish Russian-owned diner in Soho, which is "super for impressing your guest". Sceptics say its comfort food is "poor for the price", but a number of reporters note that it's "miles better than it was" under chef Anna Haugh (appointed in late 2016). / W1F 9DF; www.bobbobricard.com; @BobBobRicard; 11.15 pm, Sat midnight, Sun 11.15 pm; closed Sat L; Jacket required.

The Bobbin SW4 £52 4️⃣4️⃣4️⃣
1-3 Lillieshall Rd   020 7738 8953   11–1D
"A cool Clapham crowd underpin this trendy gastropub", drawn by its "way-above-average" food, and it manages to be "romantic and ambient" as well. "Awesome" Sunday roasts rate mention as does the "indulgent Bobbin's burger (it's the spicy mayo that does it"!). / SW4 0LN; www.thebobbinclapham.com; @bobbinsw4; 10 pm, Sun 9 pm.

Bobo Social W1 £45 3️⃣3️⃣3️⃣
95 Charlotte St   020 7636 9310   2–1C
Fans say "top burgers" (using rare-breed meat) and an extensive cocktail-menu accompaniment are the highlights at this small town-house conversion in Fitzrovia. Survey feedback has its highs and lows, but the best reviews are enthusiastic: "I will be back!" / W1T 4PZ; www.bobosocial.com; @BoboSocial; 10.30 pm; closed Sun.

Bocca Di Lupo W1 £62 4️⃣4️⃣3️⃣
12 Archer St   020 7734 2223   4–3D
"Unexpected, distinctive regional dishes" and staff who are "knowledgeable" and "brilliantly friendly" continue to win a major thumbs up for Jacob Kenedy's "energetic" Italian, near Piccadilly Circus. "Noise is a big issue here – it can be hard to hold a conversation". And the "stimulating" setting can feel too "crowded", both in the rear section and at the front counter (which is "hated" by a few, but for most reporters "a favourite place, where you can watch the chefs and see what other people are eating"). "There are two very wise policies – all options come in half/main portions, and many of the interesting wines are available by the glass or in 500cc pichets". / W1D 7BB; www.boccadilupo.com; @boccadilupo; 11 pm, Sun 9.30 pm; booking max 10 may apply.

Bocconcino W1 £88 3️⃣3️⃣3️⃣
19 Berkeley St   020 7499 4510   3–3C
"Expensive but good" is actually the least enthusiastic endorsement of this agreeable, bare-brick-walled, Russian-owned Italian and pizzeria in Mayfair's eurotrashiest of enclaves. / W1J 8ED; www.bocconcinorestaurant.co.uk; @BocconcinoUK; 11.30 pm, Sun 10.30 pm.

Al Boccon di'vino TW9 £66 3 4 5
14 Red Lion St 020 8940 9060 1–4A
"Starve yourself before going!" – "A real 'Venetian wedding'-style feast" greets diners at this "completely different" operation in Richmond. "Beautiful Italian food is made from fresh ingredients, and while there's no choice of menu, there are so many dishes that you walk out with a warm glow, feeling like you've just left Nonna's house". / TW9 1RW; www.nonsolovinoltd.co.uk; 11 pm; closed Mon, Tue L & Wed L; No Amex.

Bodean's £51 2 2 2
10 Poland St, W1   020 7287 7575   4–1C
25 Catherine St, WC2   020 7257 2790   5–3D
4 Broadway Chambers, SW6   020 7610 0440   6–4A
348 Muswell Hill Broadway, N10   020 8883 3089   1–1C
225 Balham High St, SW17   020 8682 4650   11–2C
169 Clapham High St, SW4   020 7622 4248   11–2D
201 City Rd, EC1   020 7608 7230   13–1A
16 Byward St, EC3   020 7488 3883   10–3D
These Kansas City-style BBQ joints were some of the first to mine the capital's enthusiasm for Americana, and their "cookie-cutter feel" is arguably all part of the "fun". The large, "all-American menu" seems to follow the principle of "pile it high and sell it cheap" – results are "decent, but not great". / www.bodeansbbq.com; 11 pm, Sun 10.30 pm, NW10 10 pm, Fri & Sat 11 pm; booking: min 8.

La Bodega Negra Cafe W1 £48 3 2 4
16 Moor St   020 7758 4100   5–2B
This low-lit Soho basement Mexican wins converts mainly for its "buzzy" atmosphere, but reporters are perfectly satisfied with the food on offer, too. / W1D 5NH; www.labodeganegra.com; midnight, Thu-Sat 1 am, Sun 11 pm.

Boisdale of Belgravia SW1 £65 3 2 4
15 Eccleston St   020 7730 6922   2–4B
With its "plush jockinese decor and fabulous bar", Ranald Macdonald's "always fun" and "very clubbable" Belgravian provides "an excellent all-round experience", bolstered by its "great selection of wines and spirits", regular jazz, and cigar terrace. The "traditional, meaty Scottish fare" is "pricey" but consistently well rated. / SW1W 9LX; www.boisdale.co.uk/belgravia; @boisdale; midnight; closed Sat L & Sun.

Boisdale of Bishopsgate EC2 £72 3 2 3
Swedeland Court, 202 Bishopsgate   020 7283 1763   10–2D
"A great atmosphere" (by the standards of City restaurants) helps win fans for this outpost of the Caledonian Victoria original, down an alley near Liverpool Street, which has a ground floor bar and basement dining room, and serves a similar modern Scottish formula, with an emphasis on wines and whiskies. / EC2M 4NR; www.boisdale.co.uk; @Boisdale; 11 pm; closed Sat & Sun; set pre theatre £48 (FP).

Boisdale of Canary Wharf E14 £62 3 3 4
Cabot Place   020 7715 5818   12–1C
"Good fun" (a rare commodity in Canary Wharf) is to be had at this "surprisingly enjoyable" (including at the weekend) Scottish themed venue, whose meaty fare, "great live music and selection of drinks" follow a similar formula to the Belgravia original. "If you can grab a space on the terrace, it's an ideal place for an after work bevvie too". / E14 4QT; www.boisdale.co.uk/canary-wharf; @boisdaleCW; 11 pm, Wed-Sat midnight, Sun 4 pm; closed Sun D.

Boisdale of Mayfair W1 NEW £77 333
12 North Row   020 3873 8888   2–2A
This bistro-style new Mayfair addition to the Boisdale clan is off to a good start, and wins very respectable ratings for its Scottish-slanted cuisine, plus the usual indulgences: wine, whisky and regular jazz. / W1K 7DF; www.boisdale.co.uk/mayfair; @Boisdale; 11 pm, Sun 6 pm; closed Sun D.

Bokan E14 NEW £70
40 Marsh Wall   020 3530 0550   12–2C
Located on the 37th floor of the new Novotel Canary Wharf, this 65-cover restaurant features modern European cuisine from Aurelie Altemaire, formerly of L'Atelier de Joël Robuchon. Limited feedback to-date, but such as there is praises "thoroughly enjoyable cooking without silly prices", but with splendid views. / E14 9TP; bokanlondon.co.uk; 10 pm.

Bombay Brasserie SW7 £65 343
Courtfield Rd   020 7370 4040   6–2B
"Excellent food in a somewhat formal setting" – an elegant conservatory with colonial decor – elevates this South Kensington stalwart beyond "run-of-the-mill curry houses". Reports have dwindled in recent years, but consistently high ratings suggest it's worth a second look. / SW7 4QH; www.bombayb.co.uk; @bbsw7; 11 pm, Sun 10.30 pm; closed Mon L.

Bombay Palace W2 £41 442
50 Connaught St   020 7723 8855   7–1D
This long-time Bayswater favourite reopened at long last after a fire closed the doors for over a year, sparking concern among the many fans of its "fabulous Indian flavours". "After the initial hiccups, they've got it just right", is the relieved verdict shared by most – if not quite all – reporters. The interior, always the weak point at this venue, is "a marked improvement, and the food still of consistent high quality". / W2 2AA; www.bombay-palace.co.uk; @bombaypalaceW2; 10.45 pm; booking essential.

Bombetta E11 £51 342
Station Approach   020 3871 0890   1–1D
This "charming and well-meaning", "cheap 'n' cheerful" Puglian newcomer on the "outer reaches of the Central Line" – near Snaresbrook station in Wanstead – "is no ordinary Italian". For one, there's "no pizza". Instead, "a small-plates menu with lots of meaty and good vegetarian options" followed by the signature "bombetta" (cheesy-meaty bites). / E11 1QE; www.bombettalondon.com; @bombettaLondon.

Bon Vivant WC1 NEW £57 333
75-77 Marchmont St   020 7713 6111   9–4C
"A brave and useful addition to an increasingly buzzy corner of Bloomsbury" – this "minimalist" newcomer is "more intimate and grown-up than many offerings in this part of town" with "well-executed and presented" Gallic fare. / WC1N 1AP; www.bonvivantrestaurant.co.uk; set weekday L £33 (FP).

Bone Daddies £42 433
Nova, Victoria St, SW1   no tel   2–4B
14a, Old Compton St, W1   020 7734 7492   5–2A
30-31 Peter St, W1   020 7287 8581   4–2D
46-48 James St, W1   020 3019 7140   3–1A NEW
Whole Foods, Kensington High St, W8   020 7287 8581   6–1A
The Bower, Baldwin St, EC1   020 7439 9299   13–1A
"Good lord, that stock they use in the ramen!" – Aussie restaurateur, Ross Shonhan's funky fusion chain offers "noodles served in lovely, rich broths, as well as some fantastic salads and small dishes" to create a "superb all-round experience"; branches are regularly "heaving". / www.bonedaddies.com/restaurant/bermondsey/; 10 pm, Thu-Sat 11 pm, Sun 9.30 pm; W1 no bookings.

Bonhams Restaurant,
Bonhams Auction House W1   £75   4 5 2
101 New Bond St   020 7468 5868   3–2B
Tom Kemble's "amazing food" won instant renown for this "intimately
proportioned, if rather steriley decorated" three-year-old, at the back of the
famous Mayfair auction house (and also with its own, separate entrance).
Of equal attraction is the "incredible wine list that leverages the wines at the
auction house's disposal" – "the wine markups, or lack thereof, are unheard
of in their generosity", with many available by the glass. Top Tip – "wander
round the auction rooms post meal". / W1K 5ES; www.bonhamsrestaurant.com;
@dineatbonhams; 8.30 pm; L only, Fri L & D, closed Sat & Sun.

La Bonne Bouffe SE22 NEW   £53   3 2 3
49 North Cross Rd   020 3730 2107   1–4D
"New on the block, with French bistro food harking back to the '70s": this
East Dulwich arrival evokes mostly supportive reviews. There are critics who
feel "more polish is required", but fans – while acknowledging some "not-
quite-knowing-how-things-work moments" – say "it's not trying anything too
clever", but can be "brilliant". / SE22 9ET; www.labonnebouffe.co.uk;
@laBonneBouffe49.

Bonnie Gull W1   £57   4 3 3
21a Foley St   020 7436 0921   2–1B
"A wide range of fresh fish is cooked with flair and skill" in this "bright and
cheerful" Fitzrovia dining room, whose small size is at odds with its huge
following. Conditions are "so cramped", but "it's compact nature makes
it cosy", as does the "very friendly service". / W1W 6DS; www.bonniegull.com;
@BonnieGull; 9.45 pm, Sun 8.45 pm.

Bonnie Gull Seafood Shack W1 NEW   £52   5 3 3
22 Bateman St   020 7436 0921   5–2A
For "very fresh fish and seafood from a changing menu" it's worth
discovering this "cosy and slightly cramped" Fitzrovia dining room – "a quiet
corner of London not far from the bustle of Oxford Street",
with "an enjoyable, familial feel to it". / W1D 3AN;
www.bonniegull.com/seafood-shack/soho; @BonnieGull; 11 pm, Sun 9 pm.

Bonoo NW2   £42   5 4 3
675 Finchley Rd   020 7794 8899   1–1B
"What a find! Finally a fabulous local restaurant in NW2!" – "this friendly,
neighbourhood tapas-style Indian in Childs Hill surpasses many swanky
competitors" with "fantastic street food dishes, plus a few usual old
favourites". / NW2 2JP; www.bonoo.co.uk; @bonoohampstead; 10.30 pm.

The Booking Office,
St Pancras Renaissance Hotel NW1   £67   2 2 4
Euston Rd   020 7841 3566   9–3C
The hugely characterful, former St Pancras station ticket office makes
a "lovely location" for calm all-day refuelling (at nights it can be "rocking").
Food reports are a tad uneven, but it's a good bet for a "quality afternoon
tea". / NW1 2AR; www.bookingofficerestaurant.com; @StPancrasRen; 11 pm.

Boqueria   £46   4 4 4
192 Acre Ln, SW2   020 7733 4408   11–2D
278 Queenstown Rd, SW8   020 7498 8427   11–1C
"Fresh, light tapas dishes, with influences from Asia" provide a "different
take on the usual fare" at these "stylish", "buzzy and fun" neighbourhood
places, in Battersea and on the Clapham/Brixton border; "charming
service" too.

Il Bordello E1 £56 ③③④
81 Wapping High St 020 7481 9950 12–1A
"Love the place!" – a fixture in Wapping, this *"very traditional Italian"*
is *"always thrumming, which gives it a terrific atmosphere"*. *"Always good
value"*, it's *"unchanged for years – including the waiters..."*. / E1W 2YN;
www.ilbordello.com; 11 pm, Sun 10.30 pm; closed Sat L.

Boro Bistro SE1 £44 ③④③
Montague Cl, 6-10 Borough High St 020 7378 0788 10–3C
"A hidden gem" in Borough Market worth remembering as a good *"cheap
'n' cheerful"* option and whose *"basic"* Gallic decor is part of its charm.
It serves *"great sharing boards, plus a surprisingly good cheese and wine
selection"*. #NotReeling / SE1 9QQ; www.borobistro.co.uk; @borobistro; 10.30 pm,
Mon & Sun 9 pm; closed Mon & Sun; booking max 6 may apply.

The Botanist £68 ②②②
7 Sloane Sq, SW1 020 7730 0077 6–2D
Broadgate Circle, EC2 020 3058 9888 13–2B
"A Sloaney spot for ladies who lunch" – the well-known, *"very lively"*
Chelsea branch right on Sloane Square that's also convenient for *"business
lunches or drinks"* (no-one talks about its City offshoot). The food avoided
the drubbing of prior surveys and won consistent support this year.
/ thebotanist.uk.com; SW1 breakfast 8, Sat & Sun 9, SW1 & EC2 11 pm.

The Bothy E14 NEW £53
16 Hertsmere Rd 020 3907 0320 12–1C
An enviable waterside location in Canary Wharf (in the same former
warehouse buildings as the Docklands Museum) provides the setting for this
large new Drake & Morgan's outlet; all-day dining, Sunday roasts, cocktails,
plenty of outside seating and weekend brunch complete the picture.
/ E14 4AX; drakeandmorgan.co.uk/the-bothy; @TheBothyW1Q; 10 pm, Sun 9 pm.

Boudin Blanc W1 £58 ③③④
5 Trebeck St 020 7499 3292 3–4B
"Classic Gallic food and service in a lovely old building" (with extensive
al fresco seating) draws a steady crowd to this *"romantic"* and *"cosy Mayfair
staple"* in picturesque Shepherd Market. / W1J 7LT; www.boudinblanc.co.uk;
11 pm.

Boulestin SW1 £71 ③③②
5 St James's St 020 7930 2030 3–4D
Joel Kissin's three-year-old brasserie (on the site that was L'Oranger,
long RIP) revives the name of a famous 1920s fine dining Gallic basement
in Covent Garden. Perhaps unsurprisingly given its swanky location it seems
"slightly pricey" for what it is, but attractions do include *"one of the
best breakfasts in St James's"*, plus *"a super little courtyard for outdoor
dining in summer"*. / SW1A 1EF; www.boulestin.com; @BoulestinLondon; 10.30 pm;
closed Sun; No trainers.

The Brackenbury W6 £56 ④④③
129-131 Brackenbury Rd 020 8741 4928 8–1C
The epitome of *"an excellent neighbourhood restaurant"* – chef/patron
Humphrey Fletcher's *"lovely local"* in the backstreets of Hammersmith
provides *"frequently changing seasonal fare"*, very *"charming"* service and
a civilised atmosphere, enhanced by a sizeable terrace in summer. The re-
jigged layout – with a bar in one of its two rooms – seems to be working
well too. / W6 0BQ; www.brackenburyrestaurant.co.uk; @BrackenburyRest; 9.30 pm;
closed Mon & Sun D.

Brackenbury Wine Rooms W6 £57 3 3 4
Hammersmith Grove 020 3696 8240 8–1C
"A very good range of wine by the glass as well as bottle" is just one attraction at this Hammersmith corner-spot – others include very decent cooking, *"friendly"* staff, very attractive styling, and a large outside terrace. Inviting neighbouring café/deli too, with *"exceptional coffee"*. / W6 0NQ; winerooms.london/brackenbury; @Wine_Rooms; 11.30 pm, Sun 10.30 pm.

Bradley's NW3 £62 3 2 2
25 Winchester Rd 020 7722 3457 9–2A
"Convenient for the Hampstead Theatre", this *"off-the-beaten-track"* Swiss Cottage stalwart serves a modern British menu of some ambition, and offers *"especially good value pre-show menus"*. At other times, prices are *"a bit steep"*, service can lag, and it can seem *"curiously unmemorable"* even though *"objectively the food is good, and the room tastefully restrained"*. / NW3 3NR; www.bradleysnw3.co.uk; 10 pm; closed Sun D.

Brady's SW18 £39 3 3 3
39 Jews Row 020 8877 9599 11–2B
"Still loving it after over 20 years" – *"The Brady's family-owned fish 'n' chip shop may have changed location a few years ago"*, but even if *"it's not as lively as it used to be"* in its *"posh"* new Thames-side home (*"rather hidden away near Wandsworth Bridge"*) this is *"a simple formula that's survived the test of time and the move"* – *"superb fish 'n' chips"* (with *"a grand choice of specials alongside old favourites"*) and *"a warm welcome"*. Top Menu Tip – *"Mr Brady's famous desserts are a big draw too"*. / SW18 1DG; www.bradysfish.co.uk; @Bradyfish; 10 pm; Tue-Thu D only, Fri & Sat L & D, Sun L only, closed Mon; no booking.

Brasserie Blanc £56 1 3 2
'Brasserie Bland' would unfortunately be a better title for Raymond Blanc's modern brasserie chain. To be sure there are less enjoyable standbys out there, and for an *"OK pre-theatre meal"* they could be worse, but the fare is *"formulaic"* and *"the ambience AWOL"*. / www.brasserieblanc.com; most branches close between 10 pm & 11 pm; SE1 closed Sun D, City branches closed Sat & Sun.

Brasserie Toulouse-Lautrec SE11 £56 3 3 3
140 Newington Butts 020 7582 6800 1–3C
"Surprisingly good" cooking is to be found at this genuinely Gallic brasserie (and popular live music venue) in a thinly-provided corner of Kennington (*"convenient for the nearby cinema museum"*). / SE11 4RN; www.btlrestaurant.co.uk; @btlrestaurant; 10.30 pm, Sat & Sun 11 pm.

BRASSERIE ZÉDEL W1 £40 1 3 5
20 Sherwood St 020 7734 4888 4–3C
"Why bother with any restaurant chain when you can actually eat here cheaper and get the Corbin & King experience on a budget!" Their *"breathtaking refurbishment of the Regent Palace Hotel's Art Deco basement grill room"* provides a *"dramatic and unexpected setting in a fantastic location, just off Piccadilly Circus"*, that's *"very evocative of a true Parisian brasserie"* (*"democratic and wonderful!"*). The trade-off is the *"conveyor-belt"* classic brasserie fare which can utterly *"lack spark"*, but even so *"at these prices you can't go wrong"*. Top Menu Tips – *"stick to the classics like steak haché"* or the *"incredible value set options"*. / W1F 7ED; www.brasseriezedel.com; @brasseriezedel; 11.45 pm, Sun 10.45 pm.

Bravas E1 £46 3 4 3
St Katharine Docks 020 7481 1464 10–3D
Prettily located overlooking the marina at St Katharine dock, this *"favourite"* modern Basque three-year-old provides *"excellent high-quality tapas"*. / E1W 1AT; http://www.bravasrestaurant.com; @Bravas_Tapas; 10 pm.

Brawn E2 £62
49 Columbia Rd 020 7729 5692 14–2A
*"Skilled and seasonal" small plates, plus "a funky and sometimes
challenging (in a good way) list of natural wines" have earned exalted foodie
status for Ed Wilson's rough-hewn venue in a former Bethnal Green
workshop. Scores have slipped off their high peak here though, amidst the
odd gripe that "its former zip and precision are missing". / E2 7RG;
www.brawn.co; @brawn49; 11 pm; closed Mon L & Sun D; No Amex.*

Bread Street Kitchen EC4 £64
10 Bread St 020 3030 4050 10–2B
*The "great fit-out" of this Gordon Ramsay operation in a City shopping mall
makes it "a surprisingly welcoming environment for such a huge space",
and its sizeable fan club like its "buzzy atmosphere" and "varied menu"
of food that's "good without being great but not bad value". But while
it escaped harsh critiques, for some tastes it's all just too "formulaic".
/ EC4M 9AJ; www.breadstreetkitchen.com; @breadstreet; 11 pm, Sun 8 pm.*

Breakfast Club £43
33 D'Arblay St, W1 020 7434 2571 4–1C
2-4 Rufus St, N1 020 7729 5252 13–1B
31 Camden Pas, N1 020 7226 5454 9–3D
12-16 Artillery Ln, E1 020 7078 9633 13–2B
*"Delicious breakfasts: English, American, Antipodean (the waffles are
a must!), …" supply "food that's worth getting up for" at this growing group
of "consistently high-quality" cafés. There is a snag though: "go off-peak
to avoid the crowds and long waiting times". Top Menu Tip – the "ever-
popular huevos rancheros". / www.thebreakfastclubcafes.com; SRA-Food Made
Good – 3 stars.*

Breddos Tacos EC1 NEW £41
82 Goswell Rd 020 3535 8301 10–1B
*"Mouthwatering tacos" – "an innovative take on Mexican food in a City with
few good Mexicans" – draw a strong fanclub to this "fun and vibrant"
Clerkenwell cantina, which started out as a stall in E8, and is about to open
a second Soho branch in September 2017 on the former site of Shotgun
(RIP). / EC1M 7AH; www.breddostacos.com; @breddostacos; no booking.*

Brew House Café,
Kenwood House NW3 £31
Hampstead Heath 020 8348 1286 9–1A
*"If you can just muster enough patience to manage the queues at the
check-out, there's nowhere better on a sunny day in North London for
a delicious piece of cake and a cup of tea than this stunning garden", which
adjoins the self-service café within the stable blocks of this stately home,
on Hampstead Heath; "wonderful breakfasts" too. / NW3 7JR;
www.english-heritage.org.uk/visit/places/kenwood/facilities; @EHKenwood; 6 pm
(summer), 4 pm (winter); L only.*

Briciole W1 £50
20 Homer St 020 7723 0040 7–1D
*"Excellent, authentic Italian cooking" wins high popularity for this deli-
trattoria favourite in the backwoods of Marylebone (a spin-off from Latium),
aided by its "buzzy atmosphere" and "charming staff". It's "a bit pricey"
though – at times, "while the quality is there, the quantity isn't". / W1H 4NA;
www.briciole.co.uk; @briciolelondon; 10.15 pm.*

Brick Lane Beigel Bake E1 £6
159 Brick Ln 020 7729 0616 13–1C
*"Long waits, hectoring staff" and "imperious queue marshalling" do nothing
to diminish the rockstar status of this epic, 24/7 Brick Lane veteran, which
sells the "best beigels ever, and they're SO cheap". / E1 6SB; open 24 hours;
Cash only; no booking.*

Brigadiers EC2 NEW
Bloomberg Arcade, Queen Victoria St awaiting tel 10–2C
JKS Restaurants (AKA the Sethi siblings), the founders of Gymkhana and Hoppers, are behind this Indian BBQ restaurant inspired by traditional Indian Army mess halls. It is slated to open autumn 2017 alongside nine other eateries in the new Bloomberg City HQ. / EC2R; www.jksrestaurants.com.

The Bright Courtyard W1   £62   4 2 2
43-45 Baker St 020 7486 6998 2–1A
Consistently high ratings again this year for this comparatively little-known, contemporary Marylebone Chinese, tipped particularly for its dim sum. / W1U 8EW; www.lifefashiongroup.com; @BrightCourtyard; 10.45 pm, Thu-Sat 11.15 pm.

Brilliant UB2   £46   4 4 3
72-76 Western Rd 020 8574 1928 1–3A
A "Southall institution" that "never disappoints" – this big and bustling 'burbs Punjabi is "certainly not resting on its laurels", providing "finely spiced" food ("with an East African bias as the owners are from Kenya"). "I hesitated for 40 years before coming and it was worth the wait!". / UB2 5DZ; www.brilliantrestaurant.com; @brilliantrst; 11 pm, Fri & Sat 11.30 pm; closed Mon, Sat L & Sun L.

Brinkley's SW10   £62   2 2 3
47 Hollywood Rd 020 7351 1683 6–3B
"A lively spot, with an excellent wine list" – key selling points of John Brinkley's Chelsea perennial, near the C&W hospital. "The food isn't bad, but it's unlikely to be the main attraction to the twenty-something, local bright-young-things that seem so attracted to the place". / SW10 9HX; www.brinkleys.com; @BrinkleysR; 11.30 pm; closed weekday L.

Bronte WC2   £69   2 3 4
Grand Buildings, 1-3 Strand 020 7930 8855 2–3C
Even critics of this big and ambitious yearling off Trafalgar Square confess it looks "amazing" ("an Aladdin's cave of to-die-for Tom Dixon design-treasures"). "When fusion food goes wrong, it goes really wrong" however, and even though the "Asian-ish fare" can impress, it can also be "atrocious". Perhaps try it out first for a "lovely cocktail" ("it's a stunning place for a drink, particularly if you grab the outdoor table with a through-the-arch view of Nelson's Column"), or try the "top notch brunch". / WC2N 5EJ; www.bronte.co.uk; @bronte_london.

Brookmill SE8 NEW   £50   3 3 3
65 Cranbrook Rd 020 8333 0899 1–4D
Recently-refurbished Deptford gastropub, "definitely worth a visit if you're passing" for its superior cooking and "nice city garden". / SE8 4EJ; www.thebrookmill.co.uk; @thebrookmillpub; 10 pm, Sun & Mon 9 pm.

The Brown Dog SW13   £46   3 3 3
28 Cross St 020 8392 2200 11–1A
A "gem" tucked away in the cute backstreets of Barnes's 'Little Chelsea', this "reliable local gastropub" dishes up "the best roasts in the vicinity (based on extensive testing!)". Children and dogs are welcome. / SW13 0AP; www.thebrowndog.co.uk; @browndogbarnes; 10 pm, Sun 9 pm.

Brown's Hotel,
The English Tea Room W1   £74   3 4 4
Albemarle St 020 7493 6020 3–3C
"A great balance between cosy comfort and formality" – Rocco Forte's "classic" Mayfair hotel lounge haven is renowned for its "memorable afternoon tea", which is one of London's 'greats' in this department. / W1S 4BP; www.roccofortehotels.com; No trainers.

Brown's Hotel, HIX Mayfair W1 — £69 — 2 2 **3**

Albemarle St   020 7518 4004   3–3C

For fans this civilised Mayfair chamber provides "a quintessential London dining experience", and it wins particular praise both as a "power" lunch or "delicious breakfast" spot. Mark Hix's régime here has almost as many detractors as fans however, who feel the traditional cuisine is too "average" and "overpriced". / W1S 4BP; www.thealbemarlerestaurant.com; 11 pm, Sun 10.30 pm.

Brunswick House Café SW8 — £56 — **3** 3 **5**

30 Wandsworth Rd   020 7720 2926   11–1D

The "improbable" and "eccentrically wonderful" setting of an architectural salvage and antiques shop inside the former Duke of Brunswick's Georgian mansion on Vauxhall roundabout hosts this modern British dining room. "A regularly changing menu of delicious and innovative food" makes any meal here a "quirky treat". Top Tip – "lunch is a steal". / SW8 2LG; www.brunswickhouse.co; 10 pm; closed Sun D.

Bubbledogs, Kitchen Table W1 — £134 — **5** 3 **4**

70 Charlotte St   020 7637 7770   2–1C

"One of the best experiences ever" – James Knappett's "truly unique" venture, tucked away behind his and his wife's adjoining hot dog place – is as "absolutely fascinating" as it is unexpected. Seated at stools around the 20-seat kitchen table creates "great intimacy with the team" and the daily changing 12-course array of dishes ("on the whole sourced from the UK, and very well explained") are "from another world". "It's cosy, it's unpretentious, it's delicious, it's friendly, it's excellent value". / W1T 4QG; www.kitchentablelondon.co.uk; @bubbledogsKT; seatings only at 6 pm & 7.30 pm; D only, closed Mon & Sun.

Buen Ayre E8 — £62 — **4** 4 2

50 Broadway Market   020 7275 9900   14–2B

"Top steaks (and a couple of vegetarian BBQ options too)" seal high satisfaction with this well-established and popular Argentinian 'parilla' in the heart of Hackney's happening Broadway Market. / E8 4QJ; www.buenayre.co.uk; 10 pm, Fri & Sat 10.30 pm, Sun 10 pm; No Amex.

The Builders Arms SW3 — £54 — 2 2 **3**

13 Britten St   020 7349 9040   6–2C

"Fun, with reliable, simple grub" – this modernised pub (part of the Geronimo Inns chain) in a cute Chelsea backstreet wins very consistent praise, especially for its "relaxed ambience". / SW3 3TY; www.thebuildersarmschelsea.co.uk; @BuildersChelsea; 10 pm, Thu-Sat 11 pm, Sun 9.30 pm; no booking.

Bukowski Grill — £38 — **3** 3 2

10-11 D'Arblay St, W1   020 3857 4756   4–1C
Brixton Market, Unit 10 Market Row, SW9   020 7733 4646   11–2D
Boxpark, Unit 61, 4-6 Bethnal Green Rd, E1   020 7033 6601   13–2B

"Good for carnivores", these "friendly", "reasonably priced" American-style grills with branches in Soho, Brixton and Shoreditch max out on burgers and ribs. / W1 10.30 pm, E1 10 pm, Sun 6 pm, SW9 11 pm, Sun 9 pm, Croydon 11 pm, Sun 10 pm; SW9 closed Mon; W1 online bookings.

The Bull N6 — £53 — **3** 4 **4**

13 North Hill   020 8341 0510   9–1B

"Homely and welcoming with a very good menu", this microbrewery pub in Highgate has brought its food up a notch in the past year or so. / N6 4AB; thebullhighgate.co.uk; @Bull_Highgate.

Bull & Last NW5 £65 3 3 3
168 Highgate Rd   020 7267 3641   9–1B
This "quintessential gastropub" in Kentish Town feels "more like a homely
local than a high class place" but remains north London's most popular
hostelry – "the food is amazingly consistent" ("lovely for a big Sunday
lunch" after a walk on the heath) and "served with infectious enthusiasm".
/ NW5 1QS; www.thebullandlast.co.uk; @thebullandlast; 10 pm, Sun 9 pm.

Bumpkin £59 2 2 2
119 Sydney St, SW3   020 3730 9344   6–3C
102 Old Brompton Rd, SW7   020 7341 0802   6–2B
Westfield Stratford City, The St, E20   020 8221 9900   14–1D
This "comfy and slightly rustic" West London mini-chain featuring British
fare is reduced in numbers nowadays and its performance "continues
to vary wildly". Fans, though, say the service "may be chaotic but is always
cheerful", "love the farm-to-table options", and find it OK value.
/ www.bumpkinuk.com; 11 pm; closed Mon.

Buona Sera £45 3 3 3
289a King's Rd, SW3   020 7352 8827   6–3C
22 Northcote Rd, SW11   020 7228 9925   11–2C
"Basic Italian cooking done to a satisfactory standard" along with a "family-
friendly atmosphere" have established this "busy" and incredibly
"consistent" café as a Clapham institution; it has a Chelsea spin-off too
at the King's Road 'Jam' – an age-old place with fun double-decker booths.
/ SW11 11.30 pm, Sun 10.30 pm; SW3 11 pm; SW3 closed Mon L.

Burger & Lobster £59 3 2 3
Harvey Nichols, 109-125 Knightsbridge, SW1   020 7235 5000   6–1D
26 Binney St, W1   020 3637 5972   3–2A
29 Clarges St, W1   020 7409 1699   3–4B
36 Dean St, W1   020 7432 4800   5–2A
6 Little Portland St, W1   020 7907 7760   3–1C
195-198 High Holborn, WC1   020 7432 4805   2–1D
18 Hertsmere Rd, E14   020 3637 6709   12–1C NEW
40 St John St, EC1   020 7490 9230   10–1B
Bow Bells Hs, 1 Bread St, EC4   020 7248 1789   10–2B
"For a straightforward, relaxed meal with a bit of pizzazz", these "buzzy"
joints maintain their massive popularity with a "simple" formula executed
"with style": "awesome lobster rolls" are "excellent value" – the burgers
"are rather expensive, albeit well-executed". / www.burgerandlobster.com;
10.30 pm-11pm, where open Sun 8 pm-10 pm; WC1 & EC2 closed Sun; booking:
min 6.

Busaba Eathai £39 2 2 3
"Original and unique decor" has always helped distinguish these communal
canteens (who share the same founder as Wagamama). Critics feel its
cooking has "really gone downhill" over the years, but most reporters still
say its "westernised Thai food" provides "a good formula for a quick, cheap
meal". / www.busaba.co.uk; 11 pm, Fri & Sat 11.30 pm, Sun 10 pm; W1 no booking;
WC1 booking: min 10.

Butler's Restaurant,
The Chesterfield Mayfair W1 £83 2 4 3
35 Charles St   020 7958 7729   3–3B
Traditional Mayfair dining room, where fans applaud its "relaxed" style and
Nathan Hindmarsh's dependable (if, some would say, pricey) British cuisine.
The hotel's star turn actually takes place in the adjoining "lovely"
'Conservatory' – "a fun all-you-can-eat afternoon tea themed around Charlie
and the Chocolate Factory". / W1J 5EB; www.chesterfieldmayfair.com;
@chesterfield_MF; 10 pm; Jacket required; booking max 8 may apply; set pre theatre
£54 (FP).

Butlers Wharf Chop House SE1   £65   2 2 **3**
36e Shad Thames   020 7403 3403   10–4D
*A "good riverside location" near Tower Bridge is what most qualifies this
D&D London venue as "a decent option", as its "high-end comfort food"
is "never special, and pricey for what you get". Its better-known stablemate,
Le Pont de la Tour, is next door but one. / SE1 2YE;
www.chophouse-restaurant.co.uk; @bwchophousetowerbridge/; 11 pm, Sun 10 pm.*

La Buvette TW9   £45   **3** **3** **3**
6 Church Walk   020 8940 6264   1–4A
*"Hidden away up an alleyway in a charming location" beside a churchyard
in the heart of Richmond, this "good-value French bistro" is "the perfect
local". "Good game (duck and venison), with traditional starters (fish soup)
and desserts" are highlights of the menu. / TW9 1SN; www.labuvette.co.uk;
@labuvettebistro; 10 pm; booking max 8 may apply.*

by Chloe WC2 NEW
34-43 Russell St   awaiting tel   5–2D
*The first overseas site from this American, plant-based restaurant brand
arrives in Covent Garden. Its London flagship (a roll-out no doubt is on its
way) will seat 70 and offers a grab and go service too. / WC2B 5HA;
www.eatbychloe.com; @eatbychloe.*

Byron   £36   2 2 2
*Supporters say "hats off to an unformulaic formula", but enthusiasm
is waning fast for this 'posh patties' group, which seems increasingly
"overtaken by the independent burger joints", and whose ratings are
heading inexorably south. Supporters do still applaud its "upmarket burgers
and good choice of sides", but there are too many former fans who –
amidst gripes over "slipping standards" and "soulless" branches – say its
"descent to chain-dom" is nearly complete. (Whether Tom Byng its founder
stepping down as CEO at the end of the 2016 is causative or symptomatic
is hard to read). / www.byronhamburgers.com; most branches 11 pm.*

C London W1   £95   1 1 **3**
25 Davies St   020 7399 0500   3–2B
*"Maybe I'm just not the target audience, but that still doesn't justify the
bill!" – this eurotrashy Mayfair scene (forced to drop the [C]'ipriani' from its
name in a lawsuit a few years ago) continues to live down to the low
expectations formed by former surveys: "service is slow and condescending",
and "prices are outrageous for ordinary dishes" (think of a number,
then double it). / W1K 3DE; www.crestaurant.co.uk; 11.45 pm.*

C&R Cafe   £30   **4** 2 2
3-4 Rupert Ct, W1   020 7434 1128   4–3D
52 Westbourne Grove, W2   020 7221 7979   7–1B
*"Ignore the Formica! The flavours and smells are pure Malaysia" at this
"café-style" venue, in Chinatown (with a glossier offshoot in Bayswater).
"If you like South East Asian food, this is the place to find it" – "made fresh
and brought quickly" – and it's "fantastic value for money".
/ www.cnrrestaurant.com; W1 10 pm, Fri & Sat 11 pm; W2 10.30 pm, Fri & Sat
11 pm, Sun 10 pm; W2 closed Tue.*

Cabotte EC2 NEW £67 **4 5 4**
48 Gresham St 020 7600 1616 10–2C
"Working equally well for a quick bite and business chat, or a long, slow afternoon of indulgence with one of London's most astonishing wine lists" – this "refined" newcomer near the Guildhall is one of the best restaurants to have hit the Square Mile in recent years, certainly of a more traditional nature. "There's a distinct Burgundian feel" to the "elegant and full flavoured" cuisine which is the counterpoint to "an exemplary wine list from the region, with very fair markups headed up by not one but two Master Sommeliers." The "delightful" atmosphere is uncharacteristic for the ECs too – "buzzy but not macho". / EC2V 7AY; www.cabotte.co.uk; @Cabotte_; 9.30 pm.

Cacio & Pepe SW1 £58 **3 2 2**
46 Churton St 020 7630 7588 2–4B
"There's bar seating upstairs and more tables in the vaulted cellar" (the former is preferred) at this year-old Italian, in a Pimlico backwater. A couple of misfires, particularly on the food front hit its ratings this year, but fans applaud its "authentic" and "friendly" style. / SW1V 2LP; www.cacioepepe.co.uk; 10.30 pm, Fri & Sat 11 pm, Sun 10 pm.

Café Below EC2 £43 **3 2 3**
St Mary-le-Bow, Cheapside 020 7329 0789 10–2B
"Shhh, don't tell anyone", but this "busy, noisy café in the crypt of St Mary-Le-Bow" (and, weather permitting, al fresco in the churchyard) is "surely one of the City's best-kept secrets". The "good food" includes "decent, reasonably priced breakfasts", "nice salads and hot dishes". / EC2 6AU; www.cafebelow.co.uk; 2.30 pm; L only.

Café del Parc N19 £45 **4 5 3**
167 Junction Rd 020 7281 5684 9–1C
"A perfect local" that "never fails to deliver" – this "charming oasis on the Archway Road" is a "terrific partnership between the chef and the head waiter" and "whizzes out" an "inventive" set menu of Spanish and North African tapas: "there's no choice, but none is needed as everything is fresh, interesting and delicious". / N19 5PZ; www.delparc.com; 10.30 pm; open D only, Wed-Sun; No Amex; booking D only.

Café du Marché EC1 £57 **3 3 5**
22 Charterhouse Sq 020 7608 1609 10–1B
It can feel "magical", especially when the pianist is playing, at this "romantic, candle-lit and cosy" old Gallic bistro, just off Charterhouse Square, which has been a "reassuringly unchanging" feature of the area since long before the environs of Smithfield became fashionable, and its "classic (if perhaps unadventurous) cuisine" is "always a great pleasure". / EC1M 6DX; www.cafedumarche.co.uk; @cafedumarche; 10 pm; closed Sat L & Sun.

Café East SE16 £24 **5 2 2**
100 Redriff Rd 020 7252 1212 12–2B
This Bermondsey canteen is "mostly full of Vietnamese" for a good reason: "the best pho in London", according to its devotees. And it's not just the pho: "everything tastes so fresh" – "and at bargain-basement prices". / SE16 7LH; www.cafeeastpho.co.uk/; @cafeeastpho; 10.30 pm, Sun 10 pm; closed Tue; No Amex; no booking.

**Cafe Football,
Westfield Stratford E20** £47 **2 2 2**
The St 020 8702 2590 14–1D
With its "football-themed menu names and the multi-screens tuned to Sky Sports", this big Stratford diner doesn't aim for gastronomy, but wins solid praise for a "cheap 'n' cheerful" night, especially in a group. / E20 1EN; www.cafe-football.com; @cafefootballuk; 10 pm.

Café in the Crypt,
St Martin in the Fields WC2 £30 2 1 4
Duncannon St 020 7766 1158 2–2C
"Huge" crypt, beneath St Martin-in-the-Fields and right on Trafalgar Square.
To some its self-service cafeteria style is too "soulless", but fans adore the
setting and that you can get "tasty snacks at really good prices" so centrally.
/ WC2N 4JJ; stmartin-in-the-fields.org/cafe-in-the-crypt; @smitf_london; 8 pm,
Wed 10.30 pm, Thu-Sat 9 pm, Sun 6 pm; L & early evening only; No Amex;
no booking.

Café Monico W1 £62 2 2 4
39-45 Shaftesbury Avenue 020 3727 6161 5–3A
"At last! A grown-up oasis of pleasure and calm amidst the hustle and bustle
of theatreland" – the Soho House group's carefully distressed, retro-vibe
brasserie is a welcome "addition to the dining desert that is Shaftesbury
Avenue". "A firm favourite for business in the heart of London", it's "great
for lunch" and "pre or post theatre", despite food that's no better than
"solid". / W1D 6LA; www.cafemonico.com; @cafemonico; midnight, Fri & Sat 1 am;
set weekday L £40 (FP).

Cafe Murano £69 3 2 3
33 St James's St, SW1 020 3371 5559 3–3C
34 Tavistock St, WC2 020 3535 7884 5–3D NEW
36 Tavistock St, WC2 020 3371 5559 5–3D
"Proper decent Italian food without needless bells and whistles – just as
you'd expect from Angela Hartnett, plus some surprisingly good (and well-
priced) wines" help win a huge fan club for her "more relaxed" Theatreland
and St James's outposts, especially amongst business-lunchers who like their
"reliable and low-key" style. The cooking "lacks the magic of the Murano
mothership" however, and the "welcoming" staff can be off the case.
/ www.cafemurano.co.uk; 11 pm, Sun 4 pm, Pastificio 9 pm, Sun closed.

Café Spice Namaste E1 £55 5 5 3
16 Prescot St 020 7488 9242 12–1A
"Every mouthful is a joy", say fans of Cyrus Todiwala's "airy and bright"
(somewhat "eccentrically decorated") City-fringe Indian, where "extremely
attentive service" is a hallmark, and where "the man himself usually does
the rounds in a clubbable fashion". The "wide variety of unusual Parsi
dishes" – "quite different food to standard Indian fare" – "are spicy rather
than just hot (though you can have that too)". / E1 8AZ; www.cafespice.co.uk;
@cafespicenamast; 10.30 pm; closed Sat L & Sun.

Caffè Caldesi W1 £61 2 3 3
118 Marylebone Ln 020 7487 0754 2–1A
This congenial "old-school Italian" in Marylebone Lane provides antipasti,
light meals and wine in the downstairs bar and full-scale dining upstairs.
Many reporters praise the "exceptional and good-value" Tuscan cuisine,
but marks were hit this year by a couple of "disappointing" reports.
/ W1U 2QF; www.caldesi.com; 10.30 pm, Sun 9.30 pm.

La Cage Imaginaire NW3 £48 2 2 3
16 Flask Walk 020 7794 6674 9–1A
This "tiny and close-packed" old spot on a super-cute Hampstead
backstreet knocks out "delightful traditional French cuisine", albeit without
pushing back any gastronomic frontiers. Service is not always on-the-ball,
but amiable. / NW3 1HE; www.la-cage-imaginaire.co.uk; 11 pm.

Cah-Chi £37 3 4 3
394 Garratt Ln, SW18 020 8946 8811 11–2B
34 Durham Rd, SW20 020 8947 1081 11–2B
"Brilliant, fresh, full-flavoured Korean food" attracts Asian expats as well
as adventurous south west London foodies to these "great value", "busy and
friendly" venues in Raynes Park and Earlsfield. "BYO is a bonus". / SW18
midnight, SW20 11 pm; SW18 & SW20 closed Mon; cash only.

The Camberwell Arms SE5 £54 4 3 3
65 Camberwell Church St   020 7358 4364   1–3C
*"They pack in the umami flavour here", with "inspired British cooking"
at this Camberwell gastro-boozer that retains the "slightly grubby", "rough-around-the-edges decor" of the traditional pub. There's an argument that
"the little sibling is finally outgunning SE1's Anchor & Hope: the food's more
interesting and original" – "and you can even get a table!". / SE5 8TR;
www.thecamberwellarms.co.uk; @camberwellarms; 10 pm; closed Mon L & Sun D.*

Cambio de Tercio SW5 £71 3 3 2
161-163 Old Brompton Rd   020 7244 8970   6–2B
*The "superb modern cooking" at Abel Lusa's Earl's Court Hispanic is of
a "quality that vies with Barrafina". There's also "an astonishingly broad and
interesting range of Spanish wines", although "the wine prices are
in nosebleed territory" (hence the "very well-heeled Eurobanker crowd").
/ SW5 0LJ; www.cambiodetercio.co.uk; @CambiodTercio; 11.15 pm, Sun 11 pm.*

Cambridge Street Kitchen SW1 £56 3 4 4
52 Cambridge St   020 3262 0501   2–4B
*"For a delightful and friendly brunch", this "busy and vibrant"
neighbourhood spot is just the ticket – a converted boozer in the side streets
of Pimlico that's a key hang-out in the locality. / SW1V 4QQ;
www.cambridgestreetcafe.co.uk; @TheCambridgeSt; 9 pm, Sat 9.30 pm, Sun 8 pm.*

Camino £50 3 3 2
3 Varnishers Yd, Regent Quarter, N1   020 7841 7330   9–3C
The Blue Fin Building, 5 Canvey St, SE1   020 3617 3169   10–4A
15 Mincing Ln, EC3   020 7841 7335   10–3D
33 Blackfriars Ln, EC4   020 7125 0930   10–2A
*"Lovely", "well-sourced" tapas is the straightforward appeal of this Spanish
group, much favoured for business lunching. Staff manage to be both
"attentive" and "unobtrusive", but branches can get "noisy" at busy times.
/ www.camino.uk.com; 11pm, EC3 Sat 10 pm, Sun 10pm; EC3 closed Sun, EC4 closed
Sat & Sun.*

Campania & Jones E2 NEW
23 Ezra St   020 7613 0015   14–2A
*Columbia Road's Campania Gastronomia has moved around the corner into
this idyllic-looking former cowshed and dairy; it's still serving up handmade
pasta, hearty Italian dishes and breakfasts to locals and market visitors
alike. / E2 7RH; campaniaandjones.com; 10.30 pm.*

Cannizaro House, Hotel du Vin SW19 £58 1 2 3
West Side, Wimbledon Common   0871 943 0345   11–2A
*With its "beautiful position on Wimbledon Common" and "stunning views
over Cannizaro Park", this Hotel du Vin venue should be a winner and
"it's hard to believe you're half an hour from central London". But eating
here is an "unpredictable experience", with too many complaints:
"the Caesar salad was neither Caesar nor salad"... "the location is so
special, but the food is so average". / SW19 4UE;
www.hotelduvin.com/locations/wimbledon; @HotelduVinBrand; 10 pm.*

Cannons N8 £35 4 4 2
4-6 Park Rd   020 8348 3018   9–1C
*"Cooked to order fish", "brilliant chips" and "helpful staff" help win a small
but very enthusiastic fan club for this Crouch End chippy; they have one
in Southgate too. / N8 8TD; www.cannons-fish.co.uk; @CannonsFish; 10 pm, Fri &
Sat 11.30 pm, Sun & Mon 9 pm.*

Cantina Laredo WC2 £58 3 2 3
10 Upper St Martin's Lane   020 7420 0630   5–3C
*Limited feedback on this heart-of-Theatreland outpost of the relatively
upmarket US Mexican chain. For fans, "the guacamole made at the table
is fab" and emblematic of the "good fun and food", but doubters "don't
understand the crowds, given bland dishes and (perhaps understandably)
under-pressure service". / WC2H 9FB; www.cantinalaredo.co.uk;
@CantinaLaredoUK; 10 pm, Fri & Sat 10.30 pm, Sun 9 pm.*

Canto Corvino E1 £65 4 3 3
21 Artillery Lane   020 7655 0390   13–2B
*"Very good quality pasta" heads the list at this "solid" modern Italian
by Spitalfields Market, which serves "a rather limited but good quality
menu" of "interesting dishes". Unusually for an Italian, it's also "great for
an informal business breakfast" or cocktail-fuelled brunch, when a
"full Italian" is on the menu. / E1 7HA; www.cantocorvino.co.uk; @cantocorvino1.*

Canton Arms SW8 £51 4 2 4
177 South Lambeth Rd   020 7582 8710   11–1D
*"Fantastic British produce from a pretty much daily changing menu" makes
this an "excellent", even "ideal" Stockwell gastroboozer (it's sibling to SE1's
stellar Anchor & Hope). "Service can be a bit slow at busy times, although
it doesn't matter for a lazy Sunday lunch". / SW8 1XP; www.cantonarms.com;
@cantonarms; 10.30 pm; closed Mon L & Sun D; No Amex; no booking.*

Capote Y Toros SW5 £50 3 4 4
157 Old Brompton Rd   020 7373 0567   6–2B
*"Close your eyes and imagine you're in Sevilla" at Cambio de Tercio's
neighbouring bar, where at times "the great atmosphere is helped
by someone strumming away on a guitar". "It's not a cheap night out for
tapas, but you get the best croquetas this side of the Pyrenees!" / SW5 0LJ;
www.cambiodetercio.co.uk; @CambiodTercio; 11.30 pm; D only, closed Mon & Sun;
booking D only.*

Capricci SE1 £55 4 4 3
NEO Bankside Unit C South, 72 Holland St   020 7021 0703   10–3B
*"Perfect for coffee or lunch while visiting Tate Modern" – a "tiny space"
within an upscale Italian food store nearby, offering "a great choice
of wines" and small but good (if sometimes expensive) menu. / SE1 9NX;
www.capricciforlondon.co.uk; 10.30 pm, Fri & Sat 11 pm.*

Le Caprice SW1 £81 2 4 4
20 Arlington St   020 7629 2239   3–4C
*"A very special place" for many of the most blasé of Londoners – this "slick
oasis of sophistication" near The Ritz owes its enduring success to the
"elegance of the interior with its superb lighting", "the comfort of the piano
playing", and staff under Jesus Adorno who "make you feel like a million
dollars (even if you're far from it)". "The food is hardly the point here" and
never really has been, but "prices have gone up under Richard Caring"
making what has always seemed "well executed and unfussy dishes" now
seem "fairly ordinary and expensive for what they are". / SW1A 1RJ;
www.le-caprice.co.uk; @CapriceHoldings; 11.30 pm, Sun 10.30 pm; May need 6+ to
book; set weekday L £51 (FP).*

Caraffini SW1 £61 3 5 3
61-63 Lower Sloane St   020 7259 0235   6–2D
*"You always leave feeling you have been well looked after", after a visit
to this veteran trattoria near Sloane Square, whose "old school, wonderfully
welcoming staff remember everyone". The food is "reliable (if unambitious)"
and even if "the tables are rather close to each other", "there always seems
to be a happy crowd". "Nice terrace in summer". / SW1W 8DH;
www.caraffini.co.uk; 11 pm; closed Sun.*

Caravaggio EC3   £62   **3** 2 2
107-112 Leadenhall St   020 7626 6206   10–2D
"The food doesn't let you down, even if it's a little pricey" at this "smart"
City Italian, whose location right by Leadenhall Market helps earn it strong
nominations "for a business lunch". On the downside, the atmosphere can
seem "slightly dull" and an unusual number of service glitches were
reported this year. / EC3A 4DP; www.etruscarestaurants.com; 10 pm; closed
Sat & Sun.

Caravan   £57   **3** **3** **4**
1 Granary Sq, N1   020 7101 7661   9–3C
30 Great Guildford St, SE1   020 7101 1190   10–4B
11-13 Exmouth Mkt, EC1   020 7833 8115   10–1A
Bloomberg Arcade, Queen Victoria St, EC2   no tel   10–2C **NEW**
"London's most interesting brunch dishes" – "light pastries and wholesome
porridge to unusual spicy and savoury options" (not to mention "fabulous
speciality coffees") – help drive a "vibrant" buzz at these "funky" hang-outs,
with the "bustling industrial-style" Granary Square outlet vying for top
popularity with the smaller Exmouth Market original (Bankside has yet
to make many waves; and there's also a new City branch is opening
in October 2017, in the new 'Bloomberg Arcade'). The eclectic dishes can
seem too "keen to be innovative at the expense of polish" though,
or just plain "weird". / www.caravanonexmouth.co.uk; 10.30 pm,
Sun 8 pm; closed Sun.

Carob Tree NW5   £36   **3** **4** **3**
15 Highgate Rd   020 7267 9880   9–1B
"Grilled fish prepared on charcoal" is the highpoint of the "reliable,
sometimes exceptional" Greek fare at this Dartmouth Park local, where
"they treat everyone entering as their favourite customer". Top Tip –
"Fish dish of the day is pricey, but will feed two or three and is usually very
well cooked". / NW5 1QX; www.carobtree.in; 10.30 pm, Sun 9 pm; closed Mon;
No Amex.

Carousel W1   £57   **5** **4** **4**
71 Blandford St   020 7487 5564   3–1A
An "inspiring" programme of guest chefs from around the world (who take
over the kitchen for two weeks at a time) makes for some "superb" meals
at this unique Marylebone merry-go-round – a "brilliant" and "laudable
concept" ("you eat some amazing food you wouldn't have come across
otherwise"). Be prepared to be "squashed at sharing tables" amid
"high noise levels". / W1U 8AB; www.carousel-london.com; @Carousel_LDN;
one seating only, at 7 pm; closed Mon L & Sun L.

Cartel SW11 **NEW**   £39
517-519 Battersea Park Rd   020 8610 9761   11–1C
You can sample 100 different Mezcals in the dedicated Mezcaleria room
of this new Battersea Mexican, serving quesadillas and tacos to accompany
the wide range of latino spirits. We're not sure whether they ran the name
past the good taste committee first... / SW11 3BN; cartelbattersea.co.uk;
@cartelbattersea.

Casa Brindisa SW7   £49   2 2 2
7-9 Exhibition Rd   020 7590 0008   6–2C
For foodies, the Brindisa name casts a halo around this South Kensington
café (with large outside terrace) and they salute its "high-quality fresh
tapas". A more realistic view perhaps is that the food here is "not earth-
shattering, but fine" – "ideal before/after a visit to the Royal Albert Hall
or one of the museums on Exhibition Road". / SW7 2HE;
www.brindisatapaskitchens.com/casa-brindisa; @TapasKitchens; 11 pm, Sun 10 pm;
booking max 8 may apply.

Casa Cruz W11 — £80 — 2 3 4
123 Clarendon Rd   020 3321 5400   7–2A
"Gaucho-size portions" of "top-quality beef" ("there's even a kilo steak
on the menu") and "extremely stylish decor" make Juan Santa Cruz's lavish
Argentinian pub conversion on the edge of Notting Hill "a brilliant night
out"… "if you can get a table". But even fans concede it is "extremely
expensive" – "at £36 for a main course this is a place to go when someone
else is paying". / W11 4JG; www.casacruz.london; @CasaCruzrest; 12.30 am,
Sun 5 pm; closed Mon.

Casita Andina W1 — £37 — 4 3 4
31 Great Windmill St   020 3327 9464   4–3D
"Unusual, flavoursome small plates" with big Latino flavours win consistently
high ratings for Martin Morales's year-old 'picantería' in Soho – his fourth
opening in the capital. / W1F 9UE; www.andinalondon.com/casita; @CasitaAndina.

Casse-Croute SE1 — £54 — 4 3 4
109 Bermondsey St   020 7407 2140   10–4D
"Think of the film 'Amélie'", and you won't be a million miles off this
"cramped", "more-French-than-France" bistro in Bermondsey (where
"you leave expecting to see the Eiffel Tower, but instead it's The Shard").
"On the blackboard, a selection of three starters, mains and desserts" –
"the simplicity of choice means it's modern cuisine grand-mère is always
fresh and well-prepared". / SE1 3XB; www.cassecroute.co.uk; @CasseCroute109;
10 pm, Sun 4 pm; closed Sun D.

Catford Constitutional Club SE6 — £38 — 3 4 4
Catford Broadway   020 8613 7188   1–4D
"This semi-derelict former Conservative Club has been converted into
a popular pub with a garden (of sorts) by Antic". The food's good and
"the local cool cats are loving it". / SE6 4SP; catfordconstitutionalclub.com;
@CatfordCClub; 10 pm.

Cau — £54 — 2 2 2
10-12 Royal Pde, SE3   020 8318 4200   1–4D
33 High St, SW19   020 8318 4200   11–2B
1 Commodity Quay, E1   020 7702 0341   10–3D
"Gaucho's little brother chain" offers a stripped down version of the main
brand, featuring "reasonably priced steaks" and burgers plus an "interesting
range of other Argentinian-derived dishes" and "a good choice of South
American wines". Ratings overall are middling however, reflecting a feeling
in some quarters that the offer is "pleasant but lacking something". / 11 pm,
Sun 10 pm.

Caxton Grill SW1 — £75 — 2 3 3
2 Caxton St   020 7227 7773   2–4C
This hotel dining room, tucked away in Westminster, is still readjusting
to Adam Handling's departure in May 2016 and reports tend to include
highs and lows. It's a characterful space however, that's worth remembering.
/ SW1H 0QW; www.caxtongrill.co.uk; 10.30 pm.

Cây Tre — £43 — 3 3 2
42-43 Dean St, W1   020 7317 9118   5–2A
301 Old St, EC1   020 7729 8662   13–1B
"Brilliant value and authentic Vietnamese" venues in Soho and Shoreditch.
The interiors might be "inauspicious", but staff are "helpful" and the food
is "warming and packed with taste". / www.vietnamesekitchen.co.uk; 11 pm,
Fri & Sat 11.30 pm, Sun 10.30 pm; booking: min 8.

Cecconi's W1   £78   2 2 **3**
5a Burlington Gdns   020 7434 1500   4–4A
Soho House's "vibrant" all-day Venetian-style brasserie near Old Bond Street makes "a great place to relax, take your time, and watch the world go by" and is well liked – except by a few who find it "snotty" and "arrogant" – for its "professional and fun" approach. Even many fans think its food ("pleasant in a simple sort of way") is "expensive", but this place is a particular favourite "for an upmarket business breakfast". / W1S 3EP; www.cecconis.co.uk; @SohoHouse; 11.30 pm, Sun 10.30 pm.

The Cedar   £43   **3 3 3**
65 Fernhead Rd, W9   020 8964 2011   1–2B
202 West End Lane, NW6   020 3602 0862   1–1B
81 Boundary Rd, NW8   020 3204 0030   9–3A
"The variety of Lebanese dishes from mezzes to mains is one of the best in town" (including Lebanese-style breakfasts and pizza) at these agreeable, brick-walled ventures in Hampstead, Maida Vale and St John's Wood.

Céleste,
The Lanesborough SW1   £107   2 **3** 5
Hyde Park Corner   020 7259 5599   2–3A
In over 25 years of its existence, the incredibly "impressive" dining room of this ultra-swanky Hyde Park Corner hotel has never really hit a full stride, and has been through a succession of incarnations. The management of Paris's Le Bristol are the latest to have a go, and their version is doing better than most to date, with "elegant looks presaging a traditional style of service", and cuisine that "puts an emphasis on British ingredients and French technique". Service is "expert" – perhaps a little "over-attentive" – and other than that it's "generally expensive" most reports are upbeat. Top Tip – "set menus are good value, if with limited choice". / SW1X 7TA; www.lanesborough.com/eng/restaurant-bars/celeste; @TheLanesborough; 10.30 pm; set weekday L £71 (FP).

Cepages W2   £50   **3 3 3**
69 Westbourne Park Rd   020 3602 8890   7–1B
"Small, noisy (the only drawback), Bayswater bistro with a loyal (partly French) customer-base", of note for its "exceptional wine list, with many fine wines sourced directly from small growers", and backed up by some "consistently accomplished, small, tapas-type dishes". "The place is, unsurprisingly, always full". / W2 5QH; www.cepages.co.uk; @cepagesWPR; 11 pm, Sun 10 pm.

Ceru SW7 NEW   £39   **4 3** 2
7-9 Bute St   020 3195 3001   6–2C
"Excellent Levantine cuisine at very reasonable prices" win consistent praise for this middle eastern newcomer. Some fans "are puzzled at by the decor choices" but for a "cheap and cheerful" option "convenient to South Kensington and the museums" it fits the bill. / SW7 3EY; www.cerurestaurants.com; @cerulondon; 11 pm, Sun 10 pm.

Ceviche   £55   **4 3 3**
17 Frith St, W1   020 7292 2040   5–2A
Alexandra Trust, Baldwin St, EC1   020 3327 9463   13–1A
"Amazing, seriously tasty dishes, with lots of fresh tastes", and washed down with "perfect Pisco sours" instill high esteem for these "buzzy" (if "rather noisy") Latino ventures, in Soho and near Old Street. / www.cevicheuk.com; W1D 11.30 pm, Sun 10.15 pm, EC1V 10.45 pm, Fri & Sat 11.30 pm, Sun 9.30 pm.

Chai Thali NW1 NEW   £33   3 3 4
Centro 3, 19 Mandela St   020 7383 2030   9–3C
"A fun place to have a gathering" with "non-clichéd, fresh-tasting Indian dishes" – a big, "attractive" pan-Indian street food and bar operation, "tucked away" in a new development near Mornington Crescent. / NW1 0DU; chaithali.com; @ChaiThaliCamden.

Chakra W8   £57   3 3 3
33c Holland St   020 7229 2115   7–2B
"Beautiful cooking with a high-level modern twist" wins consistent praise for this comfortable Indian, "in a pretty locale" near High Street Ken tube – not at all a standard curry house. / W8 4LX; www.chakralondon.com; @ChakraLondon; 11 pm, Sun 10.30 pm.

Champor-Champor SE1   £54   4 4 4
62 Weston St   020 7403 4600   10–4C
Colourful, eclectic decor and distinctive "fresh tasting" Thai-Malay cuisine (the name means 'mix and match') still win an enthusiastic, if small fanclub for this "old-favourite, little oasis, tucked away in an unassuming location", near the Shard. / SE1 3QJ; www.champor-champor.com; @ChamporChampor; 10 pm; D only.

Charlotte's   £52   3 4 3
6 Turnham Green Ter, W4   020 8742 3590   8–2A
"An excellent cocktail bar" with "a lovely gin selection" helps set a "friendly and homely" tone at the W4 Charlotte's – a "buzzy bistro and bar" near Turnham Green Tube, whose "tasty" fare suits an "informal" get-together. In W5, in Ealing's new Dickens Yard development, its younger sibling is also "a good local venue" popular with business-lunchers and families at weekends. (Both are spin-offs from Charlotte's Place, also in W5 – see also). / www.charlottes.co.uk; W4 midnight, Sun 11 pm, W53 10 pm, W5 11.30 pm.

Charlotte's Place W5   £52   3 3 4
16 St Matthew's Rd   020 8567 7541   1–3A
"You can always find something delicious to enjoy" at Alex Wrethman's "pleasantly quiet" long-established (1984) fixture by Ealing Common – acclaimed by its local fanclub as "the best restaurant in Ealing by a long way" (although dishes which are "amazing and creative" to some tastes are a little "complicated" to others). / W5 3JT; www.charlottes.co.uk; @CharlottesW5; 10.30 pm, Fri & Sat 11 pm, Sun 9 pm; booking max 10 may apply.

Chelsea Cellar SW10 NEW   £40   4 4 3
9 Park Walk   020 7351 4933   6–3B
"Charming basement newcomer", in a side street near the Chelsea & Westminster hospital, which "features Pugliese cooking (delicious burrata, antipasti, and pasta) and an excellent, wide selection of interesting Pugliese wines" (250 bins). "It's not expensive, service is engaging" and "the room's reasonably quiet even when full". / SW10 0AJ; www.thechelseacellar.co.uk; midnight.

Chettinad W1   £40   4 3 3
16 Percy St   020 3556 1229   2–1C
"Proper south Indian fare" ("yummy" Tamil specialities including dosas and dishes served on fresh banana leaves) win praise for this busy venue in Fitzrovia. / W1T 1DT; www.chettinadrestaurant.com; @chettinadlondon; 11 pm, Sun 10 pm; No Amex.

Cheyne Walk Brasserie SW3 £74 2 2 3
50 Cheyne Walk   020 7376 8787   6–3C
Beautiful-people Chelsea brasserie, whose chic interior is arranged around
the central open wood fire grill. As ever, prices can seem "rather dear",
but the high quality BBQ dishes are consistently well-rated. / SW3 5LR;
www.cheynewalkbrasserie.com; @CheyneWalkBrass; 10.30 pm, Sun 9.30 pm; closed
Mon L.

Chez Abir W14 £39 3 3 2
34 Blythe Rd   020 7603 3241   8–1D
"High quality, reliable Lebanese food" makes it worth truffling out this
"cheap 'n' cheerful" backstreet café behind Olympia (that some still
remember as Chez Marcelle… she's retired.) / W14 OHA; www.chezabir.co.uk;
11 pm; closed Mon.

CHEZ BRUCE SW17 £86 5 5 4
2 Bellevue Rd   020 8672 0114   11–2C
"So professional, but without any of the usual nonsense!" – Bruce Poole's
"wonderful neighbourhood restaurant" by Wandsworth Common is, for the
13th year in a row, the survey's No. 1 favourite destination. It's by no means
a flash place – "the understated atmosphere is of a comfortable local" –
but for legions of Londoners it provides "perfection where it counts",
not least the "immaculate service", and "inspiring food": dishes are "fine,
but not fussy", and with "enough innovation to surprise you each time"
thanks to their "exceptional, and deft flavour combinations". "AND, it's
affordable! For once you don't need a second mortgage…" / SW17 7EG;
www.chezbruce.co.uk; @ChezBruce; 10 pm, Fri & Sat 10.30 pm, Sun 9 pm;
set weekday L £57 (FP), set Sun L £63 (FP).

Chicama SW10 £59 2 2 3
383 King's Rd   020 3874 2000   6–3C
"Outstanding fish comes at a cost in this Peruvian newcomer" in Chelsea
(from the team behind Marylebone's Pachamama) – an enjoyably "vibrant"
(if "crowded and noisy") place. The approach doesn't please everyone
though: "dishes arrived in any order, which might suit the kitchen,
but resulted in some not-so-good flavour combinations". / SW10 0LP;
www.chicamalondon.com; @chicamalondon.

Chick 'n' Sours £42 3 3 3
1 Earlham St, WC2   020 3198 4814   5–2B
390 Kingsland Rd, E8   020 3620 8728   14–2D
"Everything you could wish for in a crunchy-fried, tender, perfectly cooked
chicken" gets a big thumbs up for this "really fun" Dalston joint (now with
a Covent Garden branch); "accoutrements to die for" too ("surprisingly,
the outstanding dish didn't involve chicken – the amazing Sichuan aubergine
stole the show").

Chicken Shop £34 3 3 3
199-206 High Holborn, WC1   020 7661 3040   2–1D
5 Oak Rd, W5   020 3859 1120   1–3A NEW
274-276 Holloway Rd, N7   020 3841 7787   9–2D
46 The Broadway, N8   020 3757 4848   9–1C NEW
79 Highgate Rd, NW5   020 3310 2020   9–1B
128 Allitsen Rd, NW8   020 3757 4849   9–3A
7a Chestnut Grove, SW12   020 8102 9300   11–2C
141 Tooting High St, SW17   020 8767 5200   11–2B
9 Brighton Terrace, SW9   020 3859 1130   11–2D NEW
27a Mile End Rd, E1   020 3310 2010   13–2D
Arguably they're just "a fancy version of Nandos", but Soho House's
"deliciously moreish and quite addictive" pit stops "do one thing, and do
it well": "succulent moist chicken, piping hot salty chips, melt in your mouth
corn on the cob and the grand finale, the spongy light apple pie". / Mon-Thu
11 pm, Fri & Sat midnight, Sun 10-10.30 pm; WC1V closed Sun.

Chik'n W1 NEW £18
134 Baker St   020 7935 6648   2–1A
*From the people who brought us Chick 'n' Sours, a new idea along similar,
but pared down lines – the first branch appeared in Baker Street in July
2017. It's very fast food style: you grab and go. / W1U 6SH; www.chikn.com;
@lovechikn; 11.30 pm; no booking.*

Chilli Cool WC1 £34   5 2 1
15 Leigh St   020 7383 3135   2–1D
*"Wonderfully spicy" Sichuan cooking is the reason to discover this "brilliant
find in Bloomsbury". Forget the "plain" surroundings and the "hit-and-miss
service": "you can put up with all that to eat such fantastic dishes!"
/ WC1H 9EW; www.chillicool.co.uk; 10.15 pm; No Amex.*

The Chiltern Firehouse W1 £96   1 1 3
1 Chiltern St   020 7073 7676   2–1A
*"If you're not a C-Z lister, don't go" to this Marylebone haunt –
"a stunningly decorated old firehouse" where only "people watching is top
of the menu". True, there is a minority of fans who applaud its "imaginative
food", but even they can find it "incredibly overpriced" and there are
nowadays far too many sceptics for whom it's a bad case of "Emperor's
New Clothes", providing "very odd food combinations" and "staff who
wander around looking fabulous, but not attending on customers".
/ W1U 7PA; www.chilternfirehouse.com; 10.30 pm.*

Chin Chin Club W1 NEW
54 Greek St   no tel   5–2A
*Camden Town's 'instant' ice cream bar (made on-the-spot with nitrogen and
seasonal, sometimes bonkers, ingredients) arrived in Soho in summer 2017,
with this white marble and gold outlet. The options here are similarly
'out there', but some flavours are pre-made rather than, as at the original,
zapped on the spot. / W1D 3DS; www.chinchinicecream.com; @chinchinicecream;
9 pm, Fri & Sat 10 pm.*

China Tang, Dorchester Hotel W1 £84   4 3 3
53 Park Ln   020 7629 9988   3–3A
*The "classy cocktail bar" is a big highlight of Sir David Tang's
(RIP) recreation of '30s Shanghai in the basement of a Mayfair hotel, whose
main dining room surprisingly can "lack atmosphere", particularly at lunch.
The food (with Peking Duck the speciality) has been lacklustre over the
years, but was very highly rated in this year's survey. / W1K 1QA;
www.chinatanglondon.co.uk; @ChinaTangLondon; 11.45 pm.*

The Chipping Forecast W11 £42   3 3 3
29 All Saints Rd   020 7460 2745   7–1B
*"The fish is fab" at this new Notting Hill take on the trad fish 'n' chip shop,
using sustainable fish landed in Cornwall less than 48 hours earlier. Having
started out as a street stall in Soho's Berwick Street Market, it has a "great
supper club feel". "Friendly, quirky and bound to become stupidly expensive,
so get there now while it's fresh and fun!" Cute garden too. / W11 1HE;
www.chippingforecast.com; @CForecast; 9.30 pm, Fri & Sat 10 pm, Sun 9pm; closed
Mon; no booking.*

Chisou £56   4 3 2
4 Princes St, W1   020 7629 3931   4–1A
31 Beauchamp Pl, SW3   020 3155 0005   6–1D
*"Excellent sushi, sashimi and tempura" are the stars of the show at this
"long-established and quite smart – though not unduly expensive – Mayfair
Japanese" (with an offshoot near Harrods), which boasts a "great sake list,
too". The "quiet" original is "a civilised retreat from the fray of Regent
Street", and its chichily-located Knightsbridge branch is in a similar vein.
/ www.chisourestaurant.com; Mon-Sat 10.30 pm, Sun 9.30 pm.*

Chiswell Street Dining Rooms EC1 £63 2 2 2
56 Chiswell St   020 7614 0177   13–2A
*"Usefully placed for City meetings", this outfit near the Barbican
is consistently well-rated "reasonably priced" and fairly "convivial",
"if perhaps with tables a little close together". / EC1Y 4SA;
www.chiswellstreetdining.com; @chiswelldining; 11 pm; closed Sat & Sun; set pre
theatre £42 (FP).*

Chit Chaat Chai SW18 £45 4 3 2
356 Old York Rd   020 8480 2364   11–2B
*"Extremely authentic Indian street food bites" served "in funky
surroundings" draws fans, young and old, to this local "gem",
near Wandsworth Town station. / SW18 1SS; chitchaatchai.com;
@ChitChaatChai; 10 pm, Sun 9 pm.*

Chotto Matte W1 £60 4 3 5
11-13 Frith St   020 7042 7171   5–2A
*"The surprising fusion of different cuisines works very well" at this
impressively "buzzy" and "clubby" Japanese-Peruvian haunt in Soho, which
– aided by "quirky decor" and "excellent Peruvian-styled cocktails" –
"somehow really works", even if "the final bill is a bit heavy". / W1D 4RB;
www.chotto-matte.com; @ChottoMatteSoho; 1 am, Sun 11 pm; set pre theatre
£32 (FP).*

Chriskitch £59 4 3 3
7 Tetherdown, N10   020 8411 0051   1–1C
5 Hoxton Market, N1   020 7033 6666   13–1B
*The "intense and interesting flavours" of Christian Honor's "inventive"
cuisine have won a host of admirers for his two-year-old café in a converted
Muswell Hill front room, and his follow-up open-kitchen venture in Hoxton:
"it's a funky experience but someone here knows how to cook" and
"the welcome is very warm". "Fabulous cakes, too". / N10 6 pm, Sat-Mon
5 pm; N1 10.30pm; N1 closed L and Sun & Mon; N10 min 3 people.*

Christopher's WC2 £78 2 2 3
18 Wellington St   020 7240 4222   5–3D
*"Discreet, classy, American (so 1/3rd like Trump)" – this stalwart 25-year-
old occupies a huge and particularly beautiful Covent Garden townhouse.
The food on the surf 'n' turf-dominated menu has always divided views –
to fans "fabulous", to foes "average" and "overpriced". Top Tips –
good brunch and downstairs bar. / WC2E 7DD; www.christophersgrill.com;
@christopherswc2; May need 6+ to book; set weekday L & pre-theatre £45 (FP).*

Chucs £82 3 3 3
30b Dover St, W1   020 3763 2013   3–3C
226 Westbourne Grove, W11   020 7243 9136   7–1B
*Owned by an Italian luxury brand of 'resort' wear, these "cozy and calm"
cafés adjoining shops in Mayfair and Chelsea aim to inspire the yachtie life
of the Riviera in the 1960s. There's "excellent service and solid food",
although some reporters favour breakfast over lunch. / W1 11.30 pm,
Sat midnight, Sun 4.30 pm; W11 11 pm, Sun 10 pm; W1 closed Sun D.*

Churchill Arms W8 £35 3 2 5
119 Kensington Church St   020 7792 1246   7–2B
*"Unbeatable value for a very good nosh-up" is to be had at this "quirky-but-
real pub", just off Notting Hill Gate, whose "butterfly-themed conservatory"
makes a feature of "great, simple Thai food", and provides "a good deal in a
normally expensive area". "Service can be brusque, but the place is so busy
it's hard to see how it could be otherwise". / W8 7LN;
www.churchillarmskensington.co.uk; @ChurchilArmsW8; 10 pm, Sun 9.30 pm.*

Chutney Mary SW1 £84 4 4 4
73 St James's St   020 7629 6688   3–4D
*In its "lavish and beautifully decorated" St James's home for over two years
now, this "very glam" relocated stalwart (which for over two decades was
on the fringe of Chelsea) remains one of London's foremost 'posh' Indians,
serving "brilliantly spiced" contemporary cuisine, plus "fantastic cocktails"
("the Pukka bar is great for a clandestine drink"). / SW1A 1PH;
www.chutneymary.com; @thechutneymary; 10.30 pm; closed Sat L & Sun; booking
max 4 may apply; set weekday L £55 (FP), set brunch £57 (FP).*

Chutneys NW1 £27 3 2 2
124 Drummond St   020 7388 0604   9–4C
*"A Mecca for veggie Indian cuisine near Euston" ("especially the ridiculously
cheap Sunday night and weekday lunchtime buffet") – "for the money,
this place just can't be beaten". "The decor upstairs is acceptable, less so
the slightly scruffy downstairs". / NW1 2PA; www.chutneyseuston.co.uk; 11 pm;
No Amex; May need 5+ to book.*

Ciao Bella WC1 £45 2 3 4
86-90 Lamb's Conduit St   020 7242 4119   2–1D
*"The perfect trat'" is a typically affectionate tribute to this "merry"
Bloomsbury Italian, where "the food is not spectacular" but "unbelievably
good value" and served in "an ambience reminiscent of 1960s Fellini and
Antonioni films". "It was my staple when I was poor and first moved
to London, then I got marginally richer and moved on, but I recently went
back and was reminded how great it is". / WC1N 3LZ;
www.ciaobellarestaurant.co.uk; @CiaobellaLondon; 11.30 pm, Sun 10.30 pm.*

Cibo W14 £58 4 5 3
3 Russell Gdns   020 7371 6271   8–1D
*"Lovely, authentic cuisine" ("pasta as it should be" and other "great, simple
dishes") and "an owner who goes out of his way to make sure you have
a good time" is the recipe for longevity at this "slightly cramped" Italian
stalwart on a side street near Olympia (a favourite of the late Michael
Winner). Fans feel "it deserves to be busier". / W14 8EZ;
www.ciborestaurant.net; 10.30 pm; closed Sat L & Sun D.*

Cigala WC1 £48 3 3 3
54 Lamb's Conduit St   020 7405 1717   2–1D
*"Every neighbourhood should be blessed with somewhere as friendly and
reliable as this", say happy regulars of this long-serving Bloomsbury
Spaniard. Its "classic tapas and Iberian gastronomy" make it "the sort
of place where you get ideas to go home and try yourself". On the negative
side, "the surroundings are ordinary". / WC1N 3LW; www.cigala.co.uk; 10.45 pm,
Sun 9.45 pm.*

Cigalon WC2 £58 3 4 4
115 Chancery Lane   020 7242 8373   2–2D
*"In an area not overstocked with restaurants", this "airy and charming"
fixture on Chancery Lane (built as a book auction room, and with
a "huge rooflight, which lets in lots of sunshine at lunchtime") really stands
out with its "skilful service", and "excellent, interesting Provençal cuisine"
(from the team behind Club Gascon). / WC2A 1PP; www.cigalon.co.uk;
@cigalon_london; 10 pm; closed Sat & Sun.*

Cinnamon Bazaar WC2 NEW £40 2 3 3
28 Maiden Lane   020 7395 1400   5–4D
*The latest Cinnamon Club spin-off occupies the "quirky and appealing", two-
floor Covent Garden site that was formerly La Perla (RIP). But while fans
praise its "exciting and tasty fusion food", critics say "it was well-cooked but
bordering on bland – they need to up the heat/spice!" / WC2E 7NA;
www.cinnamon-bazaar.com; @Cinnamon_Bazaar.*

THE CINNAMON CLUB SW1 £84 3️⃣3️⃣4️⃣
Old Westminster Library, Great Smith St 020 7222 2555 2–4C
Vivek Singh's "refined cuisine" served in the "magnificent" (slightly "cavernous") setting of the old Westminster Public Library still creates a winning formula for London's grandest nouvelle Indian, which is nowadays one of the Top-40 most-mentioned restaurants in town. If it were not quite so "expensive", its ratings would reach even loftier heights. / SW1P 3BU; www.cinnamonclub.com; @cinnamonclub; 10.30 pm; closed Sun; No trainers; booking max 14 may apply; set weekday L £61 (FP); SRA-Food Made Good – 2 stars.

Cinnamon Kitchen EC2 £59 4️⃣3️⃣3️⃣
9 Devonshire Sq 020 7626 5000 10–2D
"Excellent Indian food that's reasonably priced for the City" is the mainstay of the Cinnamon Club's easterly cousin – "a most enjoyable" destination in an attractive, large covered atrium near Liverpool Street. / EC2M 4YL; www.cinnamon-kitchen.com; @cinnamonkitchen; 10.45 pm; closed Sat L & Sun.

Cinnamon Soho W1 £46 3️⃣2️⃣2️⃣
5 Kingly St 020 7437 1664 4–2B
The casual operation, behind Regent Street, "may not be up there with the Cinnamon Club", but "it has an interesting menu of well-cooked Indian food" and "is really affordable". / W1B 5PE; www.cinnamon-kitchen.com/soho-home; @cinnamonsoho; 11 pm, Sun 4.30 pm; closed Sun D.

City Barge W4 £51 3️⃣2️⃣3️⃣
27 Strand-on-the-Green 020 8994 2148 1–3A
This is "a great little bistro-pub" in a "lovely spot on the river" at Strand-on-the-Green, Chiswick, and where "the food is really rather good". / W4 3PH; www.citybargechiswick.com; @citybargew4; 11 pm, Fri & Sat midnight, Sun 10.30 pm.

City Càphê EC2 £18 3️⃣3️⃣2️⃣
17 Ironmonger St no tel 10–2C
Limited but enthusiastic reports on this popular Vietnamese pit stop near Bank – you may have to queue at lunch. / EC2V 8EY; www.citycaphe.com; 4.30pm; L only, closed Sat & Sun; no booking.

City Social EC2 £86 2️⃣3️⃣5️⃣
Tower 42 25 Old Broad St 020 7877 7703 10–2C
"You do pay for the vista", but Jason Atherton's 24th floor perch, in the City's Tower 42 boasts "thrilling views" and "plenty of wow factor", hence it's often "first choice for a business lunch" ("clients love it!"). "The food won't take your breath away, but you won't complain either". / EC2N 1HQ; www.citysociallondon.com; @CitySocial_T42; 10.30 pm; closed Sat & Sun; booking max 4 may apply.

Clarette W1 NEW £81
44 Blandford St 020 3019 7750 3–1A
Set in a chicly revamped Tudorbethan pub, this plush new Marylebone wine bar has an impressive pedigree – for example, one of the owners is Alexandra Petit-Mentzelopoulos, daughter of Corinne Mentzelopoulos, who owns Château Margaux! The focus is on the wines (with a whole page of the list dedicated to Margaux), and to offset this there is a menu of Mediterranean small plates. / W1U 7HS; www.clarettelondon.com; @ClaretteLondon; set weekday L £51 (FP).

Clarke's W8 £71 554
124 Kensington Church St   020 7221 9225   7–2B
"Although a classic of the neighbourhood, it doesn't rest on its laurels" and "how standards have stayed so high here over all these years is a testament to the omnipresent and charming Sally Clarke". "Superb ingredients are cooked with a light touch", in the Californian style that first inspired her, while "professional-without-hovering" service is "absolutely spot on". "If you are under thirty, the only downside is that it can be full of 'old timers'". / W8 4BH; www.sallyclarke.com; @SallyClarkeLtd; 10 pm; closed Sun; booking max 14 may apply.

Claude's Kitchen,
Amuse Bouche SW6 £58 444
51 Parsons Green Lane   020 7371 8517   11–1B
Claude Compton's "quirky neighbourhood gem", upstairs from the "heaving" Amuse Bouche fizz bar by Parsons Green station, serves "interesting but tasty food in generous portions". "The cooking is confident and the service charming" – "I went home feeling inspired and satisfied". / SW6 4JA; www.amusebouchelondon.com/claudes-kitchen; @AmuseBoucheLDN; 11 pm; D only, closed Sun.

Clerkenwell Cafe £38 344
80a Mortimer St, W1   020 7253 5754   10–1A
St Christopher's Place, W1   020 7253 5754   3–1A
27 Clerkenwell Rd, EC1   020 7253 5754   10–1A
60a Holborn Viaduct, EC1   no tel   10–2A
Fans hail "by far the best coffee in town" at this small chain with its own roastery – "don't let the lack of comfort put you off!". Along with a "range of different brews to try", they also serve snacks and pastries, while the Clerkenwell original goes a step further, with a full brunch and lunch menu. / workshopcoffee.com/; EC1M 6 pm, Tue-Fri 7 pm; W1U & W1W 7 pm, Sat & Sun 6 pm; EC1A 6 pm; EC1 closed Sat & Sun; no bookings.

The Clifton NW8 NEW
96 Clifton Hill   020 7625 5010   9–3A
This gorgeous, tucked-away St John's Wood pub (famously where Edward VII used to hook up with Lillie Langtry) has re-opened after three years, having been rescued from the developers by brothers Ben and Ed Robson (ex Boopshi's). The menu doesn't attempt culinary fireworks, but that's never been the point of a visit here. / NW8 0JT; www.thecliftonnw8.com; @thecliftonnw8.

Clipstone W1 £60 443
5 Clipstone St   020 7637 0871   2–1B
"An equally fantastic experience as at Portland (same team)", say the many fans of this Fitzrovia newcomer, lauding its "very inventive, beautifully prepared small plates from the open kitchen" and "really outstanding wine list (full of remarkable, little known options)", all delivered by "a super-friendly and attentive young team". The "buzzy" setting is too "austere" for some tastes however, and there is a minority who feel that "although all the major food critics have eulogised, the cuisine is not quite as cosmic as has been suggested, albeit good". / W1W 6BB; www.clipstonerestaurant.co.uk; @clipstonerestaurant; 11 pm.

CLOS MAGGIORE WC2 £77 **3** **4** **5**
33 King St   020 7379 9696   5–3C
"You feel that love is in the air!" at this *"very special"* destination (yet again
the survey's No. 1 choice for a romantic occasion), especially in *"the inner
sanctum"* – *"the lovely glass-roofed courtyard at the back, hung with
blossom, a roof that opens in fine weather, and with an open fire for chilly
nights"*. *"Amidst the dross of Covent Garden"*, not only is it *"an oasis
of calm"*, but staff are *"charming"* and *"professional"*, the French-inspired
cuisine is *"very enjoyable"* and the *"daunting"* wine bible – one of London's
most extensive lists – is *"really something else"*. *"Securing one of the
courtyard seats is a challenge"*, but *"the experience in the somewhat
blander upstairs is still memorable"*. / WC2E 8JD; www.closmaggiore.com;
@closmaggiorewc2; 11 pm, Sun 10 pm; set pre theatre £55 (FP).

THE CLOVE CLUB EC1 £108 **5** **4** **4**
Shoreditch Town Hall, 380 Old St   020 7729 6496   13–1B
*Isaac McHale's temple to "fine dining Shoreditch-style" sits in London's
culinary Top-5 nowadays, and his "theatrically presented" 5-course and 10-
course menus offer "an absolute balance between sophistication, simplicity,
and creativity". The space itself within the fine old town hall is "a bit urban-
ascetic" (no table cloths, of course), but is "not too archly hipster" and the
"relaxed yet professional service" creates an appropriately "chilled out" yet
"truly memorable" experience. Very progressively, there's a "brilliant non-
alcoholic drink match" alongside the more conventional wine pairings.
/ EC1V 9LT; www.thecloveclub.com; @thecloveclub; 9.30 pm; closed Mon L & Sun.*

Club Gascon EC1 £98
57 West Smithfield   020 7600 6144   10–2B
"Special", *"extremely elaborate"* Gascon cuisine (*"the dish arrives and looks
like a Matisse"*) – famously featuring oodles of foie gras – has carved
a huge name for Pascal Aussignac and Vincent Labyrie's ambitious 20-year-
old, in a fine Smithfield corner site (a former Lyon's Tea House). Despite
consistently maintaining standards, its profile has waned somewhat in recent
years and in August 2017 the restaurant closed for a major revamp, prior
to an autumn re-launch with a new look and tweaked concept (hence we've
removed what were good ratings). / EC1A 9DS; www.clubgascon.com;
@club_gascon; 9 pm, Fri & Sat 9.30 pm; closed Sat L & Sun; set weekday L £67 (FP).

Coal Rooms SE15 NEW
11a Station Way   020 7635 6699   1–4D
*Meat and fish are grilled in a special coal oven at this newly restored former
Grade II listed ticket office at Peckham Rye station, which opens from
breakfast on, and serves a flat-bread based lunch menu. / SE15 4RX;
www.coalrooms.com; @coalrooms; 10 pm, Sun 6 pm.*

The Coal Shed SE1 NEW
One Tower Bridge   01273 322998   10–4D
*Overlooking the recently completed public piazza at the centre of the new
One Tower Bridge development, Brighton's favourite steak joint is heading
up to the Smoke in autumn 2017. / SE1 2AA; www.coalshed-restaurant.co.uk.*

CôBa N7 £40 **4** **4** **3**
244 York Way   07495 963336   9–2C
*Damon Bui's Vietnamese BBQ dishes come with an Aussie twist at his pub
conversion in Barnsbury – a "young and vibrant" joint whose "simple menu"
and "great cocktails" earn solid scores across the board. / N7 9AG;
www.cobarestaurant.co.uk; @cobafood; 10 pm; booking D only.*

Cocotte W2 £48 **4** **3** **4**
95 Westbourne Grove   020 3220 0076   7–1B
"Fantastic chicken" is the only option at this year-old rotisserie concept, on the Notting Hill/Bayswater border, with poultry from the French team's own farm in Normandy. Fans say it's "the best roast chicken ever eaten", accompanied by a "delicious" choice of potatoes, salads and sauces. / W2 4UW; www.mycocotte.uk; @cocotte_rotisserie; 10 pm, Fri & Sat 11 pm.

Colbert SW1 £62 **2** **2** **3**
51 Sloane Sq   020 7730 2804   6–2D
"There's plenty of buzz" at Corbin & King's "busy" Parisian-style brasserie on a prime Sloane Square corner. A "reliable breakfast" is its highest claim to culinary fame though – otherwise its "competent but unexciting" fodder and "erratic service" make it a handily situated but "underwhelming" destination. / SW1W 8AX; www.colbertchelsea.com; @ColbertChelsea; 11 pm, Fri & Sat 11.30 pm, Sun 10.30 pm.

La Collina NW1 £54 **3** **4** **3**
17 Princess Rd   020 7483 0192   9–3B
"Piedmontese cuisine that's unusual and very well executed" and some "very good house wines" have carved a dedicated following for this "traditional Italian with a modern twist", tucked away on the fringes of Primrose Hill – a "romantic" spot, whose "ambience is exceptional in the garden in summer". / NW1 8JR; www.lacollinarestaurant.co.uk; @LacollinaR; 10.15 pm, Sat-Sun 9.15 pm; closed Mon L; booking max 8 may apply.

The Collins Room, The Berkeley Hotel SW1 £99 **2** **4** **5**
Wilton Place   020 7107 8866   6–1D
"Exquisite attention to detail" – particularly the "fabulous miniature-styled cakes" – help create an "elegant, refined and beautiful" experience, when you sample the "fashion-inspired 'Pret-a-Portea'" at the Berkeley hotel in Knightsbridge. "I go twice a year with my mother, and we simply adore the new designs each season (the prices creep up, too, but we are always able to justify it by taking advantage of the unlimited supplies…!)". / SW1X 7RL; www.the-berkeley.co.uk; @TheBerkeley; 10.45 pm, Sun 10.15 pm.

Le Colombier SW3 £69 **3** **5** **4**
145 Dovehouse St   020 7351 1155   6–2C
"Totally French, with bags of Gallic charm!" – Didier Garner's "perfect brasserie" on a tucked-away corner near the King's Road, particularly benefits from "wonderfully welcoming" service. "Patrons may not be so young" but the ambience is very "authentique", and "while the menu is unadventurous, it does what it does very well indeed"; "excellent value wine list". / SW3 6LB; www.le-colombier-restaurant.co.uk; 10.30 pm, Sun 10 pm.

Colony Grill Room, Beaumont Hotel W1 £78 **3** **3** **3**
8 Balderton Street, Brown Hart Gardens   020 7499 9499   3–2A
"You feel like you are stepping onto the set of a Hollywood movie with dim lighting, booths and decadent atmosphere" at Corbin & King's "luxurious" Mayfair dining room: "a proper, traditionally wood-panelled room" which provides "a Gatsby-worthy setting for Alaïa-clad blue-bloods to gorge on classic US comfort food" – "meatloaf and mac 'n' cheese, as well as excellent grills". On the downside, critics feel the menu is "boring" – "fine so far as it goes, but rather overpriced for what it is" – and the setting "a little stuffy". / W1K 6TF; www.colonygrillroom.com; @ColonyGrillRoom; midnight, Sun 11 pm.

The Colton Arms W14 NEW £45   2 3 4
187 Greyhound Rd   020 3757 8050   8–2C
At the rear of Queen's Club, this Baron's Court boozer has been transformed by Hippo Inns from one of London's more quirkily characterful and old-fashioned backstreet pubs into a particularly stylish modern gastro' haunt (with fab back garden). Ratings are undercut by the odd uneven report, but all agree the straightforward cooking here has potential. / W14 9SD; www.thecoltonarms.co.uk; @thecoltonarms; 10 pm, Sun 8 pm.

Como Lario SW1 £70   2 3 2
18-22 Holbein Pl   020 7730 2954   6–2D
This "true neighbourhood Italian near Sloane Square" is, to its loyal (older) fans, a "throwback" of the best sort – "it's so much fun" and "you feel you're in safe hands" with the "friendly and professional" staff and "charmingly unspecial but adequate 'cucina'". / SW1W 8NL; www.comolario.co.uk; 11 pm, Sun 9.30 pm.

Comptoir Café & Wine W1 NEW £55
Weighhouse St   0207 499 9800   3–2B
Xavier Rousset, of the hugely successful Blandford Comptoir and Cabotte, opened a third venue, this time near Bond Street in May 2017; an all-day brasserie, cafe and wine shop (open from breakfast on), it features over 2000 wines. / W1K 5AH; comptoir-cafe-and-wine.co.uk.

Comptoir Gascon EC1 £51   3 3 2
63 Charterhouse St   020 7608 0851   10–1A
"Duck, duck and more duck, plus BBQ meats and other delights (the deluxe burger is a joy)" from southwest France continue to inspire all-round praise for this "very enjoyable" Smithfield bistro, including as a business lunch destination. Even so, a number of fans noted "a slight going off the boil" this year – the distractions of preparing for a refurb at its parent, Club Gascon? / EC1M 6HJ; www.comptoirgascon.com; @ComptoirGascon; 10 pm, Thu & Fri 10.30 pm; closed Mon & Sun.

Comptoir Libanais £36   2 2 2
"Choose the right dish and you can have a good meal" at this Lebanese chain, which "makes you feel welcome as you arrive, and plies you with free baklava as you leave". Brightly decorated, perhaps they "don't seem entirely authentic", but they're solid standbys. / www.lecomptoir.co.uk; 10 pm (SW 8 pm), W1C & E20 Sun 8 pm; W12 closed Sun D; no bookings.

Il Convivio SW1 £70   4 3 4
143 Ebury St   020 7730 4099   2–4A
"Superb, high-quality Italian fare" is served in a "timelessly attractive room" at this Belgravia stalwart, which combines "consistent" favourite dishes with a changing weekly menu. (There's another space upstairs that is "very good for business events.") / SW1W 9QN; www.etruscarestaurants.com/il-convivio; 10.45 pm; closed Sun.

Coopers Restaurant & Bar WC2 £49   2 3 3
49 Lincoln's Inn Fields   020 7831 6211   2–2D
"Handy for legal eagles and academics from the LSE", this understated operation arguably "benefits from not having much competition nearby", but by-and-large "does what it says on the tin" and "is good for clients and business discussions". / WC2A 3PF; www.coopersrestaurant.co.uk; @coopers_bistro; 10.30 pm; closed Sat & Sun; no booking; set weekday L £30 (FP).

Coq d'Argent EC2 £86 223

1 Poultry 020 7395 5000 10–2C

"Whisking up in a lift and having it open onto a gorgeous rooftop" helps set up good vibes – especially for expense-accounters – at D&D London's well-known landmark, "in the heart of the City" (right by Bank). "You are paying for the view" to some extent, but its current culinary performance is "sound – perfectly OK without being exceptional". / EC2R 8EJ; www.coqdargent.co.uk; @coqdargent1; 9.45 pm; closed Sun D; booking max 10 may apply; set brunch £50 (FP), set weekday L & pre-theatre £56 (FP).

Corazón W1 NEW £41 343

29 Poland St 020 3813 1430 4–1C

"Away from the increasing chain-ification of Wahaca", Laura Sheffield's new Soho taqueria scratches a similar itch with its "fabulously flavourful", "fluffy light tacos" with "friendly service in cheerful surroundings at a great price" – "what more could you ask for in W1?" / W1F 8QN; www.corazonlondon.co.uk; @corazon_uk.

Core by Clare Smyth W11 NEW

92 Kensington Park Rd 020 3937 5086 7–2B

Clare Smyth, former 'chef patron' at Restaurant Gordon Ramsay – and the first British woman to hold three Michelin stars – chose this well-known site (previously Notting Hill Kitchen, RIP, and once the site of the original Leith's) to launch her first solo venture in summer 2017. / W11 2PN; www.corebyclaresmyth.com.

Cork & Bottle WC2 £58 235

44-46 Cranbourn St 020 7734 7807 5–3B

"The perfect bolt-hole in the West End" – this atmospheric, charmingly dated cellar is, for those who know it, a much-loved haven, just off Leicester Square. "It's the comprehensive wine list that shoots it up the scale", but there's some "decent", if "slightly safe" grub too. Tip Tips: "cheese and ham pie is super" (but not for slimmers). / WC2H 7AN; www.thecorkandbottle.co.uk; @corkbottle1971; 11.30 pm, Sun 10.30 pm; no booking D.

Corner Kitchen E7 £43 333

58 Woodgrange Rd 020 8555 8068 14–1D

"A great local in up-and-coming Forest Gate" – this all-day outfit is "not just a pizzeria", but that's the highlight, with a "genuine Italian pizzaiolo at the oven serving up pizza using sourdough". / E7; cornerkitchen.london; @CornerKitchenE7; 10 pm, Fri & Sat 10.30 pm, Sun 9 pm; no booking.

Corner Room E2 £53 344

Patriot Sq 020 7871 0461 14–2B

"Hidden away at the back of the hotel", this "tiny", "sparse" chamber shares a kitchen with the better-known Typing Room; for fans, it's "a wonderful fashionista inside secret" and a "splendid gastronomic delight", but for sceptics "the food doesn't taste quite as good as hoped". / E2 9NF; www.townhallhotel.com/cornerroom; @townhallhotel; 9.30 pm, Thu-Sat 10 pm.

Corrigan's Mayfair W1 £91 343

28 Upper Grosvenor St 020 7499 9943 3–3A

"There's just the right balance of fine dining and a relaxed approach" at Richard Corrigan's "masculine and clubby", and business-friendly, Mayfair HQ, "whose honest cooking of first-rate ingredients avoids the over-elaboration that often mars restaurants that are trying to win gongs". Top Tips – "the Sunday set lunch menu stands out as good value for the posh location" and the "private dining room experience is outstanding, be it at the Chef's Table or in the Library". / W1K 7EH; www.corrigansmayfair.com; @CorriganMayfair; 10 pm; closed Sat L; booking max 12 may apply; set Sun L £58 (FP), set weekday L £64 (FP).

Côte £48 2 2 2

"You know what you're going to get" from this ubiquitous French brasserie chain: a formula that's "classier than Café Rouge's", and whose "easy and convenient, if uninspiring" virtues nowadays make it the survey's most-mentioned multiple. The "classic bistro fare" is "formulaic but edible" (steak-frites is a popular choice) and while service is "hit or miss" and conditions often "noisy", the "sensible pricing" especially of lunch or pre-theatre deals underpins its massive popularity. / www.cote-restaurants.co.uk; 11 pm.

Counter Culture SW4 £54 4 3 3

16 The Pavement 020 8191 7960 11–2D

A year-old offshoot from Robin Gill's well-known Dairy next door, this "very little restaurant" (15 seats) knocks out "great-tasting", "well-sourced" small dishes on the Pavement in Clapham; "very friendly" service too. / SW4 0HY; www.countercultureclapham.co.uk; @culturesnax; no booking.

Counter Vauxhall Arches SW8 £59 4 3 4

Arch 50, South Lambeth Pl 020 3693 9600 11–1D

"The new head chef has kicked the kitchen up several levels" at this "rocking" two-year-old in a Vauxhall railway arch (at 60m long, its claim-to-fame is as London's longest restaurant). "From oysters to lobster burger and chateaubriand, this arch now stands shoulder-to-shoulder with the grand brasseries of the West End" (well, nearly!). / SW8 1SP; www.counterrestaurants.com; @eatatcounter; 12.30 am, Fri & Sat 1.30 am.

The Cow W2 £58 3 3 4

89 Westbourne Park Rd 020 7221 0021 7–1B

"Exceptional seafood" is the gastronomic draw at Tom Conran's "really relaxed and friendly" Irish pub in the Notting Hill-Bayswater hinterland. "The fish stew is highly recommended", alongside the oysters and Guinness. / W2 5QH; www.thecowlondon.co.uk; @TheCowLondon; 11 pm, Sun 10 pm; No Amex.

Coya W1 £83 4 3 5

118 Piccadilly 020 7042 7118 3–4B

"Wow! What a lot of fun". This "exciting" Peruvian in Mayfair is "that rare restaurant" which can deliver "a truly spectacular meal", with an "amazing atmosphere (especially when the band starts playing)" and "exquisite flavour combinations" that "set the palette alight". Even fans though say "the prices are as outstanding as the cuisine". / W1J 7NW; www.coyarestaurant.com; @coyalondon_; 11 pm, Sun-Wed 10.30 pm.

Craft London SE10 £61 4 4 2

Peninsula Square 020 8465 5910 12–1D

"Quelle surprise! A real restaurant at the O2" – Stevie Parle has created one of his better places on the Greenwich Peninsular. The first-floor kitchen serves "inspired, locally sourced food in a beautiful room with impeccable service", while the café downstairs makes "top pizza". Top Tip – "try the tester (not taster) menu", served on Tuesdays. / SE10 0SQ; www.craft-london.co.uk; @CraftLDN; 10.30 pm (cafe 6pm); cafe L only; restaurant D only, Sat L & D, closed Mon & Sun.

Crate Brewery and Pizzeria E9 £27 3 2 4

7, The White Building, Queens Yard 020 8533 3331 14–1C

"Our go-to place for pizza, with fantastic atmosphere and great service" – this "cracking", consciously grungy hipster craft brewery and pizzeria beside the canal by the Olympic Park is "still as popular as ever with the Hackney Massive". / E9 5EN; www.cratebrewery.com; @cratebrewery; 10 pm, Fri & Sat 11 pm.

Crazy Bear Fitzrovia W1 £71 3 3 4
26-28 Whitfield St   020 7631 0088   2–1C
"Quirky and plush" – this idiosyncratic Thai, hidden away off Tottenham
Court Road "doesn't stand out from the street", but is "gorgeous once
inside". The beautifully presented food was well-rated this year, and no meal
here is complete without a visit to the superb, "funky" basement bar.
/ W1T 2RG; www.crazybeargroup.co.uk/fitzrovia; @CrazyBearGroup; 10.45 pm,
Sun 10 pm; closed Mon; No shorts.

Crocker's Folly NW8 £64 2 2 4
23-24 Aberdeen Pl   020 7289 9898   9–4A
"This most impressive and original of London's 19th-century pubs" –
a monumental pile built by the said Mr Crocker in the misplaced belief that
a huge railway terminus would be built in St John's Wood – "could be really
wonderful". Its owners of the last few years, Maroush Group, have struggled
to make their mark, but – bizarre as it may seem – its recent ditching of a
British menu to focus on the Lebanese cuisine that made the group's name
seems like a good first step. / NW8 8JR; www.crockersfolly.com; @Crockers_Folly;
10.30 pm; set weekday L £40 (FP).

The Crooked Well SE5 £48 3 2 3
16 Grove Ln   020 7252 7798   1–3C
"High-quality cooking in this tucked-away corner of town" sums up the
appeal of this "lovely neighbourhood pub" in Camberwell. Plenty of space
means it's "really comfortable for all the family", with a "nicely buzzing
atmosphere". / SE5 8SY; www.thecrookedwell.com; @crookedwell; 10.30 pm; closed
Mon L; No Amex; booking max 6 may apply.

The Cross Keys SW3 £54 3 4 4
1 Lawrence St   020 7351 0686   6–3C
Chelsea's oldest boozer is nowadays a stablemate of the Sands End
in Fulham, and it wins consistently good scores with its "friendly local
atmosphere" and some "excellent" pub nosh. / SW3 5NB;
www.thecrosskeyschelsea.co.uk; @CrossKeys_PH; 10 pm, Sun 9 pm.

The Culpeper E1 £51 2 2 3
40 Commercial St   020 7247 5371   13–2C
An "inventive" approach helps win fans for this Spitalfields two-year-old –
a wittily updated old corner boozer, with a more upscale dining room over
the happening bar. However, it's not the fave rave it was when
it first burst on the scene. / E1 6LP; www.theculpeper.com; @TheCulpeper;
midnight, Fri & Sat 2 am, Sun 11 pm; SRA-Food Made Good – 0 stars.

Cumberland Arms W14 £48 4 4 3
29 North End Rd   020 7371 6806   8–2D
"The best pub for food in the area around Olympia" – this "very friendly"
gastropub serves a "cracking" Med-inspired menu and "makes a good place
to meetup and discuss the world". "Nice outdoor space" in summer.
/ W14 8SZ; www.thecumberlandarmspub.co.uk; @thecumberland; 10 pm,
Sun 9.30 pm.

Cut,
45 Park Lane W1 £124 2 2 2
45 Park Ln   020 7493 4545   3–4A
US celebrity chef Wolfgang Puck's "very expensive" London outpost, tucked
inside a boutique hotel on Park Lane, again earnt a mixed rep this year.
It does have its fans, who say that "steaks don't get better than this",
but not that many of them, and almost as numerous are those who find
it "stuffy and rather disappointing" or even "a total waste of money".
/ W1K 1PN; www.45parklane.com; @45ParkLaneUK; 10.30 pm; set pre theatre
£87 (FP).

Cut The Mustard SW16 £23 3 2 3
68 Moyser Rd 07725 034101 11–2D

The decor's distressed, but customers aren't at this "little Streatham café", serving "a good selection of brunches", plus a "great array of breads and pastries". / SW16 6SQ; cutthemustardcafe.com; @WeCutTheMustard; 5.30 pm, Sun 4 pm; L only.

Cyprus Mangal SW1 £38 3 2 2
45 Warwick Way 020 7828 5940 2–4B

For a "cheap 'n' cheerful" blow out, this well-established Pimlico café is just the job: "delicious Turkish barbecue meat and kebabs, with fresh salads, washed down with a good range of wines and beers". / SW1V 1QS; www.cyprusmangal.co.uk; 10.45 pm, Fri & Sat 11.45 pm.

Da Mario SW7 £48 3 3 4
15 Gloucester Rd 020 7584 9078 6–1B

For "an efficient and cheerful meal, especially before a visit to the Royal Albert Hall" this "buzzing Italian pizza-fest" ("there's a wide selection including vegetarian, gluten-free, halal and per bambini") is "so good, you can forgive them their kitsch, Princess Di-themed decor!" "It's not overpriced for the location and always entertaining". / SW7 4PP; www.damario.co.uk; 11.30 pm.

Da Mario WC2 £53 3 4 3
63 Endell St 020 7240 3632 5–1C

"Superb pasta" tops the bill at this "cosy, traditional family-run Italian in Covent Garden" ("and there ain't many of those left in central London"), which has a big fanclub thanks to its "welcoming" (if "noisy") style and "excellent value". / WC2H 9AJ; www.da-mario.co.uk; 11.15 pm; closed Sun.

The Dairy SW4 £49 4 4 4
15 The Pavement 020 7622 4165 11–2D

"Wow... double wow!" – Robin Gill's "quirky, amazing value and ever changing" small plates are "bursting with flavour", according to most reports on this "very casual and so popular" Clapham hangout, which fans cross town for. As it matures though, it's drawing increasing flak, for seeming "too cool for school and charging ridiculous prices". / SW4 0HY; www.the-dairy.co.uk; @thedairyclapham; 9.45 pm; closed Mon, Tue L & Sun D.

Dalloway Terrace, Bloomsbury Hotel WC1 £56 3 2 4
16-22 Great Russell St 020 7347 1221 2–1C

An exceptional al fresco dining space – a leafy terrace, complete with fully retractable roof – is the special reason to truffle out this year-old eatery, whose bucolic nature is utterly at odds with the grungy environs of Centre Point. Limited but consistent feedback on its cooking too. / WC1B 3NN; www.dallowayterrace.com; @DallowayTerrace; 10.30 pm.

La Dame de Pic London EC3 NEW £100 3 3 2
10 Trinity Square 020 7297 3799 10–3D

An "excellent addition to the City" – this high-ceilinged arrival occupies the gobsmackingly grand, ex-HQ of the old Port of London Authority, near the Tower of London: since January 2017, the second outpost of Four Seasons Hotels in the capital. The dining room – run by the Pic family, who run a much-fêted, Gallic dining empire dating to 1889 in Valence, SE France – is an instant hit with expense-accounters, and wins bouquets from most foodies too for the "sophisticated" and "intense" cuisine from ex-Apsleys chef Luca Piscazzi. There are niggles too: the space – "romantic" to fans – can seem too "blingy" to critics, flavour combinations strike some reporters as "odd", and, perhaps inevitably, it can all seem "way overpriced". / EC3N 4AJ; ladamedepiclondon.co.uk; @FSTenTrinity; No shorts; set weekday L £66 (FP).

Dandy N16 [NEW] £50 [4][4][3]
20 Newington Green 020 8617 1930 1–1C
"Carrying across the real joy and passion for food to this bigger place in Newington Green" – this Aussie-owned communal canteen (the new incarnation of Hackney's Dandy Café) provides simple, funky (lots of Asian and middle eastern spicing) dishes alongside coffee and breads from their bakery. / N16 9PU; www.dandycafe.co.uk; @DandyCaf; 11 pm, Sun-Tue 5 pm; Sun-Tue L only.

Daphne's SW3 £80 [2][2][2]
112 Draycott Ave 020 7589 4257 6–2C
Once a favourite of Princess Di's, this "romantic" Italian stalwart in Chelsea is "just about keeping up appearances" but doesn't delight everyone. To its fans it's "great fun" ("not too noisy but not too silent") and with acceptable cuisine, but to detractors service is so so and "the food has been a disappointment of late". / SW3 3AE; www.daphnes-restaurant.co.uk; @DaphnesLondon/; 11 pm, Sun 10 pm; set weekday L £50 (FP).

Daquise SW7 £49 [2][3][2]
20 Thurloe St 020 7589 6117 6–2C
This 70-year-old South Ken institution "is a time-warp, but in a good way". Old fans as well as one-off visitors love coming here for the "charming service and good, solid Polish fare". "Excellent stuffed eggs and delicious stuffed cabbage with potato vodka – all without having to travel to Poland". / SW7 2LT; www.daquise.co.uk; @GesslerDaquise; 11 pm; No Amex.

Darbaar EC2 £62 [4][3][2]
1 Snowden St 020 7422 4100 13–2B
"Subtle spicing" is key to ex Cinnamon Kitchen chef, Abdul Yaseen's very superior take on Indian cuisine at this Liverpool Street yearling – a "fine", but slightly cold site inherited from svelte Japanese, Chrysan (Long RIP). / EC2A 2DQ; www.darbaarrestaurants.com; @DarbaarbyAbdul; 10.45 pm.

Darjeeling Express W1 [NEW] £48 [4][3][3]
6-8 Kingly St 020 7287 2828 4–2B
From supper club star, to pop-up favourite (at The Sun and 13 Cantons), Asma Khan's Darjeeling Express has finally found a permanent station atop Kingly Court in Soho, serving an array of north Indian dishes that are "generous, interesting and so delicious". / W1B 5PW; www.darjeeling-express.com; @AsmaKhanCooks; 10 pm, Sun 4 pm.

Dartmouth Arms NW5
35 York Rise 020 7485 3267 9–1B
This well-liked pub in Parliament Hill, was rescued from the developers by Andy Bird and his London Public House Group (Fanny Nelson's, The Chesham Arms in Hackney and co-owner of Happiness Forgets in Hoxton). Now restored, its kitchen is due to reopen in summer 2017. / NW5 1SP; www.dartmoutharms.uk; @dartmoutharms; 10 pm; No Amex.

The Dartmouth Castle W6 £47 [3][4][4]
26 Glenthorne Rd 020 8748 3614 8–2C
There's "always a fun vibe" at this "hustling and bustling gastropub" with cute terrace, a short walk from Hammersmith Broadway. "The food's always a notch above the rest", service is "super-fast", and it's "a great place to relax and unwind". / W6 0LS; www.thedartmouthcastle.co.uk; @DartmouthCastle; 9.30 pm, Sun 9 pm; closed Sat L

FSA

Darwin Brasserie EC3 £69 `2` `3` `4`
1 Sky Garden Walk   033 3772 0020   10–3D
"That you can wander among tropical foliage in the Sky Garden all the while surrounded by the most breathtaking views of the capital…" is the big draw to this all-day operation at the top of the Walkie-Talkie. *"Not as bad or overpriced as some restaurants with a view"* is a fair, if slightly grudging summary of its culinary performance this year, with breakfast particularly recommended. / EC3M 8AF; skygarden.london/darwin; @SG_Darwin; 10.30 pm.

Dastaan KT19 `NEW` £39 `5` `4` `3`
447 Kingston Rd   020 8786 8999   1–4A
In the depths of South London 'burbs, this simple newcomer from a duo of ex-Gymkhana chefs leaves early reporters *"blown away"*: *"it's a small menu, but everything was marvellous; the fish was wonderfully hot, spicy and fresh, and lamb chops are a must!"* / KT19 0DB; dastaan.co.uk; @Dastaan447; Booking weekdays only.

Daylesford Organic £51 `3` `2` `3`
44b Pimlico Rd, SW1   020 7881 8060   6–2D
Selfridges & Co, 400 Oxford St, W1   0800 123 400   3–1A
6-8 Blandford St, W1   020 3696 6500   2–1A
208-212 Westbourne Grove, W11   020 7313 8050   7–1B
"Great healthy brunches" help draw a busy crowd to Lady Bamford's rus-in-urbis organic cafés. Service can be variable and even *"sniffy"* however, and high prices are a recurring concern: *"the food is nice, but it is SO expensive that I always feel a little bit ripped off!"* / www.daylesfordorganic.com; SW1 & W11 9.30 pm, Mon 7 pm, Sun 4 pm; W1 9 pm, Sun 6.15 pm; W11 no booking L.

Dean & DeLuca W1 `NEW`
11 Mount St   awaiting tel   3–3A
In the former heart-of-Mayfair premises of Allen's the Butchers, this most chichi (and expensive!) of NYC lifestyle brands (a global business now, of which a chunk is still held by founder Giorgio DeLuca, who opened his first SoHo store in 1977) aims to storm the capital in the second half of 2017. So many US businesses founder on overpricing when they hit London – perhaps having a British chairman (Charles Finch) will help them judge the market better than some of their peers. / W1K 2AP; www.deandeluca.com; @deandeluca.

Dean Street Townhouse W1 £66 `2` `2` `4`
69-71 Dean St   020 7434 1775   4–1D
"Watching the parade of Soho media types" can make for good sport at this *"smooth"* operation – an *"atmospheric"* brasserie with *"a great buzz to it"*. True to form for owners Soho House, *"it's a bit variable food and service-wise"*, but generally it's found *"it's an uplifting place to visit"*, especially for *"a great breakfast in cool surroundings"*. / W1D 3SE; www.deanstreettownhouse.com; @deanstreettownhouse; 11.30 pm, Fri & Sat midnight, Sun 10.30 pm; set weekday L £41 (FP).

Defune W1 £72 `3` `2` `1`
34 George St   020 7935 8311   3–1A
Even fans of this decades-old veteran have always conceded that the interior feels *"barren"*, and that *"it might be cheaper to fly to Tokyo for lunch"*, but still they acclaim its *"fantastic sushi"* and other *"top, no-fusion-nonsense, Japanese dishes"*. A couple of reporters sounded a warning note this year though: *"it used to be our treat, but we found its quality had gone down"*. / W1U 7DP; www.defune.com; 10.45 pm, Sun 10.30 pm.

80   FSA RATINGS: FROM `1` POOR — `5` EXCEPTIONAL

Dehesa W1 £52 3 2 3
25 Ganton St 020 7494 4170 4–2B
"Awesome Spanish and Italian tapas" has made this "convivial" dining room
with terrace off Carnaby Street a "firm favourite" for many ("I always feel
at home here even with the crowds shopping!"). But food scores are down
this year, as they are for several Salt Yard group stablemates – not helped
by the Spring 2017 departure of chef-director Ben Tish? / W1F 9BP;
www.saltyardgroup.co.uk/dehesa; @SaltYardGroup; 10.45 pm, Sun 9.45 pm.

THE DELAUNAY WC2 £58 2 4 5
55 Aldwych 020 7499 8558 2–2D
"Not as grand as its sibling The Wolseley", Corbin & King's "glamorous"
outpost on Aldwych "is in a similar vein, but feels less frantic", and in its own
more "intimate" way is "one of the classiest rooms in town". "The cooking,
in an Austrian bent, is OK without being fantastic", majoring in "jolly gigantic
schnitzel" and other "stodgy" (slightly "complacent and expensive") fare.
As with its Piccadilly stablemate, breakfast here is a prime strength –
"a very civilised way to start the day" – and its "well-spaced", comfortable
and "old-fashioned" style similarly makes it a major business favourite, being
"smart enough to impress, without being overbearing". It's "brilliantly
convenient for pre-theatre too." Next door, its spin-off, 'The Counter', "serves
a great coffee and the pastries are to die for!" / WC2B 4BB;
www.thedelaunay.com; @TheDelaunayRest; midnight, Sun 11 pm.

Delfino W1 £53 4 3 2
121a Mount St 020 7499 1256 3–3B
"Amazing prices for Mayfair" help evoke the spirit of "Italian-as-they-used-
to-be" at this squashed, "really busy and noisy" outfit, just along the road
from the Connaught, serving "great pizzas". / W1K 3NW; www.finos.co.uk;
10 pm; closed Sun.

Delhi Grill N1 £25 3 2 2
21 Chapel Mkt 020 7278 8100 9–3D
"Still the best simple curries in Islington" – "succulent, spicy" and with
"tender meat" – this Chapel Market canteen is "better than
most restaurants at double the price" (with lunch particularly good value).
/ N1 9EZ; www.delhigrill.com; @delhigrill; 10.30 pm; Cash only.

Delisserie NW8 £40 3 2 2
87 Allitsen Rd 020 7722 7444 9–3A
"The Temple Fortune branch of this small chain of NYC-style delis is always
full of families at lunch". Kids in particular love the "gargantuan portions,
of tasty American New York Jewish deli food" ("don't go if you're afraid
of calories or cholesterol!") / NW8 7AS; www.delisserie.com/st-johns-wood; 10 pm.

La Delizia Limbara SW3 £44 3 3 3
63-65 Chelsea Manor St 020 7376 4111 6–3C
This "little neighbourhood pizza joint", just off the Kings Road – "unchanged
in 30+ years" – serves "wonderful thin-crust pizzas" ("I just love this
intimate, cheap and cheerful place"). / SW3 5RZ; www.ladelizia.org.uk;
@ladelizia; 11 pm, Sun 10.30 pm; No Amex.

Department of Coffee, and Social Affairs EC1 £13 3 4 4
14-16 Leather Ln 020 7419 6906 10–2A
"What it claims to be: a good coffee stop!" – the "no frills" but
straightforward proposition at this Leather Lane original of what is now
a mini-chain of coffee bars. "It's small and not always easy to get a seat,
but always good", with "great cakes". / EC1N 7SU;
www.departmentofcoffee.co.uk; @DeptOfCoffee; 5.30 pm, Sat 4 pm; L only;
no booking.

The Dining Room,
The Goring Hotel SW1 £91 3 4 4

15 Beeston Pl 020 7396 9000 2–4B

"One of the last bastions of the English style of the old days" – this "time-warp" family-run hotel between Victoria and Buckingham Palace provides "the quintessential country house experience in London", with "smartly dressed staff with many years of service" and a "hugely traditional, well-spaced interior". It's shot to prominence in recent years – both since the Middletons stayed here prior to the Royal Wedding and since Michelin (slightly bafflingly) awarded the "classic" British cuisine a star, although in truth the top culinary attractions are its superb breakfasts and afternoon tea ("just how it should be – comfy sofas and chairs, endless streams of sandwiches and scones, followed by dainty cakes"). But "oh dear, is it starting to rest on its regal laurels?" It took more flak this year for being "very expensive". / SW1W 0JW; www.thegoring.com; @TheGoring; 9.30 pm; closed Sat L; No jeans; booking max 8 may apply; set brunch £52 (FP), set pre-theatre £61 (FP).

Dinings £68 5 4 2

22 Harcourt St, W1 020 7723 0666 9–4A

Walton House, Walton St, SW3 020 7723 0666 6–2C NEW

"Don't be put off by the simplicity of the dining room" – "a noisy concrete basement" (although you can also sit at the ground floor bar): Tomonari Chiba's sushi and other Japanese fare is "genius", albeit "spectacularly expensive" at his original Marylebone venture of over ten years standing. In May 2017 he opened a considerably swankier offshoot in the beautiful and chichi premises vacated by Toto's (RIP) which seem likely to become the dominant member of the duo hereafter. It features a mashup of Japanese and Western ingredients and ideas – early press reviews are mixed. / dinings.co.uk.

Dinner,
Mandarin Oriental SW1 £112 2 3 2

66 Knightsbridge 020 7201 3833 6–1D

"I am perplexed as to how it achieved a second Michelin Star and made it onto the World's 50 Best!" – verdicts are ever-harsher on Heston's "historically inspired" Knightsbridge dining room, which increasingly "trades on the Blumenthal name". Yes, many reporters do still enjoy "an amazing taste sensation" from its "delicious Olde Worlde English recipes with a twist". And yes it has "stunning views over Hyde Park". But far too many refuseniks nowadays report "terrifying bills" for food that's "simply OK", from a menu that reads like "a marketing con" (and barely changes), in a room with all the ambience of "a plush hotel foyer". "If I want a modern take on 15th century chicken, in future I think I'll go to Chicken Cottage!" Top Menu Tip – "the Meat Fruit is cool". / SW1X 7LA; www.dinnerbyheston.com; 10.30 pm; set weekday L £69 (FP).

Dip & Flip £34 3 3 3

87 Battersea Rise, SW11 no tel 11–2C

115 Tooting High St, SW17 no tel 11–2C

62 The Broadway, SW19 no tel 11–2B

64-68 Atlantic Rd, SW9 no tel 11–2D

For fans – and there are plenty – this burger-'n'-gravy concept with four outlets across southwest London (Battersea, Brixton, Tooting and Wimbledon) offers "the best burgers in town by far!". By no means everyone agrees though: "Maybe I just don't get it, but I wasn't impressed by the quality of the burger or by the messy gravy". / 10 pm, Thu-Sat 11 pm; SW9 & SW17 booking: 8 min.

Dirty Burger £33
78 Highgate Rd, NW5 020 3310 2010 9–2B
Arch 54, 6 South Lambeth Rd, SW8 020 7074 1444 2–4D
13 Bethnal Green Rd, E1 020 7749 4525 13–1B
27a, Mile End Rd, E1 020 3727 6165 13–2D
"Curiously satisfying burgers served in a hipster shed" sums up the appeal of these funky snack-shacks. "When you do something right, there's no need for other options!" / www.eatdirtyburger.com; 10 pm-midnight, Fri & Sat 11pm-2 am, Sun 8 pm-11 pm; no bookings.

Dishoom £41
22 Kingly St, W1 020 7420 9322 4–2B
12 Upper St Martins Ln, WC2 020 7420 9320 5–3B
The Barkers Building, Derry St, W8 awaiting tel 8–1D **NEW**
Stable St, Granary Sq, N1 020 7420 9321 9–3C
7 Boundary St, E2 020 7420 9324 13–1B
"My daughter in law (born in Delhi) says it reminds her so much of Bombay food – and that is really high praise!" These "high energy" replicas of Mumbai's Parsi cantinas are "quite exceptional" for a chain, with Indian reporters feeling "nostalgia for my childhood… the noise, the bustle, the products on display in the loos!" "The evening queues are deeply tedious" ("you can only book for 6 or more") but the payoff is "exceptionally flavoursome Indian street-food with a difference", "a fun cocktail list" and "a real buzz". "Breakfast with a twist" is another option and it's easier to get a table. Top Menu Tips – black dhal, or, for breakfast, their "reinvented bacon butty" – "a bacon naan with spicy ketchup is a great start to the day!" / www.dishoom.com; 11pm, Thu-Sat midnight; breakfast 8, Sat & Sun 9; booking: min 6 at D.

Diwana Bhel-Poori House NW1 £27
121-123 Drummond St 020 7387 5556 9–4C
"The best bargain meal in London" – an "incredibly good lunchtime buffet for very little cash" – is to be found at this battered veggie "institution", in the 'Little India' behind Euston station. "You can't beat their de luxe dosas" and the eponymous Bhel-Poori are also well worth a try, but "forget the decor!". "I've been coming since 1972, and it's always a safe bet!" Top Tip – BYO. / NW1 2HL; www.diwanabph.com; @DiwanaBhelPoori; 11 pm, Sun 10 pm; No Amex; May need 10+ to book.

Diyarbakir Kitchen N4 £37
52-53 Green Lanes 020 8802 5498 1–1C
"Vast amounts" of "terrific" Turkish scoff "for comparatively little money" win praise for this "busy and atmospheric" Haringey ocakbasi. / N4 1AG; www.diyarbakir.co.uk; @DiyarbakirKtchn; 1 am.

**The Dock Kitchen,
Portobello Dock W10** £60
342-344 Ladbroke Grove, Portobello Dock 020 8962 1610 1–2B
Stevie Parle's "creative" and "ever-changing" menu from all points of the globe has earned a loyal following for this Victorian warehouse conversion, by the canal (lovely in summer) at the 'wrong' end of Ladbroke Grove. At its worst though, the end-result is "mundane imitations of a variety of styles of cuisine". / W10 5BU; www.dockkitchen.co.uk/contact.php; @TheDockKitchen; 9.30 pm; closed Sun D.

Dokke E1 **NEW** £44
Ivory House, 50 St Katharine's Way 020 7481 3954 10–3D
Healthy small plates and brunch are a focus at Niel Wager's open kitchen, all-day café newcomer, in the heart of St Katharine's Dock. / E1W 1LA; www.dokke.co.uk; @dokkelondon; 10 pm; booking max 10 may apply.

F S A

Dominique Ansel Bakery London SW1   £24   5 4 3
17-21 Elizabeth St   020 7324 7705   2–4B
"The long awaited opening of this globally renowned pâtissier" in Belgravia last year has gone down a storm, bringing London not only his trademarked 'cronut' – a croissant crossed with a doughnut – but other "cakes to die for", such as the Ansel take on Brit classics like Eton mess. / SW1W 9RP; www.dominiqueansellondon.com; @DominiqueAnsel; no booking.

The Don EC4   £67   3 3 2
The Courtyard, 20 St Swithin's Lane   020 7626 2606   10–3C
"A perfect business venue"; this "well oiled machine", tucked away near the Bank of England, is one of the City's prime choices for entertaining thanks to its "discreet" and "prompt" service, "well-spaced tables", "outstanding wine list" and cuisine that's "very dependable" – all "minus the bling and over-charging". See also Sign of the Don. / EC4N 8AD; www.thedonrestaurant.com; @thedonlondon; 10 pm; closed Sat & Sun; No shorts.

The Don Bistro and Bar EC4   £55   3 3 4
21 St Swithin's Ln   020 7626 2606   10–3C
"My go-to place in the Square Mile"; this "reliable" basement brasserie occupies the "atmospheric old cellars" that once housed the Sandeman wine and sherry importers. "Cheerful and relatively cheap", with a "small but perfectly formed menu", it "avoids the style over substance of many City restaurants" and is "less stuffy than The Don next door". / EC4N 8AD; www.thesignofthedon.com; @signofthedon; 10 pm; closed Sat & Sun.

Donostia W1   £53   4 4 4
10 Seymour Pl   020 3620 1845   2–2A
"Exceptional pintxos and tapas" have earned a cult following for this "buzzy" Basque outfit near Marble Arch, sibling to nearby Lurra. "One of the better Spanish restaurants in the capital" – "sit at the bar around the open kitchen to watch the chefs at work" (or there are a couple of tables in the small rear space). "The wine list is also extensive and intriguing". / W1H 7ND; www.donostia.co.uk; @DonostiaW1; 11 pm; closed Mon L; booking max 8 may apply.

Doppio NW1   £6   3 3 3
177 Kentish Town Rd   020 7267 5993   9–2B
"Exceptional coffee from experts" who "take real pride in making an outstanding brew" can be sampled at these on-trend espresso bars, operated by a coffee wholesaler in Camden Town, Shoreditch and Battersea. NB they "sell and service coffee machines", but "they don't serve food"! / NW1 8PD; www.doppiocoffee.co.uk; @doppiocoffeeltd; 6 pm; L only; no booking.

Dorchester Grill, Dorchester Hotel W1   £107   3 4 4
53 Park Lane   020 7629 8888   3–3A
Chapeau! to Alain Ducasse who has successfully turned around this formerly lacklustre traditional dining room in Mayfair, to create "a most enjoyable experience" with "expensive but faultless" modern French cuisine, charmingly served in tasteful, luxurious surroundings. / W1K 1QA; www.thedorchester.com; @TheDorchester; 10.15 pm, Sat 10.45 pm, Sun 10.15 pm; No trainers; set pre-theatre £64 (FP), set Sun L £74 (FP).

Dotori N4   £33   4 3 2
3a Stroud Green Rd   020 7263 3562   9–1D
Squeezing into this popular East Asian outfit near Finsbury Park station is "a bit like eating in a corridor". But it's worth it: "the sushi is brilliant and the Korean food out of this world". / N4 2DQ; www.dotorirestaurant.wix.com/dotorirestaurant; 10.30 pm, Sun 10pm; closed Mon; No Amex; no booking.

The Dove W6 £50 3️⃣3️⃣4️⃣
19 Upper Mall   020 8748 5405   8–2B
"An atmospheric 18th-century hostelry right by the river on Chiswick Mall", a short walk from Hammersmith. There's "excellent pub food" – "true English fare" – "and local London Pride ale on tap", but it's really all about the location: "lovely outside on the terrace in the summer, or cosy by the fire in winter". / W6 9TA; www.fullers.co.uk; @thedovew6; 11 pm; closed Sun D.

Dozo W1 £48 3️⃣3️⃣3️⃣
32 Old Compton St   020 7434 3219   5–2A
"The perfect neighbourhood sushi stop" – "reasonably priced for the location" near South Kensington tube too. (There's also a branch in Soho, but no-one reports on it). / W1D 4TP; www.dozosushi.co.uk; @DozoLondon; 10 pm, Thu-Sat 11 pm.

Dragon Castle SE17 £48 4️⃣3️⃣3️⃣
100 Walworth Rd   020 7277 3388   1–3C
"Amazing and authentic Chinese cuisine" – particularly "top dim sum" – wins consistent acclaim this year for this "barn-like" but "buzzy" Cantonese venue, stuck out near Elephant & Castle, which is "full of Chinese families, especially at weekends". "It's back on song after a dip in recent times, with some interesting new regional dishes on the menu". / SE17 1JL; www.dragoncastlelondon.com; @Dragoncastle100; 11 pm, Sun 10 pm.

Dragon Palace SW5 £42 4️⃣2️⃣2️⃣
207 Earls Court Rd   020 7370 1461   6–2A
"Plenty of Chinese frequent" this inconspicuous modern café "right on the Earl's Court Road" near the tube, where by all accounts the all-day dim sum is "excellent". / SW5; www.thedragonpalace.com/; 11 pm.

Drakes Tabanco W1 £49 3️⃣2️⃣2️⃣
3 Windmill St   020 7637 9388   2–1C
"Authentic tapas", "sherries from the cask and good Spanish wine" draw a steady crowd to this "bustling Fitzrovia cantina", named after the sherry taverns of Andalucia. / W1T 2HY; www.drakestabanco.com; @drakestabanco; 10 pm; booking max 7 may apply.

The Drapers Arms N1 £53 3️⃣2️⃣3️⃣
44 Barnsbury St   020 7619 0348   9–3D
"A nice balance between pub and restaurant" – this well-known Islingtonian knocks out an "interesting seasonal menu", although "service can be patchy". "The wine list is a real delight, with a huge range of bottles priced to invite exploration". / N1 1ER; www.thedrapersarms.com/; @DrapersArms; 10.30 pm; No Amex.

The Duck & Rice W1 £59 3️⃣3️⃣4️⃣
90 Berwick St   020 3327 7888   4–2C
Design-wise it looks "really cool", and this Soho two-year-old is the latest prototype format of restaurant impresario Alan Yau, combining "interesting, small Chinese dishes" with the great British boozer. It doesn't yet look like a hit on the scale of Hakkasan or Wagamama, but the food's "really tasty" and the place has "a great atmosphere". / W1F 0QB; www.theduckandrice.com; @theduckandrice; 11 pm, Fri & Sat 11.30 pm, Sun 10 pm.

Duck & Waffle Local SW1 NEW £50
No 2, St. James's Market, 52 Haymarket   0203 900 4444   4–4D
London's highest restaurant (on the 40th floor of 110 Bishopsgate, alongside Sushisamba) has a new sibling: one with its feet firmly on the ground this time, at Haymarket's new St James's Market development. Although it shares some dishes with its City namesake, this is a fast-food café operation: you can't book, you order at the counter, and food (and cocktails) come quickly. / SW1Y 4RP; duckandwafflelocal.com; @duckwafflelocal; 1 am.

Duck & Waffle EC2 £75 [2][2][5]

110 Bishopsgate, Heron Tower   020 3640 7310   10–2D

"The view is jaw-dropping" on the 40th floor of the Heron Tower (next to Sushisamba) – "an ideal date spot" that's "worth it for the lift-ride alone" (the fastest in western Europe). "No doubt this is factored into the bill", but most reporters feel it's "not overpriced" all-things-considered. Some of the combinations on its meaty, calorie-laden menu sound "insane", and views divide on the end-result: "unusual and delicious" in most cases, but "really awful" in a few. Brunch is the best bet. / EC2N 4AY; www.duckandwaffle.com; @DuckandWaffle; open 24 hours.

Duckroad SW8 NEW

Battersea Power Station, 188 Riverlight Quay   awaiting tel   11–1C

Sibling to Soho's Ducksoup and Hackney's Rawduck, this newcomer is set to open in January 2018, in the Circus West Village at Battersea Power Station. / SW8 5BN; www.ducksoupsoho.co.uk.

Ducksoup W1 £61 [3][3][4]

41 Dean St   020 7287 4599   5–2A

"Inventive" dishes with Italian and North African influences, "friendly (and informative) service" and "an impressive selection of natural wines (by the glass on frequent rotation)" are the makings of a "lovely evening" at this Soho spot. "You have to relish its super-buzzy crowded spaces", but most reporters "love every minute". / W1D 4PY; www.ducksoupsoho.co.uk; @ducksoup; 10.30 pm; closed Sun D; May need 3+ to book.

Duddell's SE1 NEW

6 St Thomas St   awaiting tel   10–4C

Hong Kong comes to London in autumn 2017 when this authentic Cantonese/dim sum chain (with 10 sites across HK) opens its first UK branch, in St Thomas Church in London Bridge. Chef Daren Liew was, until recently, executive sous chef with the Hakkasan Group. / SE1 9RY; www.duddells.co; @DuddellsHK.

Duke of Sussex W4 £49 [2][3][4]

75 South Pde   020 8742 8801   8–1A

"Lovely pub food with a Spanish twist" ("there's always something interesting and new on the menu") ensures the grand rear dining room is kept busy at this Victorian tavern beside Acton Common Green. Why are its marks not higher? – even fans say "it can be hit or miss". / W4 5LF; www.metropolitanpubcompany.com; @thedukew4; 10.30 pm, Sun 9.30 pm.

Duke's Brew & Que N1 £51 [4][3][4]

33 Downham Rd   020 3006 0795   14–2A

"Amazing beef ribs the size of your forearm and the best burgers around" are real crowd-pleasers at this "loud and hopping" Texan BBQ in Dalston. "An excellent selection of beers on tap" ("but be warned: some of the imports are very pricey") make for a "fantastic evening of meat and ale". / N1 5AA; www.dukesbrewandque.com; @dukesJoint; 10 pm, Sun 9.30 pm.

Dum Biryani W1 NEW £53 [4][4][3]

187 Wardour St   020 3638 0974   3–1D

Limited but positive feedback on this walk-in, late 2016 newcomer in a small Soho basement: fans say it "deserves to be successful, delivering the best biryani in a long time" (cooked in a heavy pot, the 'dum' and with a pastry top). / W1F 8ZB; dumlondon.com; 10.30 pm, Sun 10 pm; May need 5+ to book.

Dynamo SW15 £42 3 3 3
200-204 Putney Bridge Rd   020 3761 2952   11–2B
"Built for cyclists but cooking for everyone!" – this cycle-themed café in Putney seems "set to last in a funny location that has failed in previous guises". The sense of permanency stems not least from the "consistently good brunches and fabulous sourdough pizzas" and "popularity with MAMILS (middle-aged men in lycra) means excellent coffee!". / SW15; www.the-dynamo.co.uk; @WeAreTheDynamo; 10 pm, Thu-Sat 11 pm.

The Dysart Petersham TW10 £70 3 4 4
135 Petersham Rd   020 8940 8005   1–4A
A "trusted favourite" to its sizeable fanclub – this "smart and spacious" Arts & Crafts pub between Richmond Park and the Thames serves Kenneth Culhane's "imaginative food in a beautiful setting" and "manager Barney and his team are always very attentive". It provoked a couple of 'off' reports this year however, accusing it of being "prissy, expensive and not that exciting". / TW10 7AA; www.thedysartarms.co.uk; @dysartpetersham; Mon - Tue closed, Wed - Sat 9.30 pm, Sun 3.30 pm; closed Sun D.

E&O W11 £57 3 3 3
14 Blenheim Cr   020 7229 5454   7–1A
It's no longer the A-lister magnet it once was, but Will Ricker's buzzy Notting Hill haunt still "keeps a high standard" of "great cocktails" and "wonderful" pan-Asian tapas. / W11 1NN; www.rickerrestaurants.com; 11 pm, Sun 10.30 pm; booking max 6 may apply.

The Eagle EC1 £37 4 2 5
159 Farringdon Rd   020 7837 1353   10–1A
"Loud... crowded... open kitchen... stubbly chefs... short Anglo-Mediterranean menu on the blackboard... good beer"; that's the "dreamy and simple" formula that made London's original gastropub near Exmouth Market "a benchmark", and for its very many fans "it still rocks" – "ace" dishes are "generous and full-flavoured", and enjoyed "in a rough-and-tumble, everyone-having-a-good-time atmosphere". / EC1R 3AL; www.theeaglefarringdon.co.uk; @eaglefarringdon; 10.30 pm; closed Sun D; No Amex; no booking.

Ealing Park Tavern W5 £54 3 4 3
222 South Ealing Rd   020 8758 1879   1–3A
"A fantastic mix of pub and restaurant" – this spacious former coaching inn in South Ealing has its own on-site microbrewery. Quality has varied in the past, but it's "consistently back on form". / W5 4RL; www.ealingparktavern.com; @Ealingpark; 10 pm, Sun 9 pm.

Earl Spencer SW18 £48 3 2 4
260-262 Merton Rd   020 8870 9244   11–2B
This substantial early 20th-century roadhouse on a trafficky route through Wandsworth is a "great local gastropub" with an impressively large following: a "fun place" with "good, daily-changing gastro-fare". / SW18 5JL; www.theearlspencer.co.uk; @TheEarlSpencer; 11 pm; Mon-Thu D only, Fri-Sun open L & D.

Eat 17 £43 3 4 3
28-30 Orford Rd, E17   020 8521 5279   1–1D
64-66 Brooksbys Walk, E9   020 8986 6242   14–1C
"A lovely spot in Walthamstow Village" – an "enjoyable" British kitchen whose "attentive staff" provide "locally sourced" fare that's "great value for money". Bacon jam was invented here, so take a jar home with you and "check out the Spar next door which is run by Eat 17 and specialises in supplies from interesting small producers". / www.eat17.co.uk; E17 10 pm, Sun 9 pm, E9 9 pm, Fri & Sat 9.30 pm, Sun 8 pm.

Eat Tokyo £29 4 3 2
16 Old Compton St, W1   020 7439 9887   5–2A NEW
50 Red Lion St, WC1   020 7242 3490   2–1D
15 Whitcomb St, WC2   020 7930 6117   5–4B
27 Catherine St, WC2   020 3489 1700   5–3D NEW
169 King St, W6   020 8741 7916   8–2B
18 Hillgate St, W8   020 7792 9313   7–2B
14 North End Rd, NW11   020 8209 0079   1–1B
628 Finchley Rd, NW11   020 3609 8886   1–1B NEW
"The mostly Japanese clientele speaks volumes" for the virtues of these
"busy and cramped" canteens ("like a typical Tokyo dive"), which serve
"excellent sushi and have plenty of other dishes to choose from": "portions
are generous and the price is good for the quality". Top Tip – a wide variety
of "great value bento boxes". / www.eattokyo.co.uk; Mon-Sat 11.30 pm,
Sun 10.30 pm.

Ebury Restaurant & Wine Bar SW1 £59 2 2 3
139 Ebury St   020 7730 5447   2–4A
Consistent (if limited) praise for this age-old, traditional wine bar on a
picturesque corner near Victoria station, whose performance is "as it's
always been", with solid, if not spectacular cooking and wine that's "fairly
priced" for this posh 'hood. / SW1W 9QU; www.eburyrestaurant.co.uk;
@EburyRestaurant; 10 pm; closed Sat L & Sun L; booking max 14 may apply.

Eco SW4 £36 3 3 3
162 Clapham High St   020 7978 1108   11–2D
"Consistently good food and cheerful service" keep this "popular Clapham
hangout" impressively busy ("it's usually packed and noisy") after over
20 years in business. / SW4 7UG; www.ecorestaurants.com; @ecopizzaLDN;
11 pm, Fri & Sat 11.30 pm.

Edera W11 £65 3 4 3
148 Holland Park Ave   020 7221 6090   7–2A
"Authentic" Sardinian cuisine from an "interesting menu" backed up by
"very obliging service" have long made this "quiet" Holland Park fixture
a very "professional" kind of local (although of course "it's not cheap"). Top
Tip – "go in the truffle season". / W11 4UE; www.edera.co.uk; 11 pm,
Sun 10 pm.

Edwins SE1 £56 3 4 4
202-206 Borough High St   020 7403 9913   10–4B
"A hidden gem near Borough tube station", this bistro upstairs from a mock-
Tudor pub has "tasty grub, excellent cocktails and lovely service". / SE1 1JX;
www.edwinsborough.co.uk; @edwinsborough; 10 pm, Sun 4 pm; closed Sun D.

8 Hoxton Square N1 £52 3 3 3
8-9 Hoxton Sq   020 7729 4232   13–1B
"Interesting, tasty food" from a menu changing daily, "friendly service,
and tables where you can talk quietly over lunch" all help make this "highly
recommended" destination a Hoxton favourite. / N1 6NU;
www.8hoxtonsquare.com; @8HoxtonSquare; 10.30 pm; closed Sun D.

Eight Over Eight SW3 £56 3 3 4
392 King's Rd   020 7349 9934   6–3B
"Delicious southeast Asian food and a fun vibe" draws a lively crowd to Will
Ricker's clubby Chelsea hang-out: nowadays the best known of his small
group, and "always consistent". / SW3 5UZ;
www.rickerrestaurants.com/eight-over-eight; 11 pm, Sun 10.30 pm.

Electric Diner W11   £49   2 2 3
191 Portobello Rd   020 7908 9696   7–1B
*Brunch with the trustafarian crowd at this "fun" Notting hill hangout
(nowadays part of Soho House), whose plush interior – homage à the
US diner – sits at the base of one of London's oldest cinemas (a landmark
of Portobello). / W11 2ED; www.electricdiner.com; @ElectricDiner; 11 pm, Fri & Sat
midnight, Sun 10 pm.*

No.11 Cadogan Gardens SW3   £64
11 Cadogan Gardens   020 7730 7000   6–2D
*"A hidden gem in the heart of Chelsea" – this swish boutique hotel (formerly
operated on a club basis) has been taken over by the team behind Chewton
Glen and Cliveden, and its ground-floor restaurant serving a brasserie-style
menu is now open to the public. Too little feedback for a rating so far,
but its afternoon tea, complete with edible flowers, has already had the
thumbs up. / SW3 2RJ; www.11cadogangardens.com.*

Ella Canta W1
InterContinental London Park Lane   020 7318 8715   3–4A
*World's 50 Best chef, Martha Ortiz, of Mexico City's Dulce Patria, opened
her first London venture alongside Theo Randall at The Intercontinental Park
Lane's second restaurant. The new dining room, designed by David Collins
Studio, serves the chef's take on Mexican cuisine. The name by the way
means 'She Sings'. / W1J 7QY; www.ellacanta.com; @ellacantalondon.*

Elliot's Café SE1   £55   3 3 3
12 Stoney St   020 7403 7436   10–4C
*Limited but all-round positive feedback on Brett Redman's bare-brick café,
whose tapas-style dishes and all-natural list of wines are a staple of Borough
Market. / SE1 9AD; www.elliotscafe.com; @elliotscafe; 10 pm; closed Sun.*

Ellory,
Netil House E8   £59   3 5 3
1 Westgate St   020 3095 9455   14–2B
*"A fab place run by fab people!" – "passionate staff" breath lots of life into
Matthew Young's "hipster hangout" in London Fields (part of a set
of creative studios) which has a strong wine offering, and where
on most (if not quite all) accounts "the food has bags of flavour too".
"When full, all the high ceilings and hard surfaces can make it deafening".
/ E8 3RL; www.ellorylondon.com; @ellorylondon; 11 pm, Sun 9 pm; booking max 6
may apply.*

Elystan Street SW3   £98   4 4 2
43 Elystan St   020 7628 5005   6–2C
*"A vast improvement over the late and not-lamented Restaurant Tom Aikens
that previously occupied this space" – Phil Howard's Chelsea yearling
(in partnership with restaurateur Rebecca Mascarenhas) has proved one
of the better openings of the year, with a "mature reinvention" of his style
at The Square: a seasonal, 'Flexitarian' approach that's "bang-up-to-date,
light, fresh, modern and exciting!" Feedback is not totally free of quibbles
though – in particular even for the area it's "pricey" (especially given the
more fuss-free style) – and the interior is a tad "sexless". / SW3 3NT;
www.elystanstreet.com; @elystanstreet; set weekday L £69 (FP), set Sun L £78 (FP).*

Ember Yard W1   £53   2 3 3
60 Berwick St   020 7439 8057   3–1D
*"Very accomplished" small plates, cooked over charcoal (hence the name),
have carved a reputation for this stylish Soho sibling to Salt Yard. But,
as with a number of Salt Yard properties this year, marks are down this
year, especially for food, amid the odd report of a "shameful decline from
early acclaim". / W1F 8SU; www.emberyard.co.uk; @emberyard; 11 pm,
Sat midnight, Sun 10 pm; booking max 13 may apply.*

Emilia's Crafted Pasta E1 NEW   £44   4|3|3
Unit C3 Ivory House, St Katharine Docks   020 7481 2004   10–3D
"A table outside overlooking the dock is perfect, and I haven't even
mentioned the delicious pasta!" – this St Katharine's Dock newcomer does
what it says on the tin, and early reports are full of praise for its "authentic
homemade dishes at a great price". / E1W 1AT; www.emiliaspasta.com;
@emiliaspasta.

The Empress E9   £49   4|3|4
130 Lauriston Rd   020 8533 5123   14–2B
"This ideal local" – "a sort of bistro-pub hybrid" beside Victoria Park that
was one of east London's first dining destinations – still "never disappoints".
"There's an interesting and always spot-on seasonal menu, good beer and
a varied and lively crowd". / E9 7LH; www.empresse9.co.uk; @elliottlidstone;
10 pm, Sun 9 pm; closed Mon L; No Amex.

Encant WC2   £55   4|2|3
16 Maiden Ln   020 7836 5635   5–4D
Victor Garvey's Covent Garden two-year-old serves "innovative and
most importantly delicious modern Spanish food" ("sometimes overly fussy,
but the flavours are strong"). It's "fun" (if "noisy") too, and "warmly
welcoming", but "ridiculously small – they put four people on a table which
seemed just OK for two!". / WC2E 7NJ; www.encantlondon.com; @encantlondon;
11.30 pm.

Eneko at One Aldwych, One Aldwych Hotel WC2   £76   3|3|2
1 Aldwych   020 7300 0300   2–2D
Fans of this year-old régime of a much-fêted Spanish chef, hail this Aldwych
basement as an "undiscovered gem" with "inventive Basque food" that's
"very modern, but not over-complex". However, even though "they've
evidently spent a lot of money on refurbishing the old Axis site" (RIP),
the venture can still seem "rather let down by its unconventional and rather
uncongenial space", and even many supporters have concerns about
"inflated prices" and food that's "a mix of the incredible and the rather
boring". / WC2B 4BZ; www.eneko.london; @OneAldwych; 11 pm, Sun 10 pm;
set pre theatre £54 (FP).

Enoteca Turi SW1   £74   3|4|3
87 Pimlico Rd   020 7730 3663   6–2D
"If you like Italian wine there is nowhere better in London" than Giuseppe
and Pamela Turi's Pimlico venture which – having lost their SW15 premises
of decades standing due to a rent review – "has magnificently managed the
tumultuous move from Putney to near Sloane Square", and offers Sig. Turi's
"wonderful wine list, embellished by his own personal remarks". Its new
home is more "elegant" than its last, but it's the "family touch that elevates
the place above the norm" and "preserves what was good about its original
incarnation, while becoming smarter". The "trusty northern Italian menu
augmented by seasonal daily specials" has also transplanted well, although
some old regulars note that "overall it seems more expensive now, making
it more of a special occasion than a regular treat". / SW1W 8PH;
www.enotecaturi.com; @EnotecaTuri; 10.30 pm, Fri & Sat 11 pm; closed Sun; booking
max 8 may apply; set weekday L £48 (FP).

The Enterprise SW3   £54   3|3|5
35 Walton St   020 7584 3148   6–2C
Where the 'Made in Chelsea' crowd go when they become older singles! –
this chichi stalwart in a gorgeous enclave near Knightsbridge is a cosy
rendezvous with very dependable cooking. / SW3 2HU; www.theenterprise.co.uk;
10.30 pm, Sun 10 pm.

L'Escargot W1   £70   4 4 4
48 Greek St   020 7439 7474   5–2A
"Everything is quite perfect" at this "civilised" but also "quirky" Gallic classic that has notched up 90 years in the heart of Soho (nowadays under owner Brian Clivaz). Though not as high profile as once it was, it remains by all accounts "a very special destination", with "brilliant, non-intrusive service", a "wonderful" and "romantic" room, and "excellent" French cuisine. / W1D 4EF; www.lescargot.co.uk; @LEscargotSoho; 11.30 pm; closed Sun D; set weekday L & pre-theatre £42 (FP).

Essenza W11   £68   3 4 3
210 Kensington Park Rd   020 7792 1066   7–1A
This "reliable Italian with good wine and friendly staff" is a smartly turned-out Notting Hill fixture, with a solid menu of classic dishes. Many of the ingredients used are imported from Italy – including the black and white truffles which are a house speciality. / W11 1NR; www.essenza.co.uk; 11.30 pm; set weekday L £43 (FP).

Est India SE1   £39   3 3 3
73-75 Union Street, Flat Iron Square   020 7407 2004   10–4B
"New age Indian" dishes in a "fun underground space" in the Flat Iron Square development. / SE1 1SG; www.estindia.co.uk; @EstIndiaLondon; 11 pm, Sun 10.30 pm.

Estiatorio Milos SW1   £122   3 2 4
1 Regent St   020 7839 2080   4–4D
"The setting is impressive and dramatic... as are some of the prices" at Costas Spiladis's glamourous West End yearling, where the centrepiece is "a terrific display and choice of Mediterranean fish flown in daily" ("you choose your fish and pay by weight"). All the many reports it inspires are of "masterfully prepared and sensational" dishes using "sublimely fresh" ingredients, and – leaving aside the "eyewatering expense" – the consensus is that it's "worth a visit" and emerging as one of London's top addresses for fish and seafood. / SW1Y 4NR; www.milos.ca/restaurants/london; 11 pm; set weekday L £62 (FP), set pre-theatre £85 (FP).

Ethos W1   £54   3 3 3
48 Eastcastle St   020 3581 1538   3–1C
"I'm not vegetarian but the wide-ranging offerings here could (almost) make me one!" – limited but positive feedback on this self-service veggie near Oxford Circus. "Food is charged by weight (not yours thankfully!)". / W1W 8DX; www.ethosfoods.com; @ethosfoods; 10 pm, Sat 9.30 pm, Sun 4 pm; May need 6+ to book.

L'Etranger SW7   £70   3 3 2
36 Gloucester Rd   020 7584 1118   6–1B
This French restaurant with Japanese influences is most acclaimed for its extremely impressive wine list and represents a "good option in an otherwise difficult part of town", near the Royal Albert Hall. Top Tip – "the under-advertised set pre-theatre menu is excellent value for the area". / SW7 4QT; www.etranger.co.uk; @letrangerSW7; 11 pm; credit card required to book; set weekday L £46 (FP).

Everest Inn SE3   £43   3 2 3
41 Montpelier Vale   020 8852 7872   1–4D
"Great-tasting gurkha curries" and good tandoor-oven specials ensure that this Blackheath Nepalese is "better than the average curry house". Even some fans however concede that "it's a little bit expensive". / SE3 0TJ; www.everestinnblackheath.co.uk; 11.30 pm, Fri & Sat midnight.

FSA

Eyre Brothers EC2 £67 **4** **3** **3**
70 Leonard St 020 7613 5346 13–1B
Don't be deceived by its English name – "posh tapas", and other "top-notch" Spanish and Portuguese dishes are matched with "very good wine" from the Iberian peninsula at this still-stylish Shoreditch joint, which has been around for yonks but can still seem like a "surprise find". / EC2A 4QX; www.eyrebrothers.co.uk; @eyrebrothers2; 10.30 pm, Sat 11 pm; closed Sat L & Sun.

Faanoos £31 **3** **3** **2**
472 Chiswick High Rd, W4 020 8994 4217 8–2A
11 Bond St, W5 020 8810 0505 1–3A
481 Richmond Rd, SW14 020 8878 5738 1–4A
"One of the best local cheap eats" – this pair of Persian kitchens in Chiswick and East Sheen are "not to be missed if in the locale". / SW14 11 pm; W4 11 pm; Fri & Sat midnight.

Fairuz W1 £45 **3** **3** **2**
3 Blandford St 020 7486 8108 2–1A
No fireworks at this "favourite" Mayfair Lebanese – just solidly rated and affordable mezze, plus more substantial fare. / W1H 3DA; www.fairuz.uk.com; 11 pm, Sun 10.30 pm.

Falafel King W10 £8 **3** **3** **2**
274 Portobello Rd 020 8964 2279 7–1A
It's "worth going out of your way for the best freshly cooked falafel" at this simple and popular Notting Hill pit stop. / W10 5TE; 7 pm; L & early evening only; Cash only; no booking.

La Famiglia SW10 £63 **2** **2** **3**
7 Langton St 020 7351 0761 6–3B
"Always fun and typically Italian" is how many long-term fans still regard this long-standing Chelsea favourite, renowned for its family-friendly style ("it's full of groups with kids at the weekend"), and "delightful" back garden. It's always been "inclined to be rather expensive" though, and – now long in the tooth – the odd former fan feels it's becoming "a shadow of what it was in its heyday". / SW10 0JL; www.lafamiglia.co.uk; @lafamiglia_sw10; 11 pm, Sun 9 pm.

Fancy Crab W1 NEW
92 Wigmore St 020 3096 9484 3–1A
Although the name suggests the opposite, this all-day Marylebone restaurant promises 'accessibly priced' seafood – with Red King Crab as the star dish. Have this North Pacific Ocean crustacean cold on ice with dipping sauce and pickle; grilled with butter, thyme and hollandaise sauce; tempura-style crab claws; crab salad; Singaporean chilli crab or as a Fancy Crab Burger! / W1U 3RD; www.fancycrab.co.uk; @fancycrabuk.

Farang N5 £37 **4** **4** **3**
72 Highbury Park 0207 226 1609 9–1D
"Terrific food" – "zesty" and "unusual" dishes "from a relatively short menu" – have won instant acclaim for Seb Holmes's "very buzzy" Thai pop-up, near Arsenal. In what is a slightly "weird set up", "they've kept the Italian decor from the previous restaurant" (the much loved San Daniele RIP) but it only "adds to the charm". / N5 2XE; www.faranglondon.co.uk; @farangLDN; 10.30 pm, Sun 5 pm; closed Mon & Sun D.

Farmacy W2 £57 **3** **3** **4**
74 Westbourne Grove 020 7221 0705 7–1B
Camilla Al Fayed's health-conscious yearling, complete with pharmacist-inspired decor, wins strong (if not quite universal) support for its "very imaginative" vegan cuisine. Its "really buzzy" atmosphere also wins particular praise, even before its recent introduction of 'High' tea – afternoon tea that not only avoids refined sugars, but uses hemp leaf infusions! / W2 5SH; www.farmacylondon.com; @farmacyuk; 11 pm, Sun 7 pm.

Fenchurch Restaurant, Sky Garden EC3 £91 **3** *2* **3**
20 Fenchurch St 033 3772 0020 10–3D
"The view is great (well it should be at these prices!)", perched on top of the City's 'Walkie-Talkie' tower. Sceptics say the food is "overpriced for what it is", but harsh critiques are notable by their absence, and fans by contrast are enthusiastic, saying the cuisine (overseen since April 2017 by ex Square head chef, Dan Fletcher) is "superlative, creative, and well-judged". / EC3M 3BY; skygarden.london/fenchurch-restaurant; @SG_Fenchurch; 10.15 pm; booking max 7 may apply; set weekday L £69 (FP).

FERA AT CLARIDGE'S, CLARIDGE'S HOTEL W1 £108
49 Brook St 020 7107 8888 3–2B
"Here's hoping it sustains its magic post Simon Rogan" – In April 2017, the L'Enclume chef terminated his tenure at this "beautiful Art Deco chamber", leaving his head chef Matt Starling to maintain the "exotic and quixotic" dishes ("delicately balanced between being intriguing and not daunting") that have placed this famously elegant hotel's dining room firmly in London's first rank. Claridge's had a good record of running this restaurant prior to any celebrity involvement, and – though there may be some bumps after his departure – we'd wager this "superb" all-rounder will maintain its appeal. / W1K 4HR; www.feraatclaridges.co.uk; @FeraAtClaridges; 10 pm; set weekday L £73 (FP).

Ferdi W1 NEW £78 **1** **1** *2*
30 Shepherd Market 073 7553 8309 3–4B
"There's nothing wrong with this place… other than its ridiculous small size, average food and crazy prices!" Paris comes to London – not in a good way – at this new Shepherd Market spin-off from an über-trendy 1er arrondissement brasserie (Kim Kardashian's go-to spot when in the City of Light). "It's terrible and they're still snotty"… "I'd rather be a sardine than be packed in here". / W1J 7QN; www.ferdi-restaurant.com; @ferdi.london; 11.30 pm.

La Ferme London EC1 £45 **3** **3** **3**
102-104 Farringdon Rd 020 7837 5293 10–1A
"Possibly the Frenchest restaurant ever" – this "cosy", rustique-style deli/restaurant near Exmouth Market has a small but enthusiastic fan club for its fairly ambitious Gallic cuisine. / EC1R 3EA; www.lafermelondon.com; @lafermelondon; 10 pm.

Fernandez & Wells £54 **3** **3** **3**
43 Lexington St, W1 020 7734 1546 4–2C
55 Duke St, W1 020 7042 2774 3–2A NEW
1-3 Denmark St, WC2 020 3302 9799 5–1A NEW
Somerset Hs, Strand, WC2 020 7420 9408 2–2D
8 Exhibition Rd, SW7 020 7589 7473 6–2C
Although they almost pre-date the 'hipster', these high-quality, funky little cafés, with their "superb coffee, great tapas, freshly squeezed juices, breads, cakes and toasties" hold their own well against newer competitors.
"The best F&W is at Somerset House, where on a sunny day you can sit outside and look at the beautiful architecture and fountains, just a minute from the Courtauld and the Strand". / www.fernandezandwells.com; 11 pm, Sun 6 pm; St Anne's Court closed Sun.

Fez Mangal W11 £26 **5** **4** **3**
104 Ladbroke Grove 020 7229 3010 7–1A
"Top notch meat and super-tasty salads and dips", plus the chance to BYO "makes for a cheap but great dinner" at this "exceptional" Turkish kebab house in Ladbroke Grove. It's "small and very crammed": "the queues out of the door speak volumes…" / W11 1PY; www.fezmangal.com; @FezMangal; 11.30 pm; No Amex.

Fifteen N1 £69

15 Westland Place   020 3375 1515   13–1A

If it were not for Jamie Oliver's celebrity, it would be hard to justify a listing nowadays for this once-famous Hoxton Italian, which seems increasingly ignored by reporters, and which continues to inspire deeply mixed opinions. / N1 7LP; www.fifteen.net; @JamiesFifteen; 10.30 pm, Sun 9.30 pm; booking max 12 may apply.

Fischer's W1 £64

50 Marylebone High St   020 7466 5501   2–1A

"You feel like you are in a grand coffee shop in Vienna", at Corbin & King's "beautiful, wood-panelled" Marylebone venture, whose "buzzy" (quite "noisy") quarters are particularly "ideal for a winter meal". The food splits opinion – to fans its schnitzel and wurst are "a stodgy, warm embrace", but there's also quite a feeling that "while it's fun for a change, at the price, it needs more polish". / W1U 5HN; www.fischers.co.uk; @FischersLondon; 11 pm, Sun 10 pm.

Fish Central EC1 £32

149-155 Central St   020 7253 4970   13–1A

"Freshly fried fish", "the warmest of welcomes" and "great value for money" all strike the right note at this "reliable" Clerkenwell chippie. There's "some creativity in the specials" – "the fish of the day is always interesting and beautifully cooked". / EC1V 8AP; www.fishcentral.co.uk; @fishcentral1968; 10.30 pm, Fri 11 pm; closed Sun.

Fish in a Tie SW11 £36

105 Falcon Rd   020 7924 1913   11–1C

A "good-value" and "varied selection" of Mediterranean dishes is on the menu at this slightly "kitsch" local bistro near Clapham Junction station, where service is "cheerful" and the "atmosphere is always great". / SW11 2PF; www.fishinatie.com; midnight, Sun 11 pm.

Fish Market EC2 £57

16a New St   020 3503 0790   10–2D

"Reasonably priced fresh fish cooked perfectly" is the promise of this lesser-known D&D London warehouse conversion, near Bishopsgate. Even those who feel "the room itself is nothing special" say "the fish is excellent". / EC2M 4TR; www.fishmarket-restaurant.co.uk; @FishMarketNS; 10.30 pm; closed Sun.

fish! SE1 £54

Cathedral St   020 7407 3803   10–4C

"Still going strong in its atmospheric Borough Market location" – this "noisy, echoey and crammed-in" glazed shed is arguably a bit touristy and pricey, but generally lives up to its name with "fresh fish, simply and deliciously cooked". / SE1 9AL; www.fishkitchen.com; @fishborough; 11 pm, Sun 10.30 pm.

Fishworks £62

7-9 Swallow St, W1   020 7734 5813   4–4C
89 Marylebone High St, W1   020 7935 9796   2–1A

"An excellent selection of very fresh, simply cooked fish" inspires very consistent satisfaction with these straightforward bistros in Marylebone and near Piccadilly Circus (survivors of what was once a medium-sized chain); "a mixed West End crowd makes for a jolly atmosphere". / www.fishworks.co.uk; W1B 10.30 pm, Fri & Sat 11 pm; W1U 10.30 pm.

Fiume SW8 NEW

Circus West Village, Sopwith Way   awaiting tel   11–1C

Hot on the heels of opening Radici, Francesco Mazzei and D&D London are set to open this modern Italian, in the revamped Battersea Power Station site, in autumn 2017. That's the headline anyway, but the man actually in the kitchen day-to-day is Francesco Chiarelli (who worked with Mazzei at L'Anima). / SW8 4NN; www.danddlondon.com/restaurant/fiume.

THE FIVE FIELDS SW3 £89 5 5 4
8-9 Blacklands Ter   020 7838 1082   6–2D
"The Elysian Fields?" – Taylor Bonnyman's "graceful and intimate dining room", tucked away in Chelsea offers an "exemplary experience", which for all-round quality and consistency has few rivals in the capital. "Phenomenal cooking" – from either the prix fixe or tasting menu – is delivered by "faultless, thoroughly attentive yet unpretentious" staff and "a contented buzz in the room ensures the ambience is never hushed". / SW3 2SP; www.fivefieldsrestaurant.com; @The5Fields; 10 pm; D only, closed Mon & Sun; No trainers.

Five Guys £19 3 2 2
1-3 Long Acre, WC2   020 7240 2657   5–3C
71 Upper St, N1   020 7226 7577   9–3D
"A guilty pleasure" that's "a real step up in fast food" ("no table service") – this US-based chain may look "Spartan", but serves "the juiciest, most delicious burgers" ("it must be the peanut oil they fry them in"), alongside "yummy fries in huge portions" and "top shakes". Also, "it's ideal for fussy people as you build your own (with multiple free topping choices)". "Sure, it's expensive, but leagues ahead of McDonald's and Burger King; but with none of the pretence of Byron". / 11 pm, Thu-Sat midnight.

500 N19 £52 3 3 2
782 Holloway Rd   020 7272 3406   9–1C
"Beautifully cooked Italian and Sicilian dishes" at this "excellent" little local near Archway make it "so much better than the generic pizza and pasta joints in the Holloway area": "a real find, and well worth a journey to visit". / N19 3JH; www.500restaurant.co.uk; @500restaurant; 10.30 pm, Sun 9.30 pm; Mon-Thu D only, Fri-Sun open L & D.

500 Degrees SE24 £24 3 3 2
Herne Hill, 153a Dulwich Rd   020 7274 8200   11–2D
Above-average wood-fired pizza wins consistent ratings for this straightforward Herne Hill yearling (a business with family connections back to a famous Naples pizzeria). / SE24; www.500degrees.co; @500degreesuk; 11 pm, Sun 10 pm.

Flat Iron £32 4 4 3
17 Beak St, W1   020 3019 2353   4–2B
17 Henrietta St, WC2   020 3019 4212   5–3C
9 Denmark St, WC2   no tel   5–1A
46 Golborne Rd, W10   7–1A NEW
77 Curtain Rd, EC2   no tel   13–1B
"If you are only going to do one thing, do it well ...and they do!" Charlie Carroll's small chain offers "a limited menu but a great piece of steak" (plus a veggie alternative), which is "simply and perfectly cooked" and "free homemade ice cream is a lovely surprise" to finish. "You don't go for an intimate meal, but service is straightforward and effective". (Expect more expansion, as he just raised £10m from Piper private equity to grow the brand.) / www.flatironsteak.co.uk; midnight, Sun 11.30pm; EC2 11 pm; W1F 11 pm, Thu 11.30 pm, Fri & Sat midnight, Sun 10.30 pm; no bookings.

Flat Three W11 £88 4 4 3
120-122 Holland Park Ave   020 7792 8987   7–2A
With its funky six-course tasting menus of experimental Japanese and Nordic fusion menu – with a 100% vegan option – this good-looking, Holland Park haunt deserves to be better discovered, and, though feedback is limited, fans "love it". 'Cook like Pavel' masterclasses are a feature – a 90-minute demo, followed by lunch. / W11 4UA; www.flatthree.london; @infoflat3; 9.30 pm; set weekday L £60 (FP).

Flavour Bastard W1 NEW £54
63-64 Frith St 020 7734 4545 5–2A
Yes, they really called it that! So what's in a name – it seems that chef-patron Pratap Chahal is keen to use a fusion of flavours – gleaned from his time at Claridge's, Chez Bruce, Cinnamon Club and Galvin Bistrot – to create an international menu with 'no attempt at authenticity'. It opens in September 2017, taking over the former site of Arbutus in Soho. / W1D 3JW; www.flavourbastard.com; @flavourbastard; 10.30 pm, Fri & Sat 11 pm, Sun 10 pm.

Flesh and Buns WC2 £53 4 3 3
41 Earlham St 020 7632 9500 5–2C
"A taste sensation" – this "party vibe" Japanese izakaya in a Soho basement (part of the Bone Daddies group) wins consistently rave reviews for its steamed buns, loaded with "high quality meat". Top Tip – "Sunday brunch is a firm favourite": "an amazing amount of food and drink for the price". / WC2H 9LX; www.bonedaddies.com/restaurant/flesh-and-buns; @FleshandBuns; 10 pm, Wed-Sat 11 pm, Sun 9.30 pm; booking max 8 may apply.

Flora Indica SW5 £47 3 2 3
242 Old Brompton Rd 020 7370 4450 6–2A
"Sophisticated Indian cuisine at the right price point" makes this yearling an appealing option on the two-floor (ground and basement) Earl's Court site that some oldies still remember as Mr Wing (now long RIP). / SW5 0DE; www.flora-indica.com; @Flora_Indica; 1 am.

Flotsam and Jetsam SW17 £26 3 4 4
4 Bellevue Parade 020 8672 7639 11–2C
"It's a little too popular with the yummy mummies of Wandsworth Common", but that's the worst folk have to say about this "lovely buzzing cafe" towards its edge, whose "generally speedy service" and "well-prepared fresh food" make it a "great local coffee shop". / SW17 7EQ; www.flotsamandjetsamcafe.co.uk; @_flotsam_jetsam; 5 pm; L only; no booking.

FM Mangal SE5 £32 3 3 2
54 Camberwell Church St 020 7701 6677 1–4D
A "proper old-style grill bar" – this Camberwell Turk delivers "magnificent grilled onions, spiced flat breads and meaty treats", and "carnivores should look no further for food that's well-cooked and inexpensive". / SE5 8QZ; midnight; No Amex; no booking.

Foley's W1 £44 4 4 4
23 Foley St 020 3137 1302 2–1B
"Buzzing with energy and wonderful, eclectic food" – that's the dominant view on ex-Palomar chef Mitz Vora's Fitzrovia venue, which serves "an enticing, really interesting and unusual menu" combining myriad influences, and where there's the option of eating at the counter by the open kitchen. Ratings would be even higher, were it not for a couple of disappointing reports. / W1W 6DU; www.foleysrestaurant.co.uk; @foleyslondon.

Fortnum & Mason,
The Diamond Jubilee Tea Salon W1 £67 **3 3 3**
181 Piccadilly 020 7734 8040 3–3D

For "a quintessential afternoon tea" in the heart of the West End,
the "delightfully traditional" third-floor chamber of Piccadilly's world-famous
grocer slugs it out with the nearby Ritz (and to a lesser extent The Wolseley)
as London's best-known destination. Naturally "it's a tourist trap, but not
overwhelmingly so", and – although some reporters feel "there is better
elsewhere for a fraction of the cost" – the majority view remains that the
"non-stop sandwiches and delicious cakes-with-a-twist" are "still special"
here (there are also "lots of savoury and dairy free options"). "The choice
of teas is extensive too, and you can sample different ones throughout the
afternoon". "You will not need an evening meal…". Top Tip – "the scones
are a piece of heaven: fresh, fluffy and warm with a dusting of sugar
alongside their own dream-come-true jams". / W1A 1ER;
www.fortnumandmason.com; @fortnumandmason; 7 pm, Sun 6 pm; L & afternoon
tea only.

45 Jermyn Street SW1 £66 **3 4 4**
45 Jermyn Street, St. James's 020 7205 4545 3–3D

Fortnum & Mason's "very positive" relaunch of the all-day eatery at the rear
of the store, whose "chic" looks are in stark contrast to its former traditional
style (as the long-running Fountain, RIP). No longer consigned to maiden
aunts and their godchildren, "the cocktail chaps shake up an irresistible
storm" at the bar, and it offers a "consistently interesting menu and service
to match". Top Tip – some traditions have been maintained –
breakfast here goes down a treat. / SW1Y 6DN; www.45jermynst.com;
@Fortnums; 11 pm, Sun 6 pm; closed Sun D.

40 Maltby Street SE1 £54 **4 4 3**
40 Maltby St 020 7237 9247 10–4D

"The cooks work miracles in a tiny kitchen" tucked under the railway arches
at this wine warehouse in one of Southwark's foodiest of enclaves near
London Bridge. Chef Steve Williams uses "imaginative combinations
of seasonal ingredients" in the daily menu he chalks up on a blackboard.
Ironically, "while certainly interesting, the natural wines are arguably the
least enjoyable aspect of the offer" (they can be "very challenging!").
/ SE1 3PA; www.40maltbystreet.com; @40maltbystreet; 9.30 pm; closed Mon,
Tue, Wed L, Thu L, Sat D & Sun; No Amex; no booking.

The Four Seasons £46 **4 1 1**
12 Gerrard St, W1 020 7494 0870 5–3A
23 Wardour St, W1 020 7287 9995 5–3A
84 Queensway, W2 020 7229 4320 7–2C

"Succulent and not too fatty" – the "excellent roast duck" lining the window
of these "dingy", "shabby", "shouty" canteens in Chinatown and Bayswater
is some "the tastiest in town". There are "absolutely no frills" and
"rude service is part of the traditional charm" but even so you'll "leave with
a smile on your face". Top Menu Tip – the crispy pork belly here also rates
mention. / www.fs-restaurants.co.uk; 11pm-midnight.

The Fox & Hounds SW11 £48 **4 3 4**
66-68 Latchmere Rd 020 7924 5483 11–1C

"This atmospheric old corner pub in Battersea" is a "buzzy, friendly,
traditional spot" serving "a Med-inspired menu that never disappoints".
"Cosy and warm in winter, with stunning Christmas decorations, it also has
a fabulous rose-clad garden in summer". / SW11 2JU;
www.thefoxandhoundspub.co.uk; @thefoxbattersea; 10 pm; Mon-Thu D only, Fri-Sun
open L & D.

The Fox and Anchor EC1 £53 3 3 4
115 Charterhouse St   020 7250 1300   10–1B
A "great Smithfield institution" – this imposing Victorian tavern is one of a
handful in London to be licensed from the early hours to serve workers
in the nearby meat market, and is known for its traditional, hearty cooked
breakfast washed down with a pint – "a wonderful way to start a day". It's
moved with the times, too: "they do a great avocado on toast!" / EC1M 6AA;
www.foxandanchor.com; @foxanchor; 9.30 pm, Sun 6 pm.

Foxlow £50 2 2 2
Lower James St, W1   020 7680 2710   4–3C **NEW**
11 Barley Mow Pas, W4   020 7680 2702   8–2A
15-19 Bedford Hill, SW12   020 7680 2700   11–2C
St John St, EC1   020 7014 8070   10–2A
For a "cheap 'n' cheerful" steak, most reporters do commend these
Hawksmoor-lite spin-offs as a "fun" and affordable option (including for
brunch). But while "it's a decent standard of food, nothing is out-of-the-
ordinary". / www.foxlow.co.uk; 10 pm, Fri & Sat 10.30 pm, Sun 9 pm;
EC1 10.30 pm, Sun 3.30 pm; EC1 closed Sun D; SRA-Food Made Good – 2 stars.

Franco Manca £27 3 3 2
"If this is what passes for chain-pizza these days, we are indeed living in fine
times!" From humble Brixton Market origins, these "frenetic" and "rather
basic" cafés have embarked on "a mammoth roll-out" and even if ratings
don't equal the early days, most reporters marvel at how steady quality has
remained. It's the sourdough bases – "crispy on the outside with a fine,
chewy taste towards the centre" – that make dishes "so much better than
bog standard", along with "bold" toppings ("away from the run-of-the-mill")
all at "keen prices". / www.francomanca.co.uk; 10 pm, Wed-Sat 11 pm;
no bookings.

Franco's SW1 £74 3 3 3
61 Jermyn St   020 7499 2211   3–3C
A "smart" interior where white linen abounds, and "very good" and
courteous service are the badges of distinction at this St James's institution
(one of London's oldest Italians, est 1946). "It's very pleasant, even if the
lack of space between tables is not ideal" and a major favourite
amongst local pinstripes. "Perfect for a working breakfast too… unless you
find the whole concept abhorrent!" / SW1Y 6LX; www.francoslondon.com;
@francoslondon; 10.30 pm; closed Sun.

Franklins SE22 £56 3 3 2
157 Lordship Ln   020 8299 9598   1–4D
"The trad British menu, brilliantly done – if sometimes a leap of faith" has
put this pub conversion (with a farm shop opposite) on the south London
map. "East Dulwich is lucky to have such a great local". / SE22 8HX;
www.franklinsrestaurant.com; @frankinsse22; 10.30 pm, Sun 10 pm; No Amex;
set brunch £32 (FP).

Frantoio SW10 £61 3 3 4
397 King's Rd   020 7352 4146   6–3B
The owner Bucci "makes the place, he couldn't be more welcoming" at this
World's End "gem", which inspires a small but passionate fan club.
"Standards are high" and results from the menu (enhanced by blackboard
specials) are delivered in "huge portions". "We've been going for years and
the whole family feel at home here – young and old". / SW10 0LR;
www.frantoio.co.uk; 11 pm.

Frederick's N1   £64   3 4 4
106 Camden Passage   020 7359 2888   9–3D
*"An old favourite" that "never disappoints" – this Islington veteran with
a "lovely conservatory" and cocktail bar is run with high "professionalism"
and has a "great buzz". The "unexciting but safe food" has been "resting
on its laurels" for at least a couple of decades now. / N1 8EG;
www.fredericks.co.uk; @fredericks_n1; 11 pm; closed Sun; set weekday L &
pre-theatre £39 (FP).*

Frenchie WC2   £79   4 2 2
18 Henrietta St   020 7836 4422   5–3C
*"Interesting but ungimmicky" modern French cuisine has helped win a big
following for Grégory Marchand's Parisian import – a "chilled" Gallic yearling
on the Covent Garden site that was for aeons Porters: nowadays
an "informal" contemporary bistro, with ground floor dining room,
plus basement (the latter complete with open kitchen). Service can lapse
however, and the interior is "very noisy". / WC2E 8QH;
www.frenchiecoventgarden.com; @frenchiecoventgarden; 10.30 pm; set weekday L
£57 (FP).*

The Frog   £49   5 3 2
35 Southampton St, WC2   020 7199 8370   5–3D NEW
Old Truman Brewery, Hanbury St, E1   020 3813 9832   13–2C
*"Bold British tapas, with interesting combinations, textures and flavours"
goes down a storm at Adam Handling's "superb newcomer" – an "echoey",
rather "Spartan" operation in Brick Lane's Truman Brewery, where
"you observe the fierce concentration of the chefs, who also serve you";
and which achieved top marks for food in spite of significant grumbling even
from fans over its "unbelievably high bills". He must be doing something
right, as in September 2017 he's already opened branch number two,
in Covent Garden. Top Menu Tip – "the best mac 'n' cheese in London".
/ www.thefrogrestaurant.com.*

La Fromagerie   £45   3 2 2
2-6 Moxon St, W1   020 7935 0341   3–1A
52 Lamb's Conduit St, WC1   awaiting tel   2–1D NEW
30 Highbury Park, N5   020 7359 7440   9–2D
*Superior café for light bites (soups, sandwiches, salads) and brunches
attached to one of London's foremost cheese stores in Marylebone.
A Bloomsbury branch opened in September 2017 with its most ambitious
food operation yet, incorporating a seafood bar. / www.lafromagerie.co.uk.*

The Frontline Club W2   £54   2 2 4
13 Norfolk Pl   020 7479 8960   7–1D
*"Useful in the culinary desert that is Paddington", this "stylish" and "buzzy"
venue is part of a club for war reporters (with pics on the walls providing
"reminders of the big news events from the start of the Cold War to the fall
of the Berlin Wall"). Most reports praise its "well-prepared classic food",
but there's also a feeling that "erratic cooking can let down an otherwise
sensible option in an area that needs it". / W2 1QJ; www.frontlineclub.com;
@frontlineclub; 11 pm; closed Sat L & Sun; booking max 6 may apply.*

Fucina W1 NEW   £47   1 2 4
26 Paddington St   020 7058 4444   2–1A
*"Overwhelming design, underwhelming food" seems to be the diagnosis
at Kurt Zdesar's "buzzy and really cool-looking" Marylebone newcomer,
whose organic Italian cooking is too often "disappointing" and "average-
tasting". / W1U 5QY; fucina.co.uk.*

Fumo WC2 £61 3 2 3
37 St Martin's Lane   020 3778 0430   5–4C
This "attractive", year-old, all-day Italian in Covent Garden, near the ENO
(part of the national San Carlo group) wins pretty consistent praise for its
"good value". Service is a bit hit-and-miss, though, with different reporters
complaining of either "interminable waits" or of food arriving "too quickly".
/ WC2N 4JS; www.sancarlofumo.co.uk/fumo-london/; @sancarlo_fumo.

Gabeto Cantina NW1 NEW
Chalk Farm Rd   020 7424 0692   9–3B
On the first floor of Camden Stables, this new Camden Town brasserie,
which includes a weatherproof roof terrace, opened in July 2017, complete
with an ex-Chiltern Firehouse chef, and self-confessed 'design swagger'.
/ NW1 8AH; www.gabeto.co.uk; booking max 8 may apply.

Gaby's WC2 £36 3 2 2
30 Charing Cross Rd   020 7836 4233   5–3B
"Ignore the unappealing, grot hole façade" – this "cramped and rather
tatty" theatreland relic by Leicester Square tube is "an institution you need
to try", serving authentic Jewish and Middle Eastern specials, including
"the best falafels in the West End" (possibly a first when it opened in 1965)
and perfect for "salt beef, latkes and a pickle with retsina before a show".
Apparently Jeremy Corbyn's favourite pit stop, it won major kudos for
thwarting its aristocratic landlord's efforts to redevelop in 2011.
/ WC2H 0DE; midnight, Sun 10 pm; No Amex.

Galley N1 £56 3 2 3
105-106 Upper St   020 3670 0740   9–3D
An "interesting menu" of modern European dishes, "especially seafood",
makes this a "welcome and upmarket addition" to Upper Street in Islington
– although "it's not cheap". There's an impressive sharing platter of hot
seafood, crab and fish, and they also deliver a superior "fish 'n' chip fix".
/ N1 1QN; www.galleylondon.co.uk; @Galleylondon; 11 pm; set weekday L £36 (FP).

Gallipoli £32 2 3 4
102 Upper St, N1   020 7359 0630   9–3D
107 Upper St, N1   020 7226 5333   9–3D
120 Upper St, N1   020 7226 8099   9–3D
"Real old Upper Street favourites", these Ottoman-themed Turkish cafés are
"buzzy, bustling and loud – so you have to be in the right mood". Arguably
the cheap scoff is a tad "routine" nowadays, but on most accounts, you still
get "plentiful food at reasonable prices" and a fair dose of "fun".
/ www.cafegallipoli.com; 11 pm, Fri & Sat midnight.

Galvin at the Athenaeum W1 £65 3 4 2
Athenaeum Hotel, 116 Piccadilly   020 7640 3333   3–4B
Plusses and minuses for the Galvin Bros new more "casual" and "café-style"
regime at this hitherto rather overlooked dining room (whose 2016 relaunch
is part of a programme to boost the profile of this Art Deco hotel, facing
Green Park). To its credit, it does inspire much more feedback nowadays,
with praise for its "friendly staff and bistro cooking". On the downside
though, "much of its previously characterful atmosphere was lost in the
massive refurb" leaving the space feeling "humdrum and hotel-y". Top Tip –
"fab value lunchtime menu". / W1J 7BJ; www.athenaeumhotel.com;
@galvinathenaeum; 10.30 pm.

Galvin at Windows,
Park Lane London Hilton Hotel W1   £111   2 2 5
22 Park Ln   020 7208 4021   3–4A

"The view would melt anyone's heart" at this 28th-floor eyrie, overlooking Buckingham Palace's gardens and Hyde Park. But whereas many fans see it as a "fantastic all-rounder", particularly for business or romance, refuseniks rail at food that's "somewhat pedestrian" and service that's surprisingly "hit 'n' miss". Top Tip – the neighbouring bar actually has a better outlook! / W1K 1BE; www.galvinatwindows.com; @GalvinatWindows; 10 pm, Thu-Sat 10.30 pm, Sun 3 pm; closed Sat L & Sun D; No trainers; booking max 5 may apply; set weekday L £61 (FP), set Sun L £84 (FP).

Galvin Bistrot de Luxe W1   £69   3 3 3
66 Baker St   020 7935 4007   2–1A

"It never lets you down", say fans of this "staple favourite" south of Baker Street tube – the Galvin brothers first venture, known for its "sophisticated and well-presented" bistro cuisine and "bustling, business-like and atmospheric" style. Top Tip – "the set menu is an absolute steal". / W1U 7DJ; www.galvinbistrotdeluxe.com; @bistrotdeluxe; 10.30 pm, Thu-Sat 10.45 pm, Sun 9.30 pm; set weekday L £33 (FP), set pre-theatre £37 (FP), set Sun L £48 (FP).

Galvin HOP E1   £57   2 3 3
35 Spital Sq   020 7299 0404   13–2B

"Not so much has changed since Café à Vin was converted into a pub", but views differ as to whether that's a good thing for this "busy bar". For fans the Galvin Bros' posh gastro-fare ("a decent steak" in particular) is "brilliantly adaptable", but it can also be "hit 'n' miss" and critics "are not sure the overall concept works: it's not really a bistro, not really a gastropub either". / E1 6DY; www.galvinrestaurants.com/section/62/1/galvinhop; @Galvin_brothers; 10.30 pm, Sun 9.30 pm; booking max 5 may apply; set pre theatre £38 (FP).

GALVIN LA CHAPELLE E1   £85   3 2 4
35 Spital Sq   020 7299 0400   13–2B

"A sumptuous and dramatic setting" – the "elegant" conversion of a Victorian school chapel – provides "one of the best dining rooms in London" at the Galvin's celebrated Spitalfields fixture. At its best it's still a "fabulous all-rounder" for business or pleasure, with "superb French food, served with flair". Its ratings have slipped in the last couple of years however – "disjointed service" is the biggest bugbear. / E1 6DY; www.galvinlachapelle.com; @galvin_brothers; 10.30 pm, Sun 9.30 pm; No trainers; booking max 8 may apply; set weekday L, pre-theatre & Sun L £54 (FP).

The Game Bird at The Stafford London SW1 £70   3 4 4
16-18 St James's Place   020 7518 1234   3–4C

"Very comfortable, discreet luxury hotel, hidden away in St James's" that's always been curiously off the radar from a culinary standpoint. Under chef James Durrant, it's "light, airy and opulent, marbled dining room around a large bar" was relaunched in 2017 aiming to showcase UK produce, with a particular focus on game, and wins solid support, particularly from business diners, thanks to its "fabulous" cuisine and "professional and dependable" standards. Top Menu Tip – "chicken Kiev with lashings of truffle butter... what more could you want?" / SW1A 1NJ; thestaffordlondon.com/the-game-bird; @TheGameBirdLON; 10 pm.

Ganapati SE15 £45 **5** **4** **3**
38 Holly Grove   020 7277 2928   1–4C
"South India comes to South London" at this "friendly and cosy" Peckham
"perennial" – the area's longest serving foodie hotspot – which is "untypical,
as you sit at long wooden tables and are served by female, non-Asian staff"
(it's run by Brit Claire Fisher who was inspired to open it after her return
from travelling). "Fabulous spicing, good quality ingredients, and a regularly
changing menu ensure fresh surprises at each visit!" / SE15 5DF;
www.ganapatirestaurant.com; 10.30 pm, Sun 10 pm; closed Mon; No Amex.

The Garden Cafe at the Garden Museum SE1 **NEW**
5 Lambeth Palace Rd   020 7401 8865   2–4D
Lambeth's very civilised Garden Museum, highly favoured by ladies who
lunch, is converted from one of London's oldest churches, by Lambeth
Palace, and its café re-opened in summer 2017, with a new copper-and-
glass pavilion building as its home. Chefs Harry Kaufman (St John Bread
& Wine) and George Ryle (Padella, Primeur) present a menu of seasonal
British fare – initial press feedback is very upbeat. / SE1 7LB;
www.gardenmuseum.org.uk; @GardenMuseumLDN; 5 pm, Sat 3.30 pm; L only.

Le Garrick WC2 £54 **2** **3** **4**
10-12 Garrick St   020 7240 7649   5–3C
"Warm and welcoming staff" and an inviting interior ("improved after
a recent refit") add to the appeal of this "reliable old favourite" in Covent
Garden. "The menu comprises the usual French suspects and even if the
cooking won't rock your world, the pre-theatre menu is good value for
money". / WC2E 9BH; www.legarrick.co.uk; @le_garrick; 10.30 pm, Sun 5pm;
closed Sun; set pre theatre £34 (FP).

The Garrison SE1 £51 **3** **3** **3**
99 Bermondsey St   020 7089 9355   10–4D
This "very enjoyable and busy, buzzy ex-pub" was one of the first gastro-
destinations in Bermondsey, and "remains a favourite", thanks in no small
part to its "ever-changing seasonal menu". / SE1 3XB; www.thegarrison.co.uk;
@TheGarrisonSE1; 10 pm, Fri & Sat 10.30 pm, Sun 9 pm.

Gastronhome SW11 £71 **4** **4** **2**
59 Lavender Hill, London   020 3417 5639   11–2C
"Brilliantly done!" Damien Fremont's contemporary take on classic French
cuisine has built a small but enthusiastic following for the venue he founded
on Lavender Hill with Christopher Nespoux. But while fans say its "five-
course 'surprise' tasting menu is a sublime lesson in elegant simplicity",
the odd reporter has the opposite reservation: "too chefy looking –
everything looks pretty, with smears and flower sprinkles, but it detracts
from the food". / SW11; www.gastronhome.co.uk; @gastronhome1; 10:15 pm;
closed Mon & Sun; No jeans.

The Gate £52 **4** **3** **3**
22-24 Seymour Place, W1   020 7724 6656   2–2A **NEW**
51 Queen Caroline St, W6   020 8748 6932   8–2C
370 St John St, EC1   020 7278 5483   9–3D
"I'm not a veggie but this was one of the best meals I've had in the
last year" – typical praise for these "ingenious" veggies, which offer
"an unmatched range of such accomplished dishes, beautifully sourced and
expertly presented". From the "lovely hidden-gem original in Hammersmith"
(behind the Hammy-O), they added a similarly "top notch" branch in trendy
Seymour Place this year. Islington is probably the weakest performer of the
three – "it's let down by a noisy environment" – but even so it's "decent and
very handy for Sadlers Wells". / www.thegaterestaurants.com; 10.30 pm; W1 Sun
9.45 pm; W6 Sun 9.30 pm; SRA-Food Made Good – 3 stars.

Gaucho £82 ② ② ②

As "a place to impress", especially on business, these well-known Argentinian steak houses are still well-recommended by some reporters for their "fine steaks" and "fabulous South American wines". Even fans can find the bill "noticeably painful" however, particularly given the "indifferent" service, and critics feel the overall offering is "bland" and "outrageously overpriced". / www.gauchorestaurants.co.uk; 11 pm, Thu-Sat midnight; EC3 & EC1 closed Sat & Sun, WC2 & EC2 closed Sat L & Sun.

GAUTHIER SOHO W1 £79 ⑤ ⑤ ④

21 Romilly St 020 7494 3111 5–3A

"The charming necessity to ring the doorbell to get in" helps "to whisk you miles from Soho" at this "intimate" and "elegant" townhouse, whose "calm and quiet atmosphere is amazing for somewhere just one street away from Shaftesbury Avenue". Alexis Gauthier's "mind-blowingly fantastic" seasonal cuisine is "some of the best French cooking in London" – "classic, but never old fashioned" – and backed up by an "unusual and interesting wine selection"; while "uncloying" service is of the "nothing-is-too-much-trouble" variety. "The absence of a Michelin Star since 2012 is baffling" and starkly calls into question the judgement of the tyre men. Top Tip – "lunch is a real snip". / W1D 5AF; www.gauthiersoho.co.uk; @GauthierSoho; 9.30 pm, Fri & Sat 10.30 pm; closed Mon & Sun; booking max 7 may apply.

LE GAVROCHE W1 £134 ④ ⑤ ④

43 Upper Brook St 020 7408 0881 3–2A

"A well-oiled, old-school machine that still delivers!" The Roux dynasty's Mayfair icon "never goes out of fashion" to its army of fans for whom it's "simply the best". Founded in Chelsea in 1967, it moved to its current "cosy" site round the corner from the American Embassy in 1982, and even if the occasional reporter "wishes it wasn't in a basement" the general effect "oozes class and charm". Michel Roux Jr succeeded his father as the helm in 1991, and "the regular presence of the great man himself adds value; he takes time with his customers and actually talks!" (Currently his daughter Emily is being primed as next in line.) The Gallic cuisine – under head chef Rachel Humphrey – is "rich and sumptuous", while the "polished but un-condescending" service under Emmanuel Landré is "almost other-worldly good". "A hefty chunk out of the wallet" is of course de rigueur, but even so gripes about "arm-and-a-leg" bills increased this year, contributing to the food grade missing a 5/5 for the first time in a few years. Top Tip – "The fixed price lunch menu is still the best deal in London!" / W1K 7QR; www.le-gavroche.co.uk; @michelrouxjr; 10 pm; closed Sat L & Sun; Jacket required; booking essential; set weekday L £101 (FP).

Gay Hussar W1 £51 ① ② ④

2 Greek St 020 7437 0973 5–2A

"Another year of hearty Hungarian fare" has passed by at this venerable Soho institution – "a haven on a cold winter's day" with lashings of "old fashioned atmosphere" and decades of Labour Party legend on the side. For some reporters, the "tasty goulash" never fails to delight, but it's really not a culinary hotspot: "the quality of the caricatures on the walls is far higher than the dishes on the table". / W1D 4NB; www.gayhussar.co.uk; @GayhussarsSoho; 10.45 pm; closed Sun.

Gaylord W1 £60 ④ ④ ③

79-81 Mortimer St 020 7580 3615 2–1B

Half a century and counting, and this stately and "impeccably run" Fitzrovia veteran is "still always enjoyable" according to reports. Praise too for "new menu additions with a modern twist", such as "Golgappa street-food shots – a food journey transporting you straight to the lanes of Old Delhi or beaches of Chowpatty!" / W1W 7SJ; www.gaylordlondon.com; @gaylord_london; 10.45 pm, Sun 10.30 pm.

Gazette £47 2️⃣2️⃣3️⃣
79 Sherwood Ct, Chatfield Rd, SW11   020 7223 0999   11–1C
100 Balham High St, SW12   020 8772 1232   11–2C
147 Upper Richmond Rd, SW15   020 8789 6996   11–2B
"Trying and largely succeeding" is a fair view on these jolly Gallic "neighbourhood bistros" in Balham, Clapham and Putney, particularly praised for their "excellent value set price deals". Disasters are not unknown here though, and it's also true to say that they can be "middling and inconsistent" ("I will return… but only with friends who know it!)". / www.gazettebrasserie.co.uk; 11 pm.

GBR SW1 NEW £70
St James's St   020 7491 4840   3–4D
Launched in May 2017 simultaneously in Duke's London (St James's) and Duke's Dubai (Jumeirah Palm), GBR – Great British Restaurant – is an all-day homage to British scoff, open from breakfast time through lunch to afternoon tea and dinner. / SW1A 1NA; www.gbrrestaurantslondon.com; @gbr_london.

Geales £56 2️⃣2️⃣2️⃣
1 Cale St, SW3   020 7965 0555   6–2C
2 Farmer St, W8   020 7727 7528   7–2B
This fish 'n' chip veteran (est 1939) just off Notting Hill Gate (with a more recent spin-off in Chelsea) still has a few fans, but dwindling feedback can make it seem surprisingly obscure nowadays. / www.geales.com; 10.30 pm, Sun 4 pm; W8 closed Mon; SW3 closed Sun & Mon.

Gelupo W1 £8 5️⃣2️⃣2️⃣
7 Archer St   020 7287 5555   4–3D
"The best ice cream in London, simple as that", say addicts of Jacob Kenedy's little Soho gelateria (opposite his Bocca di Lupo) where the selection is "not quite your traditional Italian flavours" but rather a series of "adventurous (but not actually bonkers) flavour combos". / W1D 7AU; www.gelupo.com; @GelupoGelato; 11 pm, Fri & Sat midnight; No Amex; no booking.

Gem N1 £32 3️⃣4️⃣2️⃣
265 Upper St   020 7359 0405   9–2D
"It's not flash", but "unusually good value" enthuses reports on this "no-frills" Turkish-Kurdish local near Angel, which offers "lovely mezze" in "generous portions", and whose "super staff make families very welcome". "BYO if you ask". / N1 2UQ; www.gemrestaurant.org.uk; @Gem_restaurant; 11 pm, Sun 10 pm; No Amex.

George in the Strand WC2
213 Strand   020 7353 9638   2–2D
Too few reports for a rating for the traditionalist-looking, first-floor restaurant (with open kitchen) of this revamped, black and white, half-timbered pub opposite the Royal Courts of Justice, but one early report suggests the chef is helping its gastropub menu punch well above its weight, as do many initial online reviews. / WC2R 1AP; www.georgeinthestrand.com; @thegeorgestrand; 10pm, Fri & Sat 10.30pm, Sun 9pm.

German Gymnasium N1 £72 2️⃣2️⃣3️⃣
1 King's Boulevard   020 7287 8000   9–3C
"What a stunner!" A former Victorian gymnasium right next to King's Cross station was converted two years ago into this "impressive and unique" D&D London venue, and, especially given its unusual Teutonic formula, it has all the elements for a smash hit… except the execution: too often the "solid German fare" feels "average and significantly overpriced", which – not helped by "slow" service – can create "a let-down given all the hype". Still, there's always solace in the "joy" of a wine list – being focused on Germany and Austria "forces you to veer away from the standard and what discoveries that brings". / N1C 4BU; www.germangymnasium.com; @TheGermanGym; 11 pm, Sun 9 pm; set weekday L & pre-theatre £48 (FP).

Giacomo's NW2 £40 **3** **3** **2**
428 Finchley Rd   020 7794 3603   1–1B
For a "cheap 'n' cheerful" nosh up Child's HIll way, bear in mind this cosy, consistently well-rated, family-run Italian of over fifteen year's standing. / NW2 2HY; www.giacomos.co.uk; 10 pm.

Gifto's Lahore Karahi UB1 £25 **3** **2** **2**
162-164 The Broadway   020 8813 8669   1–3A
This large, well-known Pakistani canteen on one of Southall town centre's main roads offers "great value" – "especially for its grills". / UB1 1NN; www.gifto.com; 11.30 pm, Sat & Sun midnight; booking weekdays only.

The Gilbert Scott NW1 £74 **2** **3** **4**
Euston Rd   020 7278 3888   9–3C
"Even the splendour of the dining room does not explain the bill" at Marcus Wareing's "airy" and "atmospheric" venue, near the Eurostar Platforms – even those who feel the British cuisine is good can find prices "excessive", and its worst critics feel the mismatch is "ridiculous". / NW1 2AR; www.thegilbertscott.co.uk; @Thegilbertscott; 11 pm, Sun 9 pm; booking max 7 may apply.

Ginger & White £13 **3** **4** **3**
2 England's Ln, NW3   020 7722 9944   9–2A
4a-5a, Perrins Ct, NW3   020 7431 9098   9–2A
"Top-quality coffee", "great breakfasts" and "excellent cakes" are the winning formula for these "casual" Antipodean-style caffeine stops off Hampstead High Street and Belsize Park. They can be "cramped and busy", but "you feel somebody is making food you like, just for you". / www.gingerandwhite.com; 5.30 pm; W1 closed Sun.

Ginza Onodera SW1 NEW £86 **4** **5** **2**
15 Bury St   020 7839 1101   3–3D
"Recently refurbished and renamed from Matsuri" (RIP after 23 years but same owners) – this ambitious fixture (part of an international chain) in a large basement near Piccadilly Circus recently emerged from a £2.5m renovation, and the 128-seat space continues to provide a wide array of eating options (from sushi to teppan and robata, from private rooms to the Chef's Table). Even if it has been overlooked in recent years, this has always been a top quality, traditional Japanese and early reports suggest it's on fine form: "gobsmackingly expensive, but equally gobsmackingly delicious". / SW1Y 6AL; onodera-group.com/uk/#menu; @Onodera_London; 10 pm.

Giraffe £40 **2** **2** **2**
"The free giraffe-shaped drinks stirrers are always a winner" for amusing youngsters at these supremely family-friendly diners, where "staff are happy to work around balloons and colouring". Its world food menu offers "great choice" but divides views – a sizeable minority feel results are plain "dispiriting" nowadays, but parents in particular still say it's "good value and fun". / www.giraffe.net; 11 pm, Sun 10.30 pm; no booking, Sat & Sun 9 am-5 pm.

The Glasshouse TW9 £82 **5** **4** **3**
14 Station Pde   020 8940 6777   1–3A
"Interesting cuisine in the style of sister establishments, Chez Bruce and La Trompette" help distinguish this bright, contemporary ("slightly bland") dining room by Kew Gardens as "a real treat of a local". Ratings recovered this year, thanks to consistent praise for its "discreet and polite service" and "food that's always bang on". / TW9 3PZ; www.glasshouserestaurant.co.uk; @The__Glasshouse; 10.30 pm, Sun 10 pm; booking max 8 may apply.

Globe Tavern SE1 £51 **3** **3** **3**
8 Bedale St   020 7407 0043   10–4C
Bridget Jones's Diary was filmed above this Borough Market boozer – an atmospheric spot in the heart of the area, with dishes sourced from the market traders. / SE1 9AL; www.theglobeboroughmarket.com; @TheGlobeSE1.

Go-Viet SW7 NEW £57 4 3 3
53 Old Brompton Rd   020 7589 6432   6–2C
"Fun and casual" spin-off from Jeff Tan's Soho Viet Food – "the food tastes great and looks magic too" at this a 60-cover café near South Kensington tube. / SW7 3JS; vietnamfood.co.uk/go-viet; 10 pm, Fri & Sat 10.30 pm.

Goddards At Greenwich SE10 £15 3 4 4
22 King William Walk   020 8305 9612   1–3D
"There's a good selection, but why would you want anything other than the most traditional pie, mash and liquor, plus a mug of tea?", if you visit this Greenwich veteran (est 1890) – one of London's dying breed of traditional pie 'n' mash shops. / SE10 9HU; www.goddardsatgreenwich.co.uk; @GoddardsPieMash; 7.30 pm, Fri & Sat 8 pm; L & early evening only.

Gogi W2 £40 3 3 3
451 Edgware Rd   020 7724 3018   9–4A
Moody, "slightly clubby" decor adds to the atmosphere of this consistently well-rated Korean BBQ, well positioned near the canal in Little Venice. / W2 1TH; www.gogi-restaurant.com; 10.30 pm, Sun 10 pm.

Gökyüzü N4 £33 3 3 3
26-27 Grand Pde, Green Lanes   020 8211 8406   1–1C
The "super-fresh ingredients", "tip-top grilled meats", "vast portions and terrific prices" at this "very slick operation" on Harringay's Grand Parade "set the Turkish standard". "You can feed the whole family for less than £40". / N4 1LG; www.gokyuzurestaurant.co.uk; @Gokyuzulondon; midnight, Fri & Sat 1 am.

Gold Mine W2 £38 4 2 2
102 Queensway   020 7792 8331   7–2C
"Nobody does it better" say fans of the "top crispy roast duck" at this Bayswater Cantonese, which they claim vies with the more famous Four Seasons next door. "Don't expect fab service or elegant ambience, but foodwise you won't be disappointed". / W2 3RR; 11 pm.

Golden Chippy SE10 £14 3 4 2
62 Greenwich High Rd   020 8692 4333   1–3D
You definitely get the "best fish 'n' chips in the area" at Chris Kanizi's Greenwich chippy. We mean it no disrespect when we say that TripAdvisor's November 2016 ranking of '#1 out of 17,372 Restaurants in London' was over-egging it a tad. / SE10 8LF; www.thegoldenchippy.com; 11 pm.

Golden Dragon W1 £31 4 2 2
28-29 Gerrard St   020 7734 1073   5–3A
"If in doubt in Chinatown, you won't go far wrong" if you choose this busy staple which is "worth the ten minute wait for dim sum and decent noodles" (and there's also "a very interesting menu in Chinese"). "I took some fussy Chinese friends there and they were pleasantly surprised!". STOP PRESS: A Colindale outpost opened summer 2017 (see Bang Bang Oriental). / W1 6JW; goldendragonlondon.com; 11.30 pm, Fri-Sun midnight; no booking.

Golden Hind W1 £36 3 3 2
73 Marylebone Ln   020 7486 3644   2–1A
"You won't find fresher fish or better (greaseless) chips anywhere else in London", say fans of this well-loved Marylebone institution, founded in 1914. But while on most accounts it's "still a classic", ratings slipped a tad this year, and some regulars still "miss the previous owner" ("under the new management you can no longer BYO, which was one of its best features!"). / W1U 2PN; www.goldenhindrestaurant.com; 10 pm; closed Sat L & Sun.

Good Earth £63 222
233 Brompton Rd, SW3 020 7584 3658 6–2C
143-145 The Broadway, NW7 020 8959 7011 1–1B
11 Bellevue Rd, SW17 020 8682 9230 11–2C
"A very old friend that continues to please" is how many long-term fans still
see these "comfortable" Chinese stalwarts in Balham, Knightsbridge and
Mill Hill, where the prix/qualité verdict has traditionally been that they're
"slightly overpriced, but worth it". Ratings overall remain on the wane
however, and – even if harsh critiques are rare – there's a feeling that
they're "not as good as they used to be". / www.goodearthgroup.co.uk; Mon-Sat
10.45 pm, Sun 10 pm; NW7 11.15 pm, Sun 10.45 pm.

The Good Egg N16 £53 443
93 Church St 020 7682 2120 1–1C
"It's worth braving the queues", in particular at brunch, for this white-brick-
walled Stokey deli. The odd dish can seem "strange", but the Middle
Eastern/American cooking is "exceptional quality", and service is from
"genuine staff who clearly love the place". STOP PRESS: A Soho offshoot
is slated to open November 2017. / N16 0AS; www.thegoodeggn16.com;
@TheGoodEgg_; 10.30 pm, Sun 3.30 pm; no booking; SRA-Food Made Good –
3 stars.

Goodman £93 442
24-26 Maddox St, W1 020 7499 3776 3–2C
3 South Quay, E14 020 7531 0300 12–1C
11 Old Jewry, EC2 020 7600 8220 10–2C
"Every cut is served exactly the way it should be" at these testosterone-
heavy, NYC-style steak-houses, which – amongst the multiples (including
Hawksmoor) – serve "the best steak in London full stop", and are naturally
"ideal for business". "Staff are personable which keeps the atmosphere
buzzing", and "while they are far from cheap, the meat is top quality,
ranging from UK, US and further afield; matched with an excellent, varied
wine list, with US bottles very well represented".
/ www.goodmanrestaurants.com; 10.30 pm; W1 closed Sun, EC2 closed Sat & Sun,
E14 closed Sat L & Sun.

Gordon Ramsay SW3 £157 222
68-69 Royal Hospital Rd 020 7352 4441 6–3D
"The old standard of cooking is long gone, yet the bill defies gravity…" –
that's the overall verdict on the TV chef's "chic" (but some would say
"surprisingly small and claustrophobic") Chelsea flagship, whose long
overdue turnaround would provide great material for one of his TV shows.
On the plus-side, there are many loyal fans who say Matt Abe's cuisine can
be "fabulous" and who continue to laud Jean-Claude Breton's "impeccable"
service. Criticisms that the place is "stuck up", "down a notch on previously"
or just "quite underwhelming overall" are far too prevalent however, which
given the "shocking prices" can lead to a sense of "crushing
disappointment". Mr Michelin Man wake up – this is not a three star
performance. / SW3 4HP; www.gordonramsay.com; @GordonRamsay; 10.15 pm;
closed Sat & Sun; No jeans; booking max 9 may apply; set weekday L £106 (FP).

Gordon's Wine Bar WC2 £38 225
47 Villiers St 020 7930 1408 5–4D
"Dark cave-like cellars" create a superb atmosphere at this epic old wine
bar (dating from 1890) by Embankment Gardens, which also boasts one
of central London's nicest outside terraces (with BBQ in summer). The
"excellent choice of wine and sherries" is another reason the world and his
dog flock to the place – the self-service pies, cold cuts, cheeses and salads
are certainly no incentive to hurry along. / WC2N 6NE;
www.gordonswinebar.com; @GordonsWineBar; 11 pm, Sun 10 pm.

The Goring
See 'Dining Room, The Goring Hotel'

Gourmet Burger Kitchen   £28   3 2 2
"Hard to beat, even with all the new competition" – this "always reliable"
stalwart (the first of the upmarket burger chains to hit the capital) still
"does what it says on the tin": "the burgers here are great, and as a venue
for a no-fuss meal when the family are hungry and in a hurry" it's
"good value" and "very tasty". / www.gbkinfo.com; most branches close 10.30 pm;
no booking.

Gourmet Goat SE1   £12   4 4 2
Borough Market, Unit 27a Rochester Walk   020 8050 1973   10–4C
Sustainable kid goat, rose veal and mutton are cooked Greek-Cypriot style
by Nadia and Nick Stokes at this Borough Market specialist, which again
earned consistently high grades from reporters. / SE1 9AH;
www.gourmetgoat.co.uk; @gourmet_goat; no booking; SRA-Food Made Good – 3 stars.

The Gowlett Arms SE15   £37   4 3 4
62 Gowlett Rd   020 7635 7048   1–4D
"Decent pizzas in a back-street boozer" is an accurate but understated
description of a combination that's gone down a treat for many years at this
wood-panelled Peckham hotspot, also serving meats home-smoked in the
cellar. / SE15 4HY; www.thegowlett.com; @theGowlettArms; 10.30 pm, Sun 9 pm;
Cash only.

Goya SW1   £46   3 3 2
34 Lupus St   020 7976 5309   2–4C
"Genuine, tasty tapas" and "friendly" service ensure this family-run Pimlico
Spaniard is "always busy", even though "the tables are too tight". Try to sit
upstairs ("the basement dining room is less charming"). / SW1V 3EB;
www.goyarestaurant.co.uk; midnight, Sun 11.30 pm.

The Grand Imperial,
Guoman Grosvenor Hotel SW1   £62   3 2 2
101 Buckingham Palace Rd   020 7821 8898   2–4B
"A surprising location for a quiet and spacious Chinese" – this hotel dining
room by Victoria station does "superb dim sum", and some other
"very good" Cantonese fare. "While the food remains above average,
it's now very expensive for what it is though, and service sometimes
struggles". / SW1W 0SJ; www.grandimperiallondon.com; 10.30 pm; set weekday L
£39 (FP).

Grand Trunk Road E18   £59   4 4 3
219 High St   020 8505 1965   1–1D
"The depth of flavour of the dishes is incredible" say fans of this
comparatively elegant high street Indian yearling in Woodford: brainchild
of Rajesh Suri and Dayashankar Sharma, the ex-manager and ex-head chef
of Mayfair's Tamarind. / E18 2PB; www.gtrrestaurant.co.uk; @GT_Road; 10.30pm;
closed Mon & Sun D.

Granger & Co   £53   3 3 3
237-239 Pavilion Rd, SW1   020 3848 1060   6–2D **NEW**
175 Westbourne Grove, W11   020 7229 9111   7–1B
Stanley Building, St Pancras Sq, N1   020 3058 2567   9–3C
The Buckley Building, 50 Sekforde St, EC1   020 7251 9032   10–1A
"Friends have returned from Australia full of the joys of Bill Granger, now we
can get the real thing!" – so say fans of these "cool and airy", "posh-brunch
heavens" who are prepared to endure the savage queues and "sometimes
indifferent service" for his "brilliant and very different breakfasts", and other
"healthy and innovative food (although a menu which requires a dictionary
might be seen as a bit pretentious!)". However, at the W11 original
in particular, there are critics who say: "it's not worth the wait given plenty
of alternatives nearby". / Mon-Sat 10 pm, Sun 5pm.

The Grazing Goat W1 £60 2 3 3
6 New Quebec St   020 7724 7243   2–2A
The "lovely venue" can outshine the other elements of the experience at this extremely popular dining pub (in fact with no space for drinking only any more), a short walk from Marble Arch. / W1H 7RQ; www.thegrazinggoat.co.uk; @TheGrazingGoat; 10 pm, Sun 9.30 pm.

Great Nepalese NW1 £38 3 4 3
48 Eversholt St   020 7388 6737   9–3C
"A valiant survivor (I've been going here for 50 years!)" – this veteran "no frills" curry house on a grotty Euston side street serves "some very unusual dishes", with plenty of choice for veggies. Some long term fans however fear it's "not quite so special as it was before". / NW1 1DA; www.great-nepalese.co.uk; 11.30 pm, Sun 10 pm.

Great Queen Street WC2 £54 3 2 2
32 Great Queen St   020 7242 0622   5–1D
Seasonal British cooking that's "unusual and always interesting" has won a big foodie following for this Covent Garden gastropub. A 'Curate's Egg' quality to reports has emerged in recent times however: "borderline good, but lacking the punchiness of the past"... "great food, but complacent on the service". / WC2B 5AA; www.greatqueenstreetrestaurant.co.uk; @greatqueenstreet; 10.30 pm, Sun 3.30 pm; closed Sun D; No Amex.

The Greek Larder, Arthouse N1 £58 3 2 2
1 York Way   020 3780 2999   9–3C
In ever-more-"arty" King's Cross, Theodore Kyriakou's "fun and trendy" two-year-old offers his "modern take on Greek cuisine" and is "smaller than some of its more impersonal and noisy competitors nearby". Upbeat feedback is sometimes tinged with "inconsistencies" of both food and service, but "when you can eat in the sun, it's a welcome reminder of Aegean island life". / N1C 4AS; www.thegreeklarder.co.uk; @thegreeklarder; 10.30 pm, Sun 5 pm; set weekday L £38 (FP).

The Green EC1 £48
29 Clerkenwell Grn   020 7490 8010   10–1A
Prominently-sited on a corner of Clerkenwell Green, this attractive new pub shares the superior design DNA of its sibling The Culpeper, and a similar setup with ground floor bar and first floor restaurant. / EC1R 0DU; www.thegreenclerkenwell.com; 10 pm, Sun 6 pm.

Green Cottage NW3 £38 3 2 2
9 New College Pde   020 7722 5305   9–2A
This longstanding "neighbourhood Chinese" in a parade of shops in Swiss Cottage endures thanks to its "reliably good" and "inexpensive" chow – expect neither a cheery welcome nor a scintillating atmosphere. / NW3 5EP; 11 pm; No Amex.

The Green Room, The National Theatre SE1 £46 2 2 2
101 Upper Ground   020 7452 3630   2–3D
Decorated with props and scenery from prior productions, the NT's ("very noisy") 'neighbourhood diner' is an airy space (surrounded by a sustainable garden). Some reports are lukewarm at best, but most consider the food "decent", certainly for a pre-show bite. / SE1 9PP; www.greenroom.london; @greenroomSE1; 10.30 pm, Sun 7 pm.

Greenberry Café NW1 £54 3 3 3
101 Regents Park Rd 020 7483 3765 9–2B
"Good daily specials and a reasonable, weekday prix fixe menu" along with "popular breakfasts and weekend brunch" help keep things busy at this all-day Primrose Hill local ("always crowded with babies and dog-owners"). It's "not entirely cheap, but there's an excellent price/quality ratio", and it's "run very graciously and effectively". / NW1 8UR; greenberrycafe.co.uk; @Greenberry_Cafe; 10 pm; closed Mon D & Sun D; No Amex; set weekday L £33 (FP).

The Greenhouse W1 £110 4 4 4
27a Hays Mews 020 7499 3331 3–3B
Marlon Abela's "serene oasis tucked away in the midst of bustling Mayfair is a delight", and was one of London's highest-rated all-rounders this year. Arnaud Bignon's "terrific cuisine" has "the hallmarks of impressive refinement and precision", but even so risks being eclipsed by arguably "the biggest and most-in-depth wine list in the country". Service is "exceptional", in particular the "charming and knowledgeable sommelier", and "a well-spaced interior that ought to be very corporate is actually lovely and memorable". "The only downer is the eye-popping prices" but on practically all accounts they are worth it. / W1J 5NY; www.greenhouserestaurant.co.uk; @greenhouse27a; 10.30 pm; closed Sat L & Sun; booking max 12 may apply; set weekday L £45 (FP).

Greenwood SW1 NEW £49
170 Victoria St 020 3058 1000 2–4B
Another new opening (alongside Aviary) for the ETM Group, this time in the Nova mega-development in Victoria – a split level venue with a sports lounge upstairs, all-day dining on the ground floor, and (possibly a first for us) an in-house barber and brow 'n' lashes bar for those can't-wait grooming needs. / SW1E 5LB; www.greenwoodlondon.com.

Gremio de Brixton, St Matthew's Church SW2 £44 3 3 3
Effra Rd 020 7924 0660 11–2D
Fun, "friendly" tapas haunt in the atmospheric crypt under Brixton's St Matthew's Church, fuelled by cocktails and a decent wine selection; DJs at the weekend. / SW2 1JF; www.gremiodebrixton.com; @gremiobrixton; 10.30 pm, Sat 11 pm, Sun 10 pm.

The Grill at McQueen EC2 £70 3 4 3
59-61 Tabernacle St 020 7036 9229 13–1A
All things Steve McQueen provide the theme for this comfortable and plushly decked out Shoreditch grill, which has "upped its game since a revamp last October", serving very decent steaks and "killer cocktails". Top Tip – BYO free on Tuesdays. / EC2A 4AA; www.thegrillmcqueen.co.uk; @TheGrillMcQueen; No shorts.

Ground Coffee Society SW15 £30 3 4 3
79 Lower Richmond Rd 0845 862 9994 11–1B
"The coffee's fantastic" at this Antipodean outfit, also with cakes and light bites, but even in sedate Putney "there can be long queues" ("I can no longer even get a table!"). / SW15 1ET; www.groundcoffeesociety.com; @groundcoffeesociety; 6 pm; L only; no booking.

Guglee £38 3 2 2
7 New College Pde, NW3 020 7722 8478 9–2A
279 West End Ln, NW6 020 7317 8555 1–1B
"Original", street food-influenced cooking wins solid praise for this modern Indian duo in West Hampstead and Swiss Cottage. / www.guglee.co.uk; 11 am.

The Guildford Arms SE10 £51 3 4 3

55 Guildford Grove   020 8691 6293   1–3D

"A hidden gem we hope stays hidden" – this three-storey Georgian pub in Greenwich offers "great cooking and attentive but not intrusive service" in the upstairs dining room. Chef-director Guy Awford previously ran "the wonderful Inside" (RIP, long considered "the best in Greenwich"). / SE10 8JY; www.theguildfordarms.co.uk; @GuildfordArms_; 10 pm, Sun 9 pm; closed Mon.

The Guinea Grill W1 £75 4 4 4

30 Bruton Pl   020 7409 1728   3–3B

"Suddenly fashionable despite its old school ambience" – this "surprising" grill room, behind a pub in a picturesque Mayfair mews, provides some of London's best steaks and pies (albeit at "very expensive" prices) in a well-preserved, traditional setting. / W1J 6NL; www.theguinea.co.uk; @guineagrill; closed Sat L & Sun; booking max 8 may apply.

Gul and Sepoy E1 NEW

65 Commercial St   020 7247 1407   13–2C

The latest Indian restaurant from Harneet and Devina Baweja, the duo behind the flavoursome Gunpowder and Madame D's (also located on Commercial Street), arrives in the City in October 2017. / E1 6BD; www.gulandsepoy.com; @GulandSepoy.

The Gun E14 £65 3 3 4

27 Coldharbour   020 7515 5222   12–1C

This historic Docklands tavern has "a wonderful atmosphere right on the Thames" and views directly across to the O2. "Long established as a riverside gastropub", it serves "imaginative, distinctive food" in the "classy dining room" or al fresco on a heated terrace. / E14 9NS; www.thegundocklands.com; @thegundocklands; 10 pm, Sun 7.30 pm.

Gunpowder E1 £44 4 3 3

11 Whites Row   020 7426 0542   13–2C

"Surprising" flavours help "put a great spin on Indian food" at this "tiny" Spitalfields yearling, whose "fantastic tapas-style dishes" seem "completely authentic, based on family recipes". Top Tips – "venison doughnut" and "wild rabbit pulao – a thing of beauty". / E1 7NF; www.gunpowderlondon.com; @gunpowder_ldn; 10.30 pm.

Gustoso Ristorante & Enoteca SW1 £47 3 4 3

33 Willow Pl   020 7834 5778   2–4B

"Continuing to enchant…" – this "wonderful Italian" is "a jolly place, really hidden away in Pimlico, but with a very local feel to it as it's off-the-beaten-track". Staff are "exceptionally friendly" and "the food is good and doesn't cost an arm and a leg" ("after a hiccough in recent times, it's had a definite return to form"). "And they adore kids… it's very Italian". / SW1P 1JH; ristorantegustoso.co.uk; @GustosoRist; 10.30 pm, Fri & Sat 11 pm, Sun 9.30 pm.

GYMKHANA W1 £61 4 4 4

42 Albemarle St   020 3011 5900   3–3C

"Absolutely the bee's knees" – the Sethi family's "classy" Mayfair five-year-old near The Ritz remains London's best-known nouvelle Indian by dint of mixing "terrifically-spiced" cuisine ("whose refinement doesn't detract from powerful punchy flavours") and "heroic wine pairings", with a good pinch of "old-colonial glamour" ("very in keeping with the India I grew up in"). There's also a superb cocktail bar in the basement. Top Tip – "goat brains are a must try!" / W1S 4JH; www.gymkhanalondon.com; @GymkhanaLondon; 10.30 pm; closed Sun.

Haché £38 3 4 4

95-97 High Holborn, WC1   020 7242 4580   2–1D NEW
329-331 Fulham Rd, SW10   020 7823 3515   6–3B
24 Inverness St, NW1   020 7485 9100   9–3B
37 Bedford Hill, SW12   020 8772 9772   11–2C
153 Clapham High St, SW4   020 7738 8760   11–2D
147-149 Curtain Rd, EC2   020 7739 8396   13–1B

Amongst the elite of the posh burger groups – this "cheerful" small group
"never lets you down" with its "great variety" ("awesome by itself, or go
mad with the toppings!") and yummy sides (including "the best sweet potato
fries ever"). "And a focus on quality enables them to serve the real thing"
(it's one of the few chains that will do burgers medium rare).
/ www.hacheburgers.com; 10.30 pm, Fri-Sat 11 pm, Sun 10 pm; WC1 9 pm;
WC1 Sat & Sun.

Hai Cenato SW1 NEW £55 3 3 2

2 Sir Simon Milton Square, 150 Victoria St   020 3816 9320   2–4B
"Fantastic sourdough pizzas-with-a-twist" are the main event at Jason
Atherton's much-heralded newcomer, and they "almost make up for the
dreadful ambience of the soulless new Nova development". Overall,
its ratings are middling though, and sceptics feel that "notwithstanding the
well-presented food, Hai Cenato commits the crime of just not being very
interesting". Maybe try the bar upstairs first. / SW1H 0HW; haicenato.co.uk;
@haicenato; 10 pm, Sun 9.30 pm; booking max 6 may apply; set pre theatre
£37 (FP).

Hakkasan £96 3 2 4

17 Bruton St, W1   020 7907 1888   3–2C
8 Hanway Pl, W1   020 7927 7000   5–1A
"Fast paced, seductive, club-like" – these "wonderfully vibey" operations may
be "so busy and very noisy" but have founded a global brand on the
strength of their "feel-good" ambience and "brilliantly executed
Chinese/pan-Asian cuisine". However, even some fans concede that they can
also seem "hideously expensive" and "brusque" service ("we were kept
waiting, only then to be hassled to order or risk being kicked off the table
at the end of our 2-hour slot") is a perennial gripe. Top Tip – "Their Dim
Sum Sunday is exquisite". / www.hakkasan.com; 12.30 am, Sun 11.15 pm;
W1 12.30 am, Thu-Sat 12.45 am, Sun midnight; no trainers, no sportswear.

Ham Yard Restaurant, Ham Yard Hotel W1 £67 2 3 5

1 Ham Yd   020 3642 1007   4–3D
"Sit outside in the quiet courtyard and enjoy a civilised lunch away from the
bustle of Soho" at this "lovely" Firmdale hotel ("the set deal is fab value"),
which provides an amazingly tranquil "haven" for the West End,
and particularly comes into its own for a "fun, delicious and affordable"
afternoon tea. In the evenings (including pre-theatre) feedback is less
positive, with accusations of "style with no substance" ("very beautiful,
but nothing that earnt the price demanded"). / W1D 7DT;
www.firmdalehotels.com; @Ham_Yard; 11.30 pm, Sun 10.30 pm; set pre theatre
£43 (FP).

The Hampshire Hog W6 £51 3 2 4

227 King St   020 8748 3391   8–2B
Unusually attractive, "always busy" gastropub, on a grotty bit of highway
near Hammersmith Town Hall, which also benefits from a large garden.
It inspired the odd critique this year, but overall is well-rated for its decent
level of cooking. / W6 9JT; www.thehampshirehog.com; @TheHampshireHog;
10 pm, Sun 4 pm; closed Sun D.

Hanger SW6 £50 **3** **4** **3**
461-465 North End Rd   020 7386 9739   6–4A
"A great steak formula – specialising in this undervalued cut of beef, cooked rare with triple-cooked chips, plus a glass of Malbec – for under £30 its a steal!" Top Tip – 'bottomless' basement brunch. / SW6 1NZ; www.hangersteak.co.uk; @hanger_sw6; 10 pm, Sun 9 pm.

The Harcourt W1 £58 **4** **3** **4**
32 Harcourt St   020 3771 8660   7–1D
"Only a gastropub by dint of its decor, as the cuisine is restaurant quality" – this excellent Marylebone yearling provides "terrific Scandi food" and while the cooking is distinctive "it makes a welcome change from over-inventive eclectic menus you see elsewhere". One gripe – "the music can be deafening!" / W1H 4HX; www.theharcourt.com; @the_harcourt; 11 pm, Fri & Sat 11.30 pm, Sun 10 pm.

Hard Rock Café W1 £64 **3** **3** **4**
150 Old Park Ln   020 7514 1700   3–4B
Drugs and nuclear weapons are still forbidden (as they have been since 1971) at this aging rocker, near Hyde Park Corner – the cradle of the global franchise – where the noise level and queue still show no sign of abating. Perhaps surprisingly the burgers here are pretty decent – "huge and a real mouthful." / W1K 1QZ; www.hardrock.com/london; @HardRockLondon; 12.30 am, Fri & Sat 1 am, Sun 10.30 pm; May need 20+ to book.

Hardy's Brasserie W1 £59 **3** **3** **3**
53 Dorset St   020 7935 5929   2–1A
"I go there whenever I'm in the neighbourhood – I love it!" – this old-school, independent wine bar and brasserie is tucked away in Marylebone, and though it's never going to set the world on fire its welcoming charm and modest prices maintain a loyal fan club. / W1U 7NH; www.hardysbrasserie.com; @hardys_W1; 10 pm; closed Sat & Sun.

Hare & Tortoise £42 **3** **2** **2**
11-13 The Brunswick, WC1   020 7278 9799   2–1D
373 Kensington High St, W14   020 7603 8887   8–1D
156 Chiswick High Rd, W4   020 8747 5966   8–2A
38 Haven Grn, W5   020 8810 7066   1–2A
296-298 Upper Richmond Rd, SW15   020 8394 7666   11–2B
90 New Bridge St, EC4   020 7651 0266   10–2A
"A regular when the fridge is empty" – this "casual" pan-Asian chain is a "cheap 'n' cheerful" staple thanks to its "diverse range of dishes from quality, fresh ingredients" and "buzzy" ("loud") atmosphere. Ratings slipped a little this year though on a couple of disappointing reports. / www.hareandtortoise-restaurants.co.uk; 11 pm; EC4 10.30, Fri 11 pm; EC4 closed Sun; W14 no bookings.

Harry Morgan's NW8 £43 **2** **2** **2**
29-31 St John's Wood High St   020 7722 1869   9–3A
This "friendly and cheerful" kosher institution in St John's Wood keeps its many fans happy with Jewish deli classics, including "chicken soup just like Mum used to make", latkes and salt beef. Perennially there are gripes however that it's "going downhill". / NW8 7NH; www.harryms.co.uk; @morgan_hm; 10 pm.

Harwood Arms SW6 £68 **4** **3** **3**
Walham Grove   020 7386 1847   6–3A
"Worth a taxi-ride from central London!" – this "good old-fashioned pub" in a quiet Fulham backstreet has won renown (including from the tyre men) for its "adventurous" British cooking, particularly of game (culinary oversight comes from Brett Graham of The Ledbury and Mike Robinson of Berkshire's Pot Kiln). Top Tip "go for the venison and try one of the Scotch eggs". / SW6 1QP; www.harwoodarms.com; 9.30 pm, Sun 9 pm; closed Mon L; credit card required to book.

F S A

Hashi SW20 £37 **3 4 2**
54 Durham Rd   020 8944 1888   11–2A
*This "reliable and friendly local Korean/Japanese" joint in suburban Raynes
Park is "a gem, despite the look from outside", delivering "really good sushi
and other Japanese fare", and "good value for money". Top Tip – option
to BYO £4 corkage. / SW20 0TW; 10.30 pm; closed Mon; No Amex.*

Hatchetts W1 £56 **2 3 2**
5 White Horse St   020 7409 0567   3–4B
*Set over two floors near lovely Shepherd Market, this year-old bar/restaurant
with regular live music still only generates limited feedback, but even those
who feel it draws "an uninspiring crowd" rate it well for its "great food and
great value". / W1J 7LQ; www.hatchetts.london; @hatchettslondon; 10 pm;
set weekday L £35 (FP).*

The Havelock Tavern W14 £51 **3 2 3**
57 Masbro Rd   020 7603 5374   8–1C
*"One of the top gastropubs around" – this backstreet Olympia hotspot
is "past its best" according to some age old aficionados, but "the crowds
don't seem to have noticed" as its "buzzing every evening and for Sunday
lunch"; "steak is a highlight" of an "interesting" menu. / W14 0LS;
www.havelocktavern.com; @HavelockTavern; 10 pm, Sun 9.30 pm.*

Haven Bistro N20 £49 **2 3 2**
1363 High Rd   020 8445 7419   1–1B
*Fans of this Whetstone "oasis" vaunt it for its "well presented and
interesting food" and say "there's nowhere like it in the area". Sceptics
though say it's over popular: "the grub's not bad, but it suffers from a lack
of local competition". / N20 9LN; www.haven-bistro.co.uk; 10.30 pm, Sun 10 pm;
No shorts.*

Hawksmoor £79 **3 3 3**
5a Air St, W1   020 7406 3980   4–4C
11 Langley St, WC2   020 7420 9390   5–2C
3 Yeoman's Row, SW3   020 7590 9290   6–2C
16 Winchester Walk, SE1   020 7234 9940   10–4C **NEW**
157 Commercial St, E1   020 7426 4850   13–2B
10-12 Basinghall St, EC2   020 7397 8120   10–2C
*Huw Gott and Will Beckett's zeitgeisty steakhouse chain still hits just the
right vibe for many savvy Londoners with their "casual but professional"
service of "sublime" British-bred meat and "superb" cocktails, and for cooler
business-types in particular "they never fail to impress". Some "whopping
price tags" give rise to complaints, but even though ratings have ebbed
a little over the years with the roll-out of branch after branch
(the latest in spring 2017 was a new "hipster" branch near Borough
Market) the brand's legions of fans remain very loyal: "It costs an arm and
a leg, but you can rest assured that the arm and leg will be perfectly
cooked!" / www.thehawksmoor.com; 10.30 pm; W1 & WC2 Fri & Sat 11 pm,
Sun 9pm-10 pm; EC2 closed Sat & Sun; SRA-Food Made Good – 2 stars.*

Haz £45 **2 2 2**
9 Cutler St, E1   020 7929 7923   10–2D
34 Foster Ln, EC2   020 7600 4172   10–2B
64 Bishopsgate, EC2   020 7628 4522   10–2D **NEW**
112 Houndsditch, EC3   020 7623 8180   10–2D
6 Mincing Ln, EC3   020 7929 3173   10–3D
*"Still a decent option in the City" for a cheapo bite – these "functional"
Turkish operations offer "tasty grills" and "a wide selection of mezze". They
are "aimed at the business crowd and perhaps tourists" – particularly the
"lovely, large venue at St Paul's". / www.hazrestaurant.co.uk; 11.30 pm;
EC3 closed Sun.*

114   FSA RATINGS: FROM **1** POOR — **5** EXCEPTIONAL

Heddon Street Kitchen W1 £62 112
3-9 Heddon St 020 7592 1212 4–3B
It's potentially a "lovely big space" just off Regent Street, but Gordon Ramsay's West End operation is another one of his very own Kitchen Nightmares. There are fans for whom it's "quick, cheerful, buzzy and does what it sets out to do", but there are also too many critics who say to "avoid at all costs": "it feels like a conveyor belt", with "indifferent and chaotic service" and "laughably bad food". / W1B 4BE; www.gordonramsayrestaurants.com/heddon-street-kitc; @heddonstkitchen; 11 pm, Sun 9 pm; set pre theatre £41 (FP).

Hedone W4 £118 332
301-303 Chiswick High Rd 020 8747 0377 8–2A
"You either 'get' this restaurant or you don't", and views on Mikael Jonsson's "innocuous" and "homely"-looking Chiswick project remain somewhat divided. For a strong majority, "the best ingredients in the UK, coupled with sophisticated cooking technique" provides a "thought-provoking" and "most exciting" tasting menu experience that's "just about perfect... not too heavy, not too showy, very well balanced, surprising… from a master just riffing in his open kitchen and passing you something like he's just thought it up, which always tastes great". Ratings are undercut however, by a vociferous minority, who just "don't see it", or who feel a meal is "30-50% overpriced". / W4 4HH; www.hedonerestaurant.com; @HedoneLondon; 9.30 pm; closed Mon, Tue L, Wed L & Sun; booking max 7 may apply; set weekday L £73 (FP).

Heirloom N8 £53 333
35 Park Rd 020 8348 3565 9–1C
"Love the ethos! (as much produce as possible from their own farm in Bucks) and the cooking lives up to it", say fans of this field-to-fork operation, in Crouch End. / N8 8TE; www.heirloomn8.co.uk; @HeirloomN8; 11 pm, Sun 7 pm.

Hélène Darroze,
The Connaught Hotel W1 £136 344
Carlos Pl 020 3147 7200 3–3B
With its "laser-like precision", Hélène Darroze's Gallic cuisine is "simply stunning" in this plush and "stylish" Mayfair chamber, whose "perfectly attentive" service adds a lot to the experience. Just one gripe – it's "unbelievably expensive" – but fans say "those who complain about the prices are missing the point!" / W1K 2AL; www.the-connaught.co.uk; @TheConnaught; 10 pm, Sun 9 pm; closed Mon & Sun; No trainers; set weekday L £87 (FP).

Heliot Steak House WC2 £64 444
Cranbourn St 020 7769 8844 5–3B
For a surprisingly high quality steak at a very good price, check out this glitzily glam' grill – in the circle of the original theatre – which nowadays has a birds-eye view over the gambling tables of the UK's biggest casino (right over Leicester Square tube). Top Tip – great 2-course, pre-theatre deal at £14.95. / WC2H 7AJ; www.hippodromecasino.com; @HippodromeLDN; midnight, Sat 1 am, Sun 11 pm; set pre theatre £37 (FP).

Henrietta WC2 NEW
Henrietta St 020 3794 5314 5–3C
This late spring 2017 dining room opening from the Experimental Group (who own this plush, new hotel – sibling to Grand Pigalle in Paris) is most notable for the consultancy of Ollie Dabbous in the kitchen. It opened too late for survey feedback on his trademark exotic small plates – press reviews report the odd miss, but mostly hits. / WC2E 8NA; www.henriettahotel.com.

Hereford Road W2 £48 4 4 3
3 Hereford Rd 020 7727 1144 7–1B
Chef/Patron Tom Pemberton's "hearty, fresh, seasonal British cooking"
is "very reasonably priced for London" and maintains his "elegant and low
key" Bayswater venture as "a fabulous neighbourhood restaurant" (but one
which draws fans from across town). Top Tip – "the good value lunch menu,
which cuts no corners". / W2 4AB; www.herefordroad.org; @3HerefordRoad;
10.30 pm, Sun 10 pm.

High Road Brasserie W4 £59 2 2 2
162-166 Chiswick High Rd 020 8742 7474 8–2A
Fans of this slightly self-conscious all-day hang-out in Chiswick (part of
a boutique hotel in the Soho House group) laud it as a "handy local",
especially for a see-and-be-seen brunch on its prominent terrace, but it's
always seemed a bit "pretentious and overpriced for food that's nothing
special". / W4 1PR; highroadbrasserie.co.uk; @HRBrasserie; 11 pm, Fri & Sat
midnight, Sun 10 pm; booking max 8 may apply; set weekday L £34 (FP).

High Timber EC4 £68 3 5 3
8 High Timber St 020 7248 1777 10–3B
This "relaxed" 'wine-dining' spot beside the Wobbly Bridge is an "oasis of joy
in the City", with a "fantastic view of the Thames" and across the river
to Tate Modern. A "big part of the fun" is "the ability to mooch around the
wine cellar and cheese room" (the "excellent wine list" has a focus on South
Africa, thanks to the ownership by a Stellenbosch vineyard). / EC4V 3PA;
www.hightimber.com; @HTimber; 10 pm; closed Sat & Sun; set weekday L £43 (FP).

Hill & Szrok E8 £55 4 4 4
60 Broadway Mkt 0207 254 8805 14–2B
Very positive all-round, if limited feedback this year on this vibey Broadway
Market butchers, which transforms at night into a counter-style diner, selling
grills, with a small number of sides, plus a small but high quality array
of wines. / E8 4QJ; www.hillandszrok.co.uk; @hillandszrok; Mon - Sat 11pm,
Sun 9pm; No Amex; no booking.

Hilliard EC4 £25 4 4 4
26a Tudor St 020 7353 8150 10–3A
"Sandwiches above the usual cut" and "especially good salads and tarts
(savoury as well as sweet)" meet the brief at this "well executed"
coffeehouse, ensuring it is always "full of lawyers from the local legal scene".
/ EC4Y 0AY; www.hilliardfood.co.uk; @hilliardcafe; 5.30 pm; L only, closed Sat & Sun;
no booking.

Hispania EC3 £66 3 2 2
72-74 Lombard St 020 7621 0338 10–3D
This Spanish two-year-old, over two floors right opposite the Bank
of England, "caters for all types of business wining and dining", "be it
private dining, a formal meal, tapas or bar snacks over wine". It's
"just informal enough to feel relaxed", but it can get very busy. / EC3V 9AY;
www.hispanialondon.com; @hispanialondon; 10pm, Mon 9.30 pm; closed Sat & Sun.

Hix W1 £64 1 2 3
66-70 Brewer St 020 7292 3518 4–3C
Mark Hix's flagship Soho venture inspires limited feedback nowadays,
and continues to disappoint as much as it delights, although "it's not
so much bad as underwhelming". Top Tip – "there's a great buzz about the
basement bar". / W1F 9UP; www.hixrestaurants.co.uk/restaurant/hix-soho/;
@HixRestaurants; 11.30 pm, Sun 10.30 pm.

Hix Oyster & Chop House EC1 £62 2 2 2
36-37 Greenhill Rents, Cowcross St 020 7017 1930 10–1A
Mark Hix's original solo operation, near Smithfield, excels at "the simple things" – specifically "everyday and special-occasion steaks (sometimes with a Hix-ian twist)". On the debit side, "some of the specials don't work too well", "the waiting staff are pleasant but inefficient", and it's a bit "pricey". / EC1M 6BN; www.hixrestaurants.co.uk/restaurant/hix-oyster-cho; @hixchophouse; 11 pm, Sun 9 pm; closed Sat L; set pre theatre £38 (FP).

HKK EC2 £74 5 5 3
88 Worship St, Broadgate Quarter 020 3535 1888 13–2B
"Probably the best Chinese food in London" (not least "the best Peking Duck this side of Beijing") inspires a hymn of praise to this "calm and relaxed" Hakkasan-cousin, north of Liverpool Street. Despite some "whopping" prices, no quibbles are raised – "it's just fantastic". Top Tip – "the amazing and excellent value Duck and Bubbles lunch". / EC2A 2BE; www.hkklondon.com; @HKKlondon; 10 pm; closed Sun.

Hoi Polloi, Ace Hotel E1 £62 3 2 3
100 Shoreditch High St 020 8880 6100 13–1B
For the "best brunch my miles..", fans tip this trendy hangout in a hip Shoreditch hotel, also a useful all-day option hereabouts (including for afternoon tea). / E1 6JQ; hoi-polloi.co.uk; @wearehoipolloi; midnight, Thu-Sat 1 am.

Holborn Dining Room WC1 £70 3 3 4
252 High Holborn 020 3747 8633 2–1D
This "lovely, grand dining room" on the edge of the City is designed to impress, and provides "a great buzz", and "classic staple dishes" to a largely business clientele, including first thing when it's "an excellent breakfast venue". Sartorially speaking, views divide on the "amusing trousers" which are standard issue for the waiting staff. STOP PRESS: In autumn 2017 a dedicated pie hatch is due to open. / WC1V 7EN; www.holborndiningroom.com; @HolbornDining; 11.15 pm, Sun 10.15 pm; set pre theatre £46 (FP).

Homeslice £34 4 4 4
52 Wells St, W1 020 3151 7488 2–1B
13 Neal's Yd, WC2 020 7836 4604 5–2C
Television Centre, W12 awaiting tel 8–1C **NEW**
374-378 Old St, EC1 020 3151 1121 13–1B
Bloomberg Arcade, Qn Victoria St, EC4 awaiting tel 10–2C **NEW**
"Excellent, enormous pizzas with a decent variety of toppings" wins a major fanbase for these buzzy and cheery pit stops. "It's quick and dirty with paper plates and plastic cutlery - lingering is not encouraged". (Fascinating fact: it's owned by the late Terry Wogan's sons!) / www.homeslicepizza.co.uk; 11 pm, EC1 & W1 Sun 10 pm; no booking.

Honest Burgers £28 3 3 3
"The best and most distinctive of the upmarket burger chains": they "dare to serve them medium-rare as standard", alongside those "deliciously moreish rosemary fries, which deserve mention as a stand out simple side"; all this plus "warm and welcoming staff and a cool vibe"... "what more can a girl want?" / www.honestburgers.co.uk; 10 pm-11 pm; SW9 closed Mon D; EC3 closed Sat & Sun; no booking.

Honey & Co W1 £46 3 3 2
25a Warren St 020 7388 6175 2–1B
"Food straight from the streets and markets of the Middle East" –
"absolutely divine, regularly changing Israeli-inspired recipes with surprising
twists on very simple dishes" (and, in particular, marvellous cakes) –
has won impressive fame for this "delightfully friendly" Warren Street
"hideaway". Even some fans now admit however that "it's on the expensive
side considering that it's more of a café than a restaurant" (and a mightily
"cramped" one at that). Top Tip – "the breakfast mezze is enough for the
whole day". / W1T 5JZ; www.honeyandco.co.uk; @Honeyandco; 10.30 pm; closed
Sun; No Amex.

Honey & Smoke W1 NEW £49 5 4 2
216 Great Portland St 020 7388 6175 2–1B
"Whoa, brilliant!" – "Honey & Co's bigger sibling" opened to rightful
acclaim in late 2016, south of Great Portland Street tube. A modern take
on a Middle Eastern grill house, it serves a "seemingly endless array"
of "spectacular but completely honest" mezze ("you rediscover dishes you
thought you knew like hummus or falafel, and you marvel at simple raw veg
which feels re-invented"). On the downside, the site is "a bit lacking
in ambience", but given its "upbeat" and "enthusiastic" staff most reporters
don't quibble . Top Menu Tip – "I'd run a marathon just for the
cheesecake!" / W1W 5QW; www.honeyandco.co.uk/smoke; @Honeyandco;
11.30 pm; closed Mon & Sun.

Hood SW2 £50 4 3 2
67 Streatham Hill 020 3601 3320 11–2D
"A great find in the heart of Streatham", this "fantastic" two-year-old bases
its "regularly changing" menu around "locally sourced produce and fabulous
English wine", with "increasingly exciting flavours" as the kitchen develops.
"We went as a family of 11 and sampled most of the menu between us –
we were all thrilled!" / SW2 4TX; www.hoodrestaurants.com; @HoodStreatham;
11 pm.

Hoppers £49 5 4 3
49 Frith St, W1 no tel 5–2A
77 Wigmore St, W1 020 3319 8110 3–1A NEW
"I went over 15 times last year. I can't get enough!" The Sethi family's
"tiny", "fun" Soho two-year-old punches well above its weight with its "ultra-
tasty" Sri Lankan and Tamil street food – "perfectly spiced bites" (majoring
in rice pancake 'hoppers') that "burst with flavour and texture" ("I was born
in Sri Lanka, and this place is pretty authentic"). Given the no-bookings
policy, "it's a disaster to get into, but damn it, it's worth it!" In mid-
September 2017, they opened a much-anticipated spin-off in Marylebone
which, thankfully, does take bookings..

The Horseshoe NW3 £53 3 3 4
28 Heath St 020 7431 7206 9–2A
This atmospheric gastro-boozer is "rather more buzzy than
most Hampstead restaurants or pubs". The menu comprises
Mediterranean-influenced classics, while the bar stocks the entire range
of the Camden Town Brewery – founded on-site before moving down the
road. / NW3 6TE; www.thehorseshoehampstead.com; @TheHorseShoeCTB; 10 pm,
Fri & Sat 10.30pm, Sun 9.30 pm.

Hot Pot W1 NEW £39
Wardour St 020 7287 8881 4–2D
Authentic communal Asian dining comes to Chinatown, thanks
to Taechaubol Group, owners of 148 hot pot or 'huo guo' restaurants
in Bangkok; the new, two-floor, 148-seat Wardour Street branch is the
upmarket version, using British free-range ingredients where possible.
/ W1F 8ZP; www.hotpotrestaurants.co.uk; @HotPotLondon_; 12.30 am, Sat 1.30 am,
Sun midnight.

Hot Stuff SW8 £23 3 5 3
19-23 Wilcox Rd   020 7720 1480   11–1D
"You're treated as a friend" at this *"old favourite"* curry house in the 'Little Portugal' stretch near Vauxhall (immortalised in the film, My Beautiful Laundrette). It's been scoring well for its *"really well spiced fresh food"* for years; and the *"terrific value"* is increased if you BYO. / SW8 2XA; www.welovehotstuff.com; 10 pm; closed Mon; No Amex.

The Hour Glass SW3 £53 3 4 2
279-283 Brompton Rd   020 7581 2497   6–2C
"Top-quality bar dishes" and *"efficient young staff"* inspire warm vibes for this *"bright and cheerful old pub"* in South Ken, run for the past year by the duo behind Brompton Food Market. / SW3 2DY; hourglasspub.co.uk; @TheHourGlassSK; 10 pm, Sun 4 pm; closed Sun D.

House of Ho W1 £60 3 3 3
1 Percy St   020 7323 9130   2–1C
This modern Vietnamese/Japanese mashup occupies the decadent and vibey Fitzrovia townhouse vacated by Bam-Bou (RIP), and though feedback is still quite limited, its enthusiastic small fanclub says it's beginning to live up both to its predecessor and to the extensive hype at launch. Top Tip – *"Saturday bottomless brunch, with a high-end Vietnamese twist"*. / W1T 1DB; www.houseofho.co.uk; @HouseOfHo; 11 pm.

House Restaurant, National Theatre SE1 £52 2 3 2
National Theatre, South Bank   020 7452 3600   2–3D
"Useful before or after a performance", the National Theatre's in-house venue is a bit of a *"glorified cafeteria"* but benefits from *"quick and efficient service"*, which means *"you're out in time for the show without being rushed or pushed to the wire"*. The food perhaps does rely on its *"captive audience"*, but most feel it's *"a good option"*. / SE1 9PX; house.nationaltheatre.org.uk; @NT_House; 11 pm; D only (L served on matinee days), closed Sun.

Hubbard & Bell, Hoxton Hotel WC1 £57 3 2 3
199-206 High Holborn   020 7661 3030   2–1D
"Dude food plus" (*"great pancakes"*; *"classic burgers"*) and *"a very cool vibe"* win a food thumbs up for this *"canteen-type eatery in a trendy and expensive hotel"* (from Soho House) which despite its name is actually in Holborn. *"Whatever your thoughts on the clientele, which can make it feel a bit dystopian and/or like an Apple advert, the food is really rather good"*. / WC1V 7BD; www.hubbardandbell.com; @HubbardandBell; midnight, Sun 11 pm.

Humble Grape £49 3 4 4
Theberton St, N1   020 3904 4480   9–3D NEW
2 Battersea Rise, SW11   020 3620 2202   11–2C
1 Saint Bride's Passage, EC4   020 7583 0688   10–2A
A *"great selection of interesting small-batch wines"* is served by the glass, bottle or case at this popular yearling – an offshoot of a Battersea wine bar in the lovely crypt of St Bride's, Fleet Street (with a new Islington branch, which opened in summer 2017). *"The simple food and platters complement the vino nicely"*. Top Tip – *"go on a Monday, and you can drink at retail prices"*. / www.humblegrape.co.uk.

Hunan SW1 £93 5 2 1
51 Pimlico Rd 020 7730 5712 6–2D
"The food keeps on coming until you stay 'stop'!" – "a seemingly never-ending stream of perfectly judged dishes" – at this Pimlico veteran, where "Mr Peng decides what you'll eat, and my goodness he is right!" It's "Russian roulette but fantastic if you're not a fussy eater" and regularly scores as "the best Chinese in London (if not the planet)". The room itself is "slightly odd" and "minor language problems" can impede the service, but overall it's "a genius way to have a social meal". "The wine list is pretty amazing too!" – "thoughtfully matched, with lots of Germanic and other aromatic whites, including a number of excellent mature Rieslings".
/ SW1W 8NE; www.hunanlondon.com; 11 pm; closed Sun; set weekday L £66 (FP).

Hush £81 2 2 3
8 Lancashire Ct, W1 020 7659 1500 3–2B
95-97 High Holborn, WC1 020 7242 4580 2–1D
A "magical location" (a cute courtyard just off Bond Street) creates "a little oasis in the middle of the London mêlée" for this all-day Mayfair brasserie, which – "refreshed after a recent refurb" – is "great for business or fun in the West End". But the setting outstrips the food, with reports on the latter ranging from "first class" to merely "average". Limited feedback on its handily-located sibling, by Holborn tube. / www.hush.co.uk; W1 11 pm, Sat 10 pm, Sun 9 pm; WC1 11 pm; WC1 closed Sun.

Hutong,
The Shard SE1 £88 1 2 5
31 St Thomas St 020 3011 1257 10–4C
"Try to get a window seat at dusk and watch the sun go down over London: it's magic", at this "lush" and "romantic" 33rd floor eyrie. It helps to be starry eyed though – "you don't go for the Chinese food", which critics feel comes at utterly "outrageous" prices for such an "ordinary" standard ("I've had better at M&S!"), nor the "patchy" and "brusque" service. STOP PRESS: in July 2017 Sifu Fei Wang was appointed as the new head chef – perhaps he can at last take the cooking here to real heights... / SE1 9RY; www.hutong.co.uk; @HutongShard; 10 pm; No shorts; set weekday L £62 (FP).

Iberia N1 £36 3 3 2
294-296 Caledonian Rd 020 7700 7750 9–2D
The 'Iberia' in question is Georgia not Spain (who knew!), and this simply decorated Islingtonian is a low key but pleasant way to discover a cuisine that's "quite a cultural melting pot and not as heavy as might be feared".
/ N1 1BA; www.iberiarestaurant.co.uk; 11 pm, Sun 9 pm; closed Mon, Tue-Fri D only, Sat & Sun open L & D.

Ibérica £53 2 2 3
Zig Zag Building, 70 Victoria St, SW1 020 7636 8650 2–4B
195 Great Portland St, W1 020 7636 8650 2–1B
12 Cabot Sq, E14 020 7636 8650 12–1C
89 Turnmill St, EC1 020 7636 8650 10–1A
"I don't know if they're really all that special, but they're terrifically enjoyable" – so say fans of these "vibrant", contemporary Spanish operations, whose City and Canary Wharf branches are "good for business".
/ 11pm, SW1 Sun 10.30 pm; W1 closed Sun D.

Ikoyi SW1 NEW
1 St James's Market   020 3583 4660   4–4D
West African-influenced cuisine – a modern take on traditional Nigerian, Ghanaian and Senegalese flavours, without particular reference to indigenous dishes – comes to St James's, thanks to (Canadian-Chinese) chef Jeremy Chan (who has previously worked at Dinner by Heston Blumenthal, Noma and Hibiscus) and native Nigerian, Iré Hassan-Odukale (born in Ikoyi, Lagos's most affluent suburb). The venture – part of the extensive redevelopment of St James's Market, and by far London's swankiest African-inspired venture to-date – follows a successful pop-up career (including at Carousel). / SW1Y 4AH; www.ikoyilondon.com.

Il Guscio N5   £50   3 4 3
231 Blackstock Rd   020 7354 1400   9–1D
"We're lucky to have such a great local!" – so say fans of this "courteous", three-year-old Highbury haunt. "The interior is a little cramped, but all their authentic Sardinian food is excellent (pizza is particularly good)". / N5 2LL; www.ilguscihighbury.co.uk; 10.30 pm, Fri & Sat 11 pm.

India Club, Strand Continental Hotel WC2   £28   2 2 1
143 Strand   020 7836 4880   2–2D
This veteran near the Indian High Commission in the Strand "has been around for more than 50 years" and "hardly changes". "So basic it's almost a parody", it is reached via an "unappealing entrance and up two flights of stairs", but "very good value and authentic" scoff still justifies the trip. "A miracle it has survived in redeveloping London – if it ever goes, we will miss it!". BYO, or buy beer from the hotel bar. STOP PRESS: Redevelopment is now threatened here with news that the lease is expiring in 2019, and plans to modernise the site have been submitted. Join the online petition to save the place! / WC2R 1JA; www.strand-continental.co.uk; @hostelstrandcon; 10.50 pm; Cash only; booking max 6 may apply.

Indian Accent W1 NEW
16 Albemarle St   awaiting tel   3–3C
On the former site of Chor Bizarre (RIP, but from the same owner, Old World Hospitality) – another nouvelle Indian restaurant with sibling venues in New York and New Delhi. The New Delhi original is on the World's 50 Best List. / W1S 4HW; www.indianaccent.com/indianaccent/london/; @indianaccentlon.

Indian Moment SW11   £42   3 3 2
47 Northcote Rd   020 7223 6575 / 020 7223 1818   11–2C
The "delicious and varied menu" at this "friendly" Indian, on the 'Nappy Valley' main drag near Clapham Junction station, means "you can always find something you want, whatever your mood" (and it's "not designed to blow your head off" either). / SW11 1NZ; www.indianmoment.co.uk; @indianmoment; 11.30 pm, Fri & Sat midnight.

Indian Ocean SW17   £36   3 3 2
214 Trinity Rd   020 8672 7740   11–2C
"Unusual spicing takes the food a cut above the average", according to the big local fanclub of this "old-school Indian" near Wandsworth Common, which is "reliable, friendly and great value". / SW17 7HP; www.indianoceanrestaurant.com; 11.30 pm, Sat 11.45 pm, Sun 11 pm.

Indian Rasoi N2   £36   3 3 2
7 Denmark Terrace   020 8883 9093   1–1B
This "tiny local Indian" in Muswell Hill specialises in Mughal-era cuisine, producing "unusual dishes, that are always delicious". "Looks like nothing from the outside, but don't be fooled – it's great". / N2 9HG; www.indian-rasoi.co.uk; 10.30 pm; No Amex.

Indian Zing W6 £53 4 4 2

236 King St   020 8748 5959   8–2B

"It's well worth the tube ride" to Manoj Vasaikar's well-known, "wonderful" little Indian, a short walk from Ravenscourt Park. "It's still right up there as one of the best Indians in West London" with "consistently superb", "non-mainstream" cuisine all "at a reasonable price point", delivered by "willing and thoughtful staff". / W6 0RS; www.indian-zing.co.uk; @IndianZing; 11 pm, Sun 10 pm.

Indigo,
One Aldwych WC2 £65 3 4 3

1 Aldwych   020 7300 0400   2–2D

This hotel mezzanine boasts a "brilliantly convenient" West End location – "get a table overlooking the Lobby Bar for atmosphere and fun" – and "makes a great place for meetings" of many kinds. "It's especially a joy to be able to take people who are coeliac or can't eat dairy to a decent restaurant" – the "clever" menu is entirely dairy-free and gluten-free. / WC2B 4BZ; www.onealdwych.com; @OneAldwych; 10.15 pm.

Ippudo London £43 3 2 2

1 Crossrail Pl, E14   020 3326 9485   12–1C

"Decent ramen and one of the better food options on the Wharf" – twin selling points of this global, Japan-based noodle outfit (whose unit in WC2's Central St Giles Piazza doesn't incite any feedback). / WC2 10.30 pm; E14 9.30 pm, Sun 8.30 pm; no bookings.

Isabel W1 NEW

26 Albemarle St   020 3096 9292   3–3C

On the Mayfair site that was Sumosan (RIP), Juan Santa Cruz opened this sibling to Notting Hill's eurotrash favourite, Casa Cruz in late spring 2017. It serves a long, modern Mediterranean menu of meat and fish plates plus accompaniments in very glam surroundings, all day from breakfast to late night. / W1S 4HQ; isabelw1.london.

Isarn N1 £46 4 4 2

119 Upper St   020 7424 5153   9–3D

The "pretty authentic food" and attentive staff win consistent praise for this Islington fixture. The "modern decor is a cut above the normal high street Thai", making the best of what could be a tricky narrow space. / N1 1QP; www.isarn.co.uk; 11 pm, Sat & Sun 10 pm.

Ishtar W1 £51 3 4 2

10-12 Crawford St   020 7224 2446   2–1A

"Excellent Anatolian food – a level above the usual local Turkish" – has won this Marylebone fixture "a big local following". Top Tip – "the fixed-price set lunch and early evening dinner is unbeatable for quality and value". / W1U 6AZ; www.ishtarrestaurant.com; 11.30 pm, Sun 10.30 pm; set weekday L £29 (FP).

The Ivy WC2 £69 3 4 5

1-5 West St   020 7836 4751   5–3B

"When you step through the doors, it's reassuring to know you'll be well-fed and treated like a king" at Richard Caring's "sophisticated" Theatreland legend, whose revamp a year ago stemmed years of decline, and where "so long as you don't expect to be challenged by the grown-up comfort food, the old favourite dishes don't disappoint". True, the celeb crowd primarily frequent the neighbouring Ivy Club nowadays, and true, it's no longer in the survey's Top 40 Most Mentioned restaurants, and true, this is now the flagship for a fast-expanding chain of spin-offs, so it's no surprise a few reporters now dismiss it as "just a chain restaurant for out-of-towners", but actually catty comments are most notable by their absence. / WC2H 9NQ; www.the-ivy.co.uk; @TheIvyWestSt; 11.30pm, Thu-Sat midnight, Sun 10.30 pm; No shorts; booking max 6 may apply.

The Ivy Café £57 1️⃣2️⃣3️⃣
96 Marylebone Ln, W1   020 3301 0400   2–1A
120 St John's Wood High St, NW8   020 3096 9444   9–3A
75 High St, SW19   020 3096 9333   11–2B
9 Hill St, TW9   020 3146 7733   1–4A NEW

Bistro fare that's "deeply average at best", particularly at the
newest St John's Wood branch (on the site of Megan's, RIP) of these still-
young spin-offs from the legendary original – plus "snobbish and unhelpful
service" – do not bode well for Richard Caring's rapid roll-out
of (ie shameless cashing-in on) this celebrated brand, of which these The
'Ivy Cafés' are the sub-sub-brand (compared with the slightly more upmarket
sub-brand 'The Ivy Grills & Brasseries'). The West End outlets are better,
and fans do say their atmosphere generally "lifts them out of the ordinary",
but "with this caché surely they can afford better chefs?" / 11 pm, Fri & Sat
11.30 pm, Sun 10.30 pm; SW19 11 pm, Sun 10.30 pm; midnight.

Ivy Grills & Brasseries £58 2️⃣2️⃣3️⃣
26-28 Broadwick St, W1   020 3301 1166   4–1C NEW
1 Henrietta St, WC2   020 3301 0200   5–3D
197 King's Rd, SW3   020 3301 0300   6–3C
96 Kensington High St, W8   020 3301 0500   6–1A
One Tower Bridge, 1 Tower Bridge, SE1   020 3146 7722   10–4D
69 Old Broad St,, EC2   020 3146 7744   10–2C NEW

The vote remains fairly equally split on Richard Caring's burgeoning bevy
of Ivy spin-offs which are popping up like mushrooms 'in carefully selected
locations' across the country. (These – the 'Grills & Brasseries' are not to be
confused with the mere 'Cafés', and aim for a more faithful reproduction
of the original's magic). For 'The Ayes', they make "a great local addition"
providing "great British food in a buzzy setting" ("I keep expecting to be
disappointed, and I'm not!"). For 'The Nays', "hugely underwhelming food"
and "uneven" standards generally make it "feel like they are trying to milk
the franchise, but are destroying it in the process". The most popular is the
"ladies-who-lunch" favourite on the King's Road, whose "garden is to die for"
(although "it's an uphill struggle actually being seated in it") – a "super,
bustling and tastefully decorated venue with fabulous people watching
opportunities" (and where the Top Tip is "its great breakfast: it's much
quieter so service is spot on!)". / ivycollection.com.

Jackson & Rye £56 1️⃣2️⃣2️⃣
56 Wardour St, W1   020 7437 8338   4–2D
219-221 Chiswick High Rd, W4   020 8747 1156   8–2A
Hotham House, 1 Heron Sq, TW9   020 8948 6951   1–4A

"Decent brunch options" are the best bet at these well-resourced American-
style diners, and the riverside branch at Richmond makes good use of its
"great location". But, more generally, too many punters report "uninteresting
food" leaving them "most disappointed". / www.jacksonrye.com; 11 pm,
Sun 10.30 pm; EC2 closed Sat & Sun.

Jaffna House SW17 £23 5️⃣2️⃣2️⃣
90 Tooting High St   020 8672 7786   11–2C

"Mind-bogglingly hot Sri Lankan and South Indian curries", all at "bargain
prices" make this family-run outfit in Tooting a must-visit. "Cafeteria-style
by day and licensed restaurant (which resembles a suburban dining-room)
by night". Top Tip – "the lunchtime deal is astonishing value: a selection
of vegetarian or non-veggie dishes and a soft drink for a fiver". / SW17 0RN;
11.30 pm.

Jamavar W1 £88 **5 4 4**
8 Mount St 020 7499 1800 3–3B

Leela Palace's "stunning" newcomer in Mayfair's most fashionable restaurant row has immediately established itself as "the best Indian restaurant in town, indeed it's amongst the best restaurants of any cuisine".
Ex Gymkhana chef, Rohit Ghai's "expert" and "exquisite" dishes are "genuinely top class" (while "still remaining properly authentic to the flavours you might find in New Delhi or Mumbai") and the interior (modelled, apparently, on the Viceroy's House of New Delhi) is a picture of "elegance and sophistication". STOP PRESS: In December 2017 a sequel, Dabbawala is to open at 29 Maddox Street (formerly Hibiscus, RIP).
/ W1K 3NF; www.jamavarrestaurants.com; @JamavarLondon.

James Cochran £53 **5 1 2**
21 Parkfield St, N1 020 3489 2090 9–3D **NEW**
19 Bevis Marks, Liverpool St, EC3 020 3302 0310 10–2D **NEW**

"Superb cooking is in evidence" at ex-Ledbury chef, James Cochran's newcomer, a couple of minutes from Liverpool Street, where his British small plates are "the stuff of dreams" and "at prices seldom seen for food of this quality in the City". There are negatives – too often "it is let down by very amateur service", and "the decor is not terribly inspiring", but all-in-all it's still highly recommended. In July 2017, he announced a second 60-seater at Angel Central.

Jamie's Italian £49 **1 1 1**

"Jamie get out!" – "you can do better" than this "dreadful, truly dreadful" Italian chain that "used to be enjoyable, but has gone downhill badly" and is "not much better, perhaps no better than school dinners" nowadays. / www.jamiesitalian.com; 11.30 pm, Sun 10.30 pm; booking: min 6.

JAN SW11 £37
78 Northcote Rd 0207 525 9446 11–2C

"A new addition to Northcote Road offering Caspian cuisine that replaces the missed Lola Rojo (RIP)" – limited but positive feedback so far on this funkily and expensively decorated year-old corner-site. / SW11 6QL; www.myjan.co.uk; @jan_restaurant; 9.30 pm.

Japan Centre Food Hall SW1 **NEW**
35b Panton St 020 3405 1246 5–4A

Since 1976, Tak Tokumine's Japanese cultural centre, complete with food hall and canteen, has occupied a variety of sites near Piccadilly Circus. This latest 6,000 sq ft incarnation is planned to open in September 2017, with 100-seater dining hall, surrounded by open kitchens. / SW1Y 4EA; www.japancentre.com; @JapanCentre.

Jar Kitchen WC2 £50 **2 5 3**
Drury Ln 020 7405 4255 5–1C

At its best (although mis-fires are not unknown), this sweet (if somewhat "done on the cheap") two-year-old café in Covent Garden supplies "lovely" farm-to-fork cooking, "even lovelier service and a warm, friendly atmosphere". "Don't worry, the jars are just the lighting decor, which works well… you get your food on plates!". / WC2B 5QF; www.jarkitchen.com; @JarKitchen; 9 pm; booking max 6 may apply.

Jashan N8 £32 **4 4 2**
19 Turnpike Ln 020 8340 9880 1–1C

This "lovely local Indian" attracts fans from across London to unlovely Turnpike Lane for another fix of its "awesome food". Lamb chops are a particular crowd favourite, but there are also many "excellent" dishes not found on menus elsewhere. / N8 0EP; www.jashan.co.uk; 10.15 pm, Fri & Sat 10.30 pm; D only; No Amex; May need 6+ to book.

Jean-Georges at The Connaught W1 NEW
The Connaught, Carlos Place 020 7107 8861 3–3B
No-one comes to The Connaught to save money, but early press reviews on this summer 2017 revamp of the hotel's 'second' restaurant (the slightly less informal one) under star Jean-Georges Vongerichten, are slightly guarded when it comes to the NYC chef's haute-comfort food here: not because it's bad, but because £25-£30 is a lot for a pizza or burger, even if the former has truffle on it. (The launch PR also insists that you can now order pizza take-out from The Connaught – go on we dare you...) / W1K 2AL; www.the-connaught.co.uk/mayfair-restaurants/jean-georges; @TheConnaught; 11 pm.

Jikoni W1 £64 334
21 Blandford St 020 70341988 2–1A
"Marina's review was spot on: this clubbable and laid-back newcomer is a triumphant, kick-you-in-the-crotch winner where diners spontaneously rave to neighbours about their meals!" – so say fans of food writer Ravinder Bhogal's "cosy" Marylebone debutante, which mashes up flavours from East Africa, the Middle East, Asia and Britain. A big minority though are nonplussed – they say that "when you read the menu it looks adventurous" but claim the end result is "overhyped" and "bland". / W1U 3DJ; www.jikonilondon.com; @JikoniLondon.

Jin Kichi NW3 £46 543
73 Heath St 020 7794 6158 9–1A
"This cosy, cramped little Japanese stalwart in Hampstead is absolutely great" ("I always leave feeling the world is a better place"). "The seats upstairs near the grill are best", and there's a wide-ranging menu incorporating "top quality sushi and tempura", which are arguably "the best in north London". "Service is very fast (almost too fast)". / NW3 6UG; www.jinkichi.com; 11 pm, Sun 10 pm; closed Mon L

Jinjuu W1 £61 334
16 Kingly St 0208 1818887 4–2B
Fom Korean-American TV chef Judy Joo, this "buzzy" Korean bar (with DJ some nights) and basement restaurant off Regent Street, "instantly wipes away the cares of a busy work week". "Great Korean fried chicken and prawn lollipops" are the standout items on a menu which is "that little bit different". / W1B 5PS; www.jinjuu.com; @JinjuuSoho; 11.30 pm, Thu-Sat 1 am, Sun 9.30 pm.

Joanna's SE19 £47 354
56 Westow Hill 020 8670 4052 1–4D
"Just the sort of place you want on your doorstep", this family-owned Crystal Palace institution celebrates its 40th anniversary next year. It serves American-style food and cocktails, kicking off every morning with a "great casual breakfast". / SE19 1RX; www.joannas.uk.com; @JoannasRest; 10.45 pm, Sun 10.15 pm.

Joe Allen WC2 £53 124
2 Burleigh St 020 7836 0651 5–3D
In September 2017, this "always buzzing" 40-year-old "West End institution" (no longer co-owned with its NYC cousin) moved to a new site just 25m from the original, to accommodate Robert de Niro's new Wellington hotel (opening in 2018). They've taken everything with them from the panelling to the posters and piano, and we've rated it assuming nothing changes, that is: "you go for the bustle and the showbiz feel" and by-and-large "forget the food" ("little better than an upmarket TGI Fridays"). Top Menu Tip – "the favourite staple is the off-menu burger that's always available". / WC2E 7PX; www.joeallen.co.uk; @JoeAllenWC2; 11.30 pm, Fri & Sat 12.30 am, Sun 10 pm; set weekday L & pre-theatre £34 (FP).

Joe Public SW4 £17 **4**3**3**
4 The Pavement   020 7622 4676   11–2D
A former WC by Clapham Common (geddit?), is the spot for this hip, year-
old pizza-by-the-slice operation – "it might be only a tiny, essentially
takeaway or eat outside joint, but you'll go a long way to get a better piece
of pizza!". / SW4 7AA; www.joepublicpizza.com; @JoepublicSW4; midnight,
Sun 11pm; no booking.

The Joint SW9 £28 **3**3**3**
87 Brixton Village, Coldharbour Ln   07717 642812   11–2D
"There's a long queue but it's worth it" insist fans of this Brixton Market
BBQ, known for its "gorgeous pulled pork and brisket". Service can
be "brusque" though, and the odd reporter felt very short-changed here:
"maybe they'd run out, because we were passed off with rubbish".
/ SW9 8PS; www.the-joint.co/; @thefoodjoint; 10 pm.

Jolly Gardeners SW18 £52 **3**3**3**
214 Garratt Ln   020 8870 8417   11–2B
"Such a good spot – but no-one really knows its there!"; a "nice, airy room
at the back" of an Earlsfield gastropub, where "former MasterChef winner
Dhruv Baker puts his skills to good use", with an "interesting menu" that
"gets rather more elaborate later in the week". / SW18 4EA;
www.thejollygardeners.com; @Jollygardensw15; 9.30 pm.

Jones & Sons N16 £51 **4**4**4**
Stamford Works, 3 Gillett St   020 7241 1211   14–1A
It's "worth crossing London for the beautiful steaks, excellent flavours and
great atmosphere" at this "utterly brilliant" venture, which recently moved
into "fabulous" new open-plan premises in Dalston. "A constantly changing
menu keeps me coming back but I often end up ordering the sharing rib-eye
– Hawksmoor at half the price!" / N16 8JH; www.jonesandsonsdalston.com;
@JonesSons; 10 pm, Fri & Sat 11 pm, Sun 7 pm; booking max 7 may apply.

The Jones Family Project EC2 £58 **4**4**4**
78 Great Eastern St   020 7739 1740   13–1B
"Heartily recommended" – this Shoreditch basement beneath a cocktail bar
is renowned for "excellent steak (sourced from the Ginger Pig)" and
"a diverse wine list served by knowledgeable staff". / EC2A 3JL;
www.jonesfamilyproject.co.uk; @JonesShoreditch; 10.30 pm, Sun 6 pm; set weekday
L & Sun L £33 (FP).

José SE1 £48 **5**4**5**
104 Bermondsey St   020 7403 4902   10–4D
"I'd travel here from Spain for the pluma Iberica!" – José Pizarro's original
Bermondsey tapas bar "somehow has the edge over the competition"
serving some of "the best tapas you will find"... "if you can get
in (it's always heaving)". / SE1 3UB; www.josepizarro.com; @Jose_Pizarro;
10.15 pm, Sun 5.15 pm; closed Sun D; no booking.

José Pizarro EC2 £59 **3**3**2**
Broadgate Circle   020 7256 5333   13–2B
Tapas king, José P's "quick and easy" two-year-old is "well-located in the
revamped Broadgate Circle", and can become extremely busy ("it was too
loud to hear one another talk"). But while fans do extol its "excellent food",
overall feedback is a little middling and muted for such a hallowed name.
/ EC2M 2QS; www.josepizarro.com/jose-pizarro-broadgate; @JP_Broadgate; 10.45 pm,
Sat 9.45 pm; closed Sun; set pre theatre £39 (FP).

Joy King Lau WC2 £37 3 2 2
3 Leicester St 020 7437 1132 5–3A
"Very much better than the average for Chinatown" – this "old school",
three-floor operation just north of Leicester Square delivers just what you
hope for in the area (but is so often hard to find) with its "no frills and great
value". Top billing goes to its "fantastic dim sum" but "evening hits the spot
too, with plenty for the adventurous diner: sea cucumber, ducks' beaks,
drunken chicken feet, curry whelks…" / WC2H 7BL; www.joykinglau.com;
11.30 pm, Sun 10.30 pm.

Jugemu W1 NEW £42 5 2 3
3 Winnett St 020 7734 0518 4–2D
A diminutive new 'Japanese tapas bar' in Soho – there are a few tables but
the Top Tip is to sit up at the bar and watch chef Yuya Kikuchi (previously
at Kirazu) in action. "The authentic (slightly bewildering), Japanese food's
quite an adventure… and I thought I was a Japanese restaurant pro";
but it's brilliantly "well made" ("the sushi rivaled the best I've ever had"!).
/ W1D 6JY; jugemu-uk.crayonsite.com.

The Jugged Hare EC1 £63 3 2 3
49 Chiswell St 020 7614 0134 13–2A
"A meat-eater's delight" – this "quirky" City-fringe gastropub serves "proper
British food" and "they know their game here" (as the "animals hanging
in the window" hint). It's "always busy" and "noisy" and as a result service
can be "perfunctory". / EC1Y 4SA; www.thejuggedhare.com; @juggedhare; 11 pm,
Thu-Sat midnight, Sun 10.30 pm.

Jules SW15 NEW £42
5 Lacy Rd 020 8780 3033 11–2B
Straightforward new all-day brasserie in Putney aiming to deliver
a neighbourhood-y cocktails and tapas formula. (It's the first business
venture of George Herbert, heir to Downton Abbey, aka Highclere).
/ SW15 1NH; julesputney.co.uk.

Julie's W11 £61
135 Portland Rd 020 7229 8331 7–2A
For the third year, this seductive 48-year-old – a lush, subterranean warren
in a gorgeous Holland Park street that was an A-lister magnet in the '70s
and '80s – remains closed, with its website promising a forthcoming re-
launch for which the date is perennially pushed-out (currently it reads
'we hope to open in September 2017'). We don't know the backstory here,
but hopefully it will re-appear one day as promised. / W11 4LW;
www.juliesrestaurant.com; 11 pm.

Jun Ming Xuan NW9 £44 2 3 2
28 Heritage Ave 020 8205 6987 1–1A
"Very strong dim sum" still justifies the trip for some fans of this Cantonese,
in a "strange, rather soulless new development" in Colindale – hailed in The
Times a couple of years ago as the UK's best. There is also a school
of thought though which says "don't bother!" / NW9 5GE; www.junming.co.uk;
@jun_ming_xuan; 11 pm.

The Junction Tavern NW5 £49 3 3 3
101 Fortess Rd 020 7485 9400 9–2B
Limited but all-round upbeat feedback on this popular gastropub on the
Tufnell Park/Kentish Town borders, complete with conservatory and small
garden. / NW5 1AG; www.junctiontavern.co.uk; @JunctionTavern; 11 pm, Fri & Sat
midnight, Sun 11 pm; Mon-Thu D only, Fri-Sun open L & D; No Amex.

Juniper Tree NW3 NEW £58 | 3 | 2 | 2 |
72 Belsize Lane   020 3019 7303   9–2A
*Organic British cooking (of some ambition) is the self-appointed mission
of this Belsize Park newcomer, decorated in pleasant if slightly anodyne
modern style – early reports on culinary results vary from "just OK"
to "fantastic". / NW3 5BJ; www.junipertree.london; @JuniperTreeLDN; 10 pm;
closed Mon.*

K10 £35 | 3 | 4 | 2 |
3 Appold St, EC2   020 7539 9209   13–2B
Minster Ct, Mincing Ln, EC3   020 3019 2510   10–3D
*"The sushi's always fresh, and the hot food's worth a look too" as it circulate
on the conveyor belt of these handy city operations. The Copthall Avenue
original copped it this year at the hands of the developers, but the
remaining branches are "a good option for a quick lunch". / www.k10.com;
3 pm; Appold 9 pm; Closed D, closed Sat & Sun; no booking at L.*

Kaffeine £13 | 3 | 5 | 4 |
15 Eastcastle St, W1   020 7580 6755   3–1D
66 Great Titchfield St, W1   020 7580 6755   3–1C
*"Consistently incredible coffee" (and "superb salads and sarnies" too) give
this incredibly "welcoming" Aussie/Kiwi-owned duo a serious claim to being
"London's top independent coffee houses". "Both branches are fabulous;
the Eastcastle one is a bit more relaxed". / kaffeine.co.uk/Eastcastle/; 6 pm,
Sun 5 pm; no bookings.*

Kai Mayfair W1 £108 | 3 | 2 | 2 |
65 South Audley St   020 7493 8988   3–3A
*"A very modern take on Chinese cuisine" excites devotees of Bernard Yeoh's
"stylish and contemporary" Mayfair fixture, one of London's top Asian
venues. "I'm not sure it is genuine Chinese rather than influenced by China,
but presentation is artistic and there are really interesting menu choices".
"Eyewatering" prices "befit the location" however, as does the heavyweight
wine list which features many famous French names. / W1K 2QU;
www.kaimayfair.co.uk; @kaimayfair; 10.45 pm, Sun 10.15 pm.*

Kaifeng NW4 £69 | 3 | 3 | 3 |
51 Church Rd   020 8203 7888   1–1B
*"Good Kosher Chinese" is the USP of this Hendon stalwart. There's the odd
gripe that it's "overpriced", but on most accounts its "high standards
continue to be maintained" with food that's "excellent and authentic".
/ NW4 4DU; www.kaifeng.co.uk; 10 pm; closed Fri & Sat.*

Kanada-Ya £29 | 5 | 2 | 2 |
3 Panton St, SW1   020 7930 3511   5–4A
64 St Giles High St, WC2   020 7240 0232   5–1B
*"Delicious ramen, unsurpassed in London" ("the broth is clearly a labour
of love, so rich and silky") is the verdict on these "authentic" outposts of a
noodle chain, based in Japan: "no wonder there's always a queue out the
door!". Top Tip – "the eggs are also amazing – order an extra one to add
to your bowl". / 10.30 pm; WC2 no bookings.*

Kaosarn £28 | 4 | 3 | 3 |
110 St Johns Hill, SW11   020 7223 7888   11–2C
Brixton Village, Coldharbour Ln, SW9   020 7095 8922   11–2D
*"Fresh spicy flavours" ("they're not afraid of chillies") ensure this "rustic",
"family-run Thai group" in southwest London is "still firing on all cylinders".
"Good value" and with a "busy", "studenty" feel, "they're always hopping".
And they're "BYO to boot". / SW9 10 pm, Sun 9 pm; SW11 closed Mon L*

LONDON'S HOTTEST NEW RESTAURANTS 2018

JAMAVAR W1

TOP NEWCOMER AT THE HARDEN'S LONDON RESTAURANT AWARDS

108 GARAGE, W10

TIDBITS BANKSIDE, SE1

MOTHER, SW11

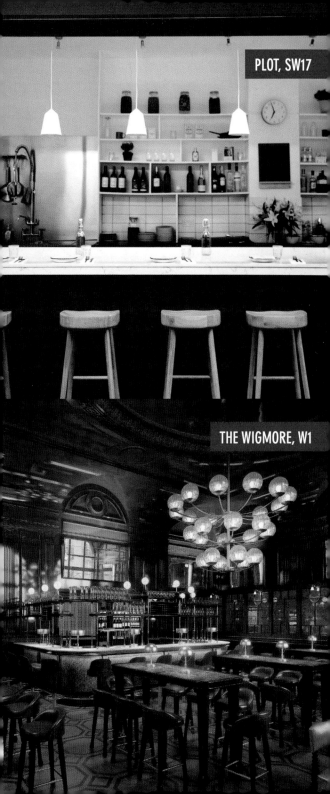

PLOT, SW17

THE WIGMORE, W1

TOM SIMMONS, SE1

HOPPERS MARYLEBONE, W1

DUDDELL'S, SE1

LAPHET, E8

FLAVOUR BASTARD

FLAVOUR BASTARD, W1

RADICI, N1

MINNOW, SW4

DUCK & WAFFLE LOCAL, SW1

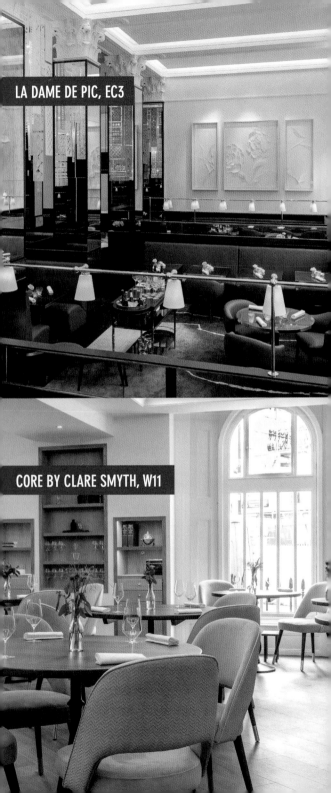

LA DAME DE PIC, EC3

CORE BY CLARE SMYTH, W11

HENRIETTA, WC2

KRICKET, W1

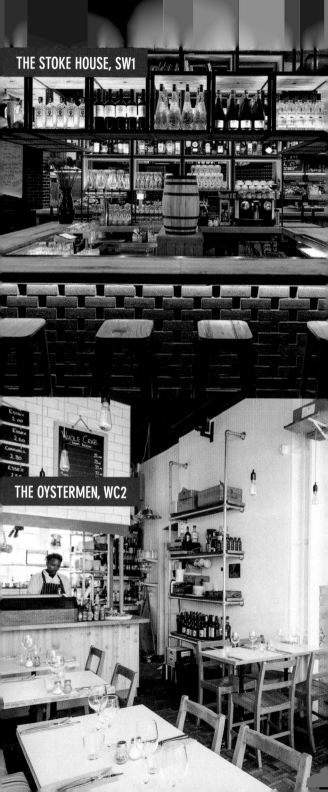

THE STOKE HOUSE, SW1

THE OYSTERMEN, WC2

HONEY & SMOKE, W1

RED ROOSTER, EC2

NOBU SHOREDITCH EC2

ASTER, SW1

TEMPER CITY, EC2

IKOYI, SW1

Harden's

LONDON
RESTAURANT
AWARDS 2017

SEPTEMBER 11 2017

Top Gastronomic Experience Award:
Marianne W2
SPONSORED BY NYETIMBER

A "tiny but lovely" 14-seater restaurant where
"cooking is peerless perfection."

*Marianne Lumb and her team with Raymond Blanc
and Peter Harden*

Top Newcomer Award:

Lifetime Achievement Award:
Corbin & King

SPONSORED BY THE HIPPODROME CASINO

"For success in a business partnership, it helps to look for the strengths in your partner's argument before you look for its weaknesses"

Jeremy King with Peter Harden and 2016 winner Bruce Poole (Chez Bruce SW17)

Kappacasein SE16 £8 **5** **3** **2**

1 Voyager Industrial Estate   07837 756852   12–2A

"Elevating melted cheese into high art" – this wizard Borough Market stall uses a mix of cheeses, leek, onions, shallots and sourdough bread to create "the best cheese toastie in the world, bar none!!". Expect to queue at busy times. / SE16 4RP; www.kappacasein.com; @kappacasein; 2pm; Sat L only; Cash only; no booking.

Karma W14 £44 **4** **3** **1**

44 Blythe Rd   020 7602 9333   8–1D

"Never-failing" curries at this Indian local, tucked away behind Olympia, help it consistently exceed expectations; less so the atmosphere, which more rarely takes flight. / W14 0HA; www.k-a-r-m-a.co.uk; @KarmaKensington; 11 pm; No Amex.

Kashmir SW15 £42 **4** **3** **3**

18-20 Lacy Rd   07477 533 888   11–2B

"On the site of longstanding Samratt" (RIP), on a side street off Putney High Street, this "extremely hospitable" yearling "has raised the bar for Indian cuisine in SW15". "A short but interesting and carefully prepared menu, and a calm atmosphere makes for a good combination, albeit at the pricier end of the range". / SW15 1NL; www.kashmirrestaurants.co.uk; @KashmirRestUK; 10.30 pm, Fri & Sat 11 pm.

**Kaspar's Seafood and Grill,
The Savoy Hotel WC2** £88 **3** **3** **4**

100 The Strand   020 7836 4343   5–3D

"Lovely fish served in a beautiful room" – in prior decades known as The Savoy's River Restaurant – has won a renewed following and consistent high praise for this convenient Thames-side chamber. Top Tip – "ideal for a pre/post theatre set deal" and lunch too. / WC2R 0EU; www.kaspars.co.uk; @KasparsLondon; 11 pm; set pre theatre £58 (FP).

Kateh W9 £66 **3** **2** **3**

5 Warwick Pl   020 7289 3393   9–4A

"The well executed dishes are just delicious" at this jolly modern Iranian joint in Little Venice, where you squish in cheek-by-jowl. Top Tip – "the upstairs dining room is preferable to the basement". / W9 2PX; www.katehrestaurant.co.uk; @RestaurantKateh; 11 pm, Sun 9.30 pm; closed weekday L.

Kazan £44 **3** **3** **3**

77 Wilton Rd, SW1   020 7233 8298   2–4B
93-94 Wilton Rd, SW1   020 7233 7100   2–4B

"A long-standing, beautifully run Pimlico gem" – this Turkish café (and its offshoot across the road) provides "reliably good value" at a "handy address close to Victoria station". "Comfortable, with always cheerful service… it's popular for good reason". / www.kazan-restaurant.com; 10 pm, Fri & Sat 10.30 pm, Sun 9.30 pm.

**The Keeper's House,
Royal Academy W1** £66 **2** **2** **2**

Royal Academy of Arts, Burlington House,   020 7300 5881   3–3D

"OK post-culture", but "could do better" remains a fair assessment of this popular operation, hidden in the vaults of the Royal Academy (which is reserved at lunchtime for RA members and their guests). "It's a useful location" (if a slightly "gloomy" one), but while fans say it's "lovely" it disappoints too often to be a totally recommendable one. / W1J 0BD; www.royalacademy.org.uk/keepers-house; @KHRestaurant; closed Sun.

Ken Lo's Memories SW1 £60 3 3 2
65-69 Ebury St 020 7730 7734 2–4B
Ken Lo's traditional Belgravia operation not far from Victoria Station "doesn't change much: but if it ain't broke, why fix it?" The odd reporter does feel "it has gone down over the years", but more commonly there's praise for "consistently good food in a very convivial atmosphere". / SW1W 0NZ; www.memoriesofchina.co.uk; 11 pm, Sun 10.30 pm.

Kennington Tandoori SE11 £54 4 4 4
313 Kennington Rd 020 7735 9247 1–3C
"The mix of locals, politicians, and a convivial owner and staff ensure a happy evening" at "this most political of restaurants" – a Kennington curry house notoriously popular with MPs from nearby Westminster. Expect "high quality Indian fare, with not too many fussy frills but large doses of flavour, a warm atmosphere and low lighting!" / SE11 4QE; www.kenningtontandoori.com; @TheKTLondon; No Amex.

Kensington Place W8 £62 3 2 2
201-209 Kensington Church St 020 7727 3184 7–2B
This "glass-fronted bastion" – in its day, a seminal icon of the 1990s restaurant scene near Notting Hill – nowadays, under D&D London, specialises in fish with its own fishmonger next door. "Not as slick or smart as it was" in its heyday – and "not cheap" – but the food is "fresh and well-cooked". (Avoid the place if you don't like "distracting acoustics" – it can get far "too noisy".) / W8 7LX; www.kensingtonplace-restaurant.co.uk; @KPRestaurantW8; 10 pm, Fri & Sat 10.30 pm; closed Mon L & Sun D.

Kensington Square Kitchen W8 £37 3 4 3
9 Kensington Sq 020 7938 2598 6–1A
"Perfect breakfasts", "brilliant brunch", and "really good coffee" ensure that this cute, little two-storey café in one of Kensington's oldest squares has a "regular and loyal clientele". "If you're not into a Full English there are masses of other yummy things on the menu", along with "great-value fresh and seasonal lunches". / W8 5EP; www.kensingtonsquarekitchen.co.uk; @KSKRestaurant; 4.30 pm, Sun 4 pm; L only; No Amex.

The Kensington Wine Rooms W8 £56 2 3 3
127-129 Kensington Church St 020 7727 8142 7–2B
This modern wine bar (with branches in Fulham and Hammersmith) gives you the chance to sample an "excellent range" of more than 40 "high-end wines by the glass". The food is a bit of a supporting act, but even those who feel it's "slightly uninventive" find it "perfectly satisfactory". / W8 7LP; www.greatwinesbytheglass.com; @wine_rooms; 11.30 pm.

Kerbisher & Malt £24 3 3 2
53 New Broadway, W5 020 8840 4418 1–2A
164 Shepherd's Bush Rd, W6 020 3556 0228 8–1C
170 Upper Richmond Road West, SW14 020 8876 3404 1–4A
50 Abbeville Rd, SW4 020 3417 4350 11–2D
This "hipsters' take on the urban chippy", founded six years ago in Brook Green, now also boasts branches in East Sheen and Clapham (Ealing and Islington are no more). They're "unpretentious, the fresh fish is superb, and the chips aren't half bad either". / www.kerbisher.co.uk; 10-10.30 pm, Sun & Mon 9-9.30 pm; W6 closed Mon; no booking.

Khan's W2 £23 3 2 2
13-15 Westbourne Grove 020 7727 5420 7–1C
"Rather down-to-earth, but always excellent" sums up the Khan family's popular and fast-paced Indian canteen in Bayswater, founded in 1977 (which, for the past 18 years, has been alcohol-free). / W2 4UA; www.khansrestaurant.com; @KhansRestaurant; 11.30 pm.

Kiku W1 £62 3 3 2
17 Half Moon St 020 7499 4208 3–4B
"Very enjoyable (if slightly expensive) dishes" are the hallmark of this veteran Japanese in Mayfair, served in traditionally austere and formal surroundings. / W1J 7BE; www.kikurestaurant.co.uk; 10.15 pm, Sun 9.45 pm; closed Sun L.

Kikuchi W1 £76 4 3 2
14 Hanway St 020 7637 7720 5–1A
This little izakaya in the backstreets near Tottenham Court Road tube attracts a small but dedicated fan club, who say: "don't look at the bill whatever you do, but prepare to be amazed by the food!" / W1T 1UD; 10.30 pm, Sat 9.30 pm; closed Sun; no booking.

Killer Tomato W12 £24 4 3 2
18 Goldhawk Rd 020 8743 0082 8–1C
"East London comes to the Goldhawk Road" with this street food yearling in Shepherds Bush, whose tacos and burritos deliver "fresh Mexican flavours from a short, focused menu", and whose "mezcal margaritas alone are worth a visit". Coming soon – a second branch on Portobello Road. / W12 8DH; killertomato.co.uk; @eatkillertomato; 9.30 pm, Thu-Sat 10 pm, Sun 9 pm; no booking.

Kiln W1 £33 5 4 4
58 Brewer St no tel 4–3C
"A rare London venture that feels genuinely different" – Ben Chapman's "vibey", "little" Soho haunt is "the best casual opening of the year" and its "inspired", "palate-searing" small plates ("taking a bite is like travelling abroad") are "made totally unique by dint of their incredible sourcing, ballsy spicing and cooking everything over charcoal". "No reservations + very popular = annoyingly large wait times though". / W1F 9TL; www.kilnsoho.com.

Kintan WC1 £42 3 2 3
34-36 High Holborn 020 7242 8076 10–2A
This Japanese/Korean tabletop BBQ near Holborn wins consistent praise for its yakiniku (grilled meat) dishes. / WC1V 6AE; www.kintan.uk; @kintanuk; 10.30 pm, Sun 9.30 pm.

Kipferl N1 £46 3 2 3
20 Camden Passage 020 77041 555 9–3D
"Great strudel, and the best sachertorte north of Vienna!" help score fans for this modern Austrian coffee house in Islington (with a new branch in Ladbroke Grove), and there's also a "small, unusual menu" of more substantial dishes like Viennese sausages, dumplings and schnitzels. / N1 8ED; www.kipferl.co.uk; @KipferlCafe; 9.25 pm; closed Mon; booking weekdays only.

Kiraku W5 £37 4 4 2
8 Station Pde 020 8992 2848 1–3A
This low-key café near Ealing Common tube station – heavily patronised by west London's Japanese expat community – doesn't win the raves it once did, but is still regularly praised for top-value dishes. / W5 3LD; www.kiraku.co.uk; @kirakulondon; 10 pm; closed Mon; No Amex.

Kiru SW3 £52 4 4 3
2 Elystan St 020 7584 9999 6–2D
"In the ever-growing range of Asian fusion restaurants", this year-old, neighbourhood Japanese on Chelsea Green "is a great new addition". The prices raise the odd complaint however – "it's good, but for these prices it would have to be the best in London..." / SW3; www.kirurestaurant.com; @KiruRestaurant; 10 pm, Fri & Sat 10.30 pm.

Kitchen W8 W8 £71 443
11-13 Abingdon Rd 020 7937 0120 6–1A
"The cuisine has recently gone up another notch: it was always top quality, but is even subtler now", at this unexpectedly fine neighbourhood restaurant, just off Kensington's main drag, where Phil Howard's consultancy helps yield a "very slick and professional" approach. Ambience-wise, it generally rates well, but even fans can find it "a little empty emotionally". / W8 6AH; www.kitchenw8.com; @KitchenW8; 10.30 pm, Sun 9.30 pm; booking max 6 may apply; set weekday L £46 (FP), set pre-theatre £49 (FP).

Kitty Fisher's W1 £75 333
10 Shepherd Mkt 020 3302 1661 3–4B
No-one disputes that this "gorgeous quirky restaurant" in cute Shepherd Market provides "lovely" British dishes and an "intimate" ("squashed") setting. But having been the place about which Le Tout Londres raved non-stop a couple of years ago, even many fans now feel that "while it's perfectly good, it's not as exceptional as some reviews might lead you to believe". / W1J 7QF; www.kittyfishers.com; @kittyfishers; 9.30 pm; closed Sun.

Knife SW4 NEW £57 544
160 Clapham Park Rd 020 7627 6505 11–2D
"Elegantly cooked steaks, beautifully presented with deep umami flavours" make Matt-'The Dairy'-Wells's new "small put perfectly formed" 'neighbourhood steak restaurant' an "absolutely fantastic" addition to SW4. The first part of a planned local chain – all the meat is British, from the Lakes – and there's Cornish fish and seafood too. / SW4 7DE; knifrestaurant.co.uk; @KnifeLondon; 10 pm, Sun 4 pm; closed Mon, Tue & Sun D.

Koba W1 £44 433
11 Rathbone St 020 7580 8825 2–1C
"New Malden may boast the highest concentration of Korean BBQs, but Koba in Fitzrovia is the chicest – it offers delicious, authentic tabletop cooking in an elegant room and a pure Seoul vibe!" Staff are "welcoming" and the experience "reasonably priced". / W1T 1NA; kobalondon.com; @kobalondon; 10.45 pm; closed Sun L.

Koji SW6 £80 444
58 New King's Rd 020 7731 2520 11–1B
"Sushi, ceviche and a robata grill" earn high marks for Pat & Mark Barnett's smart modern Japanese fusion joint in Parsons Green (which for ages, they ran as Mao Tai, long RIP), whose "cocktails are a great motor-starter!" / SW6 4LS; www.koji.restaurant; @koji_restaurant; D only, Sun open L & D.

Kolossi Grill EC1 £32 333
56-60 Rosebery Ave 020 7278 5758 10–1A
This "tiny, welcoming Greek" off Exmouth Market "hasn't changed in 40 years". The "real taverna feel" makes it an eternal "great favourite" for regulars, even if, in contemporary culinary terms, it is arguably no more than "hanging in there". / EC1R 4RR; www.kolossigrill.com; 10.30 pm; closed Sat L & Sun.

Koya £32 333
50 Frith St, W1 020 7434 4463 5–2A
Bloomberg Arcade, Queen Victoria St, EC2 no tel 10–2C NEW
"Excellent udon noodles, just like in Japan", are "worth the wait" – there's no booking at this Soho destination (with a City outpost opening in late 2017), so be prepared to queue at busy times. There are also "nice additional starters like the pork belly or tempura – all delicious, simple food done well and served by friendly staff". / www.koyabar.co.uk; W1 10.30 pm, Thu-Sat 11 pm, Sun 10 pm; no booking; SRA-Food Made Good – 1 star.

Kricket W1 £47 **5** **4** **4**

12 Denman St 020 7734 5612 4–3C

"Living up to all the rave reviews... and then some!" Rik Campbell and Will Bowlby's "fun dive, off increasingly gaudy Shaftesbury Avenue" (the Soho successor to the wildly popular Brixton prototype in a shipping container) is "a whole new ball game!" offering "a great experience, even if it's mad and rushed". The "design is simple but sophisticated", with much of the seating on stools at a long counter; and the "profoundly original dishes" – "derived largely from Mumbai street food but either elevated a notch or transformed imaginatively" – is "spicy without being overpowering" and "quite exceptional". / W1D 7HH; www.kricket.co.uk; @kricketlondon; 10 pm.

Kulu Kulu £34 **3** **2** **1**

76 Brewer St, W1 020 7734 7316 4–3C

51-53 Shelton St, WC2 020 7240 5687 5–2C

39 Thurloe Pl, SW7 020 7589 2225 6–2C

"My go-to for cheap, reliable Japanese food" – these "unchanging" (read dated and drab) conveyor-belt sushi dives (Kulu Kulu means 'sushi-go-round') "feel authentic" and "won't break the bank". / 10 pm, SW7 10.30 pm; closed Sun; no Amex; no booking.

Kurobuta £63 **3** **2** **2**

312 King's Rd, SW3 020 7920 6442 6–3C

17-20 Kendal St, W2 020 7920 6444 7–1D

"A great punky Australian/Asian mashup" characterises the menu at these "fun" izakaya-style venues, where "stunning grill dishes" are the highlights of the "funky" fare. On the downside they're "not all that cheap" and "loud". In July 2017 (post survey) founder Scott Hallsworth sold out to his business partners, so change may be afoot. / www.kurobuta-london.com; 10.30 pm; SW3 closed Mon-Thu L.

The Ladbroke Arms W11 £53 **3** **3** **3**

54 Ladbroke Rd 020 7727 6648 7–2B

This attractive and atmospheric "gourmet pub", at the Holland Park end of Ladbroke Grove, "definitely requires a reservation, especially on weekends", but it's "worth the aggravation" for the "delicious food" and "great local beer". Top Tip – "the real draw is the terrace on a nice day". / W11 3NW; www.ladbrokearms.com; @ladbrokearms; 10 pm, Sat 10.30 pm, Sun 9 pm; no booking after 8 pm.

Lady Mildmay N1 NEW £40 **3** **4** **3**

92 Mildmay Park 020 7241 6238 1–1C

"A great addition to local eateries" – this handsome, "recently refurbished pub" on the corner of Newington Green was relaunched in February 2016 and provides "excellent food" from an open kitchen at good prices. / N1 4PR; www.ladymildmay.com; @theladymildmaypub; 10 pm, Sun 9 pm; May need 6+ to book.

Lahore Karahi SW17 £26 **4** **2** **2**

1 Tooting High Street, London 020 8767 2477 11–2C

"Fabulous Pakistani cooking at ridiculously inexpensive prices" makes this "quirky" BYO canteen one of the best in Tooting. "Expect to have to wait for a table." / SW17 0SN; www.lahorekarahirestaurant.co.uk; 11.45 pm; No Amex.

Lahore Kebab House £25 **4** **3** **2**
668 Streatham High Rd, SW16   020 8765 0771   11–2D
2-10 Umberston St, E1   020 7481 9737   12–1A

"Still dishing up exceptional value Punjabi cuisine after all these years (despite the various changes in setup and clientele)"; this "cheap and no-nonsense" Whitechapel dive is a legend for its "amazing curries" and lamb chops, and – "despite a swathe of competitors now" – for fans "it's still the winner". That said, the "cavernous" upstairs has "all the ambience of a school canteen rented out to a stag do operator" – "if you get a table downstairs it's a bit calmer". Meanwhile, its Streatham cousin inspires only a tiny amount of feedback, but it's just as upbeat: "fantastic, fresh dishes – efficient and friendly service – and nicer than the E1 aircraft hangar". / midnight.

Lamberts SW12 £55 **4** **5** **3**
2 Station Parade   020 8675 2233   11–2C

"Superb in every respect" and "extremely good value" – Joe Lambert's "Balham gem" is renowned locally for its "informal-but-never-sloppy service" and a "very high standard of seasonal cooking" that, for its most ardent fans, "classes it as a competitor to Chez Bruce". A couple of regulars reported a "loss of mojo" here this year however – "it was disappointing, but we hope this let-down was a one off". / SW12 9AZ; www.lambertsrestaurant.com; @lamberts_balham; 10 pm, Sun 5 pm; closed Mon & Sun D; No Amex.

The Landmark, Winter Garden NW1 £77 **2** **4** **5**
222 Marylebone Rd   020 7631 8000   9–4A

The "very beautiful surroundings" of this romantic, light-filled Marylebone atrium make it a "top-notch" choice for Sunday brunch or afternoon tea treats, when the "sheer volume and amazing range" of the food impress. "Service is excellent", with waiters who "keep the Champagne flowing" (it's 'all-you-can-drink' at brunch). / NW1 6JQ; www.landmarklondon.co.uk; @landmarklondon; 10.15 pm; No trainers; booking max 12 may apply.

Langan's Brasserie W1 £67 **2** **3** **4**
Stratton St   020 7491 8822   3–3C

"Like an old pair of slippers, you just feel comfortable with!" – this famous and "fun" brasserie near The Ritz, celebrating its 40th year, remains, for its older fan club, "something magical, steeped in gastronomic history, and never failing to impress". The less rose-tinted view is that it looks "tired" and serves "nursery food gone wrong". / W1J 8LB; www.langansrestaurants.co.uk; @langanslondon; 11 pm, Fri & Sat 11.30 pm; closed Sun.

Palm Court, The Langham W1 £75 **3** **3** **4**
1c Portland Place   020 7965 0195   2–1B

The "quintessentially English" afternoon tea in the civilised lounge of this well-known hotel is "so beautifully crafted you feel it's a shame to bite in!", with "portions so generous you might need a doggy bag". "Super location and staff and a great cocktail menu make it a winner for meeting up with friends" at other times too. / W1B 1JA; www.palm-court.co.uk; @Langham_London; 10.30 pm; No trainers.

Lantana Cafe £43 **3** **3** **3**
13-14 Charlotte Pl, W1   020 7323 6601   2–1C
45 Middle Yd, Camden Lock Pl, NW1   020 7428 0421   9–2B
Ground Floor West, 44-46 Southwark St, SE1   no tel   10–4C
Unit 2, 1 Oliver's Yd, 55 City Rd, EC1   020 7253 5273   13–1A

"One of the first to do an Aussie brunch and still one of the best" – these "funky" Antipodean hangouts also serve an "interesting" and "super-tasty" choice of "bistro-style food" at lunchtime. / lantanacafe.co.uk; EC1 9.30 pm, Sat & Sun 3 pm; W1 3.30 pm, Sat & Sun 5 pm; NW1 5.30 pm; NW1 closed Sun; W1 no booking Sat & Sun.

Lao Cafe WC2 NEW £38 3 3 2

60 Chandos Place   020 3740 4748   5–4C

In another successful transition from pop-up to permanent, Saiphin Moore's (of Rosa's Thai) dim-lit café just off the Strand, follows the popularity of a temporary home in Victoria last year. "Whether this is really Lao or northern Thai/Isarn food is an open question, and the menu is small, but the dishes are delicious and at the right spice level." / WC2N 4HG; laocafe.co.uk; May need 8+ to book.

Laphet E8 NEW £42 3 3 3

5 Helmsley Place   020 3883 5629   14–2B

"A great chance to try an underrepresented cuisine" – this new Burmese communal canteen in Hackney (previously a Maltby Street stall) is well-rated in reports: "traditional dishes like the tea salad are the best options". / E8 3SB; www.lahpet.co.uk; @Lahpet; 10.30 pm, Sun 5 pm.

Lardo £50 3 3 2

158 Sandringham Rd, E8   020 3021 0747   14–1B
197-201 Richmond Rd, E8   020 8533 8229   14–1B

"A short list of properly made thin-crust pizzas" pack in the hip crowd at this Italian in the Arthaus building near London Fields – a "must-visit before the Hackney Empire". Good, if limited, feedback on the second branch, Bebè, nearby. / 10.30 pm, Sun 9.30 pm.

LASSCO Bar & DIning SE1 NEW £50

Ropewalk, 37 Maltby St   020 7394 8061   10–4D

From one overcrowded hipster market to another – bar manager Jerome Slesinski and chef James Knox Boothman worked together at The Royal Oak in Columbia Road's Flower Market, and now they have teamed up again to run the restaurant and bar at LASSCO's (London Architectural Salvage and Supply Company) Ropewalk warehouse, in the heart of über-trendy Maltby St Market. It's a not-dissimilar idea to LASSCO's well-established operation at Brunswick House. / SE1 3PA; www.lasscobar.co.uk; @lassco_bar; 10 pm; closed Mon-Wed D & Sun D.

Latium W1 £58 3 3 2

21 Berners St   020 7323 9123   3–1D

"A solid choice if you are seeking a classic Italian" – this "tranquil" and "white-table-clothed" Fitzrovia fixture has "lost a bit of wow-factor since the change of personnel" a couple of years ago, but with its "subtle dishes, and unobtrusive service" it's still seen by most reporters as "a stalwart of very good Italian cuisine"; and the fact that it's "blessedly un-noisy at lunchtime" makes it "perfect for business discussions". / W1T 3LP; www.latiumrestaurant.com; @LatiumLondon; 10.30 pm, Sat 11 pm, Sun 9.30 pm; closed Sat L & Sun L; set weekday L £37 (FP).

Laughing Gravy SE1 £56 3 4 3

154 Blackfriars Rd   020 7998 1707   10–4A

Billing itself as 'London's best-kept secret' – this tucked-away bar/restaurant in Southwark can be "a lovely find" despite its "unexceptional location", thanks to its "top cocktails" and consistently good cooking – in particular "stand out steak" and "stunning puddings". / SE1 8EN; www.thelaughinggravy.co.uk; @laughinggravyuk; 10 pm, Fri & Sat 10.30 pm, Sun 4.30 pm; closed Sun D; no booking.

The Laughing Heart E2 NEW £64 3 2 3

277 Hackney Rd   020 7686 9535   14–2A

"It's been a favourite with the critics" and fans find it "bangin' on all fronts", but the overall view is more nuanced when it comes to Charlie Mellor's "dark and moodily-lit" new Hackney wine bar and off-licence. True, nearly all reports do acknowledge the "interesting food" and "inventive wine list" (featuring many top biodynamic wines), but even fans can feel that "the price and pretensions are not that laughable", given the "expensive and small" dishes. / E2 8NA; thelaughingheartlondon.com.

Launceston Place W8 £73 **3**4**4**

1a Launceston Pl 020 7937 6912 6–1B

This "lovely townhouse tucked away in the back streets of Kensington" has "had several recent changes of chef/patron under D&D group", of which the latest is Ben Murphy, who arrived from The Woodford in early 2017. Fans say his "modern, inventive and delicious cuisine is taking them back into Michelin territory" but there are also those who feel "it's now more expensive and impressive rather than compelling". Top Tip – "excellent value early bird menu". / W8 5RL; www.launcestonplace-restaurant.co.uk; @LauncestonPlace; 10 pm, Sun 9.30 pm; closed Mon & Tue L.

THE LEDBURY W11 £142 **5**5**4**

127 Ledbury Rd 020 7792 9090 7–1B

"Wow! I didn't think this place could possibly live up to the hype, but it did… and easily!" Brett Graham's "sophisticated" Notting Hill HQ delivers a pitch-perfect performance and again topped the survey's nominations for offering London's best meal of the year. But for all his "stunningly well-crafted" cuisine ("so many dishes that were so memorable") and "perfectly matched wines", it's the "unpretentious, customer-first attitude that makes a meal here that much more enjoyable": "everyone's relaxed and having a great time!" / W11 2AQ; www.theledbury.com; @theledbury; 9.45 pm; closed Mon L & Tue L; booking max 6 may apply; set weekday L £97 (FP).

Legs E9 £50 **3**4**4**

120 Morning Lane 020 3441 8765 14–1B

This hip yearling from Aussie chef Magnus Reid (founder of Shoreditch coffeehouse C.R.E.A.M.) "never disappoints", with "great" modern dishes and a "relaxing" boho atmosphere. Diners perch facing the window looking across to the new Hackney Walk fashion hub, and there's an interesting list of small producer wines (the name, 'Legs', is wine lingo). / E9 6LH; www.legsrestaurant.com; @legsrestaurant; 11 pm; D only, Sat L & D, Sun L only, closed Mon & Tue; no booking L.

Lemonia NW1 £49 **1**3**4**

89 Regent's Park Rd 020 7586 7454 9–3B

This "vast Greek taverna" has become a landmark after 40 years on Primrose Hill, and is "extraordinarily busy" due to the "unique experience and family atmosphere" it offers. But the cooking "is average at best, and less-than-average of late"; "I've been coming here for 25 years and the food is nothing like it used to be, which is very sad because it's a fun place". / NW1 8UY; www.lemonia.co.uk; @Lemonia_Greek; 11 pm; closed Sun D; No Amex.

The Lido Café, Brockwell Lido SE24 £43 **2**2**4**

Dulwich Rd 020 7737 8183 11–2D

"Great for a brunch watching the swimmers" – getting wet is not compulsory if you visit this all-day café attached to Brixton's wonderfully characterful and lovingly preserved Lido. / SE24 0PA; www.thelidocafe.co.uk; @thelidocafe; 4 pm; closed Sun D; No Amex; booking max 8 may apply.

The Light House SW19 £54 **3**3**2**

75-77 Ridgway 020 8944 6338 11–2B

"What a neighbourhood restaurant should strive to be", this long-running, bare-walled (hence "noisy") Wimbledon indie has a "slightly quirky menu" with "seasonal produce to the fore". Fans feel it's "seemingly underrated", but there's also always been a "hit 'n' miss" element to reports here. / SW19 4ST; www.lighthousewimbledon.com; 10.30 pm; closed Sun D; set weekday L £35 (FP).

The Lighterman N1 £59 3 4 4
3 Granary Square   020 3846 3400   9–3C
"A terrific location at Granary Square" – with "stunning views overlooking the canal", "a sunny terrace with lots of outside space" and attractive first-floor dining room – win massive popularity for this "very atmospheric" King's Cross yearling. And it's "well-run" too – staff are "surprisingly efficient and personable" and its "typical British dishes" are "well-executed and tasty" with impressive consistency. / N1C 4BH; www.thelighterman.co.uk; @TheLightermanKX; 10.30 pm, Sun 9.30 pm.

Lima Fitzrovia £70 3 2 2
31 Rathbone Pl, W1   020 3002 2640   2–1C
14 Garrick St, WC2   020 7240 5778   5–3C
"Very pretty and delicious food in a fun setting" is the promise of these modern Peruvians, in Fitzrovia and Covent Garden ('Lima Floral'). On the downside, they can feel "understaffed" or "a little basic given the price", and sceptics feel that "the food looks like a picture, but can taste a little underwhelming". / www.limalondongroup.com/fitzrovia; 10.30 pm, Sun 9.30 pm; Mon L closed.

Lisboa Pâtisserie W10 £8 3 3 4
57 Golborne Rd   020 8968 5242   7–1A
"Simply the best pastéis de nata in London, and excellent coffee too" make it worth adding this "truly unpretentious" and "good value" Portuguese café into a trip down Portobello way, although NB "it's very crowded most of the time". / W10 5NR; 7 pm; L & early evening only; no booking.

The Little Bay NW6 £33 2 3 4
228 Belsize Rd   020 7372 4699   1–2B
"An intimate and romantic interior and low prices" have long sustained this theatre-themed bistro, "hidden" off Kilburn High Road, complete with little balconies for couples. / NW6 4BT; www.littlebaykilburn.co.uk; midnight, Sun 11pm.

Little Bird £58 2 2 4
1 Station Parade, W4   020 3145 0894   1–3A
1 Battersea Rise, SW11   020 7324 7714   11–2C **NEW**
Lorraine Angliss's (Annie's, Rock & Rose) latest exercise in neighbourhood glam combines eclectic, exotic decor, with "excellent cocktails" and a (slightly rootless) Asian/European menu. Good vibes from locals to the first branch, "in a quiet backwater, right by Chiswick Station" – there's now also a second in the heart of Battersea.

Little Georgia Cafe £40 3 2 3
14 Barnsbury Rd, N1   020 7278 6100   9–3D
87 Goldsmiths Row, E2   020 7739 8154   14–2B
"Interesting wines and lots of garlic" enliven the "reliable" hearty fodder at this duo of Georgian cafés, in Islington and Hackney, which inspire limited but positive feedback. / www.littlegeorgia.co.uk; N1 11 pm, Sun 10 pm; E2 11 pm, Mon 5 pm; N1 closed Mon, E2 closed Mon D.

Little Social W1 £79 2 2 2
5 Pollen St   020 7870 3730   3–2C
Across the road from Pollen Street, Jason Atherton's more informal second 'Social' is "enjoyable, but nowhere near as good as over the road", "with some interesting dishes but all-in-all a bit expensive". / W1S 1NE; www.littlesocial.co.uk; @_littlesocial; 10.30 pm; closed Sun; booking max 6 may apply; set pre theatre £51 (FP).

Little Taperia SW17 £42 3 3 3
143 Tooting High St   020 8682 3303   11–2C
"A Tooting find", this "fun and buzzy" Spanish two-year-old provides "plate after plate of fresh tapas, all served with friendly advice" ("it's so good, you just keep on ordering!") / SW17; www.thelittletaperia.co.uk; @littletaperia; 10 pm, Fri & Sat 11 pm, Sun 9.30 pm; May need 6+ to book.

Lluna N10 £43 **3 3 3**
462 Muswell Hill Broadway   020 8442 2662   3–3B
*Right on the Broadway in Muswell Hill, this bright, modern Spanish
bar/restaurant serves a "very varied menu" from breakfast onwards,
including "delicious tapas". "It can get very loud at the front when it's busy."
/ N10 1BS; lalluna.co.uk; @lallunalondon; 9 pm.*

LOBOS Meat & Tapas SE1 £50 **4 4 2**
14 Borough High St   020 7407 5361   10–4C
*"Outstanding and inventive, meat-based tapas" – "served with attitude"
(in a good way) – make it well worth seeking out this "hard-to-find" two-
year-old "squashed under a rail viaduct" at Borough Market. Set up by
alumni of nearby Brindisa, whose "passion shines through", it is "chaotic and
busy" – but "somehow it works". / SE1 9QG; www.lobostapas.co.uk;
@LobosTapas; 11 pm, Sun 10 pm; booking max 8 may apply.*

Locanda Locatelli, Hyatt Regency W1 £85 **4 3 3**
8 Seymour St   020 7935 9088   2–2A
*"Classic food is beautifully presented and served with an understated aura
of luxury" in Giorgio Locatelli's "dim-lit" (slightly '90s) Marylebone HQ –
one of London's most "polished" Italian dining rooms ("at its best, nowhere
else matches it"). Service is "slick" but prone sometimes to hitting the wrong
note. / W1H 7JZ; www.locandalocatelli.com; 11 pm, Thu-Sat 11.30 pm,
Sun 10.15 pm; booking max 8 may apply.*

Locanda Ottomezzo W8 £67 **3 3 3**
2-4 Thackeray St   020 7937 2200   6–1B
*"Excellent, genuine Italian cuisine" helps makes this an "atmospheric" local
in a backstreet near Kensington Square Garden. "Everything is homemade
from the grissini to the pasta", and they also do a "great breakfast and top
pizzas". / W8 5ET; www.locandaottoemezzo.co.uk; 10.30 pm; closed Mon L,
Sat L & Sun.*

Loch Fyne £43 **2 3 3**
*"A good variety of nicely cooked fish" is a perhaps lukewarm but fair
estimation of this "dependable" national chain, liked also for its well-
appointed branches and "polite" service. / www.lochfyne-restaurants.com; 10 pm,
WC2 Mon-Sat 10.30 pm.*

Lockhouse W2 NEW £38 **3 2 3**
3 Merchant Square   020 7706 4253   7–1D
*"Newly opened in Paddington Quay" – and with "a great ambience from
being by the canal's waterside" – this large operation offers "a fine range
of trendy ales and lagers" and a menu headlining with 'award winning
Lockhouse Loaded burgers'. The odd early report says it's "excellent value".
/ W2 1AZ; www.lockhouselondon.co.uk; @Lockhouselondon; 23.30, Sat 5pm.*

London House SW11 £60 **2 2 2**
7-9 Battersea Sq   020 7592 8545   11–1C
*Gordon Ramsay's Battersea venue wins some praise for "decent food and
cocktails", but its ratings have suffered as a result of an apparent identity
crisis: "It doesn't know if it's a restaurant or a pub, which made it feel like
it was neither…"; "Bring back the white tablecloths! It's much less special
than when it first opened. What went wrong?" / SW11 3RA;
www.gordonramsayrestaurants.com/london-house; @londonhouse; 11 pm, Sun 9 pm.*

London Shell Co. W2 NEW £66 455
Sheldon Square 07818 666005 7–1C
"A highly original dining experience!" – a converted wide beam canal boat ('The Prince Regent') moored in the Paddington Central development, offering a simple, "very seasonal and carefully sourced menu of amazingly fresh and perfectly cooked fish". "It's fun and they're very friendly." / W2 6EP; www.londonshellco.com; @LondonShellCo; dinner cruises depart at 7.30 pm; closed Mon, Sun & Sat L.

Lorne SW1 NEW £60 453
76 Wilton Rd 020 3327 0210 2–4B
"A triumph from the River Café/Chez Bruce/The Square's Katie Exton and Peter Hall" – this "confident, new modern British kid on the ever-more-interesting Pimlico culinary block" (on the same street as A Wong) is yet another reason to brave the "grimy streets surrounding Victoria station". "The seasonal menu is expertly created and cooked" and matched with a "concise but astonishingly tempting wine list" in a "light", simple space. / SW1V 1DE; www.lornerestaurant.co.uk; 9.30 pm; closed Sun.

Louie Louie SE17 NEW £43 333
347 Walworth Rd 020 7450 3223 1–3C
"Exponentially raising the attractiveness of SE17 as a culinary destination!" – this white-walled, all-day café opened as a result of a successful 2016 crowdfund by the owners of nearby Fowlds, and transforms (four nights a week) into a hip restaurant with guest chefs and DJ nights. / SE17 2AL; louielouie.london; @LouieLouie_Ldn; closed Mon D & Sun D.

Luardos EC1 £9 54-
Pitch 39, Whitecross St Market no tel 13–1A
"You don't go for ambience, but those burritos are the stuff of dreams" – so say addicted fans of this 10-year-old Mexican food truck biz, who have added a KERB Camden stall to the original Whitecross Street pitch, where they still sell from their first Citroën H van, 'Jesus'. / EC1Y 8JL; luardos.co.uk.

Luca EC1 NEW £73 344
88 St John St 020 3859 3000 10–1A
"It's not the Clove Club: get over it!" – this new Clerkenwell sibling to Shoreditch's legendary foodie temple takes a totally different culinary tack, delivering a menu of "high quality, refined Italian dishes" using the best British produce. Not everyone loves it (especially those burdened by Clove Club expectations), but most reports are of "outstanding" cooking, "extremely accommodating staff" and a "beautiful" and "romantic" interior (the rambling site once known as Portal (long RIP), with a cosy bar at the front and conservatory and private rooms towards the rear). Top Menu Tip – "the Parmesan fries are truly the work of angels (addictively moreish!)". / EC1M 4EH; luca.restaurant; @LucaRestaurant.

Luce e Limoni WC1 £59 443
91-93 Gray's Inn Rd 020 7242 3382 10–1A
"Service with passion and a smile" from "great host" Fabrizio matched with "fantastic, freshly cooked Sicilian food and wine" is a winning combination at this Bloomsbury Italian: "it's not very near anywhere, but worth a trip". / WC1X 8TX; www.luceelimoni.com; @Luce_e_Limoni; 10 pm, Fri & Sat 11 pm.

Luciano's SE12 £52 333
131 Burnt Ash Rd 020 8852 3186 1–4D
This "fabulous family-run (and family-friendly) pizza and pasta joint in Lee is always full". Arguably "it's nothing more than a friendly neighbourhood place" but the worst anyone has to say about the food is that it's "OK". / SE12; www.lucianoslondon.co.uk; @LucianosLondon; 10.30 pm, Sun 10 pm.

Lucio SW3   £75   3 4 3
257 Fulham Rd   020 7823 3007   6–3B
A "family-owned" Chelsea trattoria "run with real professionalism", and with "a calm and relaxing" style. Pasta dishes are particularly good. Top Tip – go for the "amazing value set lunch". / SW3 6HY; www.luciorestaurant.com; 10.45 pm.

Lupins SE1 NEW   £48
66 Union St   020 3617 8819   10–4B
Chefs Lucy Pedder and Natasha Cooke met working at Medlar and set up a catering collective together; this is their first permanent restaurant venture, which opened in mid 2017 in Flat Iron Square food hub, a short walk from Borough Market, with a menu full of 'seasonal British produce with a splash of sunshine' (on which early press reviews are upbeat). / SE1 1TD; www.lupinslondon.com; 10.30 pm; closed Mon D & Sun D.

Lupita   £46   3 2 2
13-15 Villiers St, WC2   020 7930 5355   5–1C
7 Kensington High St, W8   020 3696 2930   6–1A
60-62 Commercial Street, Spitalfields, E1   020 3141 6000   13–2C
This "fun", budget dive is "a cut above most Mexicans" serving "authentic" dishes ("excellent guacamole") just where you expect them least – on the grotty street, right next to Charing Cross station. Very limited but positive feedback on its City-fringe and Kensington branches too.

Lure NW5   £37   3 5 3
56 Chetwynd Rd   020 7267 0163   9–1B
"How all fish 'n' chip shops ought to be!", say fans of Aussie Philip Kendall's Dartmouth Park three-year-old – "a lovely neighbourhood restaurant" with "friendly and humorous service" producing "a simple menu of good-quality fresh produce, well cooked and served". "Smell-free too – no fears about eating in!" / NW5 1DJ; www.lurefishkitchen.co.uk; @Lurefishkitchen; 10 pm, Sun 9.30 pm; booking weekends only.

Lurra W1   £55   3 3 3
9 Seymour Place   020 7724 4545   2–2A
"A mouthful of Galician aged beef, or unbelievably tender and succulent, grilled octopus" represent "Basque grills at their best" to the many fans of this stylish "slice of San Sebastian in London", near Marble Arch, whose "outstanding steak" is amongst the best in town. Ratings have slipped since it opened a couple of years ago however, with growing fears that it risks seeming "over-rated" and "not justifying its prices". / W1H 5BA; www.lurra.co.uk; @LurraW1; 10.30 pm, Sun 3.30 pm; closed Mon L & Sun D.

Lutyens EC4   £78   2 2 2
85 Fleet St   020 7583 8385   10–2A
Sir Terence Conran's business-centric brasserie off Fleet Street is a "solid" performer focused on a City-based market: even fans admit "the ambience is decidedly corporate" – there's "nothing wrong here, except the daft prices" (and the "slightly dull room"). / EC4Y 1AE; www.lutyens-restaurant.com; 9.45 pm; closed Sat & Sun.

Lyle's E1   £78   4 2 2
The Tea Building, 56 Shoreditch High St   020 3011 5911   13–1B
"A pioneer in the new world of London restaurants and the UK scene generally" – James Lowe's "so-very-trendy Shoreditch fixture" is much more than a "casual" hipster haven, and for most reporters his "always surprising, frequently stunning" cuisine, "with incredible intensity of flavours" makes it a "five-star all-round experience". Ratings here came off the boil a tad this year however, with reservations creeping in regarding "off-hand service", the "very, very stark setting" and some meals that were "clever, but lacked wow-factor". / E1 6JJ; www.lyleslondon.com; @lyleslondon; 10 pm; closed Sat L & Sun.

M Restaurants £89   2 2 2
Zig Zag Building, Victoria St, SW1   020 3327 7776   2–4B
Brewery Wharf, London Rd, TW1   020 3327 7776   1–4A NEW
2-3 Threadneedle Walk, EC2   020 3327 7770   10–2C
"When you want to impress your companions" many reporters
do recommend these *"swanky and shiny"*, Vegas-style operations in the City
and Victoria (and very recently opened in Twickenham, too), applauding the
"superb" steaks, and *"innovative and original wine list"*. To their critics
however, it's *"massively a case of style over substance"*, with *"food that's
designed to sound fancy and exotic"* but which seems *"mediocre at the
inflated prices"*: *"I went on a deal, which brought the cost for the albeit
good meal down from outrageous to merely expensive"*. / midnight; EC2 closed
Sat L & Sun, SW1 closed Sun.

Ma Goa SW15 £41   4 4 3
242-244 Upper Richmond Rd   020 8780 1767   11–2B
"Still producing exceptional cooking" after all these years – this *"excellent"*
family-run Goan delights its Putney regulars who consider themselves *"lucky
to have this as a local"*, with food that's *"consistently fresh, aromatic and
spicy without being OTT"*. Now the family have opened a wine shop next
door, they also offer one of *"the best affordable wine lists of any local
Indian"*. / SW15 6TG; www.ma-goa.com; @magoarestaurant; 10.30 pm, Fri & Sat
11 pm, Sun 10pm.

Ma La Sichuan SW1 £58   4 3 1
37 Monck St   020 7222 2218   2–4C
*"The level and authenticity of the spicy Sichuanese cooking are entirely
unexpected"* (and *"you can have the degree of spice and heat altered
to taste"*) at this Westminster venture, which serves an array of *"unusual,
non-routine dishes, not usually found in Chinese restaurants"*.
Notwithstanding the *"rather bland"* decor and *"unlikely location"*, reports
say it *"deserves more recognition"*. / SW1P 2BL; malasichuan.co.uk; 11 pm,
Sun 10.30 pm.

Mac & Wild £52   4 3 4
65 Great Titchfield St, W1   020 7637 0510   3–1C
9a Devonshire Square, EC2   020 7637 0510   10–2D NEW
"Really good venison" is the star turn at this Fitzrovia two-year-old
specialising in Scottish game (much of it from the family estate of owner
Andy Waugh), delivering *"very tasty, gamey flavours for not terribly high
prices"*. Having started out as a street stall, the venture now has a second
branch at Devonshire Square, near Liverpool Street.

Macellaio RC £56   3 2 3
84 Old Brompton Rd, SW7   020 7589 5834   6–2B
Arch 24, 229 Union St, SE1   07467 307682   10–4B
124 Northcote Rd, SW11   020 3848 4800   11–2C NEW
38-40 Exmouth Market, EC1   020 3696 8220   10–1A
"A wacky way of issuing cutlery (plunging the steak knives into the table!)"
adds a further frisson to these *"memorable venues"* – *"an interesting
concept where the butcher's counter sits in the middle of the restaurant"*.
"Steak or tuna, that's your only choice", but the former in particular
is *"superb"*, *"melt-in-the-mouth"* Piemontese Fassone meat matched with
"delicious Italian wines". There are two 'flies in the ointment' – *"prices are
now approaching 'rip off' levels"*, and hit unlucky and service can be *"rude,
arrogant and slow"*. / 11 pm.

Machiya SW1 NEW £45
5 Panton St   020 7925 0333   5–4A
Positive early reports on this "yummy new Japanese from the folks behind Kanada-Ya" (just down the street). Upstairs it's a neutrally decorated café with a to-the-point short menu – downstairs a bar serves a wide range of sakes and whiskys. / SW1Y 4DL; machi-ya.co.uk; @MachiyaLondon; 10.30 pm, Fri & Sat 11 pm, Sun 10 pm.

Madame D's E1 NEW £34
76 Commercial St   awaiting tel   13–2C
"Original Himalayan sharing plates, most with a great chilli kick" feature in one early report on this "small dining den" (from the founders of Gunpowder) – a room above a pub, near Spitalfields. / E1 6LY; madame-d.com; @madame_d_london.

Made in Italy £40   3 2 3
50 James St, W1   020 7224 0182   3–1A
249 King's Rd, SW3   020 7352 1880   6–3C
141 The Broadway, SW19   020 8540 4330   11–2B
"Great elongated pizza" (sold by the metre) make it worth remembering these crowded cafés in Chelsea and Wimbledon. / www.madeinitalygroup.co.uk; SW3 11.30 pm; W1 11.30 pm, Sun 10.30 pm; SW19 11 pm; SW3 closed Mon L.

Made of Dough SE15 NEW £33
182 Bellenden Rd   020 7064 5288   1–4D
Pop Brixton's buzzing Made of Dough pizzeria grew permanent roots with this bright new café which opened in Peckham in June 2017. The dough in question is fermented for over 60 hours before being zapped in a wood fire oven. / SE15 4BW; www.madeofdough.co.uk; @MadeOfDoughLDN; 10.30 pm, Sun 9 pm; no booking.

Madhu's UB1 £42   4 4 3
39 South Rd   020 8574 1897   1–3A
Sanjay Anand's legendary Southall curry house is "simply the best", say fans of its Kenyan-influenced Punjabi cooking. It is now the flagship of a catering empire that takes in Harrods and Harvey Nichols, among others. / UB1 1SW; www.madhus.co.uk; 11.30 pm, Fri-Sun midnight; closed Tue, Sat L & Sun L; no booking.

The Magazine Restaurant, Serpentine Gallery W2 £59   3 3 4
Kensington Gdns   020 7298 7552   7–2D
This Zaha Hadid-designed gallery restaurant in Hyde Park "deserves more recognition" according to reporters, who think it "a great space", with "interesting food" (maybe only being open for lunch and afternoon tea is what keeps it under the radar). Perhaps a new team, scheduled to take over its management in late 2017, will finally put it properly on the map? / W2 2AR; www.magazine-restaurant.co.uk; @TheMagazineLDN; 10.45 pm, Tue & Sun 6 pm; closed Mon, Tue D & Sun D.

Maggie Jones's W8 £61   2 2 5
6 Old Court Pl   020 7937 6462   6–1A
"You can hide in the booths and hold hands" at this eccentric, extremely "romantic", rustic-style operation near Kensington Palace (named after the pseudonym Princess Margaret once used here). The dated Gallic cooking is "average for the price", but only those with the hardest hearts "are surprised there are really so many first dates looking for novelty decor and uneven staircases?" / W8 4PL; www.maggie-jones.co.uk; 11 pm, Sun 10.30 pm.

    FSA RATINGS: FROM **1** POOR —— **5** EXCEPTIONAL

Magpie W1 NEW
10 Heddon St   020 7254 8311   4–3B
Co-founders of Hackney's stellar Pidgin (James Ramsden and Sam Herlihy) have headed West, just off Regent Street, for their latest newcomer, opened in July 2017. The revolutionary concept is British dim sum, with diners choosing plates (and cocktails!) straight off circulating trolleys. / W1B 4BX; www.magpie-london.com.

Maguro W9 £57   3 4 2
5 Lanark Pl   020 7289 4353   9–4A
"Tiny" Japanese outfit near Little Venice where "lovely" service helps offset the "cramped and uncomfortable" interior. "There is better sushi in London, but the price, selection and relaxed style ensure this is a top pick". / W9 1BT; www.maguro-restaurant.com; 10.30 pm, Sun 10 pm; No Amex.

Maison Bertaux W1 £8   3 4 4
28 Greek St   020 7437 6007   5–2A
"Still unique" – this 'Patisserie Francaise' in Soho, opened in 1871, and, run (slightly "eccentrically") by sisters Michelle and Tania Wade since the late 1980s, seems ever-more precious in a world of ubiquitous Starbucks and Costa Coffees. "I'm always a bit shocked at the prices, but the quality is top notch", and it's "surprisingly good for quiet conversation". / W1D 5DQ; www.maisonbertaux.com; @Maison_Bertaux; 10.15 pm, Sun 8.45 pm.

Malabar W8 £47   5 4 3
27 Uxbridge St   020 7727 8800   7–2B
"Amazing Indian food" – "still inventive and fresh", "even after well over 30 years" – maintains this distinctive (it looks more like an Italian restaurant) and distinguished curry house off Notting Hill Gate as "a real gem". "Staff are nearly as lovely as the delicious menu." / W8 7TQ; www.malabar-restaurant.co.uk; 11 pm.

Malabar Junction WC1 £41   3 3 2
107 Gt Russell St   020 7580 5230   2–1C
"Ignore the unpromising exterior: it belies an airy atrium within" at this "easygoing" Indian, "handy for the British Museum nearby". "Modern decor combines with southern Indian cuisine", provided by "very charming staff." / WC1B 3NA; www.malabarjunction.com; 11 pm.

MAM W11 NEW
16 All Saints Rd   awaiting tel   7–1B
Colin Tu, owner of Salvation in Noodles, opened this street-food-inspired Vietnamese BBQ in the second half of 2017; expect skewers cooked on a robata grill, pho and fish sauce wings. MAM is pronounced 'mum' and means fermentation in Vietnamese. / W11 1HH; mamlondon.com.

Mamma Dough £39   3 3 4
179 Queen's Rd, SE15   020 7635 3470   1–4D
76-78 Honor Oak Pk, SE23   020 8699 5196   1–4D
354 Coldharbour Ln, SW9   020 7095 1491   11–2D
Despite all the competition in the pizza market, this small South London group (Brixton, Peckham and Honor Oak Park) won very high ratings this year. The interiors are all stripped-down wood and brickwork, and the main event is complemented by local craft beer, coffee roasted in Shoreditch, and ginger beer brewed on site. Top Tip – half-sized plates available for kids. / www.mammadough.co.uk; SE23 10 pm, SW9 11 pm, SE15 10.30 pm; Mon-Thu closed L

Mandarin Kitchen W2 £41 4 2 1
14-16 Queensway   020 7727 9012   7–2C
"It's always full (the sign of a great place)", but don't go to this crowded Bayswater Chinese expecting much in the way of ambience. Stick to the "consistently outstanding" seafood dishes – "the best lobster noodles in the world" are the "must-try" signature dish – but "in truth, the Peking duck is a bit less good". / W2 3RX; 11.15 pm.

Mangal I E8 £28 5 4 2
10 Arcola St   020 7275 8981   14–1A
"Absolutely the best kebabs this side of Istanbul" have turned this Turkish grill into a "Dalston institution" over 20 years. "Exceptional meat from the barbecue" is backed up by "good salads and BYO (keeping the price down)". "Despite the proliferation of Mangal offshoots, the Arcola street original is still the best!" / E8 2DJ; www.mangal1.com; @Mangalone; midnight, Sat & Sun 1 am; Cash only; no booking.

Manicomio £68 2 3 3
85 Duke of York Sq, SW3   020 7730 3366   6–2D
6 Gutter Ln, EC2   020 7726 5010   10–2B
Although their prime locations – next to the Saatchi Gallery off Sloane Square in Chelsea and in the City – mean they are "not cheap", these "good-natured" Italians provide a "solid" level of cooking and a "fun" atmosphere. Top Tip – lovely outside terrace in SW3. / www.manicomio.co.uk; SW3 10 pm, Sun 4 pm; EC2 10 pm; EC2 closed Sat & Sun.

Manna NW3 £56 2 2 2
4 Erskine Rd   020 7722 8028   9–3B
From "exceptional" to "slightly off the boil" – the UK's oldest veggie (Primrose Hill, 1968) perennially attracts inconsistent and fairly middling feedback. If you like meat-free food and are in north London give it a try, but it's not a certain bet. / NW3 3AJ; www.mannav.com; @mannacuisine; 10 pm, Sun 7.30 pm; closed Mon.

The Manor SW4 £58 3 3 3
148 Clapham Manor St   020 7720 4662   11–2D
"Weird… in a good way!", say fans of Robin Gill's "buzzy, bare and loud" venture in a Clapham backstreet (a sibling to the nearby Dairy), who extol its "truly memorable modern British cooking". To its detractors, though, it's simply "too hyped" – "so hipster it hurts, with too many misses for the price". / SW4 6BS; www.themanorclapham.co.uk; 10 pm, Sun 4 pm.

Manuka Kitchen SW6 £53 3 4 3
510 Fulham Rd   020 7736 7588   6–4A
"Cosy", "little" New Zealand-inspired bistro near Fulham Broadway with a "great open kitchen, good food and nice atmosphere" – probably best for "brunch rather than a full meal, but most enjoyable" (and with a downstairs gin bar). / SW6 5NJ; www.manukakitchen.com; @manukakitchen; 10 pm, Tue-Sat 11 pm, Sun 4 pm; closed Sun D; booking max 8 may apply.

Mar I Terra SE1 £43 3 4 3
14 Gambia St   020 7928 7628   10–4A
"Tapas that's a cut above-the-norm" helps makes this "slightly cramped" former boozer in a Southwark backstreet a favourite pre-theatre pit stop, and "great after-work place". / SE1 0XH; www.mariterra.co.uk; 11 pm; closed Sat L & Sun.

Marcus,
The Berkeley SW1   £122   3 2 3
Wilton Pl   020 7235 1200   6–1D
Marcus Wareing's "spacious" and "peaceful" Belgravia chamber
is "the epitome of what a special restaurant should be" for its very many
admirers, not least when it comes to the "incredible" cooking with
"maximum flavours to the fore", be it from the à la carte, or 5- and 8-
course tasting options. However, its ratings are dragged down by a
vociferous minority who diss the "disengaged" service and an experience
where "everything is fine but nothing is great": is that second Michelin star
just boosting expectations too high? / SW1X 7RL; www.marcusrestaurant.com;
@marcusbelgravia; 10 pm; closed Sun; No trainers; booking max 6 may apply;
set weekday L £88 (FP).

Mare Street Market E8 NEW
89-115 Mare St   awaiting tel   14–2B
Star ex-Viajante, Chiltern Firehouse, etc chef Nuno Mendes teams up with
Barworks to launch a new neighbourhood venue in Hackney's Keltan House,
incorporating a bar, restaurant, deli and café. / E8 4RU.

Margot WC2   £56   4 5 5
45 Great Queen St   020 3409 4777   5–2D
"An instant classic, bravo!" This "very elegant Italian on the edge of Covent
Garden" proved one of the best arrivals of 2016 and although the odd
report complains it's been "hyped" the vast majority say it's plain "stunning".
"Quality and service are in abundance" – the comfortable interior feels
enjoyably "superior", and "staff make the meal into an occasion –
they make you feel very special". "Most of the menu is of traditional dishes
with a twist" and it's "damned good too". Top Menu Tip – "the best ever
Osso Buco". / WC2B 5AA; www.margotrestaurant.com; @MargotLDN; 10.45 pm,
Sun 9.30 pm.

Mari Vanna SW1   £79   3 3 4
116 Knightsbridge   020 7225 3122   6–1D
This "romantic" and luxurious Knightsbridge fixture attracted few reports
this year, but all of them highly upbeat regarding its simple Russian cooking
(and huge range of vodkas). / SW1X 7PJ; www.marivanna.co.uk;
@marivannalondon; 11.30 pm.

Marianne W2   £128   5 4 4
104 Chepstow Rd   020 3675 7750   7–1B
"Marianne Lumb nails it, spot on, time and time again" at her "very special,
petite restaurant" (just 14 covers) in Bayswater. La patronne herself "is not
only a brilliant chef, but also a charming and welcoming host" and the
"tiny but lovely" set-up is "perfect for a romantic evening" (if "without a lot
of buzz"). "The set menu is chosen with good taste rather than
extravagance, and the cooking is peerless perfection" ("it is rare that
a tasting menu is all hits but this place manages it"). Finally, "the wine
list is a real draw too – a terrific selection at prices that are actually
affordable". / W2 5QS; www.mariannerestaurant.com; @Marianne_W2; 10 pm;
closed Mon; booking max 6 may apply; set weekday L £71 (FP).

The Marksman E2   £62   4 3 4
254 Hackney Rd   020 7739 7393   14–2A
"Ignore the hipster-beards!" – this "relaxed East End boozer serving top
notch nosh" is "too good to be written-off as just-another-hangout-of-the-
terminally-trendy!" "Impeccably cooked, thoroughly modern British dishes"
are "cheerfully and efficiently served" and while "it's always crowded",
"it's got a good buzz, still feels like a pub (almost)" and "it's great that its
old character and charm still thrive". / E2 7SJ; www.marksmanpublichouse.com;
@marksman_pub; 10 pm, Sun 8 pm; closed weekday L & Sun D.

Maroush £52 3 2 2
I) 21 Edgware Rd, W2 020 7723 0773 7–1D
II) 38 Beauchamp Pl, SW3 020 7581 5434 6–1C
V) 3-4 Vere St, W1 020 7493 5050 3–1B
VI) 68 Edgware Rd, W2 020 7224 9339 7–1D
'Garden') 1 Connaught St, W2 020 7262 0222 7–1D
"It's the starters and mezze that hold centre stage" (although the mains are
"tasty" too) at this successful Lebanese chain, whose café sections with
excellent menus of wraps (part of I and II) are better known than the
adjoining more formal (rather "stiff and impersonal") restaurants. Head
to the Marble Arch original for regular music and belly dancing.
/ www.maroush.com; most branches close between 12.30 am-5 am.

Masala Zone £37 3 3 4
"We always go for the Grand Thali and it's a knockout!" – These "ever-
buzzing" contemporary Indians make a very "handy backstop", with WC2
in particular "an excellent pre-theatre option" for a "fast and delicious"
meal. "We thought it might be chain-bland, but the food was good and quite
authentic… and good value too!" / www.realindianfood.com; 11 pm,
Sun 10.30 pm; W1U 9 pm, Sun 4 pm; booking: min 8.

MASH Steakhouse W1 £81 2 2 2
77 Brewer St 020 7734 2608 4–3C
This Danish-owned, American-style steakhouse, occupying a "massive
basement" near Piccadilly Circus, divides opinion. To fans, it's an "awesome"
place full of "old-fashioned" qualities. Critics, though, complain
of "very disappointing beef, cooked merely adequately", "highly overpriced
wine" and "dire surroundings". / W1F 9ZN; www.mashsteak.co.uk;
@mashsteaklondon; 11.30 pm; closed Sun L; set pre-theatre £47 (FP), set weekday
L £51 (FP).

**Massimo,
Corinthia Hotel WC2** £80 2 2 3
10 Northumberland Ave 020 7321 3156 2–3D
Few restaurants can match the truly "special", "sumptuous", "spacious"
decor of this "simply stunning" Italian dining room (designed by David
Collins) in a luxury hotel off Trafalgar Square. It's never really caught
on however, and though it has a few fans and avoids harsh criticism is still
sometimes "empty". / WC2N 5AE; www.massimo-restaurant.co.uk; @massimorest;
10.45 pm; closed Sun.

Masters Super Fish SE1 £24 3 2 2
191 Waterloo Rd 020 7928 6924 10–4A
"Being full of black cab drivers adds to the atmosphere of this traditional
chippie", which is both handy for Waterloo, and also serves "fish and chips
that are really VERY good", "in generous portions, with crispy batter",
all "at reasonable prices". "If you like napiery, etc this isn't for you: it's basic
Formica". Top Tip – BYO (£4.50 corkage). / SE1 8UX; masterssuperfish.com;
10.30 pm; closed Sun; No Amex; no booking, Fri D.

Matsuba TW9 £46 3 4 2
10 Red Lion St 020 8605 3513 1–4A
"Very good sashimi" and sushi head the "varied menu" at this "tiny"
Korean-run Japanese joint in Richmond town centre. The location and
setting may not be perfect, but it's a "much-appreciated attraction" in the
area. / TW9 1RW; www.matsuba-restaurant.com; @matsuba; 10.30 pm; closed Sun.

Max's Sandwich Shop N4   £32   4️⃣4️⃣3️⃣
19 Crouch Hill   no tel   1–1C
*"Epic sarnies" – home-baked focaccia stuffed with hot fillings –
make "legend" Max Halley's Crouch Hill sandwich shop an entertaining
destination, whose "great value" door-stops are accompanied
by "good beers and nice grooves on the jukebox". (Now also at Birthdays
in Stoke Newington.)* / N4 4AP; www.maxssandwichshop.com; @lunchluncheon;
11 pm, Fri & Sat midnight, Sun 6 pm; closed Sun D; No Amex; no booking.

May The Fifteenth SW4   £57   3️⃣4️⃣2️⃣
47 Abbeville Rd   020 8772 1110   11–2D
*This "solid" Clapham operation (formerly Abbeville Kitchen) is "excellent for
breakfast, brunch, lunch, dinner..." – it's the sort of place locals "love to
have on the doorstep".* / SW4 9JX; www.maythe15th.com; 11 pm, Sun 9.30 pm.

Mayfair Garden W1 🆕   £62   4️⃣3️⃣2️⃣
8-10 North Audley St   020 7493 3223   3–2A
*"On the site of the Princess Garden... it's hard to tell if anything has actually
changed other than the name" at this elegant Chinese stalwart in Mayfair –
"the cooking's good, the duck exceptional, but beyond that the service and
atmosphere aren't such as to get too excited about".* / W1K 6ZD;
www.mayfairgarden.co.uk; 11.30 pm, Sun 11 pm.

Mayfair Pizza Company W1   £52   3️⃣4️⃣3️⃣
4 Lancashire Ct   020 7629 2889   3–2B
*A "great location off the beaten track" is one reason to truffle out this bright
and airy pizzeria, hidden in a cute courtyard off Bond Street – others are
friendly service and sensible prices.* / W1S 1EY; www.mayfairpizzaco.com;
@mayfairpizzaco; 11 pm, Sun 10 pm.

maze W1   £85   2️⃣2️⃣1️⃣
10-13 Grosvenor Sq   020 7107 0000   3–2A
*Gordon Ramsay's Mayfair outfit was a star of the London gastronomic scene
a decade ago, under founding chef Jason Atherton (who is now long gone),
but "has lost its way" bigtime in recent years. True, some fans do say it's
"simply amazing", but even they can find it "eye-wateringly expensive" –
and too many critics complain of a "below average" or even "awful"
experience, in "an unsympathetic room that could be an airport restaurant".*
/ W1K 6JP; www.gordonramsayrestaurants.com; @mazerestaurant; 11 pm;
No trainers; booking max 9 may apply.

maze Grill W1   £77   1️⃣2️⃣2️⃣
10-13 Grosvenor Sq   020 7495 2211   3–2A
*"Very disappointing... not great flavours... came out hungry and went for
something to eat afterwards!" – Gordon Ramsay's Mayfair grill is not
without its fans, but yet again incites too many harsh criticisms to justify
a recommendation.* / W1K 6JP; www.gordonramsay.com; @mazegrill; 11 pm;
No shorts.

maze Grill SW10   £54   2️⃣2️⃣2️⃣
11 Park Wk   020 7255 9299   6–3B
*The most eloquent comment on Gordon Ramsay's two-year-old in the
Chelsea street where he made his name is how little feedback is received.
Have people finally lost interest in him? It doesn't help that of the few
reporters who did care to opine, the majority were unimpressed: "dreadful
service...", "what a disappointment... won't be returning".* / SW10 0AJ;
www.gordonramsay.com/mazegrill/park-walk; @GordonRamsayGRP; 11 pm.

Mazi W8 £64 3 3 3
12-14 Hillgate St   020 7229 3794   7–2B
*"Exciting" dishes still win fans for this "classy" and "highly creative modern
Greek", on the site of successive Notting Hill tavernas for almost 70 years.
Scores dropped across the board this year though – it's becoming
"very expensive" and some diners felt 'processed' ("we were served
so fast we were finished in 45 minutes"). / W8 7SR; www.mazi.co.uk;
@mazinottinghill; 10.30 pm; closed Mon L & Tue L.*

MEATliquor £37 3 2 4
74 Welbeck St, W1   020 7224 4239   3–1B
6 St Chad's Place, WC1   020 7837 0444   9–3C NEW
17 Queensway, W2   020 7229 0172   7–2C NEW
133b Upper St, N1   020 3711 0104   9–3D
37 Lordship Lane, SE22   020 3066 0008   1–4D
*If and when you have "beer, bondage and burgers fantasies", these
"outlandish" grunge-fests are unparalleled with their "wild (and LOUD)
interiors" and "street food with attitude" – "legendary dirty burgers"
("the Dead Hippie is a Big Mac on steroids")... wings... chili cheese fries.
/ meatliquor.com; W1 midnight (Fri & Sat 2 am), N1 11 pm, SE22 midnight,
Sun 10.30 pm-11.30 pm; booking: min 6.*

MEATmarket WC2 £28 3 3 2
Jubilee Market Hall, 1 Tavistock Ct   020 7836 2139   5–3D
*This West End outpost of the wilfully grungy MEATliquor franchise is "quick
and tasty, fun and cheap" – "just what you want from a burger joint"...
"and in Covent Garden, too". / WC2E 8BD; www.themeatmarket.co.uk;
@MEATmarketUK; 11pm, Fri & Sat midnight, Sun 10 pm; No Amex; no booking.*

MEATmission N1 £32 3 3 4
14-15 Hoxton Market   020 7739 8212   13–1B
*If you like "dirty burgers and great cocktails", you'll "love this place". Hoxton
Square's MEATliquor outpost has all the group's signature flavours, including
Dead Hippie sauce and chili cheese fries. / N1 6HG; www.meatmission.com;
@MEATmission; 11 pm, Sun 10 pm.*

MeatUp SW18 £55 3 2 2
350 Old York Rd   020 8425 0017   11–2B
*Wandsworth Town yearling that manages to live up to its name –
a "fun place to meet up with a good choice of BBQ-type dishes", and also
a decent range of cocktail, beers and wine make it "a useful addition to the
local scene". / SW18 1SS; www.meatupgrill.com; @meatupuk.*

Mediterraneo W11 £65 3 2 3
37 Kensington Park Rd   020 7792 3131   7–1A
*This "classic Italian with great food and service" has been a Notting Hill
"favourite" for the best part of two decades. "It never changes... which is a
good thing!" / W11 2EU; www.mediterraneo-restaurant.co.uk; 11.30 pm,
Sun 10.30 pm; booking max 10 may apply.*

Medlar SW10 £76 4 4 2
438 King's Rd   020 7349 1900   6–3B
*"Joe Mercer-Nairne should have a Michelin star" and why the tyre men took
it away is bonkers given the "faultless, complex cuisine with modern flair"
and "slick and pleasant service" at this well-known and extremely popular
"hidden gem", at the 'wrong' end of the King's Road. At best the slightly
awkward interior feels "classy" and "convivial", but it can also appear
"staid" and "strangely low key". / SW10 0LJ; www.medlarrestaurant.co.uk;
@MedlarChelsea; 10.30 pm, sun 9.30pm.*

Megan's £42 2 3 3

571 Kings Rd, SW6   020 7371 7837   6–4A
57-69 Parsons Green Lane, SW6   020 7348 7139   11–1B NEW
*A "lovely outdoor space, which is covered in the winter" is the special draw
to this atmospheric all-day King's Road café, praised for its "wholesome"
fare, particularly for brunch; a new branch opened in Parsons Green
in September 2017.*

Mei Ume EC3 NEW £88

10 Trinity Square   020 3297 3799   10–3D
*Open alongside La Dame de Pic inside the City's new Four Seasons hotel,
this Chinese and Japanese fusion café opened too late for survey feedback.
The team of chefs hail from Royal China, Sake no Hana and Yauatcha,
and – in keeping with the swish setting – ambitions are high. / EC3N 4AJ;
www.meiume.com; @FSTenTrinity; 10 pm.*

Melange N8 £50 3 2 2

45 Topsfield Parade, Tottenham Lane   020 8341 1681   9–1C
*This "excellent value local" in Crouch End mixes dishes of French and Italian
inspiration. "Service is smooth and friendly, and the food consistent and
comforting after a hard day at work". / N8 8PT; www.melangerestaurant.co.uk;
@malange_malange; 10.30 pm, Fri-Sun 11 pm.*

Mele e Pere W1 £54 3 4 3

46 Brewer St   020 7096 2096   4–3C
*"Straightforward, well-prepared Italian cooking" wins praise for this central
trattoria, which is "great fun too, with very reasonable prices for Soho".
"Its bar is a super hang-out", featuring "an excellent range of Vermouth
cocktails that are quite delicious". / W1F 9TF; www.meleepere.co.uk;
@meleEpere; 11 pm, Sun 10 pm; set weekday L £33 (FP).*

Melody at St Paul's W14 £58 2 3 3

153 Hammersmith Rd   020 8846 9119   8–2C
*Limited but positive feedback (as a business destination) for this calm,
very grandly situated dining room – part of a hotel set in a grand Gothic
Victorian building at the south end of Brook Green that formed part of the
original St Paul's Boys' School. / W14 0QL; www.themelodyrestaurant.co.uk;
10 pm; set weekday L £35 (FP).*

Menier Chocolate Factory SE1 £54 2 2 3

51-53 Southwark St   020 7234 9610   10–4B
*"The meal deal tickets combining show and dinner are good value (if hard
to book)" at this theatre café in a Victorian former chocolate factory. If you
can't get the package however maybe hold off – "with foodie Borough
Market just over the road there are plenty of other nicer options nearby".
/ SE1 1RU; www.menierchocolatefactory.com; @MenChocFactory; 11 pm; closed
Mon & Sun D.*

Meraki W1 NEW

80-82 Gt Titchfield St   020 7305 7686   3–1C
*Can the Waney family (the powerhouse behind Roka, Zuma and the Arts
Club) bring their magic to contemporary Greek cuisine with this summer
2017 newcomer in Fitzrovia? A 100-cover venture boasting two al fresco
terraces; the name is a Greek term that refers to the love and passion that
someone puts into their work. / W1W 7QT; www.meraki-restaurant.com.*

Mercato Metropolitano SE1 £25 3 2 5

42 Newington Causeway   020 7403 0930   1–3C
*This year-old, 45,000 sq ft street food centre, just south of Elephant
& Castle, makes "a fab hangout whatever the weather" – the food can
be "hit and miss" and it's "slow when busy", but there's "so much choice"
and it's "great for a chilled evening in a group". / SE1 6DR;
www.mercatometropolitano.co.uk; @mercatometropol; 11pm, Sun 9pm.*

The Mercer EC2 £62 2️⃣2️⃣2️⃣
34 Threadneedle St 020 7628 0001 10–2C
"Classic British dishes in a smart dining room" is the understated offer
in this converted banking hall, *"tucked away on Threadneedle Street"*.
"It doesn't shout about its presence" and even fans can find it *"a little
boring"*, but it makes a *"reliable choice for business lunches, without melting
the credit card"*. / EC2R 8AY; www.themercer.co.uk; @TheMercerLondon; 9.30 pm;
closed Sat & Sun.

Merchants Tavern EC2 £61 3️⃣2️⃣4️⃣
36 Charlotte Rd 020 7060 5335 13–1B
*"A terrific bar at the right price-point, kitchen on display and live vinyl in the
background"* all contribute to the *"terrific atmosphere"* at Angela Hartnett's
stylish, big Shoreditch gastropub (the conversion of a former warehouse).
Some feedback is mixed, but the overall verdict is of *"lovely"* food and solid
value for money. / EC2A 3PG; www.merchantstavern.co.uk; @merchantstavern;
11 pm, Sun 9 pm.

Le Mercury N1 £34 2️⃣2️⃣4️⃣
154-155 Upper St 020 7354 4088 9–2D
"Terrific value" old, candle-lit bistro that's a *"cheap 'n' cheerful"* and
"romantic" Islington classic, and also *"handy for the Almeida Theatre
opposite"*. *"I'm not surprised it's always packed"*, but do *"request a table
downstairs to make the most of the evening"*. / N1 1QY; www.lemercury.co.uk;
midnight, Sun 10 pm; Mon-Thu D only, Fri-Sun open L & D.

Mere W1 £89 3️⃣5️⃣3️⃣
74 Charlotte St 020 7268 6565 2–1B
MasterChef: The Professionals judge, Monica Galetti's Fitzrovia newcomer
opened shortly before our 2017 survey and gives the impression of still
settling down. On the plus side, the service (overseen by husband, ex-
Gavroche sommelier, David) is *"exceptionally friendly and top notch"* and
the *"comfortable"* basement setting feels *"classy"* and *"perfectly relaxed"*.
A number of reports find the (primarily Gallic) cuisine *"needing to improve"*
or *"lacking in wow factor"*, but *"excellent"* meals are also noted and the
fairest view is *"this is one to watch and likely to get more polished with
time"*. / W1T 4QH; www.mere-restaurant.com; @mererestaurant; Jacket & tie
required; set weekday L £67 (FP).

Meson don Felipe SE1 £40 2️⃣2️⃣3️⃣
53 The Cut 020 7928 3237 10–4A
"Reminiscent of a holiday in Spain", this *"fun"* tapas-veteran, conveniently
located for the Old and Young Vics, may have an *"unprepossessing exterior,
but inside it's buzzy, lively and nicely decorated"* (if *"a bit 1960s
nowadays"*), and you eat pretty well without spending a packet too. Top Tip
– *"avoid the evening when a guitarist blows you away"*. / SE1 8LF;
www.mesondonfelipe.com; 10 pm; closed Sun; No Amex; no booking after 8 pm.

Messapica NW10 🆕 £23
109 Chamberlayne Rd 020 8964 3200 1–2B
New to Kensal Rise from the owners of nearby Ostuni, an all-day 'café, deli,
bombetteria and juice bar' (named for a town in Puglia) which is open daily
for breakfast, lunch and dinner. An Italian charcoal grill produces the
'bombetta' – bite-sized meaty street food snacks – and stonebaked pizzas.
/ NW10 3NS; 10 pm, Thu-Sat 10.30 pm.

Mews of Mayfair W1 £70 3️⃣3️⃣3️⃣
10 Lancashire Court, New Bond St 020 7518 9388 3–2B
"Arrive early to get a table in the cobbled courtyard", which are the
best seats during the summer months at this versatile Mayfair charmer,
owned by Roger Moore's son. Other attractions include *"professional and
enjoyable brasserie-style food"*, a well-stocked bar, and afternoon tea.
/ W1S 1EY; www.mewsofmayfair.com; @mewsofmayfair; 10.45 pm; closed Sun D.

Meza   £37   **3** **3** **2**

34 Trinity Rd, SW17   07722 111299   11–2C
70 Mitcham Rd, SW17   020 8672 2131   11–2C
"Fresh and tasty mezze" at *"good-value"* prices have built a strong
reputation for these two tiny cafés in Tooting. Softer ratings mirror reports
of *"some falling off in quality"* but on most accounts they're still *"reliably
good"*. / www.mezarestaurant.co.uk; 11 pm, Fri & Sat 11.30 pm.

Michael Nadra   £60   **4** **3** **2**

6-8 Elliott Rd, W4   020 8742 0766   8–2A
42 Gloucester Ave, NW1   020 7722 2800   9–3B
"Excellent modern French cuisine and a variable atmosphere" are the
common themes which unite feedback on Michael Nadra's accomplished
but disparate duo of ventures. Both occupy *"difficult"* sites – the Chiswick
original is notably tightly packed, while Camden Town (right next to Regent's
Canal) has an unusual lay-out. In more mainstream locations, he would
enjoy a much higher profile. / www.restaurant-michaelnadra.co.uk; W4 10 pm,
Fri-Sat 10.30 pm, NW1 10.30 pm, Sun 9 pm; NW1 closed Mon, W4 closed Sun D.

Mien Tay   £37   **4** **3** **2**

180 Lavender Hill, SW11   020 7350 0721   11–1C
122 Kingsland Rd, E2   020 7729 3074   14–2A
"Goat and galangal – just love it!" The signature dish at this *"great value"*
Vietnamese group in Battersea, Fulham and Shoreditch is a legend.
"The place may look a bit rough and ready but the food's hard to resist!"
and they're always *"rammed"*. / 11 pm, Sun 10 pm; E2 Sun 10.30 pm.

Mildreds   £46   **3** **3** **3**

45 Lexington St, W1   020 7494 1634   4–2C
200 Pentonville Rd, N1   020 7278 9422   9–3D **NEW**
9 Jamestown Rd, NW1   020 7482 4200   9–3B **NEW**
Upper Dalston Sq, E8   020 8017 1815   14–1A **NEW**
That *"it's always over-crowded, with never-a-free table"* speaks volumes for
this long-enduring veggie café in Soho, whose *"simple and delicious recipes"*
have been packing 'em in for decades. All of a sudden they've decided
to 'go for it' expansion-wise though: there is also one near King's Cross now,
as well as Camden Town (*"unlike the original, you can book, thus avoiding
the horrendous waits!"*) and a Dalston branch opened in summer 2017.

Milk SW12   £21   **4** **3** **3**

20 Bedford Hill   020 8772 9085   11–2C
"The best breakfast in town", with *"great staples and specials that deliver
on flavour"*, has earned cult status for this Antipodean café in Balham,
now branching into evening service. *"You have to pick your times to get
a seat"*, though – *"my absolute favourite place to be at 10.30am on a
Saturday morning; unfortunately, I'm not the only one..."*. A cynical minority
do loathe the place though: *"it's masquerading as some sort of high-end
funky elite dining experience"* for *"wannabe hipsters"*. / SW12 9RG;
www.milk.london; @milkcoffeeldn; 10 pm; booking D only.

Min Jiang,
The Royal Garden Hotel W8   £81   **4** **4** **5**

2-24 Kensington High St   020 7361 1988   6–1A
"Never failing to impress my Chinese wife or anyone we invite here" –
this *"very professional and impressive"* 8th-floor operation is not only one
of London's very best Chinese dining rooms, but – *"despite being in a hotel"*
– it also manages not to be blighted by its *"stunning views"* (*"go in daylight
to get the best of the panorama over Kensington Gardens"*). *"If you want
excellent dim sum or Peking duck look no further"*: the food is *"fresh and
totally engrossing"* – particularly the wood-fired duck which is *"incredible"* –
and *"given the quality and freshness of the ingredients it is money well
spent"*. / W8 4PT; www.minjiang.co.uk; @minjianglondon; 10 pm.

F S A

Minnow SW4 NEW   £54
21 The Pavement 020 7720 4105 11–2C
British food with an International twist is promised at this new Clapham Common dining spot (literally a little fish in a big pond, hence the name); chef Jake Boyce formerly headed up the team at Jason Atherton's Social Wine and Tapas. The all-day restaurant has a range of tricks to attract the local hipsters – not just brunch and a Robata grill, but also breakfast cocktails, 'pay-as-you-drink' wine by the bottle, a walled garden and an honesty box. / SW4 0HY; minnowclapham.co.uk; @minnowclapham; 10 pm.

Mint Leaf   £69   4 4 4
Suffolk Pl, Haymarket, SW1 020 7930 9020 2–2C
Angel Ct, Lothbury, EC2 020 7600 0992 10–2C
The "wonderful and imaginative cuisine" matches the snazzy contemporary décor at this Indian duo, in a basement off Trafalgar Square and near Bank, which scored well across the board this year. "Praise was unanimous in our party of 30"; "we love this place!" / www.mintleafrestaurant.com; 10.45 pm; SW1 closed Sat L & Sun D, EC2 closed Sat & Sun.

Mirch Masala SW17   £26   4 2 1
213 Upper Tooting Rd 020 8767 8638 11–2D
"Great flavours at very low prices" make it "well worth travelling to Tooting" for this "no-nonsense" Pakistani canteen, whose BYO policy, "bold and chilli-hot flavours, and generous portions" create "such great value". Top Tip – "weekends (which can be busy) also offer some amazing slow-cooked meat specials". / SW17 7TG; www.mirchmasalarestaurant.co.uk; midnight; Cash only.

MNKY HSE W1   £86   1 2 3
10 Dover St 020 3870 4880 3–3C
"A great, happening vibe, and the food's not bad either!" – so say fans of this large, "luxurious", Latino dining and drinking den with resident DJ on the Mayfair site that for decades was The Dover Street Wine Bar (RIP). A significant minority find it seriously disappointing however, particularly in the food department. / W1S 4LQ; www.mnky-hse.com; @mnky_hse; set weekday L £46 (FP).

The Modern Pantry   £64   2 2 2
47-48 St Johns Sq, EC1 020 7553 9210 10–1A
The Alphabeta Bldg, 14 Finsbury Sq, EC2 020 3696 6565 13–2A
Aussie chef, Anna Hansen's "somewhat Spartan" looking fusion ventures in Clerkenwell ("the better of the two") and Finsbury Square are "great for brunch", when options like "miso pancakes (who knew?)" draw a major fan club. More generally though her funky fusion dishes divide views – fans praise "enjoyable combinations confounding any bias against fusion fare", but critics disparage "over-fussy straining with exotic ingredients doing nothing for taste". / www.themodernpantry.co.uk; 10.30 pm, Sun 10 pm.

MOMMI SW4   £45   3 4 3
44 Clapham High St 020 3814 1818 11–2D
"Fun, buzzy local" in Clapham High Street offering a "sensibly priced Asian-fusion menu and good cocktails" – it seems to have bedded-in in its second year, with improving scores for both food and service. / SW4 7UR; www.wearemommi.com; @wearemommi; 11 pm.

Momo W1   £72   3 3 4
25 Heddon St 020 7434 4040 4–3B
Twenty years on, the smart crowd have forgotten it but the party's still going strong at Mourad Mazouz's "chaotic but charming Moroccan" in the Heddon Street foodie enclave off Regent Street, whose couscous, tagines and other North African dishes earn solid marks. / W1B 4BH; www.momoresto.com; @momoresto; 11.30 pm, Sun 11 pm; credit card required to book.

Mon Plaisir WC2 £52 2 3 5
19-21 Monmouth St 020 7836 7243 5–2B
"I've been coming with friends since the '60s, and though it's nothing too fancy (escargots, steak-frites, excellent cheese) it never disappoints" – that's the kind of loyalty which keeps this "very cosy", 70-year-old bistro in business, and even if "maybe it's past its best", "it's still hard not to fall in love with it". Much-extended over the years, "there are lots of small rooms, and although I can never decide if the food is as good as the decor, the eccentric layout is certainly all part of its charm". Top Tip – "pre-theatre it's a steal". / WC2H 9DD; www.monplaisir.co.uk; @MonPlaisir4; 11 pm; closed Sun.

Mona Lisa SW10 £40 3 4 2
417 King's Rd 020 7376 5447 6–3B
"Great value for money in Chelsea" is to be had at this veteran, Italian-run greasy spoon near World's End, which has "a super feel to it". Service starts at 7am with "the best old-fashioned classic English trucker's breakfast" and runs through to 11pm. Top Tip – miraculously for SW10, you can still get a "hearty" three-course evening meal for £10: no wonder it's "always packed". / SW10 0LR; monalisarestaurant.co.uk; 11 pm, Sun 5.30 pm; closed Sun D; No Amex.

Monkey Temple W12 £30 3 4 3
92 Askew Rd 020 8743 4597 8–1B
"Delicious Nepali curries" make this newish cuzza a welcome addition on ever-more "happening Askew Road" (in deepest Shepherds Bush). They're "building a loyal local clientele" with their speciality dishes but also do the "usual suspects" of Indian cuisine, all at good prices. / W12 9BL; monkeytempleonline.co.uk; 10 pm, Fri & Sat 10.30 pm, Sun 9.30 pm.

Monmouth Coffee Company £7 4 5 4
27 Monmouth St, WC2 020 7232 3010 5–2B
btwn Dockley Rd & Spa Rd, SE16 020 7232 3010 12–2A
2 Park St, SE1 020 7232 3010 10–4C
"It's cramped, it's busy", but "you'll never get bored of the variety of coffee flavours on offer", at these epic caffeine-stops – the best-known of London's top tier coffee house chains – where "excellent recommendations" from the "really knowledgeable" staff ("who will let you sample and taste different growths") really add to the experience. Borough Market is the definitive branch, and – as well as the pastries offered elsewhere in the group – also has bread and jam on hand to soak up the brews. / www.monmouthcoffee.co.uk; WC2 6:30 pm; SE1 6 pm; SE16 Sat 1.30 pm; WC2 & SE1 closed Sun; no Amex; no booking.

Monty's Deli N1 NEW £36 3 4 4
225-227 Hoxton St 020 7729 5737 14–2A
After many years in Bermondsey and a £50k crowdfund, Mark Ogus and Owen Barratt now have a stylish, boothed (if "noisy") Hoxton diner in which to serve their "great sandwiches and bagels" and other 'Jewish soul food'. / N1; montys-deli.com; @MontysDeli.

Morada Brindisa Asador W1 £50 3 2 2
18-20 Rupert St 020 7478 8758 4–3D
"Excellent meat from the asador" – a Castilian-style wood-fire roasting oven – "is the main point" at this stylish, but slightly clinical two-year-old off Shaftesbury Avenue (from the Brindisa group), but its other "tasty" tapas dishes generally also get the thumbs up. / W1D 6DE; www.brindisatapaskitchens.com/morada; @Brindisa; 11 pm.

The Morgan Arms E3 £49 3 2 3
43 Morgan St 020 8980 6389 14–2C
This "high-end gastropub" in Mile End is "often rammed" and "a bit noisy due to lack of soft furnishings". But you usually (if not quite always) get "great food here" – "especially Sunday lunch". / E3 5AA; www.morganarmsbow.com; @TheMorganArms; 10 pm.

Morito   £44   4 4 4
195 Hackney Rd, E2   020 7613 0754   14–2A
32 Exmouth Mkt, EC1   020 7278 7007   10–1A
*"Moro's little sister two doors down from Moro itself" nowadays also has
a Hackney outpost, near Columbia Road Flower Market, and although the
newer branch is "more roomy" and "less frenetic than the original",
"pressure on tables is fierce" at both of these "crowded, small eateries".
That said, they "run like clockwork" on the whole, and service is "incredibly
helpful and knowledgeable". The draw? – "scrumptious" Spanish/North
African tapas with "imaginative modern twists" at prices that are "terrific
value". / EC1 11 pm, Sun 4 pm; E2 10.30 pm, Sun 9 pm; EC1 closed Sun D;
no booking.*

MORO EC1   £61   4 3 3
34-36 Exmouth Mkt   020 7833 8336   10–1A
*"I've been going for 20 years but it still surprises me" – Samuel and
Samantha Clark's epic Exmouth Market "institution" remains "a regular
haunt" for hordes of reporters thanks to its "sunshine-filled" neo-Spanish
and north African dishes, even if "the poor acoustics of this former
supermarket make it hard to maintain a conversation when it's busy".
By and large it "goes from strength to strength" – if ratings aren't quite
as stratospheric as once they were maybe it's just "no longer so different
from the competition as to be as remarkable as it was". / EC1R 4QE;
www.moro.co.uk; 10.30 pm; closed Sun D.*

Motcombs SW1   £55   2 2 3
26 Motcomb St   020 7235 6382   6–1D
*That it's "stuck somewhere in the '70s" is a good thing for most (if not quite
all) who report on this "Belgravia stalwart", applauding its "always reliable"
standards (both in the upstairs wine bar and downstairs restaurant).
/ SW1X 8JU; www.motcombs.co.uk; @Motcombs; 10 pm; closed Sun D.*

Mother SW11 NEW
2 Archers Lane   020 7622 4386   11–1C
*From Copenhagen's meatpacking district – the first UK venture of this
hugely popular pizza concept in Denmark, is one of the first outlets to have
opened in Battersea Power Station's Circus West Village in July 2017,
occupying a moodily, low-lit railway arch near Chelsea Bridge. The website
promises 'Italian pizza without all the nonsense'… but still notes its
'signature sourdough', 'seawater' and 'manufacturing its own mozzarella'.
/ SW11 8AB; www.motherrestaurant.co.uk; @mother_ldn.*

Mr Bao SE15   £35   4 3 3
293 Rye Ln   020 7635 0325   1–4D
*"Cute and cool, with interesting cocktails" – this "small and friendly"
Taiwanese yearling in Peckham inspires "absolute love" with its "great bao
buns and sides" that are "cheap, filling and really, really delicious".
/ SE15 4UA; www.mrbao.co.uk; @MrBaoUK; 11 pm.*

Mr Chow SW1   £88   2 2 2
151 Knightsbridge   020 7589 7347   6–1D
*Scant reports this year at this datedly-glamorous A-lister of yesteryear near
1 Hyde Park, which built an international brand in the '60s with its formula
of Chinese cuisine served by Italian waiters. In recent years its food has been
consistently tolerable, but very pricey, so we have felt able to keep last year's
rating, although feedback was too thin to rate it properly. / SW1X 7PA;
www.mrchow.com; @mrchow; midnight; closed Mon L.*

Murano W1 £99 5 5 4
20-22 Queen St 020 7495 1127 3–3B
As it enters its tenth year, Angela Hartnett's "understatedly brilliant" Mayfair haven is an unusual example of a swanky, celeb-backed restaurant just getting better and better as it approaches middle age. Though not enormously distinctive in design, "the dining room is beautifully set up – you don't feel crowded" – and the "charmingly kind staff" help "create a wonderful and romantic atmosphere". Head chef Pip Lacey's Italian-inspired cooking is taking the food quality here to new heights – "fantastically good" – and reporters "love that you can construct your own tasting menu", whereby you select any number of dishes from the menu's five sections in the order of your choosing. STOP PRESS: in July 2017, Pip Lacey left Murano, to be replaced by Oscar Holgado. Here's hoping he can keep up the good work. / W1J 5PP; www.muranolondon.com; @muranolondon; 11 pm; closed Sun; credit card required to book; set weekday L £57 (FP).

Mustard W6 £44 3 3 3
98-100 Shepherd's Bush Rd 020 3019 1175 8–1C
Smart brasserie decor (superior to the Café Rouge it replaced) and a professional attitude up the tone of this neighbourhood yearling north of Brook Green. The affordable cuisine? – it's mostly decent, but can also be a little "comme ci, comme ça". / W6 7PD; www.mustardrestaurants.co.uk; @mustarddining; 10 pm, Sun 5 pm; closed Mon & Sun D.

My Neighbours The Dumplings E5 £41 4 2 2
165 Lower Clapton Rd 020 3327 1556 14–1B
"Excellent and innovative" Chinese dumplings win praise for this engaging if sometimes "chaotic" Clapton canteen – a year-old pop-up-turned-permanent, which in summer 2017 opened a large lantern-lit 'Hanging Garden' space. / E5 8EQ; www.myneighboursthedumplings.com; @my_neighbours; 10.30 pm, Fri & Sat 11 pm, Sun 9.30 pm; closed Mon.

Namaaste Kitchen NW1 £43 3 3 2
64 Parkway 020 7485 5977 9–3B
"Everything seems to be cooked from scratch" at this Camden Town curry house, "so be prepared to wait, especially if you don't have a starter!". "The cooking can miss its mark, but is often very good." / NW1 7AH; www.namaastekitchen.co.uk; @NamaasteKitchen; 11 pm.

Nanashi EC2 NEW £61
14 Rivington St 020 7686 0010 13–2B
"Top notch sushi with some great accompaniments" feature in one early report on this 'environmentally conscious modern Japanese', newly opened in Shoreditch. / EC2A 3DU; www.nanashi.co.uk; 10 pm, Sat 11 pm.

Nanban SW9 £44 4 3 3
Coldharbour Ln 020 7346 0098 11–2D
"The food is so different!" – "very unusual combos that you don't think are going to work, but which they pull off" – at former MasterChef winner Tim Anderson's "thoroughly interesting Japanese-soul-food-fusion" venue beside Brixton market. "Staff are great and really work hard too, but there can be delays in getting attention". / SW9 8LF; www.nanban.co.uk; @NanbanLondon; 11 pm, Sun 10 pm.

The Narrow E14 £57 3 3 4
44 Narrow St 020 7592 7950 12–1B
*Is Gordon Ramsay's Limehouse pub finally, after all these years, starting to live up to its "lovely riverside setting"? Even a reporter who can't resist a swipe at the "****" food admits that "the building and location make it great for a family-and-friends lunch" and all other feedback this year praises "tasty food at quite reasonable prices". / E14 8DP; www.gordonramsayrestaurants.com/the-narrow; @thenarrow; 10.30 pm, Sun 8 pm.*

Native WC2 £55 4 3 2
3 Neal's Yd 020 3638 8214 5–2C
*With an emphasis on game and foraging dishes, this "bijou" Covent Garden
yearling is "right on trend". There's a small upstairs, and larger basement
whose "minimalist decor gives rise to poor acoustics", but "stick with it,
as the unusual combinations work well and are full of flavour". / WC2H 9DP;
www.eatnative.co.uk; @eatnativeuk; 10 pm.*

Naughty Piglets SW2 £56 5 5 3
28 Brixton Water Ln 020 7274 7796 11–2D
*That "every dish is a stand out, every time", plus the "really exciting natural
wine list" has made a smash hit of this "personal and friendly" two-year-old,
"tucked away in a Brixton side street" and "run by a charming husband-
and-wife team", Margaux Aubry and Joe Sharratt. On the strength of this
debut, Andrew Lloyd Webber recently scouted them to open 'The Other
Naughty Piglets', see also. / SW2 1PE; www.naughtypiglets.co.uk; 10 pm,
Sun 3 pm.*

Nautilus NW6 £35 4 3 1
27-29 Fortune Green Rd 020 7435 2532 1–1B
*"It has seen better days in terms of décor" (and we've been saying that for
over 20 years), but no-one is put off at this classic West Hampstead chippy,
where "plaice fried in matzo" is a highlight of the "excellent, fresh fish". Top
Tip – "best for takeaway!" but eat in and you can BYO. / NW6 1DU; 10 pm;
closed Sun; No Amex.*

The Ned EC2 NEW
27 Poultry 020 3828 2000 10–2C
*If Cecil B DeMille had designed a City food court, it might have looked
something like Soho House & Co's and Sydell Group's gob-smacking
refurbishment of the banking hall of the former, Lutyens-designed, Grade
I, Midland Bank HQ, just next to the Bank of England. With 850 covers
split between seven different operations, it is long on glamour, short
on cosiness, and feels like the ginormous hotel foyer that it now is. The food
offering mixes existing brands – like Cecconi's – with those created for the
operation: Millie's Lounge (British), The Nickel Bar (American), Zobler's
Delicatessen ('NYC'-Jewish), Malibu Kitchen (Californian), Kaia (Asian-
Pacific) and Café Sou (French). Members bypass all that 'open air' eating for
the cosier 'Lutyens Grill' (a steakhouse) or head for one of the two club
bars, either in the roof, or the old bank vaults. / EC2R 8AJ; www.thened.com;
@TheNedLondon.*

Needoo E1 £25 4 3 2
87 New Rd 020 7247 0648 13–2D
*"It's like eating a great curry in a school cafeteria", say fans of this East End
Pakistani BYO (a rival to nearby Tayyab's) – "the food is awesome! Please
pass the lamb chops…" / E1 1HH; www.needoogrill.co.uk; @NeedooGrill;
11.30 pm.*

Neo Bistro W1 NEW £54
11 Woodstock St 0207 499 9427 3–1B
*On paper, this summer 2017 newcomer near the top of New Bond Street
has a fine pedigree – Alex Harper was formerly head chef at The Harwood
Arms and Mark Jarvis is chef-patron of Anglo. As the name hints,
it's inspired by the modern bistros of Paris, offering a short à la carte plus,
in the evening, a 6-course tasting menu. Early press reports on its creative
modern European dishes wax lyrical. / W1C 2JF; www.neobistro.co.uk;
@neo_bistro; 9.45 pm.*

New World W1 £35 2 1 2
1 Gerrard Place   020 7734 0677 / 020 7734 0396   5–3A
"Dim sum still served from old-fashioned trolleys" ensure this massive fixture is still "fabulous fun!" – "in and out as quick as you like, with a little bit of theatre". "Otherwise the food is average for Chinatown." / W1D 5PA; www.newworldlondon.com; 10.30 pm, Sun 9.30 pm.

Niche EC1 £53 2 3 2
197-199 Rosebery Avenue   020 7837 5048   9–3D
"You wouldn't know it from the pastries" but this casual spot, "well-placed for Sadler's Wells and Angel" is 100% gluten free and Grade A certified by Coeliac UK, and "offers a good mix of choices from healthy (salads) to less so (pie and mash, burgers etc)". Most reports say it's "a great choice for a quick bite", but even a critic who claimed the fare was "absolutely tasteless" said: "my friend with strict dietary requirements loved having a choice of whatever she wanted". / EC1R 4TJ; www.nichefoodanddrink.com; @Nichefooddrink; 9.45 pm, Fri & Sat 10.15 pm, Sun 3.30 pm.

The Ninth London W1 £68 4 3 3
22 Charlotte St   020 3019 0880   2–1C
Jun Tanaka's "consistently brilliant food – simple but immaculately presented, with amazing flavours" – wins rave reviews for his "shabby-chic-meets-modern-industrial" Fitzrovia yearling, also praised also for its "lovely" staff. Having said that, there is a minority who feel it has been hyped: "it was good, but after all the raves, I somehow expected more". / W1T 2NB; www.theninthlondon.com; @theninthlondon; 10 pm, Thu-Sat 10.30 pm; closed Sun.

Ninth Ward EC1 £32 2 3 4
99-101 Farringdon Rd   020 7833 2949   10–1A
"A very good range of craft beers and interesting decor" are perhaps the highlights of this dark and divey, southern US-themed hangout near Farringdon station, but its filling dude food can be "great value" too. / EC1R 3BN; www.ninthwardlondon.com; @9thWardLondon; 10 pm.

Nirvana Kitchen W1 £69 4 2 2
61 Upper Berkeley St   020 7958 3222   7–1D
There's relatively limited feedback so far – but all of it positive – for this glossy pan-Asian yearling adjoining a hotel near Marble Arch, which combines cuisines stretching from India eastwards to Korea and Japan... sometimes within a single dish; service seems to be the weakest link. / W1H 7PP; www.nirvana.restaurant; @KitchensNirvana; 10.45 pm; closed Sun; set weekday L £42 (FP).

No 197 Chiswick Fire Station W4 £53 2 2 4
197-199 Chiswick High Rd   020 3857 4669   8–2A
A "re-invention of the old fire station in Chiswick" – from neighbourhood bar chain Darwin & Wallace – "an open airy space, successfully divided into various differing areas". Its Aussie-style menu generally produces "well thought-out" and "tasty" dishes, but although service is "friendly" its speed can be "very slack". / W4 2DR; www.no197chiswickfirestation.com; @No197Chiswick; midnight, Fri & Sat 1 am, Sun 11 pm; booking max 9 may apply.

Noble Rot WC1 £66 3 3 4
51 Lamb's Conduit St   020 7242 8963   2–1D
The "ridiculously comprehensive and thoughtful wine list" has established Mark Andrew and Daniel Keeling's "knockout" Bloomsbury yearling as London's No. 1 destination for œnophiles. Housed in the "buzzy", "dark-wooded" premises which traded for decades as Vats, the variety of vintages is "fascinating", with "some exceptional rarities, many in per glass portions". "They take pride in the food too", but it's relatively "simple" and no criticism to say this is "more a wine bar than a restaurant". Top Menu Tip – fish dishes in oxidized white burgundy. / WC1N 3NB; www.noblerot.co.uk; @noblerotbar; 10 pm; set weekday L £42 (FP).

Nobu,
Metropolitan Hotel W1   £99   3 2 1

19 Old Park Ln   020 7447 4747   3–4A

Celebrating its 20th anniversary this year – this once-trailblazing Japanese fusion icon, overlooking Hyde Park, "doesn't pull the crowds the way it used to" ("go if you like loud groups of celebratory thirtysomethings, or watching people taking endless selfies") but "the food can still sparkle" to the extent fans find "incredible". "There are IKEA salesrooms that look more luxurious than this place", however, "prices are eyewatering", and "it's insulting how staff's main aim seems to be turning tables faster than you can eat"… at least some things never change. / W1K 1LB; www.noburestaurants.com; @NobuOldParkLane; 10.15 pm, Fri & Sat 11 pm, Sun 10 pm; set weekday L £69 (FP).

Nobu Berkeley W1   £88   3 2 3

15 Berkeley St   020 7290 9222   3–3C

"It still has it on the fusion-food front", and this 'newer Nobu' in Mayfair inspires much more feedback and is rated considerably higher nowadays than the original Park Lane branch, particularly the ambience. The criticisms it attracts haven't changed since day one – it's above "a pretentious bar", some tables are "cramped" and "canteen"-like, it can seem "grossly overpriced", and critics feel "it's one for the tasteless 'in' crowd". / W1J 8DY; www.noburestaurants.com; @NobuBerkeleyST; 11 pm, Thu-Sat midnight, Sun 9.45 pm; closed Sun L.

Nobu Shoreditch EC2 NEW

10-50 Willow St   020 3818 3790   13–1B

Inside the brand's newly opened (July 2017) Shoreditch hotel, the 240-seat restaurant incorporates a sushi counter, bar and outdoor courtyard, and occupies almost an entire floor of the building. It opened too late for survey feedback, but aside from the odd exclusive dish here, a repeat of the cooking at the other two London Nobus is our expectation. / EC2A 4BH; www.nobuhotelshoreditch.com; @NobuShoreditch.

Noizé W1 NEW

39 Whitfield St   2–1C

Opening in early October 2017, on the former site of Ollie Dabbous's "loft-style", industrial-chic restaurant, Dabbous, comes a rustic French bistro (quite a departure!) from former co-owner and manager of Pied à Terre, Mathieu Germond (and Pied à Terre owner, David Moore, is also involved). / W1T 2SF; @NoizeRestaurant.

Noor Jahan   £43   3 3 3

2a Bina Gdns, SW5   020 7373 6522   6–2B
26 Sussex Pl, W2   020 7402 2332   7–1D

"A sure thing after over 20 years" – this "unfailing and very traditional" (and "sensibly priced") Earl's Court curry house is "the perfect Indian" for its well-heeled regular crowd, and is perpetually "buzzing" and "crowded". It has a lesser-known Bayswater spin-off, which is likewise a "cut above the norm". / W2 11.30 pm, Sun 11 pm; SW5 11.30 pm.

Nopi W1   £74   4 3 3

21-22 Warwick St   020 7494 9584   4–3B

"The flavours in the food just leap out and astound you" at Yotam Ottolenghi's "bustling and deservedly popular" (if "slightly clinical") Soho flagship, serving a "sensational" selection of the Middle Eastern/Mediterranean small plates that have made him a household name, with "lovely fresh ingredients and wonderful combinations of flavour, colourfully presented". / W1B 5NE; www.nopi-restaurant.com; @ottolenghi; 10.30 pm, Sun 4 pm; closed Sun D.

Nordic Bakery £13
14a Golden Sq, W1   020 3230 1077   4–3C
37b New Cavendish St, W1   020 7935 3590   2–1A
48 Dorset St, W1   020 7487 5877   2–1A
55 Neal Street, Seven Dials, WC2   020 7836 4996   5–3C
"You can't better the cinnamon buns, rye rolls and coffee" served at this quartet of Scandi cafés in Soho, Marylebone and now also Covent Garden, which – leaving aside a hint of *"design mag self-consciousness"* – are *"great for a sweet or savoury treat"*. / nordicbakery.com; Golden Square 8 pm, Sat & Sun 7 pm; Cavendish Street & Dorset Street 6.30 pm, Sun 6 pm.

The Norfolk Arms WC1 £46
28 Leigh St   020 7388 3937   9–4C
The Spanish-accented scoff is "surprisingly good" at this "noisy and unattractive pub" near King's Cross: "it can seem a bit disorganised", but "the quality of the food belies the absence of sophistication" and "makes it worth sticking it out". / WC1H 9EP; www.norfolkarms.co.uk; 11pm, Sun 10.30 pm; No Amex.

North China W3 £43
305 Uxbridge Rd   020 8992 9183   8–1A
"Whenever the itch comes for a Chinese", Acton folk head for this above-average neighbourhood stalwart – "the food's just right and the welcome is real". / W3 9QU; www.northchina.co.uk; 11 pm, Fri & Sat 11.30 pm.

North Sea Fish WC1 £44
7-8 Leigh St   020 7387 5892   9–4C
"One of London's better chippies" – this "traditional family-run" outfit in Bloomsbury remains hugely popular thanks to its big variety of "very fresh, totally reliable fish" (all deep-fried) in "large portions". It has "generally freshened itself up since the new generation took the reins", bringing a "slightly smarter ambience and decor". / WC1H 9EW; www.northseafishrestaurant.co.uk; 10 pm, Sun 9.30 pm; closed Sun D; No Amex.

**The Northall,
Corinthia Hotel WC2** £89
10a Northumberland Ave   020 7321 3100   2–3C
Given its "giant" and – to many tastes – "wonderful" interior, this plush five-star hotel dining room near Trafalgar Square is surprisingly "not on the radar", and especially "if you want somewhere with understated class in which to do business", and with "good-quality modern British cuisine", it can be ideal. On the debit side, "some dishes lack oomph", and, particularly when empty, it can "lack ambience" ("it felt like we were eating in a provincial railway station waiting room"). / WC2N 5AE; www.thenorthall.co.uk; @CorinthiaLondon; 10.45 pm; set pre-theatre £52 (FP); set weekday L £53 (FP).

Northbank EC4 £58
One Paul's Walk   020 7329 9299   10–3B
"Food with a view" across the Thames is a "real treat" at this 10-year-old City stalwart beside the Wobbly Bridge, directly opposite Tate Modern. After a wobble in last year's survey, marks for food have revived under new chef John Harrison. / EC4V 3QH; www.northbankrestaurant.co.uk; @NorthbankLondon; 10 pm; closed Sun.

Novikov (Asian restaurant) W1 £94
50a Berkeley St   020 7399 4330   3–3C
"Sod the bill!" – "The buzz is electric and the pan-Asian small plates delectable" at this "brassy" and "theatrical" Russian-owned scene near Berkeley Square, where the crowd's "always very glamorous". / W1J 8HA; www.novikovrestaurant.co.uk; @NovikovLondon; 11.15 pm; set weekday L £49 (FP).

F S A

Novikov (Italian restaurant) W1   £106   1 2 2
50a Berkeley St   020 7399 4330   3–3C
*"Come to see and be seen" – "but not on an empty stomach, as you pay
so much for the location not the food" – if you visit the Italian rear dining
room of this glam, Russian-owned eurotrash-magnet in Mayfair, which serves
"unexceptional Italian fare at exceptional prices". / W1J 8HA;
www.novikovrestaurant.co.uk; @NovikovLondon; 11.45 pm.*

Nukis Kitchen W13   £27   3 2 2
58 Northfield Avenue   020 8579 2113   1–3A
*"You must book in advance for this local Thai yearling" – the best eating
option in Northfields: "it's always packed" (but then it is tiny…) / W13 9RR;
10 pm.*

Numero Uno SW11   £54   3 4 3
139 Northcote Rd   020 7978 5837   11–2C
*"Consistently good over 20 years" – this Italian stalwart in Battersea's
Nappy Valley has "very friendly staff who love children" and is "always
packed". The food? "not in 'wow'-factor territory but more-than-competent".
/ SW11 6PX; 11.30 pm; No Amex.*

Nuovi Sapori SW6   £49   3 4 3
295 New King's Rd   020 7736 3363   11–1B
*Limited but upbeat feedback on this "friendly local Fulham trattoria" near
Parsons Green – "always a pleasant experience with food that doesn't
disappoint". / SW6 4RE; www.nuovisaporilondon.co.uk; 11 pm; closed Sun; booking
max 6 may apply.*

Nutbourne SW11 NEW   £59   3 3 4
29 Ransomes Dock, 35-37 Parkgate Rd   020 7350 0555   6–4C
*"A worthy successor to Ransome's Dock" (long RIP) – the Gladwin brothers'
Battersea haunt has a very pleasant "backwater" location in docks by the
Thames and provides "rather good, rustic" 'farm-to-table' British small plates
alongside some "amazing English wine" (the restaurant is named for the
family vineyard in Sussex). / SW11 4NP; www.nutbourne-restaurant.com;
@NutbourneSW11; set weekday L £37 (FP).*

O'ver SE1   £51   4 3 3
44-46 Southwark St   020 7378 9933   10–4C
*Sea water is a key ingredient of the "perfect pizza" at Tommaso
Mastromatteo's popular, new white-walled Neapolitan café in Southwark,
which also serves other "really interesting" regional dishes. / SE1 1UN;
www.overuk.com; 10.30 pm.*

Oak   £50   3 3 4
243 Goldhawk Rd, W12   020 8741 7700   8–1B
137 Westbourne Park Rd, W2   020 7221 3355   7–1B
*"Delicious, light, crispy pizza" in a "retired pub" remains a "winning
formula", both at the "lovely, cosy and very atmospheric" Notting Hill haunt,
and its sizeable and "relaxing" Shepherd's Bush follow-up. / W12 10.30pm,
Fri & Sat 11 pm Sun 9.30pm; W2 10.30pm, Fri & Sat 11 pm, Sun 10 pm.*

Oak N4 N4 NEW   £31
5-7 Wells Terrace   07710 761606   9–1D
*You can select from 150 wines by the bottle to drink-in or take-away at this
new indie wine store and tasting rooms. Limited feedback to-date say it's
"a great addition to the area and presumably will find a larger audience
once the developments at nearby Finsbury Park station have been
completed". The "the simple nibbly platters" very much play second fiddle
however. / N4 3JU; oakn4.co.uk; @oak_n4; 11 pm, Fri & Sat midnight; closed Mon.*

Obicà £56 **3** 2 2
11 Charlotte St, W1   020 7637 7153   2–1C
19-20 Poland St, W1   020 3327 7070   4–1C
96 Draycott Ave, SW3   020 7581 5208   6–2C
1 West Wintergarden, 35 Bank St, E14   020 7719 1532   12–1C
4 Limeburners Lane, 1 Ludgate Hill, EC4   020 3327 0984   10–2A
This Rome-based chain is inspired by Japanese sushi-bars and serves "tasty
small plates of Italian food". The five "efficiently run" London branches,
from South Ken to Canary Wharf, provide a "surprisingly good experience…
so long as you like mozzarella or burrata". / obica.com; 10 pm - 11 pm; E14 Sat
8 pm; E14 & EC4 Closed Sun.

Oblix SE1 £87 2 2 **3**
Level 32, The Shard, 31 St. Thomas St   020 7268 6700   10–4C
"Yes the views are amazing and that is what you go for" (including
on business), but this 32-floor venue is "living off its location" – the food
is "expensive and nothing to write home about" and service – though more
amiable of late – still so so. / SE1 9RY; www.oblixrestaurant.com;
@OblixRestaurant; 11 pm; booking max 6 may apply.

Odette's NW1 £68 **4** 3 **4**
130 Regents Park Rd   020 7586 8569   9–3B
Bryn Williams's "consistently excellent" cuisine is "really good value for the
quality" and ensures that this well-known venue maintains its long-held
reputation as "the best in Primrose Hill". It's "a good place for
a celebration", especially of the "romantic" variety; "book yourself in a
corner and the atmosphere is lovely". / NW1 8XL; www.odettesprimrosehill.com;
@Odettes_rest; 10 pm, Sat 10.30 pm, Sun 9.30 pm; closed Mon; No Amex;
set weekday L £42 (FP).

Ognisko Restaurant SW7 £50 **3** 3 **5**
55 Prince's Gate, Exhibition Rd   020 7589 0101   6–1C
The "very beautiful time-warp setting" of an impressive old émigrés club,
complete with "clubby" bar and "high-ceilinged dining room", helps create
a "very relaxing" experience at Jan Woroniecki's South Kensington gem
(whose "terrace at the rear is a hidden secret for outdoor summer dining").
The "Polish comfort food" is "lighter than you expect", and there's "a huge
range of vodkas". / SW7 2PN; www.ogniskorestaurant.co.uk; @OgniskoRest;
11.15 pm, Sun 10.30 pm; closed Mon L; No trainers.

Oka £49 **4** 2 2
Kingly Court, 1 Kingly Court, W1   020 7734 3556   4–2B
251 King's Rd, SW3   020 7349 8725   6–3C
71 Regents Park Rd, NW1   020 7483 2072   9–3B
"Sushi that is inventive and spankingly fresh" along with "delicious" Asian
fusion dishes deliver "great value for money" at these little Japanese outlets
– "the only problem is that they're so small you often can't get in!".
/ www.okarestaurant.co.uk; 10.30 pm.

Oklava EC2 £56 **4** 2 **3**
74 Luke St   020 7729 3032   13–1B
Selin Kiazim showcases her "superb, generous, tasty and thought-through
Turkish food" in this "small but elegant", tile-and-brick two-year-old,
complete with open kitchen, in Shoreditch. / EC2A 4PY; www.oklava.co.uk;
@oklava_ldn; 10.30 pm, Sun 4 pm; booking max 6 may apply.

Oldroyd N1 £51 **4** 3 2
344 Upper St   020 8617 9010   9–3D
That "it's a bit of a basic, tiny space" colours feedback on Tom Oldroyd's
accomplished but "crushed" Islington yearling. On most accounts his
"fabulously tasty, daily changing (if limited) menu" is full compensation,
but there's a noticeable minority for whom "though it's undeniably good",
the size hinders appreciation. / N1 0PD; www.oldroydlondon.com; @oldroydlondon;
10.30 pm, Fri 11 pm, Sun 9.30 pm; booking max 4 may apply.

Oliver Maki W1 £69 3 3 3

33 Dean St 020 7734 0408 5–2A

Mixed views on this two-floor Soho yearling – first London branch of a Gulf-based fusion chain: fans say the "sushi's delicious to eat and beautiful to look at", but doubters find the whole approach "a bit too cookie cutter". / W1D 4PW; www.olivermaki.co.uk; @OliverMakiUK; 10.30 pm, Fri & Sat 11 pm, Sun 9.30 pm.

Oliveto SW1 £60 4 2 1

49 Elizabeth St 020 7730 0074 2–4A

"You can't go wrong", say fans of this "very busy" Sardinian, which provides pizza and pasta "of a consistently high standard" and which is "good value for money" too, at least by the standards of pricey Belgravia; it's also "excellent for families with children". / SW1W 9PP; www.olivorestaurants.com/oliveto; 10.30 pm, Sun 10 pm; booking max 7 may apply.

Olivo SW1 £75 3 3 2

21 Eccleston St 020 7730 2505 2–4B

"The original of this Belgravia chain of Sardinian stalwarts" – this "friendly and efficient" fixture is a "classic Italian" which provides a "failsafe choice, with excellent seasonal specials". "A very welcome refurbishment means it's even now possible to hold a conversation while eating!" / SW1W 9LX; www.olivorestaurants.com; 10.30 pm; closed Sat L & Sun L.

Olivocarne SW1 £64 3 3 2

61 Elizabeth St 020 7730 7997 2–4A

Part of the local Olivo, Oliveto, etc empire – this offbeat but upscale Belgravian continues in the good-but-pricey mould of Mauro Sanna's other venues – here the traditional Sardinian cuisine puts more of an emphasis on meat. / SW1W 9PP; www.olivorestaurants.com; 11 pm, Sun 10.30 pm.

Olivomare SW1 £69 3 2 2

10 Lower Belgrave St 020 7730 9022 2–4B

"Memorably succulent fish" is the acclaimed highlight of Mauro Sanna's "cosmopolitan" Sardinian in Belgravia, which on many accounts is an accomplished and "enjoyably hustling and bustling" all-rounder. To some tastes however, the idiosyncratic decor is more soulless than it is stylish, and the odd blip on service also hit ratings this year. / SW1W 0LJ; www.olivorestaurants.com; 11 pm, Sun 10.30 pm; booking max 10 may apply.

Olympic,
Olympic Studios SW13 £50 2 2 3

117-123 Church Rd 020 8912 5161 11–1A

This "lively" all-day brasserie forms part of Barnes's indie cinema and members' club, in a former recording studio (famous amongst '60s/'70s rock anoraks for many iconic tracks). For the well-heeled locals "it ticks all the boxes" – "great for breakfast/brunch, both healthy and indulgent", and "perfect before or after a film". It does run the risk of being "complacent" though, and "the cooking is a bit ordinaire". / SW13 9HL; www.olympiccinema.co.uk; @Olympic_Cinema; 11 pm, Fri & Sat midnight, Sun 10 pm.

Olympus Fish N3 £35 4 5 2

140-144 Ballards Ln 020 8371 8666 1–1B

"Outstanding fresh fish cooked on a charcoal grill" – and tablecloths! – ensure this "delightful" family-run fixture in Finchley is "definitely the best fish 'n' chips in the area". / N3 2PA; www.olympusrestaurant.co.uk; @Olympus_London; 11 pm.

On The Bab £36 3 2 2

39 Marylebone Ln, W1   020 7935 2000   2–1A
36 Wellington St, WC2   020 7240 8825   5–3D
305 Old St, EC1   020 7683 0361   13–1B
9 Ludgate Broadway, EC4   020 7248 8777   10–2A

"Amazingly tasty bites" ("very good chicken" is the standout) keeps these
"fun, modern and minimalist", K-pop-styled street food joints "crowded and
bustling"; expect "lots of directional haircuts among fellow diners".
/ onthebab.co.uk; EC1 & WC2 10.30 pm, Sun 10 pm; W1 & EC4 4 pm; EC4 closed
Sat & Sun; W1 closed Sun.

One Canada Square E14 £62 2 4 3

1 Canada Square   020 7559 5199   12–1C

In the lobby of Canary Wharf's most iconic building, it's no surprise that this
modern European outfit is geared towards business dining – a function
it generally performs well. On Friday and Saturday nights, it caters for post-
office excess with a "bottomless dinner". / E14 5AB;
www.onecanadasquarerestaurant.com; @OneCanadaSquare; 10.45 pm; closed Sun.

108 Brasserie W1 £59 3 3 3

108 Marylebone Ln   020 7969 3900   2–1A

Attractive, spacious hotel dining room at the top end of Marylebone Lane,
which wins praise as an "efficient and useful option" serving a wide variety
of consistently well-rated brasserie fare, much of it from the Josper Grill.
/ W1U 2QE; www.108brasserie.com; @108Marylebone; 10.30pm.

108 Garage W10 NEW £60 5 4 5

108 Golborne Rd   020 8969 3769   7–1A

Just about "the hottest newcomer of the year": "chef Chris Denny is truly
talented, and a name to remember!". This "wacky, noisy and stimulating",
"NYC-vibe" debutante is a "laid-back", cooly grungy garage-conversion,
on "one of West London's most interesting streets" (at the top end
of Portobello Market). The food is "to die for" – "light but satisfying cooking
with brilliant use of herbs and greens". It's just "a pity you can't get in any
more". (In September 2017, they are set to open a second venture nearby:
Southam Street.) / W10 5PS; www.108garage.com.

100 Wardour Street W1 £69 2 2 3

100 Wardour St   020 7314 4000   4–2D

Latest, year-old incarnation of this two-floor venue – once famous as the
Marquee Club, and which since 1995 under D&D London has been multiply
re-launched (as Mezzo, Floridita, Carom... maybe others we've forgotten).
All the feedback we have for its latest, plus-ça-change mix of DJs, cocktails,
Asian/European cuisine and dancing are OK, but given its massive central
Soho site, what's most striking is how little interest it piques. / W1F 0TN;
www.100wardourst.com; @100WardourSt.

1 Lombard Street EC3 £71 2 2 3

1 Lombard St   020 7929 6611   10–3C

"A great central location" – a former banking hall "right in the heart of the
City" – is key to the success of Soren Jessen's well-known expense-accounter
favourite. The jaundiced view is that it's "a boring place" for "City types who
can't think of anywhere else": a more upbeat take is that while it's
"overpriced", it's "decent and trusty". / EC3V 9AA; www.1lombardstreet.com;
10 pm; closed Sat & Sun; booking max 10 may apply.

One-O-One,
Park Tower Knightsbridge SW1 £98 431
101 Knightsbridge   020 7290 7101   6–1D
"I want to get a petition going to get more people to eat here!". Pascal Proyart's cuisine "when it is on song, is majestic" at this Knightsbridge hotel dining room, known particularly for his "fabulous and beautifully presented fish and seafood". "Sadly the room can be empty" – it has "an awful ambience, akin to an airport lounge" – "which just drags down the mood". / SW1X 7RN; www.oneoonerestaurant.com; @OneOOneLondon; 10 pm; closed Mon & Sun; booking max 7 may apply; set weekday L £47 (FP).

Les 110 de Taillevent W1 £72 443
16 Cavendish Square   020 3141 6016   3–1B
"The wine is second to none" – a "fabulous selection" of 110 vintages "available by the glass and without melting your wallet" – at this London outpost of the famous Parisian venue, which occupies a "smart (without being overbearing)" converted banking hall on the square behind Oxford Street's John Lewis. "There's a very good kitchen here" too, producing "high quality", "classic" Gallic cuisine, while service is "delightful" and "prompt". / W1G 9DD; www.les-110-taillevent-london.com; @110London; 10.30 pm; closed Sat L & Sun; set weekday L & pre-theatre £45 (FP).

Opera Tavern WC2 £52 443
23 Catherine St   020 7836 3680   5–3D
"Exceptional tapas" tastes like "it's been beamed over straight from Spain", according to fans of the Salt Yard group's two-floor Covent Garden pub-conversion – an "always welcoming" venue that's "perfect for a light meal before or after the theatre". / WC2B 5JS; www.saltyardgroup.co.uk/opera-tavern; @saltyardgroup; 11.15 pm, Sun 9.45 pm.

Opso W1 £48 333
10 Paddington St   020 7487 5088   2–1A
Limited and uneven feedback on this casual Marylebone three-year-old. Fans are delighted with its modern Greek-with-a-twist dishes and cleanly designed interior, but its detractors rate it as average on both these counts. / W1U 5QL; www.opso.co.uk; @OPSO_london; 10:30pm, Sun 10 pm; closed Sun D.

The Orange SW1 £60 334
37 Pimlico Rd   020 7881 9844   6–2D
"In a pretty part of Pimlico", overlooking Orange Square, this attractive boozer can usually be relied upon to provide "good pub grub", including wood-fired pizza. / SW1W 8NE; www.theorange.co.uk; @theorangesw1; 10 pm, Sun 9.30 pm.

Orange Pekoe SW13 £35 344
3 White Hart Ln   020 8876 6070   11–1A
"The best tea shop in existence" may be stretching it, but this Barnes tea room is permanently rammed to overflowing onto the pavement. "It's my favourite place for a reasonably priced 'full English' tea", with excellent coffee and "mouthwatering cakes supported by unusual lunchtime salads". / SW13 0PX; www.orangepekoeteas.com; @OrangePekoeTeas; 5 pm; L only.

Orchard SE4 £55 222
5 Harefield Rd   020 8692 4756   1–4D
"A Brockley meeting place which copes with families, digital hipsters and friends without being defined by them" – this "convivial" gastropub is the best in these parts, although "some dishes missed their mark this past year". / SE4 1LW; www.thebrockleyorchard.com; @The_Orchard_; 11 pm, Sun 10.30 pm.

Orée £12 | 3 | 2 | 3

275-277 Fulham Rd, SW10   020 3813 9724   6–3B

65 King's Rd, SW3   020 3740 4588   6–3D NEW

147 Kensington High St, W8   020 3883 7568   6–1A NEW

"An on-site bakery ensures everything is super-fresh" at this "lovely, light and bright location" near the Chelsea & Westminster Hospital: "great coffees, cakes and French-styles brunches". They must be doing something right as in mid 2017 they launched new stores on the King's Road and in Kensington. / www.oree.co.uk.

Ormer Mayfair W1 £120 | 4 | 3 | 3

Half Moon St   020 7016 5601   3–4B

Star Channel Islands chef, Shaun Rankin "brings Jersey flavours to the heart of London" at this year-old venture: the new occupant of a classically smart, basement dining room of a Mayfair hotel. It's one of the highest-rated openings of recent times: "the food looks fabulous but even better is its exceptional flavour". / W1J 7BH; www.ormermayfair.com; @ormermayfair; No shorts; set weekday L £93 (FP).

Oro Di Napoli W5 £34 | 4 | 3 | 2

6 The Quadrant, Little Ealing Lane   020 3632 5580   1–3A

That it's "marginally better even than Santa Maria" is a claim sometimes made of this South Ealing Neapolitan, even if its "very good wood-fired pizza" isn't (yet) quite as highly rated as its famous local rival. / W5 4EE; www.lorodinapoli.co.uk; 11 pm.

Orrery W1 £90 | 3 | 3 | 2

55 Marylebone High St   020 7616 8000   2–1A

"You can hear each other speak" in this "quiet" and "pleasant" first-floor dining room over Marylebone's Conran Shop, which makes "stylish" use of a slightly "odd" space, and is best-visited when the roof terrace is open in summer. Long renowned as "one of the better D&D establishments", its profile has lessened of late, but its modern French cuisine still wins reasonable support from reporters. A strong wine list is a feature. / W1U 5RB; www.orreryrestaurant.co.uk; @orrery; 10 pm, Fri & Sat 10.30 pm; booking max 8 may apply; set weekday L £53 (FP), set Sun L £56 (FP).

Oscar Wilde Bar at Cafe Royal W1 £82

68 Regent St   020 7406 3333   4–4C

Famous for its rococo decor, this truly dazzling room, a short hop from Piccadilly Circus, is one of London's most venerable restaurant spaces (dating from 1865), but – despite various reformattings by different owners – has sunk from view in recent times. More change may be on the cards in 2018, but for the time being it's mainly worth visiting for its award winning afternoon tea. / W1B; www.hotelcaferoyal.com/oscarwildebar; @HotelCafeRoyal; 6 pm; L & afternoon tea only.

Oslo Court NW8 £64 | 4 | 5 | 5

Charlbert St   020 7722 8795   9–3A

"How restaurants used to be" – this "fun throwback to the 1970s", "quirkily located at the foot of a Regent's Park apartment block" perfectly preserves the plush pink style of the era; while its "wonderful happy atmosphere" is buoyed along by celebratory parties of septuagenarian north Londoners bantering with long-serving staff for whom "nothing is too much trouble". The generous dishes are "old-fashioned, but superb if you like the style" ("where else can you find a proper veal Holstein?") and "there's always a full house because it's such good value" ("it's booked well ahead by those who know it"). Be sure to leave space for Neil's dessert trolley. / NW8 7EN; www.oslocourtrestaurant.co.uk; 11 pm; closed Sun; No jeans.

Osteria, Barbican Centre EC2 £57 2 2 3
Level 2 Silk St   020 7588 3008   10–1B
"Super views" make this "quiet and unobtrusive venue" at the Barbican Centre a "really handy and pleasant" option for theatre and concert-goers for whom there's a "reasonable set menu". Judged as a foodie destination however, "the food continues to disappoint" despite the arrival of chef Anthony Demetre (late of Soho's Arbutus, RIP) to boost the Italian cuisine provided by contract caterer Searcys. / EC2Y 8DS; osterialondon.co.uk; @osterialondon; 10.30 pm, Sat 11.30 pm; closed Sun; set weekday L £38 (FP).

Osteria Antica Bologna SW11 £47 3 2 2
23 Northcote Rd   020 7978 4771   11–2C
A "friendly, long-established local near Clapham Junction", well-known in the area for its "competent North Italian cooking and pleasant ambience". "Wild boar ragu on black pepper spaghetti is one highlight from a menu of simple authenticity". / SW11 1NG; www.osteria.co.uk; @OsteriaAntica; 10.30 pm, Sun 10 pm.

Osteria Basilico W11 £63 3 3 4
29 Kensington Park Rd   020 7727 9957   7–1A
An enduring pillar of the Notting Hill restaurant scene, this fun Italian isn't as high profile as once it was, but still knows how to please its clientele, with authentic pizzas, homemade pasta or more sophisticated specials. / W11 2EU; www.osteriabasilico.co.uk; 11.30 pm, Sun 10.30 pm; no booking, Sat L.

Osteria Dell'Angolo SW1 £59 3 3 1
47 Marsham St   020 3268 1077   2–4C
"A good standby for politicos trapped in the Westminster bubble" – this "comfortable" Italian "just opposite the Home Office" can seem very "quiet" (although some reporters find it "romantic"). The "authentic" cooking is "very acceptable", and "as it never appears too busy, you get plenty of attention!" / SW1P 3DR; www.osteriadellangolo.co.uk; @Osteria_Angolo; 10 pm; closed Sat L & Sun.

Osteria Tufo N4 £48 3 3 2
67 Fonthill Rd   020 7272 2911   9–1D
"Rich and interesting Neapolitan home cooking" makes this "delightful and idiosyncratic neighbourhood Italian" in Finsbury Park a "real find": an "all-female outfit" run by the owner, Paola, who shares with you her "enthusiasm and love of food". Just one request: "the savoury tomato-based sauces can all blend into one another – a tweak to differentiate them would unlock even more potential in the place". / N4 3HZ; www.osteriatufo.co.uk; @osteriatufo; 10.30 pm, Sun 9.30 pm; closed Mon & Sun L; No Amex.

Ostuni £58 2 3 3
1 Hampstead Lane, N6   020 7624 8035   9–1B
43-45 Lonsdale Rd, NW6   020 7624 8035   1–2B
This four-year-old Italian in Queen's Park – and its more recent Highgate sibling – specialise in the cuisine of Puglia in southern Italy. Service is "friendly" and there's a "great atmosphere", but while fans report "thoroughly enjoyable cooking on every visit" critics are "not so impressed with all the dishes". / 10.30 pm; N6 closed Mon L; no booking at D.

The Other Naughty Piglet SW1 NEW £60 4 4 3
12 Palace St   020 7592 0322   2–4B
"What a great addition to the otherwise pretty dreary dining scene around Victoria" – Andrew Lloyd Webber's has teamed up to good effect with Brixton's Naughty Piglets for the 'small plates' restaurant on the first floor of his 'The Other Palace Theatre' (formerly the St James's Theatre): "the food's stunning and the staff charming" and even if "the location and decor don't really match", the interior's "been nicely refitted and it's great fun to sit up at the kitchen counter and watch the chefs". / SW1E 5JA; www.theothernaughtypiglet.co.uk; booking max 10 may apply.

Otto's WC1 £72 **4** **5** **4**
182 Gray's Inn Rd 020 7713 0107 2–1D

"For a superb, Escoffier-style dining experience", this "quirky", unpromising-looking fixture on a grungy, out-of-the-way Bloomsbury street might seem an improbable destination, but it's something of a "dream restaurant". "Proper, old-school, luxurious French gastronomic dishes" are "served with charm and wit by Otto himself" in an "attractive and old-fashioned" room ("where you can hear yourself speak"). Top Menu Tip – "everyone should go here for the pressed duck at least once in their lives". / WC1X 8EW; www.ottos-restaurant.com; 9.30 pm; closed Mon, Sat L & Sun.

Ottolenghi £57 **4** **3** **2**
13 Motcomb St, SW1 020 7823 2707 6–1D
63 Ledbury Rd, W11 020 7727 1121 7–1B
287 Upper St, N1 020 7288 1454 9–2D
50 Artillery Pas, E1 020 7247 1999 10–2D

"The salads on display as you enter get your gastric juices moving!" at Yotam Ottolenghi's communal cafés, whose "enterprising" Middle Eastern dishes remain "fresh, delicious and interesting" ("cakes and desserts are not to be missed" either). If there are drawbacks, it's "variable service", "terrible acoustics" and the wait to be seated. Nor is it cheap, but it's worth it ("cook books are all very well, but the prep takes hours!"). / www.ottolenghi.co.uk; N1 10.30 pm, Sun 7 pm; W11 & SW1 8 pm, Sat 7 pm, Sun 6 pm; E1 10.30 pm, Sun 6 pm; N1 closed Sun D; Holland St takeaway only; W11 & SW1 no booking.

Outlaw's at The Capital SW3 £91 **4** **4** **2**
22-24 Basil St 020 7591 1202 6–1D

"A lot easier to get to than Cornwall!" – Nathan Outlaw's "small and intimate dining room" near the back of Harrods lives up to his renown as one of the UK's top fish and seafood chefs with "superb and superbly fresh dishes" delivering "delightful" and "delicate" flavours. That it's a "quiet space (so hard to find in central London)" is valued by some, although others feel "atmosphere can be lacking". Note, the hotel – a rare independent – was sold to a small American group in January 2017. Top Tips – value-wise "the lunchtime menu is hard to beat" and "you can BYO with no corkage on Thursdays". / SW3 1AT; www.capitalhotel.co.uk; @OUTLAWSinLondon; 10 pm; closed Sun; credit card required to book; set weekday L £59 (FP).

Over Under SW5 NEW £13 **4** **4** **2**
181a Earl's Court Rd 07944 494555 6–2A

This "new Antipodean coffee shop" near Earl's Court tube "feels different to others out there" – "a small space run by a great young team producing familiar-with-a-twist and yummy breakfast fare (bircher muesli, porridge, avocado toast, generous granola etc) and importantly, exceptional brews". / SW5 9RB; www.overundercoffee.com; @overundercoffee.

Oxo Tower, Restaurant SE1 £86 **1** **1** **2**
Barge House St 020 7803 3888 10–3A

"A real tourist conveyor belt" on the South Bank, where "prices, relative to the quality of the food, are ridiculous". "How do they get away with it year after year? The wonderful view!!" / SE1 9PH; www.harveynichols.com/restaurant/the-oxo-tower; @OxoTowerWharf; 11 pm, Sun 10 pm; booking max 8 may apply; set weekday L £57 (FP); SRA-Food Made Good – 2 stars.

Oxo Tower, Brasserie SE1 £75 1 1 2

Barge House St   020 7803 3888   10–3A

"Great views" – ("among the best in London") – tempt diners to this brasserie section of the landmark South Bank tower. But, oh dear, "everything else is not good" ("don't go, unless you are compelled to as a guest"). / SE1 9PH; www.harveynichols.com/restaurants/oxo-tower-london; 11 pm, Sun 10 pm; May need 2+ to book.

The Oystermen Seafood Kitchen & Bar WC2 NEW £50

32 Henrietta St   020 7240 4417   5–3D

A June 2017 opening from former pop-up caterers, The Oystermen; their new, simple, tightly packed Covent Garden home features shellfish and seafood, fresh from the boats, or pickled, smoked and cured by the owners Matt Lovell and Rob Hampton. Top Tip – 'Bubbles 'n' Oysters Happy Hour' (3pm-5pm every day; six oysters and a glass of fizz for £10). / WC2E 8NA; oystermen.co.uk; @theoystermen.

Ozone Coffee Roasters EC2 £40 4 4 4

11 Leonard St   020 7490 1039   13–1A

"Unbeatable… except for the queues in the morning"; the habit-forming smell from the big roasting machines in the basement is justification enough for a trip to this superbly hip, Kiwi-owned Shoreditch haunt, which provides exceptional brews and does a "fab" brunch too. / EC2A 4AQ; ozonecoffee.co.uk; @ozonecoffeeuk; 9 pm, Sat & Sun 4.30 pm; May need 8+ to book.

P Franco E5 £48 4 3 3

107 Lower Clapton Rd   020 8533 4660   14–1B

"Wonderful, innovative food cooked up on two hot plates at the end of a communal table" makes this in-the-know Clapton wine shop a really interesting dining destination. The wine, from the people behind Noble Fine Liquor on Broadway Market, is not your standard plonk, either. / E5 0NP; www.pfranco.co.uk; @pfranco_e5; Thu-Sat 10 pm, Sun 9 pm; closed Mon-Wed, Thu-Sat D only, Sun L & D; No Amex; no booking.

Pachamama W1 £65 3 2 2

18 Thayer St   020 7935 9393   2–1A

"Innovative and delicious" Peruvian-inspired fusion dishes combined with cocktails based on pisco and mezcal to create a buzz at this Marylebone three-year-old. / W1U 3JY; www.pachamamalondon.com; @pachamama_ldn; 10.45 pm, Sun 10 pm; closed Mon L; set brunch £38 (FP).

Padella SE1 £28 5 4 4

6 Southwark St   no tel   10–4C

"Oh wowza! pasta perfection!!!!!" – "the best in town and so incredibly cheap" – "no wonder the capital has gone mad for this gem of a Borough Market yearling" from the team behind Trullo: "a simple concept brilliantly executed". Staff are "engaging" and "efficient" too but getting in is a challenge: "queues are longer than an economy-class check-in to Ibiza". / SE1 1TQ; www.padella.co; @padella_pasta; 10 pm, Sun 5 pm; no booking.

The Painted Heron SW10 £57 5 4 2

112 Cheyne Walk   020 7351 5232   6–3B

A "slightly awkward location" is no barrier to enjoyment of this "out-of-the-way gem", just off Chelsea Embankment. "Staff try to please" and the Indian cuisine represents "exceptional value" – "well-prepared with a light and individual touch" and "with unusual layers of flavours and spicing". / SW10 0DJ; www.thepaintedheron.com; @thepaintedheron; 10.30 pm.

Palatino EC1 NEW   £58   4 5 3

71 Central St   020 3481 5300   10–1B

Stevie Parle's "hip, urban (and urbane) newcomer in trendy Clerkenwell" is one of his best openings yet. An "airy", warehouse-y corner-site that's part of FORA (a 'pro-working' space) – "once you get past the office-style reception", the "incredibly friendly" service is "low key and efficient" and the "straightforward", "authentically Roman" cooking is "delicious" and "surprisingly good value" too ("I thought the bill was wrong, it was so cheap!"). / EC1V 8AB; palatino.london; @PalatinoLondon; 10 pm; closed Sun.

The Palmerston SE22   £56   4 3 3

91 Lordship Ln   020 8693 1629   1–4D

This "East Dulwich gastropub consistently gets things right" – a "fantastic old-fashioned boozer with terrific beer", but also whose "adventurous" food hints at "real talent in the kitchen" ("you can take foodie friends with confidence that they won't snark"). / SE22 8EP; www.thepalmerston.co.uk; @thepalmerston; 10 pm, Sun 9.30 pm; No Amex; set weekday L £33 (FP).

The Palomar W1   £62   4 4 3

34 Rupert St   020 7439 8777   4–3D

"The Israeli answer to Barrafina" – this "compact" ("squashed", "noisy" and sometimes "boiling") Tel Aviv import is a "joyous" and "horizon-opening" experience, where "the good humour of the staff is infectious" and the "clever" (if sometimes "miniscule") small plates dish up "whizz-bang" flavours that "demand to be noticed". "Sitting at the counter, interacting with the chefs" is the way to go – you can only book for the much less funky dining room. / W1D 6DN; www.thepalomar.co.uk; @palomarsoho; 11 pm, Sun 9 pm; closed Sun L.

Pamban NW1 NEW

North Yard, Chalk Farm Rd   no tel   9–3B

A new all-day chai and coffee house in Camden Market, owned by Mayhul Gondhea and Aruna Sellahewa, opened in July 2017. The food offering includes curry, stuffed pancakes and sweet buns. / NW1 8AH; www.camdenmarket.com/food-drink/pamban.

Il Pampero SW1 NEW   £75

20 Chesham Place   020 3189 4850   6–1D

With an interior aiming to 'embody chic and vintage glamour', this new hotel dining room in Belgravia delivers a traditional Italian menu, under chef Claudio Covino – only limited feedback so far, but all positive. / SW1X 8HQ; www.ilpampero.com; @ilPamperoLondon; 22.30pm.

The Pantechnicon SW1 NEW

18 Motcomb St   6–1D

This superb, neo-classical 1830 Grade II listed building in Belgravia, owned by Grosvenor Estates, is to take on a new lease of life in 2018 as a new 10,000 sq ft retail and restaurant space, the latter incorporating a basement café/bar, second floor restaurant and roof terrace. / SW1X 8LA; www.thepantechnicon.com; 9.30 pm, Sun 9 pm; booking max 12 may apply.

Pappa Ciccia   £36   3 3 3

105 Munster Rd, SW6   020 7384 1884   11–1B
41 Fulham High St, SW6   020 7736 0900   11–1B

"Delicious crispy thin pizzas" and "particularly good antipasti" are "a substantial cut above average" at these stalwart Fulham and Putney cafés – and they're "well priced for southwest London". They also do good gluten-free pizza and pasta options, but "sadly they've stopped BYO at the weekends". / www.pappaciccia.com; SW6 5RQ 11 pm, Sat & Sun 11.30 pm; SW6 3JJ 11 pm.

Parabola,
Design Museum W8   £70   3 2 3
224-238 Kensington High St   020 7940 8795   6–1A
*Off the airy foyer of the new design museum – and named for the curve
of its roof – this minimalist yearling "serves interesting food in a part
of Kensington that's a bit of a food desert", along with "an excellent
selection of wine". However, it also expresses some of Prescott & Conran's
less desirable restaurant DNA with its "variable service" and some prices
that "are not really justified". Perhaps that will change for the good with the
September 2017 appointment of well-known chef, Rowley Leigh
as permanent chef – previously there was a roster of guest chefs (of which
he had been one). Top Tip – "pick a window seat" for the best views
of Holland Park.* / W8 6AG; www.parabola.london; @ParabolaLondon; 9.45 pm.

Paradise by Way of Kensal Green W10   £48   3 3 4
19 Kilburn Lane   020 8969 0098   1–2B
*"A wonderful unexpected find in an offbeat location" – this huge, rambling
shabby-chic tavern in Kensal Green has been a magnet for the local cool
crowd for over 20 years, with gardens, roof-terraces and bars a go-go; and a
large rear dining room that's very atmospheric.* / W10 4AE;
www.theparadise.co.uk; @weloveparadise; 10.30 pm, Fri & Sat 11 pm, Sun 9 pm;
closed weekday L; No Amex.

Paradise Garage E2   £54   4 4 3
254 Paradise Row   020 7613 1502   14–2B
*"Tucked under the arches in Bethnal Green" – this "fantastic" two-year-old
from chef Robin Gill (of hip Clapham duo Manor and Dairy) has
an "outstanding and inventive menu" packed with "unusual delights".*
/ E2 9LE; www.paradise254.com; @ParadiseRow254; 10 pm; closed Mon,
Tue L & Sun D; booking max 6 may apply.

Paradise Hampstead NW3   £38   4 5 4
49 South End Rd   020 7794 6314   9–2A
*This veteran Hampstead Heath curry house is now run by the founder's son,
but has lost none of its legendary welcome: "they pretend to know you like
an old friend!" "It looks a bit dated now" and the food may be very
traditional, but it's "always delicious – with never a bad meal".* / NW3 2QB;
www.paradisehampstead.co.uk; 10.45 pm.

El Parador NW1   £40   3 2 3
245 Eversholt St   020 7387 2789   9–3C
*"Rich and authentic tapas" in "generous portions" makes it worth
discovering this "busy but friendly" Hispanic, near Mornington Crescent.
Some sections of the "small" interior are "noisy", but there's a great garden
for sunny days.* / NW1 1BA; www.elparadorlondon.com; 11 pm, Fri & Sat 11.30 pm,
Sun 9.30 pm; closed Sat L & Sun L; No Amex.

Park Chinois W1   £95   2 2 4
17 Berkeley St   020 3327 8888   3–3C
*"The opulence is astonishing and so seductive", say fans of Alan Yau's ultra-
"glamorous" homage to 1920's Shanghai, complete with live music,
in Mayfair – "you could lose yourself here for hours". Even those who
acknowledge a "wonderful experience" however, find it "shockingly
expensive" given the unexceptional Chinese cuisine and to a few reporters
the vibe is plain "horrible" – "like a brothel for billionaires".* / W1S 4NF;
www.parkchinois.com; 11 pm, Sun 10.15 pm; No jeans.

Parlez SE4 NEW
16 Coulgate St   020 8691 0202   1–4D
*This new all-day restaurant is aiming to make Brockley the envy of all of its
South London neighbours, with a mantra of 'local is gospel', seasonal menus
and local artist involvement.* / SE4 2RW; www.parlezlocal.com; @parlezlocal.

Parlour Kensal NW10   £49   4 5 4
5 Regent St   020 8969 2184   1–2B
*"Chef Jesse Dunford Wood's food just goes from strength to strength" at this
Kensal Rise pub conversion, which, as well as more typical options,
goes further down serious dining options than most gastroboozers:
"the Chef's Table overlooking the kitchen is an experience second to none".
/ NW10 5LG; www.parlourkensal.com; @ParlourUK; 10 pm; closed Mon.*

Passione e Tradizione N15 NEW   £36   4 3 2
451 West Green Rd   020 8245 9491   1–1C
*"Note-perfect Italian cooking and stylish presentation left us blown away –
it was more reminiscent of a seasoned, high end establishment in Central
London than a small, reasonably priced eatery around Turnpike Lane!" –
Mustapha Mouflih's "offshoot of Anima e Cuore" feels like an "overdue and
hugely welcome arrival" in Haringey, serving "wonderful pizzas from
a woodfired oven alongside many of the favourite dishes from the sister
restaurant". / N15 3PL; spinach.london; 11 pm.*

Pasta Remoli N4   £35   3 2 2
7 Clifton Terrace   020 7263 2948   9–1D
*"A brilliant pasta café next door to the Park Theatre" – "everything's freshly
cooked, and there are delicious sauces". / N4 3JP; www.pastaremoli.co.uk;
@PastaRemoli; 11 pm, Sun 10.30 pm.*

Pastaio W1 NEW
19 Ganton St   awaiting tel   4–2B
*The latest venture from chef/restaurateur Stevie Parle (Dock Kitchen,
Rotorino, Craft, Palatino) – a freshly made pasta spot, on the former site
of Alan Yau's Cha Cha Moon in Soho's Kingly Court, to open in autumn
2017. / W1F 7BU; www.pastaio.london; @pastaiolondon.*

El Pastór SE1   £44   4 3 4
7a Stoney St   no tel   10–4C
*"Just like being in Mexico" – the Hart Bros brick-lined new Borough Market
taqueria delivers "stunning tacos" that are "up there with the best of the
best" in conditions of "glorious managed chaos". No bookings, of course.
/ SE1 9AA; www.tacoselpastor.co.uk; @Tacos_El_Pastor; 11 pm; no booking.*

Patara   £60   4 4 4
15 Greek St, W1   020 7437 1071   5–2A
5 Berners St, W1   020 8874 6503   3–1D
7 Maddox St, W1   020 7499 6008   4–2A
181 Fulham Rd, SW3   020 7351 5692   6–2C
9 Beauchamp Pl, SW3   020 7581 8820   6–1C
82 Hampstead High St, NW3   020 7431 5902   9–2B NEW
18 High St, SW19   020 3931 6157   11–2B NEW
*"Time and again we get fine Thai tastes!" This enduring chain is, in a low
key way, one of London's most consistent performers, combining "well-above
average food", with "very attentive service" and "beautiful decor".
/ www.pataralondon.com; 10.30 pm, Thu-Sat 11 pm; Greek St closed Sun L.*

Paternoster Chop House EC4   £56   2 1 2
1 Warwick Court   020 7029 9400   10–2B
*That its main claim to fame nowadays is as the location for TV show
First Dates speaks volumes for the unimpressive performance of this
modern steakhouse, by St Paul's, which has never really made the grade
with its natural City business-dining constituency. "Of all the D&D London
places, this is near the bottom, with impossibly slow service, tables too close,
little ambience or magic to the room itself, and average food". (And in real-
life, heart-throb maître d' Fred Sirieix doesn't work here, but at Galvin
at Windows on Park Lane.) / EC4M 7DX; www.paternosterchophouse.co.uk;
@paternoster1; 10.30 pm; closed Sat & Sun D; booking max 12 may apply.*

Patogh W1 £13 **4** **3** **2**
8 Crawford Pl 020 7262 4015 7–1D
*"Some might feel the decor is a bit basic" but don't let that put you off this
"shabby but very friendly" Edgware Road BYO – a "cheap 'n' cheerful"
classic thanks to its "simple Persian food, invariably perfectly cooked".
/ W1H 5NE; 11 pm; Cash only.*

Patron NW5 £59 **2** **3** **3**
26 Fortess Rd 020 7813 2540 9–2C
*"Frogs' legs, snails, pâté and duck confit – and how we've missed them…"
makes this "buzzy" little Kentish Town two-year-old a nostalgic "trip down
memory lane to what French restaurants used to be". But while fans
applaud its "classic flavours" sceptics fear that a significant amount of its
output is "not brilliantly cooked". / NW5 2HB; www.patronlondon.com;
@PatronNW5; 11 pm, Sun 10 pm.*

Patty and Bun £27 **4** **3** **3**
18 Old Compton St, W1 020 7287 1818 5–2A
54 James St, W1 020 7487 3188 3–1A
14 Pembridge Rd, W11 020 7229 2228 7–2B **NEW**
36 Redchurch St, E2 020 7613 3335 13–1C
205 Richmond Rd, E8 020 8525 8250 14–1B **NEW**
22-23 Liverpool St, EC2 020 7621 1331 10–2D
8 Brown's Bdgs, Saint Mary Axe, EC3 020 3846 3222 10–2D **NEW**
*"Be prepared to use loads of napkins, it gets too messy without a plate…"
at these "quirky and cool cafés" whose "delicious-beyond-compare dirty
burgers are just the right side of sloppy" and in contention for "London's
best". / www.pattyandbun.co.uk; 10 pm-11.30 pm, Sun 9 pm-10pm.*

Pavilion Cafe & Bakery E9 £14 **3** **2** **4**
Victoria Park, Old Ford Rd 020 8980 0030 14–2C
*This quaint looking domed structure, "overlooking the boating lake
at Victoria Park" is "a wonderful setting for a locally-sourced, full English, all-
day breakfast, and serves superlative coffee too". / E9 7DE;
www.pavilionbakery.com; @pavilionbakery; 3 pm; L only.*

The Pear Tree W6 £48 **3** **3** **4**
14 Margravine Rd 020 7381 1787 8–2C
*This cute, little Victorian free house (rare in London) is hidden away
in Baron's Court, behind Charing Cross Hospital, and on most (if not quite
all) accounts, is well worth remembering for its "fab" food from a short
menu. / W6 8HJ; www.thepeartreefulham.com; 9.30 pm, Fri-Sun 9 pm;
Mon-Thu D only, Fri-Sun open L & D.*

Pearl Liang W2 £46 **3** **2** **2**
8 Sheldon Square 020 7289 7000 7–1C
*"Fabulous dim sum" has helped earn this big basement in Paddington Basin
a reputation as one of London's top Cantonese spots. But marks have
slipped this year across the board, perhaps because "the location has
transformed from a wasteland to a happening destination, so service has
suffered under the pressure". / W2 6EZ; www.pearlliang.co.uk; @PearlLiangUK;
11 pm.*

Peckham Bazaar SE15 £51 **5** **3** **4**
119 Consort Rd 020 7732 2525 1–4D
*"Finally, some decent Greek food in London!", extol fans of this "fun" and
brilliant Peckham venue serving dishes inspired by the eastern Med from the
Balkans to the Middle East. There's "great chargrilled seafood and meat",
"delivered to your table as it is cooked", and an "interesting wine list at fair
prices", including hard-to-find bottles from the Greek islands. / SE15 3RU;
www.peckhambazaar.com; @PeckhamBazaar; 10 pm, Sun 8 pm; closed Mon,
Tue-Fri D only, Sat & Sun open L & D; No Amex.*

Peckham Refreshment Rooms SE15   £50   3 3 3
12-16 Blenheim Grove   020 7639 1106   1–4D
Behind Peckham Rye station, this chilled all-day café/bar is worth knowing about for coffee or a light bite – it attracts only limited feedback, but to the effect that it's an all-round good place. / SE15 4QL;
www.peckhamrefreshment.com; @peckhamrefresh; midnight; closed Sun D.

Pedler SE15   £44   3 3 4
58 Peckham Rye   020 3030 1515   1–4D
"Intimate and super-cool" Peckham two-year-old bistro, with "engaging food" and a "great bar"; its headline attraction is its "seriously interesting brunch, well worth lingering over". / SE15 4JR; www.thebeautifulpizzaboy.london; @pizzaboylondon1; 10.15 pm, Sun 8.30 pm; closed Mon, Tue L, Wed L, Thu L & Sun D; May need 6+ to book.

Pellicano Restaurant SW3   £58   3 4 3
19-21 Elystan St   020 7589 3718   6–2C
"You're always assured a good welcome when going to this lively Italian" in a quiet Chelsea backwater, which serves a "limited, primarily Sardinian menu". "Gold star to them for making visits with children and/or grandparents so relaxed!" / SW3 3NT; www.pellicanorestaurant.co.uk; 11 pm, Sun 9.30 pm.

E Pellicci E2   £16   3 4 5
332 Bethnal Green Rd   020 7739 4873   13–1D
"A piece of London history" – this Bethnal Green caff (the wood-panelled Art Deco interior is listed) has "not yet been captured by hipsters (who probably think the coffee is awful) and attracts a real mix of locals". Fans say breakfast "is the best in town… and you'll never feel a stranger here". / E2 0AG; epellicci.com; 4 pm; L only, closed Sun; Cash only.

Pentolina W14   £51   4 5 4
71 Blythe Rd   020 3010 0091   8–1C
"We love it!" – neighbourhood restaurants "don't come much better" than this "lovely" (and affordable) contemporary Italian in the backstreets of Olympia, where "Michele in the kitchen always delivers wonderful food, while Heidi is always charming as front of house". One gripe: "please could they vary their menu a bit more – we'd eat there far more if we hadn't already seen it all!" / W14 0HP; www.pentolinarestaurant.co.uk; 10 pm; closed Mon & Sun; No Amex.

The Pepper Tree SW4   £33   2 3 3
19 Clapham Common South Side   020 7622 1758   11–2D
For a "cheap 'n' cheerful" bite, long-term fans still tip this Thai canteen stalwart in Clapham; it's no longer the area's 'go-to' standby though. / SW4 7AB; www.thepeppertree.co.uk; @PepperTreeSW4; 10.45 pm, Sun & Mon 10.15 pm; no booking.

Percy & Founders W1   £57   3 3 3
1 Pearson Square, Fitzroy Place   020 3761 0200   2–1B
"Tables are well-spaced for business", at this "smart, urban dining pub" – a large "bustling" space with kitchen on view occupying the ground floor of a Fitzrovia development on the site of the old Middlesex Hospital; in particular "breakfast is always very good". / W1W 7EY; www.percyandfounders.co.uk; @PercyFounders; 10.30 pm, Sun 9.30 pm; closed Sun D.

Perilla N16   £62   4 4 3
1-3 Green Lanes   07467 067393   1–1C
"A youthful team in the kitchen is pulling out all the stops" at Ben Marks and Matt Emerson's new permanent venture near Newington Green – "one of the least stuffy upmarket restaurants ever", which "makes the most of a slightly odd L-shaped room". "Beautiful, fresh ingredients are 'zhooshed up' to great heights" – with the options of "a small but carefully calibrated menu" or an "amazing" 10-course taster menu plus matching wines – "although not every dish is 100% successful, each is interesting and well-priced enough that all can be forgiven." "Thoughtful and intelligent service" completes an impressive debut. / N16 9BS; www.perilladining.co.uk; @perilladining; 10.30 pm, Sun 8.30 pm.

The Perry Vale SE23   £58   3 4 3
31 Perry Vale   020 8291 0432   1–4D
Limited but positive feedback on this sibling to Camberwell's Crooked Well in up-and-coming Forest Hill – "someone in the kitchen really knows and loves their food, and the service is also excellent!" / SE23 2AR; www.theperryvale.com; @theperryvale.

Persepolis SE15   £23   4 3 2
28-30 Peckham High St   020 7639 8007   1–4D
"Quirky, a bit shabby, maybe not for everyone... but the food is top notch!" – cookery book author Sally Butcher's well-known, eccentric corner shop in Peckham delivers zesty, eclectic, Persian, African and Middle Eastern-influenced dishes and a lot of personality in its in-store café 'Snackistan'. / SE15 5DT; www.forataste ofpersia.co.uk; @PersiainPeckham; 9 pm.

Pescatori W1   £75   2 4 3
57 Charlotte St   020 7580 3289   2–1C
Especially by the standards of West End Italians, this traditional-ish, fish-focussed Fitzrovian is a favourite for a good number of fans, inspiring consistent feedback across the board. / W1T 4PD; www.pescatori.co.uk; 10.30 pm; closed Sat L & Sun; set weekday L £49 (FP).

The Petersham WC2   NEW
Floral Court, off Floral St   020 8940 5230   5–3C
The Boglione family, owners of Richmond's Petersham Nurseries, venture into central London, with this newcomer in the courtyard of the 'Floral Court' new CapCo property development between Floral Street and King Street. The menu is primarily Italian-led and when it's warm you can eat alfresco. They are also opening a deli, and adjoining bar and small plates restaurant, 'La Goccia'. / WC2E 9DJ; petershamnurseries.com; midnight.

Petersham Hotel TW10   £65   3 3 4
Nightingale Lane   020 8939 1084   1–4A
"A window table for lunch is one of the nicest spots in London", at this old-fashioned Richmond hotel, with "incredible views over the Thames", and whose "rather formal" style suits its older clientele. "The food is good by hotel standards, especially the Sunday lunch, but it's advisable to book." / TW10 6UZ; petershamhotel.co.uk/restaurant; @thepetersham; 9.45 pm.

Petersham Nurseries Cafe TW10   £77   2 1 5
Church Lane (signposted 'St Peter's Church')   020 8940 5230   1–4A
"It looks so magical", and there's "genuinely nowhere else like" this "secret-garden-style" venue near Richmond Park – a "truly enchanting" candle-lit greenhouse, within a garden centre – and the fact that "you can take a riverside stroll before or after your meal is heaven!". "On a dull day however, the wobbly tables and chairs, untrained waiters, and ridiculous queues for the toilets make you feel that at these prices, you're being ripped off", especially as when it comes to the ambitious cuisine nowadays, while "the ingredients are interesting, their realisation is only fair". / TW10 7AB; www.petershamnurseries.com; 2 pm, Sat & Sun 3.30 pm; L only, closed Mon; SRA-Food Made Good – 3 stars.

Petit Ma Cuisine TW9 £50 2 2 **3**
8 Station Approach   020 8332 1923   1–3A
This "proper little French bistro" with a "nice local feel" is "tucked away in a side street near Kew Gardens station". Fans still say "they really know their way around a cassoulet" or "wonderful boudin blanc", but ratings have dipped due to views that – since they moved in 2016 to the smaller neighbouring site – "prices have moved up, while the quality has gone down". / TW9 3QB; www.macuisinebistrot.co.uk; 10 pm, Fri & Sat 10.30 pm; No Amex; set weekday L £32 (FP).

Petit Pois Bistro N1 £53 **3 3** 2
9 Hoxton Square   020 7613 3689   13–1B
"Small and quite crowded, but friendly" year-old bistro (with terrace) in hip Hoxton Square offering a "short menu, well cooked to order" of "decent Gallic fare" (steak-frites, etc). / N1 6NU; www.petitpoisbistro.com; @petitpoisbistro; 10.30 pm, Sun 9 pm.

The Petite Coree NW6 £41 **4 4** 2
98 West End Lane   020 7624 9209   1–1B
'Modern bistro with a Korean twist' characterises the distinctive cuisine at this husband-and-wife outfit in West Hampstead, and results in "delicious and interesting dishes" and at "very low prices" too. Top Tip – the evening set menu (not Friday or Saturday) is brilliant value. / NW6 2LU; www.thepetitecoree.com; @thepetitecoree; 9.30 pm; booking max 6 may apply.

La Petite Maison W1 £90 **4** 3 3
54 Brook's Mews   020 7495 4774   3–2B
"Stunning French (but not stereotypically French) sharing plates" that really "taste of their ingredients" help induce a happy, if "noisy" buzz at this little piece of the Côte d'Azur, just around the corner from Claridges. "It caters to a Mayfair clientele, who obviously love it (and can afford it)", and "whilst it's ridiculously expensive, it's always enjoyable". / W1K 4EG; www.lpmlondon.co.uk; @lpmlondon; 10.45 pm, Sun 9.45 pm.

Pétrus SW1 £118 **3 3** 2
1 Kinnerton St   020 7592 1609   6–1D
Gordon Ramsay's "luxurious and well-spaced" Belgravian – whose centrepiece is a circular, glass-walled wine vault – is arguably his best London restaurant nowadays, winning consistent praise for its "faultless" cuisine and "efficient but unobtrusive" service. "The dining room is very pleasant and comfortable – just not quite as spectacular as some others at this price level". Top Tip – "excellent lunch deal". / SW1X 8EA; www.gordonramsayrestaurants.com; @petrus; 10 pm; closed Sun; No trainers; set weekday L £65 (FP).

Peyote W1 £82 **3 3** 2
13 Cork St   020 7409 1300   4–4A
Arjun Waney's fashionably located Latino, just off Bond Street; it continues to attract surprisingly little feedback to the effect that although the quality is OK "the menu needs an overhaul – it needs to figure out if it's a restaurant or a club". / W1S 3NS; www.peyoterestaurant.com; @peyotelondon; 1 am, Fri & Sat 2 am; closed Sat L & Sun; set weekday L & pre-theatre £47 (FP).

Peyotito W11 £56 2 2 2
31 Kensington Park Rd   020 7043 1400   7–1A
Uneven reviews for this Mexican yearling in Notting Hill, featuring mezcal cocktails and sharing plates: all reports find something to praise and something to criticise (different in each case). / W11 2EU; www.peyotitorestaurant.com; @peyotitolondon; midnight, Fri & Sat 1 am, Sun 10.30 pm.

PF Chang's Asian Table WC2 NEW
10 Great Newport St   01923 555161   5–3B
Already a household name in the States, this pan-Asian powerhouse brings its popular dumplings and Dynamite shrimp to the heart of the West End. Ex-Nobu chef Deepak Kotian heads up the kitchen. / WC2H 7JA; www.pfchangs.co.uk; @PFChangs.

Pham Sushi EC1   £39   4 3 2
159 Whitecross St   020 7251 6336   13–2A
"Excellent value and authenticity" make this Japanese duo near the Barbican and Silicon Roundabout well worth knowing about. "It's not about the ambience, but the sushi and fresh sashimi remain really good quality." / EC1Y 8JL; www.phamsushi.com; @phamsushi; 10 pm; closed Sat L & Sun.

Pharmacy 2,
Newport Street Gallery SE11   £62   2 3 3
Newport St   020 3141 9333   2–4D
Mark Hix's wilfully "sterile" dining room in Damien Hirst's Vauxhall art gallery splits reporters – sometimes in the same sentence! "Tiny portions make for a disappointing and overpriced experience – but the food is lovely and the room is amazing" is one example. Another is: "this could be a disastrous concept, but in fact it seems to work quite well". / SE11 6AJ; www.pharmacyrestaurant.com; @Ph2restaurant; midnight, Sun 6 pm; credit card required to book.

Pho   £38   2 2 2
"Very passable pho" and other "generous and healthy dishes" maintain the appeal of these Vietnamese street-food outlets, which, even if they're "not as good as they were" when the chain was younger, are still "OK as a pit stop". / www.phocafe.co.uk; 10 pm-11pm, Sun 6.30 pm-10 pm; EC1 closed Sat L & Sun; no booking.

Pho & Bun W1   £46   4 3 2
76 Shaftesbury Ave   020 7287 3528   5–3A
"Fabulous pho" or Vietnamese steamed bun burgers make for a "great, cheap 'n' cheerful snack" at this simple café in the heart of Theatreland. / W1D 6ND; vieteat.co.uk/pho-bun; @phoandbun; 10.30 pm, Sat 11 pm, Sun 9.30 pm; booking max 8 may apply.

Phoenix Palace NW1   £56   3 2 2
5-9 Glentworth St   020 7486 3515   2–1A
This well-established Cantonese near Baker Street is something of a dim sum Mecca, and although it's arguably "rather dated" and has seen "erratic swings in quality over the years", it wins nothing but praise this year for "food that's always good". "Brusque" service "is a reminder you're in a Chinese venue" but "staff are patient with kids". / NW1 5PG; www.phoenixpalace.co.uk; 11.30 pm, Sun 10.30 pm.

Picture   £67   3 3 2
110 Great Portland St, W1   020 7637 7892   2–1B
19 New Cavendish St, W1   020 7935 0058   2–1A
"Together with The Portland, this group has made local dining worthwhile!" – So say Fitzrovia foodies, who applaud the "brilliant selection of small plates, good choice of wine and very friendly service" at these low-key but accomplished ventures, near Broadcasting House and in Marylebone. Even supporters concede that they are "a bit pricey" however, and that "the stripped back interiors and rather hard chairs will not be to everyone's taste". / 10.30 pm; closed Sun.

Pidgin E8 £66 **5 4 3**
52 Wilton Way 020 7254 8311 14–1B
*"What a fascinating dining experience – if it wasn't so hyped, I would
probably have enjoyed it even more!" This "tiny" Hackney yearling has
instantly won gigantic acclaim for "heavenly, delicate and inventive" cuisine,
bringing a "substantial Asian influence onto modern British ideas". "Space
is very tight" and though "you get to know your fellow diners intimately" the
end result seems "so special, cosy and romantic" to most reporters –
"it's like eating in your friend's front room, it just turns out your friend is a
top chef!". Founding chef Elizabeth Allen moved on in February 2017
to open Shibui (see also), but early reports say "nothing has been lost from
the cooking here during the change". See also Magpie. / E8 1BG;
www.pidginlondon.com; @PidginLondon; 11 pm; closed Mon & Tue,
Wed & Thu D only, Fri-Sun L & D.*

Piebury Corner £20 **3 4 3**
3 Caledonian Rd, N1 020 7700 5441 9–3C **NEW**
209-211 Holloway Rd, N7 020 7700 5441 9–2D
*"Food and service really warm the cockles of your heart!", at this popular
'pie deli' near The Emirates, providing well-stuffed pies (with weird, Arsenal-
related names) and craft beers to Gunners fans and foodies alike. The
formula has now also spread to King's Cross with a slightly grander, but still
bare-brick 'n' tiles spin-off. / www.pieburycorner.com; N7 9 pm, N1 11 pm;
N7 closed Mon-Wed & Sun D, N1 closed Sun D.*

Pied à Terre W1 £112 **4 4 3**
34 Charlotte St 020 7636 1178 2–1C
*"David Moore runs a tight ship to maintain standards" and his
"comfortable" Fitzrovia townhouse represents "perfection" for its many fans
on account of its "unfailingly impressive" cuisine, "awesome" wines,
and "good but not overly solicitous service". There's an undertow on ratings
however, from sceptics who are slightly less wowed – they say "it's not a bad
place, but for these prices perhaps a bit, well... beige". The griping is from
a small minority though – overall this remains one of London's highest-
achieving foodie temples. (There has been a lot of change afoot here post-
survey. Popular sommelier and co-owner Mathieu Germond announced
he was to leave to establish nearby Noize, and in September 2017 chef
Andy McFadden moved on, with Asimakis Chaniotis moving up within the
ranks.) / W1T 2NH; www.pied-a-terre.co.uk; @PiedaTerreUK; 10.45 pm; closed
Sat L & Sun; booking max 7 may apply; set weekday L £64 (FP), set pre-theatre
£66 (FP).*

Pig & Butcher N1 £52 **4 5 4**
80 Liverpool Rd 020 7226 8304 9–3D
*"Mighty meaty matey!" – this "lovely spacious and airy Islington gastropub
on the corner of one of the area's nicest streets" is "brilliant for carnivores",
serving "generous portions of lovingly sourced meat" (which they butcher on-
site), but "veggie options are superb" too, and there's a good selection
of craft beer. Top Tip – "it's worth it just for the beef dripping and bread!"
/ N1 0QD; www.thepigandbutcher.co.uk; @pigandbutcher; 10 pm, Sun 9 pm;
Mon-Fri D only, Fri-Sun open L & D.*

Pilpel £11 **4 3 2**
38 Brushfield Street, London, E1 020 7247 0146 13–2B
60 Alie St, E1 0207 952 2139 10–2D **NEW**
Old Spitalfields Mkt, E1 020 7375 2282 13–2B
146 Fleet St, EC4 020 7583 2030 10–2A
Paternoster Sq, EC4 020 7248 9281 10–2B
*"Brilliantly fresh and zingy falafel wraps and salads are the point" at these
"bright and busy" Middle Eastern cafés, whose "efficient and friendly staff
seem to really want you to enjoy the food". / www.pilpel.co.uk; EC4 4 pm;
E1 6 pm; Brushfield St & Alie St 9pm, Fri 4pm, Sun 6pm; Paternoster Sq 9 pm,
Fri 4 pm; EC4 branches closed Sat & Sun; no booking.*

Pique Nique SE1 £58
32 Tanner St 020 7403 9549 10–4D
This proper, French rotisserie from the backers of Bermondsey's little Parisian bistro Casse-Croute opened just as the survey concluded in May 2017. Just across the road from its sister restaurant, this 40-seater café in Tanner Street Park revolves around spit-roast chicken (geddit), specialising in designer breed Poulet de Bresse. / SE1 3LD; pique-nique.co.uk; @piquenique32.

El Pirata W1 £42 3|3|4
5-6 Down St 020 7491 3810 3–4B
"Classic tapas served well" and at "extremely reasonable prices for the location" make this busy old Hispanic haunt a good option in Mayfair, especially for lunch. There's a "great atmosphere" and "lovely waiters". Top Tip – "try to get a table upstairs". / W1J 7AQ; www.elpirata.co.uk; @elpirataw1; 11.30 pm; closed Sat L & Sun.

Pisqu W1 NEW £54
23 Rathbone Place 020 7436 6123 5–1A
"A small, casual newcomer near Charlotte Street" dedicated to Peruvian cuisine – limited feedback so far, but one early report endorses its "unique and excellent food and cocktails!" / W1T 1HZ; www.pisqulondon.com; @PisquLondon; set weekday L & pre-theatre £32 (FP).

Pitt Cue Co EC2 £58 4|3|3
1 The Ave, Devonshire Sq 020 7324 7770 10–2D
Designed "for hearty appetites", Tom Adams's American-style BBQ remains a big hit in its "newish, large and glamorous" premises near Liverpool Street (although "everyone in suits at lunchtime doesn't feel 100% right for this sort of food"). The menu is "unusual but worth grappling with" and excels through "the quality of the ingredients and the subtle simplicity of the cooking, which delivers special results". / EC2; www.pittcue.co.uk; @PittCueCo; 10.30 pm.

Pizarro SE1 £60 3|3|3
194 Bermondsey St 020 7256 5333 10–4D
"In the creative quarter that is Bermondsey St", Sr. P's busy sibling to his nearby José "is a far cry from the tapas bar down the road, with more substantial dishes and a very modern design". On most accounts it delivers "extremely flavoursome Spanish dishes to a very high level", but a hint of resistance is creeping into its prices and a perceived "sense of entitlement, as it's so busy and popular". Top Tip – "The Presa Iberica was superb and so tender". / SE1 3TQ; www.josepizarro.com; @Jose_Pizarro; 10.45 pm, Sun 9.45 pm.

Pizza East £52 3|2|4
310 Portobello Rd, W10 020 8969 4500 7–1A
79 Highgate Rd, NW5 020 3310 2000 9–1B
56 Shoreditch High St, E1 020 7729 1888 13–1B
"If you can tolerate the noise and the hipsters" (particularly at the "cavernous and noisy" Shoreditch original), these "slick" Soho House-owned haunts provide "decent pizza" with "interesting toppings and flavours" and "have a good vibe as well". / www.pizzaeast.com; E1 midnight, .

Pizza Metro Pizza £40 3|3|3
147-149 Notting Hill Gate, W11 020 7727 8877 7–2B
64 Battersea Rise, SW11 020 7228 3812 11–2C
There's "always a great night out" at this Battersea Neapolitan (now with a Notting Hill sibling), which pioneered rectangular pizza in London, selling it 'al metro'. Recommended for groups, "it's fun having a whole metre-long pizza to share". / pizzametropizza.com/battersea/; 11 pm, Fri & Sat midnight.

Pizza Pilgrims £37 🄸🄸🄸

102 Berwick St, W1   0778 066 7258   4–1D
11-12 Dean St, W1   020 7287 8964   4–1D
Kingly Ct, Carnaby St, W1   020 7287 2200   4–2B
23 Garrick St, WC2   020 3019 1881   5–3C
12 Hertsmere Rd, E14   020 3019 8020   12–1C NEW
136 Shoreditch High St, E1   020 3019 7620   13–1B NEW
15 Exmouth Mkt, EC1   020 7287 8964   10–1A
8 Brown's Buildings, Saint Mary Axe, EC3   no tel   10–2D NEW
"Believe the hype!" – "If you have a craving for pizza", the Elliot brothers'
"no-nonsense" pit stops are some of the capital's best antidotes: "the menu
is simple but they use top quality ingredients" and "what a hit – YUM!"
/ pizzapilgrims.co.uk; 10.30pm, Sun 9.30 pm; WC2 11 pm, Sun 10 pm;
Dean St booking: min 8.

PizzaExpress £46 🄸🄸🄸

For the first 20 years of this guide, this famous pizza chain with its
"surprisingly distinctive branches" was – with tedious regularity –
the survey's most mentioned group: constantly re-inventing itself to remain
everyone's favourite standby, especially with kids in tow. Competition
is sharper nowadays however, and since its ownership changed a couple
of years ago (to Hony Capital) ratings and the volume of feedback have
slipped well below their historical average. Yes, it is still much-mentioned,
and still "as reliable as ever" to armies of loyal supporters, but harsher
critics "are stunned by the complacency and staleness of the brand: even
the ubiquitous, good value voucher deals are starting to lose their shine".
/ www.pizzaexpress.co.uk; 11.30 pm - midnight; most City branches closed all or part
of weekend; no booking at most branches.

Pizzastorm SW18 NEW £27 🄸🄸🄸

Southside Shopping Centre, 4 Garratt Lane   020 8877 0697   11–2B
"First pizza choice for anyone who's fussy about their toppings" – you select
pick 'n' mix style at this efficient shopping centre fast-food outlet: "bases are
thin and crispy, the toppings super fresh and everything is done to order".
/ SW18 4TF; www.pizzastorm.pizza; @PizzaStormUK; 10 pm, Thu-Sat 11 pm,
Sun 9 pm.

Pizzeria Pappagone N4 £35 🄸🄸🄸

131 Stroud Green Rd   020 7263 2114   9–1D
This "traditional Italian trattoria" in Finsbury Park "is a proper
neighbourhood favourite". Locals love "the lively atmosphere, reliable food
from a vast menu, and a nice mixed crowd". "Super-speedy service makes
it an easy family choice" – despite having no kids' menu, they're happy
to make half-portions or plain pizzas". / N4 3PX; www.pizzeriapappagone.co.uk;
@pizza_pappagone; midnight.

Pizzeria Rustica TW9 £40 🄸🄸🄸

32 The Quadrant   020 8332 6262   1–4A
"It may look cheap 'n' cheerful, but the pizzas are very good" at this
convenient outlet in Richmond town centre, next to the station. / TW9 1DN;
www.pizzeriarustica.co.uk; @RusticaPizzeria; 11 pm, Sun 10 pm; No Amex.

Pizzicotto W8 £50 🄸🄸🄸

267 Kensington High St   020 7602 6777   6–1A
Directly opposite the new Design Museum in Kensington High Street,
this more casual offshoot of the venerable, family-run Il Portico five doors
away is two years old. The "fantastic young and enthusiastic staff" "exude
Italian hospitality", and there's a "short but interesting menu", majoring
in "excellent wood-fired pizza". / W8 6NA; www.pizzicotto.co.uk; @pizzicottow8;
10.30 pm, Sun 9.30 pm.

Plaquemine Lock N1 NEW
139 Graham St   020 7688 1488   9–3D
Despite the very English-looking exterior overlooking Regent's Canal, Jacob Kenedy's (Bocca di Lupo, Gelupo) pub-newcomer, which opened in June 2017, aims to serve up authentic Cajun and Creole dishes in a fairly sparse, jazzily muralled interior; very encouraging press reviews so far. / N1 8LB; plaqlock.com.

Plateau E14   £73
4th Floor, Canada Sq   020 7715 7100   12–1C
Spectacular cityscape views have always established this D&D London operation as one of the "go-to business lunch venues in Canary Wharf". It still take occasional knocks for being "overpriced", but Chef Jeremy Trehout's "great French cooking" won consistent praise this year. / E14 5ER; www.plateau-restaurant.co.uk; @plateaulondon; 10.30 pm; closed Sat L & Sun.

Platform1 SE22   £49
71 Lordship Lane   020 3609 2050   1–4D
"A great little (read: very tiny) joint in East Dulwich run by two amazing women who give exceptional, attentive and tailored service, and whose main focus is curating a small wine list that is altogether intriguing, exotic and excellent. The kitchen is manned by creative chefs who do a few months at a time, so the menu is always fresh." / SE22 8EP; www.platform1.london; @Platform_1ldn; 10.30 pm; D only, closed Sun-Wed.

Plot SW17 NEW   £39
Broadway Market, Tooting High St   020 8767 2639   11–2C
"You can eat at narrow tables with benches or perched at the bar" at this 'British Kitchen' in Tooting's Broadway Market. "Market life goes on around you, which is amusing if not particularly comfortable" – the key draw is the consistently well-rated selection of small plates. / SW17 0RL; plotkitchen.com; @plot_kitchen.

The Plough SW14   £44
42 Christ Church Rd   020 8876 7833   11–2A
"Always busy with good vibes" – this attractive hostelry (with large terrace) occupies a picturesque corner of East Sheen and is perfect after a yomp with your dog through neighbouring Richmond Park. "It does many traditional pub staples, as well as 'smarter' dishes, and the food is restaurant quality." / SW14; www.theplough.com; 9.30 pm, Fri & Sat 10 pm, Sun 9 pm; 12 – 3pm and 6.30pm – 9.30pm, Fri - Sat - 12 – 5pm and 6.30pm – 10pm, Sun - 12 – 9pm.

Plum + Spilt Milk,
Great Northern Hotel N1   £73
King's Cross St Pancras Station, Pancras Rd   020 3388 0818   9–3C
Right by King's Cross, this "well-located" hotel brasserie (named for the livery of the 'Flying Scotsman') is attractively "slightly out-of-the-ordinary" and has a good atmosphere. At best it's a "professional" spot with "decent food", but inevitably "it trades on its location" a bit: it can seem "reasonable but pricey" or merely "pleasant enough". / N1C 4TB; plumandspiltmilk.com; @PlumSpiltMilk; 11 pm, Sun 10 pm.

POLLEN STREET SOCIAL W1   £101
8-10 Pollen St   020 7290 7600   3–2C
"Slick" and "always buzzing" – Jason Atherton's first Mayfair building block of his expanding restaurant empire mixes "serious" cuisine ("exquisitely presented dishes on a different level to most you encounter") with a "relaxing but smart" atmosphere that lives up to its 'Social' branding. Mind you, even fans note that "it can be very expensive", but – on most accounts the pain is "worth it for that special occasion". / W1S 1NQ; www.pollenstreetsocial.com; @PollenStSocial; 10.30 pm; closed Sun; booking max 7 may apply; set weekday L £66 (FP).

Polpetto W1 £48 3 3 3
11 Berwick St   020 7439 8627   4–2D
Surprisingly limited feedback this year for Russell Norman's little heart-of-
Soho 'bacaro' behind what used to be called Raymond's Revue Bar, although
such as there is continues to laud its "delicious small plates". / W1F 0PL;
www.polpetto.co.uk; @polpettoW1; 11 pm, Sun 10.30 pm; booking L only.

Polpo £50 2 2 2
41 Beak St, W1   020 7734 4479   4–2B
142 Shaftesbury Ave, WC2   020 7836 3119   5–2B
6 Maiden Ln, WC2   020 7836 8448   5–3D
Duke Of York Sq, SW3   020 7730 8900   6–2D
126-128 Notting Hill Gate, W11   020 7229 3283   7–2B
2-3 Cowcross St, EC1   020 7250 0034   10–1A
"Delicious Venetian-style tapas" is still applauded by the big fanclub
of Russell Norman's "rammed-and-noisy or buzzy (you take your pick)"
cicchetti cafés, which can still offer "a fun time" without breaking the bank.
However there's also a significant sceptical minority, who nowadays view
their performance as "a bit tired" or even "oh-so-disappointing".
/ www.polpo.co.uk; 10 pm-11.30 pm, EC1 Sun 4 pm; EC1 closed D Sun; no bookings.

Pomaio E1 NEW £42 3 4 3
224 Brick Lane   020 3222 0031   13–2C
Bravissimo! Named after their winery Podere di Pomaio in Arezzo, brothers
Marco & Iacopo Rossi opened this Brick Lane enoteca in late 2016.
Feedback is thin but effusive regarding its "top wine list – from new wave
to Tuscan classics – a real find at great prices too", soaked up with
authentic Tuscan tapas. / E1 6SA; www.enotecapomaio.com; @pomaiobrickln;
11 pm, Fri midnight, Sun 7 pm; closed Mon & Sun D.

Pomona's W2 NEW £68 3 3 3
47 Hereford Rd   020 7229 1503   7–1B
"Bright LA-style newcomer" occupying a converted Notting Hill pub once
known as The Commander, complete with garden. The zingy fare 'with an
emphasis on fresh veg', grains and charcoal grills is "surprisingly good".
/ W2 5AH; www.pomonas.co.uk; @PomonasLondon; 10 pm, Fri & Sat 10.30 pm,
Sun 9 pm.

Le Pont de la Tour SE1 £78 2 2 3
36d Shad Thames   020 7403 8403   10–4D
"It's wonderful if you get a table outside in good weather" at this smart
D&D London Thames-sider, named for its superb views of Tower Bridge.
When it was first opened by Sir Terence Conran it was the hottest ticket
in town, but – despite a major refurb last year – only a dwindling number
of fans still see it as "a special place for special occasions", and increasingly
it is viewed as "overpriced and coasting along on its past reputation".
/ SE1 2YE; www.lepontdelatour.co.uk; @lepontdelatour; 10.30 pm, Sun 9.30 pm;
No trainers.

Pop Brixton SW9 £14 5 4 3
49 Brixton Station Rd   07725 230995   11–1D
Over 50 traders help transform this formerly disused plot in Brixton into
a funky community space with numerous street-food options (a partnership
with Lambeth Council currently planned to run till August 2018). Survey
favourites include Baba G's Bhangra Burger ("a well thought out Indian take
on burgers", with "phenomenal mango chips and lamb jalfrezi burger"),
Duck Duck Goose ("simple but excellent duck, rice and greens")…
"if nothing else, come and marvel at how 3 not-small blokes manage in a
kitchen that size in a sea container"), Donostia Social Club and Koi Ramen.
See also Smoke & Salt. / SW9 8PQ; www.popbrixton.org; 10 pm.

Popeseye £51 3 2 2

108 Blythe Rd, W14   020 7610 4578   8–1C
36 Highgate Hill, N19   020 3601 3830   9–1B
277 Upper Richmond Rd, SW15   020 8788 7733   11–2A

"You can keep your Hawksmoors and Goodmans: this is the real deal for me": so say fans of this "time-warp" Olympia steak-bistro (the 1994 original branch), whose Highgate spin-off (the newest, opened in 2015), also inspires a fair amount of (more up-and-down) feedback. All deliver a "no pretensions" formula combining a short selection of cuts supported by a well-chosen list of affordable reds. / www.popeseye.com; W14 11.30 pm; SW15 11 pm; N19 10.30 pm, Sun 9 pm; W14 & SW15 closed Sun; N19 closed Mon.

Popolo EC2 NEW £52 5 4 3

26 Rivington St   020 7729 4299   13–1B

"Precious moments" are created by Jonathan Lawson's superb small plates ("pasta is especially wonderful") at this artfully worn-looking and laid back newcomer in Shoreditch (where else?), comprising a compact ground floor bar area, and "nice but slightly cramped" upstairs room. / EC2A 3DU; popoloshoreditch.com; @popolo_EC2; no booking.

Poppies £40 3 2 3

59 Old Compton St, W1   020 7482 2977   4–2D
30 Hawley Cr, NW1   020 7267 0440   9–2B
6-8 Hanbury St, E1   020 7247 0892   13–2C

"Excellent, fresh-cooked fish 'n' chips" is served with lashings of nostalgia, provided by the post-war memorabilia on the walls at these "great fun" venues in Spitalfields, Camden Town and Soho. East Ender Pat "Pops" Newland, the founder, entered the trade aged 11 in 1952, and he has created "a great vibe". / 11 pm, Fri & Sat 11.30 pm, Sun 10.30 pm.

La Porchetta Pizzeria £41 2 3 2

33 Boswell St, WC1   020 7242 2434   2–1D
141-142 Upper St, N1   020 7288 2488   9–2D
147 Stroud Green Rd, N4   020 7281 2892   9–1D
74-77 Chalk Farm Rd, NW1   020 7267 6822   9–2B
84-86 Rosebery Ave, EC1   020 7837 6060   10–1A

After 27 years and with five branches across north London, these old school, family-owned pizza cafés have built a fan base on "large and delicious portions" and "exceptionally family-friendly" staff. "In an area now drowning in pizzerias, Porchetta is still ace!" / www.laporchetta.net; N1, NW1 & EC1 11pm, Fri & Sat midnight, Sun 10 pm; N4 11 pm, Sun 10 pm; WC1 11 pm, Fri midnight; WC1 closed Sat & Sun; NW1, N1 & N4 closed Mon-Fri L; EC1 closed Sat L; no Amex.

La Porte des Indes W1 £75 3 2 4

32 Bryanston St   020 7224 0055   2–2A

Rather "a fascinating place" – this Tardis-like, converted underground Edwardian ballroom near Marble Arch serves "fresh and original, French influenced" Indian cuisine in a "tropical and lush", foliage-filled interior. At times "service could be sharper" though, and even many fans would concede that eating here costs a "lotta loot". / W1H 7EG; www.laportedesindes.com/london/; @LaPorteDesIndes; 11.30 pm, Sun 10.30 pm; No Amex; set weekday L £45 (FP).

Il Portico W8 £60 3 5 4

277 Kensington High St   020 7602 6262   8–1D

"Very few restaurants can claim the staying power" of this "busy and noisy" family-run trattoria in Kensington. Its "honest", "traditional" Italian dishes come in "huge portions", "but it's the wonderful and caring service that is really outstanding". / W8 6NA; www.ilportico.co.uk; 11 pm; closed Sun.

Portland W1 £84 **4 4 3**

113 Great Portland St   020 7436 3261   2–1B

"An unpretentious Michelin winner" – this Fitzrovia two-year-old offers "modern, informal dining at its very best" and "although it looks a little sparse from the outside, inside the welcome is warm". "Polite and eloquent" staff offer dishes "combining creativity with attention to detail, plus brilliantly chosen wines" ("ask for the specials list for some well priced fun"). "Success has bred a bit more cockiness with the pricing" however, so it's no longer quite the ace bargain it debuted as. / W1W 6QQ; www.portlandrestaurant.co.uk; 9.45 pm; closed Sun.

Portobello Ristorante Pizzeria W11 £52 **3 4 4**

7 Ladbroke Rd   020 7221 1373   7–2B

"Very friendly, and full of Italians" – this "good value" neighbourhood spot with an outside terrace, just off Notting Hill Gate, remains "on good form", serving more than just pizza and pasta. "A favourite with families", it can be "very noisy". / W11 3PA; www.portobellolondon.co.uk; 10 pm, Fri & Sat 11 pm, Sun 10 pm.

The Portrait,
National Portrait Gallery WC2 £67 **2 2 3**

St Martin's Place   020 7306 0055   5–4B

"Views over the rooftops lend a very spacy and special ambience" to this top-floor dining room above the gallery and "justify the trip alone". "You pay a premium" for "mainstream" cooking, but it's "not bad" and "great for guests from out of town". / WC2H 0HE; www.npg.org.uk/visit/shop-eat-drink/restaurant.php; @NPGLondon; 8.30 pm; Sun-Wed closed D; set pre theatre £44 (FP).

Potli W6 £43 **4 4 3**

319-321 King St   020 8741 4328   8–2B

"The menu changes regularly and is really worth exploring" at this "fun and busy Indian" on the 'restaurant row' near Ravenscourt Park – its "well judged" and "unusual" street food dishes deliver "vibrant" tastes that fans find "quite unbelievable". "I've taken at least 50 friends there in the last 12 months and all have returned to eat there!". Top Menu Tip – "black daal that's cooked for 24 hours". / W6 9NH; www.potli.co.uk; @Potlirestaurant; 10.15 pm, Fri & Sat 10:30 pm, Sun 10 pm; booking essential.

La Poule au Pot SW1 £62 **2 2 5**

231 Ebury St   020 7730 7763   6–2D

"The deliciously dark and candle-lit interior is romance personified", at this "sensual French delight" in Pimlico, whose intimate nooks and crannies have made it a famed trysting spot for as long as anyone can remember. The food "has come off the boil" in recent times: "just in case you notice it, it's old fashioned, bistro fare, and not particularly cheap, but no-one cares". Service meanwhile is very Gallic – "they respond more favourably to Francophones!" Top Tip – "fab outside space in summer". / SW1W 8UT; www.pouleaupot.co.uk; 10 pm.

Prawn on the Lawn N1 £58 **4 4 3**

292-294 St Paul's Rd   020 3302 8668   9–2D

This "small but perfectly formed" Highbury Corner outfit "can't make up its mind whether it's a fish shop, wine bar or restaurant". But "don't be put off" – the tapas-style fish and platters of Cornish crab, lobster and fruits de mer on ice are "delicious, fresh and moreish". / N1 2LY; prawnonthelawn.com; @PrawnOnTheLawn; 11 pm; closed Mon & Sun; No Amex.

Primeur N5 £55 444
116 Petherton Rd   020 7226 5271   1–1C
"Busy" (sometimes "overcrowded") Highbury local that offers "a daily
changing menu with good combinations of well-executed food" and
an "esoteric, if expensive wine list". Sharing plates are selected from
a blackboard: "we ordered everything on the menu… and enjoyed it all!"
/ N5 2RT; www.primeurN5.co.uk; @Primeurs1; 10.30 pm, Sun 5 pm; closed Mon,
Tue L, Wed L, Thu L & Sun D; booking max 7 may apply.

Princess of Shoreditch EC2 £55 322
76 Paul St   020 7729 9270   13–1B
One of the first gastropubs on the City's Shoreditch border, this place takes
old-timers "back to the early '00s!". What they do, "they do well", whether
you're eating in the bar or on the upstairs mezzanine. / EC2A 4NE;
www.theprincessofshoreditch.com; @princessofs; 10.30 pm, Sun 9 pm; No Amex;
booking D only.

Princi W1 £37 323
135 Wardour St   020 7478 8888   4–1D
Smart Soho outlet of a Milanese bakery, whose self-service and restaurant-
service areas both get "extremely busy". Breakfast/brunch is "joy", at other
times pizza is more to the fore. "Grab a seat by the window, and it's great
for people-watching". / W1F 0UT; www.princi.com; 11 pm, Sun 10 pm; no booking.

Prix Fixe W1 £45 332
39 Dean St   020 7734 5976   5–2A
"For the price, it is hard to find anything better in central London" than this
"always reliable" venue "in the heart of Soho", whose "classic French bistro
dishes" represent "extraordinarily good value". / W1D 4PU; www.prixfixe.net;
@prixfixelondon; 11.30 pm.

The Promenade at The Dorchester W1 £124 244
The Dorchester Hotel, 53 Park Lane   020 7629 8888   3–3A
"For a fantastic afternoon tea in plush surroundings", it's worth trying the
swagged, padded and cushioned environs of this opulent Mayfair hotel
lounge, which provides "superb service and an endless amount
of sandwiches and sweet treats!" / W1K 1QA;
www.dorchestercollection.com/en/london/the-dorchester/restaurant-bars/afternoon-tea;
@TheDorchester; 10.30 pm; No shorts.

Provender E11 £42 344
17 High St   020 8530 3050   1–1D
"Yes, it is worth the trek!", say fans of this latest venture from veteran
restaurateur Max Renzland – an "authentic" bistro, whose "old style French
cuisine" makes it "a safe and happy choice for those out and about
in Wanstead and Snaresbrook". Top Tip – "good value set menu". / E11 2AA;
www.provenderlondon.co.uk; @ProvenderBistro; 10 pm, Fri & Sat 10.30 pm,
Sun 9 pm; booking max 10 may apply.

The Providores and Tapa Room W1 £73 432
109 Marylebone High St   020 7935 6175   2–1A
"The menu knocks your socks off!" – "Peter Gordon continues to excel",
at the renowned Kiwi chef's Pacific fusion venue in Marylebone; still serving
"beautiful, inventive and original dishes" well into its second decade,
with marks for its food riding higher than ever. "The tables are too close
together and it's pricey, but I keep going back…" / W1U 4RX;
www.theprovidores.co.uk; @theprovidores; 10 pm, Sun 9.45 pm; SRA-Food Made Good
– 2 stars.

Prufrock Coffee EC1 £13 **3**|**2**|**4**
23-25 Leather Ln 07852 243470 10–2A
"Leading the pack in coffee (and its new stoneground oolong tea is amazing!)" – this caffeine haven near Chancery Lane offers "a great value brunch for a City location, but it's always packed so arrive early". / EC1N 7TE; www.prufrockcoffee.com; @PrufrockCoffee; L only; No Amex.

Pulia SE1 £34 **3**|**4**|**3**
36 Stoney St 020 7407 8766 10–4C
"Really interesting and different Italian food" and "knowledgeable staff" win praise for this "friendly, buzzing and modern" deli/café "on the borders of Borough Market" (the first outside Italy for a Puglian-based group). / SE1 9AD; www.pulia.com; @Puliauk; 10.30 pm, Sun 8.30 pm.

The Punchbowl W1 £61 **3**|**4**|**3**
41 Farm St 020 7493 6841 3–3A
Once owned by film director Guy Ritchie, Madonna's ex, this atmospheric 18th-century Mayfair boozer has dropped out of sight a little since he sold up, but it's a good all-rounder in this pricey 'hood. / W1J 5RP; www.punchbowllondon.com; @ThePunchBowlLDN; 11 pm, Sun 10.30 pm; closed Sun D.

Punjab WC2 £35 **3**|**2**|**3**
80 Neal St 020 7836 9787 5–2C
"Good food at good prices… but then they rush you out"; "especially considering its location", this long-lived Covent Garden curry house avoids (most of) the pitfalls of its tourist trap potential and is resolutely "free of the gimmicks that plague more modern Indians!" / WC2H 9PA; www.punjab.co.uk; 11 pm, Sun 10 pm; booking max 8 may apply.

Pure Indian Cooking SW6 £50 **4**|**3**|**2**
67 Fulham High St 020 7736 2521 11–1B
A "hidden gem" behind a little shopfront north of Putney Bridge – this "slightly austere" three-year-old is a first venture as boss for chef Shilpa Dandekar, who used to work for Raymond Blanc, and her contemporary dishes are consistently "interesting and well presented". / SW6 3JJ; www.pureindiancooking.com; @PureCooking.

QP LDN W1 £102 **3**|**3**|**3**
34 Dover St 020 3096 1444 3–3C
The "subdued and romantic" Mayfair showcase for Amalfitan chef Antonio Mellino's cooking offers a "top dining experience", with "wonderful Italian cuisine" presented by "staff who go the extra mile". It inspires only limited feedback however, perhaps something to do with its not-inconsiderable prices. / W1S 4NG; www.quattropassi.co.uk; @quattropassiuk; 10.30 pm; closed Sun D; set pre theatre £60 (FP).

Quaglino's SW1 £74 **1**|**2**|**3**
16 Bury St 020 7930 6767 3–3D
This vast and "plush" St James's basement – an age-old venue (est 1929) that became an icon of the '90s restaurant boom when it was relaunched by Sir Terence Conran in 1993 – can still seem like a "smashing environment" for an occasion. "It could aim higher in the food department" though – the cuisine is "acceptable but no more" and comes at intimidating prices – and while fans love the music and entertainment, it can be so loud as "to kill the conversation". / SW1Y 6AJ; www.quaglinos-restaurant.co.uk; @quaglinos; 10.30 pm, Fri & Sat 11 pm; closed Sun; No trainers.

The Quality Chop House EC1 £64 **3** **3** **3**
94 Farringdon Rd 020 7278 1452 10–1A
*"If you can tolerate the discomfort" of the "terrible", bum-numbing benches,
the "authentic Victorian wooden booths lend charm" to this restored Grade
II listed 'Working Class Caterer', which in the '90s helped establish the
environs of Exmouth Market as the foodie hotspot it has become. Nowadays
with Shaun Searley at the stoves, it continues in the oft-"excellent" but
sometimes "variable" vein that it has under his predecessors, offering
a meaty menu "clearly influenced by Henderson and St John" and a wine
list "full of interesting gems (some on Coravin)". / EC1R 3EA;
www.thequalitychophouse.com; @QualityChop; 10.30 pm; closed Sun.*

Quantus W4 £56 **4** **5** **3**
38 Devonshire Rd 020 8994 0488 8–2A
*"Passionate and exceptional service from Leo Pacarada and his team" lifts
the experience at this little venture in a Chiswick side street – a "favourite"
amongst its small fan club thanks to its "excellent" Latin-influenced modern
European cooking. / W4 2HD; www.quantus-london.com; 10 pm; closed Mon L,
Tue L & Sun.*

Quartieri NW6 NEW £37 **4** **3** **3**
300 Kilburn High Rd 020 7625 8822 1–2B
*"A great addition to the neighbourhood" – this new, small but stylish Kilburn
pizza-stop is owned by Neapolitans and it shows: despite the odd report
that it was "shambolic in its early days", all agree that "the pizza
is amazing". / NW6 2DB; www.quartieri.co.uk; @quartierilondon; 11 pm.*

Le Querce SE23 £42 **4** **4** **3**
66-68 Brockley Rise 020 8690 3761 1–4D
*"Customers are welcomed like old friends" at this family-run neighbourhood
Italian in Brockley, which is "only improved by being Sardinian, with great
specials, fish and burrata". (For years, it won some of southeast London's
highest ratings – nowadays its scores are very respectable but not quite
as earth shattering.) / SE23 1LN; www.lequerce.co.uk; 9.30 pm, Sun 8.15 pm;
closed Mon & Tue L.*

Quilon SW1 £71 **5** **4** **3**
41 Buckingham Gate 020 7821 1899 2–4B
*Sriram Aylur's "glorious, creative, original take on Keralan cuisine, with great
integrity to its origins, but enough latitude to feel very unusual and special"
has long established Taj Group's luxurious venue near Buckingham Palace
as one of London's top subcontinentals ("My Indian colleagues swear by it
when they're in the UK"). Staff "go out of their way to be polite and helpful
too", and the only reservation is that the "spacious" interior can seem "a bit
sterile". / SW1E 6AF; www.quilon.co.uk; @thequilon; 11 pm, Sun 10.30 pm;
SRA-Food Made Good – 2 stars.*

Quirinale SW1 £64 **4** **3** **2**
North Ct, 1 Gt Peter St 020 7222 7080 2–4C
*"Precise and elegant" Italian cuisine, "lovely wine", "exemplary discreet
service" and "a rarity – a quiet interior", make this "airy" ("but dull")
basement a perfect venue for entertaining MPs or senior civil servants from
nearby Westminster; hence "it's great for parliamentarian-spotting".
/ SW1P 3LL; www.quirinale.co.uk; @quirinaleresto; 10.30 pm; closed Sat & Sun.*

Quo Vadis W1 £60 **4** **5** **5**
26-29 Dean St 020 7437 9585 4–1D
*"Benefitting from its reduction in size to accommodate Barrafina's move
from Frith Street, QV is now more intimate" than it was before, and the
ground floor of the Hart Bros' Soho classic also feels even more "relaxed
and convivial", aided by its "sublimely attentive, yet also informal staff".
Appreciation for Jeremy Lee's cuisine has stepped up a notch too –
"sensational British food using the best seasonal produce". / W1D 3LL;
www.quovadissoho.co.uk; @QuoVadisSoho; 11 pm; closed Sun.*

Rabbit SW3 £46 3 3 2
172 King's Rd 020 3750 0172 6–3C

"You squeeze in on wobbly chairs, next to cramped wobbly tables" at the Gladwin brothers (Shed, Nutbourne) quirky Chelsea venture, serving distinctive, farm-to-table British tapas. Critics (more numerous this year) say *"the novelty of eating expensive, tiny bits of food wears off pretty quickly"*, but most reporters still applaud its *"interesting small dishes concept"*. / SW3 4UP; www.rabbit-restaurant.com; @RabbitResto; midnight, Mon 11 pm, Sun 6 pm; closed Mon L & Sun D.

Rabot 1745 SE1 £63 2 2 2
2-4 Bedale St 020 7378 8226 10–4C

"The huge vat of melted chocolate is the big draw" at this *"curious concept"* in Borough Market: *"a cafe styled like a St Lucian cocoa plantation"*. There are cakes for afternoon tea, *"chocolate fusion cuisine"*, and *"a proper bar at night in case you fancy a cocoa-infused beer or gin"*. The only unqualified success, however, is the *"wonderful hot chocolate!"* / SE1 9AL; www.rabot1745.com; @rabot1745; 9.30 pm; closed Mon & Sun.

Radici N1 NEW £61 2 2 3
30 Almeida St 020 7354 4777 9–3D

"Newly rooted near the Almeida Theatre", this rustically-themed, south Italian newcomer – D&D London's replacement for The Almeida (RIP) – has made a tepid debut, despite the much-hyped involvement of Francesco Mazzei, and although its *"competent cooking"* isn't terribly rated, Islingtonians in particular preferred its fairly middling predecessor: *"I really wanted to like this place and I love the chef, but this looks like a chain using a famous name without being prepared to source quality ingredients or cook them with real love"*. End result – *"too expensive for a casual local, but not good enough for a special occasion"*. / N1 1AD; www.radici.uk; @radici_n1.

Ragam W1 £28 4 2 1
57 Cleveland St 020 7636 9098 2–1B

"Spectacularly good South Indian meals" at a *"wonderfully cheap"* price won renewed acclaim this year for this grungy Keralan stalwart, near the Telecom Tower. Especially since its recent makeover it can seem even more *"drab and harshly-lit"*, but on all accounts it's still *"a tremendous recommendation"*. / W1T 4JN; www.ragam.co.uk; 11 pm.

Rail House Café SW1 £60 2 2 2
Sir Simon Milton Sq 020 3906 7950 2–4B

The task of feeding 300-plus diners over two floors of Victoria's new Nova development was never going to be a doddle, and Adam White's year-old venue has yet to make a consistent go of it: there are fans, but too many critics feel *"it doesn't live up to its sibling Riding House Café, on any front"* – *"the food is all over the place, and service is either too keen or just disappears!"* / SW1H 0HW; www.railhouse.cafe; @railhouse_cafe.

Rainforest Café W1 £61 2 3 3
20-24 Shaftesbury Ave 020 7434 3111 4–3D

"I'm a parent get me out of here!... but I admit they cater for large groups including children very well..."; this lavish Piccadilly Circus venue – complete with animatronic animals and indoor rain storms – isn't a foodie choice, but it is a very kid-friendly one. / W1V 7EU; www.therainforestcafe.co.uk; @RainforestCafe; 9.30 pm, Sat 10 pm; credit card required to book.

Rambla W1 NEW
64 Dean St awaiting tel 5–2A

Named for Barcelona's famous restaurant strip, this third opening from Victor 'Encant' Garvey is set to open in October 2017, promising a Catalan menu in a larger (60 cover) space than his openings to date. / W1D 4QG; @ramblasoho.

Randall & Aubin W1 £60 3 3 4

14-16 Brewer St 020 7287 4447 4–2D

"The epitome of a Soho lifestyle" is to be found at this "fun" classic, near The Box Soho, where "great people watching" helps whet the appetite for some "brilliant fruits de mer and fabulous fish", enjoyed while nattering and perched on high bar stools. "Service is warm, friendly and, occasionally, quirky in a good way". "Be prepared to queue but it's worth the wait". / W1F 0SG; www.randallandaubin.com; @randallandaubin; 11 pm, Fri & Sat 11.30 pm, Sun 9.30 pm; booking L only.

Randy's Wing Bar E15 £34 4 3 3

28 East Bay Lane, The Press Centre, Here East, Queen Elizabeth Olympic Park 020 8555 5971 14–1C

Olympic Park outlet doling out a variety of catchily-named burgers and wings with funky flavourings and lashings of fun attitude – limited reports as yet, but all of them positive. / E15 2GW; www.randyswingbar.co.uk; @randyswingbar; 11 pm, Thu-Sat 11.30 pm, Sunday 6 pm; closed Sun D.

Rani N3 £34 4 2 2

7 Long Lane 020 8349 4386/2636 1–1B

The "outstanding buffet" is a decades-old feature and continues to inspire enthusiastic (if limited) feedback for 'London's oldest Gujarati' in Finchley. / N3 2PR; www.raniuk.com; 10.30 pm.

Raoul's Café £44 3 2 3

105-107 Talbot Rd, W11 020 7229 2400 7–1B
13 Clifton Rd, W9 020 7289 7313 9–4A

"Still the best eggs in the world", with "the most amazing deep-yellow yolks", are the signature attraction at these "very busy" brunch hangouts in Maida Vale and Notting Hill. / www.raoulsgourmet.com; W9 10.15 pm, W11 10 pm; booking after 5 pm only.

Rasa £35 3 3 3

6 Dering St, W1 020 7629 1346 3–2B
Holiday Inn Hotel, 1 Kings Cross, WC1 020 7833 9787 9–3D
55 Stoke Newington Church St, N16 020 7249 0344 1–1C
56 Stoke Newington Church St, N16 020 7249 1340 1–1C

"Enough to make a believer of the most ardent meat-eater": these "rather basic" and primarily veggie Keralans are so good, especially the Stoke Newington original, that "it's hard not to overeat". But while they remain "great value" there's a feeling amongst long-term fans that "a little extra would be needed to regain full marks" – "it's still good, but the menu never changes, and doesn't excite me like it did". / www.rasarestaurants.com; N16 & Travancore N16 10.45 pm, Fri & Sat 11.30 pm, W1 11 pm, Sun 9 pm; WC1 closed L, Sun L&D, N16 closed Mon-Fri L, Travancore closed L.

Ravi Shankar NW1 £30 3 2 2

132-135 Drummond St 020 7388 6458 9–4C

"Really tasty food at amazing prices" makes this vegetarian stalwart one of the stars of the Little India curry zone near Euston station. Value is best – and dishes tastiest – at the lunchtime and weekend buffet, "when staff add items from the à la carte menu". The surroundings are definitely "bargain basement". / NW1 2HL; www.ravishankarbhelpoori.com; 10.30 pm.

Red Fort W1 £72 4 3 2

77 Dean St 020 7437 2525 4–1D

"Still excelling after all this time", say fans of this long-established Soho North Indian, whose contemporary looks postdate a fire a few years ago. But while it's consistently well-rated, the volume of feedback it attracts is quite low these days. / W1D 3SH; redfort.co.uk; @redfortlondon; 10.30 pm; closed Sat L & Sun L; No shorts; set pre theatre £45 (FP).

The Red Lion & Sun N6 £52 3|2|3
25 North Rd 020 8340 1780 9–1B

"An unpretentious country pub in a leafy part of London" – Highgate locals say it's *"just what a gastropub should be"*, with *"reasonably priced"* food *"consistent with the character of the environment, but very well cooked"*. / N6; www.theredlionandsun.com; @redlionandsun; 10 pm.

The Red Pepper W9 £50 3|2|2
8 Formosa St 020 7266 2708 9–4A

Cramped café in Maida Vale, consistently well-rated for its wood-fired pizza. / W9 1EE; www.theredpepperrestaurant.co.uk; 10.30 pm, Fri & Sat 11 pm, Sun 10 pm; closed weekday L; No Amex.

Red Rooster EC2 NEW £69
45 Curtain Rd 020 3146 4545 13–1B

Ethiopian-Swedish chef, Marcus Samuelsson brings his southern-soul-food-via-Scandinavia cuisine to the eclectically decorated basement of an oh-so-hip Shoreditch boutique hotel and members club. It opened in mid 2017 – early press feedback is positive. / EC2A 4PJ; www.thecurtain.com; @RoosterHarlem; midnight, Wed 1 am, Thu-Sat 2 am, Sun 5 pm; closed Sun D.

Le Relais de Venise L'Entrecôte £47 3|2|2
120 Marylebone Ln, W1 020 7486 0878 2–1A
50 Dean St, W1 020 3475 4202 5–3A NEW
18-20 Mackenzie Walk, E14 020 3475 3331 12–1C
5 Throgmorton St, EC2 020 7638 6325 10–2C

"You know what you are getting" at this Gallic steakhouse chain whose *"unique formula"* delivers *"excellence through simplicity"* – the only menu option is *"tasty"* steak-frites (with unlimited seconds), garnished with their *"to-die-for secret sauce"*. / www.relaisdevenise.com; 10.45 pm-11 pm, Sun 9 pm-10.30 pm; EC2 closed Sat & Sun; no booking.

Restaurant Ours SW3 £78 1|2|3
264 Brompton Rd 020 7100 2200 6–2C

It's "amusingly eurotrashy" – if you like that kind of thing – but this *"buzzing and vibrant"* South Kensington yearling *"doesn't quite hit the mark"* (and it's no huge surprise that über-chef Tom Sellers decided to move on just a year after its much-hyped launch). True to the form of predecessors on this site, the design-values may be *"inspirational"*, but even fans say *"it's not one to go to on a budget"* and given *"food that doesn't always match up"* it too often seems *"dire"*. / SW3 2AS; www.restaurant-ours.com; @restaurant_ours; midnight, Fri & Sat 1.30 am; closed Mon & Sun.

Reubens W1 £57 2|2|2
79 Baker St 020 7486 0035 2–1A

"Salt beef is still excellent" at this long-running kosher deli-diner in Marylebone, while other dishes vary from merely *"OK"* to *"good"*. *"The downstairs restaurant a bit of a squeeze."* / W1U 6RG; www.reubensrestaurant.co.uk; 10 pm; closed Fri D & Sat; No Amex.

The Rib Man E1 £12 5|4–
Brick Lane, Brick Lane Market no tel 13–2C

"The best rib rolls in London", made by the legendary Mark Gevaux, are *"just extraordinarily good street food"* – and, for aficionados, *"the only reason to go to Brick Lane on a Sunday"*. You'll have to get there early, because his *"perfect"* pulled pork always sells out. The rest of the week, fans make do with one of his trademark condiments, led by Holy F**k hot sauce. *"You cannot fault this guy: he loves what he produces and it shows"*. / E1 6HR; www.theribman.co.uk; @theribman; Cash only; no booking.

Rib Room,
Jumeirah Carlton Tower Hotel SW1 £100
Cadogan Pl   020 7858 7250   6–1D

This luxurious Sloane Street address, long known as a temple to roast beef and steak – will reopen in late 2017 as the new London vehicle for Marlow's 'Hand & Flowers' chef, Tom Kerridge. What we know from the PR so far: it will keep the name, it will evoke the spirit of Knightsbridge in the swinging '60s (groovy baby), and it will aim to be good value (not something the site has achieved hitherto). STOP PRESS: in early October 2017, the deal with Tom Kerridge was called off and the Rib Room re-opened in its existing guise. / SW1X 9PY; www.theribroom.co.uk; @RibRoomSW1; 9.30 pm, Sat 10 pm; set weekday L, dinner & pre-theatre £65 (FP).

Riccardo's SW3 £47   2 2 3
126 Fulham Rd   020 7370 6656   6–3B

A "reliable if not exciting" Chelsea local which offers a "great choice of genuine Italian food and wine in an informal environment". While nowadays it may not seem as notable as it once was, "it provides value for money" in a posh part of town. / SW3 6HU; www.riccardos.it; @ricardoslondon; 11.30 pm, Sun 10.30 pm.

Rick Stein SW14 NEW £67   3 2 5
Tideway Yard, 125 Mortlake High St   020 8878 9462   11–1A

"Little changed in decor since its days as The Depot" (now RIP) – the Stein empire's new (and first) foray into the capital inhabits a well-known neighbourhood spot, near Barnes Bridge, never known for its gastronomy. Sceptics feel that "confused if well-meaning service" is one plus-ça-change reminder of the old days, as is the fact that "you get a substantial bill for what amounts to enthusiastic brasserie fare" but the more positive (and also oft-expressed view) is that it produces "wonderful fish that finally lives up to this terrific riverside location". / SW14 8SN; www.rickstein.com/eat-with-us/barnes; @SteinBarnes; 9.30 pm.

Riding House Café W1 £58   2 2 4
43-51 Great Titchfield St   020 7927 0840   3–1C

"Cool" Fitzrovia haunt, exuding all the right design pheromones, whose "interesting breakfast choices (both healthy and less so)" and "informal vibe" make it "spot on for weekend brunch". Fans do recommend it at other times too, but service is "uneven" and the overall food offering can seem "rather uninspiring". A sibling, Rail House Café, opened in Nova Victoria in early 2017. / W1W 7PQ; www.ridinghousecafe.co.uk; 10.30 pm, Fri & Sat 11 pm, Sun 9.30 pm.

Rigo' SW6 NEW
277 New King's Rd   020 7751 3293   11–1B

New ambitious modern Italian which opened its doors post-survey in Fulham in July 2017; chef Gonzalo Luzarraga and Francesco Ferretti are the owners – Luzarraga trained with Alain DuCasse and has cooked all over the world. / SW6 4RD; rigolondon.com.

The Rising Sun NW7 £58   3 2 3
137 Marsh Ln   020 8959 1357   1–1B

"A local pub in Mill Hill, run by a very friendly Italian family" ("they know all about entertaining children"): sounds a good formula, and, though "sometimes it's too busy for their own good" fans from across north London say it's "definitely a winner", with "very good quality Italian cooking". / NW7 4EY; www.therisingsunmillhill.com; @therisingsunpub; 10 pm, Fri & Sat 11 pm, Sun 8.30 pm; closed Mon L.

Ristorante Frescobaldi W1   £82   3 3 2
15 New Burlington Pl   020 3693 3435   4–2A
*This pricey two-year-old Mayfair Tuscan has yet to make waves, but on
(practically) all accounts is "most enjoyable", with a "nice interior and
friendly service". Its top feature is a wine list reflecting its ownership by a
700-year-old Florentine wine and banking dynasty, for whom this is a
first UK venture. / W1S 5HX; www.frescobaldirestaurants.com; @frescobaldi_uk;
11 pm.*

The Ritz W1   £132   3 4 5
150 Piccadilly   020 7493 8181   3–4C
*"The most beautiful dining room on the planet" – this "stunning" Louis XVI
chamber is "a wonderful place for a celebratory experience", especially
a romantic one. The "glorious classical cuisine" has "stepped up a notch"
in recent years, and "even though it's eye-wateringly expensive it's always
impressive", and delivered by "knowledgeable and passionate staff". Top Tip
– "the latest incarnation of its weekend dinner dance is also excellent".
/ W1J 9BR; www.theritzlondon.com; @theritzlondon; 10 pm; Jacket & tie required;
booking essential; set weekday L £101 (FP); SRA-Food Made Good – 3 stars.*

The Ritz, Palm Court W1   £87   2 4 5
150 Piccadilly   020 7493 8181   3–4C
*Even those who find this famous afternoon tea experience "a bit cheesy",
feel "it has to be done" given its status as the benchmark that has for
so long epitomised the occasion, and it's "possibly the best of its type
in grand surroundings". Yes, it's "expensive – but if you're going to do it, do it
in style". Top Tip – "you'll need to book months ahead for that special
event". / W1J 9BR; www.theritzlondon.com; Jacket & tie required.*

Riva SW13   £64   3 3 2
169 Church Rd   020 8748 0434   11–1A
*Andreas Riva's enduring destination in out-of-the-way Barnes is known as a
very "understated" stalwart, whose "simple, seasonal north Italian cooking"
has long made it a clandestine Mecca for in-the-know foodies, and bizarrely
means the venue can be "great for spotting celebs" (but only the kind you
might hear on Radio 4). But while it's a genuine "favourite" for many
habitués, occasional visitors can feel "let down" by "snooty" service (it can
feel like "the owner spends all his efforts on regulars"), or perceive it as
"overpriced". / SW13 9HR; 10.30 pm, Sun 9 pm; closed Sat L.*

Rivea, Bulgari Hotel SW7   £80   3 4 3
171 Knightsbridge   020 7151 1025   6–1C
*Alain Ducasse's luxe Knightsbridge dining room offers "exceptionally skilful"
and "exquisitely presented" Italian-French small plates, with "the smooth
and charming service you would expect" of the French superchef.
"Not everyone likes the hotel decor and basement setting" (with "lots of
cold chrome and heavily lacquered wood") but some do "love it".
/ SW7 1DW; www.bulgarihotels.com; @bulgarihotels; 10.30 pm; booking max 7 may
apply.*

THE RIVER CAFÉ W6 £97 ⬛3⬛3⬛3

Thames Wharf, Rainville Rd 020 7386 4200 8–2C

"The sheer genius and simplicity of always-exciting Tuscan food prepared from ingredients of unparalleled quality" have won global renown for this "unique", "off-the-beaten-track Italian, in the obscure backstreets of Hammersmith. Its prices, however, are "daylight robbery" – and while its army of fans say that "if you believe it's overpriced, you don't get its concept of provenance, care and integrity", an equally large band of sceptics "appreciate the top-quality sourcing, but still think charges are absurd for rustic dishes (it might be cheaper to fly to Italy for the day, dine and fly back...")". And the atmosphere? "On a summer evening you could not ask for a better location" than its Thames-side terrace, but when it comes to eating inside first-timers can be surprised at how "hectic and noisy" its canteen-like set-up can be; service meanwhile veers from "charming" to "indifferent". Still, it's always full, so you can't blame them" and "if I was a billionaire I'd go every week!" / W6 9HA; www.rivercafe.co.uk; @RiverCafeLondon; 9 pm, Sat 9.15 pm; closed Sun D; set weekday L £59 (FP).

Rivington Grill SE10 £54 2⬜2⬜2⬜

178 Greenwich High Rd 020 8293 9270 1–3D

Ironically this Greenwich grill is now the sole bearer of the 'Rivington' brand as the Rivington Street original in Shoreditch shut up shop in August 2017. Critics see this straightforward British restaurant as a tad "mundane", but as "there's just about nowhere really decent to eat in SE10", its supporters boost it as arguably "the best option in the area" – "go for the grilled meats and excellent selection of gins". / SE10 8NN; www.rivingtongrill.co.uk; 11 pm, Sun 10 pm; closed Mon, Tue L & Wed L.

Roast SE1 £68 2⬜2⬜3⬛

Stoney St 0845 034 7300 10–4C

"The marvellous space is exhilarating" – and ideal for business – at this potentially brilliant fixture over Borough Market (partially constructed from a glazed Victorian structure that was originally a portico of the Royal Opera House's Floral Hall). When it comes to the traditional British meat dishes, however, "the food's OK, but nothing special for the hefty price tag" with enjoyment often "dependent on whether you make a good menu choice" ("some dishes show good promise, others are simply no more than the sum of their ingredients"), and "service can be slow". Top Tip – "magnificent Full English breakfast – there's no need to eat again that day!" / SE1 1TL; www.roast-restaurant.com; @roastrestaurant; 10.45 pm; closed Sun D.

Rocca Di Papa £38 ⬛3⬛3⬛4

73 Old Brompton Rd, SW7 020 7225 3413 6–2B
75-79 Dulwich Village, SE21 020 8299 6333 1–4D

These "cosy, busy and good-value" local Italians in South Kensington and Dulwich do the simple things well: "handmade pasta, great pizzas and lovely service". "Perfect for families – kids are well-treated" (so "it can be a bit of a creche if you go at the wrong time"). / www.roccarestaurants.com; SW7 11.30 pm; SE21 11 pm.

Rochelle Canteen E2 £59 ⬛3⬛3⬛4

Rochelle School, Arnold Circus 020 7729 5677 13–1C

"A hidden treat" in Spitalfields – this offbeat (and on a sunny day "amazing"), venue from Melanie Arnold and Margot Henderson – wife of St John's Fergus – occupies the converted bike sheds of a former school ("just lovely on a summer's day sitting outside in what was the playground, now a walled courtyard") and offers "simple, well-cooked food for those in-the-know" (NB it's no longer BYO, they now have a license). In September 2017, a new 'Rochelle' was announced taking over the bar/café at the ICA on the Mall – spiritually speaking, the two locations seem poles apart. / E2 7ES; www.arnoldandhenderson.com; 4.30 pm, Thu-Sat 9 pm; L only, Thu-Sat L & D; No Amex.

Rök   £53   4 2 2
149 Upper St, N1   no tel   9–3D
26 Curtain Rd, EC2   020 7377 2152   13–2B
"Lovely combinations of Scandinavian food", much of it brined or smoked,
is the calling card at this *"great little bar"* in Shoreditch, now with
an Islington offshoot. *"It's un-glossy and unpretentious, but don't be fooled
by appearances."* / N1 midnight, EC2 11 pm, Fri & Sat 1 am; EC2 closed Sun.

Roka   £80   4 3 3
30 North Audley St, W1   020 7305 5644   3–2A
37 Charlotte St, W1   020 7580 6464   2–1C
Aldwych House, 71-91 Aldwych, WC2   020 7294 7636   2–2D
Unit 4, Park Pavilion, 40 Canada Sq, E14   020 7636 5228   12–1C
"Some of the best fusion fare that will pass your lips" – these *"always
buzzy"* and *"vibey"* Japanese-inspired operations dazzle with their
"beauteous robata dishes", *"amazing black cod"*, sushi and other *"superb
Asian dishes"*, and even if *"the prices are as incredible as the food"* it's
"money well spent". That they are perennially ignored by Michelin
is incomprehensible. / www.rokarestaurant.com; 11.30 pm, Sun 10.30 pm;
E14 11pm, Sun 8.30 pm; WC2 11 pm, Sun 8 pm; booking: max 5 online.

Rola Wala E1   NEW
36 Brushfield St   13–2B
After a long residency at Street Feast, this spicy street food concept (already
rooted in Leeds since 2014) is adding a permanent London branch
in Spitalfields, with a menu including low-calorie, low-carb and gluten-free
options. / E1 6AT; www.rolawala.com; @RolaWala.

Romulo Café W8   £58   3 3 3
343 Kensington High St   020 3141 6390   6–1A
Limited reports to-date on this year-old venture – one of London's few
Filipino restaurants – decorated with portraits of the owner's ancestors,
but all feedback says it's a *"great new arrival"*. / W8 6NW;
www.romulocafe.co.uk; @romulolondon; 10 pm.

Rosa's   £42   2 2 2
5 Gillingham St, SW1   020 3813 6773   2–4C
23a Ganton St, W1   020 7287 9617   4–2B
48 Dean St, W1   020 7494 1638   5–3A
246 Fulham Rd, SW10   020 7583 9021   6–3B
6 Theberton St, N1   020 3393 2482   9–3D   NEW
152a West End Lane, NW6   020 3773 1568   1–1B   NEW
36 Atlantic Rd, SW9   020 3393 8562   11–2D
Westfield Stratford City, E15   020 8519 1302   14–1D
12 Hanbury St, E1   020 7247 1093   13–2C
This *"hectic"* and *"cheerful"* Thai café chain has grown apace over the
years. Compared with the early days (when *"the original E1 branch set the
standards for the roll-out"*) its spicy fare is probably *"nothing to write home
about"*, but most reports still say it's *"tasty and fresh"* and *"really well
priced"*. / rosasthaicafe.com; 10.30 pm, Fri & Sat 11 pm; E15 9 pm, Sat 10 pm,
Sun 6 pm; W1F & W1D Sun 10 pm; E1, SW1 & SW9 6+ to book, W1 4+ to book.

The Rosendale SE21   £52   3 4 3
65 Rosendale Rd   020 8761 9008   1–4D
Handsome Victorian coaching inn (with a large garden) in West Dulwich,
consistently well-rated for its quality gastropub cooking. / SE21 8EZ;
www.therosendale.co.uk; @threecheerspubs; 10 pm, Sat 9.30 pm, Sun 9 pm;
No Amex.

Rossopomodoro £45
John Lewis, 300 Oxford St, W1 020 7495 8409 3–1B
50-52 Monmouth St, WC2 020 7240 9095 5–3B
214 Fulham Rd, SW10 020 7352 7677 6–3B
1 Rufus St, N1 020 7739 1899 13–1B
10 Jamestown Rd, NW1 020 7424 9900 9–3B
46 Garrett Ln, SW18 020 8877 9903 11–2B
"They know how to make a decent pizza" (wood-fired) – as indeed they
should! – at this "affordable" global chain, which is based in Naples,
and where many of the ingredients (and staff and customers) are imported
from Italy. / www.rossopomodoro.co.uk; 11 pm, Fri & Sat 11.30 pm, Sun 10 pm.

Roti Chai W1 £46 4 3 4
3 Portman Mews South 020 7408 0101 3–1A
The "spicy" dishes are "damned good" at this "original and interesting"
Indian operation near Selfridges, serving street-hawker-style small plates
on the "more casual", "grab-and-go" ground floor and tandoori grills plus
regional specialities in the "more formal" basement. Both options are
"very good value for central London". / W1H 6HS; www.rotichai.com; @rotichai;
10.30 pm; booking D only.

**Roti King,
Ian Hamilton House NW1** £22 5 2 1
40 Doric Way 020 7387 2518 9–3C
"Fabulous rotis" – "the best in town" – and "really good Malaysian street
food at bargain prices" mean this "crowded basement dive" in Euston is one
of the few places "worth queuing for". Don't let "the location put you off",
and come prepared to share a table with the "students and Malaysians"
who flock here. / NW1 1LH; www.rotiking.in; no booking.

Rotorino E8 £49 2 4 2
434 Kingsland Rd 020 7249 9081 14–1A
Stevie Parle's Italian-inspired outfit in Dalston can still impress, but all
feedback this year (which was quite limited) was shot through with pluses
and minuses: "great local eatery, maybe losing its shine", was typical; "it felt
technically great but could do with some more soul" was another. / E8 4AA;
www.rotorino.com; @Rotorino; 10 pm.

**Rotunda Bar & Restaurant,
Kings Place N1** £55 3 4 4
90 York Way 020 7014 2840 9–3C
"Especially on a sunny day, overlooking the canal" (by which it has a large
terrace), this "buzzy" arts centre brasserie provides a "beautiful setting".
Some dishes can seem "run-of-the-mill", but, Top Tip – "they serve
wonderful meat" from their own Northumberland farm (and it's "very good
for Sunday lunch"). / N1 9AG; www.rotundabarandrestaurant.co.uk;
@rotundalondon; 10.30 pm, Sun 6.30 pm; closed Sun.

**Roux at Parliament Square,
RICS SW1** £91 5 5 3
12 Great George St 020 7334 3737 2–3C
"Perfection!" – "I enjoyed every single mouthful!" – "wonderful food and
service in the Roux tradition" is the consistent accolade for this formal
Parliament Square venue, where the kitchen is run by MasterChef winner
Steve Groves. "It's a bit quiet and sedate… but that's not a criticism."
/ SW1P 3AD; www.rouxatparliamentsquare.co.uk; @RouxAPS; 9 pm; closed
Sat & Sun; No trainers; set weekday L £71 (FP).

Roux at the Landau, The Langham W1 £101

1c Portland Pl   020 7965 0165   2–1B

Fans of the Roux's management of this "calm and elegant" chamber truly adore its "quiet" and "romantic" style, while also praising its "polite and seriously attentive service" and "superb French cuisine". Its ratings have waned in the last couple of years however, as a small but vociferous minority give it flak for "unadventurous" food they consider "average for the price". / W1B 1JA; www.rouxatthelandau.com; @Langham_Hotel; 10.30 pm; closed Sat L & Sun; No trainers; set brunch £61 (FP), set weekday L, dinner & pre-theatre £63 (FP).

Rowley's SW1 £70

113 Jermyn St   020 7930 2707   4–4D

"The (unlimited!) fries are a treat" at this venerable St James's steakhouse, set in the original Wall's sausages and ice cream premises. Though dogged in the past by inconsistent standards, all feedback this year says it's a "reliable" option that's "great for Chateaubriand". / SW1Y 6HJ; www.rowleys.co.uk; @rowleys_steak; 10.30 pm.

Rox Burger SE13 £32

82 Lee High Rd   020 3372 4631   1–4D

"Top burgers" washed down with craft beers win rave reviews from far and wide for this popular little outfit in Lewisham. Don't despair if you can't get a seat: "they do takeaway…" / SE13 5PT; www.roxburger.com; @RoxburgerUK; 10 pm, Fri & Sat 11 pm.

Royal China £54

24-26 Baker St, W1   020 7487 4688   2–1A
805 Fulham Rd, SW6   020 7731 0081   11–1B
13 Queensway, W2   020 7221 2535   7–2C
30 Westferry Circus, E14   020 7719 0888   12–1B

"My Chinese friend will not go anywhere else!"; these "garish black and gold" Cantonese stalwarts (particularly the Baker Street and Bayswater branches) remain many Londoners 'go-to' choice for "particularly authentic and economical dim sum" ("never had a bad dish in 20 years!"), although the full menu is less of an attraction. "Expect a queue at the weekend" and prepare for "abrupt" service and a setting that's "lively without being very convivial". / www.royalchinagroup.co.uk; 11 pm, Sun 10 pm; W1 Fri & Sat 11.30 pm; no booking Sat & Sun L.

Royal China Club W1 £68

40-42 Baker St   020 7486 3898   2–1A

"Delectable dim sum" that's "comparable to the best in HK" ensures the accomplished Marylebone flagship of the China Club group is "always packed". Especially given "an interior that could be improved" however, even fans can find it "overpriced". / W1U 7AJ; www.royalchinagroup.co.uk; 11 pm, Sun 10.30 pm; booking weekdays only.

The Royal Exchange Grand Café, The Royal Exchange EC3 £51

The Royal Exchange Bank   020 7618 2480   10–2C

For an informal business bite (including a "top quality breakfast") it's worth remembering the café in the "very handsome" covered courtyard of this Victorian pile, right at the heart of the City of London. / EC3V 3LR; www.royalexchange-grandcafe.co.uk; @rexlondon; 10 pm; closed Sat & Sun; credit card required to book.

Rucoletta EC2 £48 222
6 Foster Lane   020 7600 7776   10–2C
*"Simple, well-prepared Italian food in a City backstreet" near St Paul's
makes this a useful lunch spot in a busy part of town. But reporters are split
over the quality of the offer, with comments ranging from "great" to "totally
careless". / EC2V 6HH; www.rucoletta.co.uk; @RucolettaLondon; 9.30 pm, Thu & Fri
10 pm; closed Sat D & Sun; No Amex.*

Rugoletta £41 332
308 Ballards Ln, N12   020 8445 6742   1–1B
59 Church Ln, N2   020 8815 1743   1–1B
*These "cramped Italian" local favourites in Barnet and East Finchley are
"well worth knowing" and "excellent value" for their traditional dishes,
especially the pasta. / www.la-rugoletta.com; 10.30 pm; N12 Fri & Sat 11 pm;
N2 closed Sun.*

Rules WC2 £78 235
35 Maiden Ln   020 7836 5314   5–3D
*"Step into London's history" on entering the capital's oldest restaurant
(established 1798), whose "stunning" panelled premises near Covent
Garden have a "timeless feel – Victorian diners wouldn't look out of place,
nor modern, open-collared business folk". For "so-traditional British fare"
("wonderful game" and "top steak puddings") it can still deliver "old-school
perfection", and though "foreign visitors love it", it's still "an absolute
favourite" for many locals. That said, they need to watch the ever-more
"inflated prices" here: "step this way and empty your wallet!" / WC2E 7LB;
www.rules.co.uk; 11.45 pm, Sun 10.45 pm; No shorts.*

Sabor W1 NEW
35 Heddon St   awaiting tel   4–3A
*Nieves Barragán Mohacho and José Etura, who met working at Barrafina
(where the former was the executive head chef), have unsurprisingly chosen
a Spanish style for their autumn newcomer, which – with additional bar and
asador (wood-fired oven), will open in Heddon Street. The ground-floor will
feature a fresh seafood counter and an open kitchen producing regional
dishes from across Spain, while the upstairs restaurant will focus on the
cuisine of Galicia and Castile. / W1B 4BP; @NievesBarragan1.*

Le Sacré-Coeur N1 £39 222
18 Theberton St   020 7354 2618   9–3D
*Mixed views this year on this Gallic veteran, north of Angel. Supporters
continue to hail it as a "lovely bistro" with "reasonably priced" fare,
but sceptics feel "it's lost some of its old charm" of late, and become
"very average". / N1 0QX; www.lesacrecoeur.co.uk; @LeSacreCoeurUK; 11 pm,
Fri & Sat 11.30 pm, Sun 10.30 pm.*

Sacro Cuore £37 542
10 Crouch End Hill, N8   020 8348 8487   1–1C
45 Chamberlayne Rd, NW10   020 8960 8558   1–2B
*"Authentic" Neapolitan-style pizza is the single main course offered at this
Kensal Rise pizzeria (now with a Crouch End branch). But what a pizza it is:
"brilliant" – "one of the best outside Italy". "The only con is that you can't
eat anything else" – although there is a short and tasty menu of starters
and desserts.*

Sagar £35 321
17a Percy St, W1   020 7631 3319   3–2B
31 Catherine St, WC2   020 7836 6377   5–3D
157 King St, W6   020 8741 8563   8–2C
*"Fresh South Indian vegetarian food", including "monster-sized dosas", all at
low prices wins a sizeable fan club this small chain (Covent Garden,
Tottenham Court Road, Hammersmith and Harrow) despite its incredibly
"ordinary" decor. / www.sagarveg.co.uk; W1 10.45 pm-11pm, Sun 10 pm.*

Sagardi EC2 £62 2️⃣2️⃣2️⃣
Cordy House, 95 Curtain Rd 020 3802 0478 13–1B
*"The meat is delicious", say fans of this Basque yearling in Shoreditch
(part of an international chain specialising in Galician Txuleton beef cooked
on a charcoal grill). The problem here can be the price: "while the food and
wine selection was very good, the small-plates concept meant costs soared
very quickly". / EC2A 3AH; www.sagardi.co.uk; @Sagardi_UK; 11 pm.*

Sager + Wilde £62 2️⃣4️⃣4️⃣
193 Hackney Rd, E2 020 8127 7330 14–2A
250 Paradise Row, E2 020 7613 0478 14–2B
*A "funky wine selection" is a feature of both these Hackney haunts,
although only the Paradise Row venue – set in a hip railway arch, and with
"a lovely outside space" – serves substantial food (it's just tiny bites
in Hackney Road). Chris Leach (formerly of Kitty Fisher's) took over the
stoves in February 2017, and reports (mostly) say the cooking is also
an attraction in itself.*

Saigon Saigon W6 £36 2️⃣3️⃣3️⃣
313-317 King St 020 8748 6887 8–2B
*"Always crowded", long-serving Hammersmith Vietnamese with
atmospheric, if faded, decor and serving "a huge menu" of flavoursome
dishes – if you're flummoxed by the choice, "just order appetizers and
a bowl of pho". / W6 9NH; www.saigon-saigon.co.uk; @saigonsaigonuk; 10.30 pm,
Fri & Sun 11 pm.*

Sail Loft SE10 £51 2️⃣3️⃣4️⃣
11 Victoria Parade 020 8222 9310 1–3C
*"Lovely views across the Thames to Canary Wharf" are the highlight at this
Fullers pub in Greenwich. No surprises on the pub grub, but it's dependably
well-rated. / SE10 9FR; www.sailloftgreenwich.co.uk; @SailLoftLondon; 11 pm,
Sun 10.30 pm.*

St John Bread & Wine E1 £62 3️⃣3️⃣2️⃣
94-96 Commercial St 020 7251 0848 13–2C
*"It looks basic, but that's because every single dish speaks for itself,
or should that be SHOUTS!" – the accepted view on this engaging, if slightly
"bleak" Spitalfields canteen – "younger sibling to the Smithfield veteran",
whose "lip smacking" menu of offal-centric British "delights" has long made
it "a real favourite". Several meals this year however "didn't live up to its
reputation", and ratings have dipped as a result. / E1 6LZ;
www.stjohngroup.uk.com/spitalfields; @StJBW; 10.30 pm, Mon 8 pm.*

St John Smithfield EC1 £64 5️⃣4️⃣3️⃣
26 St John St 020 7251 0848 10–1B
*"You either love or hate the austerity of the dining room, and the
uncompromising nature of the 'nose to tail' offal-heavy approach" that's
made this "stark", white-walled ex-smokehouse in Smithfield "the high altar"
of challenging British cuisine. "The extraordinary longevity of the place
suggests that most people do get it" and "Fergus Henderson and his team
continue to turn the humdrum off-cuts into something magical" – "it's hard
to better such straightforward heavenly food" – with "something that's
always new or different to tempt regulars back and to intrigue the
uninitiated." Top Menu Tips – game in season, "brilliant suckling pig",
bone marrow salad ("dem bones, dem bones…"), and the Eccles cakes.
/ EC1M 4AY; www.stjohngroup.uk.com; @SJRestaurant; 11 pm, Sun 4 pm; closed
Sat L & Sun D.*

St Johns N19 £52 345

91 Junction Rd   020 7272 1587   9–1C

"Unrivalled in this neck of the woods"; this "genuine gastropub" has a particularly "convivial" atmosphere, both in the "more formal rear dining room" – a lovely, striking space built as a ballroom, and serving "hearty modern British cooking" – and in the bar, where there are "excellent tapas-style options". / N19 5QU; www.stjohnstavern.com; @stjohnstavern; 10 pm, Tue-Sat 11 pm, Sun 9 pm; Mon-Thu D only, Fri-Sun open L & D; No Amex; booking max 12 may apply.

St Luke's Kitchen,
Library WC2 £59 333

112 Saint Martin's Lane   020 3302 7912   5–4C

Limited reports on this boutique-guesthouse near the Coliseum, which launched in 2016 (and which took on new head chef, Daniel Petitta in spring 2017): fans though "love the quality, presentation and awesome surroundings". / WC2N 4BD; www.lib-rary.com; @LibraryLondon; midnight; No trainers; booking essential.

St Moritz W1 £55 334

161 Wardour St   020 7734 3324   4–1C

A "hilarious evening of kitsch" ("the cow bells are too tempting not to ring") is guaranteed at this long-running tribute to all things Swiss, set in a chalet-style interior in the heart of Soho. "Cheese fondue is great", although the odd reporter feels the accompanying dishes are "stuck in the 1970s" (ie, pretty genuine). "It would probably treble profits in Fulham full of folk just back from 'Verbs', but it's a fun time nonetheless". / W1F 8WJ; www.stmoritz-restaurant.co.uk; 11.30 pm, Sun 10.30 pm.

Saiphin's Thai Kitchen E8 NEW £35

381 Railway Arches, Mentmore Terrace   020 3603 9968   14–1B

Saiphin and Alex Moore are at it again: their Rosa's Thai Cafe group is now ten-strong, with further openings expected for 2018; Lao Cafe opened in December 2016, and they launched this new proto-chain in London Fields in late spring 2017, featuring a similar menu to Rosa's. No reports as yet. / E8 3PH; www.saiphinsthaikitchen.com; 10 pm, Fri & Sat 10.30 pm.

Sakagura W1 £58 443

8 Heddon St   020 3405 7230   4–3B

"Excellent, authentic Japanese food with a modern twist" inspires numerous enthusiastic reports for this year-old operation (where the sake collection is a feature) just off Regent Street, from the group behind Shoryu Ramen and the Japan Centre. Wagyu beef is made quite a highlight, but equally there's a dedicated vegetarian menu. / W1B 4BU; www.sakaguralondon.com; @sakaguraldn; 10.30 pm, Thu-Sat 11.30 pm, Sun 10 pm.

Sake No Hana SW1 £62 433

23 St James's St   020 7925 8988   3–4C

Though part of the can't-put-a-step-wrong Hakkasan Group, this wackily impressive modern Japanese, in a deeply 1960s St James's building next to The Economist, has divided opinion in the past, not helped by the fact that its "closely packed" interior "can lack ambience when empty". Still, its "delicate", "melt-in-the-mouth" cuisine wins over all reporters this year. / SW1A 1HA; www.sakenohana.com; @sakenohana; 11 pm, Fri & Sat 11.30 pm; closed Sun.

Sakonis HA0 £24 521

127-129 Ealing Rd   020 8903 9601   1–1A

"You don't go to impress!" when you visit this grungy veggie canteen in Wembley, but "the food is top notch from the fresh and large-ranging menu" (including some Chinese and Hakka dishes). / HA0 4BP; www.sakonis.co.uk; @sakonis; 9.30 pm; No Amex.

Salaam Namaste WC1 £47 3 3 2
68 Millman St 020 7405 3697 2–1D
This "good-quality mid-range Indian offering intelligent cooking" is handily central (but "off the beaten track") in Bloomsbury. Reasonable prices too for somewhere so conveniently located. / WC1N 3EF; www.salaam-namaste.co.uk; @SalaamNamasteUK; 11.30 pm, Sun 11 pm.

Sale e Pepe SW1 £67 3 4 4
9-15 Pavilion Rd 020 7235 0098 6–1D
"Such fun, and unchanged in 30 years" – this "lively" veteran trattoria near Harrods thrives on its "very friendly" service ("we were welcomed like long lost friends on our first visit!"), and it's also "not bad value for money in this busy neighbourhood". Any negatives? – can be "noisy" and "a bit cramped". / SW1X 0HD; www.saleepepe.co.uk.

Salloos SW1 £55 4 2 2
62-64 Kinnerton St 020 7235 4444 6–1D
"Divine Pakistani food" has maintained the popularity of this dated (and eternally pricey) veteran, hidden in a Belgravia mews venue, for decades. Top Tip – classic lamb chops. / SW1X 8ER; www.salloos.co.uk; 11 pm; closed Sun; May need 5+ to book.

Salon Brixton SW9 £53 3 3 3
18 Market Row 020 7501 9152 11–2D
Hip-ly located upstairs at Brixton Market (with a new ground floor bar), this crammed-in café wins limited but all-round very upbeat feedback for its seasonal British grub, nowadays primarily veg-focussed, but with meat and fish accompaniments also available. / SW9 8LD; www.salonbrixton.co.uk; @Salon_Brixton; 10 pm.

Le Salon Privé TW1 £52 4 3 4
43 Crown Rd 020 8892 0602 1–4A
"Perfectly pitched" St Margaret's bistro – "relaxed yet smart, attentive yet discreet, understated yet amicable"; its "classic French cooking" helps make it "delightful for a cosy romantic meal or for a special occasion". / TW1 3EJ; lesalonprive.net; @lesalon_tweet; 10.30 pm.

Salt & Honey W2 £53 3 3 2
28 Sussex Pl 020 7706 7900 7–1D
This tiny and "inventive" two-year-old near Paddington station does a good job of "spicing up French bistro standards" (it's run by the Kiwi couple behind Fulham's popular Manuka Kitchen). / W2 2TH; www.saltandhoneybistro.com; @SaltHoneyBistro; 10 pm, Sun 9 pm; closed Mon; booking max 8 may apply; set weekday L £31 (FP).

Salt Yard W1 £52 3 3 2
54 Goodge St 020 7637 0657 2–1B
"Tapas slightly outside the normal offerings (courgette flowers and squid croquettes are especially good)" have made a big name for Simon Mullins's "always packed and squeezed in" Fitzrovia "favourite" (the original member of his group). It's no longer a 'wow' nowadays though, and some fear "the bill's always a bit bigger than expected". / W1T 4NA; www.saltyard.co.uk; @SaltYardGroup; 10.45 pm, Sun 9.45 pm; booking max 8 may apply.

Salut N1 £61 4 4 4
412 Essex Rd 020 3441 8808 9–3D
"Worth the trip to the fringes of Islington", says (a Hammersmith-based) fan of this quite ambitious yearling, at the wrong end of the Essex Road – "the people couldn't be nicer", it has a "great vibe" and its Nordic-influenced modern cuisine is consistently highly rated. / N1 3PJ; www.salut-london.co.uk; @Salut_London; 11 pm, Sun 10 pm.

Salvation in Noodles £38
122 Balls Pond Rd, N1   020 7254 4534   14–1A
2 Blackstock Rd, N4   020 7254 4534   9–1D
"Authentic tasting pho" wins limited but positive feedback for these modern Vietnamese noodle cafés, in Dalston and Finsbury Park.
/ www.salvationinnoodles.co.uk; 10.30 pm; closed Mon-Fri L.

San Carlo Cicchetti £56
215 Piccadilly, W1   020 7494 9435   4–4C
30 Wellington St, WC2   020 7240 6339   5–3D
"You feel like you're in a smart Venetian brasserie" at these "classy and sassy" – if "hectic and noisy" – Italians (part of a national chain) which successfully create "a brilliant vibe in tourist hellhole locations", particularly the "buzzy, buzzy, buzzy" branch a few feet from Piccadilly Circus. Service is "on the ball" and you get "proper" cooking from "an interesting selection of Italianate tapas-style dishes". / www.sancarlocicchetti.co.uk/; W1 11.30 pm; WC2 midnight; M1 11 pm, Sun 10 pm.

The Sands End SW6 £51
135 Stephendale Rd   020 7731 7823   11–1B
One of Prince Harry's favourites (and owned by one of his greatest pals) – this "very busy" backstreet gastroboozer attracts the young Fulham set and wins consistently high ratings for its "well-sourced" British scoff. / SW6 2PR; www.thesandsend.co.uk; @thesandsend; 10 pm, Sun 9 pm.

Santa Maria £37 **5** **3** **3**
"The best pizza in London" – "similar to what you'd get in Naples" – ensures these "basic but cool" cafés are "always busy whatever the time of day". The 14-seat Ealing original has just "had a great expansion into the pub next door – now it's easier to get in!" / 10.30 pm; W5 no booking.

Santini SW1 £72 **2** **3** **3**
29 Ebury St   020 7730 4094   2–4B
This swanky Belgravia stalwart was a big-hitter in the 80s, but attracts mixed praise these days. "Competent Italian food with good professional service and some style" is the majority view, but even fans can find it "surprisingly pricey for what it offers" and to critics "what used to be justified by fine cooking and a sense of verve, now seem expensive for something that's slapdash and fraying at the edges". / SW1W 0NZ; www.santini-restaurant.com; @santinirest; 10 pm, Sat 11 pm.

Santo Remedio SE1 **NEW**
152 Tooley St   10–4D
Husband and wife team, Edson and Natalie Diaz-Fuentes are back with their trendy Mexican street-food spot following a successful Kickstarter campaign. The new Bermondsey location features a tequila and mezcal bar, a new charcoal grill and Mexican wines. There will even be reservations! Santo Remedio's original (queue-tastic) Shoreditch site closed in August 2016. / SE1 2TU; www.santoremedio.co.uk; @santoremediouk; 10 pm, Sat 11 pm.

Santore EC1 £51 **4** **3** **3**
59-61 Exmouth Mkt   020 7812 1488   10–1A
'Traditional wood-fired pizza al metro' (plus some pasta) is the proposition at this agreeable Neapolitan – a handy, fairly "cheap 'n' cheerful" option in trendy Exmouth Market. / EC1R 4QL; www.santorerestaurant.london; @Santore_london; 11 pm.

Sapori Sardi SW6 £56 **3** **3** **3**
786 Fulham Rd   020 7731 0755   11–1B
Fulham neighbourhood Italian run by a husband-and-wife team, whose Sardinian cooking is highly rated by a small but enthusiastic fan club. / SW6 5SL; @saporisardi; 10.30 pm; No Amex.

Saravanaa Bhavan HA0   £32   5️⃣ 2️⃣ 1️⃣

531-533 High Rd   020 8900 8526   1–1A
"Top dosas" are a highlight at this *"exceptional cheap 'n' cheerful"* veggie,
mixing north and south Indian dishes – one of the better bets in Wembley.
/ HA0 2DJ; www.saravanabhavanuk.com; Mon - Thurs 10.30pm, Fri-Sun 11pm.

Sardine N1   £57   3️⃣ 2️⃣ 2️⃣

15 Micawber St   020 7490 0144   13–1A
"A short but interesting menu inspired by the south of France" realised
by Alex Jackson generated gushing press reviews for the opening of this
"slightly hard-to-find yearling, just off City Road" (part of Stevie Parle's
empire), but while reporters generally judge it to be *"authentic and
delicious"* they can also find it *"something of a let down after all the
publicity"*. The naming of the venture is all too apt, and even fans can find
this *"small, high-ceilinged space"* to be *"too crowded"* and *"very noisy with
all the hard surfaces"*. / N1 7TB; www.sardine.london; @sardinelondon; 10 pm.

Sardo W1   £58   3️⃣ 3️⃣ 2️⃣

45 Grafton Way   020 7387 2521   2–1B
"Sardinian regional cooking with an excellent list of Sardinian wines" have
carved a foodie reputation for this *"well established"* Fitzrovia venue, and it's
consistently well-rated for its *"unfussy, well-cooked fare"*. / W1T 5DQ;
www.sardo-restaurant.com; 11 pm; closed Sat L & Sun.

Sarracino NW6   £45   4️⃣ 3️⃣ 2️⃣

186 Broadhurst Gdns   020 7372 5889   1–1B
A West Hampstead stalwart, this rustic-style Neapolitan trattoria
(best known for its pizza) has scored consistently well for its food over
a number of years. There's a sibling, Sole d'Oro, in Palmers Green.
/ NW6 3AY; www.sarracinorestaurant.com; closed weekday L.

Sartoria W1   £76   3️⃣ 3️⃣ 3️⃣

20 Savile Row   020 7534 7000   4–3A
"When you need quiet to have a good business conversation",
this *"very comfortable and well-spaced"* Mayfair Italian, with its
"very refined Calabrian cucina", *"very smart"* decor and *"particularly
professional"* service is just the ticket. All this comes at a price naturally,
and while the overall offer escapes any serious criticisms, and draws a good
degree of praise, the overall verdict value-wise is really quite muted,
especially measured by Francesco Mazzei's involvement and its much-
publicised revamp two years ago. / W1S 3PR; www.sartoria-restaurant.co.uk;
@SartoriaRest; 10.45 pm; closed Sat L & Sun.

Satay House W2   £35   3️⃣ 3️⃣ 3️⃣

13 Sale Pl   020 7723 6763   7–1D
For a dependable meal, not of the cutting edge variety, fans continue
to recommend this Malaysian stalwart (est 1973), just off Edgware Road.
/ W2 1PX; www.satay-house.co.uk; 11 pm; booking max 9 may apply.

Sauterelle,
Royal Exchange EC3   £62   3️⃣ 3️⃣ 4️⃣

Bank   020 7618 2483   10–2C
The marvellous backdrop of the Royal Exchange's internal courtyard sets the
tone at this business-friendly mezzanine, *"whose good acoustic means you
don't have to bellow, and whose well-spaced tables mean you needn't fear
being overhead"*. A D&D London operation, its food wins consistently solid
ratings. / EC3V 3LR; www.sauterelle-restaurant.co.uk; 9.30 pm; closed Sat & Sun;
No trainers.

Savini at Criterion W1 £87 ②②**5**
224 Piccadilly   020 7930 1459   4–4D
*Too often branded "a disappointment… and an expensive disappointment
at that" – this incredible, gilded neo-Byzantine chamber on Piccadilly Circus
has been through a succession of owners, of which this year-old Milanese
régime is the latest. By-and-large ignored by Londoners nowadays,
such feedback as there is talks of "bland food, poorly presented". / W1J 9HP;
www.saviniatcriterion.co.uk; @SaviniMilano; midnight; set weekday L £59 (FP), set
pre-theatre £62 (FP).*

Savoir Faire WC1 £45 **3**4**3**
42 New Oxford St   020 7436 0707   5–1C
*Long-established Gallic bistro near the British Museum (plastered with
posters from West End shows) which "never disappoints". Even those who
say the food's "never exciting", see it as "an efficient and good value staple"
and more commonly there's praise for its "generous portions and keenly
priced wines". / WC1A 1EP; www.savoir.co.uk; 10 pm.*

The Savoy Hotel,
Savoy Grill WC2 £94 ②**3**3
Strand   020 7592 1600   5–3D
*"Discretion is assured" in this "smooth" and "comfortable" panelled
chamber, whose "well-spaced tables" and "formal" styling have made it a
power-dining favourite since time immemorial. Run by Gordon Ramsay for
nearly 15 years now, the celeb chef's operation puts in a middling
performance: the traditional British fare is arguably "too expensive", and can
be "uninspired", but is generally "competently cooked" and of "high quality".
/ WC2R 0EU; www.gordonramsayrestaurants.com; @savoygrill; 11 pm, Sun 10.30 pm;
set weekday L & pre-theatre £56 (FP).*

Savoy Thames Foyer WC2 £97 ②**3**4
The Savoy, The Strand   020 7420 2111   5–3D
*The "sensational" setting beneath a glass dome, with a pianist tinkling the
ivories while you eat, complements the "exquisitely prepared and presented"
afternoon tea at this grand London landmark. The staff are
"very welcoming", and make "extra effort to accommodate dietary
requests". / WC2R; www.fairmont.com/savoy-london; @fairmonthotels; 11 pm.*

Scalini SW3 £76 **3**3**3**
1-3 Walton St   020 7225 2301   6–2C
*"I love Scalini's!" – this "buzzy" (perennially "noisy") stalwart on the fringes
of Knightsbridge is "a great, traditional Italian": "it's not the best food in the
world" ("respectable but at stratospheric prices") "but the staff are super,
the atmosphere is fun, and it's not pretentious or showy". / SW3 2JD;
www.scalinilondon.co.uk; 11 pm; No shorts.*

Scandinavian Kitchen W1 £17 **3**4②
61 Great Titchfield St   020 7580 7161   2–1B
*"As a Dane, I go when I'm homesick for my local food". This "charming"
Nordic café/grocer is a handy destination in Fitzrovia, serving "attractive
open sandwiches" and other smorgasbord offerings. "With 'Abba Nice Day'
on the T-shirts it's strong on Scandi-Blanc humour too." / W1W 7PP;
www.scandikitchen.co.uk; @scanditwitchen; 7 pm, Sat 6 pm, Sun 3 pm; L only;
no booking.*

SCOTT'S W1 £85 **4**4**5**
20 Mount St   020 7495 7309   3–3A
*"Possibly the best all-round dining experience in London" – James Bond's
favourite lunch-spot remains, under Richard Caring's ownership,
a "sophisticated" Mayfair institution that's "worth it if you can afford it"
thanks to its "classic" seafood (it's "a paradise for fish lovers"), "exemplary"
service and "perfect atmosphere". Its "effortless" style suits all occasions,
but in particular it's a "power-brokers' favourite". / W1K 2HE;
www.scotts-restaurant.com; 10.30 pm, Sun 10 pm; booking max 6 may apply.*

F S A

Sea Containers,
Mondrian London SE1 £68 222
20 Upper Ground   020 3747 1063   10–3A
"Top-floor prices with a ground-floor view" makes for an often unhappy combination in the "trying-to-be-über-cool" dining room of this Thames-side, US-owned hotel, near Blackfriars Bridge. The odd fan does applaud its "fabulous Eurofusion fare", but the whole "bizarre sharing concept" seems like "too much style-over-substance" and "hugely overpriced: even with someone else paying it seemed like a rip off". / SE1 9PD; www.seacontainersrestaurant.com; @MondrianLDN; 11 pm.

Seafresh SW1 £45 332
80-81 Wilton Rd   020 7828 0747   2–4B
"Not to be compared with Sheekey or Scott's, but the fish 'n' chips are better!". This age-old Pimlico veteran has "become quite upmarket" nowadays, "serving lobster, oysters, and very fresh plaice alongside its excellent fish 'n' chips". The interior though remains fairly "basic". / SW1V 1DL; www.seafresh-dining.com; @SeafreshLondon; 10.30 pm; closed Sun.

The Sea Shell NW1 £49 322
49 Lisson Grove   020 7224 9000   9–4A
"If you just want good old fashioned fish 'n' chips", what is probably London's most famous chippie (certainly one of its oldest) "is the place to come to introduce the national dish to your foreign guest". Top Tip – "it's best for take-away – the restaurant area is good, but somehow the food's not quite the same". / NW1 6UH; www.seashellrestaurant.co.uk; @SeashellRestaur; 10.30 pm; closed Sun.

Season Kitchen N4 £49 332
53 Stroud Green Rd   020 7263 5500   9–1D
A "neighbourhood gem" in Finsbury Park, where "food is cooked with expertise and love" and served "with charm" from a small menu. A flat cash mark-up is charged on wine instead of the traditional percentage (it's not every restaurant where you can enjoy Saint-Emilion Grand Cru at £36) – "excellent, should be the norm!" / N4 3EF; www.seasonkitchen.co.uk; @seasonkitchen; 10.30 pm, Sun 8 pm; D only.

Señor Ceviche W1 £48 324
Kingly Ct   020 7842 8540   4–2B
A "fun" Peruvian street-food hang-out in Soho's Kingly Court gastro hub that's generally well-rated. As well as the eponymous raw fish, it serves Peruvian-Japanese BBQ dishes and pisco cocktails. / W1B 5PW; www.senor-ceviche.com; @SenorCevicheLDN; 11.30 pm, Sat midnight, Sun 10.30 pm; booking max 6 may apply.

Seven Park Place SW1 £103 454
7-8 Park Pl   020 7316 1615   3–4C
"The food actually reduced my husband to tears (in a good way!)…" The "quirky but cosy" dining room of this luxurious St James's hotel deserves a much higher profile – "staff take real pride in their work and take such good care of you", and William Drabble's "consistently reliable and refined" cooking is "too delicious for words". / SW1A 1LS; www.stjameshotelandclub.com; @SevenParkPlace; 10 pm; closed Mon & Sun; set weekday L £59 (FP).

Sexy Fish W1 £91 1 1 3
1-4 Berkeley Sq 020 3764 2000 3–3B
"It's certainly an experience", and no-one disputes that Richard Caring's "flashy and brassy" Mayfair venture is "good for people-watching". But while for fans the "amazing" interior and "sublime and sexy" sushi, robata and Asian seafood, all justify the monumental expense, there are too many critics for whom it's "the most overpriced, over-rated restaurant in London" – "a trashy, vulgar hellhole filled to the brim with people dressed for cameos in a cheap US cable-TV soap opera, and not for anyone with the slightest disinclination for being fleeced rotten!" Maybe the best advice is "go once, get it out of your system, then leave it to those where money isn't an issue..." / W1J 6BR; www.sexyfish.com; @sexyfishlondon; 11 pm, Sun 10.30 pm; booking max 6 may apply.

Shackfuyu W1 £48 4 3 3
14a, Old Compton St 020 7734 7492 5–2A
"Genuinely fantastic", westernised-Japanese joint in Soho – "a busy, bright, well-staffed sister to the wonderful Bone Daddies", offering "a great all-round experience". Top Menu Tip – "that dessert! Kinako French Toast with the Matcha soft serve! Got me into green tea!" / W1D 4TH; www.bonedaddies.com; @shackfuyu; 11 pm, Mon & Tue 10 pm, Sun 9 pm; no booking.

Shake Shack £29 2 2 2
Nova, Nova, Victoria St, SW1 awaiting tel 2–4B
80 New Oxford St, WC1 01925 555171 5–1B
24 The Market, WC2 020 3598 1360 5–3D
The Street, Westfield Stratford, E20 01923 555167 14–1D
"Top burgers for texture and taste" ("with potato rolls flown specially in from the US!") win numerous fans for Danny Meyer's "no fuss no fancy" burger operations. Even supporters can find them "bloody pricey" however, and critics gripe about "anaemic" portions, and "long waits". / WC2 & E14 11 pm, Sun 9 pm-10.30 pm; E20 9.30 pm, Fri & Sat 11 pm.

Shampers W1 £47 2 4 5
4 Kingly St 020 7437 1692 4–2B
A perfectly preserved, "proper" 1970s wine bar in Soho, where the atmosphere always fizzes "with a good buzz of conversation" and you'll always find a "warm welcome". Great for "not-too-serious business", it has a "sensibly priced wine list that's a pleasure to work your way through" and "classic, albeit old-school food" that's "pretty good". "Been coming here for well nigh 30 years, and it's home from home: Simon and his team always deliver. Bravo!" / W1B 5PE; www.shampers.net; @shampers_soho; 11 pm; closed Sun.

The Shed W8 £55 4 4 4
122 Palace Gardens Ter 020 7229 4024 7–2B
"Bonkers, quirky but delicious" – the Gladwin family's "oddball" farm-to-table venture in Notting Hill has won many converts to its seasonal British small plates, aided by its "charming" staff and "attractive" (if "slightly uncomfortable") rustic-style interior. / W8 4RT; www.theshed-restaurant.com; @theshed_resto; 11 pm; closed Mon L & Sun; SRA-Food Made Good – 3 stars.

J SHEEKEY WC2 £81 3 3 4
28-34 St Martin's Ct   020 7240 2565   5–3B
"Well deserving its status as a West End Institution", Richard Caring's "very classy" Theatreland Icon (est 1896) offers "plenty of star gazing after the theatre", and remains both the survey's most talked-about destination, and its No. 1 tip for fish (eclipsing its stablemate Scott's for nominations as London's best). Sitting in a narrow, Dickensian alleyway off St Martin's Lane, you pass its doorman and etched-glass façade to enter a series of snug ("poky") panelled chambers, where "white-aproned waiters deliver whip-sharp service and a menu that sings of the sea: from shellfish platters and superior classics (eg lobster thermidor) to creamy, comforting fish pie". "Nothing is experimental or over fussy": "it's without fripperies, foams and smears – just perfectly sourced and cooked seafood". The ongoing drive to expand the business (including here the September 2016 rebranding of the bar into the 'Atlantic Bar') seemed to put some pressure on ratings this year however, with a tiny but tangible proportion of reports saying "expansion has hit standards a bit" (hence a slight dip in grades). The general verdict however? "Always magical!" / WC2N 4AL; www.j-sheekey.co.uk; @JSheekeyRest; 11.30 pm, Sun 10 pm; booking max 6 may apply; set weekday L £53 (FP).

J Sheekey Atlantic Bar WC2 £68 3 4 4
28-34 St Martin's Ct   020 7240 2565   5–3B
"A sense of excitement and glamour" has long given Sheekey's adjacent bar a distinct identity from the restaurant – hence its relaunch last year under the new 'Atlantic' brand. Its performance is not quite as stellar as a few years ago when it felt less discovered, but "its tasty fish tapas is lovely for sharing pre-theatre" and still "delivered with style and panache in a wonderful old-fashioned room". "Fresh oysters and champagne on the doorstep of Covent Garden – what more could you ask for?" / WC2N 4AL; www.j-sheekey.co.uk; @JSheekeyRest; 11.30 pm, Sun 10.30 pm; booking max 3 may apply.

Shepherd's SW1 £56 3 4 4
Marsham Ct, Marsham St   020 7834 9552   2–4C
This traditional British stalwart – resurrected a couple of years ago after a period of closure – is something of a "Westminster favourite", on account of its "well spaced tables, calm atmosphere and good comfort food", all of which make it "ideal for a business lunch" (particularly of a politico nature). / SW1P 4LA; www.shepherdsrestaurant.co.uk; @shepherdsLondon; 10.30 pm; closed Sat & Sun.

Shikumen, Dorsett Hotel W12 £56 4 3 2
58 Shepherd's Bush Grn   020 8749 9978   8–1C
In the unusual setting of an upmarket new hotel by grungy Shepherd's Bush Green, this contemporary dining room has won recognition of a name as "one of London's better Chinese restaurants". More downbeat reports say it's "vibeless, not bad but not that good, and not cheap", but more commonly it's praised for "unexpectedly authentic cooking" – in particular "dim sum that comprehensively beats much more expensive places". / W12 5AA; www.shikumen.co.uk; @ShikumenUK; 10.30 pm, Sun 10 pm.

Shilpa W6 £31 5 2 1
206 King St   020 8741 3127   8–2B
"Lip-smackingly delicious Keralan food" at "unbelievably low prices" ("incredible for food of this quality") is the surprise find at this "very basic" South Indian, easily missed in an anonymous row of shops in Hammersmith. "Staff mean well, but don't expect too much in the way of service." / W6 0RA; www.shilparestaurant.co.uk; 11 pm, Thu-Sat midnight.

Shoryu Ramen £48 **3** 2 2
9 Regent St, SW1   no tel   4–4D
3 Denman St, W1   no tel   4–3C
5 Kingly Ct, W1   no tel   4–2B
Broadgate Circle, EC2   no tel   13–2B
"Super-tasty ramen soups and moreish meat-filled buns" still win praise for
these "very cramped" Japanese pit stops. Fans say "they put pretenders like
Wagamama to shame", but overall ratings here are not as stratospheric
as once they were. / 11 pm-midnight, Sun 9.30 pm-10 pm; E14 9 pm, Sun 6 pm;
no booking (except Kingly Ct).

Sibarita WC2 NEW £45
7 Maiden Lane   020 7497 0999   5–3D
Even with Rambla (opening later this year) still in the pipeline, Encant's
Victor Garvey found time to open this cosy, closely packed, small (26 seats)
wine, cheese, and tapas bar almost next door (with his dad!) in July 2017;
early press reviews are very upbeat. / WC2E 7NA; www.sibaritalondon.com;
@sibaritalondon; Jacket required.

The Sichuan EC1 £57 **4** **3** **3**
14 City Rd   020 7588 5489   13–2A
"A real find", near the Honourable Artillery Company, this "cracking"
yearling serves "palate-blasting" Sichuan dishes from chef Zhang Xiao
Zhong that "really hit the spot", and prices are "great" for food of this
quality. / EC1Y 2AA; www.thesichuan.co.uk; 11 pm.

Sichuan Folk E1 £45 **3** **3** 2
32 Hanbury St   020 7247 4735   13–2C
"The very good traditional Sichuan food" at this Brick Lane canteen makes
a trip "way better than a visit to Chinatown". Conditions are "pretty basic",
but staff are "very helpful to newcomers to the cuisine". / E1 6QR;
www.sichuan-folk.co.uk; 10.30 pm; No Amex.

Signor Sassi SW1 £76 **3** **3** **3**
14 Knightsbridge Green   020 7584 2277   6–1D
That it "can be noisy" is all part of the charm of this classic trattoria near
Harrods, which continues to do what it does with a fair amount of pizzazz.
/ SW1X 7QL; www.signorsassi.co.uk; @SignorSassi; 11.30 pm.

Silk Road SE5 £23 **5** 2 2
49 Camberwell Church St   020 7703 4832   1–3C
"Awesome food from the northwest frontier province of Xinjiang" at this
"noisy and ridiculously good-value" canteen in Camberwell presents
a "whole new take on Chinese cuisine". It's "spicy and fiery", "closer to the
sub-continent than typical Chinese", and "the homemade noodles are silky
and chewy and incredible". Top Tips: "amazing offal", "melt-in-the-mouth
lamb", and "the chicken plate is one of the best dishes in London!".
/ SE5 8TR; 10.30 pm; closed Sat L & Sun L; Cash only.

Simpson's in the Strand WC2 £76
100 Strand   020 7420 2111   5–3D
After too many years in the wilderness, this "tired war horse of British
cuisine" underwent a 10-week revamp in summer 2017 in a bid to restore
its "faded elegance". Having been consigned in recent decades to tourists
and breakfasting businessmen, it remains to be seen whether its legendary
trolley-service of roasts will cease to "trade on its historic reputation".
/ WC2R 0EW; www.simpsonsinthestrand.co.uk; @simpsons1828; No trainers.

Simpson's Tavern EC3 £35 234
38 1/2 Ball Ct, Cornhill 020 7626 9985 10–2C
*"I imagine Billy Bunter would have enjoyed Simpson's!". This
"City institution" dating back to 1757 is tucked down a Dickensian alleyway
and has "barely changed for a century", making it well worth a visit, even if
the food – "simple British stodge" – "is not really the point". / EC3V 9DR;
www.simpsonstavern.co.uk; @SimpsonsTavern; 3.30 pm; L only, closed Sat & Sun.*

Sinabro SW11 £59 343
28 Battersea Rise 020 3302 3120 11–2C
*"Cosy" (under 30 seats), husband-and-wife team, Battersea bistro, whose
local fan club applauds "delicious Asian-French fusion fare executed with
great care", plus "attentive service and a pleasing ambience". On Friday and
Saturday evenings, only the most ambitious tasting menu is available.
/ SW11 1EE; www.sinabro.co.uk; @SinabroLondon; 10 pm, Fri & Sat 10.30 pm.*

Singapore Garden NW6 £48 332
83a Fairfax Rd 020 7624 8233 9–2A
*The very definition of "a solid performer" – this "reliable" and "reasonably
priced" Asian in a tucked-away Swiss Cottage parade of shops has long
been a big north London favourite (including with Giles Coren). It offers
a mix of Chinese, Malaysian and Singaporean dishes – "be adventurous
in ordering to get the most benefit". / NW6 4DY; www.singaporegarden.co.uk;
@SingaporeGarden.*

Six Portland Road W11 £57 443
6 Portland Rd 020 7229 3130 7–2A
*"Clever without being pretentious" (with "something always tempting on the
specials board") characterises the somewhat "unusual" Gallic-influenced
modern cuisine at this "classy" (if "cramped and noisy") neighbourhood spot
in Holland Park, where supporting attractions include "well-chosen wine and
a warm welcome". / W11 4LA; www.sixportlandroad.com; @SixPortlandRoad;
10 pm; closed Mon & Sun D; set weekday L £35 (FP).*

Sketch,
Lecture Room W1 £147 445
9 Conduit St 020 7659 4500 4–2A
*"Take your sense of humour and embrace the place", say fans of this
"crazy, wonderful" chamber – "a stunning" space on the first floor of a
huge Mayfair palazzo. That it's "shockingly expensive" occasions less
outrage nowadays, and when it comes to the tasting menus (overseen
by Pierre Gagnaire), while "there may be a few more components in each
dish too many" there are "some nice marriages of flavours" and results can
be "remarkable". "It's not everyone's cup of tea, but the trick is to admire
the quality and meticulousness, while not taking the ponciness too seriously."
/ W1S 2XG; www.sketch.uk.com; @sketchlondon; 10.30 pm; closed Mon,
Sat L & Sun; No trainers; booking max 6 may apply; set weekday L £65 (FP).*

Sketch,
Gallery W1 £85 123
9 Conduit St 020 7659 4500 4–2A
*"Everything from the David Shrigley sketches covering the candy-pink walls
to the teacups are witty and whimsical" at this Mayfair fashionista favourite
– and the famous egg-shaped pods in the "space-age loos" are "worth the
queue" too. Was there something else? Ah yes, the food… "also completely
OTT, and not in a good way, and eye-wateringly expensive with no reason
to be". Top Tip – the "fun-filled" afternoon tea. / W1S 2XG;
www.sketch.uk.com; @sketchlondon; booking max 6 may apply.*

Skewd Kitchen EN4 NEW £47 333
12 Cockfosters Parade 020 8449 7771 1–1C
*"Fantastic kebabs" win praise for this attempt to modernise the Turkish grill
experience in Cockfosters. / EN4 0BX; www.skewdkitchen.com; @SkewdKitchen;
11 pm.*

Skylon,
South Bank Centre SE1   £75   2 2 2
Belvedere Rd   020 7654 7800   2–3D
*"Terrific views of the Thames", particularly from the window tables, are the
star feature of this striking and "spacious" chamber within the Southbank
Centre, earning it nominations for both business and romance.
"You shouldn't just have to pay for the vista" though, so it's a shame about
the "boring food, mediocre service and sky high prices". See also Skylon
Grill. / SE1 8XX; www.skylon-restaurant.co.uk; @skylonsouthbank; closed Sun D;
No trainers; set Sun L £49 (FP).*

Skylon Grill SE1   £69   2 2 3
Belvedere Rd   020 7654 7800   2–3D
*Like its more expensive adjacent sibling, this D&D London venue should
be "the perfect venue to take visitors to London", given its amazing views.
But even more enthusiastic reports concede that "it doesn't justify the price
tag" however, and too often it serves food that's "very poor for the price".
/ SE1 8XX; www.skylon-restaurant.co.uk; @skylonsouthbank; 11 pm; closed Sun D.*

Smith & Wollensky WC2   £102   2 1 2
The Adelphi Building, 1-11 John Adam St   020 7321 6007   5–4D
*"A little bit of NYC in London… but at what a frightening price". This
"huge", two-year-old outpost of the famous US brand in the ground floor
of the Adelphi has a slight feel of the "white elephant" to it, and to
a surprising extent has wholly failed to gain traction as a business-dining
mecca. Yes, the meat is top quality and there's "an amazing US wine list",
but the menu can seem "predictable", service is "very poor quality" for this
level, and "there are better places in town to go to for a good steak".
/ WC2N 6HT; www.smithandwollensky.co.uk; @sandwollenskyuk; 10.30 pm, Fri & Sat
11 pm; booking max 12 may apply; set weekday L & pre-theatre £50 (FP).*

Smith's Wapping E1   £71   4 4 4
22 Wapping High St   020 7488 3456   12–1A
*"The view of Tower Bridge and The Shard is stunning" from this Wapping
brasserie (offshoot from the long-established Ongar original), which has
a "wonderful location by the Thames". "They do serve meat, but the fish
or seafood is the way to go" – "it's exceptional, very fresh and well-
presented". / E1W 1NJ; www.smithsrestaurants.com; @smithswapping; 10 pm;
closed Sun D; No trainers; set weekday L £44 (FP), set dinner £48 (FP).*

Smiths of Smithfield,
Top Floor EC1   £77   3 3 4
67-77 Charterhouse St   020 7251 7950   10–1A
*The "wonderful rooftop location", with "old London lit up all around and
visible from all parts of the restaurant", makes this an "excellent night-time
venue". "The food is first-class", too, with a focus on rare-breed British beef,
appropriate for the meat-market setting, while service is "attentive without
being overbearing". "With a little more care this has the potential to be
really outstanding." / EC1M 6HJ; www.smithsofsmithfield.co.uk; @thisissmiths;
10.45 pm; closed Sat L & Sun; booking max 10 may apply; set weekday L &
pre-theatre £45 (FP).*

Smiths of Smithfield,
Dining Room EC1   £69   2 2 2
67-77 Charterhouse St   020 7251 7950   10–1A
*"The steaks are OK (if nothing to write home about)" at this first-floor
dining room by Smithfield meat market. It's "quite pricey for what's on offer"
though, not helped by the challenging acoustics of the space which can
make it very noisy. / EC1M 6HJ; www.smithsofsmithfield.co.uk; @thisissmiths;
10.45 pm; closed Sat L & Sun; booking max 12 may apply; set weekday L &
pre-theatre £39 (FP).*

Smiths of Smithfield,
Ground Floor EC1   £32   2 2 **3**

67-77 Charterhouse St   020 7251 7950   10–1A

This big and once-famous brunch destination across the road from
Smithfield Market is still a "favourite breakfast spot" for some, thanks to its
all-day breakfasts and 'bottomless' brunch. / EC1M 6HJ;
www.smithsofsmithfield.co.uk; @thisissmiths; 5 pm; L only; no booking.

Smokehouse Chiswick W4   £51   **3** 2 **3**

12 Sutton Lane North   020 3819 6066   8–2A

"The meat is right on the money" – "beautifully cooked" – at this "relaxed"
two-year-old Chiswick outpost of Islington's Smokehouse, in a converted pub
with very cute garden. It's "dog-friendly", too, although your poor canine
may drool with envy in this environment! / W4 4LD;
www.smokehousechiswick.co.uk; @smokehouseN1; 10 pm, Sun 9 pm;
Mon-Thu D only, Fri-Sun open L & D.

Smokehouse Islington N1   £55   **3 3** 2

63-69 Canonbury Rd   020 7354 1144   9–2D

"A carnivore's heaven"; this Canonbury gastro-boozer serves "brilliant
meat", smoked or roasted, backed up by a "great wine list". There is a sister
branch in Chiswick. / N1 2RG; www.smokehouseislington.co.uk; @smokehouseN1;
10 pm, Sun 9 pm; closed weekday L.

Smokestak E1   £48   **5 3 3**

35 Sclater St   020 3873 1733   13–1C

David Carter's "super-on-trend" yearling has left its street food origins
behind, "taking smoked meats to a more civilised level" at the 2m wide
charcoal grill of this "well-designed and stripped-back" site, just off Brick
Lane. "The smokey room adds to the atmosphere" and although "it's so
much more expensive now that it's gone permanent" the "very imaginative
BBQ" served tapas-style makes it "arguably the best smokehouse
in London" right now. Just one thing: "the interior's extremely dark
(your camera phone lights may be needed to read the menu!)". Top Menu
Tips – the brisket ("like butter"), and the crispy pig tail ("taking pork
scratchings to supreme heights!"). / E1 6LB; www.smokestak.co.uk.

Smoking Goat   £47   **4 3** 2

7 Denmark St, WC2   no tel   5–1B
64 Shoreditch High St, E1   no tel   13–1B **NEW**

"Small plates maybe, but with big, big flavours": Ben Chapman's "zingy"
Thai-inspired BBQ delivers "some real standout dishes" in a "dark and
atmospheric" – if "hipster-infested" – Soho setting, where "they also serve
decent beers on tap". "Now and again they miss, but when they get it right
they really nail it". 'Smoking Goat 2.0' opens in its spiritual home
of Shoreditch in October 2017; the new place will be bigger, and the menu
will focus on serving just a couple of signature Thai dishes each day. Top
Menu Tip – "fiery chicken wings and scallop with chilli".
/ www.smokinggoatsoho.com.

Snaps & Rye W10   £59   **3 4 3**

93 Golborne Rd   020 8964 3004   7–1A

"Unique, fresh combos of Scandi flavours, particularly fish" score well at this
"highly commendable" Danish diner in North Kensington; also "great for
breakfast or brunch" ("really good coffee"), "informal lunch", and the
"weekly set four-course dinner", with "an extensive selection of akvavit".
/ W10 5NL; www.snapsandrye.com; @snapsandrye; 10 pm; L only, Fri open L & D,
closed Mon.

Social Eating House W1 £72 5 5 4
58-59 Poland St 020 7993 3251 4–1C
"Living up to its name" – Jason Atherton's Soho 'Social' provides "one of the most enjoyable dining experiences" in town, with its "rare combination" of "exceptional value" dishes ("such modern, interesting yet 'familiar' food, focussed on flavour and pure pleasure") delivered by "really attentive yet un-pushy staff" in "a casual and buzzy setting". / W1F 7NR; www.socialeatinghouse.com; @socialeathouse; 10 pm; closed Sun; set weekday L £46 (FP).

Social Wine & Tapas W1 £53 3 4 4
39 James St 020 7993 3257 3–1A
An "extensive and great value wine list" presided over by a "fantastic sommelier" is perhaps the biggest attraction at Jason Atherton's Marylebone two-year-old – "buzzy upstairs, cosier downstairs" – but it scored extremely strongly all-round this year, including for its "really top small plates". / W1U 1EB; www.socialwineandtapas.com; @socialwinetapas; 10.30 pm; closed Sun; credit card required to book; set weekday L £32 (FP).

Soif SW11 £59 3 4 3
27 Battersea Rise 020 7223 1112 11–2C
A sibling of the better-known Terroirs, this "enterprising", "noisy and buzzy" Battersea bistro offers the same "amazing organic wine list" ("tread carefully"), "plus a mix of small tasting plates". It's "not the place to go if you are dieting – the food is extremely rich… but just so good!" / SW11 1HG; www.soif.co; @Soif_SW11; 10 pm, Sun 4 pm; closed Mon L & Sun D.

Som Saa E1 £51 5 4 4
43a Commercial St 020 7324 7790 13–2C
"Your eyes water and it feels like steam is fizzing out of your ears, but with tons of amazing, aromatic flavours that make your taste buds literally zing" at this "terrific" Thai yearling in Spitalfields – "possibly London's best, with many dishes not often seen outside Thailand". "Friendly service too" in "a hip East End space" with "a great vibrant buzz". / E1 6BD; www.somsaa.com; @somsaa_london; 11.30 pm, Sat midnight, Sun 10.30 pm; May need 4+ to book.

Sông Quê E2 £32 3 3 2
134 Kingsland Rd 020 7613 3222 14–2A
"Very keen pricing" ensures that this "long-standing Vietnamese" canteen on a busy stretch of Shoreditch's Kingsland Road is always hopping, its sharing tables crammed with customers wolfing down pho and other Viet dishes. / E2 8DY; www.songque.co.uk; 11 pm, Sun 10.30 pm; No Amex.

Sonny's Kitchen SW13 £56 2 2 2
94 Church Rd 020 8748 0393 11–1A
Rebecca Mascarenhas's long-serving Barnes local retains a devoted following for whom it has always been "a great neighbourhood restaurant". It's not the stand-out it once was however, and views differ on whether partnership with Phil Howard (who lives nearby and is now a part-owner) has put it back on track: cynics still "prefer the Olympic across the way" but optimists feel that "after some years in the wilderness, it's much improved". / SW13 0DQ; www.sonnyskitchen.co.uk; @sonnyskitchen; 10 pm, Fri & Sat 10.30 pm, Sun 9 pm; booking max 5 may apply.

Sophie's Steakhouse £65 2 3 3
42-44 Great Windmill St, W1 awaiting tel 4–3D **NEW**
311-313 Fulham Rd, SW10 020 7352 0088 6–3B
A new 120-cover Soho opening – in the renovated Moulin Theatre – looks set to raise the profile of this long-running steakhouse brand (which closed its Covent Garden branch this year). Founded in Fulham over 10 years ago, it serves decent steaks, but wins higher ratings for its "enthusiastic" service. / www.sophiessteakhouse.com; SW10 11.45 pm, Sun 10.45 pm; WC2 12.45 am, Sun 10.45 pm; no booking.

FSA RATINGS: FROM 1 POOR — 5 EXCEPTIONAL

Sosharu,
Turnmill Building EC1 £79 **3**|**3**|**3**
63 Clerkenwell Rd   020 3805 2304   10–1A
"One of the best places in London to sit at the counter and watch the chefs at work" is how fans see Jason Atherton's izakaya-themed Japanese in Clerkenwell, whose formerly lacklustre ratings improved this year. It's still an "almost, but not quite" for some reporters however, and in August 2017, Atherton announced he is looking to shift the concept to a new location (like Mayfair or Soho) in the coming months, acknowledging that it is not really working out in its original form. / EC1M 5NP; www.sosharulondon.com; @SocialCompany; 10 pm, Fri & Sat 10.30 pm; set weekday L £52 (FP).

Southam Street W10 NEW
36 Golborne Rd   awaiting tel   7–1A
The co-founders of Notting-Hill's awesome 108 Garage are to launch a second venture nearby, on the former site of Victorian boozer West Thirty Six (RIP) in late 2017; the new place will cover three storeys and include a Japanese robata grill, a private BBQ area, a raw bar serving Nikkei (Peruvian-Japanese fusion) cuisine and a private member's champagne bar. / W10 5PR.

Sparrow SE13 NEW £54
Rennell St   020 8318 6941   1–4D
Is this Lewisham's first proper neighbourhood spot? Close to the station, it opened in late spring 2017, too late to garner survey feedback, but early media reviews of its seasonal small plates with Sri Lankan influences are upbeat. / SE13 7HD; sparrowlondon.co.uk; @sparrowlondon.

The Spencer SW15 £51 **3**|**4**|**3**
237 Lower Richmond Rd   020 8788 0640   11–1A
A huge outside area across the road, with picnic tables on Putney Common (where you can order food), is a hard-to-beat summer feature of this "great South London gastropub", which serves very dependable scoff to all-and-sundry (including dog-lovers). / SW15 1HJ; www.thespencerpub.co.uk; 10 pm, Sun 9 pm.

Spinach SE22 NEW £53 **3**|**3**|**3**
161 Lordship Lane   020 8299 3344   1–4D
"A lively and ambitious spot that outshines many of its more established local rivals" – this "pleasant", bright, white-walled Dulwich café offers enjoyable cooking of the "I could cook this at home but I'll eat out tonight" variety, with an emphasis on veg. / SE22 8HD; spinach.london; 11 pm; closed Mon D & Sun D; set weekday L £32 (FP).

Spring Restaurant WC2 £85 **3**|**3**|**4**
New Wing, Lancaster Pl   020 3011 0115   2–2D
"The most beautiful interior (is it the prettiest in London?)", sets up a "very elegant and refined" atmosphere – ideal for romance or business entertaining – at this "bright" and serene chamber in Somerset House, and most feedback applauds Skye Gyngell's "light and delicate" cuisine too. "You do pay for it though", and some reporters diagnose "style over substance", or find the cooking a tad "poncy" or "pedestrian". / WC2R 1LA; www.springrestaurant.co.uk; @Spring_Rest; 10.30 pm; closed Sun D; credit card required to book; set pre-theatre £41 (FP), set weekday L £54 (FP).

Spuntino W1 £45 **3**|**3**|**3**
61 Rupert St   020 7734 4479   4–2D
Grab a stool at Russell Norman's industrial chic bar in Soho, which makes a "very welcoming spot for a solo luncher" (there are only about 30 seats), and serves Italian-American bites. / W1D 7PW; www.spuntino.co.uk; @Spuntino; 11.30 pm, Sun 10.30 pm; no booking.

The Square W1   £140   **3** **3** **1**
6-10 Bruton St   020 7495 7100   3–2C
"New owners and chef have a lot to do to reclaim the plaudits of old!"
at this "grown up" foodie temple in Mayfair, where owner Marlon Abela
took over a year ago from Phil Howard and Nigel Platts Martin: post-sale
sceptics felt you "paid two star prices for nothingy food that wasn't star
quality", and felt the switch had done nothing for the "sterile" ambience
(never exactly a riot here). It seems that Abela has 'smelt the coffee'
because replacement chef Yu Sigimoto left in August 2017 as the restaurant
closed for a total revamp to re-open in October 2017 with 'a new concept
[that] will reflect an energetic, urban and contemporary attitude
underpinned by elegant and luxurious style'. [Did he really write that? Ed]
/ W1J 6PU; www.squarerestaurant.com; @square_rest; 9.45 pm, Sat 10.15 pm,
Sun 9.30 pm; closed Sun L; booking max 8 may apply; set weekday L £66 (FP).

Sree Krishna SW17   £32   **4** **3** **2**
192-194 Tooting High St   020 8672 4250   11–2C
The "best dosas in London" are menu highlights at this "consistently good,
long-established Keralan on Tooting's main drag of curry houses" which
offers "extremely good South Indian classics for the prices". "Unlike many
of its competitors, it is spacious and comfortable enough for an evening out
as opposed to a quick bite". / SW17 0SF; www.sreekrishna.co.uk;
@SreeKrishnaUk; 10.45 pm, Thu 12.45 am, Fri & Sat 11.30 pm.

The Stable   £37   **2** **2** **3**
Unit 12, 8 Kew Bridge Rd, TW8   020 8568 8667   1–3A
16-18 Whitechapel Rd, E1   020 7377 1133   13–2D
Expanding, 17-strong national chain, with recent openings in Whitechapel
and in the new riverside development right by Kew Bridge. Fans like the
"beautifully crafted thin bases and wide variety of craft ciders and beers",
but there's some concern "quality is dropping now the roll-out to the capital
has begun".

Stagolee's SW6 NEW   £34
453 North End Rd   020 3092 1766   6–4A
A new southern-US style 'hot chicken and liquor joint', near Fulham
Broadway – a stripped-back café also serving cornmeal-battered fried fish
alongside various finger-lickin' sides. / SW6 1NZ; stagolees.co.uk; @stagoleesldn.

Star of India SW5   £55   **4** **3** **3**
154 Old Brompton Rd   020 7373 2901   6–2B
This "old favourite" – one of London's first curry houses – on the Earl's
Court-Kensington border, is an unflagging provider of "good value, great
quality and interesting flavours", serving "modern, evolved Indian food
including game". "Service has improved, but some of the decor is looking
tired." / SW5 0BE; www.starofindia.eu; 11.45 pm, Sun 11.15 pm.

Stecca SW10 NEW
14 Hollywood Rd   020 7460 2322   6–3B
A new Chelsea Italian from Stefano Stecca (Toto's, Baglioni, Zafferano)
on cute Hollywood Road, near the Chelsea & Westminster Hospital; a small
rear garden adds charm. / SW10 9HY; www.stecca.co.uk; 10 pm.

Stick & Bowl W8   £24   **5** **3** **1**
31 Kensington High St   020 7937 2778   6–1A
This "unreconstructed noodle bar" – whose "pretty tatty" looks are in sharp
contrast to ever-more chichi High Street Ken – is "the real thing, for when
you're tired of Wagamama" (which it predates by decades). "Service is fast",
providing "a large choice of delicious Chinese chow to take away or eat in,
at bargain prices". / W8 5NP; 10.45 pm; Cash only; no booking.

Sticks'n'Sushi £52 4 2 2

3 Sir Simon Milton Sq, Victoria St, SW1   020 3141 8810   2–4B NEW
11 Henrietta St, WC2   020 3141 8810   5–3D
Nelson Rd, SE10   020 3141 8220   1–3D
58 Wimbledon Hill Rd, SW19   020 3141 8800   11–2B
Crossrail Pl, E14   020 3141 8230   12–1C

"They come from Denmark (of all places!)" and these large Scandi-Asian-fusion venues serve a "winning combination" of "delicious sushi, beautifully tender sticks of meat, and enjoyable cocktails" to create an "innovative" and "really fun" concept. Even those who say it's "a bit of a gimmick" and "doesn't justify the price tag" concede the food's "quite good".
/ www.sticksnsushi.com; 10 pm, Wed-Sat 11 pm.

Sticky Mango at RSJ SE1 NEW £46

33 Coin St   020 7803 9733   10–4A

The "unchanging" style of this South Bank stalwart has – for over 30 years – made it a "comforting" refuge near the National Theatre. But now "this longtime favourite has gone down the fusion route" (in partnership with a former chef), with an updated look, and "serving South East Asian cuisine in the place of the traditional Franco/modern British grub". There's very little feedback on its latest direction, hence we've left it unrated, but Nigel Wilkinson remains a partner in the business, and his "unbeatable" Loire wine list ("the most extensive in the UK") remains a headline attraction. / SE1 9NR; www.stickymango.co.uk; @stickymangoldn; 10.30 pm; closed Sat L & Sun.

The Stoke House SW1 NEW £49

81 Buckingham Palace Rd   020 7324 7744   2–4B

Will Ricker (of Bodega Negra, E&O, Eight over Eight) brings this new American BBQ venture to Victoria's gigantic Nova development; customers can choose their cut of meat at the counter and pay according to its weight; also offering breakfast, brunch and Sunday roasts. / SW1W 0AJ; www.thestokehouse.com; @stokehouseuk; 11 pm, Sat & Sun 9 pm.

STORY SE1 £154 4 3 3

199 Tooley St   020 7183 2117   10–4D

"I preferred it to The Fat Duck!" – Tom Sellers's "edgy, modernist culinary temple", quirkily situated near Tower Bridge, delivers some of "the most interesting meals ever", and although its ratings fell just outside London's Top 5 last year, they picked up considerably again this year (perhaps due to the ending of his Ours consultancy?), and he's once more "making a decent bid to be the capital's best restaurant". "Allow plenty of time for the show" ("as the name hints, everything has a story") – 12 courses of "experimental" cuisine, "staggeringly executed" and delivered with "real panache". "It's not the cosiest of settings, but they do give you a little footstool to put your handbag on." / SE1 2UE; www.restaurantstory.co.uk; @Rest_Story; 9.15 pm; closed Mon & Sun; set weekday L £69 (FP).

Strangers Dining Room, House of Commons SW1 NEW £99 2 3 5

St Margarets St   no tel   2–4D

The House of Commons now opens this august chamber (created in 1867) to the public, and bookings must be made on the website (max 8) – expect rigorous security checks! "It's a wonderful day out" and even if elements of the experience are a bit "clunky", it's worth it for the chance to dine in the hallowed halls of Westminster. Only a set menu formula (currently £75pp) is available; bookings currently only open up 90 days in advance. / SW1A 0AA; www.parliament.uk/dining; booking essential; set weekday L £71 (FP).

Street XO W1 NEW £98 1|1|2
15 Old Burlington St 020 3096 7555 4–3A
"The most exciting newcomer in years" or "a totally confused, fusion
concept" – views split sharply on David Muñoz's nightclubby, open-kitchen
Mayfair launch (a spin-off from his Madrid Michelin 3-star, Diver XO). Even
some who hail the "beyond original" small plates ("meat-centric with Asian
and Hispanic twists") as "genius" note "they seem double the price charged
in Spain". Critics, meanwhile, find prices plain "obnoxious" for "horrible,
flashy, irritatingly wacky" tapas-style creations served by "patronising staff"
in a "classic hipster venue with limited substance" (and "music
so thumpingly loud, you could neither hear the waiters, nor focus properly
on the interesting-looking food"). / W1X 1RL; www.streetxo.com;
@StreetXO_London; Mon - Fri 11pm, Sat 12, Sun 9.30; set weekday L £53 (FP).

Stuzzico W2 £68 3|3|3
24 Kendal St 020 7262 9122 7–1D
Luca Riccio's well-established and "friendly" Italian in Bayswater's
'Connaught Village' provides classic cuisine in a simple, stylish setting.
/ W2 2AW; www.stuzzico.co.uk; @StuzzicoLondon; 10.15 pm.

Suda WC2 £45 3|3|3
23 Slingsby Place, St Martin's Court 020 7240 8010 5–2C
"A fusion of delicious Asian flavours" secures votes for the fuss-free fare
at this "contemporary Thai", in the St Martin's Courtyard development.
/ WC2E 9AB; www.suda-thai.com; 10 pm, Thu-Sat 10.30 pm; booking max 10 may
apply.

Sukho Fine Thai Cuisine SW6 £52 5|4|3
855 Fulham Rd 020 7371 7600 11–1B
"Exceptional Thai cuisine" – among the best in London – justifies the
"very crowded" conditions at this attractive shop conversion
in deepest Fulham. Staff are full of "charm" too, and although "service
is sometimes a little slow", it holds up impressively well given the perpetually
full house. / SW6 5HJ; www.sukhogroups.com; 11 pm.

Suksan SW10 £43 4|3|2
7 Park Walk 020 7351 9881 6–3B
The "fantastic food" at this Chelsea corner café inspires consistently upbeat
feedback from reporters – it's the more casual sibling of the epic Sukho Fine
Thai Cuisine in Fulham. / SW10 0AJ; www.sukhogroups.com; 10.45 pm,
Sun 9.45 pm.

The Summerhouse W9 £62 2|2|5
60 Blomfield Rd 020 7286 6752 9–4A
"A favourite spot due to its beautiful setting and decor" – this Little Venice
fixture enjoys a "great canal-side location" and "on a sunny summer's
evening you might imagine you were in the South of France eating fish
straight from the sea". / W9 2PA; www.thesummerhouse.co; @FRGSummerhouse;
No Amex.

Summers NW6 NEW £57
264-266 Kilburn High Rd 020 7693 5443 1–2B
"Newly opened in an area crying out for good quality food" – initial vibes
are good for the "small (and, when busy, noisy)" dining room above the Sir
Colin Campbell pub, where chef Ruairidh Summers (formerly of St John
Bread and Wine) himself delivers food to the table: "the Irish-slanted menu
changes weekly and is great value for money". / NW6 2BY;
www.summersdining.co.uk; @summersdining; 10.30 pm, Sun 7.30 pm; booking max 8
may apply.

Sumosan Twiga SW1 🆕
165 Sloane St   020 7495 5999   6–1D
*Re-located from Mayfair to the Sloane Street site old-timers will recall
as Monte's and Pengelley (long RIP), this fusion Japanese – part of
a Russian-owned chain also operating in Moscow, Monte Carlo and Dubai –
now serves Italian cuisine alongside its hallmark sushi, black cod and other
Nobu-esque fare. It was formerly quite well-known, but since it reopened
here in November 2016, it seems to have fallen into the international,
Gucci-clad black hole that is central Belgravia, attracting zero survey
feedback and few press reviews.* / SW1X 9QB; www.sumosan.com;
@sumosantwiga.

Sunday N1   £43   4️⃣2️⃣3️⃣
169 Hemingford Rd   020 7607 3868   9–2D
*"Fantastic brekkies and brunches are adaptable and tailored to each
customer",* says a fan from SE13, who crosses town for this *"understandably
busy and welcoming café",* on the fringes of Islington: *"get there early if you
don't want to queue".* / N1 1DA; @sundaybarnsbury; 10.30 pm; closed Mon,
Tue D, Wed D & Sun D; No Amex.

Super Tuscan E1   £51   4️⃣4️⃣3️⃣
8a Artillery Passage   020 7247 8717   13–2B
"A great find!" – this *"small",* little-known *"hidden gem",* down an alley
on the edge of the City, is a haven of *"authentic Italian food cooked with
skill and passion"* from *"a really interesting, ever-changing menu",*
plus *"a great wine list".* *"Great welcome from the staff too, who include the
two owner brothers".* Top Tip – *"limited seating space"* and *"no email
to book – you have to ring and re-confirm your table".* / E1 7LJ;
www.supertuscan.co.uk; 10 pm; closed Sat & Sun.

Sushi Bar Makoto W4   £46   4️⃣3️⃣2️⃣
57 Turnham Green Terrace   020 8987 3180   8–2A
*A "tiny neighbourhood Japanese café" in the strip near Turnham Green tube
(recently relocated from nearby) – "the specials are good value and
interesting, but the highlight is the sublime sushi, with excellent well-
flavoured rice and beautiful fish".* / W4 1RP; www.sushibarmakoto.co.uk; 10 pm,
Sun 9 pm.

Sushi Masa NW2   £43
33b Walm Lane   020 8459 2971   1–1A
*Feedback is still very limited on this Willesden Green Japanese, but such
as there is says: "it's managing to do a very difficult thing well – to succeed
Sushi Say!" (the wonderful, authentic family-run stalwart which shut up shop
two years ago, RIP).* / NW2 5SH; 10 pm.

Sushi Tetsu EC1   £89   5️⃣5️⃣4️⃣
12 Jerusalem Pas   020 3217 0090   10–1A
"Less hyped than Araki, with great food at one-seventh the price!" –
"Toru Takahashi entertains both your taste buds and your eyes" at his
"charming" Clerkenwell 7-seater: *"a showcase for his uncompromising
attention to detail and illusionist-like skills".* *"It feels like a stellar, very special
experience"* – *"as close as you can get to authentic Japanese dining
in London"* – and delivers *"astonishingly good sushi, yet without an absurd
price tag".* The catch? – *"it's a nightmare getting a seat".* / EC1V 4JP;
www.sushitetsu.co.uk; @SushiTetsuUK; 7.45 pm, Thu-Fri 8 pm, Sat 7 pm; closed
Mon & Sun; booking essential.

Sushisamba £96 3 2 5
The Piazza, WC2 awaiting tel 5–3D
Heron Tower, 110 Bishopsgate, EC2 020 3640 7330 10–2D
"It's high up and happening" ("even the lift to get up there is brilliant!") and "you can't knock the breathtaking view, or for that matter the food" on the "impressive" 39th floor of the Heron Tower, which "shouts romance" and has "a beautiful roof balcony" to boot. Even so, whether you can justify the "astronomical" prices is debatable, and while the "bold" Japanese/South American fusion bites are "exquisitely tangy and fresh", it can seem like "there's even more emphasis on how they look than how they taste". A sibling Sushisamba is to open in Covent Garden Market's Opera Terrace as we go to press. / 1.30 am, Wed-Sat 2 am.

Sutton and Sons £35 4 4 2
90 Stoke Newington High St, N16 020 7249 6444 1–1C
356 Essex Rd, N1 020 7359 1210 14–1A
240 Graham Rd, E8 020 3643 2017 14–1B
"Fabulous fish 'n' chips" at "decent value" prices are delivered "without pretension" at these "brilliant" venues in Stokey and Hackney Central. / www.suttonandsons.co.uk; 10 pm, Fri & Sat 10.30 pm; E8 Fri 10 pm; no bookings.

The Swan W4 £52 3 4 4
1 Evershed Walk,119 Acton Ln 020 8994 8262 8–1A
Fans hail "the best pub garden in London" ("loads of tables set amongst leafy trees") at this hidden-away Chiswick-fringe gastropub, but its panelled, cosy interior is lovely too. "Charming" staff and "consistently delicious, keenly priced" food make it an impressive all-rounder. / W4 5HH; www.theswanchiswick.co.uk; @SwanPubChiswick; 9 pm, Fri & Sat 10 pm, Sun 9 pm; closed weekday L.

The Swan at the Globe SE1 £60 3 2 3
21 New Globe Walk 020 7928 9444 10–3B
"Wonderful river and City views" are the obvious draw to this mock-historic tavern attached to Shakespeare's Globe theatre. The food has had its ups and downs in recent years, but the hiring of chef Allan Pickett (after the demise of Piquet, RIP) seems to be improving matters, with reports of "some deceptively good cooking going on here". Top Tip – "arrive after theatregoers have gone in!" / SE1 9DT; www.swanlondon.co.uk; @swanabout; 10.30 pm, Sun 9 pm.

Sweet Thursday N1 £42 3 2 2
95 Southgate Rd 020 7226 1727 14–1A
This "popular" and kid-friendly local pizzeria in De Beauvoir provides "reliable" food, and has an unusually "good drinks list" as it doubles as a wine shop. / N1 3JS; www.sweetthursday.co.uk; @Pizza_and_Wine; 10 pm, Fri & Sat 10 pm, Sun 9 pm.

Sweetings EC4 £76 3 2 4
39 Queen Victoria St 020 7248 3062 10–3B
For "old school cooking in a traditional setting" few London restaurants can genuinely live up to this "unfailingly beguiling" Victorian time warp, which has served "expensive but gorgeous" fish and seafood, English puds, tankards of beer and exclusively French wines to pinstriped City gents for more than a century. "I take all my most important clients here – it's a treat!" / EC4N 4SA; www.sweetingsrestaurant.co.uk; 3 pm; L only, closed Sat & Sun; no booking.

Taberna do Mercado E1 £44 3 3 2
Spitalfields Mkt   020 7375 0649   13–2B
"Full marks for originality" to star chef Nuno Mendes' taberna, where fans extol the "inspired" petiscos from his Portuguese homeland, and overlook the "modest" interior of his two-year-old unit in Spitalfields Market. That some dishes are "challenging" and "not for everyone" has always been part of its authentic appeal, but ratings slipped this year generally, with the occasional fear that it's become too "hyped". / E1 6EW; www.tabernamercado.co.uk; @tabernamercado; 9.30 pm, Sun 7.30 pm.

Taberna Etrusca EC4 £58 2 3 3
9 -11 Bow Churchyard   020 7248 5552   10–2C
On a sunny day in particular, this central City fixture, with its tucked-away location off Bow Churchyard is just the job, thanks to its quiet setting and al fresco patio; limited but positive feedback too on its traditional Italian fare. / EC4M 9DQ; www.etruscarestaurants.com; 9.30 pm; closed Sat & Sun.

The Table SE1 £39 3 2 2
83 Southwark St   020 7401 2760   10–4B
This communal canteen to the south of Bankside is "a useful venue close to Tate Modern", and does a good line in quality breakfast and lunch dishes. / SE1 0HX; www.thetablecafe.com; @thetablecafe; 10.30 pm; closed Mon D, Sat D & Sun D; booking weekdays only.

Table Du Marche N2 NEW £54 3 3 3
111 High Rd   020 8883 5750   1–1B
"A great addition to East Finchley" – this "solidly French" bar/bistro yearling "brings some welcome culinary ambition to a high street packed with cafés and quick eats", exciting the locals with its "fantastic" food and "informal" style. / N2 8AG; www.tabledumarche.co.uk; @TableDuMarche; 11 pm.

Taiwan Village SW6 £38 4 5 3
85 Lillie Rd   020 7381 2900   6–3A
"Home Taiwanese cooking at its best" is found at this "slightly quirky, family-run restaurant" lurking unobtrusively near crossroads between Lillie Road and the North End Road, whose dedicated small fanclub has long rated it as one of London's better Chinese kitchens. Top Tip – "always take the 'leave it to the chef' option for a fantastic feast". / SW6 1UD; www.taiwanvillage.com; 11 pm, Sun 10.30 pm; closed weekday L; booking max 20 may apply.

TAKA W1 NEW
18 Shepherd Market   awaiting tel   3–4B
High-end Japanese food at affordable prices. In Mayfair's Shepherd Market? That's the promise of the pre-launch PR regarding this split-level restaurant and sake bar from restaurateur Andrey Datsenko and his sister Anastasi, due to open as we go to press. / W1J 7QH; www.takalondon.com; @takamayfair.

Takahashi SW19 £44 5 4 3
228 Merton Rd   020 8540 3041   11–2B
"I don't really want to tell people about it!" – This "tiny" yearling from an ex-Nobu chef in a parade near South Wimbledon station is "not the easiest to get to if you don't live in SW19", and has "no decor" to speak of, but the food is "just heavenly": "amazing, contemporary Japanese cuisine", "as good as anything in the West End". / SW19; www.takahashi-restaurant.co.uk; @takahashi_sw19; 10 pm, Fri & Sat 10.30 pm, Sun 9 pm.

Talli Joe WC2 £38 3 3 4
152-156 Shaftesbury Avenue   020 7836 5400   5–2B
Queue at Dishoom too large? Maybe take your chances at this heart-of-Theatreland yearling from ex-Benares chef Sameer Taneja, which – though not yet quite as highly rated – likewise provides a highly popular and consistently well-rated combo of "cleverly constructed" tapas "packing a good clout flavour-wise", and a "fun" and "really lively" setting. / WC2H 8HL; www.tallijoe.com; @tallijoe; 11 pm.

Tamarind W1 £69 5 4 3
20 Queen St 020 7629 3561 3–3B
The "subtle and fully-flavoured" modern cuisine of this "flamboyantly
decorated" Mayfair basement has returned to "exceptional" form – "it hits
a perfect balance between being authentically Indian, with Western
modernisations" and "even standard dishes are a revelation". "Caring staff"
("it's like they arrive by magic carpet") further add to the experience.
/ W1J 5PR; www.tamarindrestaurant.com; @TamarindMayfair; 10.45 pm,
Sun 10.30 pm; closed Sat L; No trainers.

Tamarind Kitchen W1 NEW £47 3 3 4
167-169 Wardour St 020 7287 4243 4–2D
On the big Soho site of Imli Street (RIP), this "semi-casual" spin-off from
posh Mayfair Indian, Tamarind, lives up to its parent's stylish looks.
On limited early reports, one diner had a couple of mixed trips, but all other
feedback is upbeat about the cooking's "sophisticated Asian flavours".
/ W1F 8WR; tamarindcollection.com.

Tamp Coffee W4 £46 3 3 4
1 Devonshire Rd no tel 8–2A
From brewing some of the "best coffee in West London" by day,
this Chiswick spot transmogrifies into a "great tapas bar" serving Spanish
cured ham and Argentinian empanadas by night, along with wines from the
two countries. / W4; www.tampcoffee.co.uk; @tampcoffee; 6 pm; L only; booking
max 6 may apply.

Tandoor Chop House WC2 NEW £49 4 3 3
Adelaide St 020 3096 0359 5–4C
"Succulent and delicious tandoori dishes, offering a different experience
of Indian cooking", win fans for this "approachable" newcomer near
Trafalgar Square, whose evocative panelled decor seems to owe a fair
amount of inspiration to Dishoom. ("A good place for sure, but I suspect the
swooning and gushing comes from people who've never visited the classics
of Tooting and Commercial Road".) / WC2N 4HW; tandoorchophouse.com;
@tandoorchop; 10 pm, Sun 9 pm; booking max 6 may apply.

**Tangerine Dream,
Chelsea Physic Garden SW3** £30 3 1 3
66 Royal Hospital Rd 020 7352 5646 6–3D
"Salads are a forte" while the fruit tarts can be "sublime" at this airy, rather
retro tea room, whose location amidst stunning gardens makes this
"a wonderful choice on a sunny day". But, oh dear, "it's all a bit disorganised
and out of control", with "very slow queues on busy days". And "prices are
fairly stratospheric, even by Chelsea standards". / SW3 4HS;
www.chelseaphysicgarden.co.uk; @TangerineDCafe; 5 pm, Sun 6 pm; closed
Mon & Sat.

Tapas Brindisa £50 2 2 2
18-20 Rupert St, W1 020 7478 8758 4–3D
46 Broadwick St, W1 020 7534 1690 4–2B
18-20 Southwark St, SE1 020 7357 8880 10–4C
The "insanely busy" Borough Market original, and also its "incredibly noisy"
Soho spin-off, inspire high loyalty with their authentic approach (from a top
firm of Spanish food importers) to "sound and unpretentious tapas". "It's no
Barrafina" however – some of the dishes are distinctly "unmemorable" –
and arguably it's "just too popular to be that good".
/ www.brindisakitchens.com; 11 pm-11.30 pm, EC2 12.30 am, Morada Sun 4 pm;
Morada closed Sun D; SE1 no booking.

Taqueria W11 £40   4 4 3
141-145 Westbourne Grove   020 7229 4734   7–1B
"Really fresh food with a genuine Mexican taste" ensures a packed crowd at this "friendly" cantina on the Notting Hill/Bayswater border. The menu is dominated by tacos, cocktails and beer. / W11 2RS; www.taqueria.co.uk; @TaqueriaUK; 11 pm, Fri & Sat 11.30 pm, Sun 10.30 pm; No Amex.

Taro £36   3 2 2
10 Old Compton St, W1   020 7439 2275   5–2B
61 Brewer St, W1   020 7734 5826   4–3C
193 Balham High Rd, SW12   020 8675 5187   11–2C **NEW**
44a Cannon St, EC4   020 7236 0399   10–3B
"Service is brusque and the venues fairly basic", but these "canteen-style" eateries (the originals in Soho are best-known) still deliver a "simple formula of good Japanese nosh and excellent value" (mostly "cheap and cheerful noodle soups and sushi"). / www.tarorestaurants.co.uk; W1F 10.30 pm, Fri & Sat 11 pm, Sun 9.30 pm; W1D 10.30 pm, Fri & Sat 10.45 pm, Sun 9.30 pm, Mon 10 pm; no Amex; Brewer St only small bookings.

Tas £43   2 2 2
Leave aside the fact that "they used to be better" – these "handy" and "down-to-earth refuelling stops" are "reliable for a cheap 'n' cheerful meal" especially pre-theatre, serving "unpolished" Turkish mezze and (on the Southbank) pide (like pizza). / www.tasrestaurant.com; 11.30 pm, Sun 10.30 pm; EC4 Sat 5 pm; 72 Borough High St 6 pm, Sat & Sun 4 pm; EC4 closed Sat D & Sun, cafe SE1 closed D.

Tas Pide SE1 £37   2 3 3
20-22 New Globe Walk   020 7928 3300   10–3B
An "ideal location", right by Shakespeare's Globe makes this "unpolished but good-value" branch of the Turkish chain a useful option beside the Thames in Southwark. The pide (Turkish pizza) are "worth trying", and the menu "nicely varied". / SE1 9DR; www.tasrestaurants.co.uk; @TasRestaurants; 11.30 pm, Sun 10.30 pm.

Tate Britain, Whistler Restaurant SW1 £60   2 2 5
Millbank   020 7887 8825   2–4C
"The room and the wine dominate" as always, when it comes to this "delightful" museum café, where "the restored Whistler murals look fantastic". The "conventional" British food "is well done, but not over-exciting" – gastronomically the main event is Hamish Anderson's scorcher of a list with "very well chosen vintages, plus beer and ciders, from all over the world, all at relatively low markups". / SW1 4RG; www.tate.org.uk/visit/tate-britain/rex-whistler-restaurant; @Tate; 3 pm, Sat & Sun 5 pm; L & afternoon tea only; booking L only.

Tate Modern Restaurant SE1 £63   2 3 4
Level 9, Blavatnik Building, Bankside   020 7401 5108   10–3B
Limited but positive feedback on Tate Modern's 9th-floor restaurant in the swish new Blavatnik Building (fka the Switch House). It is now the gallery's main eatery, having somewhat supplanted the operation on Level 6 of the main building (Boiler House, now re-christened a 'kitchen & bar'). NB no river views here – just skyline – and they're best from the non-window tables (as the genius architects put the windows at shoulder height). / SE1 9TG; www.tate.org.uk/visit/tate-modern/restaurant.

Tate Modern Kitchen & Bar SE1 £58   3 2 4
Level 6, Boiler House, Bankside   020 7887 8888   10–3B
"Keep it simple with the food, and you won't be disappointed" is good advice at this stark showcase for British produce and drink on an upper floor of the famous gallery – "it's really all about that amazing view over the Thames". / SE1 9TG; www.tate.org.uk; @TateFood; 9 pm; Sun-Thu L only, Fri & Sat open L & D.

Taylor St Baristas £11 2 3 3
"Baristas who seem to have studied caffeine to degree level or higher" help win high popularity for these hip operations serving "great artisan coffee" alongside "a limited but good quality lunch/snack offering".
/ www.taylor-st.com; most branches close 5 pm-5.30 pm, WC2 7 pm, Wed-Fri 9 pm; Old Broad ST, Clifton ST, W1, E14 closed Sat & Sun; New St closed Sat; TW9 closed Sun.

Tayyabs E1 £28 4 1 2
83 Fieldgate St 020 7247 6400 10–2D
"Brilliant as ever, despite the chaos" – this 500-seat, "noisy and rambunctious" Whitechapel "scrum" ("full of smoke and smells") is "the king of the East End" for fans of its "incredibly good value" meat platters and curries, and "is worth the trip just for the lamb chops alone". Even if you've booked however, getting a table can be an "ordeal". "It's BYO, shop for beer up the street at the Tesco Metro." / E1 1JU; www.tayyabs.co.uk; @1tayyabs; 11.30 pm.

temper £37 3 4 5
25 Broadwick St, W1 020 3879 3834 4–1C
Angel Court, EC2 020 3004 6984 10–2C NEW
"A place of worship for all carnivores!" – Neil Rankin's "underground BBQ and fire pit yearling" in Soho "is like a descent into Dante's dark and confusing world full of smoke" and "if you can sit at the bar, clustered around the firepit, you get the full-on smoke experience" – "a theatrical and fascinating evening leaving you with an understanding of the hard work that goes into flawless carnivorous cooking" (although "you may be smelling it in your clothes for days"). Most of the many reports say that "if you like flesh, it's a must" – "simply cooked smoked meats; beef, lamb, goat served on a perfectly puffed flatbread or tacos, with a range of exceptional tapas and sides, delivering a truly multi-sensory event, with beautifully complimentary flavours". Ratings are undercut however, by a disgruntled minority who just don't 'get it': "for me, it just didn't live up to the hype and the bill really stung!". In July 2017, branch two opened in the City, in Bank's Angel Court development, with more Indian/curry influences (rather than Mexican ones, as in Soho). / temperrestaurant.com.

Temple & Sons EC2 NEW £67 3 3 2
22 Old Broad St 0207 877 7710 10–2C
"Jason does it again!", say fans of Atherton's "carnivore's delight" – an "interestingly shaped" (awkward?) space near Tower 42 where "quirky starters and sides complement the meat (and fish) grills, with some unusual cocktails too" – "City friendly food but with a higher degree of quality compared to a lot of City venues". / EC2N 1HQ; templeandsons.co.uk; @templeandsons; 10 pm; closed Sun.

The 10 Cases WC2 £53 2 3 3
16 Endell St 020 7836 6801 5–2C
"An unexpected variety of affordable vintages" from "an interesting and frequently changing wine list" ("talk to them to get the best choices") is the reason to visit this "quirky", extremely popular bar near the Donmar Theatre. The "limited menu" of "simple food" plays second fiddle but inspires no complaints. / WC2H 9BD; www.the10cases.co.uk; @10cases; 11 pm; closed Sun.

10 Greek Street W1 £57 4 4 3
10 Greek St 020 7734 4677 5–2A
"No pretensions, just a pure celebration of real food" is the vibe at this simple modern wine bar in the heart of Soho, which provides "wonderful, brilliantly executed dishes, full of big flavours on every visit", plus "a dozen or so house wines available by the glass at very modest markups". "Tables are squashed in, so you have to talk to your neighbours, but it works!" / W1D 4DH; www.10greekstreet.com; @10GreekStreet; 10 pm; closed Sun; booking L only.

Tendido Cero SW5 £52 **3** **3** **3**
174 Old Brompton Rd   020 7370 3685   6–2B
Consistently delicious "designer tapas", and an "amazing wine list" make this "buzzing" venue an ongoing hit with "a sleek crowd of South Kensington thirty-somethings" but there is a catch… it's "very expensive!" But "it's also one of the most authentic Spanish bars in London… and I say this as someone who grew up in Spain!" / SW5 0BA; www.cambiodetercio.co.uk; @CambiodTercio; 11 pm.

Tendido Cuatro SW6 £52 **3** **3** **3**
108-110 New King's Rd   020 7371 5147   11–1B
This authentic if pricey Parsons Green tapas bar (sibling to Earl's Court's Cambio de Tercio) improved its scores across the board this year – fans say it's "perfect for all occasions no matter how hungry you are!" / SW6 4LY; www.cambiodetercio.co.uk; @CambiodTercio; 10.30 pm, Tue-Fri 11 pm, Sun 10.30 pm.

Terroirs WC2 £52 **3** **2** **3**
5 William IV St   020 7036 0660   5–4C
"It's hard to navigate the wine lists, but they're always exciting and full of interest" at this "handy pit stop near Charing Cross" which feels "French through and through"; and whose "really interesting, if simple, meaty and cheesy Gallic plates, and knowledgeable and friendly staff ensure it's always buzzing". (That it lacks the massive profile it once enjoyed has more to do with how far London has improved since it opened in 2009, than anything that's much changed in itself). / WC2N 4DW; www.terroirswinebar.com; @TerroirsWineBar; 11 pm; closed Sun; set weekday L £30 (FP).

Test Kitchen W1 NEW £65
54 Frith St   020 7734 8487   5–2A
Chef Adam Simmonds (Le Gavroche, Le Manoir) has opened up a year-long 'test' (some might say 'pop-up') kitchen in the Soho premises that until recently were Barrafina's legendary first site; seating is still counter-style, so you can report your thoughts directly as you eat. It opened in May 2017 – too late for survey feedback: whether it's worth the (fairly steep) prices for the honour of being chef's guinea pig remains to be seen. / W1D 4SL; www.thetestkitchen.uk.

Texture W1 £112 **4** **3** **3**
34 Portman St   020 7224 0028   2–2A
"Packed with clean Icelandic flavours and textures and presented as works of art" – Aggi Sverrisson's "Scandi-inspired" dishes, married to a list of "fabulous New World wines" have won a major reputation for this "smart" and "well-spaced" (if somewhat "low key") ten-year-old, off the foyer of a hotel near Selfridges (but with its own dedicated entrance). / W1H 7BY; www.texture-restaurant.co.uk; @TextureLondon; 10.30 pm; closed Mon & Sun; set weekday L £60 (FP).

Thali SW5 £48 **4** **4** **3**
166 Old Brompton Rd   020 7373 2626   6–2B
"A welcome change from the average Indian" – this "intimate" South Kensington café follows family recipes creating a "very original menu that's far from run-of-the-mill, and beautifully prepared". Bollywood posters and "very attentive service" add further character. It's not as famous as its nearby Indian rivals, and fans feel it "seems to fly under the radar", but "knocks its more illustrious neighbours into a cocked hat". / SW5 0BA; @ThaliLondon; 11.30 pm, Sun 10.30 pm.

Theo Randall W1 £91 **3** **3** **2**
InterContinental Hotel, 1 Hamilton Pl 020 7318 8747 3–4A
"Fabulous Italian cuisine in hearty portions" and "friendly" service delight
fans of this ex-River Café chef's "calm and quiet" HQ, off the foyer of a
luxury hotel by Hyde Park Corner. As ever, there are gripes that "it feels very
much like a brightly-lit 'hotel' restaurant", but the consensus is that
"the refurbishment to the room a couple of years ago is a definite
improvement". / W1J 7QY; www.theorandall.com; @theorandall; 11 pm,
Sun 10.30 pm; closed Sat L & Sun; set weekday L £60 (FP).

Theo's SE5 £39 **3** **4** **3**
2 Grove Ln 020 3026 4224 1–3C
"Delicious pizzas" – with a "amazing, thin sourdough base" and "super
toppings (not too overloaded)" – go down a storm at this "relaxed"
Camberwell spot, and numerous reports also applaud the "friendly" staff.
/ SE5; www.theospizzeria.com; @theospizzaldn; 10.30 pm, Fri & Sat 11 pm,
Sun 10 pm; No Amex; May need 6+ to book.

Theo's Simple Italian SW5 £69 **3** **2** **3**
34 - 44 Barkston Gardens, Kensington 020 7370 9130 6–2A
The harshest critic of acclaimed chef Theo Randall's casual snacks-and-
dining sideline, in a fairly anodyne Earl's Court hotel, says "the food's pretty
good", but thinks the overall venture "feels like an afterthought rather than
anyone's focus". Other reports though are more upbeat. / SW5 0EW;
www.theossimpleitalian.co.uk; @TRSimpleItalian; 10.30 pm.

34 Mayfair W1 £79 **3** **3** **4**
34 Grosvenor Sq 020 3350 3434 3–3A
"Very large portions of first-class and well-cooked meat at very large prices"
characterises the straightforward ("quite basic"), plutocratic "posh nosh"
at Richard Caring's upscale grill, near the old US Embassy. Inevitably it's
quite a hit with expense accounters, and does a good breakfast too.
/ W1K 2HD; www.34-restaurant.co.uk; @34_restaurant; 11 pm, Sun 10 pm;
set weekday L & dinner £48 (FP).

The Thomas Cubitt SW1 £63 **3** **4** **4**
44 Elizabeth St 020 7730 6060 2–4A
"The bright and airy upstairs dining room is more refined; the downstairs
bar is bustling" (and "very noisy"), at this "crazy busy" Belgravia pub, where
"good hearty fayre" is provided by "smiley" service throughout. / SW1W 9PA;
www.thethomascubitt.co.uk; 10 pm, Sun 9.30 pm.

Thyme and Lemon N1 £43 **3** **3** **4**
139 Upper St 020 7704 6855 9–3D
"The kind of place it can be hard to find amidst the hurly burly of Upper
Street" – a cheerful venture with "very decent, imaginative tapas and great
cocktails": "all the usual suspects are on the menu but each dish is made
with real care and attention to detail." / N1 1QP; www.thymeandlemon.co.uk;
@thymeandlemon; 11.30 pm, Fri & Sat midnight, Sun 11 pm.

tibits £35 **3** **2** **3**
12-14 Heddon St, W1 020 7758 4110 4–3B
124 Southwark St, SE1 10–4B **NEW**
"Healthy and reasonably priced!!" This Swiss cafeteria chain's attractive,
veggie-vegan self-service buffet concept – wherein you help yourself and pay
per 100g – is "a handy West End option" ("initially I thought it was pricey,
but given it's off Regent Street, I think it's worth it!"). A new branch opened
in June 2017 near Tate Modern. / www.tibits.co.uk.

Timmy Green SW1 NEW   £64   2 3 3
Nova Victoria, 11 Sir Simon Milton Square   020 3019 7404   2–4B
Mixed views on this big Nova Victoria newcomer – one of the more
ambitious outlets of the 'Daisy Green' Aussie brasserie chain, with much
of its more substantial fare produced on a Josper grill. Critics feel that "while
the marketing blurb leads you to expect a personal experience, the actual
restaurant is depressingly chain-y", but fans applaud its health-conscious
dishes for coffee or brunch. / SW1E 5BH;
www.daisygreenfood.com/venues/timmy-green; 11 pm, Sun 10 pm.

TING SE1   £98   3 3 4
Level 35, 31 St Thomas St   020 7234 8000   10–4C
"You can choose between traditional and really different Asian afternoon
teas" while enjoying "stunning views of London" on this plush perch on the
35th floor of the Shard, and its "quiet and spacious" quarters are also
"an ideal location for business". Of course it's decidedly "not cheap",
and the odd report on those paying their own way at dinner here suggests
"the electronic loos can be more memorable than the cuisine". / SE1 9RY;
www.ting-shangri-la.com; @ShangriLaShard; 11 pm; No trainers; credit card required
to book; set weekday L £64 (FP).

Toff's N10   £40   3 3 2
38 Muswell Hill Broadway   020 8883 8656   1–1B
Fans still cross north London for this "crowded and noisy" Muswell Hill
stalwart – "a high calibre, Greek Cypriot-run fish 'n' chips restaurant" whose
"notable Greek salad and homemade tartare sauce" are a foil to the
"finest fish 'n' chips". / N10 3RT; www.toffsfish.co.uk; @toffsfish; 10 pm;
closed Sun.

Tokimeite W1   £104   4 3 3
23 Conduit St   020 3826 4411   3–2C
"Layers of flavour and umami" reveal the magic of kaiseki cuisine
at renowned Japanese chef Yoshihiro Murata's Mayfair yearling (backed
by Japan's largest agricultural co-op), which, for its disciples, delivers dishes
that are "beyond fresh, and raise the pure essence of simple ingredients like
yuzu and matcha to the divine". Natch, it's "very pricey", which perhaps
is why it still hasn't built a huge fanbase. / W1S 2XS; www.tokimeite.com;
@tokimeitelondon; 10.30 pm.

Tokyo Diner WC2   £24   3 3 3
2 Newport Place   020 7287 8777   5–3B
"Just like the kind of Japanese restaurants you find in Japan" –
this "bargain" diner, on the fringe of Chinatown, is "really small, but comfy
and welcoming". "Delicious noodles and tasty sushi keep cost-conscious fans
coming, and the no-tips policy also helps keep the bill down." / WC2H 7JJ;
www.tokyodiner.com; 11.30 pm; No Amex.

Tom Simmons SE1 NEW   £60
2 Still Walk   020 3848 2100   10–4D
Pembrokeshire-born chef Tom Simmons, who appeared on MasterChef: The
Professionals, opened in the One Tower Bridge development in July 2017,
with an emphasis on the use of top Welsh ingredients. By the standards
of the area, it's one of the more foodie options. / SE1 2UP; tom-simmons.co.uk;
@TomSimmons_TB; 11 pm, Sun 6 pm; closed Sun D.

Tom's Kitchen £65 2 2 2
Somerset House, 150 Strand, WC2 020 7845 4646 2–2D
27 Cale St, SW3 020 7349 0202 6–2C
11 Westferry Circus, E14 020 3011 1555 12–1C
1 Commodity Quay, E1 020 3011 5433 10–3D
Erstwhile haute cuisine star Tom Aikens has switched his focus to these casual diners in recent years. Fans (the majority) praise their "lively" staff and "good bistro cooking at friendly prices", but ratings are still dragged down by numerous reports of "slapdash" results. / www.tomskitchen.co.uk; SW3 10.30 pm, Sun 9.30 pm; WC2 10 pm; E14 9.30 pm; E1 10.30 pm; SE1 6 pm; B1 10.30 pm, Sun 5 pm; WC2, E14, B1 & E1 closed Sun D.

Tommi's Burger Joint £29 3 3 3
30 Thayer St, W1 020 7224 3828 3–1A
37 Berwick St, W1 020 7494 9086 4–2D
342 Kings Rd, SW3 020 7349 0691 6–3C
Icelander Tomas Andres Tomason's three cool self-service venues offer "delish burgers at a good price", complemented by "fantastic sweet potato fries"; "now licensed for wine and beer". / www.burgerjoint.co.uk; 10.30 pm, Sun 9 pm; booking: min 5.

The Tommy Tucker SW6 £55 3 3 3
22 Waterford Rd 0207 736 1023 6–4A
A short walk from Fulham Broadway, this attractive gastropub provides "an interesting variety of good dishes" thanks to the involvement of the team from Parson's Green's Claude's Kitchen. / SW6 2DR; www.thetommytucker.com; @tommytuckerpub; 10 pm, Sun 9 pm.

Tomoe SW15 £41 4 2 2
292 Upper Richmond Rd 020 3730 7884 11–2B
This "underrated" Putney Japanese sits behind the "shabby exterior" inherited from its predecessor on the site, Cho-San, and although the personnel have changed, the "authentic" ethos remains the same. "The owner works the sushi bar himself", results are above-par ("proper sushi, udon and many classic dishes"), and "you know it's a good place when you always see Japanese there". / SW15; 9.30 pm.

Tonkotsu £41 3 2 3
Selfridges, 400 Oxford St, W1 020 7437 0071 3–1A
63 Dean St, W1 020 7437 0071 5–2A
7 Blenheim Cr, W11 020 7221 8300 7–1A
4 Canvey St, SE1 020 7928 2228 10–4B
382 Mare St, E8 020 8533 1840 14–1B
Arch 334, 1a Dunston St, E8 020 7254 2478 14–2A
Fans still hail "the most amazing ramen outside Japan!" at these cramped noodle stops, but for doubters they "were so good, but are more average now". A fair middle view is they are "quick and cheap, with a nice ambience". / www.tonkotsu.co.uk; 10 pm-11 pm; Selfridges 30 mins before store closing; no bookings.

Tosa W6 £36 3 3 2
332 King St 020 8748 0002 8–2B
This "good local Japanese" in Stamford Brook is "well worth a look", especially for the "fine sashimi" and yakitori (charcoal-grilled chicken skewers), the house speciality. / W6 0RR; 10.30 pm, Sun 10 pm.

Tozi SW1 £50 3 3 2
8 Gillingham St 020 7769 9771 2–4B
This "big, bustling, Italian small-plates place" attached to a hotel "works surprisingly well" and is a "great standby given the dearth of quality dining spots near Victoria". The Venetian-inspired dishes are "robustly flavoured", and staff create a "friendly atmosphere". / SW1V 1HN; www.tozirestaurant.co.uk; @ToziRestaurant; 10 pm.

The Tramshed EC2 £58 **3 3 4**
32 Rivington St   020 7749 0478   13–1B
Surprisingly limited, but consistently upbeat feedback nowadays on Mark Hix's "buzzy" converted Victorian tramshed in Shoreditch, where art from Damien Hirst et al sets the tone ("the cow in formaldehyde is stunning and really adds to the place!"). The focus is "great steaks and whole roasted chicken" (the latter served dramatically, claws poking up). / EC2A 3LX; www.hixrestaurants.co.uk/restaurant/tramshed/; @the_tramshed; 11 pm, Wed-Sat midnight, Sun 9.30 pm.

Trangallan N16 £45 **4 4 3**
61 Newington Grn   020 7359 4988   1–1C
"Authentic Spanish cooking" from a "very interesting menu" draws a steady crowd to this "rather cramped" and "slightly eccentric" Hispanic by Newington Green. Even fans can find it "a little too pricey" however. / N16 9PX; www.trangallan.com; @trangallan_n16; 10.30 pm; closed Mon; No Amex; No trainers.

Tratra E2 NEW £64
2-4 Boundary St   020 7729 1051   13–1B
Spacious and stylish Shoreditch hotel basement, formerly home to Conran's The Boundary Restaurant (RIP), which now hosts this Gallic newcomer from Parisian chef and cookery writer Stéphane Reynaud – his first venture outside France. Reynaud grew up on a pig farm in the Ardèche, and the menu majors on regional classics, with lots of pork. See also Boundary Rooftop. / E2 7DD; boundary.london.

Trawler Trash N1 NEW £46
205 Upper St   020 3637 7619   9–2D
From the company behind Fitzrovia's Firedog comes a new type of fish 'n' chip restaurant – fittingly on a Canonbury site that's been serving up Britain's favourite takeaway for over 50 years (Seafish, RIP). The 'trash' part of the name refers to the fact that they serve the less popular types of fish – pilchards, coley, sprat and grey mullet, for example – and only ever fish caught that day. / N1 1RQ; www.trawler-trash.com; @TrawlerTrashN1.

Tredwell's WC2 £60 **2 2 2**
4 Upper St Martin's Ln   020 3764 0840   5–3B
Views divide sharply on Marcus Wareing's Theatreland diner, which has yet to fully find its mojo. It does have a growing profile, and fans for whom its "clever-but-not-too-clever (fairly robust and rich) cooking" makes for "a very enjoyable night out". Even those who like its "nice buzzy feel" can feel the food is only "decent enough", however, especially as it ain't cheap, and there are still too many reports of some plain "dismal" meals. / WC2H 9NY; www.tredwells.com; @tredwells; 10 pm, Fri & Sat 11 pm.

Treves & Hyde E1 NEW £54
15-17 Leman St   020 3621 8900   10–2D
With a coffee shop and terrace downstairs, and a restaurant and bar upstairs, this new operation near Aldgate East tube – part of a boutique Aparthotel complex – covers all the bases – even brunch at weekends. No survey feedback yet, but positive press reports on its small plates from chef George Tannock. / E1 8EN; trevesandhyde.com; @trevesandhyde; 10.30 pm, Sun 3 pm.

Tried & True SW15 £25 **3 3 3**
279 Upper Richmond Rd   020 8789 0410   11–2A
"Great breakfasts in massive portions" plus a mean cup of coffee have established this Kiwi outfit on the Putney café scene. Welcoming to dogs and children – "it can be trying when Torquil and Samantha are running around expressing themselves and your quiet moment is lost". / SW15; www.triedandtrue.co.uk; @tried_true_cafe; 4 pm, Sat & Sun 4.30 pm; L only.

Trinity SW4 £75 5 5 3
4 The Polygon 020 7622 1199 11–2D

"We are privileged to have it as our local!" – Adam Byatt's Clapham landmark "goes from strength to strength", and "at last has a well deserved Michelin star" (though we're not sure what took them so long). "The whole team are so knowledgeable and committed to providing a memorable meal", and results are "exceptional" from an à la carte menu that's more "conventional" than its former multi-course tasting format. "They've greatly improved the decor since refurbishing a couple of years ago too, but it can still lack buzz." See also Upstairs at Trinity. / SW4 0JG; www.trinityrestaurant.co.uk; @TrinityLondon; 10 pm, Sun 9 pm; closed Mon L & Sun D.

Trinity Upstairs SW4 £47 5 4 4
4 The Polygon 020 3745 7227 11–2D

"Far much more casual than downstairs, but the food is AMAZING!!" – "Adam Byatt's cracking foil to the main outlet", relatively recently opened above his Clapham HQ, serves a small-plates menu "full of lip smacking choices", and "there's more buzz than below with raised counters, no white tablecloths, and quaffable rosé on a pump". "Be prepared to sit on stools all evening though!" / SW4 0JG; www.trinityrestaurant.co.uk; @trinityupstairs; 10 pm.

Trishna W1 £83 5 3 3
15-17 Blandford St 020 7935 5624 2–1A

"Even better than its slightly more glamorous sibling Gymkhana"; the Sethi family's "exceptional" Mumbai import delivers "memorably gorgeous" cuisine (most famously fish) with "lovely subtle flavours and a deft touch to the spicing". Only the food is a stand-out however: in other respects "it looks and feels like an easygoing Marylebone restaurant". / W1U 3DG; www.trishnalondon.com; @TrishnaLondon; 10.30 pm, Sun 9.45 pm.

LA TROMPETTE W4 £82 5 4 3
5-7 Devonshire Rd 020 8747 1836 8–2A

"A consistent class act, year-in-year-out" – this "perfect local" ("people of Chiswick, do you know how lucky you are?") is "pretty much on a par with Chez Bruce", its stablemate. "The sublime cooking manages to be classic, yet with exciting elements popping up in each dish", staff are "first rate" and – though "relaxed" – its "elegant" styling would not be out of place in the West End. / W4 2EU; www.latrompette.co.uk; @LaTrompetteUK; 10.30 pm, Sun 9.30 pm.

Trullo N1 £59 4 4 3
300-302 St Paul's Rd 020 7226 2733 9–2D

"Terrific food is simply but superbly realised (from a daily menu reflecting the freshest of ingredients)" at Tim Siadatan and Jordan Frieda's "top drawer Italian" – "an unexpected find in this part of Islington" ("just off Highbury Corner") – and it helps that "staff look like they enjoy their work". "Downstairs is dark and sexy, especially the booths; upstairs is light and airy and great in the summer." / N1 2LH; www.trullorestaurant.com; @Trullo_LDN; 10.15 pm; closed Sun D; No Amex.

FKA 'The Truscott Arms' W9 NEW
55 Shirland Rd 020 7266 9198 1–2B

Back with a bang! – this Maida Vale gastropub is also back from the dead as Henry Harris (formerly of Knightsbridge's Racine, long RIP) takes over the kitchen. It closed in August last year after a lengthy legal battle over rent increases, and is set to re-open in late 2017. STOP PRESS: in October 2017, it was announced that the former name, The Truscott Arms, will not be used after the re-launch for legal reasons. / W9 2JD; 10 pm, Sat & Sun 11 pm.

Tsunami SW4 £48 4 2 3
5-7 Voltaire Rd   020 7978 1610   11–1D
"Far superior to Nobu and a fraction of the price!"; this fusion Japanese is a long-running fixture on the Clapham scene thanks to its "complex menu" of "consistently delicious" fusion fare and "fabulous" cocktails. Drawbacks? – service can be "clueless" and the interior "noisy". Note, the West End branch (in Charlotte Street) is now closed, although the team has opened Yama Momo in East Dulwich. / SW4 6DQ; www.tsunamirestaurant.co.uk; 11 pm, Fri-Sun midnight; closed Sat L & Sun; No Amex.

Tulse Hill Hotel SE24 £50 3 3 3
150 Norwood Rd   020 8671 7499   1–4D
"Who'd expect such a hip hangout on the South Circular!?" – "the food is good and the vibe is great" at this trendy gastropub with a fantastic garden, between Brixton and Dulwich. / SE24 9AY; www.tulsehillhotel.com; @TulseHillHotel; 10 pm, Sun 9 pm.

Tuyo E2 NEW
129a Pritchard's Rd   020 7739 2540   14–2B
Sitting alongside the canal by Hackney's foodie Broadway Market, a new Mediterranean tapas joint serving a selection of pinchos and small bites mixing Levantine, Spanish and other influences. The backing comes from the owners of Islington perennial Gallipoli, while former Salt Yard group chef Ricardo Pimentel heads up the kitchen. / E2 9AP; www.tuyo.london; @Tuyocafebistro; 10 pm, Fri-Sun 11 pm.

28 Church Row NW3 £52 4 4 3
28 Church Row   020 7993 2062   9–2A
"A real addition to the desert of Hampstead!" This no-reservations, "very buzzy" ("it can get very full") new tapas bar – a townhouse cellar in a super-cute street – breathes a bit of much-needed life into NW3's dining options, serving "typical Spanish staples (boquerones, patatas fritas, chorizo) alongside enticing and original specials on the board". "Service is borne of a genuine enthusiasm for the place and its customers." / NW3 6UP; www.28churchrow.com; @28churchrow; 10.30 pm, Sun 9.30 pm.

28-50 £57 2 4 3
15-17 Marylebone Ln, W1   020 7486 7922   3–1A
17-19 Maddox St, W1   020 7495 1505   4–2A
140 Fetter Ln, EC4   020 7242 8877   10–2A
"Fantastic wines at fantastic prices" (in a variety of glass sizes) underlies the high ongoing popularity of these "lively" bar/bistros – to accompany, "simple" fare (like burgers) that's "enjoyable, if basic". / www.2850.co.uk; 9.30 pm-10.30 pm; EC4 closed Sat & Sun, W1S closed Sun.

Twist W1 £63 4 4 4
42 Crawford St   020 7723 3377   2–1A
"Each tapas-style dish is a delight – with crisp distinctive flavours, and fabulous for sharing", say fans of Eduardo Tuccillo's Italo-Spanish "fusion-tapas" cuisine at this Spartan but "charming" Marylebone two-year-old (on the site that was for many years Garbos, long RIP). / W1H 1JW; www.twistkitchen.co.uk; @twistkitchen; closed Sun; SRA-Food Made Good – 2 stars.

Two Brothers N3 £34 3 2 2
297-303 Regent's Park Rd   020 8346 0469   1–1B
"Consistently high quality, fresh fish" continues to win a near-universal thumbs-up for this traditional Finsbury chippy: a long-standing major favourite in the area. / N3 1DP; www.twobrothers.co.uk; 10 pm; closed Mon.

2 Veneti W1 £54 3 4 3
10 Wigmore St   020 7637 0789   3–1B
Steering clear of standard Italian cuisine, this well regarded outfit near the Wigmore Hall impresses reporters with the quality of its service and its "imaginative Venetian food". There's also a strong list of Italian wines and grappas. / W1U 2RD; www.2veneti.com; @2Veneti; 10.30 pm, Sat 11 pm; closed Sat L & Sun.

Typing Room, Town Hall Hotel E2 £95 5 5 3
Patriot Square   020 7871 0461   14–2B
Lee Westcott's "delicate but unfussy cooking, with strong flavours, and beautiful presentation" is matched with "perfectly judged" service from the open kitchen at this "unpretentious" but "pleasantly buzzing" green-walled dining room – the corner of Bethnal Green's monolithic old town hall that's nowadays a trendy boutique hotel (and which first found fame as Viajante, long RIP). "How this place doesn't have a Michelin star is beyond belief!" / E2 9NF; www.typingroom.com; @TypingRoom; 10 pm; closed Mon & Tue L; booking max 4 may apply; set weekday L £56 (FP).

Uchi E5 £41 4 2 2
144 Clarence Rd   020 3302 4670   14–1B
"Not much to look at from the outside and still a bit surprising to find even though the area is very up and coming" – this "tucked away" Japanese café is esteemed by its small fan club for "utterly delicious" sushi: "you won't even notice that you're perched on a wooden stool". / E5 8DY; www.uchihackney.com; @uchihackney; 11 pm, Sun 10 pm.

Uli W11 £46 3 3 3
5 Ladbroke Rd   020 3141 5878   7–2B
"It is great to have Uli back in a new location after an absence of a few years!" – so say numerous loyal fans of this resurrected Notting Hill pan-Asian, where "host Michael Lim is as hospitable as ever in the new flashier surroundings". It's still finding its stride however: "while the food's great, it could use more work – at times it's patchy and lacking the flair of the original". / W11 3PA; www.ulilondon.com; @ulilondon; 11.45 pm; D only, closed Sun.

Umu W1 £120 3 4 3
14-16 Bruton Pl   020 7499 8881   3–2C
The doors slide back Star Trek-style at this bijou Japanese restaurant "tucked away discreetly" in a cute Mayfair mews – one of London's leading providers of "sublime and sophisticated" Kyoto-style kaiseki cuisine… but "ye gods, the prices!" Chef Yoshinori Ishii is "the ultimate Renaissance man – he makes the pottery, does the flowers and calligraphy, teaches fisherman how to treat the catch and takes cooking to another level!" / W1J 6LX; 10.30 pm; closed Sat L & Sun; No trainers; booking max 14 may apply.

Union Street Café SE1 £62 2 2 3
47-51 Great Suffolk St   020 7592 7977   10–4B
Gordon Ramsay's "busy and bustling" casual Italian in Borough attracts a wide spectrum of very mixed views. For fans, it's "a gastronomic find" and "very special", but its worst foes say "never again" having experienced "some of the most dire food ever". Top Tip – "the lunch menu is good value". / SE1 0BS; www.gordonramsayrestaurants.com/union-street-cafe; @unionstreetcafe; 10.45 pm; closed Sun D.

Le Vacherin W4 £64 3 3 2
76-77 South Parade   020 8742 2121   8–1A
Malcolm John's "reliable local brasserie" by Acton Green feels like it's been airlifted from provincial France, and, at its best, its traditional Gallic fare can really hit the heights. Top Tip – "good value lunch". / W4 5LF; www.levacherin.co.uk; @Le_Vacherin; 10.30 pm, Sun 9 pm; closed Mon L; set weekday L & pre-theatre £41 (FP).

Vagabond Wines £32 **3** **3** **4**
Nova Building, 77 Buck' Palace Rd, SW1 020 7630 7693 2–4B
25 Charlotte St, W1 020 3441 9210 2–1C
18-22 Vanston Place, SW6 020 7381 1717 6–4A
4 Northcote Rd, SW11 020 7738 0540 11–2C
67 Brushfield St, E1 020 3674 5670 13–2C
"A very cool concept" – a 5-store chain providing "an excellent way to while
away a few hours", whereby you "you top up an Oyster-style card and then
you're able to make your way around the room, grabbing yourself samples
or large glasses from a vast array of wines". "Nibble on charcuterie and
cheeses and other sharing plates as you go" but "while the food is good,
it's really all about the vino".

Vanilla Black EC4 £63 **2** **2** **2**
17-18 Tooks Ct 020 7242 2622 10–2A
This ambitious and upmarket veggie operation near Chancery Lane has
divided opinion this year, with its food scores falling dramatically. For fans,
it still serves "vegetarian food lifted to the level of fine dining" –
"imaginative, bursting with taste and barely a lentil in sight". But there was
much unaccustomed bitter disappointment too: "fell really short…"
"landfill…", "they must hate veggies to treat us like this!" / EC4A 1LB;
www.vanillablack.co.uk; @vanillablack1; 10 pm; closed Sun; No Amex.

Vasco & Piero's Pavilion W1 £60 **3** **4** **3**
15 Poland St 020 7437 8774 4–1C
A "hidden gem" in the heart of Soho – this "cramped" old-world Italian
"ristorante" run by three generations of the same family specialises
in Umbrian cuisine. It's "not yet quite vintage but in something of a
timewarp, and offers surprisingly and genuinely good food with well
managed service". / W1F 8QE; www.vascosfood.com; @Vasco_and_Piero; 9.30 pm;
closed Sat L & Sun.

Veeraswamy W1 £78 **4** **4** **3**
Victory Hs, 99-101 Regent St 020 7734 1401 4–4B
You would never guess from its "beautiful and relaxed" interior that this
first-floor Indian veteran, near Piccadilly Circus, is London's oldest (est 1926).
Service is "professional" and the "delicate and expertly prepared" cuisine
has fully moved with the times – "it shows just how the amazing flavours
of subcontinental cooking can be elevated!" / W1B 4RS; www.veeraswamy.com;
@theveeraswamy; 10.45 pm, Sun 10:15 pm; booking max 12 may apply.

Veneta SW1 £50 **3** **3** **2**
3 Norris St 020 3874 9100 4–4D
"Choices from the fish bar are a highlight" at this year-old Salt Yard Group
venture, whose "Italian-style" small plates formula here is "mainly focussed
on Venetian dishes". Occupying a unit in the new St James's Market
development, all the "glass, flash and tourists" of this "big, chimney-like
space" are at odds with the cosy style of its stablemates. / SW1Y 4RJ;
www.saltyardgroup.co.uk/veneta; @venetastjames.

Verdi's E1 £45 **3** **4** **3**
237 Mile End Rd 020 7423 9563 14–2B
"Just how a neighbourhood restaurant should be", this "authentic, family-run
trattoria serving cuisine from Emilia Romagna" is "surprising for Stepney"
and "fantastic every time". "Prices are a little higher than average for the
area, but not excessive for such thoughtful, well-executed cooking". / E1 4AA;
www.gverdi.uk; @verdislondon.

Il Vicolo SW1 £54 **3 4 2**
3-4 Crown Passage 020 7839 3960 3–4D
"Surprisingly affordable" for St James's – this family-run Italian is tucked
down an "out-of-the-way" alley. Run with "efficiency and charm"
by "the patron and his daughters", "service is miraculous even when busy" –
which is often. Recommended for both business lunchers, and family
dinners. / SW1Y 6PP; www.ilvicolorestaurant.co.uk; 10 pm; closed Sat L & Sun.

The Victoria SW14 £53
10 West Temple Sheen 020 8876 4238 11–2A
A favourite refuelling stop after walks in Richmond Park, Paul Merrett's
"attractive gastropub" – complete with large dining conservatory and
"good facilities for children outside" – is a popular destination, serving
a "very accessible" menu. Feedback was "uneven" this year, but in
August 2017 they announced an impending facelift which seems likely
to pep the place back up to form again. / SW14 7RT; victoriasheen.co.uk;
@TheVictoria_Pub; 10 pm, Sun 9 pm; No Amex.

Viet Food W1 £32 **3 3 3**
34-36 Wardour St 020 7494 4555 5–3A
"Fresh and flavourful Vietnamese food" is the hallmark of former Hakkasan
chef, Jeff Tan's Chinatown operation: "it's rare to find quality cooking, at a
decent price, in the centre of London!" / W1D 6QT; www.vietnamfood.co.uk;
10.30 pm, Fri & Sat 11 pm.

Viet Grill E2 £45 **3 2 2**
58 Kingsland Rd 020 7739 6686 14–2A
"Clear fresh flavours" and "charming service" enable this studenty-looking
Vietnamese café to stand out among stiff competition on Kingsland Road's
'pho mile'. / E2 8DP; www.vietnamesekitchen.co.uk; @CayTreVietGrill; 11 pm, Fri &
Sat 11.30 pm, Sun 10.30 pm.

Vijay NW6 £35 **3 3 1**
49 Willesden Ln 020 7328 1087 1–1B
"Food good, decor awful": a report that could have been written any time
in the last 40 years on this "perennial Kilburn curry house favourite" –
opened in 1964 and seemingly "frozen in time", yet "consistently delivering
delicious, south Indian grub" (to a surprisingly well-heeled crowd). Top Tip –
option to BYO £2.50 corkage. / NW6 7RF; www.vijayrestaurant.co.uk; 10.45 pm,
Fri & Sat 11.45 pm; no booking.

Villa Bianca NW3 £60 **2 2 2**
1 Perrins Ct 020 7435 3131 9–2A
This stalwart Hampstead Italian is "a reassuring time warp" for fans,
bowled over by its hyper-cute village location and '70s-style glamour. A fair
assessment is that "it's not bad, not brilliant – just a nice place to be".
/ NW3 1QS; www.villabiancanw3.com; @VillaBiancaNW3; 11.30 pm, Sun 10.30 pm.

Villa Di Geggiano W4 £63 **3 3 4**
66-68 Chiswick High Rd 020 3384 9442 8–2B
"Authentic Tuscan fodder in charming surroundings" highlights this ambitious
(somewhat "pricey") three-year-old "a definite cut above the standard Italian
experience" ("given so many chains in Chiswick, it really stands out"). "It's a
brave venture too, in a large space where others have failed", and with a big
summer terrace. / W4 1SY; www.villadigeggiano.co.uk; @villadigeggiano; 10 pm;
closed Mon.

Villandry £61 1 1 3
11-12 Waterloo Pl, SW1   020 7930 3305   2–3C
170 Gt Portland St, W1   020 7631 3131   2–1B
"Great ambience" and "good locations" in St James's and Marylebone may keep these rather grand-looking cafés ticking over, but they incite complaints of "pretensions of grandeur above their station", taking flak for food and service that often seem "complacent", "formulaic" and "ordinary". / www.villandry.com/; W1 & SW1 10.30 pm, Sun 6 pm; W1 & SW1 closed Sun D.

The Vincent E8 NEW £31
3 Atkins Sq, Dalston Lane   020 8510 0423   14–1B
The trio who previously ran Bethnal Green boozer The Sebright Arms together opened this airy all-day Hackney spot in May 2017. Local beers, coffee, Sunday brunches and roasts aim to make it a linchpin of the local scene. / E8 1FN; www.thevincent-e8.com; @thevincente8; 10 pm, Sat 3 pm, Sun 5 pm; May need 6+ to book.

The Vincent Rooms,
Westminster Kingsway College SW1 £37 3 4 3
76 Vincent Sq   020 7802 8391   2–4C
"It's so enjoyable to chat with the enthusiastic trainees" at this catering college dining room in a quiet corner of Westminster, staffed by the students. Not only that, but "the set lunch menu is a steal" for "witty and beautifully presented food" delivered by "well-meaning if haphazard" servers. / SW1P 2PD; www.westking.ac.uk/about-us/vincent-rooms-restaurant/; @thevincentrooms; 7 pm; closed Mon D, Tue D, Fri D, Sat & Sun; No Amex.

Vineet Bhatia London SW3 £146 3 3 2
10 Lincoln St   020 7225 1881   6–2D
"Amid increasing competition, still London's top fine-dining Indian!" – so say most reports on Vineet Bhatia's "superbly re-invented cuisine" at this "impeccably run" Chelsea townhouse, which is "unique amongst upmarket Indians in aiming to be quiet and intimate rather than buzzy and fashionable". Formerly Rasoi, it relaunched one year ago, and fans are "extremely happy that this wonderful place is just as refined as before, but with a slightly different focus (perhaps less led by luxury ingredients)". Even supporters give "a word of warning however – don't even think about the prices" – and there is the odd critic who says "are they kidding? Just go to Gymkhana, Trishna or Jamavar for £50 less!" STOP PRESS: in October 2017, just after receiving Michelin recognition, the restaurant closed, apparently to re-open on a new site some time soon. / SW3 2TS; www.vineetbhatia.london; @VineetBhatiaLDN; 10.15 pm.

Vinoteca £55 3 3 4
15 Seymour Pl, W1   020 7724 7288   2–2A
55 Beak St, W1   020 3544 7411   4–2B
18 Devonshire Rd, W4   020 3701 8822   8–2A
One Pancras Sq, N1   020 3793 7210   9–3C
7 St John St, EC1   020 7253 8786   10–1B
Considering that the "simple" fare is "incidental" to the "terrific selection of wines at reasonable prices", the cooking is "surprisingly good" and "reasonably priced" at these "bustling" and extremely popular modern watering holes. / www.vinoteca.co.uk; 11 pm; W1H & W4 Sun 4 pm; W1F 10.45 pm, Sun 9.30 pm; EC1 closed Sun; W1H & W4 closed Sun D.

Vivat Bacchus £60 3 4 2
4 Hay's Ln, SE1   020 7234 0891   10–4C
47 Farringdon St, EC4   020 7353 2648   10–2A
A "fantastic range of mainly South African vintages" helps provide the justification for consuming the "perfectly cooked steaks" at this wine bar duo with branches in Farringdon and Bankside. Top Tip – don't miss the 'Cheese Room Experience'. / www.vivatbacchus.co.uk; 10.30 pm; closed Sun.

VIVI WC1 NEW
Centre Point   awaiting tel   5–1A
As part of the renovation of the entire, iconic Centre Point complex, London restaurateurs rhubarb (Sky Garden, Saatchi Gallery, Royal Albert Hall) will open this new flagship restaurant as part of the bridge link overlooking the new square in late 2017. / WC1A 1DD; www.rhubarb.co.uk.

VQ   £44   2 4 3
St Giles Hotel, Great Russell St, WC1   020 7636 5888   5–1A
325 Fulham Rd, SW10   020 7376 7224   6–3B
24 Pembridge Rd, W11   020 3745 7224   7–2B
9 Aldgate High St, EC3   020 3301 7224   10–2D NEW
"Very handy for early hours refuelling" – particularly the venerable SW10 original of these late night diners, which has provided "great all-day breakfasts" (and all night ones) and "service with a smile" since the '80s. / www.vingtquatre.co.uk; open 24 hours, W11 1 am, Thu-Sat 3 am, Sun midnight; booking: max 6 online.

Vrisaki N22   £35   3 3 3
73 Middleton Rd   020 8889 8760   1–1C
"The facelift hasn't spoilt it!" – this venerable Bounds Green Greek has updated its old taverna-style decor in recent times, but the food (most famously the humongous mezze special) is "still really good". / N22 8LZ; @vrisakiuk; 11.30 pm, Sun 9 pm; closed Mon; No Amex.

Wagamama   £44   2 3 2
"You know what to expect" and "you still get what you pay for" at these "good staple" Asian canteens, which "epitomise cheap and cheerful dining" and whose "reliable and reasonably healthy" noodles and curries are "great for a speedy, fresh-cooked meal", particularly with kids in tow. / www.wagamama.com; 10 pm - 11.30 pm; EC2 Sat 9 pm; EC4 closed Sat & Sun; EC2 closed Sun; no booking.

Wahaca   £37   3 3 3
"Fun and lighthearted" style – and providing "zingy" dishes at "great-value" prices, "fab cocktails" and "friendly service" – Thomasina Miers' feisty street-food chain "shows no sign of decline, despite its expansion". It's "streets ahead of other Mexican groups" and "always a solid standby when you want a quick meal". / www.wahaca.com; 11 pm, Sun 10.30 pm; W12, Charlotte St, SW19 Sun 10 pm; no booking or need 6+ to book.

Waka EC3 NEW
39a Eastcheap   no tel   10–3D
'Nikkei' cuisine – Japanese meets Peruvian – features at this City newcomer, which opened in the shadow of the Walkie Talkie in September 2017. Upstairs is 'grab and go' and there's to be a 60-cover basement dining area. / EC3M 1DT; www.waka-uk.com; @WakaLdn; 6pm; No bookings.

The Wallace,
The Wallace Collection W1   £51   2 1 5
Hertford Hs, Manchester Sq   020 7563 9505   3–1A
The "gorgeous setting" of the Wallace Collection's café, in the glass-covered atrium of one of London's most interesting smaller museums, "is delightful, especially on a bright day" – enough to transform a "teatime treat" into a "fairytale experience". But "the food and service are not much more than so-so" – "I hope it's changed since the demise of Peyton & Byrne" (the caterers who went into administration in October 2016). / W1U 3BN; www.peytonandbyrne.co.uk; 9.30 pm; Sun-Thu closed D; No Amex; booking max 10 may apply.

Walnut N4 NEW
The Arts Building, Morris Place   020 7263 5289   9–1D
This crowdfunded new neighbourhood restaurant in Finsbury Park's John Jones Arts Building opened in May 2017. Chef Emma Duggan is an Angela Hartnett protégée, and according to early reviews combines affordable scoff with a pleasing polished-concrete aesthetic. / N4 3JG; walnutdining.co.uk; @Walnut_Dining.

Waterloo Bar & Kitchen SE1   £55   222
131 Waterloo Rd   020 7928 5086   10–4A
"Handy for the Old Vic and Waterloo station", this busy brasserie provides "good portions and friendly service". Some say "the food is OK rather than great", but it's "reasonably priced". / SE1 8UR; www.barandkitchen.co.uk; @BarKitchen; 10.30 pm.

The Waterway W9   £52   222
54 Formosa St   020 7266 3557   9–4A
"The best time to go is in the summer when you can sit outside" on the big terrace of this tranquil hangout – a converted 20th century pub, attractively set on the water in Little Venice, where the food offering is "limited" but "reliable". / W9 2JU; www.thewaterway.co.uk; @thewaterway_; 11 pm, Sun 10.30 pm.

The Wells NW3   £55   223
30 Well Walk   020 7794 3785   9–1A
"Lovely after a walk on the Heath" – Hampstead's most popular pub (owned by Fay Maschler's sister, Beth Coventry) has a prime location and is "a wonderful local, full of character and charm". You can eat either in the "very civilised" upstairs room or the downstairs bar – "the food is pricey, but in fairness I always end up enjoying it". / NW3 1BX; thewellshampstead.london; @WellsHampstead; 10 pm, Sun 9.30 pm.

Westerns Laundry N5 NEW   £57
34 Drayton Park   020 7700 3700   9–2D
Primeur owners David Gingell (chef) and Jérémie Cometto-Lingenheim (manager) have opened a second restaurant, in a modishly understated, converted 1950s former laundry (hence the name) in the shadow of the Emirates Stadium in Holloway. Early press reviews are ecstatic (Grace Dent food 5/5, ambience 5/5) regarding its simply prepared seasonal small plates – 'focusing on produce from the sea' – and educated selection of natural wines. / N5 1PB; www.westernslaundry.com; @WesternsLaundry; 10.30 pm, Sun 5 pm.

The Wet Fish Café NW6   £50   334
242 West End Lane   020 7443 9222   1–1B
A "high-quality café/bistro in the heart of West Hampstead" (named after the Art Deco-tiled fishmongers premises it inherited) that's "always busy" thanks to its "relaxed" style and "good value". Top Tip – "great for brunch", especially on Sunday, when it's very popular. / NW6 1LG; www.thewetfishcafe.co.uk; @thewetfishcafe; 10 pm; No Amex; booking D only; set weekday L £32 (FP).

White Bear EC1   £33   333
57 St. John St   020 7490 3535   10–1A
"What was until last year a depressing, down-at-heel pub (although with a good fringe theatre attached) has been enlarged by Young's". "The theatre still thrives after its move upstairs", while "at the rear there's a pleasant, light dining area". "It's not gastro', but above average for pub food". / EC1M 4AN; www.thewhitebearojs.co.uk; 11.30 pm, Fri midnight.

The White Onion SW19 £65 **3**|**3**|**2**
67 High St   020 8947 8278   11–2B
"To have a consistently good restaurant in Wimbledon" is a major boon, and this high quality two-year-old enchants its very large local fan club with *"classic French cuisine"* and *"casual"* style. The worst thing anyone says about the place is that *"while very good, it's not as good as its Surbiton sibling, The French Table".* / SW19 5EE; www.thewhiteonion.co.uk; @thewhiteonionSW; 10.30 pm; closed Mon, Tue L, Wed L & Thu L; set weekday L £41 (FP).

The White Swan EC4 £62 **3**|**3**|**2**
108 Fetter Ln   020 7242 9696   10–2A
"Great bar snacks" and casual pub dishes can be had in this smart and often loud boozer, off Fleet Street. Or head upstairs for a more ambitious menu in the *"much quieter"* dining room. / EC4A 1ES; www.thewhiteswanlondon.com; @thewhiteswanEC4; 10 pm; closed Sat & Sun.

The Wigmore,
The Langham W1 NEW £48
1c Portland Pl   020 7965 0198   2–1B
Michel Roux Jr oversees the 'quintessential British pub fare' (yes, you read that right) at this 're-imagining of the Great British pub', which opened in The Langham in July 2017. / W1B 1JA; www.the-wigmore.co.uk; @Langham_London; Mon-Wed midnight, The-Sat 1 am.

Wild Honey W1 £79 **3**|**4**|**3**
12 St George St   020 7758 9160   3–2C
Anthony Demetre's agreeably *"restrained"* (and business-friendly) Mayfair venture has won renown for its *"intelligent and accomplished"* cooking and *"extensive and not outrageously priced wine list, with most available in 250ml carafes, so you can have two or three in the course of a meal".* Top Tip – *"very good lunch menu of British fare at reasonable prices"* (*"things you wouldn't necessarily choose but all well cooked and worth it if you are prepared to experiment"*). / W1S 2FB; www.wildhoneyrestaurant.co.uk; @whrestaurant; 10.30 pm; closed Sun.

Wilmington EC1 £52 **3**|**4**|**3**
69 Rosebery Avenue   020 7837 1384   10–1A
Limited feedback on this handsome corner pub in Clerkenwell, but such reports as we have particularly recommend its *"very good pre-Sadler's Wells deals on food".* / EC1R 4RL; www.wilmingtonclerkenwell.com; @wilmingtonec1; 10pm, Fri & Sat 10.30pm , Sun 9pm.

Wiltons SW1 £95 **3**|**4**|**5**
55 Jermyn St   020 7629 9955   3–3C
"The courtesy and class is evident from the moment you make the reservation" at this *"stalwart of St James"* (est 1742, here since 1984): *"a perfect and unchanging haven"* for *"the very best of British classics"* – in particular *"fabulous"* fish and seafood (and also game). *"Make sure there is plenty of money available on your credit card, as it is powerfully expensive, but it's "an ideal location for serious business discussions"* (*"I'd sign anything you put in front of me in this place, and then apologise for having the wrong sort of pen!"*). / SW1Y 6LX; www.wiltons.co.uk; @wiltons1742; 10.15 pm; closed Sat L & Sun; Jacket required; set weekday L £64 (FP).

The Windmill W1 £49 **3**|**3**|**3**
6-8 Mill St   020 7491 8050   4–2A
Looking for *"great pies"*? – You'll find 'em at this traditional Mayfair boozer where they headline the bill of *"good old-fashioned British fare"* at *"reasonable prices"* and in *"huge portions"*; cask beer, *"excellent chips"* and Sunday roasts are all tipped here too. / W1S 2AZ; www.windmillmayfair.co.uk; @tweetiepie_w1; 10 pm, Sun 5 pm; closed Sat D & Sun.

The Wine Library EC3 £40   **1** 3 5
43 Trinity Sq   020 7481 0415   10–3D
"A huge choice of wines with only a modest corkage charge" is the
irresistible draw to this ancient cellar bar near Tower Hill. *"The food
is casual party fare – pâtés, breads, cheeses, all very fresh"*. *"Only go
if you're not intending to do much work for the rest of the day."* / EC3N 4DJ;
www.winelibrary.co.uk; 7.30 pm; closed Mon D, Sat & Sun.

Winemakers Deptford SE8 NEW
209 Deptford High St   020 8305 6852   1–3D
It opened too late for survey feedback this year, but press reports
suggest this casual wine bar from Winemakers Club, a Farringdon wine
importers, is an important step in the gentrification of Deptford, providing
accomplished cooking and a superior list of biodynamic wines. / SE8 3NT;
thewinemakersclub.co.uk; 11 pm, Fri & Sat midnight, Sun 6 pm; closed Mon,
Tue-Thu D only, Fri-Sat L & D, Sun L only.

THE WOLSELEY W1 £62   3 4 5
160 Piccadilly   020 7499 6996   3–3C
"Always bustling" and *"a real occasion"* – Corbin & King's *"large,
continental and sophisticated"* Grand Café near The Ritz is *"a marvellous,
metropolitan meeting point"* not least for the capital's movers 'n' shakers
(it's *"great for subtle star-spotting!"*) for whom the *"courteous and very
professional service"* helps make it the town's No. 1 choice for business. The
"brasserie comfort food is unambitious but well done", and it's as *"a go-to
venue for breakfast"* (it's *"THE place in London"*) that it particularly shines.
Another Top Tip – *"afternoon tea to die for"*. / W1J 9EB; www.thewolseley.com;
@TheWolseleyRest; midnight, Sun 11 pm.

Wong Kei W1 £33   3 2 **1**
41-43 Wardour St   020 7437 8408   5–3A
*"Service atrocious, ambience zero... but you can't beat their steaming bowls
with change from £10 in central London!"* This famous – and famously rude
– multi-storey canteen in Chinatown *"goes from strength to strength"* thanks
to its *"ultra-cheap"*, and *"incredibly reliable"* chow. Abuse from the staff
is so institutionalised *"you can even buy a T-shirt with 'upstairs, downstairs'
which is what they bark at you when you enter"*, but in recent years some
regulars claim the treatment here is *"more polite than in the past"*.
/ W1D 6PY; www.wongkeilondon.com; 11.15 pm, Sun 10.30 pm; Cash only.

Wright Brothers £66   4 3 3
13 Kingly St, W1   020 7434 3611   4–2B
56 Old Brompton Rd, SW7   020 7581 0131   6–2B
11 Stoney St, SE1   020 7403 9554   10–4C
Battersea Power Stn, 188 Kirtling St, SW11   awaiting tel   11–1C NEW
8 Lamb St, E1   020 7377 8706   10–2D
"A haven for top notch oysters and shellfish" (they have their own Cornish
farm and wholesalers) – these *"bustling"* bistros have grown from their
Borough Market origins on the back of their *"sparklingly fresh and delicious"*
dishes, plus *"good wines by the glass"*. *"That they're cramped is all part
of the charm"*. Battersea is the latest addition to the family, and in SW7
fans tip *"the little gem of a Mermaid Bar, like a luxurious grotto with elegant
cocktails"*. / SE1 10 pm, Sat 11 pm; W1 11 pm, Sun 10 pm; E1 10.30 pm,
Sun 9 pm; SW7 10.30 pm, Sun 9.30 pm; booking: max 8.

Xi'an Impression N7 £31   4 2 2
117 Benwell Rd   020 3441 0191   9–2D
Some of *"the best authentic, lip-tingling Shaanxi food in the UK"* can
be found at this basic, Formica-tabled *"little gem in the back streets
of Holloway"* – *"bizarrely located across the road from the Emirates
Stadium"*. *"Their noodles are very fresh, incredibly tasty, beautifully cooked
and so verrrry long!"* / N7; www.xianimpression.co.uk; @xianimpression; 10 pm.

XU W1 NEW £60
30 Rupert St   020 3319 8147   4–3D
Backed by JKS Restaurants and the brains behind the hugely successful Bao chain; an elegant, wood-panelled, two-floor café serving traditional Taiwanese cooking and teas. Xu (named for co-founder and chef Erchen Chang's late grandfather) opened in Chinatown in early summer 2017 (too late for survey feedback). / W1D 6DL; xulondon.com; @XU_london; 11 pm.

Yalla Yalla £39 3 2 2
1 Green's Ct, W1   020 7287 7663   4–2D
12 Winsley St, W1   020 7637 4748   3–1C
Greenwich Peninsula Sq, SE10   0772 584 1372   9–3C
Tiny, "cheap 'n' cheerful" Lebanese street food cafés, whose "interesting" choice of "fresh and zingy" mezze and other dishes "never fails to deliver". / www.yalla-yalla.co.uk; Green's Court 11 pm, Sun 10 pm; Winsley Street 11.30 pm, Sat 11 pm; W1 closed Sun; booking min 10.

Yama Momo SE22 £53 4 2 3
72 Lordship Ln   020 8299 1007   1–4D
"Consistently delicious sushi" and inventive cocktails create the buzz at this "atmospheric local" in East Dulwich. It's an offshoot of Clapham's long-running Tsunami, bringing Pacific fusion elements to Japanese cuisine in a contemporary, clubby setting. / SE22 8HF; www.yamamomo.co.uk; @YamamomoRest; 10 pm, Fri & Sat 10.30 pm, Sun 9.30 pm; closed weekday L.

Yard Sale Pizza £35 4 3 2
54 Blackstock Rd, N4   020 7226 2651   9–1D
Hoe St, E17   020 8509 0888   1–1D NEW
105 Lower Clapton Rd, E5   020 3602 9090   14–1B
"Delicious, freshly made pizza with unusual toppings" attract raves for these hip pizzerias in Clapton, Walthamstow and Finsbury Park. They're "friendly", but "pretty basic" – "not a place to hang around". / 11 pm, Sun 10 pm; closed Mon-Thu L.

Yashin W8 £86 4 3 2
1a Argyll Rd   020 7938 1536   6–1A
This modern Japanese in Kensington inspired only a few reports this year: all of them, though, were highly complimentary regarding its ambitious cuisine. (Its lesser-known 'Ocean' branch, on the Old Brompton Road, continues to inspire thin but more feedback to the effect that "prices are nuts, there's no real atmosphere, and the whole set-up is a bit weird".) / W8 7DB; www.yashinsushi.com; @Yashinsushi; 10 pm; booking max 7 may apply.

Yauatcha Soho £81 4 3 3
Broadwick Hs, 15-17 Broadwick St, W1   020 7494 8888   4–1C
Broadgate Circle, EC2   020 3817 9888   13–2B
"Fabulously tasty dim sum with a modern twist" and "slick" styling fuel the fun at this incredibly popular and vibey, Chinese-fusion duo, with the more moody Soho original still outscoring its big and "bright" Broadgate Circle spin-off. Service is the weakest link – it can be "somewhat haphazard". / W1 10 pm, Fri & Sat 10.30 pm; EC2 11.30 pm; EC2 closed Sun.

The Yellow House SE16 £45 3 3 3
126 Lower Rd   020 7231 8777   12–2A
"Reliably yummy" wood-fired pizza and charcoal grills are the menu mainstays at this "friendly" neighbourhood indie, right next to Surrey Quays station. / SE16 2UE; www.theyellowhouse.eu; @theyellowhousejazz; 10 pm, Sun 8 pm; closed Mon, Tue-Sat D only, Sun open L & D.

Yipin China N1 £45 4 3 2
70-72 Liverpool Rd   020 7354 3388   9–3D
An "unglamorous, cash-only" operation serving "spectacular Sichuan and Hunanese food" near Angel. "It's not fancy" – "decor is functional" – "but that's part of the charm!" / N1 0QD; www.yipinchina.co.uk; 11 pm.

Yming W1 £45 3 5 2

35-36 Greek St 020 7734 2721 5–2A

This "reliable stalwart of the Soho Chinese food scene" provides "an oasis of calm" just a 1-minute walk from Chinatown. "Managed by the awesome William and Christine", its "serene" and "welcoming" style suits its older fanbase, as do the "interesting if un-challenging" dishes. Potentially under threat (like the nearby Soho Curzon) from demolition for Crossrail 2 – we hope they don't retire: "it would be the end of an institution... and some very good food!" / W1D 5DL; www.yminglondon.com; 11.45 pm.

Yolk EC2 NEW £10

Container 4, Finsbury Avenue Sq no tel 13–2B

A shipping container by Liverpool Street is the pop-up to more permanent home of this street food venture, where they know their way around an egg. / EC2M 2PA; www.yolklondon.com; @YolkLondon; 4 pm; L only, closed Sat & Sun.

York & Albany NW1 £59 2 2 3

127-129 Parkway 020 7592 1227 9–3B

Gordon Ramsay's Georgian tavern by Regent's Park is a large and handsome venue, with bags of potential, but while not totally lacking fans, its middling scores continue to confirm its performance as "nothing special". / NW1 7PS; www.gordonramsayrestaurants.com/york-and-a; @yorkandalbany; 10.30 pm, Sun 10 pm; booking essential.

Yoshi Sushi W6 £39 3 3 2

210 King St 020 8748 5058 8–2B

This nondescript-looking Korean/Japanese stalwart near Ravenscourt Park tube is worth discovering for its "reasonably priced" and dependable classic dishes. / W6 0RA; www.yoshisushi.co.uk; 11 pm, Sun 10.30 pm; closed Sun L.

Yoshino W1 £44 4 4 2

3 Piccadilly Pl 020 7287 6622 4–4C

Hiding in a side alley, this "favourite Japanese" is an "oasis of calm of the highest quality in Piccadilly". "The welcome is always amazing" ("I feel like a treasured friend"), and the food (which has had its ups and downs over the years) "very fresh and simple" but "artfully produced". There's quite a contrast in style between the ground floor counter and small upstairs space. / W1J 0DB; www.yoshino.net; @Yoshino_London; closed Sun.

Yosma W1 £51 3 3 2

50 Baker St 020 3019 6282 2–1A

It can be "off puttingly noisy" – at night, the background beats are sometimes "club-level loud" – but most reporters are "loving this new Turkish-inspired venue on Baker Street", whose "beautifully spiced" dishes "beat the old skool Turkish joints" and are "sensibly priced" too. / W1U 7BT; www.yosma.london; @Yosma_London; 11 pm, Thu-Sat midnight; set weekday L £32 (FP).

Zafferano SW1 £90 2 2 2

15 Lowndes St 020 7235 5800 6–1D

"A lovely top-class Italian" is the verdict of most reporters on this "old-fashioned" (and business-friendly) Belgravian, which in the noughties was regularly fêted as London's best and which, on most accounts, "still produces really wonderful dishes, especially fresh pasta and fish". Its ratings continue to be hampered, though, by a disgruntled minority who think "it used to be fantastic, but has become stodgy". / SW1X 9EY; www.zafferanorestaurant.com; 10.30 pm, Sun 10 pm; set weekday L £60 (FP).

Zaffrani N1 £48 3 2 2

47 Cross St 020 7226 5522 9–3D

This "excellent and above-average local Indian" off Islington's main drag boasts an "unusual and well-executed menu". / N1 2BB; www.zaffrani.co.uk; 10.30 pm.

Zaibatsu SE10 £35 **4** **3** **2**

96 Trafalgar Rd 020 8858 9317 1–3D

"Very good Japanese food" and "cheapish" prices mean you should make the effort to "book in advance" at this Greenwich café. It's "hectic, basic and BYO, but all the nosh is prepared excellently". / SE10 9UW; www.zaibatsufusion.co.uk; @ong_teck; 11 pm; closed Mon; Cash only.

Zaika of Kensington W8 £65 **3** **2** **3**

1 Kensington High St 020 7795 6533 6–1A

"Exquisite flavours" have won renown for this spacious (somewhat "cavernous") banking hall conversion by Kensington Gardens Hotel as "one of the better Indians around". But marks fell a little this year, due to gripes about "hit-and-miss service" and the odd report of food that was "not as refined as in the past". / W8 5NP; www.zaikaofkensington.com; @ZaikaLondon; 10.45 pm, Sun 9.45 pm; closed Mon L; credit card required to book; set weekday L & pre-theatre £43 (FP).

Zelman Meats £58 **5** **4** **4**

Harvey Nichols, 109-125 Knightsbridge, SW1 020 7201 8625 6–1D
2 St Anne's Ct, W1 020 7437 0566 4–1D

"The 'dirty' steak is just something else" at Misha Zelman's (of Goodman's fame) genius brainchild – a cutely tucked-away, industrial cool unit (with an offshoot in residence at Harvey Nicks), where, he has reinvented "steak as a fastish-food concept", providing "really superior steaks to share with generous side portions". There's also a "varied and not too expensive beer and wine list", which helps fuel the fun atmosphere. / W1 10.30 pm, Sun 8 pm; SW1 10 pm, Sun 7 pm; N4 midnight; W1 closed Mon L, N4 closed Mon-Fri L.

Zeret SE5 £29 **4** **5** **3**

216-218 Camberwell Rd 020 7701 8587 1–3C

"Despite the bleak location, the food is anything but!" at this Camberwell café – "a great find" thanks to its "very good value" and unusual, traditional Ethiopian dishes, and a commitment to cater for meat-eaters and vegans alike. It helps that "the people running it are incredibly nice". / SE5 0ED; www.zeretkitchen.com; 11 pm.

Zero Degrees SE3 £45 **3** **3** **4**

29-31 Montpelier Vale 020 8852 5619 1–4D

"You can't go wrong with pizza and a beer brewed in-house (and the moules frites are decent too)" at this popular Blackheath microbrewery – "it's dead cheap too and has an amazing atmosphere!" / SE3 0TJ; www.zerodegrees.co.uk; @Zerodegreesbeer; midnight, Sun 11.30 pm.

Zest, JW3 NW3 £60 **3** **3** **2**

341-351 Finchley Rd 020 7433 8955 1–1B

"Surprising and very satisfying" Middle Eastern cooking has won converts for this modern Israeli restaurant/café/bar in West Hampstead. "It may not be quite as good" (or as famous) "as the Honeys, but ingredients are always fresh and excellent". / NW3 6ET; www.zestatjw3.co.uk; @ZESTatJW3; 9.45 pm; closed Fri & Sat L.

Zheng SW3 NEW £61

4 Sydney St 020 7352 9890 6–2C

On the 'revolving doors' Chelsea site most lately occupied by Brasserie Gustave (RIP), this swish, black-walled newcomer – sibling to the renowned Oxford Chinese/Malaysian operation – opened too late for survey feedback but to excellent reviews in late spring 2017: perhaps it will finally provide a formula that 'sticks' here. / SW3 6PP; www.zhengchelsea.co.uk; 11.30 pm, Sun 10 pm.

Zia Lucia N7 £35 **4** **3** **3**
157 Holloway Rd   020 7700 3708   9–2D
"The best thing to happen around Holloway Road for some time!" –
this *"mega-busy"* yearling, built around a *"Dante-esque, wood fired oven"*,
takes *"pizza into the realm of fine dining"* with its *"unique choice
of vegetarian and easy-to-digest, 48-hour fermented doughs"* and *"perfect
toppings"*. *"Remember to book, otherwise it's hopeless"*. / N7 8LX;
www.zialucia.com; @zialuciapizza; 10.30 pm.

Ziani's SW3 £62 **2** **3** **2**
45 Radnor Walk   020 7351 5297   6–3C
"The tables are squashed together and it's hard to manoeuvre" at this
"friendly and welcoming" trattoria just off the King's Road. *"Great fun"*,
with lots of *"buzz, but not much privacy"* – *"it's full of locals"*, here for the
"good food and large portions". / SW3 4BP; www.ziani.co.uk; 11 pm, Sun 10 pm;
set Sun L £40 (FP).

Zima W1 £44 **3** **2** **3**
45 Frith St   020 7494 9111   5–2A
"Russian street food" served in a speakeasy-style venue next door to Ronnie
Scott's jazz club makes Russki celeb chef, Alexei Zimin's Soho yearling
"fun and something a bit different". / W1D 4SD; www.zima.bar; @ZimaLondon;
11.30 pm, Sun 8.30 pm; closed Mon; set weekday L £26 (FP).

Zoilo W1 £59 **4** **3** **3**
9 Duke St   020 7486 9699   3–1A
"I adore this place!" – this Argentinian bar between Selfridges and the
Wallace Collection dazzles its small and varied fanclub with its *"frequently
changing menu"* of *"very good tapas"*, complemented by an all-Argentinian
wine list. / W1U 3EG; www.zoilo.co.uk; @Zoilo_London; 10.30 pm; closed Sun.

Zuma SW7 £82 **5** **3** **3**
5 Raphael St   020 7584 1010   6–1C
"Exceptional" Japanese-fusion cuisine still wins very consistent praise for this
svelte, *"very buzzy"* Knightsbridge haunt, whose appeal – in its fifteenth
year – still stacks up well. OK, there's some *"tossing around of black credit
cards"* by its eurotrashy following, but this can make for *"awesome people-
watching"*, and even though *"it's very expensive, it's worth it"*. / SW7 1DL;
www.zumarestaurant.com; 10.45 pm, Sun 10.15 pm; booking max 8 may apply.

CUISINES

An asterisk (*) after an entry
indicates exceptional or very
good cooking

AMERICAN
Central
The Avenue *(SW1)*
Balthazar *(WC2)*
Big Easy *(WC2)*
Bodean's *(W1)*
Breakfast Club *(W1)*
The Chiltern Firehouse *(W1)*
Christopher's *(WC2)*
Colony Grill Room, Beaumont
    Hotel *(W1)*
Hai Cenato *(SW1)*
Hard Rock Café *(W1)*
Hubbard & Bell, Hoxton Hotel *(WC1)*
Jackson & Rye *(W1)*
Joe Allen *(WC2)*
Rainforest Café *(W1)*
Shake Shack *(WC1, WC2)*
Spuntino *(W1)*

West
Big Easy *(SW3)*
Bodean's *(SW6)*
Electric Diner *(W11)*
Jackson & Rye Chiswick *(W4)*
Pomona's *(W2)*
Stagolee's *(SW6)*

North
Breakfast Club Hoxton *(N1)*
Delisserie *(NW8)*
Frederick's *(N1)*

South
Bodean's *(SW17, SW4)*
Counter Vauxhall Arches *(SW8)**
Jackson & Rye Richmond, Hotham
    House *(TW9)*
The Joint *(SW9)*

East
Big Easy *(E14)*
Bodean's *(EC1, EC3)*
Breakfast Club *(E1)*
Pitt Cue Co *(EC2)**
Shake Shack *(E20)*

AUSTRALIAN
Central
Bronte *(WC2)*
Granger & Co *(SW1)*
Lantana Café *(W1)*
Timmy Green *(SW1)*

West
Granger & Co *(W11)*

North
Granger & Co *(N1)*
Lantana Cafe *(NW1)*
Sunday *(N1)**

South
Flotsam and Jetsam *(SW17)*
Lantana London Bridge *(SE1)*

East
Granger & Co, The Buckley
    Building *(EC1)*
Lantana Café *(EC1)*

BRITISH, MODERN
Central
The Alfred Tennyson *(SW1)*
Alyn Williams, Westbury Hotel *(W1)*
Andrew Edmunds *(W1)*
Aster Restaurant *(SW1)*
Aurora *(W1)*
Balthazar *(WC2)*
Barbecoa Piccadilly *(W1)*
Bellamy's *(W1)*
The Berners Tavern *(W1)*
Bob Bob Ricard *(W1)*
Bonhams Restaurant, Bonhams
    Auction House *(W1)**
The Botanist *(SW1)*
Cambridge Street Kitchen *(SW1)*
Le Caprice *(SW1)*
Caxton Grill *(SW1)*
Clipstone *(W1)**
The Collins Room *(SW1)*
Comptoir Café & Wine *(W1)*
Coopers Restaurant & Bar *(WC2)*
Daylesford Organic *(SW1, W1)*
Dean Street Townhouse *(W1)*
Dorchester Grill, Dorchester
    Hotel *(W1)*
Duck & Waffle Local *(SW1)*
Ducksoup *(W1)*
Ebury Restaurant & Wine Bar *(SW1)*
Fera at Claridge's, Claridge's
    Hotel *(W1)*
45 Jermyn Street *(SW1)*
The Frog *(WC2)**
Galvin at the Athenaeum *(W1)*
George in the Strand *(WC2)*
Gordon's Wine Bar *(WC2)*
The Grazing Goat *(W1)*
Great Queen Street *(WC2)*
Greenwood *(SW1)*
Ham Yard Restaurant, Ham Yard
    Hotel *(W1)*
Hardy's Brasserie *(W1)*
Hatchetts *(W1)*
Heddon Street Kitchen *(W1)*
Heliot Steak House *(WC2)**
Hix *(W1)*
Hush *(W1, WC1)*
Indigo, One Aldwych *(WC2)*
The Ivy *(WC2)*
The Ivy Café *(W1)*
The Ivy Market Grill *(WC2)*
Jar Kitchen *(WC2)*
The Keeper's House, Royal
    Academy *(W1)*
Kitty Fisher's *(W1)*
Langan's Brasserie *(W1)*
Little Social *(W1)*
Lorne *(SW1)**
Magpie *(W1)*
Marcus, The Berkeley *(SW1)*
Mews of Mayfair *(W1)*
Native *(WC2)**
Noble Rot *(WC1)*
The Norfolk Arms *(WC1)*
The Northall, Corinthia Hotel *(WC2)*
108 Brasserie *(W1)*
The Orange *(SW1)*
Ormer Mayfair *(W1)**
The Other Naughty Piglet *(SW1)**
The Pantechnicon *(SW1)*
Percy & Founders *(W1)*
The Petersham *(WC2)*
Picture *(W1)*
Pollen Street Social *(W1)*
Polpo at Ape & Bird *(WC2)*
Portland *(W1)**
The Portrait, National Portrait

Gallery *(WC2)*
The Punchbowl *(W1)*
Quaglino's *(SW1)*
Quo Vadis *(W1)**
Rail House Café *(SW1)*
Roux at Parliament Square,
  RICS *(SW1)**
Roux at the Landau, The
  Langham *(W1)*
Saint Luke's Kitchen, Library *(WC2)*
Savoy Thames Foyer *(WC2)*
Seven Park Place *(SW1)**
Shampers *(W1)*
Social Eating House *(W1)**
Spring Restaurant *(WC2)*
Tate Britain, Whistler
  Restaurant *(SW1)*
10 Greek Street *(W1)**
Terroirs *(WC2)*
The Thomas Cubitt *(SW1)*
Tom's Kitchen, Somerset
  House *(WC2)*
Tredwell's *(WC2)*
Villandry *(W1)*
The Vincent Rooms, Westminster
  Kingsway College *(SW1)*
Vinoteca Seymour Place *(W1)*
VIVI *(WC1)*
VQ, St Giles Hotel *(WC1)*
Wild Honey *(W1)*
The Wolseley *(W1)*

West

The Abingdon *(W8)*
The Anglesea Arms *(W6)**
Babylon, Kensington Roof
  Gardens *(W8)*
Blue Boat *(W6)*
Bluebird *(SW3)*
The Brackenbury *(W6)**
Brackenbury Wine Rooms *(W6)*
Brinkley's *(SW10)*
The Builders Arms *(SW3)*
Charlotte's Place *(W5)*
Charlotte's W4 *(W4)*
Charlotte's W5, Dickens Yard *(W5)*
City Barge *(W4)*
Clarke's *(W8)**
Claude's Kitchen, Amuse
  Bouche *(SW6)**
The Colton Arms *(W14)*
Core by Clare Smyth *(W11)*
The Cross Keys *(SW3)*
The Dartmouth Castle *(W6)*
Daylesford Organic *(W11)*
The Dock Kitchen, Portobello
  Dock *(W10)*
The Dove *(W6)*
Duke of Sussex *(W4)*
Ealing Park Tavern *(W5)*
Elystan Street *(SW3)**
The Enterprise *(SW3)*
The Five Fields *(SW3)**
The Frontline Club *(W2)*
Harwood Arms *(SW6)**
The Havelock Tavern *(W14)*
Hedone *(W4)*
High Road Brasserie *(W4)*
The Hour Glass *(SW3)*
The Ivy Chelsea Garden *(SW3)*
The Ivy Kensington Brasserie *(W8)*
Julie's *(W11)*
Kensington Place *(W8)*
Kensington Square Kitchen *(W8)*
Kitchen W8 *(W8)**
The Ladbroke Arms *(W11)*
Launceston Place *(W8)*
The Ledbury *(W11)**

The Magazine Restaurant, Serpentine
  Gallery *(W2)*
Manuka Kitchen *(SW6)*
Marianne *(W2)**
maze Grill *(SW10)*
Medlar *(SW10)**
Megan's Delicatessen *(SW6)*
Mustard *(W6)*
No 197 Chiswick Fire Station *(W4)*
Parabola, Design Museum *(W8)*
Paradise by Way of Kensal
  Green *(W10)*
The Pear Tree *(W6)*
Rabbit *(SW3)*
Restaurant Ours *(SW3)*
Salt & Honey *(W2)*
The Sands End *(SW6)*
The Shed *(W8)**
Six Portland Road *(W11)**
Tangerine Dream, Chelsea Physic
  Garden *(SW3)*
Tom's Kitchen *(SW3)*
The Tommy Tucker *(SW6)*
The Truscott Arms *(W9)*
Vinoteca *(W4)*
VQ *(SW10,W11)*
The Waterway *(W9)*

North

The Booking Office, St Pancras
  Renaissance Hotel *(NW1)*
Bradley's *(NW3)*
The Bull *(N6)*
Caravan King's Cross *(N1)*
Chriskitch *(N1, N10)**
The Clifton *(NW8)*
Dandy *(N16)**
Dartmouth Arms *(NW5)*
The Drapers Arms *(N1)*
Fifteen *(N1)*
Frederick's *(N1)*
Gabeto Cantina *(NW1)*
The Good Egg *(N16)**
Haven Bistro *(N20)*
Heirloom *(N8)*
The Horseshoe *(NW3)*
Humble Grape *(N1)*
The Ivy Café *(NW8)*
James Cochran N1 *(N1)**
The Junction Tavern *(NW5)*
Juniper Tree *(NW3)*
The Landmark, Winter Garden *(NW1)*
The Lighterman *(N1)*
Oak N4 *(N4)*
Odette's *(NW1)**
Oldroyd *(N1)**
Parlour Kensal *(NW10)**
Pig & Butcher *(N1)**
Plum + Spilt Milk, Great Northern
  Hotel *(N1)*
The Red Lion & Sun *(N6)*
Rotunda Bar & Restaurant, Kings
  Place *(N1)*
Season Kitchen *(N4)*
Walnut *(N4)*
The Wells *(NW3)*
Westerns Laundry *(N5)*
The Wet Fish Café *(NW6)*

South

Albion *(SE1)*
Aqua Shard *(SE1)*
The Avalon *(SW12)*
Babette *(SE15)*
The Bingham *(TW10)**
Bistro Union *(SW4)*
Black Prince *(SE11)*
Blueprint Café *(SE1)*

La Bonne Bouffe (SE22)
The Brown Dog (SW13)
Brunswick House Café (SW8)
The Camberwell Arms (SE5)*
Cannizaro House, Hotel du
  Vin (SW19)
Caravan Bankside (SE1)
Catford Constitutional Club (SE6)
Chez Bruce (SW17)*
Counter Culture (SW4)*
Craft London (SE10)*
The Crooked Well (SE5)
The Dairy (SW4)*
Duckroad (SW8)
The Dysart Petersham (TW10)
Earl Spencer (SW18)
Edwins (SE1)
Elliot's Café (SE1)
40 Maltby Street (SE1)*
Franklins (SE22)
The Garden Cafe at the Garden
  Museum (SE1)
The Garrison (SE1)
The Glasshouse (TW9)*
Globe Tavern (SE1)
The Green Room, The National
  Theatre (SE1)
The Guildford Arms (SE10)
Hood (SW2)*
House Restaurant, National
  Theatre (SE1)
Humble Grape (SW11)
The Ivy Café (SW19, TW9)
The Ivy Tower Bridge (SE1)
Jules (SW15)
Lamberts (SW12)*
LASSCO Bar & DIning (SE1)
Laughing Gravy (SE1)
The Lido Café, Brockwell Lido (SE24)
Louie Louie (SE17)
Lupins (SE1)
The Manor (SW4)
May The Fifteenth (SW4)
Menier Chocolate Factory (SE1)
Minnow (SW4)
Nutbourne (SW11)
Oblix (SE1)
Olympic, Olympic Studios (SW13)
Orchard (SE4)
Oxo Tower, Restaurant (SE1)
Oxo Tower, Brasserie (SE1)
The Palmerston (SE22)*
Parlez (SE4)
Peckham Refreshment Rooms (SE15)
The Perry Vale (SE23)
Petersham Hotel (TW10)
Petersham Nurseries Cafe (TW10)
Pharmacy 2, Newport Street
  Gallery (SE11)
Plot (SW17)
The Plough (SW14)
Le Pont de la Tour (SE1)
Rivington Grill (SE10)
The Rosendale (SE21)
Salon Brixton (SW9)
Sea Containers, Mondrian
  London (SE1)
Skylon, South Bank Centre (SE1)
Skylon Grill (SE1)
Soif (SW11)
Sonny's Kitchen (SW13)
Sparrow (SE13)
The Spencer (SW15)
Story (SE1)*
The Swan at the Globe (SE1)
The Table (SE1)
Tate Modern Restaurant (SE1)
Tate Modern, Restaurant, Level

6 (SE1)
Tom Simmons (SE1)
Tried & True (SW15)
Trinity (SW4)*
Trinity Upstairs (SW4)*
Tulse Hill Hotel (SE24)
Union Street Café (SE1)
The Victoria (SW14)
Waterloo Bar & Kitchen (SE1)
Winemakers Deptford (SE8)

East

Anglo (EC1)*
The Anthologist (EC2)
Bird of Smithfield (EC1)
Bistrotheque (E2)
Bob Bob Cité (EC3)
Bokan (E14)
The Botanist (EC2)
The Bothy (E14)
Bread Street Kitchen (EC4)
Café Below (EC2)
Cafe Football, Westfield
  Stratford (E20)
Caravan (EC1, EC2)
Chiswell Street Dining Rooms (EC1)
City Social (EC2)
The Clove Club (EC1)*
The Culpeper (E1)
Darwin Brasserie (EC3)
The Don (EC4)
The Don Bistro and Bar (EC4)
Duck & Waffle (EC2)
Eat 17 (E17)
Ellory, Netil House (E8)
The Empress (E9)*
Fenchurch Restaurant, Sky
  Garden (EC3)
The Frog (E1)*
Galvin HOP (E1)
The Green (EC1)
The Gun (E14)
High Timber (EC4)
Hilliard (EC4)*
Hoi Polloi, Ace Hotel (E1)
Humble Grape (EC4)
James Cochran EC3 (EC3)*
Jones & Sons (N16)*
The Jugged Hare (EC1)
Legs (E9)
Luca (EC1)
Lyle's (E1)*
Mare Street Market (E8)
The Mercer (EC2)
Merchants Tavern (EC2)
The Modern Pantry (EC1, EC2)
The Morgan Arms (E3)
The Narrow (E14)
Northbank (EC4)
One Canada Square (E14)
1 Lombard Street (EC3)
P Franco (E5)*
Paradise Garage (E2)*
Pidgin (E8)*
Princess of Shoreditch (EC2)
Rochelle Canteen (E2)
Rök (EC2)*
Sager + Wilde (E2)
St John Bread & Wine (E1)
Smith's Wapping (E1)*
Smiths of Smithfield, Top Floor (EC1)
Smiths of Smithfield, Ground
  Floor (EC1)
Tom's Kitchen (E1, E14)
Treves & Hyde (E1)
The Vincent (E8)
Vinoteca (EC1)
VQ (EC3)

The White Swan (EC4)
Wilmington (EC1)
Yolk (EC2)

BRITISH, TRADITIONAL

Central

Boisdale of Belgravia (SW1)
Brown's Hotel, The English Tea
  Room (W1)
Brown's Hotel, HIX Mayfair (W1)
Butler's Restaurant, The Chesterfield
  Mayfair (W1)
Corrigan's Mayfair (W1)
Dinner, Mandarin Oriental (SW1)
The Game Bird at The Stafford
  London (SW1)
GBR (SW1)
George in the Strand (WC2)
The Dining Room, The Goring
  Hotel (SW1)
The Guinea Grill (W1)*
Hardy's Brasserie (W1)
Holborn Dining Room (WC1)
Rib Room, Jumeirah Carlton Tower
  Hotel (SW1)
The Ritz (W1)
Rules (WC2)
The Savoy Hotel, Savoy Grill (WC2)
Scott's (W1)*
Shepherd's (SW1)
Simpson's in the Strand (WC2)
Strangers Dining Room, House of
  Commons (SW1)
Tate Britain, Whistler
  Restaurant (SW1)
The Wigmore, The Langham (W1)
Wiltons (SW1)
The Windmill (W1)

West

Bumpkin (SW3, SW7)
Maggie Jones's (W8)

North

The Gilbert Scott (NW1)
Piebury Corner (N1, N7)
St Johns (N19)
York & Albany (NW1)

South

The Anchor & Hope (SE1)*
Butlers Wharf Chop House (SE1)
Canton Arms (SW8)*
Goddards At Greenwich (SE10)
Jolly Gardeners (SW18)
Roast (SE1)
The Swan at the Globe (SE1)

East

Albion (E2)
Albion Clerkenwell (EC1)
Boisdale of Bishopsgate (EC2)
Bumpkin, Westfield Stratford
  City (E20)
The Fox and Anchor (EC1)
Hix Oyster & Chop House (EC1)
The Marksman (E2)*
Paternoster Chop House (EC4)
E Pellicci (E2)
The Quality Chop House (EC1)
St John Bread & Wine (E1)
St John Smithfield (EC1)*
Simpson's Tavern (EC3)
Sweetings (EC4)
White Bear (EC1)
Wilmington (EC1)

DANISH

Central

Sticks'n'Sushi (WC2)*

West

Snaps & Rye (W10)

South

Sticks'n'Sushi (SE10, SW19)*

East

Sticks'n'Sushi (E14)*

EAST & CENT. EUROPEAN

Central

The Delaunay (WC2)
Fischer's (W1)
Gay Hussar (W1)
The Harcourt (W1)*
The Wolseley (W1)

West

Belvedere Restaurant (W8)

North

Bellanger (N1)
German Gymnasium (N1)
Kipferl (N1)

FISH & SEAFOOD

Central

Barbecoa Piccadilly (W1)
Bellamy's (W1)
Bentley's (W1)
Black Roe (W1)
Blandford Comptoir (W1)
Bonnie Gull (W1)*
Bonnie Gull Seafood Shack (W1)*
Burger & Lobster, Harvey
  Nichols (SW1, W1)
Estiatorio Milos (SW1)
Fancy Crab (W1)
Fishworks (W1)
Hix (W1)
J Sheekey Atlantic Bar (WC2)
Kaspar's Seafood and Grill, The Savoy
  Hotel (WC2)
Olivomare (SW1)
One-O-One, Park Tower
  Knightsbridge (SW1)*
Ormer Mayfair (W1)*
The Oystermen Seafood Kitchen &
  Bar (WC2)
Pescatori (W1)
Quaglino's (SW1)
Randall & Aubin (W1)
Rib Room, Jumeirah Carlton Tower
  Hotel (SW1)
Royal China Club (W1)*
Scott's (W1)*
Sexy Fish (W1)
J Sheekey (WC2)
Wiltons (SW1)
Wright Brothers (W1)*

West

Bibendum Oyster Bar (SW3)
Big Easy (SW3)
The Chipping Forecast (W11)
The Cow (W2)
Geales (W8)
Kensington Place (W8)
London Shell Co. (W2)*
Mandarin Kitchen (W2)*
Outlaw's at The Capital (SW3)*
The Summerhouse (W9)
Wright Brothers (SW7)*

North

Bradley's (NW3)
Carob Tree (NW5)
Galley (N1)
Lure (NW5)
Olympus Fish (N3)*
Prawn on the Lawn (N1)*
Toff's (N10)
Two Brothers (N3)

South

Applebee's Fish (SE1)*
fish! (SE1)
Le Querce (SE23)*
Rick Stein (SW14)
Sea Containers, Mondrian
   London (SE1)
Wright Brothers (SE1, SW11)*

East

Angler, South Place Hotel (EC2)
Burger & Lobster (EC1, EC4)
Fish Central (EC1)
Fish Market (EC2)
Hix Oyster & Chop House (EC1)
The Royal Exchange Grand Café, The
   Royal Exchange (EC3)
Smith's Wapping (E1)*
Sweetings (EC4)
Wright Brothers (E1)*

FRENCH

Central

Alain Ducasse at The
   Dorchester (W1)
Antidote Wine Bar (W1)
L'Artiste Musclé (W1)
L'Atelier de Joel Robuchon (WC2)
The Balcon, Sofitel St James (SW1)
Bar Boulud, Mandarin Oriental (SW1)
Bellamy's (W1)
Blanchette (W1)*
Blandford Comptoir (W1)
Bon Vivant (WC1)
Boudin Blanc (W1)
Boulestin (SW1)
Brasserie Zédel (W1)
Café Monico (W1)
Céleste, The Lanesborough (SW1)
Cigalon (WC2)
Clarette (W1)
Clos Maggiore (WC2)
Colbert (SW1)
L'Escargot (W1)*
Ferdi (W1)
Frenchie (WC2)*
Galvin at Windows, Park Lane
   London Hilton Hotel (W1)
Galvin Bistrot de Luxe (W1)
Le Garrick (WC2)
Gauthier Soho (W1)*
Le Gavroche (W1)*
The Greenhouse (W1)*
Hélène Darroze, The Connaught
   Hotel (W1)
Henrietta (WC2)
maze (W1)
Mon Plaisir (WC2)
Neo Bistro (W1)
The Ninth London (W1)*
Noizé (W1)
Les 110 de Taillevent (W1)*
Orrery (W1)
Otto's (WC1)*
La Petite Maison (W1)*
Pétrus (SW1)
Pied à Terre (W1)*
La Poule au Pot (SW1)

Prix Fixe (W1)
Relais de Venise L'Entrecôte (W1)
Savoir Faire (WC1)
The Savoy Hotel, The Savoy Grill (WC2)
Seven Park Place (SW1)*
Sketch, Lecture Room (W1)*
Sketch, Gallery (W1)
The Square (W1)
Terroirs (WC2)
28-50 (W1)
Villandry (W1)
Villandry St James's (SW1)
The Wallace, The Wallace
   Collection (W1)

West

Albertine (W12)
Angelus (W2)
Bandol (SW10)
Bel Canto, Corus Hotel Hyde
   Park (W2)
Belvedere Restaurant (W8)
Bibendum (SW3)
Bibendum Oyster Bar (SW3)
Cepages (W2)
Cheyne Walk Brasserie (SW3)
Le Colombier (SW3)
L'Etranger (SW7)
Gordon Ramsay (SW3)
Michael Nadra (W4)*
Orée (SW10, SW3)
Quantus (W4)*
La Trompette (W4)*
Le Vacherin (W4)

North

L'Absinthe (NW1)
L'Aventure (NW8)
Bistro Aix (N8)*
Bradley's (NW3)
La Cage Imaginaire (NW3)
Melange (N8)
Le Mercury (N1)
Michael Nadra (NW1)*
Oslo Court (NW8)*
Patron (NW5)
Petit Pois Bistro (N1)
Le Sacré-Coeur (N1)
Table Du Marche (N2)
The Wells (NW3)

South

Augustine Kitchen (SW11)
Boro Bistro (SE1)
Brasserie Toulouse-Lautrec (SE11)
La Buvette (TW9)
Casse-Croute (SE1)*
Counter Vauxhall Arches (SW8)*
Gastronhome (SW11)*
Gazette (SW11, SW12, SW15)
Petit Ma Cuisine (TW9)
Pique Nique (SE1)
Le Salon Privé (TW1)*
Sinabro (SW11)
Soif (SW11)
The White Onion (SW19)

East

Le Bar (EC1)
Blanchette East (E1)*
Bleeding Heart Restaurant (EC1)
Cabotte (EC2)*
Café du Marché (EC1)
Club Gascon (EC1)
Comptoir Gascon (EC1)
Coq d'Argent (EC2)
La Dame de Pic London (EC3)
The Don (EC4)

La Ferme London (EC1)
Galvin La Chapelle (E1)
James Cochran EC3 (EC3)*
Lutyens (EC4)
Plateau (E14)
Provender (E11)
Relais de Venise L'Entrecôte (E14, EC2)
The Royal Exchange Grand Café, The
    Royal Exchange (EC3)
Sauterelle, Royal Exchange (EC3)
Tratra (E2)
28-50 (EC4)

FUSION
Central
Asia de Cuba, St Martin's Lane
    Hotel (WC2)
Bubbledogs, Kitchen Table (W1)*
Carousel (W1)*
La Porte des Indes (W1)
The Providores and Tapa Room (W1)*
Twist (W1)*

West
E&O (W11)
Eight Over Eight (SW3)
L'Étranger (SW7)
108 Garage (W10)*
Romulo Café (W8)

North
Caravan (N1)
The Good Egg (N16)*
The Petite Coree (NW6)*

South
Caravan (SE1)
Tsunami (SW4)*

East
Caravan (EC1)

GAME
Central
Bocca Di Lupo (W1)*
Boisdale of Belgravia (SW1)
Mac & Wild (W1)*
Rules (WC2)
Wiltons (SW1)

West
Harwood Arms (SW6)*

South
The Anchor & Hope (SE1)*

East
Boisdale of Bishopsgate (EC2)
The Jugged Hare (EC1)
Mac & Wild (EC2)*

GREEK
Central
Estiatorio Milos (SW1)
Meraki (W1)
Opso (W1)

West
Mazi (W8)

North
Carob Tree (NW5)
The Greek Larder, Arthouse (N1)
Lemonia (NW1)
Vrisaki (N22)

South
Peckham Bazaar (SE15)*

East
Kolossi Grill (EC1)

HUNGARIAN
Central
Gay Hussar (W1)

INTERNATIONAL
Central
Boulestin (SW1)
Colony Grill Room, Beaumont
    Hotel (W1)
Cork & Bottle (WC2)
Flavour Bastard (W1)
Foley's (W1)*
La Fromagerie Bloomsbury (WC1)
La Fromagerie Café (W1)
Gordon's Wine Bar (WC2)
Isabel (W1)
Jikoni (W1)
Mere (W1)
Motcombs (SW1)
The 10 Cases (WC2)
Test Kitchen (W1)

West
The Admiral Codrington (SW3)
The Andover Arms (W6)
Annie's (W4)
No.11 Cadogan Gardens (SW3)
The Kensington Wine Rooms (W8)
Melody at St Paul's (W14)
Mona Lisa (SW10)
Rivea, Bulgari Hotel (SW7)

North
Andi's (N16)
Banners (N8)
Bull & Last (NW5)
8 Hoxton Square (N1)
La Fromagerie (N5)
Haven Bistro (N20)
Primeur (N5)*
Salut (N1)*

South
Annie's (SW13)
Arthur Hooper's (SE1)
Brookmill (SE8)
Joanna's (SE19)
The Light House (SW19)
London House (SW11)
Minnow (SW4)
Pedler (SE15)
Platform1 (SE22)
Rabot 1745 (SE1)
Sparrow (SE13)
Spinach (SE22)
Tulse Hill Hotel (SE24)
Vivat Bacchus (SE1)
The Yellow House (SE16)

East
Blixen (E1)
Bokan (E14)
Dokke (E1)
Eat 17 (E9)
The Laughing Heart (E2)
Niche (EC1)
Sager + Wilde Restaurant (E2)
Typing Room, Town Hall Hotel (E2)*
Vivat Bacchus (EC4)
The Wine Library (EC3)

IRISH
West
The Cow (W2)

The Sands End (SW6)

North
Summers (NW6)

ITALIAN
Central
Al Duca (SW1)
Assunta Madre (W1)
Bar Italia (W1)
Bar Termini (W1)
Il Baretto (W1)
Bernardi's (W1)
Bocca Di Lupo (W1)*
Bocconcino (W1)
Briciole (W1)
C London (W1)
Cacio & Pepe (SW1)
Café Murano (SW1)
Café Murano Pastificio (WC2)
Caffè Caldesi (W1)
Caraffini (SW1)
Cecconi's (W1)
Chucs (W1)
Ciao Bella (WC1)
Como Lario (SW1)
Il Convivio (SW1)*
Da Mario (WC2)
Dehesa (W1)
Delfino (W1)*
Enoteca Turi (SW1)
Franco's (SW1)
Fucina (W1)
Fumo (WC2)
Gustoso Ristorante & Enoteca (SW1)
Hai Cenato (SW1)
Latium (W1)
Locanda Locatelli, Hyatt
   Regency (W1)*
Luce e Limoni (WC1)*
Made in Italy James St (W1)
Margot (WC2)*
Mele e Pere (W1)
Murano (W1)*
Novikov (Italian restaurant) (W1)
Obicà (W1)
Oliveto (SW1)*
Olivo (SW1)
Olivocarne (SW1)
Olivomare (SW1)
Opera Tavern (WC2)*
Osteria Dell'Angolo (SW1)
Il Pampero (SW1)
Pastaio (W1)
Pescatori (W1)
Polpetto (W1)
Polpo (W1,WC2)
La Porchetta Pizzeria (WC1)
Princi (W1)
QP LDN (W1)
Quirinale (SW1)*
Ristorante Frescobaldi (W1)
Rossopomodoro, John Lewis (W1,
   WC2)
Sale e Pepe (SW1)
Salt Yard (W1)
San Carlo Cicchetti (W1,WC2)
Santini (SW1)
Sardo (W1)
Sartoria (W1)
Savini at Criterion (W1)
Signor Sassi (SW1)
Theo Randall (W1)
Tozi (SW1)
2 Veneti (W1)
Vasco & Piero's Pavilion (W1)
Veneta (SW1)
Il Vicolo (SW1)

Zafferano (SW1)

West
Aglio e Olio (SW10)
L'Amorosa (W6)*
Assaggi (W2)*
Assaggi Bar & Pizzeria (W2)*
The Bird in Hand (W14)
Buona Sera (SW3)
Chelsea Cellar (SW10)*
Chucs (W11)
Cibo (W14)*
Da Mario (SW7)
Daphne's (SW3)
La Delizia Limbara (SW3)
Edera (W11)
Essenza (W11)
La Famiglia (SW10)
Frantoio (SW10)
Locanda Ottomezzo (W8)
Lucio (SW3)
Made in Italy (SW3)
Manicomio (SW3)
Mediterraneo (W11)
Mona Lisa (SW10)
Nuovi Sapori (SW6)
The Oak W12 (W12,W2)
Obicà (SW3)
Osteria Basilico (W11)
Pappa Ciccia (SW6)
Pellicano Restaurant (SW3)
Pentolina (W14)*
Polpo (SW3,W11)
Il Portico (W8)
Portobello Ristorante Pizzeria (W11)
The Red Pepper (W9)
Riccardo's (SW3)
Rigo' (SW6)
The River Café (W6)
Rossopomodoro (SW10)
Sapori Sardi (SW6)
Scalini (SW3)
Stecca (SW10)
Stuzzico (W2)
Theo's Simple Italian (SW5)
Villa Di Geggiano (W4)
Ziani's (SW3)

North
Anima e Cuore (NW1)*
Artigiano (NW3)
L'Artista (NW11)
La Collina (NW1)
500 (N19)
Giacomo's (NW2)
Il Guscio (N5)
Melange (N8)
Messapica (NW10)
Osteria Tufo (N4)
Ostuni (N6, NW6)
Passione e Tradizione (N15)*
Pasta Remoli (N4)
Pizzeria Pappagone (N4)
La Porchetta Pizzeria (N1, N4, NW1)
Quartieri (NW6)*
Radici (N1)
The Rising Sun (NW7)
Rugoletta (N12, N2)
Sarracino (NW6)*
Trullo (N1)*
Villa Bianca (NW3)

South
A Cena (TW1)
Al Forno (SW15, SW19)
Artusi (SE15)*
Bacco (TW9)
Belpassi Bros (SW17)

WESTERN | **CUISINES**

Al Boccon di'vino *(TW9)*
Buona Sera *(SW11)*
Capricci *(SE1)**
Fiume *(SW8)*
Luciano's *(SE12)*
Macellaio RC *(SE1)*
Made in Italy *(SW19)*
Mercato Metropolitano *(SE1)*
Numero Uno *(SW11)*
O'ver *(SE1)**
Osteria Antica Bologna *(SW11)*
Padella *(SE1)**
Pizza Metro *(SW11)*
Pizzeria Rustica *(TW9)*
Pulia *(SE1)*
Le Querce *(SE23)**
Riva *(SW13)*
The Table *(SE1)*

East
L'Anima *(EC2)**
L'Anima Café *(EC2)*
Apulia *(EC1)*
Bombetta *(E11)*
Il Bordello *(E1)*
Campania & Jones *(E2)*
Canto Corvino *(E1)**
Caravaggio *(EC3)*
Emilia's Crafted Pasta *(E1)**
Lardo Bebè *(E8)*
Luca *(EC1)*
Macellaio RC *(EC1)*
Manicomio *(EC2)*
The Ned *(EC2)*
Obicà *(E14, EC4)*
Osteria, Barbican Centre *(EC2)*
Palatino *(EC1)**
E Pellicci *(E2)*
Polpo *(EC1)*
Pomaio *(E1)*
Popolo *(EC2)**
La Porchetta Pizzeria *(EC1)*
Rotorino *(E8)*
Rucoletta *(EC2)*
Santore *(EC1)**
Super Tuscan *(E1)**
Taberna Etrusca *(EC4)*
Verdi's *(E1)*

MEDITERRANEAN
Central
About Thyme *(SW1)*
Blandford Comptoir *(W1)*
Massimo, Corinthia Hotel *(WC2)*
The Ninth London *(W1)**
Nopi *(W1)**
The Norfolk Arms *(WC1)*
100 Wardour Street *(W1)*
Opso *(W1)*
Riding House Café *(W1)*
Vagabond Wines *(SW1, W1)*

West
Adams Café *(W12)*
The Atlas *(SW6)**
Ceru *(SW7)**
Cumberland Arms *(W14)**
Locanda Ottomezzo *(W8)*
Made in Italy *(SW3)*
Mediterraneo *(W11)*
The Oak W12 *(W12)*
Raoul's Café *(W9)*
Raoul's Café & Deli *(W11)*
The Swan *(W4)*
Vagabond Wines *(SW6)*

North
Alcedo *(N7)*

Lady Mildmay *(N1)*
The Little Bay *(NW6)*
Sardine *(N1)*
Vinoteca *(N1)*

South
Bean & Hop *(SW18)*
The Bobbin *(SW4)**
Fish in a Tie *(SW11)*
The Fox & Hounds *(SW11)**
Gourmet Goat *(SE1)**
Peckham Bazaar *(SE15)**
Sail Loft *(SE10)*
Vagabond Wines *(SW11)*

East
Brawn *(E2)**
The Eagle *(EC1)**
Morito *(EC1)**
Tuyo *(E2)*
Vagabond Wines *(E1)*
Vinoteca *(EC1)*

ORGANIC
Central
Daylesford Organic *(SW1, W1)*

West
Daylesford Organic *(W11)*

North
Juniper Tree *(NW3)*

East
Smiths of Smithfield, Dining Room *(EC1)*

POLISH
West
Daquise *(SW7)*
Ognisko Restaurant *(SW7)*

South
Baltic *(SE1)**

PORTUGUESE
West
Lisboa Pâtisserie *(W10)*

South
Bar Douro *(SE1)**

East
Corner Room *(E2)*
Eyre Brothers *(EC2)**
Taberna do Mercado *(E1)*

RUSSIAN
Central
Bob Bob Ricard *(W1)*
Mari Vanna *(SW1)*
Zima *(W1)*

SCANDINAVIAN
Central
Aquavit *(SW1)*
Bageriet *(WC2)**
The Harcourt *(W1)**
Nordic Bakery *(W1)*
Nordic Bakery *(WC2)*
Scandinavian Kitchen *(W1)*
Texture *(W1)**

West
Flat Three *(W11)**

North
Rök *(N1)**

SCOTTISH
Central
Boisdale of Belgravia *(SW1)*
Boisdale of Mayfair *(W1)*
Mac & Wild *(W1)*

East
Boisdale of Bishopsgate *(EC2)*
Boisdale of Canary Wharf *(E14)*
Mac & Wild *(EC2)*

SPANISH
Central
About Thyme *(SW1)*
Ametsa with Arzak Instruction,
   Halkin Hotel *(SW1)*
Aqua Nueva *(W1)*
Barrafina *(W1,WC2)*
Barrica *(W1)*
Cigala *(WC1)*
Dehesa *(W1)*
Donostia *(W1)*
Drakes Tabanco *(W1)*
Ember Yard *(W1)*
Encant *(WC2)*
Eneko at One Aldwych, One
   Aldwych Hotel *(WC2)*
Goya *(SW1)*
Ibérica, Zig Zag Building *(SW1,W1)*
Kitty Fisher's *(W1)*
Lurra *(W1)*
Morada Brindisa Asador *(W1)*
Opera Tavern *(WC2)*
El Pirata *(W1)*
Rambla *(W1)*
Sabor *(W1)*
Salt Yard *(W1)*
Sibarita *(WC2)*
Social Wine & Tapas *(W1)*
Street XO *(W1)*

West
Cambio de Tercio *(SW5)*
Capote Y Toros *(SW5)*
Casa Brindisa *(SW7)*
Duke of Sussex *(W4)*
Tendido Cero *(SW5)*
Tendido Cuatro *(SW6)*

North
Bar Esteban *(N8)*
Café del Parc *(N19)*
Camino King's Cross *(N1)*
Lluna *(N10)*
El Parador *(NW1)*
Thyme and Lemon *(N1)*
Trangallan *(N16)*
28 Church Row *(NW3)*

South
Boqueria *(SW2, SW8)*
Brindisa Food Rooms *(SW9)*
Camino Bankside *(SE1)*
Gremio de Brixton, St Matthew's
   Church *(SW2)*
José *(SE1)*
Little Taperia *(SW17)*
LOBOS Meat & Tapas *(SE1)*
Mar I Terra *(SE1)*
Meson don Felipe *(SE1)*
Pizarro *(SE1)*
Tapas Brindisa *(SE1)*

East
Bravas *(E1)*
Camino Blackfriars *(EC4)*
Camino Monument *(EC3)*
Eyre Brothers *(EC2)*

Hispania *(EC3)*
Ibérica *(E14, EC1)*
José Pizarro *(EC2)*
Morito *(E2, EC1)*
Moro *(EC1)*
Sagardi *(EC2)*

STEAKS & GRILLS
Central
Barbecoa, Nova *(SW1)*
Barbecoa Piccadilly *(W1)*
Beast *(W1)*
Bentley's *(W1)*
Black Roe *(W1)*
Blacklock *(W1)*
Bodean's *(W1)*
Boisdale of Mayfair *(W1)*
Bukowski Grill *(W1)*
Christopher's *(WC2)*
Cut, 45 Park Lane *(W1)*
Flat Iron *(W1,WC2)*
Foxlow *(W1)*
Goodman *(W1)*
The Guinea Grill *(W1)*
Hawksmoor *(W1,WC2)*
Heliot Steak House *(WC2)*
M Restaurant Victoria Street, Zig Zag
   Building *(SW1)*
MASH Steakhouse *(W1)*
maze Grill *(W1)*
Le Relais de Venise L'Entrecôte *(W1)*
Rib Room, Jumeirah Carlton Tower
   Hotel *(SW1)*
Rowley's *(SW1)*
Smith & Wollensky *(WC2)*
Sophie's Steakhouse *(W1)*
34 Mayfair *(W1)*
Zelman Meats *(SW1,W1)*
Zoilo *(W1)*

West
Bodean's *(SW6)*
Flat Iron *(W10)*
Foxlow *(W4)*
Haché *(SW10)*
Hanger *(SW6)*
Hawksmoor Knightsbridge *(SW3)*
Lockhouse *(W2)*
Macellaio RC *(SW7)*
Megan's Delicatessen *(SW6)*
No 197 Chiswick Fire Station *(W4)*
Popeseye *(W14)*
Smokehouse Chiswick *(W4)*
Sophie's Steakhouse *(SW10)*

North
Haché *(NW1)*
Popeseye *(N19)*
Smokehouse Islington *(N1)*

South
Arlo's *(SW12)*
Bodean's *(SW4)*
Bukowski Grill, Brixton Market *(SW9)*
Cau *(SE3, SW19)*
Coal Rooms *(SE15)*
The Coal Shed *(SE1)*
Counter Vauxhall Arches *(SW8)*
Foxlow *(SW12)*
Hawksmoor *(SE1)*
Knife *(SW4)*
M Bar & Grill Twickenham *(TW1)*
Macellaio RC *(SW11)*
Naughty Piglets *(SW2)*
Oblix *(SE1)*
Popeseye *(SW15)*

East
Aviary (EC2)
Barbecoa (EC4)
Bodean's (EC1, EC3)
Buen Ayre (E8)*
Bukowski Grill, Boxpark (E1)
Cau (E1)
Flat Iron (EC2)*
Foxlow (EC1)
Goodman (E14)*
Goodman City (EC2)*
The Grill at McQueen (EC2)
Hawksmoor (E1, EC2)
Hill & Szrok (E8)*
Hix Oyster & Chop House (EC1)
Jones & Sons (N16)*
The Jones Family Project (EC2)*
M Restaurant Threadneedle
  Street (EC2)
Paternoster Chop House (EC4)
Relais de Venise L'Entrecôte (E14, EC2)
Simpson's Tavern (EC3)
Smith's Wapping (E1)*
Smiths of Smithfield, Top Floor (EC1)
Smiths of Smithfield, Dining
  Room (EC1)
Smiths of Smithfield, Ground
  Floor (EC1)
Temple & Sons (EC2)
The Tramshed (EC2)

SWISS
Central
St Moritz (W1)

VEGETARIAN
Central
by Chloe (WC2)
Chettinad (W1)*
Ethos (W1)
Galvin at the Athenaeum (W1)
The Gate (W1)*
Malabar Junction (WC1)
Mildreds (W1)
Ormer Mayfair (W1)*
Ragam (W1)*
Rasa (W1)
Rasa Maricham, Holiday Inn
  Hotel (WC1)
Sagar (W1)
The Square (W1)
Texture (W1)*
tibits (W1)

West
Farmacy (W2)
The Gate (W6)*
Sagar (W6)

North
Chutneys (NW1)
Diwana Bhel-Poori House (NW1)
Jashan (N8)*
Manna (NW3)
Mildreds (N1, NW1)
Rani (N3)*
Rasa (N16)
Sakonis (HA0)*
Vijay (NW6)

South
Ganapati (SE15)*
Le Pont de la Tour (SE1)
Skylon, South Bank Centre (SE1)
Spinach (SE22)
Sree Krishna (SW17)*
Tas Pide (SE1)

tibits (SE1)

East
The Gate (EC1)*
Mildreds (E8)
Vanilla Black (EC4)

AFTERNOON TEA
Central
Brown's Hotel, The English Tea
  Room (W1)
Butler's Restaurant, The Chesterfield
  Mayfair (W1)
Dalloway Terrace, Bloomsbury
  Hotel (WC1)
The Collins Room, Berkeley
  Hotel (SW1)
The Delaunay (WC2)
Fortnum & Mason, The Diamond
  Jubilee Tea Salon (W1)
La Fromagerie Café (W1)
Galvin at the Athenaeum (W1)
The Game Bird at The Stafford
  London (SW1)
The Goring Hotel (SW1)
Ham Yard, Ham Hotel (W1)
Palm Court, The Langham (W1)
Maison Bertaux (W1)
Oscar Wilde Bar at Cafe Royal (W1)
The Promenade at The
  Dorchester (W1)
The Ritz, Palm Court (W1)
Savoy Thames Foyer (WC2)
Sketch, Gallery (W1)
Villandry (W1, SW1)
The Wallace, The Wallace
  Collection (W1)
The Wolseley (W1)
Yauatcha (W1)*

West
Farmacy (W2)
No.11 Cadogan Gardens (SW3)

North
The Booking Office, St Pancras
  Renaissance Hotel (NW1)
Brew House Café, Kenwood
  House (NW3)
The Landmark, Winter Garden (NW1)

South
Cannizaro House, Hotel du
  Vin (SW19)
House Restaurant, National
  Theatre (SE1)
Oxo Tower, Brasserie (SE1)
Petersham Hotel (TW10)
Petersham Nurseries Cafe (TW10)
Rabot (SE1)
TING (SE1)

East
Hoi Polloi, Ace Hotel (E1)

BURGERS, ETC
Central
Bar Boulud, Mandarin Oriental (SW1)
Bleecker Burger (SW1)*
Bobo Social (W1)
Bodean's (W1)
Burger & Lobster, Harvey
  Nichols (SW1, W1, WC1)
Five Guys (WC2)
Goodman (W1)*
Haché (WC1)
Hard Rock Café (W1)
Hawksmoor (W1, WC2)

CUISINES | SPECIALITIES

Joe Allen (WC2)
MEATliquor (W1)
MEATliquor (WC1)
MEATmarket (WC2)
Opera Tavern (WC2)*
Patty and Bun (W1)*
Rainforest Café (W1)
Shake Shack (SW1,WC1,WC2)
Tommi's Burger Joint (W1)
Zoilo (W1)*

West
The Admiral Codrington (SW3)
Big Easy (SW3)
Bodean's (SW6)
Electric Diner (W11)
Haché (SW10)
Lockhouse (W2)
MEATliquor (W2)
Patty and Bun (W11)*
Tommi's Burger Joint (SW3)

North
Dirty Burger (NW5)
Duke's Brew & Que (N1)*
Five Guys Islington (N1)
Haché (NW1)
Harry Morgan's (NW8)
MEATLiquor Islington (N1)
MEATmission (N1)

South
Bodean's (SW4)
Dip & Flip (SW11, SW17, SW19, SW9)
Dirty Burger (SW8)
Haché (SW12, SW4)
MEATliquor ED (SE22)
Pop Brixton (SW9)*
Rivington Grill (SE10)
Rox Burger (SE13)*
Sonny's Kitchen (SW13)

East
Bleecker Burger (E1, EC4)*
Bodean's (EC1, EC3)
Burger & Lobster (E14, EC1, EC4)
Chicken Shop & Dirty Burger (E1)
Comptoir Gascon (EC1)
Dirty Burger (E1)
Goodman (E14)*
Goodman City (EC2)*
Haché (EC2)
Hawksmoor (E1, EC2)
Ninth Ward (EC1)
Patty and Bun (E2, E8, EC2, EC3)*
The Rib Man (E1)*
Shake Shack (E20)
Smiths of Smithfield, Dining Room (EC1)

FISH & CHIPS
Central
Golden Hind (W1)
North Sea Fish (WC1)
Poppies (W1)
Seafresh (SW1)

West
The Chipping Forecast (W11)
Geales (W8)
Geales Chelsea Green (SW3)
Kerbisher & Malt (W5,W6)

North
Cannons (N8)*
Nautilus (NW6)*
Olympus Fish (N3)*
Poppies Camden (NW1)

The Sea Shell (NW1)
Sutton and Sons (N1, N16)*
Toff's (N10)
Trawler Trash (N1)

South
Brady's (SW18)
fish! (SE1)
Golden Chippy (SE10)
Kerbisher & Malt (SW14, SW4)
Masters Super Fish (SE1)

East
Ark Fish (E18)
Poppies (E1)
Sutton and Sons (E8)*

ICE CREAM
Central
Chin Chin Club (W1)
Gelupo (W1)*

West
Bears Ice Cream (W12)

PIZZA
Central
Il Baretto (W1)
Delfino (W1)*
Fucina (W1)
Homeslice (W1,WC2)*
Mayfair Pizza Company (W1)
Oliveto (SW1)*
The Orange (SW1)
Pizza Pilgrims (W1,WC2)*
La Porchetta Pizzeria (WC1)
Princi (W1)
Rossopomodoro (WC2)

West
The Bird in Hand (W14)
Buona Sera (SW3)
Da Mario (SW7)
La Delizia Limbara (SW3)
Homeslice (W12)*
Made in Italy (SW3)
The Oak W12 (W12,W2)
Oro Di Napoli (W5)*
Osteria Basilico (W11)
Pappa Ciccia (SW6)
Pizza East Portobello (W10)
Pizza Metro (W11)
Pizzicotto (W8)*
Portobello Ristorante Pizzeria (W11)
The Red Pepper (W9)
Rocca Di Papa (SW7)
Rossopomodoro (SW10)
Santa Maria (SW6,W5)*

North
L' Antica Pizzeria (NW3)*
L'Antica Pizzeria da Michele (N16)
Passione e Tradizione (N15)*
Pizza East (NW5)
Pizzeria Pappagone (N4)
La Porchetta Pizzeria (N1, N4, NW1)
Rossopomodoro (N1, NW1)
Sacro Cuore (N8, NW10)*
Sweet Thursday (N1)
Yard Sale Pizza (N4)*
Zia Lucia (N7)*

South
Addomme (SW2)*
Al Forno (SW15, SW19)
Bean & Hop (SW18)
Buona Sera (SW11)
Dynamo (SW15)

Eco *(SW4)*
500 Degrees *(SE24)*
The Gowlett Arms *(SE15)**
Joe Public *(SW4)**
Made of Dough *(SE15)*
Mamma Dough *(SE15, SE23, SW9)*
Mother *(SW11)*
Numero Uno *(SW11)*
Pedler *(SE15)*
Pizza Metro *(SW11)*
Pizzastorm *(SW18)*
Pizzeria Rustica *(TW9)*
Rocca Di Papa *(SE21)*
Rossopomodoro *(SW18)*
The Stable *(TW8)*
Theo's *(SE5)*
The Yellow House *(SE16)*
Zero Degrees *(SE3)*

East
Il Bordello *(E1)*
Corner Kitchen *(E7)*
Crate Brewery and Pizzeria *(E9)*
Homeslice *(EC1, EC4)**
Pizza East *(E1)*
Pizza Pilgrims *(E1, E14, EC1, EC3)**
La Porchetta Pizzeria *(EC1)*
The Stable *(E1)*
Yard Sale Pizza *(E17, E5)**

SANDWICHES, CAKES, ETC
Central
Bageriet *(WC2)**
Bea's Cake Boutique *(WC1)*
Daylesford Organic *(W1)*
Dean & DeLuca *(W1)*
Dominique Ansel Bakery
   London *(SW1)**
Fernandez & Wells *(W1, WC2)*
Kaffeine *(W1)*
Maison Bertaux *(W1)*
Monmouth Coffee Company *(WC2)**
Nordic Bakery *(W1)*
Nordic Bakery *(WC2)*
Scandinavian Kitchen *(W1)*
Workshop Coffee *(W1)*

West
Angie's Little Food Shop *(W4)*
Fernandez & Wells *(SW7)*
Lisboa Pâtisserie *(W10)*
Oree *(W8)*
Orée *(SW3)*
Over Under *(SW5)**
Tamp Coffee *(W4)*

North
Brew House Café, Kenwood
   House *(NW3)*
Doppio *(NW1)*
Ginger & White *(NW3)*
Greenberry Café *(NW1)*
Max's Sandwich Shop *(N4)**
Monty's Deli *(N1)*

South
Cut The Mustard *(SW16)*
Ground Coffee Society *(SW15)*
Kappacasein *(SE16)**
Milk *(SW12)**
Monmouth Coffee Company *(SE1, SE16)**
Orange Pekoe *(SW13)*

East
Brick Lane Beigel Bake *(E1)**
Department of Coffee, and Social
   Affairs *(EC1)*

Ozone Coffee Roasters *(EC2)**
Pavilion Cafe & Bakery *(E9)*
Prufrock Coffee *(EC1)*
Rola Wala *(E1)*
Treves & Hyde *(E1)*
Workshop Coffee Holborn *(EC1)*

CHICKEN
Central
Bao *(W1)**
Chick 'n' Sours *(WC2)*
Chicken Shop *(WC1)*
Chik'n *(W1)*
Randall & Aubin *(W1)*

West
Chicken Shop *(W5)*
Cocotte *(W2)**
Stagolee's *(SW6)*

North
Chicken Shop *(N7, N8, NW5, NW8)*

South
Chicken Shop *(SW17, SW9)*
Chicken Shop & Dirty Burger
   Balham *(SW12)*
Pique Nique *(SE1)*

East
Chick 'n' Sours *(E8)*
Chicken Shop & Dirty Burger *(E1)*
Randy's Wing Bar *(E15)**
Red Rooster *(EC2)*
The Tramshed *(EC2)*

BBQ
Central
Bodean's *(WC2)*
The Stoke House *(SW1)*
temper Soho *(W1)*

West
MAM *(W11)*

North
Bodean's *(N10)*
CôBa *(N7)**
Smokehouse Islington *(N1)*

South
MeatUp *(SW18)*

East
Blacklock *(EC3)**
Smokestak *(E1)**
temper City *(EC2)*

ARGENTINIAN
Central
Zoilo *(W1)**

West
Quantus *(W4)**

East
Buen Ayre *(E8)**

BRAZILIAN
East
Sushisamba *(EC2)*

CAJUN/CREOLE
North
Plaquemine Lock *(N1)*

MEXICAN/TEXMEX
Central
La Bodega Negra Cafe (W1)
Cantina Laredo (WC2)
Corazón (W1)
Ella Canta (W1)
Lupita (WC2)
Peyote (W1)

West
Killer Tomato (W12)*
Lupita West (W8)
Peyotito (W11)
Taqueria (W11)*

South
Cartel (SW11)
El Pastór (SE1)*
Santo Remedio (SE1)

East
Breddos Tacos (EC1)*
Luardos (EC1)*
Lupita (E1)

PERUVIAN
Central
Casita Andina (W1)*
Ceviche Soho (W1)*
Coya (W1)*
Lima (W1)
Lima Floral (WC2)
Pachamama (W1)
Pisqu (W1)
Señor Ceviche (W1)

West
Chicama (SW10)
Southam Street (W10)

South
MOMMI (SW4)

East
Andina (E2)*
Ceviche Old St (EC1)*
Sushisamba (EC2)
Waka (EC3)

SOUTH AMERICAN
Central
MNKY HSE (W1)

West
Casa Cruz (W11)
Quantus (W4)*

South
MOMMI (SW4)

AFRO-CARIBBEAN
North
Messapica (NW10)

ETHIOPIAN
South
Zeret (SE5)*

MOROCCAN
Central
Momo (W1)

West
Adams Café (W12)

NORTH AFRICAN
Central
The Barbary (WC2)*
Momo (W1)

SOUTH AFRICAN
Central
Bbar (SW1)

TUNISIAN
West
Adams Café (W12)

WEST AFRICAN
Central
Ikoyi (SW1)

EGYPTIAN
North
Ali Baba (NW1)

ISRAELI
Central
The Barbary (WC2)
Gaby's (WC2)
Honey & Co (W1)
Honey & Smoke (W1)*
Ottolenghi (SW1)*
The Palomar (W1)*

West
Ottolenghi (W11)*

North
Ottolenghi (N1)*

East
Ottolenghi (E1)*

KOSHER
Central
Reubens (W1)

North
Kaifeng (NW4)
Zest, JW3 (NW3)

East
Brick Lane Beigel Bake (E1)*

LEBANESE
Central
Fairuz (W1)
Maroush (W1)
Yalla Yalla (W1)

West
The Cedar Restaurant (W9)
Chez Abir (W14)
Maroush (SW3)
Maroush Gardens (W2)

North
The Cedar Restaurant (NW6, NW8)
Crocker's Folly (NW8)

South
Arabica Bar and Kitchen (SE1)
Meza Trinity Road (SW17)
Yalla Yalla (SE10)

MIDDLE EASTERN
Central
The Barbary (WC2)*
Honey & Co (W1)
Honey & Smoke (W1)*

The Palomar (W1)*
Patogh (W1)*

West
Falafel King (W10)

North
The Good Egg (N16)*

South
Bala Baya (SE1)
Gourmet Goat (SE1)*
JAN (SW11)

East
Berber & Q (E8)*
Berber & Q Shawarma Bar (EC1)*
Morito (EC1)*
Pilpel (E1, EC4)*

PERSIAN
Central
Patogh (W1)*

West
Alounak (W14,W2)
Faanoos (W4,W5)
Kateh (W9)

South
Faanoos (SW14)
Persepolis (SE15)*

SYRIAN
West
Abu Zaad (W12)

TURKISH
Central
Le Bab (W1)*
Babaji Pide (W1)
Cyprus Mangal (SW1)
Ishtar (W1)
Kazan (Café) (SW1)
Yosma (W1)

West
Best Mangal (SW6,W14)*
Fez Mangal (W11)*

North
Black Axe Mangal (N1)*
Diyarbakir Kitchen (N4)
Gallipoli (N1)
Gem (N1)
Gökyüzü (N4)
Skewd Kitchen (EN4)

South
FM Mangal (SE5)
Tas Pide (SE1)

East
Haz (E1, EC2, EC3)
Mangal I (E8)*
Oklava (EC2)*

AFGHANI
North
Afghan Kitchen (N1)*
Ariana II (NW6)

BURMESE
East
Laphet (E8)

CHINESE
Central
A Wong (SW1)*
Baozi Inn (WC2)
Barshu (W1)*
The Bright Courtyard (W1)*
Chilli Cool (WC1)*
China Tang, Dorchester Hotel (W1)*
The Duck & Rice (W1)*
The Four Seasons (W1)*
Golden Dragon (W1)*
The Grand Imperial (SW1)
Hakkasan (W1)
Hunan (SW1)*
Joy King Lau (WC2)
Kai Mayfair (W1)
Ken Lo's Memories (SW1)
Ma La Sichuan (SW1)*
Mayfair Garden (W1)*
Mr Chow (SW1)
New World (W1)
Park Chinois (W1)
Royal China (W1)
Royal China Club (W1)*
Wong Kei (W1)
Yauatcha (W1)*
Yming (W1)

West
Dragon Palace (SW5)*
The Four Seasons (W2)*
Gold Mine (W2)*
Good Earth (SW3)
Mandarin Kitchen (W2)*
Min Jiang (W8)*
North China (W3)
Pearl Liang (W2)
Royal China (SW6,W2)
Shikumen, Dorsett Hotel (W12)*
Stick & Bowl (W8)*
Taiwan Village (SW6)*
Uli (W11)
Zheng (SW3)

North
Good Earth (NW7)
Green Cottage (NW3)
Kaifeng (NW4)
Phoenix Palace (NW1)
Sakonis (HA0)*
Singapore Garden (NW6)
Xi'an Impression (N7)*
Yipin China (N1)*

South
Dragon Castle (SE17)*
Good Earth (SW17)
Hutong, The Shard (SE1)
Silk Road (SE5)*

East
HKK (EC2)*
Mei Ume (EC3)
Royal China (E14)
The Sichuan (EC1)*
Sichuan Folk (E1)
Yauatcha City (EC2)*

CHINESE, DIM SUM
Central
Beijing Dumpling (WC2)*
The Bright Courtyard (W1)*
Golden Dragon (W1)*
The Grand Imperial (SW1)
Hakkasan (W1)
Joy King Lau (WC2)
New World (W1)
Novikov (Asian restaurant) (W1)

Royal China (W1)
Royal China Club (W1)*
Yauatcha (W1)*

West
Min Jiang (W8)*
Pearl Liang (W2)
Royal China (SW6,W2)
Shikumen, Dorsett Hotel (W12)*

North
Jun Ming Xuan (NW9)
Phoenix Palace (NW1)

South
Dragon Castle (SE17)*
Duddell's (SE1)

East
My Neighbours The Dumplings (E5)*
Royal China (E14)
Yauatcha City (EC2)*

FILIPINO
West
Romulo Café (W8)

GEORGIAN
North
Iberia (N1)
Little Georgia Café (N1)

East
Little Georgia Café (E2)

INDIAN
Central
Amaya (SW1)*
Benares (W1)
Chettinad (W1)*
Chutney Mary (SW1)*
Cinnamon Bazaar (WC2)
The Cinnamon Club (SW1)
Cinnamon Soho (W1)
Darjeeling Express (W1)*
Dishoom (W1,WC2)*
Dum Biryani (W1)*
Gaylord (W1)*
Gymkhana (W1)*
India Club (WC2)
Indian Accent (W1)
Jamavar (W1)*
Kricket (W1)*
Malabar Junction (WC1)
Mint Leaf (SW1)*
La Porte des Indes (W1)
Punjab (WC2)
Ragam (W1)*
Red Fort (W1)*
Roti Chai (W1)*
Sagar (W1,WC2)
Salaam Namaste (WC1)
Salloos (SW1)*
Talli Joe (WC2)
Tamarind (W1)*
Tamarind Kitchen (W1)
Tandoor Chop House (WC2)*
Trishna (W1)*
Veeraswamy (W1)*

West
Anarkali (W6)
Bombay Brasserie (SW7)
Bombay Palace (W2)*
Brilliant (UB2)*
Chakra (W8)
Dishoom (W8)*
Flora Indica (SW5)

Gifto's Lahore Karahi (UB1)
Indian Zing (W6)*
Karma (W14)*
Khan's (W2)
Madhu's (UB1)*
Malabar (W8)*
Monkey Temple (W12)
Noor Jahan (SW5,W2)
The Painted Heron (SW10)*
Potli (W6)*
Pure Indian Cooking (SW6)*
Sagar (W6)
Star of India (SW5)*
Thali (SW5)*
Vineet Bhatia London (SW3)

North
Bonoo (NW2)*
Chai Thali (NW1)
Chutneys (NW1)
Delhi Grill (N1)
Dishoom (N1)*
Diwana Bhel-Poori House (NW1)
Great Nepalese (NW1)
Guglee (NW3, NW6)
Indian Rasoi (N2)
Jashan (N8)*
Namaaste Kitchen (NW1)
Paradise Hampstead (NW3)*
Rani (N3)*
Ravi Shankar (NW1)
Sakonis (HA0)*
Saravanaa Bhavan (HA0)*
Vijay (NW6)
Zaffrani (N1)

South
Babur (SE23)*
Baluchi, Lalit Hotel London (SE1)
Bistro Vadouvan (SW15)
Chit Chaat Chai (SW18)*
Dastaan (KT19)*
Est India (SE1)
Everest Inn (SE3)
Ganapati (SE15)*
Hot Stuff (SW8)
Indian Moment (SW11)
Indian Ocean (SW17)
Kashmir (SW15)*
Kennington Tandoori (SE11)*
Lahore Karahi (SW17)*
Lahore Kebab House (SW16)*
Ma Goa (SW15)*
Mirch Masala (SW17)*
Sree Krishna (SW17)*

East
Bangalore Express (EC3)
Brigadiers (EC2)
Café Spice Namaste (E1)*
Cinnamon Kitchen (EC2)*
Darbaar (EC2)*
Dishoom (E2)*
Grand Trunk Road (E18)*
Gul and Sepoy (E1)
Gunpowder (E1)*
Lahore Kebab House (E1)*
Madame D's (E1)
Mint Leaf Lounge (EC2)*
Needoo (E1)
Rola Wala (E1)
Tayyabs (E1)*
temper City (EC2)

INDIAN, SOUTHERN
Central
Hoppers (W1)*
India Club, Strand Continental

Hotel *(WC2)*
Malabar Junction *(WC1)*
Quilon *(SW1)**
Ragam *(W1)**
Rasa *(W1)*
Rasa Maricham, Holiday Inn
Hotel *(WC1)*
Sagar *(W1, WC2)*

West
Sagar *(W6)*
Shilpa *(W6)**
Zaika of Kensington *(W8)*

North
Chutneys *(NW1)*
Rani *(N3)**
Rasa *(N16)*
Vijay *(NW6)*

South
Ganapati *(SE15)**
Jaffna House *(SW17)**
Sree Krishna *(SW17)**

JAPANESE
Central
Anzu *(SW1)*
The Araki *(W1)**
Atari-Ya *(W1)**
Bone Daddies, Nova *(SW1,W1)**
Chisou *(W1)**
Chotto Matte *(W1)**
Defune *(W1)*
Dinings *(W1)**
Dozo *(W1)*
Eat Tokyo *(W1,WC1,WC2)**
Flesh and Buns *(WC2)**
Ginza Onodera *(SW1)**
Japan Centre Food Hall *(SW1)*
Jugemu *(W1)**
Kanada-Ya *(SW1,WC2)**
Kiku *(W1)*
Kikuchi *(W1)**
Kintan *(WC1)*
Koya-Bar *(W1)*
Kulu Kulu *(W1,WC2)*
Machiya *(SW1)*
Nobu, Metropolitan Hotel *(W1)*
Nobu Berkeley *(W1)*
Oka, Kingly Court *(W1)**
Oliver Maki *(W1)*
Roka *(W1,WC2)**
Sakagura *(W1)**
Sake No Hana *(SW1)**
Shoryu Ramen *(SW1,W1)*
Sticks'n'Sushi *(SW1,WC2)**
Sumosan Twiga *(SW1)*
Sushisamba *(WC2)*
TAKA *(W1)*
Taro *(W1)*
Tokimeite *(W1)**
Tokyo Diner *(WC2)*
Tonkotsu, Selfridges *(W1)*
Umu *(W1)*
Vasco & Piero's Pavilion *(W1)*
Yoshino *(W1)**

West
Atari-Ya *(W3,W5)**
Bone Daddies, Whole Foods *(W8)**
Chisou *(SW3)**
Dinings *(SW3)**
Eat Tokyo *(W6,W8)**
Flat Three *(W11)**
Kiraku *(W5)**
Kiru *(SW3)**
Koji *(SW6)**

Kulu Kulu *(SW7)*
Kurobuta *(SW3,W2)*
Maguro *(W9)*
Oka *(SW3)**
Southam Street *(W10)*
Sushi Bar Makoto *(W4)**
Tonkotsu *(W11)*
Tosa *(W6)*
Yashin *(W8)**
Yoshi Sushi *(W6)*
Zuma *(SW7)**

North
Asakusa *(NW1)**
Atari-Ya *(N12, NW6)**
Dotori *(N4)**
Eat Tokyo *(NW11)**
Jin Kichi *(NW3)**
Oka *(NW1)**
Sushi Masa *(NW2)*

South
Hashi *(SW20)*
Matsuba *(TW9)*
MOMMI *(SW4)*
Nanban *(SW9)**
Sticks'n'Sushi *(SE10, SW19)**
Takahashi *(SW19)**
Taro *(SW12)*
Tomoe *(SW15)**
Tonkotsu Bankside *(SE1)*
Tsunami *(SW4)**
Yama Momo *(SE22)**
Zaibatsu *(SE10)*

East
Bone Daddies, The Bower *(EC1)**
Ippudo London *(E14)*
K10, Appold Street *(EC2, EC3)*
Koya *(EC2)*
Mei Ume *(EC3)*
Nanashi *(EC2)*
Nobu Shoreditch *(EC2)*
Pham Sushi *(EC1)**
Roka *(E14)**
Shoryu Ramen *(EC2)*
Sosharu, Turnmill Building *(EC1)*
Sticks'n'Sushi *(E14)**
Sushisamba *(EC2)*
Sushi Tetsu *(EC1)**
Taro *(EC4)*
Tonkotsu *(E8)*
Uchi *(E5)**
Waka *(EC3)*

KOREAN
Central
Bibimbap Soho *(W1)*
Bó Drake *(W1)*
Jinjuu *(W1)*
Kintan *(WC1)*
Koba *(W1)**
On The Bab *(WC2)*
On The Bab Express *(W1)*

West
Gogi *(W2)*
Yoshi Sushi *(W6)*

North
Dotori *(N4)**
The Petite Coree *(NW6)**

South
Cah-Chi *(SW18, SW20)*
Matsuba *(TW9)*

East
Bibimbap *(EC3)*
On The Bab *(EC1, EC4)*

MALAYSIAN
Central
C&R Café *(W1)**

West
C&R Café *(W2)**
Satay House *(W2)*

North
Roti King *(NW1)**
Singapore Garden *(NW6)*

South
Champor-Champor *(SE1)**

PAKISTANI
Central
Salloos *(SW1)**

South
Lahore Karahi *(SW17)**
Lahore Kebab House *(SW16)**
Mirch Masala *(SW17)**

East
Lahore Kebab House *(E1)**
Needoo *(E1)**
Tayyabs *(E1)**

PAN-ASIAN
Central
Hare & Tortoise *(WC1)*
Hot Pot *(W1)*
Jean-Georges at The Connaught *(W1)*
Nirvana Kitchen *(W1)**
Nopi *(W1)**
Novikov (Asian restaurant) *(W1)*
PF Chang's Asian Table *(WC2)*

West
E&O *(W11)*
Eight Over Eight *(SW3)*
Hare & Tortoise *(W14, W4, W5)*
Little Bird Chiswick *(W4)*
Uli *(W11)*
Zheng *(SW3)*

North
Bang Bang Oriental *(NW9)*
Pamban *(NW1)*

South
Hare & Tortoise *(SW15)*
Little Bird Battersea *(SW11)*
Sticky Mango at RSJ *(SE1)*

East
Hare & Tortoise *(EC4)*

THAI
Central
Crazy Bear Fitzrovia *(W1)*
Kiln *(W1)**
Lao Cafe *(WC2)*
Patara Mayfair *(W1)**
Rosa's *(SW1)*
Rosa's Soho *(W1)*
Smoking Goat *(WC2)**
Suda *(WC2)*

West
Addie's Thai Café *(SW5)*
Nukis Kitchen *(W13)*
Patara *(SW3)**

Rosa's Fulham *(SW10)*
Sukho Fine Thai Cuisine *(SW6)**
Suksan *(SW10)**
Uli *(W11)*

North
Farang *(N5)**
Isarn *(N1)**
Patara *(NW3)**
Rosa's *(N1, NW6)*

South
Awesome Thai *(SW13)*
The Begging Bowl *(SE15)**
Champor-Champor *(SE1)**
Kaosarn *(SW11, SW9)*
Patara *(SW19)**
The Pepper Tree *(SW4)*
Rosa's *(SW9)*

East
Rosa's *(E1, E15)*
Saiphin's Thai Kitchen *(E8)*
Smoking Goat *(E1)**
Som Saa *(E1)**

VIETNAMESE
Central
Cây Tre *(W1)*
House of Ho *(W1)*
Pho & Bun *(W1)**
Viet Food *(W1)*

West
Go-Viet *(SW7)**
MAM *(W11)*
Saigon Saigon *(W6)*

North
CôBa *(N7)**
Salvation In Noodles *(N1, N4)*
Singapore Garden *(NW6)*

South
Bánh Bánh *(SE15)*
Café East *(SE16)**
Mien Tay *(SW11)**

East
Cây Tre *(EC1)*
City Càphê *(EC2)*
Mien Tay *(E2)**
Sông Quê *(E2)*
Viet Grill *(E2)*

TAIWANESE
Central
Bao Fitzrovia *(W1)**
XU *(W1)*

West
Taiwan Village *(SW6)**

South
Mr Bao *(SE15)**

East
Bao Bar *(E8)**

AREA OVERVIEWS

CENTRAL

Soho, Covent Garden & Bloomsbury
(Parts of W1, all WC2 and WC1)

£110+	L'Atelier de Joel Robuchon	French	2	1	2
£100+	Smith & Wollensky	Steaks & grills	2	1	2
£90+	Savoy Thames Foyer	British, Modern	2	3	4
	The Savoy Hotel, Savoy Grill	British, Traditional	2	3	3
	Sushisamba	Japanese	3	2	5
£80+	Bob Bob Ricard	British, Modern	3	4	5
	Hush	"	2	2	3
	The Northall	"	3	3	3
	Spring Restaurant	"	3	3	4
	Kaspar's Seafood and Grill	Fish & seafood	3	3	4
	J Sheekey	"	3	3	4
	Asia de Cuba	Fusion	2	2	3
	Massimo, Corinthia Hotel	Mediterranean	2	2	3
	MASH Steakhouse	Steaks & grills	2	2	2
	Oscar Wilde Bar	Afternoon tea	–	–	–
	Yauatcha	Chinese	4	3	3
	Roka, Aldwych House	Japanese	4	3	3
£70+	Christopher's	American	2	2	3
	Balthazar	British, Modern	2	2	4
	Social Eating House	"	5	5	4
	Holborn Dining Room	British, Traditional	3	3	4
	Rules	"	2	3	5
	Simpson's in the Strand	"	–	–	–
	Clos Maggiore	French	3	4	5
	L'Escargot	"	4	4	4
	Frenchie	"	4	2	2
	Gauthier Soho	"	5	5	4
	Otto's	"	4	5	4
	Nopi	Mediterranean	4	3	3
	Eneko	Spanish	3	3	2
	Hawksmoor	Steaks & grills	3	3	3
	Lima Floral	Peruvian	3	2	2
	Red Fort	Indian	4	3	2
£60+	Bronte	Australian	2	3	4
	Dean Street Townhouse	British, Modern	2	2	4
	Ducksoup	"	3	3	4
	Ham Yard Restaurant	"	2	3	5
	Heliot Steak House	"	4	4	4
	Hix	"	1	2	3
	Indigo, One Aldwych	"	3	4	3
	The Ivy	"	3	4	5
	Noble Rot	"	3	3	4
	The Portrait	"	2	2	3
	Quo Vadis	"	4	5	5
	Tom's Kitchen	"	2	2	2

Tredwell's	"	2	2	2
J Sheekey Atlantic Bar	Fish & seafood	3	4	4
Randall & Aubin	"	3	3	4
Wright Brothers	"	4	3	3
Café Monico	French	2	2	4
Test Kitchen	International	–	–	–
Bocca Di Lupo	Italian	4	4	3
Café Murano Pastificio	"	3	2	3
Fumo	"	3	2	3
Vasco & Piero's Pavilion	"	3	4	3
100 Wardour Street	Mediterranean	2	2	3
Aqua Nueva	Spanish	2	2	3
Sophie's Steakhouse	Steaks & grills	2	3	3
Rainforest Café	Burgers, etc	2	3	3
The Palomar	Middle Eastern	4	4	3
Chotto Matte	Japanese	4	3	5
Oliver Maki	"	3	3	3
Jinjuu	Korean	3	3	4
Patara Soho	Thai	4	4	4
XU	Taiwanese	–	–	–

£50+	Big Easy	American	2	2	3
	Bodean's	"	2	2	2
	Hubbard & Bell	"	3	2	3
	Jackson & Rye	"	1	2	2
	Joe Allen	"	1	2	4
	Andrew Edmunds	British, Modern	3	4	5
	Aurora	"	3	4	4
	Great Queen Street	"	3	2	2
	The Ivy Market Grill	"	2	2	3
	Jar Kitchen	"	2	5	3
	Native	"	4	3	2
	Polpo at Ape & Bird	"	2	2	2
	Saint Luke's Kitchen, Library	"	3	3	3
	10 Greek Street	"	4	4	3
	Terroirs	"	3	2	3
	Vinoteca	"	3	3	4
	The Ivy Soho Brasserie	British, Traditional	2	2	3
	The Delaunay	Central European	2	4	5
	Bonnie Gull Seafood Shack	Fish & seafood	5	3	5
	Oystermen	"	–	–	–
	Antidote Wine Bar	French	2	2	3
	Blanchette	"	4	3	4
	Bon Vivant	"	3	3	3
	Cigalon	"	3	4	4
	Le Garrick	"	2	3	4
	Mon Plaisir	"	2	3	5
	Gay Hussar	Hungarian	1	2	4
	Cork & Bottle	International	2	3	5
	Flavour Bastard	"	–	–	–
	The 10 Cases	"	2	3	3
	Da Mario	Italian	3	4	3
	Dehesa	"	3	2	3
	Luce e Limoni	"	4	4	3
	Margot	"	4	5	5
	Mele e Pere	"	3	4	3

Obicà	"		3 2 2
Polpo	"		2 2 2
San Carlo Cicchetti	"		3 3 4
Ember Yard	Spanish		2 3 3
Encant	"		4 2 3
Morada Brindisa Asador	"		2 2 2
Opera Tavern	"		4 4 3
Foxlow	Steaks & grills		2 2 2
Zelman Meats	"		5 4 4
St Moritz	Swiss		3 3 4
Dalloway Terrace	Afternoon tea		3 2 4
Burger & Lobster	Burgers, etc		3 2 3
Fernandez & Wells	Sandwiches, cakes, etc		3 3 3
Bodean's	BBQ		2 2 2
Cantina Laredo	Mexican/TexMex		3 2 3
Ceviche Soho	Peruvian		4 3 3
Barshu	Chinese		4 2 2
The Duck & Rice	"		3 3 4
Dum Biryani	Indian		4 4 3
Flesh and Buns	Japanese		4 3 3
Sticks'n'Sushi	"		4 2 2
Bó Drake	Korean		2 2 3
£40+	Breakfast Club	American	3 3 3
	Spuntino		3 3 3
	Coopers Restaurant & Bar	British, Modern	2 3 3
	The Frog	"	5 3 2
	The Norfolk Arms	"	3 2 2
	Shampers	"	2 4 5
	VQ, St Giles Hotel	"	2 4 3
	Brasserie Zédel	French	1 3 5
	Prix Fixe	"	3 3 2
	Relais de Venise L'Entrecôte	"	3 2 2
	Savoir Faire	"	3 4 3
	La Fromagerie Bloomsbury	International	3 2 2
	Ciao Bella	Italian	2 3 4
	Polpetto	"	3 3 3
	La Porchetta Pizzeria	"	2 3 2
	Zima	Russian	3 2 3
	Barrafina	Spanish	5 5 5
	Cigala	"	3 3 3
	Sibarita	"	– – –
	Mildreds	Vegetarian	3 3 3
	North Sea Fish	Fish & chips	3 2 2
	Poppies	"	3 2 3
	Rossopomodoro	Pizza	3 2 2
	Chick 'n' Sours	Chicken	3 3 3
	La Bodega Negra Cafe	Mexican/TexMex	3 2 4
	Corazón	"	3 4 3
	Lupita	"	3 2 2
	Señor Ceviche	Peruvian	3 2 4
	The Barbary	North African	5 5 4
	Le Bab	Turkish	5 4 3
	Babaji Pide	"	3 2 2
	The Four Seasons	Chinese	4 1 1
	Yming	"	3 5 2

	Name	Cuisine	Rating
	Cinnamon Bazaar	Indian	2 3 3
	Cinnamon Soho	"	3 2 2
	Darjeeling Express	"	4 3 3
	Dishoom	"	4 4 5
	Kricket	"	5 4 4
	Malabar Junction	"	3 3 2
	Salaam Namaste	"	3 3 2
	Tamarind Kitchen	"	3 3 4
	Tandoor Chop House	"	4 3 3
	Hoppers	Indian, Southern	5 4 3
	Bone Daddies	Japanese	4 3 3
	Dozo	"	3 3 3
	Jugemu	"	5 2 3
	Kintan	"	3 2 3
	Oka, Kingly Court	"	4 2 2
	Shoryu Ramen	"	3 2 2
	Tonkotsu	"	3 2 3
	Hare & Tortoise	Pan-Asian	3 2 2
	Rosa's Soho	Thai	2 2 2
	Smoking Goat	"	4 3 2
	Suda	"	3 3 3
	Cây Tre	Vietnamese	3 3 2
	Pho & Bun	"	4 3 2
£35+	Gordon's Wine Bar	International	2 2 5
	Bar Termini	Italian	3 3 5
	Princi	"	3 2 3
	Blacklock	Steaks & grills	4 4 4
	Bukowski Grill	"	3 3 2
	Haché	Burgers, etc	3 4 4
	MEATliquor	"	3 2 4
	Pizza Pilgrims	Pizza	4 3 3
	Bea's Cake Boutique	Sandwiches, cakes, etc	3 3 3
	temper Soho	BBQ	3 4 5
	Casita Andina	Peruvian	4 3 4
	Gaby's	Israeli	3 2 2
	Yalla Yalla	Lebanese	3 2 2
	Joy King Lau	Chinese	3 2 2
	New World	"	2 1 2
	Punjab	Indian	3 2 3
	Sagar	"	3 2 1
	Talli Joe	"	3 3 4
	Rasa Maricham	Indian, Southern	3 3 3
	Taro	Japanese	3 2 2
	On The Bab	Korean	3 2 2
	Hot Pot	Pan-Asian	– – –
	Lao Cafe	Thai	3 3 2
£30+	Café in the Crypt	British, Traditional	2 1 4
	Bar Italia	Italian	2 3 5
	Flat Iron	Steaks & grills	4 4 3
	Homeslice	Pizza	4 4 4
	Chicken Shop	Chicken	3 3 3
	Chilli Cool	Chinese	5 2 1
	Golden Dragon	"	4 2 2
	Wong Kei	"	3 2 1

	Beijing Dumpling	*Chinese, Dim sum*	4 2 2
	Koya-Bar	*Japanese*	3 3 3
	Kulu Kulu	*"*	3 2 1
	C&R Café	*Malaysian*	4 2 2
	Kiln	*Thai*	5 4 4
	Viet Food	*Vietnamese*	3 3 3
£25+	MEATmarket	*Burgers, etc*	3 3 2
	Patty and Bun Soho	*"*	4 3 3
	Shake Shack	*"*	2 2 2
	Tommi's Burger Joint	*"*	3 3 3
	India Club	*Indian*	2 2 1
	Eat Tokyo	*Japanese*	4 3 2
	Kanada-Ya	*"*	5 2 2
	Bibimbap Soho	*Korean*	3 2 2
	Bao	*Taiwanese*	4 3 2
£20+	Baozi Inn	*Chinese*	– – –
	Tokyo Diner	*Japanese*	3 3 3
£15+	Five Guys	*Burgers, etc*	3 2 2
£10+	Nordic Bakery	*Scandinavian*	3 2 3
	Bageriet	*Sandwiches, cakes, etc*	4 4 3
£5+	Maison Bertaux	*Afternoon tea*	3 4 4
	Gelupo	*Ice cream*	5 2 2
	Monmouth Coffee Company	*Sandwiches, cakes, etc*	4 5 4

Mayfair & St James's (Parts of W1 and SW1)

£380+	The Araki	*Japanese*	5 5 3
£140+	Sketch, Lecture Room	*French*	4 4 5
	The Square	*"*	3 3 1
£130+	The Ritz	*British, Traditional*	3 4 5
	Alain Ducasse	*French*	2 2 2
	Le Gavroche	*"*	4 5 4
	Hélène Darroze	*"*	3 4 4
£120+	Ormer Mayfair	*British, Modern*	4 3 3
	Estiatorio Milos	*Greek*	3 2 4
	The Promenade	*International*	2 4 4
	Cut, 45 Park Lane	*Steaks & grills*	2 2 2
	Umu	*Japanese*	3 4 3
£110+	Galvin at Windows	*French*	2 2 5
	The Greenhouse	*"*	4 4 4
£100+	Dorchester Grill	*British, Modern*	3 4 4
	Fera at Claridge's	*"*	– – –
	Pollen Street Social	*"*	3 2 3
	Seven Park Place	*French*	4 5 4

Assunta Madre	*Italian*	3	3	3
Novikov (Italian restaurant)	*"*	1	2	2
QP LDN	*"*	3	3	3
Kai Mayfair	*Chinese*	3	2	2
Benares	*Indian*	2	2	2
Tokimeite	*Japanese*	4	3	3

£90+					
Alyn Williams	*British, Modern*	3	3	2
Corrigan's Mayfair	*British, Traditional*	3	4	3
Wiltons	*"*	3	4	5
Sexy Fish	*Fish & seafood*	1	1	3
La Petite Maison	*French*	4	3	3
C London	*Italian*	1	1	3
Murano	*"*	5	5	4
Theo Randall	*"*	3	3	2
Street XO	*Spanish*	1	1	2
Goodman	*Steaks & grills*	4	4	2
Hakkasan Mayfair	*Chinese*	3	2	4
Park Chinois	*"*	2	2	4
Nobu, Metropolitan Hotel	*Japanese*	3	2	1
Novikov (Asian restaurant)	*Pan-Asian*	3	2	3

£80+					
Le Caprice	*British, Modern*	2	4	4
Hush	*"*	2	2	3
Butler's Restaurant	*British, Traditional*	2	4	3
Bentley's	*Fish & seafood*	3	4	4
Scott's	*"*	4	4	5
maze	*French*	2	2	1
Sketch, Gallery	*"*	1	2	3
Bocconcino	*Italian*	3	3	3
Chucs	*"*	3	3	3
Ristorante Frescobaldi	*"*	3	3	2
Savini at Criterion	*"*	2	2	5
The Ritz, Palm Court	*Afternoon tea*	2	4	5
Peyote	*Mexican/TexMex*	3	3	2
Coya	*Peruvian*	4	3	5
MNKY HSE	*South American*	1	2	3
China Tang	*Chinese*	4	3	3
Chutney Mary	*Indian*	4	4	4
Jamavar	*"*	5	4	4
Ginza Onodera	*Japanese*	4	5	2
Nobu Berkeley	*"*	3	2	3
Roka	*"*	4	3	3

£70+					
Colony Grill Room	*American*	3	3	3
Bonhams Restaurant	*British, Modern*	4	5	2
Kitty Fisher's	*"*	3	3	3
Little Social	*"*	2	2	2
Mews of Mayfair	*"*	3	3	3
Quaglino's	*"*	1	2	3
Wild Honey	*"*	3	4	3
Brown's, English Tea Room	*British, Traditional*	3	4	4
The Game Bird	*"*	3	4	4
GBR	*"*	–	–	–
Boulestin	*French*	3	3	2
Ferdi	*"*	1	1	2

Cecconi's	Italian	2 2 3
Franco's	"	3 3 3
Sartoria	"	3 3 3
Aquavit	Scandinavian	3 3 3
Boisdale of Mayfair	Scottish	3 3 3
Barbecoa Piccadilly	Steaks & grills	2 2 2
The Guinea Grill	"	4 4 4
Hawksmoor	"	3 3 3
maze Grill	"	1 2 2
Rowley's	"	3 3 3
34 Mayfair	"	3 3 4
Momo	Moroccan	3 3 4
Veeraswamy	Indian	4 4 3

£60+			
The Avenue	American	2 4 3
Hard Rock Café	"	3 3 4
Bellamy's	British, Modern	3 4 3
Galvin at the Athenaeum	"	3 4 2
Heddon Street Kitchen	"	1 1 2
The Keeper's House	"	2 2 2
Langan's Brasserie	"	2 3 4
The Punchbowl	"	3 4 3
The Wolseley	"	3 4 5
Brown's Hotel, HIX Mayfair	British, Traditional	2 2 3
Black Roe	Fish & seafood	3 2 2
Fishworks	"	3 2 3
The Balcon, Sofitel St James	French	2 2 2
Villandry St James's	"	1 1 3
Café Murano	Italian	3 2 3
Fortnum, Diamond Jubilee	Afternoon tea	3 3 3
Mayfair Garden	Chinese	4 3 2
Gymkhana	Indian	4 4 4
Mint Leaf	"	4 4 4
Tamarind	"	5 4 3
Kiku	Japanese	3 3 2
Sake No Hana	"	4 3 3
Patara Mayfair	Thai	4 4 4

£50+			
Comptoir Café & Wine	British, Modern	– – –
Duck & Waffle Local	"	– – –
Hatchetts	"	2 3 2
The American Bar	British, Traditional	– – –
Boudin Blanc	French	3 3 4
Neo Bistro	"	– – –
28-50	"	2 4 3
Al Duca	Italian	3 3 2
Veneta	"	3 3 2
Il Vicolo	"	3 4 2
Burger & Lobster	Burgers, etc	3 2 3
Delfino	Pizza	4 3 2
Mayfair Pizza Company	"	3 4 3
Fernandez & Wells	Sandwiches, cakes, etc	3 3 3
Chisou	Japanese	4 3 2
Sakagura	"	4 4 3

£40+			
The Windmill	British, Traditional	3 3 3

FSA Ratings: from **1** (Poor) to **5** (Exceptional)

	L'Artiste Musclé	*French*	2️⃣2️⃣5️⃣
	El Pirata	*Spanish*	3️⃣3️⃣4️⃣
	Anzu	*Japanese*	– – –
	Shoryu Ramen	"	3️⃣2️⃣2️⃣
	Yoshino	"	4️⃣4️⃣2️⃣
£35+	tibits	*Vegetarian*	3️⃣2️⃣3️⃣
	Rasa	*Indian, Southern*	3️⃣3️⃣3️⃣

Fitzrovia & Marylebone (Part of W1)

£130+	Bubbledogs, Kitchen Table	*Fusion*	5️⃣3️⃣4️⃣
£110+	Pied à Terre	*French*	4️⃣4️⃣3️⃣
	Texture	*Scandinavian*	4️⃣3️⃣3️⃣
	Beast	*Steaks & grills*	1️⃣2️⃣2️⃣
£100+	Roux at the Landau	*British, Modern*	2️⃣3️⃣3️⃣
£90+	The Chiltern Firehouse	*American*	1️⃣1️⃣3️⃣
	Orrery	*French*	3️⃣3️⃣2️⃣
	Hakkasan	*Chinese*	3️⃣2️⃣4️⃣
£80+	Portland	*British, Modern*	4️⃣4️⃣3️⃣
	Clarette	*French*	– – –
	Mere	*International*	3️⃣5️⃣3️⃣
	Locanda Locatelli	*Italian*	4️⃣3️⃣3️⃣
	Trishna	*Indian*	5️⃣3️⃣3️⃣
	Roka	*Japanese*	4️⃣3️⃣3️⃣
£70+	The Berners Tavern	*British, Modern*	2️⃣3️⃣5️⃣
	Pescatori	*Fish & seafood*	2️⃣4️⃣3️⃣
	Les 110 de Taillevent	*French*	4️⃣4️⃣3️⃣
	The Providores	*Fusion*	4️⃣3️⃣2️⃣
	Il Baretto	*Italian*	2️⃣2️⃣2️⃣
	Palm Court, The Langham	*Afternoon tea*	3️⃣3️⃣4️⃣
	Lima	*Peruvian*	3️⃣2️⃣2️⃣
	La Porte des Indes	*Indian*	3️⃣2️⃣4️⃣
	Defune	*Japanese*	3️⃣2️⃣1️⃣
	Kikuchi	"	4️⃣3️⃣2️⃣
	Crazy Bear Fitzrovia	*Thai*	3️⃣3️⃣4️⃣
£60+	Clipstone	*British, Modern*	4️⃣4️⃣3️⃣
	The Grazing Goat	"	2️⃣3️⃣3️⃣
	Picture	"	3️⃣3️⃣2️⃣
	Fischer's	*Central European*	2️⃣3️⃣4️⃣
	Fishworks	*Fish & seafood*	3️⃣2️⃣3️⃣
	Galvin Bistrot de Luxe	*French*	3️⃣3️⃣3️⃣
	Villandry	"	1️⃣1️⃣3️⃣
	Twist	*Fusion*	4️⃣4️⃣4️⃣
	Jikoni	*International*	3️⃣3️⃣4️⃣
	Caffè Caldesi	*Italian*	2️⃣3️⃣3️⃣
	Blandford Comptoir	*Mediterranean*	3️⃣3️⃣3️⃣
	The Ninth London	"	4️⃣3️⃣3️⃣

	Pachamama	*Peruvian*	3	2	2
	The Bright Courtyard	*Chinese*	4	2	2
	Royal China Club	*"*	4	2	2
	Gaylord	*Indian*	4	4	3
	Dinings	*Japanese*	5	4	2
	Nirvana Kitchen	*Pan-Asian*	4	2	2
	Patara Fitzrovia	*Thai*	4	4	4
	House of Ho	*Vietnamese*	3	3	3
£50+	Daylesford Organic	*British, Modern*	3	2	3
	Hardy's Brasserie	*"*	3	3	3
	The Ivy Café	*"*	1	2	3
	108 Brasserie	*"*	3	3	3
	Percy & Founders	*"*	3	3	3
	Vinoteca Seymour Place	*"*	3	3	4
	Bonnie Gull	*Fish & seafood*	4	3	3
	28-50	*French*	2	4	3
	The Wallace	*"*	2	1	5
	Carousel	*Fusion*	5	4	4
	Bernardi's	*Italian*	3	3	4
	Briciole	*"*	3	4	3
	Latium	*"*	3	3	2
	Obicà	*"*	3	2	2
	Sardo	*"*	3	3	2
	2 Veneti	*"*	3	4	3
	Riding House Café	*Mediterranean*	2	2	4
	The Harcourt	*Scandinavian*	4	3	4
	Mac & Wild	*Scottish*	4	3	4
	Barrica	*Spanish*	3	2	2
	Donostia	*"*	4	4	4
	Ibérica	*"*	2	2	3
	Lurra	*"*	3	3	3
	Salt Yard	*"*	3	3	2
	Social Wine & Tapas	*"*	3	4	4
	Ethos	*Vegetarian*	3	3	3
	The Gate	*"*	4	3	3
	Burger & Lobster	*Burgers, etc*	3	2	3
	Daylesford Organic	*Sandwiches, cakes, etc*	3	2	3
	Zoilo	*Argentinian*	4	3	3
	Pisqu	*Peruvian*	–	–	–
	Reubens	*Kosher*	2	2	2
	Maroush	*Lebanese*	3	2	2
	Ishtar	*Turkish*	3	4	2
	Yosma	*"*	3	3	2
	Royal China	*Chinese*	3	1	2
£40+	Lantana Café	*Australian*	3	3	3
	The Wigmore, The Langham	*British, Traditional*	–	–	–
	Opso	*Greek*	3	3	3
	Foley's	*International*	4	4	4
	La Fromagerie Café	*"*	3	2	2
	Fucina	*Italian*	1	2	4
	Made in Italy James St	*"*	3	2	3
	Rossopomodoro, John Lewis	*"*	3	2	2
	Drakes Tabanco	*Spanish*	3	2	2
	Le Relais de Venise	*Steaks & grills*	3	2	2

	Bobo Social	Burgers, etc	**3**	**3**	**3**
	Fairuz	Lebanese	**3**	**3**	**2**
	Honey & Co	Middle Eastern	**3**	**3**	**2**
	Honey & Smoke	"	**5**	**4**	**2**
	Chettinad	Indian	**4**	**3**	**3**
	Roti Chai	"	**4**	**3**	**4**
	Hoppers	Indian, Southern	**5**	**4**	**3**
	Bone Daddies	Japanese	**4**	**3**	**3**
	Tonkotsu, Selfridges	"	**3**	**2**	**3**
	Koba	Korean	**4**	**3**	**3**
£35+	MEATLiquor	Burgers, etc	**3**	**2**	**4**
	Golden Hind	Fish & chips	**3**	**3**	**2**
	Workshop Coffee	Sandwiches, cakes, etc	**3**	**4**	**4**
	Yalla Yalla	Lebanese	**3**	**2**	**2**
	Sagar	Indian	**3**	**2**	**1**
	On The Bab Express	Korean	**3**	**2**	**2**
£30+	Vagabond Wines	Mediterranean	**3**	**3**	**4**
	Homeslice	Pizza	**4**	**4**	**4**
	Atari-Ya	Japanese	**4**	**2**	**1**
£25+	Patty and Bun	Burgers, etc	**4**	**3**	**3**
	Tommi's Burger Joint	"	**3**	**3**	**3**
	Ragam	Indian	**4**	**2**	**1**
	Bibimbap Soho	Korean	**3**	**2**	**2**
	Bao Fitzrovia	Taiwanese	**4**	**3**	**2**
£15+	Scandinavian Kitchen	Scandinavian	**3**	**4**	**2**
	Chik'n	Chicken	–	–	–
£10+	Nordic Bakery	Scandinavian	**3**	**2**	**3**
	Kaffeine	Sandwiches, cakes, etc	**3**	**5**	**4**
	Patogh	Middle Eastern	**4**	**3**	**2**

Belgravia, Pimlico, Victoria & Westminster (SW1, except St James's)

£120+	Marcus, The Berkeley	British, Modern	**3**	**2**	**3**
£110+	Dinner, Mandarin Oriental	British, Traditional	**2**	**3**	**2**
	Pétrus	French	**3**	**3**	**2**
£100+	Céleste, The Lanesborough	French	**2**	**3**	**5**
	Rib Room, Jumeirah Carlton Tower Hotel	Steaks & grills	–	–	–
£90+	The Collins Room	British, Modern	**2**	**4**	**5**
	Goring Hotel	"	**3**	**4**	**4**
	Roux at Parliament Square	"	**5**	**5**	**3**
	Strangers Dining Room,	British, Traditional	**2**	**3**	**5**
	One-O-One	Fish & seafood	**4**	**3**	**1**
	Zafferano	Italian	**2**	**2**	**2**
	Ametsa	Spanish	**3**	**3**	**2**

	Hunan	*Chinese*	5	2	1
£80+	M Restaurant	*Steaks & grills*	2	2	2
	Mr Chow	*Chinese*	2	2	2
	Amaya	*Indian*	4	2	3
	The Cinnamon Club	"	3	3	4
£70+	Caxton Grill	*British, Modern*	2	3	3
	Como Lario	*Italian*	2	3	2
	Il Convivio	"	4	3	4
	Enoteca Turi	"	3	4	3
	Olivo	"	3	3	2
	Il Pampero	"	–	–	–
	Santini	"	2	3	3
	Signor Sassi	"	3	3	3
	Mari Vanna	*Russian*	3	3	4
	Barbecoa, Nova	*Steaks & grills*	2	2	2
	Quilon	*Indian, Southern*	5	4	3
£60+	Timmy Green	*Australian*	2	3	3
	The Alfred Tennyson	*British, Modern*	3	3	4
	The Botanist	"	2	2	2
	45 Jermyn Street	"	3	4	4
	Lorne	"	4	5	3
	The Orange	"	3	3	4
	The Other Naughty Piglet	"	4	4	3
	Rail House Café	"	2	2	2
	Tate Britain	"	2	2	5
	The Thomas Cubitt	"	3	4	4
	Olivomare	*Fish & seafood*	3	2	2
	Bar Boulud	*French*	3	4	4
	Colbert	"	2	2	3
	La Poule au Pot	"	2	2	5
	Caraffini	*Italian*	3	5	3
	Olivocarne	"	3	3	2
	Quirinale	"	4	3	2
	Sale e Pepe	"	3	4	4
	Boisdale of Belgravia	*Scottish*	3	2	4
	Oliveto	*Pizza*	4	2	1
	The Grand Imperial	*Chinese*	3	2	2
	Ken Lo's Memories	"	3	3	2
£50+	Granger & Co	*Australian*	3	3	3
	Aster Restaurant	*British, Modern*	3	3	3
	Cambridge Street Kitchen	"	3	4	4
	Daylesford Organic	"	3	2	3
	Ebury	"	2	2	3
	Shepherd's	*British, Traditional*	3	4	4
	Motcombs	*International*	2	2	3
	Cacio & Pepe	*Italian*	3	2	2
	Hai Cenato	"	3	3	2
	Osteria Dell'Angolo	"	3	3	1
	Ottolenghi	"	4	3	2
	Tozi	"	3	3	2
	About Thyme	*Spanish*	2	3	3
	Ibérica, Zig Zag Building	"	2	2	3

	Zelman Meats	*Steaks & grills*	5 4 4
	Burger & Lobster	*Burgers, etc*	3 2 3
	Bbar	*South African*	3 4 3
	Ma La Sichuan	*Chinese*	4 3 1
	Sticks'n'Sushi	*Japanese*	4 2 2
	Salloos	*Pakistani*	4 2 2
£40+	Greenwood	*British, Modern*	– – –
	Gustoso	*Italian*	3 4 3
	Goya	*Spanish*	3 3 2
	Seafresh	*Fish & chips*	3 3 2
	The Stoke House	*BBQ*	– – –
	Kazan (Café)	*Turkish*	3 3 3
	A Wong	*Chinese*	5 5 3
	Bone Daddies, Nova	*Japanese*	4 3 3
	Machiya	*"*	– – –
	Rosa's	*Thai*	2 2 2
£35+	The Vincent Rooms	*British, Modern*	3 4 3
	Cyprus Mangal	*Turkish*	3 2 2
£30+	Vagabond Wines	*Mediterranean*	3 3 4
£25+	Shake Shack	*Burgers, etc*	2 2 2
	Kanada-Ya	*Japanese*	5 2 2
£20+	Bleecker Burger	*Burgers, etc*	5 2 2
	Dominique Ansel Baker	*Sandwiches, cakes, etc*	5 4 3

WEST

Chelsea, South Kensington, Kensington, Earl's Court & Fulham (SW3, SW5, SW6, SW7, SW10 & W8)

Price	Name	Cuisine	Ratings
£150+	Gordon Ramsay	French	2 2 2
£140+	Vineet Bhatia London	Indian	3 3 2
£100+	Bibendum	French	2 2 3
£90+	Elystan Street	British, Modern	4 4 2
	Outlaw's at The Capital	Fish & seafood	4 4 2
£80+	The Five Fields	British, Modern	5 5 4
	Rivea, Bulgari Hotel	International	3 4 3
	Daphne's	Italian	2 2 2
	Min Jiang	Chinese	4 4 5
	Koji	Japanese	4 4 4
	Yashin	"	4 3 2
	Zuma	"	5 3 3
£70+	Babylon	British, Modern	2 2 4
	Bluebird	"	3 3 3
	Clarke's	"	5 5 4
	Kitchen W8	"	4 4 3
	Launceston Place	"	3 4 4
	Medlar	"	4 4 2
	Parabola, Design Museum	"	3 2 3
	Restaurant Ours	"	1 2 3
	Cheyne Walk Brasserie	French	2 2 3
	L'Etranger	"	3 3 2
	Lucio	Italian	3 4 3
	Scalini	"	3 3 3
	Cambio de Tercio	Spanish	3 3 2
	Hawksmoor Knightsbridge	Steaks & grills	3 3 3
£60+	The Abingdon	British, Modern	3 3 4
	Brinkley's	"	2 2 3
	Harwood Arms	"	4 3 3
	Kensington Place	"	3 2 2
	Tom's Kitchen	"	2 2 2
	Maggie Jones's	British, Traditional	2 2 5
	Wright Brothers	Fish & seafood	4 3 3
	Bandol	French	3 3 3
	Belvedere Restaurant	"	2 3 4
	Le Colombier	"	3 5 4
	Mazi	Greek	3 3 3
	No.11 Cadogan Gardens	International	– – –
	La Famiglia	Italian	2 2 3
	Frantoio	"	3 3 4
	Manicomio	"	2 3 3
	Il Portico	"	3 5 4
	Theo's Simple Italian	"	3 2 3

	Ziani's	"	2	3 2
	Locanda Ottomezzo	Mediterranean	3 3 3
	Sophie's Steakhouse	Steaks & grills	2 3 3
	Good Earth	Chinese	2 2 2
	Zheng	"	– – –
	Bombay Brasserie	Indian	3 4 3
	Zaika of Kensington	Indian, Southern	3 2 3
	Dinings	Japanese	5 4 2
	Kurobuta	"	3 2 2
	Patara	Thai	4 4 4
£50+	Big Easy	American	2 2 3
	Bodean's	"	2 2 2
	The Builders Arms	British, Modern	2 2 3
	Claude's Kitchen	"	4 4 4
	The Cross Keys	"	3 4 4
	The Enterprise	"	3 3 5
	The Hour Glass	"	3 4 2
	The Ivy Chelsea Garden	"	2 2 3
	Manuka Kitchen	"	3 4 3
	maze Grill	"	2 2 2
	The Sands End	"	3 3 3
	The Shed	"	4 4 4
	The Tommy Tucker	"	3 3 3
	Bumpkin	British, Traditional	2 2 2
	Bibendum Oyster Bar	Fish & seafood	3 2 3
	The Admiral Codrington	International	2 3 4
	Kensington Wine Rooms	"	2 3 3
	Obicà	Italian	3 2 2
	Pellicano Restaurant	"	3 4 3
	Polpo	"	2 2 2
	Sapori Sardi	"	3 3 3
	The Atlas	Mediterranean	4 4 4
	Ognisko Restaurant	Polish	3 3 5
	Capote Y Toros	Spanish	3 4 4
	Tendido Cero	"	3 3 3
	Tendido Cuatro	"	3 3 3
	Hanger	Steaks & grills	3 4 3
	Macellaio RC	"	3 2 3
	Geales Chelsea Green	Fish & chips	2 2 2
	Pizzicotto	Pizza	4 4 3
	Fernandez & Wells	Sandwiches, cakes, etc	3 3 3
	Chicama	Peruvian	2 2 3
	Maroush	Lebanese	3 2 2
	Royal China	Chinese	3 1 2
	Romulo Café	Filipino	3 3 3
	Chakra	Indian	3 3 3
	The Painted Heron	"	5 4 2
	Pure Indian Cooking	"	4 3 2
	Star of India	"	4 3 3
	Chisou	Japanese	4 3 2
	Kiru	"	4 4 3
	Eight Over Eight	Pan-Asian	3 3 4
	Sukho Fine Thai Cuisine	Thai	5 4 3
	Go-Viet	Vietnamese	4 3 3

£40+					
Megan's Delicatessen	British, Modern	2	3	3
Rabbit	"	3	3	2
VQ	"	2	4	3
Mona Lisa	International	3	4	2
Aglio e Olio	Italian	3	3	3
Buona Sera	"	3	3	3
Chelsea Cellar	"	4	4	3
Da Mario	"	3	3	4
Made in Italy	"	3	2	3
Nuovi Sapori	"	3	4	3
Riccardo's	"	2	2	3
Daquise	Polish	2	3	2
Casa Brindisa	Spanish	2	2	2
La Delizia Limbara	Pizza	3	3	3
Rossopomodoro	"	3	2	2
Lupita West	Mexican/TexMex	3	2	2
Best Mangal	Turkish	4	3	3
Dragon Palace	Chinese	4	2	2
Dishoom	Indian	4	4	5
Flora Indica	"	3	2	3
Malabar	"	5	4	3
Noor Jahan	"	3	3	3
Thali	"	4	4	3
Bone Daddies, Whole Foods	Japanese	4	3	3
Oka	"	4	2	2
Rosa's Fulham	Thai	2	2	2
Suksan	"	4	3	2

£35+					
Kensington Square Kitchen	British, Modern	3	4	3
Churchill Arms	British, Traditional	3	2	5
Pappa Ciccia	Italian	3	3	3
Ceru	Mediterranean	4	3	2
Haché	Steaks & grills	3	4	4
Rocca Di Papa	Pizza	3	3	4
Santa Maria	"	5	3	3
Taiwan Village	Taiwanese	4	5	3

£30+					
Tangerine Dream	British, Modern	3	1	3
Vagabond Wines	Mediterranean	3	3	4
Stagolee's	Chicken	–	–	–
Kulu Kulu	Japanese	3	2	1
Addie's Thai Café	Thai	3	2	2

£25+					
Tommi's Burger Joint	Burgers, etc	3	3	3
Eat Tokyo	Japanese	4	3	2

£20+					
Stick & Bowl	Chinese	5	3	1

£10+					
Orée	French	3	2	3
Orée	Sandwiches, cakes, etc	3	2	3
Over Under	"	4	4	2

Notting Hill, Holland Park, Bayswater, North Kensington & Maida Vale (W2, W9, W10, W11)

£140+	The Ledbury	British, Modern	5	5	4
£120+	Marianne	British, Modern	5	4	4
£90+	Bel Canto	French	2	3	3
£80+	Chucs	Italian	3	3	3
	Casa Cruz	South American	2	3	4
	Flat Three	Japanese	4	4	3
£70+	Angelus	French	3	5	3
	Assaggi	Italian	4	5	2
£60+	Pomona's	American	3	3	3
	The Dock Kitchen	British, Modern	2	2	3
	Julie's	"	–	–	–
	London Shell Co.	Fish & seafood	4	5	5
	The Summerhouse	"	2	2	5
	108 Garage	Fusion	5	4	5
	Edera	Italian	3	4	3
	Essenza	"	3	4	3
	Mediterraneo	"	3	2	3
	Osteria Basilico	"	3	3	4
	Stuzzico	"	3	3	3
	Kateh	Persian	3	2	3
	Kurobuta	Japanese	3	2	2
£50+	Granger & Co	Australian	3	3	3
	Daylesford Organic	British, Modern	3	2	3
	The Frontline Club	"	2	2	4
	The Ladbroke Arms	"	3	3	3
	The Magazine Restaurant	"	3	3	4
	Salt & Honey	"	3	3	2
	Six Portland Road	"	4	4	3
	The Waterway	"	2	2	2
	Snaps & Rye	Danish	3	4	3
	Cepages	French	3	3	3
	The Cow	Irish	3	3	4
	Assaggi Bar & Pizzeria	Italian	4	3	2
	The Oak	"	3	3	4
	Ottolenghi	"	4	3	2
	Polpo	"	2	2	2
	Portobello Ristorante	"	3	4	4
	Farmacy	Vegetarian	3	3	4
	Pizza East Portobello	Pizza	3	2	4
	The Red Pepper	"	3	2	2
	Peyotito	Mexican/TexMex	2	2	2
	Maroush Gardens	Lebanese	3	2	2
	Royal China	Chinese	3	1	2
	Maguro	Japanese	3	4	2
	E&O	Pan-Asian	3	3	3

£40+	Electric Diner	American	2	2	3
	Paradise	British, Modern	3	3	4
	VQ	"	2	4	3
	Hereford Road	British, Traditional	4	4	3
	The Chipping Forecast	Fish & seafood	3	3	3
	Raoul's Café & Deli	Mediterranean	3	2	3
	Pizza Metro	Pizza	3	3	3
	Cocotte	Chicken	4	3	4
	Taqueria	Mexican/TexMex	4	4	3
	The Cedar Restaurant	Lebanese	3	3	3
	The Four Seasons	Chinese	4	1	1
	Mandarin Kitchen	"	4	2	1
	Pearl Liang	"	3	2	2
	Bombay Palace	Indian	4	4	2
	Noor Jahan	"	3	3	3
	Tonkotsu	Japanese	3	2	3
	Gogi	Korean	3	3	3
	Uli	Pan-Asian	3	3	3
£35+	Lockhouse	Burgers, etc	3	2	3
	MEATliquor	"	3	2	4
	Gold Mine	Chinese	4	2	2
	Satay House	Malaysian	3	3	3
£30+	Flat Iron	Steaks & grills	4	4	3
	C&R Café	Malaysian	4	2	2
£25+	Patty and Bun	Burgers, etc	4	3	3
	Alounak	Persian	3	2	3
	Fez Mangal	Turkish	5	4	3
£20+	Khan's	Indian	3	2	2
£5+	Lisboa Pâtisserie	Sandwiches, cakes, etc	3	3	4
	Falafel King	Middle Eastern	3	3	2

Hammersmith, Shepherd's Bush, Olympia, Chiswick, Brentford & Ealing (W4, W5, W6, W12, W13, W14, TW8)

£110+	Hedone	British, Modern	3	3	2
£90+	The River Café	Italian	3	3	3
£80+	La Trompette	French	5	4	3
£60+	Michael Nadra	French	4	3	2
	Le Vacherin	"	3	3	2
	Villa Di Geggiano	Italian	3	3	4
£50+	Jackson & Rye Chiswick	American	1	2	2
	The Anglesea Arms	British, Modern	4	4	4
	Blue Boat	"	2	2	3
	The Brackenbury	"	4	4	3

	Brackenbury Wine Rooms	"	3 3 4
	Charlotte's Place	"	3 3 4
	Charlotte's W4	"	3 4 3
	City Barge	"	3 2 3
	The Dove	"	3 3 4
	Ealing Park Tavern	"	3 4 3
	The Havelock Tavern	"	3 2 3
	High Road Brasserie	"	2 2 2
	No 197 Chiswick Fire Stn	"	2 2 4
	Vinoteca	"	3 3 4
	The Hampshire Hog	British, Traditional	3 2 4
	Albertine	French	3 3 4
	The Andover Arms	International	3 5 4
	Melody at St Paul's	"	2 3 3
	Cibo	Italian	4 5 3
	The Oak W12	"	3 3 4
	Pentolina	"	4 5 4
	The Swan	Mediterranean	3 4 4
	Foxlow	Steaks & grills	2 2 2
	Popeseye	"	3 2 2
	Smokehouse Chiswick	"	3 2 3
	The Gate	Vegetarian	4 3 3
	Quantus	South American	4 5 3
	Shikumen, Dorsett Hotel	Chinese	4 3 2
	Indian Zing	Indian	4 4 2
	Little Bird Chiswick	Pan-Asian	2 2 4
£40+	The Colton Arms	British, Modern	2 3 4
	The Dartmouth Castle	"	3 4 4
	Duke of Sussex	"	2 3 4
	Mustard	"	3 3 3
	The Pear Tree	"	3 3 4
	Annie's	International	2 3 4
	L'Amorosa	Italian	4 4 3
	Cumberland Arms	Mediterranean	4 4 3
	The Bird in Hand	Pizza	3 3 4
	Tamp Coffee	Sandwiches, cakes, etc	3 3 4
	Best Mangal	Turkish	4 3 3
	North China	Chinese	3 4 2
	Brilliant	Indian	4 4 3
	Karma	"	4 3 1
	Madhu's	"	4 4 3
	Potli	"	4 4 3
	Sushi Bar Makoto	Japanese	4 3 2
	Hare & Tortoise	Pan-Asian	3 2 2
£35+	Santa Maria	Pizza	5 3 3
	Chez Abir	Lebanese	3 3 2
	Anarkali	Indian	– – –
	Sagar	"	3 2 1
	Kiraku	Japanese	4 4 2
	Tosa	"	3 3 2
	Yoshi Sushi	"	3 3 2
	Saigon Saigon	Vietnamese	2 3 3
£30+	Homeslice	Pizza	4 4 4

	Oro Di Napoli	"	4	3	2
	Angie's Little Food Shop	Sandwiches, cakes, etc	3	3	3
	Chicken Shop	Chicken	3	3	3
	Adams Café	Moroccan	3	5	3
	Faanoos	Persian	3	3	2
	Monkey Temple	Indian	3	4	3
	Shilpa	Indian, Southern	5	2	1
	Atari-Ya	Japanese	4	2	1
£25+	Alounak	Persian	3	2	3
	Gifto's Lahore Karahi	Indian	3	2	2
	Eat Tokyo	Japanese	4	3	2
	Nukis Kitchen	Thai	3	2	2
£20+	Kerbisher & Malt	Fish & chips	3	3	2
	Killer Tomato	Mexican/TexMex	4	3	2
	Abu Zaad	Syrian	3	3	2
£5+	Bears Ice Cream	Ice cream	3	3	3

Hampstead, West Hampstead, St John's Wood, Regent's Park, Kilburn & Camden Town (NW postcodes)

£70+				
	The Landmark	*British, Modern*		2 4 5
	The Gilbert Scott	*British, Traditional*		2 3 4

£60+				
	The Booking Office	*British, Modern*		2 2 4
	Bradley's	"		3 2 2
	Odette's	"		4 3 4
	L'Aventure	*French*		3 4 4
	Michael Nadra	"		4 3 2
	Oslo Court	"		4 5 5
	Bull & Last	*International*		3 3 3
	Villa Bianca	*Italian*		2 2 2
	Zest, JW3	*Kosher*		3 3 2
	Crocker's Folly	*Lebanese*		2 2 4
	Good Earth	*Chinese*		2 2 2
	Kaifeng	"		3 3 3
	Patara	*Thai*		4 4 4

£50+				
	The Horseshoe	*British, Modern*		3 3 4
	The Ivy Café	"		1 2 3
	Juniper Tree	"		3 2 2
	The Wells	"		2 2 3
	The Wet Fish Café	"		3 3 4
	York & Albany	*British, Traditional*		2 2 3
	Patron	*French*		2 3 3
	Summers	*Irish*		– – –
	Artigiano	*Italian*		3 2 2
	La Collina	"		3 4 3
	Ostuni	"		2 3 3
	The Rising Sun	"		3 2 3
	28 Church Row	*Spanish*		4 4 3
	Manna	*Vegetarian*		2 2 2
	Pizza East	*Pizza*		3 2 4
	Greenberry Café	*Sandwiches, cakes, etc*		3 3 3
	Phoenix Palace	*Chinese*		3 2 2

£40+				
	Delisserie	*American*		3 2 2
	Lantana Cafe	*Australian*		3 3 3
	The Junction Tavern	*British, Modern*		3 3 3
	Parlour Kensal	"		4 5 4
	L'Absinthe	*French*		2 4 3
	La Cage Imaginaire	"		2 2 3
	Lemonia	*Greek*		1 3 4
	Anima e Cuore	*Italian*		5 4 1
	L'Artista	"		3 4 4
	Giacomo's	"		3 3 2
	La Porchetta Pizzeria	"		2 3 2
	Sarracino	"		4 3 2
	El Parador	*Spanish*		3 2 3
	Mildreds	*Vegetarian*		3 3 3

	Harry Morgan's	Burgers, etc	2	2	2
	Poppies Camden	Fish & chips	3	2	3
	The Sea Shell	"	3	2	2
	L' Antica Pizzeria	Pizza	4	4	3
	Rossopomodoro	"	3	2	2
	The Cedar Restaurant	Lebanese	3	3	3
	Skewd Kitchen	Turkish	3	3	3
	Jun Ming Xuan	Chinese, Dim sum	2	3	2
	Bonoo	Indian	5	4	3
	Namaaste Kitchen	"	3	3	2
	Jin Kichi	Japanese	5	4	3
	Oka	"	4	2	2
	Sushi Masa	"	–	–	–
	The Petite Coree	Korean	4	4	2
	Singapore Garden	Malaysian	3	3	2
	Rosa's	Thai	2	2	2
£35+	Lure	Fish & seafood	3	5	3
	Carob Tree	Greek	3	4	3
	Quartieri	Italian	4	3	3
	Haché	Steaks & grills	3	4	4
	Nautilus	Fish & chips	4	3	1
	Sacro Cuore	Pizza	5	4	2
	Green Cottage	Chinese	3	2	2
	Great Nepalese	Indian	3	4	3
	Guglee	"	3	2	2
	Paradise Hampstead	"	4	5	4
	Vijay	"	3	3	1
	Asakusa	Japanese	5	2	2
	Bang Bang Oriental	Pan-Asian	–	–	–
£30+	The Little Bay	Mediterranean	2	3	4
	Dirty Burger	Burgers, etc	3	2	2
	Brew House Café	Sandwiches, cakes, etc	2	2	3
	Chicken Shop	Chicken	3	3	3
	Chai Thali	Indian	3	3	4
	Ravi Shankar	"	3	2	2
	Saravanaa Bhavan	"	5	2	1
	Atari-Ya	Japanese	4	2	1
£25+	Ali Baba	Egyptian	3	2	2
	Ariana II	Afghani	3	2	2
	Chutneys	Indian	3	2	2
	Diwana Bhel-Poori House	"	3	2	1
	Eat Tokyo	Japanese	4	3	2
£20+	Messapica	Italian	–	–	–
	Sakonis	Indian	5	2	1
	Roti King	Malaysian	5	2	1
£10+	Ginger & White	Sandwiches, cakes, etc	3	4	3
£5+	Doppio	Sandwiches, cakes, etc	3	3	3

Hoxton, Islington, Highgate, Crouch End, Stoke Newington, Finsbury Park, Muswell Hill & Finchley (N postcodes)

£70+	Plum + Spilt Milk	British, Modern	2 2 3
	German Gymnasium	Central European	2 2 3
£60+	Fifteen	British, Modern	2 2 2
	Frederick's	"	3 4 4
	Perilla	Central European	4 4 3
	Salut	International	4 4 4
	Radici	Italian	2 2 3
£50+	Granger & Co	Australian	3 3 3
	The Bull	British, Modern	3 4 4
	Caravan King's Cross	"	3 3 4
	Chriskitch	"	4 3 3
	Dandy	"	4 4 3
	The Drapers Arms	"	3 2 3
	Heirloom	"	3 3 3
	James Cochran N1	"	5 1 2
	The Lighterman	"	3 4 4
	Oldroyd	"	4 3 2
	Pig & Butcher	"	4 5 4
	The Red Lion & Sun	"	3 2 3
	Rotunda	"	3 4 4
	Westerns Laundry	"	– – –
	St Johns	British, Traditional	3 4 5
	Bellanger	Central European	2 3 3
	Galley	Fish & seafood	3 2 3
	Prawn on the Lawn	"	4 4 3
	Bistro Aix	French	4 3 4
	Petit Pois Bistro	"	3 3 2
	Table Du Marche	"	3 3 3
	The Good Egg	Fusion	4 4 3
	The Greek Larder, Arthouse	Greek	3 2 2
	8 Hoxton Square	International	3 3 3
	Primeur	"	4 4 4
	500	Italian	3 3 2
	Il Guscio	"	3 4 3
	Melange	"	3 2 2
	Ostuni	"	2 3 3
	Ottolenghi	"	4 3 2
	Trullo	"	4 4 3
	Sardine	Mediterranean	3 2 2
	Vinoteca	"	3 3 4
	Rök	Scandinavian	4 2 2
	Camino King's Cross	Spanish	3 3 2
	Popeseye	Steaks & grills	3 2 2
	Smokehouse Islington	"	3 3 2
	Duke's Brew & Que	Burgers, etc	4 3 4
	Bodean's	BBQ	2 2 2
£40+	Breakfast Club Hoxton	American	3 3 3
	Sunday	Australian	4 2 3
	Haven Bistro	British, Modern	2 3 2

Humble Grape	"	3	4	4
Season Kitchen	"	3	3	2
Kipferl	Central European	3	2	3
Andi's	International	3	4	4
Banners	"	3	4	5
La Fromagerie	"	3	2	2
Osteria Tufo	Italian	3	3	2
La Porchetta Pizzeria	"	2	3	2
Rugoletta	"	3	3	2
Alcedo	Mediterranean	3	4	3
Lady Mildmay	"	3	4	3
Bar Esteban	Spanish	4	4	4
Café del Parc	"	4	5	3
Lluna	"	3	3	3
Thyme and Lemon	"	3	3	4
Trangallan	"	4	4	3
Mildreds	Vegetarian	3	3	3
Toff's	Fish & chips	3	3	2
Trawler Trash	"	–	–	–
Rossopomodoro	Pizza	3	2	2
Sweet Thursday	"	3	2	2
Black Axe Mangal	Turkish	5	4	2
Yipin China	Chinese	4	3	2
Little Georgia Café	Georgian	3	2	3
Dishoom	Indian	4	4	5
Zaffrani	"	3	2	2
Isarn	Thai	4	4	2
Rosa's	"	2	2	2
CôBa	Vietnamese	4	4	3
£35+ Le Sacré-Coeur	French	2	2	2
Vrisaki	Greek	3	3	3
Passione e Tradizione	Italian	4	3	2
Pasta Remoli	"	3	2	2
Pizzeria Pappagone	"	3	4	4
MEATLiquor Islington	Burgers, etc	3	2	4
Cannons	Fish & chips	4	4	2
Olympus Fish	"	4	5	2
Sutton and Sons	"	4	4	2
Sacro Cuore	Pizza	5	4	2
Yard Sale Pizza	"	4	3	2
Zia Lucia	"	4	3	3
Monty's Deli	Sandwiches, cakes, etc	3	4	4
Diyarbakir Kitchen	Turkish	3	3	3
Iberia	Georgian	3	3	2
Indian Rasoi	Indian	3	3	2
Rasa	Indian, Southern	3	3	3
Farang	Thai	4	4	3
Salvation In Noodles	Vietnamese	3	2	2
£30+ Oak N4	British, Modern	–	–	–
Two Brothers	Fish & seafood	3	2	2
Le Mercury	French	2	2	4
MEATmission	Burgers, etc	3	3	4
Max's Sandwich Shop	Sandwiches, cakes, etc	4	4	3
Chicken Shop	Chicken	3	3	3

	Gallipoli	*Turkish*	2	3	4
	Gem	*"*	3	4	2
	Gökyüzü	*"*	3	3	3
	Xi'an Impression	*Chinese*	4	2	2
	Jashan	*Indian*	4	4	2
	Rani	*"*	4	2	2
	Atari-Ya	*Japanese*	4	2	1
	Dotori	*Korean*	4	3	2
£25+	Afghan Kitchen	*Afghani*	4	3	2
	Delhi Grill	*Indian*	3	2	2
£20+	Piebury Corner	*British, Traditional*	3	4	3
	L'Antica Pizzeria da Michele	*Pizza*	3	4	3
£15+	Five Guys Islington	*Burgers, etc*	3	2	2

SOUTH

South Bank (SE1)

£150+	Story	*British, Modern*	4 3 3
£100+	Aqua Shard	*British, Modern*	1 1 2
£90+	TING	*International*	3 3 4
£80+	Oblix	*British, Modern*	2 2 3
	Oxo Tower, Restaurant	"	1 1 2
	Hutong, The Shard	*Chinese*	1 2 5
£70+	Oxo Tower, Brasserie	*British, Modern*	1 1 2
	Le Pont de la Tour	"	2 2 3
	Skylon, South Bank Centre	"	2 2 2
	Hawksmoor	*Steaks & grills*	3 3 3
	Baluchi, Lalit Hotel London	*Indian*	– – –
£60+	Sea Containers	*British, Modern*	2 2 2
	Skylon Grill	"	2 2 3
	The Swan at the Globe	"	3 2 3
	Tate Modern Restaurant	"	2 3 4
	Tom Simmons	"	– – –
	Union Street Café	"	2 2 3
	Butlers Wharf Chop House	*British, Traditional*	2 2 3
	Roast	"	2 2 3
	Applebee's Fish	*Fish & seafood*	4 3 2
	Wright Brothers	"	4 3 3
	Arthur Hooper's	*International*	– – –
	Rabot 1745	"	2 2 2
	Vivat Bacchus	"	3 4 2
	Pizarro	*Spanish*	3 3 3
	Bala Baya	*Middle Eastern*	3 2 3
£50+	Albion	*British, Modern*	2 2 2
	Caravan Bankside	"	3 3 4
	Edwins	"	3 4 4
	Elliot's Café	"	3 3 3
	40 Maltby Street	"	4 4 3
	The Garrison	"	3 3 3
	Globe Tavern	"	3 3 3
	House Restaurant	"	2 3 2
	The Ivy Tower Bridge	"	2 2 3
	LASSCO Bar & DIning	"	– – –
	Laughing Gravy	"	3 4 3
	Menier Chocolate Factory	"	2 2 3
	Tate Modern, Restaurant	"	3 2 4
	Waterloo Bar & Kitchen	"	2 2 2
	The Anchor & Hope	*British, Traditional*	4 2 2
	fish!	*Fish & seafood*	3 2 2
	Casse-Croute	*French*	4 3 4
	Capricci	*Italian*	4 4 3
	Macellaio RC	"	3 2 3

	O'ver	"	4 3 3
	Baltic	Polish	4 4 4
	Bar Douro	Portuguese	4 3 3
	Camino Bankside	Spanish	3 3 2
	LOBOS Meat & Tapas	"	4 4 2
	Tapas Brindisa	"	2 2 2
	Pique Nique	Chicken	– – –
	Arabica Bar and Kitchen	Lebanese	3 2 3
	Champor-Champor	Thai	4 4 4
£40+	Lantana London Bridge	Australian	3 3 3
	Blueprint Café	British, Modern	2 2 4
	The Green Room	"	2 2 2
	Lupins	"	– – –
	Boro Bistro	French	3 4 3
	José	Spanish	5 4 5
	Mar I Terra	"	3 4 3
	Meson don Felipe	"	2 2 3
	El Pastór	Mexican/TexMex	4 3 4
	Tonkotsu Bankside	Japanese	3 2 3
	Sticky Mango at RSJ	Pan-Asian	– – –
£35+	The Table	British, Modern	3 2 2
	tibits	Vegetarian	3 2 3
	Tas Pide	Turkish	2 3 3
	Est India	Indian	3 3 3
£30+	Pulia	Italian	3 4 3
£25+	Mercato Metropolitano	Italian	3 2 5
	Padella	"	5 4 4
£20+	Masters Super Fish	Fish & chips	3 2 2
£10+	Gourmet Goat	Middle Eastern	4 4 2
£5+	Monmouth Coffee Company	Sandwiches, cakes, etc	4 5 4

Greenwich, Lewisham, Dulwich & Blackheath
(All SE postcodes, except SE1)

£60+	Craft London	British, Modern	4 4 2
	Pharmacy 2	"	2 3 3
£50+	La Bonne Bouffe	British, Modern	3 2 3
	The Camberwell Arms	"	4 3 3
	Franklins	"	3 3 2
	The Guildford Arms	"	3 4 3
	Orchard	"	2 2 2
	The Palmerston	"	4 3 3
	Peckham Refresh' Rooms	"	3 3 3
	The Perry Vale	"	3 4 3
	Rivington Grill	"	2 2 2
	The Rosendale	"	3 4 3

	Sparrow	"	–	–	–
	Brasserie Toulouse-Lautrec	French	3	3	3
	Peckham Bazaar	Greek	5	3	4
	Brookmill	International	3	3	3
	Tulse Hill Hotel	"	3	3	3
	Luciano's	Italian	3	3	3
	Sail Loft	Mediterranean	2	3	4
	Cau	Steaks & grills	2	2	2
	Spinach	Vegetarian	3	3	3
	Babur	Indian	5	5	4
	Kennington Tandoori	"	4	4	4
	Sticks'n'Sushi	Japanese	4	2	2
	Yama Momo	"	4	2	3
£40+	The Crooked Well	British, Modern	3	2	3
	Brockwell Lido Café	"	2	2	4
	Louie Louie	"	3	3	3
	Joanna's	International	3	5	4
	Platform I	"	3	3	3
	The Yellow House	"	3	3	3
	Artusi	Italian	4	4	3
	Le Querce	"	4	4	3
	Pedler	Pizza	3	3	4
	Zero Degrees	"	3	3	4
	Dragon Castle	Chinese	4	3	3
	Everest Inn	Indian	3	2	3
	Ganapati	"	5	4	3
	The Begging Bowl	Thai	4	3	2
£35+	Babette	British, Modern	3	3	4
	Black Prince	"	3	3	3
	Catford Constitutional Club	"	3	4	4
	MEATliquor ED	Burgers, etc	3	2	4
	The Gowlett Arms	Pizza	4	3	4
	Mamma Dough	"	3	3	4
	Rocca Di Papa	"	3	3	4
	Theo's	"	3	4	3
	Yalla Yalla	Lebanese	3	2	2
	Zaibatsu	Japanese	4	3	2
	Bánh Bánh	Vietnamese	3	4	3
	Mr Bao	Taiwanese	4	3	3
£30+	Rox Burger	Burgers, etc	4	3	3
	Made of Dough	Pizza	–	–	–
	FM Mangal	Turkish	3	3	2
£25+	Zeret	Ethiopian	4	5	3
£20+	500 Degrees	Pizza	3	3	2
	Persepolis	Persian	4	3	2
	Silk Road	Chinese	5	2	2
	Café East	Vietnamese	5	2	2
£15+	Goddards At Greenwich	British, Traditional	3	4	4
£10+	Golden Chippy	Fish & chips	3	4	2

FSA Ratings: from **1** (Poor) to **5** (Exceptional)

| £5+ | Kappacasein | *Sandwiches, cakes, etc* | 5 3 2 |
| | Monmouth Coffee Company | " | 4 5 4 |

Battersea, Brixton, Clapham, Wandsworth
Barnes, Putney & Wimbledon
(All SW postcodes south of the river)

| £80+ | Chez Bruce | *British, Modern* | 5 5 4 |

| £70+ | Trinity | *British, Modern* | 5 5 3 |
| | Gastronhome | *French* | 4 4 2 |

£60+	Rick Stein	*Fish & seafood*	3 2 5
	Wright Brothers	"	4 3 3
	The White Onion	*French*	3 3 2
	London House	*International*	2 2 2
	Riva	*Italian*	3 3 2
	Good Earth	*Chinese*	2 2 2
	Patara	*Thai*	4 4 4

£50+	Bodean's	*American*	2 2 2
	Counter Vauxhall Arches	"	4 3 4
	Bistro Union	*British, Modern*	3 3 3
	Brunswick House Café	"	3 3 5
	Cannizaro House	"	1 2 3
	Counter Culture	"	4 3 3
	Hood	"	4 3 2
	The Ivy Café	"	1 2 3
	Lamberts	"	4 5 3
	The Manor	"	3 3 3
	May The Fifteenth	"	3 4 2
	Minnow	"	– – –
	Nutbourne	"	3 3 4
	Olympic, Olympic Studios	"	2 2 3
	Salon Brixton	"	3 3 3
	Sonny's Kitchen	"	2 2 2
	The Spencer	"	3 4 3
	The Victoria	"	– – –
	Canton Arms	*British, Traditional*	4 2 4
	Jolly Gardeners	"	3 3 3
	Augustine Kitchen	*French*	3 4 2
	Sinabro	"	3 4 3
	Soif	"	3 4 3
	The Light House	*International*	3 3 2
	Numero Uno	*Italian*	3 4 3
	The Bobbin	*Mediterranean*	4 4 4
	Brindisa Food Rooms	*Spanish*	2 2 2
	Cau	*Steaks & grills*	2 2 2
	Foxlow	"	2 2 2
	Knife	"	5 4 4
	Macellaio RC	"	3 2 3
	Naughty Piglets	"	5 5 3
	Popeseye	"	3 2 2
	MeatUp	*BBQ*	3 2 2

	Bistro Vadouvan	*Indian*	–	–	–
	Sticks'n'Sushi	*Japanese*	4	2	2
	Little Bird Battersea	*Pan-Asian*	2	2	4
£40+	The Avalon	*British, Modern*	2	2	3
	The Brown Dog	"	3	3	3
	The Dairy	"	4	4	4
	Earl Spencer	"	3	2	4
	Humble Grape	"	3	4	4
	Jules	"	–	–	–
	The Plough	"	3	3	5
	Trinity Upstairs	"	5	4	4
	Gazette	*French*	2	2	3
	Annie's	*International*	2	3	4
	Belpassi Bros	*Italian*	3	3	3
	Buona Sera	"	3	3	3
	Made in Italy	"	3	2	3
	Osteria Antica Bologna	"	3	2	2
	Pizza Metro	"	3	3	3
	The Fox & Hounds	*Mediterranean*	4	3	4
	Boqueria	*Spanish*	4	4	4
	Gremio de Brixton	"	3	3	3
	Little Taperia	"	3	3	3
	Arlo's	*Steaks & grills*	2	3	2
	Addomme	*Pizza*	4	3	2
	Al Forno	"	2	4	4
	Dynamo	"	3	3	3
	Rossopomodoro	"	3	2	2
	MOMMI	*Peruvian*	3	4	3
	Chit Chaat Chai	*Indian*	4	3	2
	Indian Moment	"	3	3	2
	Kashmir	"	4	3	3
	Ma Goa	"	4	4	3
	Nanban	*Japanese*	4	3	3
	Takahashi	"	5	4	3
	Tomoe	"	4	2	2
	Tsunami	"	4	2	3
	Hare & Tortoise	*Pan-Asian*	3	2	2
	Rosa's	*Thai*	2	2	2
£35+	Plot	*British, Modern*	3	3	3
	Fish in a Tie	*Mediterranean*	3	3	3
	Bukowski Grill	*Steaks & grills*	3	3	2
	Haché	*Burgers, etc*	3	4	4
	Brady's	*Fish & chips*	3	3	3
	Eco	*Pizza*	3	3	3
	Mamma Dough	"	3	3	4
	Orange Pekoe	*Sandwiches, cakes, etc*	3	4	4
	Cartel	*Mexican/TexMex*	–	–	–
	Meza Trinity Road	*Lebanese*	3	3	2
	JAN	*Middle Eastern*	–	–	–
	Indian Ocean	*Indian*	3	3	2
	Hashi	*Japanese*	3	4	2
	Taro	"	3	2	2
	Cah-Chi	*Korean*	3	4	3
	Mien Tay	*Vietnamese*	4	3	2

£30+	Vagabond Wines	*Mediterranean*	3 3 4
	Dip & Flip	*Burgers, etc*	3 3 3
	Dirty Burger	"	3 2 2
	Ground Coffee Society	*Sandwiches, cakes, etc*	3 4 3
	Faanoos	*Persian*	3 3 2
	Sree Krishna	*Indian*	4 3 2
	The Pepper Tree	*Thai*	2 3 3
£25+	The Joint	*American*	3 3 3
	Flotsam and Jetsam	*Australian*	3 4 4
	Tried & True	*British, Modern*	3 3 3
	Pizzastorm	*Pizza*	3 3 1
	Lahore Karahi	*Pakistani*	4 2 2
	Lahore Kebab House	"	4 3 2
	Mirch Masala	"	4 2 1
	Awesome Thai	*Thai*	3 4 3
	Kaosarn	"	4 3 3
£20+	Kerbisher & Malt	*Fish & chips*	3 3 2
	Cut The Mustard	*Sandwiches, cakes, etc*	3 2 3
	Milk	"	4 3 3
	Hot Stuff	*Indian*	3 5 3
	Jaffna House	*Indian, Southern*	5 2 2
£15+	Joe Public	*Pizza*	4 3 3
£10+	Bean & Hop	*Mediterranean*	3 3 2
	Pop Brixton	*Burgers, etc*	5 4 3

Outer west: Kew, Richmond, Twickenham, Teddington

£80+	The Glasshouse	*British, Modern*	5 4 3
	M Bar & Grill Twickenham	*Steaks & grills*	2 2 2
£70+	The Dysart Petersham	*British, Modern*	3 4 4
	Petersham Nurseries Cafe	"	2 1 5
£60+	The Bingham	*British, Modern*	4 5 4
	Petersham Hotel	"	3 3 4
	Al Boccon di'vino	*Italian*	3 4 5
£50+	Jackson & Rye	*American*	1 2 2
	The Ivy Café	*British, Modern*	1 2 3
	Petit Ma Cuisine	*French*	2 2 3
	Le Salon Privé	"	4 3 4
	A Cena	*Italian*	3 4 4
	Bacco	"	3 2 2
£40+	La Buvette	*French*	3 3 3
	Pizzeria Rustica	*Pizza*	3 2 2
	Matsuba	*Japanese*	3 4 2
£35+	The Stable	*Pizza*	2 2 3
	Dastaan	*Indian*	5 4 3

EAST

Smithfield & Farringdon (EC1)

£100+	The Clove Club	British, Modern	5	4	4
£90+	Club Gascon	French	–	–	–
£80+	Sushi Tetsu	Japanese	5	5	4
£70+	Luca	Italian	3	4	4
	Smiths, Top Floor	Steaks & grills	3	3	4
	Sosharu, Turnmill Building	Japanese	3	3	3
£60+	Anglo	British, Modern	5	4	2
	Chiswell St Dining Rooms	"	2	2	2
	The Jugged Hare	"	3	2	3
	The Modern Pantry	"	2	2	2
	The Quality Chop House	British, Traditional	3	3	3
	St John Smithfield	"	5	4	3
	Bleeding Heart Restaurant	French	3	3	5
	Moro	Spanish	4	3	3
	Hix Oyster & Chop House	Steaks & grills	2	2	2
	Smiths, Dining Room	"	2	2	2
£50+	Bodean's	American	2	2	2
	Granger & Co,	Australian	3	3	3
	Bird of Smithfield	British, Modern	2	2	2
	Caravan	"	3	3	4
	Vinoteca	"	3	3	4
	Wilmington	"	3	4	3
	Albion Clerkenwell	British, Traditional	2	2	2
	The Fox and Anchor	"	3	3	4
	Café du Marché	French	3	3	5
	Comptoir Gascon	"	3	3	2
	Niche	International	2	3	2
	Apulia	Italian	3	3	3
	Macellaio RC	"	3	2	3
	Palatino	"	4	5	3
	Polpo	"	2	2	2
	Santore	"	4	3	3
	Ibérica	Spanish	2	2	3
	Foxlow	Steaks & grills	2	2	2
	The Gate	Vegetarian	4	3	3
	Burger & Lobster	Burgers, etc	3	2	3
	Ceviche Old St	Peruvian	4	3	3
	The Sichuan	Chinese	4	3	3
£40+	Lantana Café	Australian	3	3	3
	The Green	British, Modern	–	–	–
	La Ferme London	French	3	3	3
	La Porchetta Pizzeria	Italian	2	3	2
	Morito	Spanish	4	4	4
	Breddos Tacos	Mexican/TexMex	4	4	4
	Berber & Q Shawarma Bar	Middle Eastern	4	3	3

	Bone Daddies, The Bower	*Japanese*	4 3 3
	Cây Tre	*Vietnamese*	3 3 2
£35+	The Eagle	*Mediterranean*	4 2 5
	Pizza Pilgrims	*Pizza*	4 3 3
	Workshop Coffee Holborn	*Sandwiches, cakes, etc*	3 4 4
	Pham Sushi	*Japanese*	4 3 2
	On The Bab	*Korean*	3 2 2
£30+	Smiths, Ground Floor	*British, Modern*	2 2 3
	White Bear	*British, Traditional*	3 3 3
	Fish Central	*Fish & seafood*	3 2 2
	Kolossi Grill	*Greek*	3 3 3
	Ninth Ward	*Burgers, etc*	2 3 4
	Homeslice	*Pizza*	4 4 4
£10+	Department of Coffee	*Sandwiches, cakes, etc*	3 4 4
	Prufrock Coffee	"	3 2 4
£5+	Luardos	*Mexican/TexMex*	5 4 –

The City (EC2, EC3, EC4)

£100+	La Dame de Pic London	*French*	3 3 2
£90+	Fenchurch Restaurant	*British, Modern*	3 2 3
	Angler, South Place Hotel	*Fish & seafood*	3 2 2
	Goodman City	*Steaks & grills*	4 4 2
	Sushisamba	*Japanese*	3 2 5
£80+	City Social	*British, Modern*	2 3 5
	Coq d'Argent	*French*	2 2 3
	M Restaurant	*Steaks & grills*	2 2 2
	Yauatcha City	*Chinese*	4 3 3
	Mei Ume	*Japanese*	– – –
£70+	Duck & Waffle	*British, Modern*	2 2 5
	1 Lombard Street	"	2 2 3
	Sweetings	*Fish & seafood*	3 2 4
	Lutyens	*French*	2 2 2
	L'Anima	*Italian*	4 4 3
	Boisdale of Bishopsgate	*Scottish*	3 2 3
	Barbecoa	*Steaks & grills*	2 2 2
	The Grill at McQueen	"	3 4 3
	Hawksmoor	"	3 3 3
	HKK	*Chinese*	5 5 3
£60+	The Botanist	*British, Modern*	2 2 2
	Bread Street Kitchen	"	2 2 2
	Darwin Brasserie	"	2 3 4
	The Don	"	3 3 2
	High Timber	"	3 5 3
	The Mercer	"	2 2 2
	Merchants Tavern	"	3 2 4

The Modern Pantry	"	2 2 2
The White Swan	"	3 3 2
Cabotte	French	4 5 4
Sauterelle, Royal Exchange	"	3 3 4
Vivat Bacchus	International	3 4 2
Caravaggio	Italian	3 2 2
Manicomio	"	2 3 3
Eyre Brothers	Spanish	4 3 3
Hispania	"	3 2 2
Sagardi	"	2 2 2
Temple & Sons	Steaks & grills	3 3 2
Vanilla Black	Vegetarian	2 2 2
Red Rooster	Chicken	– – –
Darbaar	Indian	4 3 2
Mint Leaf Lounge	"	4 4 4
Nanashi	Japanese	– – –

£50+ Bodean's	American	2 2 2
Pitt Cue Co	"	4 3 3
The Anthologist	British, Modern	2 2 3
Caravan	"	3 3 4
The Don Bistro and Bar	"	3 3 4
James Cochran EC3	"	5 1 2
Northbank	"	3 2 3
Princess of Shoreditch	"	3 2 2
Rök	"	4 2 2
Paternoster Chop House	British, Traditional	2 1 2
Fish Market	Fish & seafood	3 3 2
Royal Exchange Grand Café,	French	2 3 4
28-50	"	2 4 3
L'Anima Café	Italian	3 3 2
Obicà	"	3 2 2
Osteria, Barbican Centre	"	2 2 3
Popolo	"	5 4 3
Taberna Etrusca	"	2 3 3
Mac & Wild	Scottish	4 3 4
Camino Monument	Spanish	3 3 2
José Pizarro	"	3 3 2
Aviary	Steaks & grills	– – –
The Jones Family Project	"	4 4 4
The Tramshed	"	3 3 4
Burger & Lobster	Burgers, etc	3 2 3
Oklava	Turkish	4 2 3
Cinnamon Kitchen	Indian	4 3 3

£40+ Café Below	British, Modern	3 2 3
Humble Grape	"	3 4 4
VQ	"	2 4 3
The Wine Library	International	1 3 5
Rucoletta	Italian	2 2 2
Relais de Venise L'Entrecôte	Steaks & grills	3 2 2
Ozone Coffee Roasters	Sandwiches, cakes, etc	4 4 4
Haz	Turkish	2 2 2
Shoryu Ramen	Japanese	3 2 2
Hare & Tortoise	Pan-Asian	3 2 2

£35+	Simpson's Tavern	British, Traditional	2 3 4
	Haché	Burgers, etc	3 4 4
	Pizza Pilgrims	Pizza	4 3 3
	Blacklock	BBQ	4 4 4
	temper City	"	3 4 5
	Bangalore Express	Indian	3 3 3
	K10, Appold Street	Japanese	3 4 2
	Taro	"	3 2 2
	On The Bab	Korean	3 2 2
£30+	Flat Iron	Steaks & grills	4 4 3
	Homeslice	Pizza	4 4 4
	Koya	Japanese	3 3 3
£25+	Hilliard	British, Modern	4 4 4
	Patty and Bun	Burgers, etc	4 3 3
	Bibimbap	Korean	3 2 2
£20+	Bleecker Burger	Burgers, etc	5 2 2
£15+	City Càphê	Vietnamese	3 3 2
£10+	Yolk	British, Modern	– – –
	Pilpel	Middle Eastern	4 3 2

East End & Docklands (All E postcodes)

£90+	Typing Room	International	5 5 3
	Goodman	Steaks & grills	4 4 2
£80+	Galvin La Chapelle	French	3 2 4
	Roka	Japanese	4 3 3
£70+	Lyle's	British, Modern	4 2 2
	Smith's Wapping	"	4 4 4
	Plateau	French	2 3 3
	Bokan	International	– – –
	Hawksmoor	Steaks & grills	3 3 3
£60+	The Gun	British, Modern	3 3 4
	Hoi Polloi, Ace Hotel	"	3 2 3
	One Canada Square	"	2 4 3
	Pidgin	"	5 4 3
	Sager + Wilde	"	2 4 4
	Tom's Kitchen	"	2 2 2
	The Marksman	British, Traditional	4 3 4
	St John Bread & Wine	"	3 3 2
	Wright Brothers	Fish & seafood	4 3 3
	Tratra	French	– – –
	The Laughing Heart	International	3 2 3
	Sager + Wilde Restaurant	"	2 4 4
	Canto Corvino	Italian	4 3 3
	Brawn	Mediterranean	4 3 3
	Boisdale of Canary Wharf	Scottish	3 3 4

	Buen Ayre	*Argentinian*	4 4 2
£50+	Big Easy	*American*	2 2 3
	Bistrotheque	*British, Modern*	3 2 4
	The Bothy	"	– – –
	The Culpeper	"	2 2 3
	Ellory, Netil House	"	3 5 3
	Galvin HOP	"	2 3 3
	Jones & Sons	"	4 4 4
	Legs	"	3 4 4
	The Narrow	"	3 3 4
	Paradise Garage	"	4 4 3
	Rochelle Canteen	"	3 3 4
	Treves & Hyde	"	– – –
	Albion	*British, Traditional*	2 2 2
	Bumpkin	"	2 2 2
	Blanchette East	*French*	4 3 4
	Bombetta	*Italian*	3 4 2
	Il Bordello	"	3 3 4
	Lardo Bebè	"	3 3 2
	Obicà	"	3 2 2
	Super Tuscan	"	4 4 3
	Corner Room	*Portuguese*	3 4 4
	Ibérica	*Spanish*	2 2 3
	Cau	*Steaks & grills*	2 2 2
	Hill & Szrok	"	4 4 4
	Burger & Lobster	*Burgers, etc*	3 2 3
	Pizza East	*Pizza*	3 2 4
	Andina	*Peruvian*	4 3 3
	Ottolenghi	*Israeli*	4 3 2
	Royal China	*Chinese*	3 1 2
	Café Spice Namaste	*Indian*	5 5 3
	Grand Trunk Road	"	4 4 3
	Sticks'n'Sushi	*Japanese*	4 2 2
	Som Saa	*Thai*	5 4 4
£40+	Breakfast Club	*American*	3 3 3
	Cafe Football	*British, Modern*	2 2 2
	Eat 17	"	3 4 3
	The Empress	"	4 3 4
	The Frog	"	5 3 2
	The Morgan Arms	"	3 2 3
	P Franco	"	4 3 3
	Provender	*French*	3 4 4
	Blixen	*International*	3 3 3
	Dokke	"	– – –
	Eat 17	"	3 4 3
	Emilia's Crafted Pasta	*Italian*	4 3 3
	Pomaio	"	3 4 3
	Rotorino	"	2 4 2
	Verdi's	"	3 4 3
	Taberna do Mercado	*Portuguese*	3 3 2
	Bravas	*Spanish*	3 4 3
	Morito	"	4 4 4
	Relais de Venise L'Entrecôte	*Steaks & grills*	3 2 2
	Mildreds	*Vegetarian*	3 3 3

	Name	Cuisine	Ratings
	Poppies	Fish & chips	3 2 3
	Corner Kitchen	Pizza	3 3 3
	Chick 'n' Sours	Chicken	3 3 3
	Smokestak	BBQ	5 3 3
	Lupita	Mexican/TexMex	3 2 2
	Berber & Q	Middle Eastern	5 2 5
	Haz	Turkish	2 2 2
	Laphet	Burmese	3 3 3
	Sichuan Folk	Chinese	3 3 2
	My Neighbours The Dumplings	Chinese, Dim sum	4 2 2
	Little Georgia Café	Georgian	3 2 3
	Dishoom	Indian	4 4 5
	Gunpowder	"	4 3 3
	Ippudo London	Japanese	3 2 2
	Tonkotsu	"	3 2 3
	Uchi	"	4 2 2
	Rosa's	Thai	2 2 2
	Smoking Goat	"	4 3 2
	Viet Grill	Vietnamese	3 2 2
£35+	Bukowski Grill, Boxpark	Steaks & grills	3 3 2
	Ark Fish	Fish & chips	3 3 2
	Sutton and Sons	"	4 4 2
	Pizza Pilgrims	Pizza	4 3 3
	The Stable	"	2 2 3
	Yard Sale Pizza	"	4 3 2
	Saiphin's Thai Kitchen	Thai	– – –
	Mien Tay	Vietnamese	4 3 2
£30+	The Vincent	British, Modern	– – –
	Vagabond Wines	Mediterranean	3 3 4
	Dirty Burger	Burgers, etc	3 2 2
	Chicken Shop	Chicken	3 3 3
	Randy's Wing Bar	"	4 3 3
	Madame D's	Indian	– – –
	Sông Quê	Vietnamese	3 3 2
£25+	Patty and Bun	Burgers, etc	4 3 3
	Shake Shack	"	2 2 2
	Crate Brewery and Pizzeria	Pizza	3 2 4
	Mangal 1	Turkish	5 4 2
	Lahore Kebab House	Pakistani	4 3 2
	Needoo	"	4 3 2
	Tayyabs	"	4 1 2
	Bao Bar	Taiwanese	4 3 2
£20+	Bleecker Burger	Burgers, etc	5 2 2
£15+	E Pellicci	Italian	3 4 5
£10+	The Rib Man	Burgers, etc	5 4 –
	Pavilion Cafe & Bakery	Sandwiches, cakes, etc	3 2 4
	Pilpel	Middle Eastern	4 3 2
£5+	Brick Lane Beigel Bake	Sandwiches, cakes, etc	4 1 1

MAPS

MAP 1 – LONDON OVERVIEW

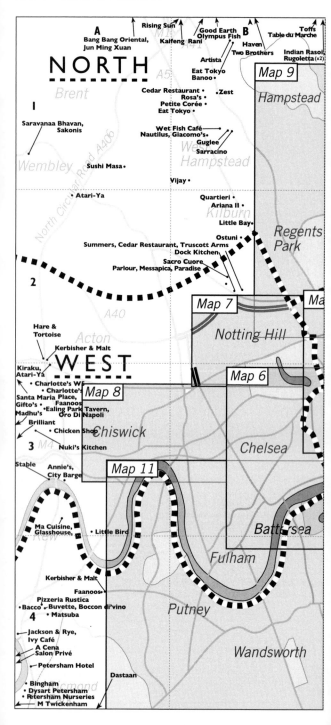

A   **B**

Bang Bang Oriental, Jun Ming Xuan

Rising Sun

Kaifeng Rani

Good Earth
Olympus Fish

Haven
Two Brothers

Toffs
Table du Marche

Indian Rasoi,
Rugoletta (x2)

NORTH

Brent

Artista

Eat Tokyo
Banoo

Map 9

Hampstead

1

Cedar Restaurant •
Rosa's •
Petite Corée •
Eat Tokyo •

• Zest

Saravanaa Bhavan,
Sakonis

Wembley

Sushi Masa •

Wet Fish Café •
Nautilus, Giacomo's •

*West
Hampstead*

Guglee
Sarracino

Vijay •

Kilburn

• Atari-Ya

Quartieri •
Ariana II •
Little Bay •

*Regents
Park*

Ostuni •

2

Summers, Cedar Restaurant, Truscott Arms
Dock Kitchen

A40

Sacro Cuore
Parlour, Messapica, Paradise

Map 7

Ma

Map 7

Notting Hill

Hare &
Tortoise

Acton

Kerbisher & Malt

WEST

Kiraku,
Atari-Ya

• Charlotte's W5
• Charlotte's
Santa Maria Place,
Gifto's •
Madhu's

Map 8

• Faanoos
•Ealing Park Tavern,
Oro Di Napoli

Map 6

Chelsea

Brilliant

• Chicken Shop

Chiswick

3 *M4*

Nuki's Kitchen

Stable

Annie's,
City Barge

Map 11

Ma Cuisine,
Glasshouse,

Kew

• Little Bird

Battersea

Fulham

Kerbisher & Malt

Faanoos•

Pizzeria Rustica
•Bacco •Buvette, Boccon di'vino

4 • Matsuba

Putney

Wandsworth

Jackson & Rye,
Ivy Café
A Cena
Salon Privé

Petersham Hotel

• Bingham
• Dysart Petersham
• Petersham Nurseries
M Twickenham

Dastaan

Richmond

MAP 1 – LONDON OVERVIEW

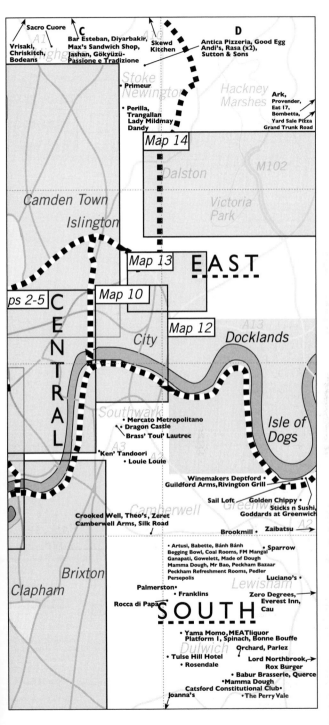

Sacro Cuore

Vrisaki, Chriskitch, Bodeans

A1

C

Bar Esteban, Diyarbakir, Max's Sandwich Shop, Jashan, Gökyüzü-Passione e Tradizione

Skewd Kitchen

D

Antica Pizzeria, Good Egg Andi's, Rasa (x2), Sutton & Sons

Stoke Newington

Hackney Marshes

Ark, Provender, Eat 17, Bombetta, Yard Sale Pizza Grand Trunk Road

• Primeur

• Perilla, Trangallan Lady Mildmay Dandy

Map 14

Dalston

M102

Camden Town

Islington

Victoria Park

Map 13

E AST

ps 2-5

C

Map 10

City

Map 12

Docklands

C E N T R A L

Southwark

Isle of Dogs

• Mercato Metropolitano
• Dragon Castle
• Brass' Toul' Lautrec

A3

• Ken' Tandoori
• Louie Louie

Winemakers Deptford Guildford Arms, Rivington Grill

Sail Loft • Golden Chippy •

Sticks n Sushi Goddards at Greenwich

Crooked Well, Theo's, Zeret Camberwell Arms, Silk Road

Camberwell

Greenwich

Brookmill • → Zaibatsu *A2*

• Artusi, Babette, Bánh Bánh Begging Bowl, Coal Rooms, FM Mangal Ganapati, Gowelett, Made of Dough Mamma Dough, Mr Bao, Peckham Bazaar Peckham Refreshment Rooms, Pedler Persepolis

• Sparrow

Luciano's •

Palmerston•

• Franklins

Zero Degrees, Everest Inn, Cau

Rocca di Papa •

S O U T H

Lewisham

Brixton

Clapham

• Yama Momo, MEATliquor Platform 1, Spinach, Bonne Bouffe

Orchard, Parlez

Dulwich

• Tulse Hill Hotel
• Rosendale

Lord Northbrook,→ Rox Burger

• Babur Brasserie, Querce
•Mamma Dough
Catsford Constitutional Club•

Joanna's •

• The Perry Vale

MAP 2 – WEST END OVERVIEW

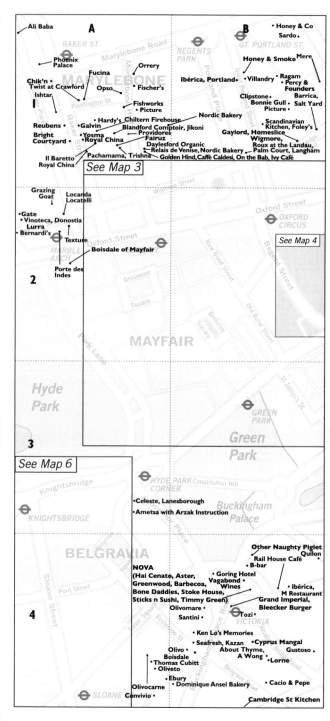

A

Ali Baba

BAKER ST.
Marylebone Road

Phoenix
Palace

Orrery

Fucina

Chik'n •
Twist at Crawford
Ishtar

MARYLEBONE

Opso

Fischer's

Paddington St.

Fishworks
• Picture

Reubens •
Galvin
Bright
Courtyard •
• Yosma
• Royal China

Hardy's Chiltern Firehouse
Blandford Comptoir, Jikoni
Providores
Fairuz
Daylesford Organic
Relais de Venise, Nordic Bakery
Golden Hind, Caffè Caldesi, On the Bab, Ivy Café

Nordic Bakery

Il Baretto
Royal China

Pachamama; Trishna

See Map 3

B

• Honey & Co
Sardo •

GT. PORTLAND ST.

REGENTS
PARK

Honey & Smoke
Mere

Ibérica, Portland
• Villandry
Ragam
• Percy &
Founders
Clipstone•
Bonnie Gull
• Picture
Barrica,
Salt Yard

Scandinavian
Kitchen, Foley's
Gaylord, Homeslice
Wigmore,
Roux at the Landau,
Palm Court, Langham

Grazing
Goat

Locanda
Locatelli

•Gate
• Vinoteca, Donostia
Lurra
• Bernardi's

Texture

Oxford Street

OXFORD
CIRCUS

See Map 4

MARBLE
ARCH

Oxford Street

Boisdale of Mayfair

Porte des
Indes

Grosvenor

New Bond Street

Regent Street

2

Grosvenor
Square

MAYFAIR

Berkeley
Square

Old Bond Street

Park Lane

Hyde
Park

GREEN
PARK

See Map 4

3

Green
Park

St. James's St.

See Map 6

Knightsbridge

HYDE PARK Constitution Hill
CORNER

Buckingham
Palace

KNIGHTSBRIDGE

•Celeste, Lanesborough

•Ametsa with Arzak Instruction

BELGRAVIA

Sloane Street

Other Naughty Piglet
Quilon
Rail House Café
• B-bar

NOVA
(Hai Cenato, Aster,
Greenwood, Barbecoa,
Bone Daddies, Stoke House,
Sticks n Sushi, Timmy Green)

• Goring Hotel
Vagabond •
Wines

• Ibérica,
M Restaurant
Grand Imperial,
Bleecker Burger

Olivomare •

Santini •

Tozi

VICTORIA

Pont Street

• Ken Lo's Memories
• Seafresh, Kazan •Cyprus Mangal
About Thyme, Gustoso •
A Wong • Lorne

Olivo •
Boisdale
•Thomas Cubitt
• Oliveto

• Ebury

Olivocarne
Convivio

• Dominique Ansel Bakery

• Cacio & Pepe

SLOANE SQ.

Cambridge St Kitchen

4

MAP 2 – WEST END OVERVIEW

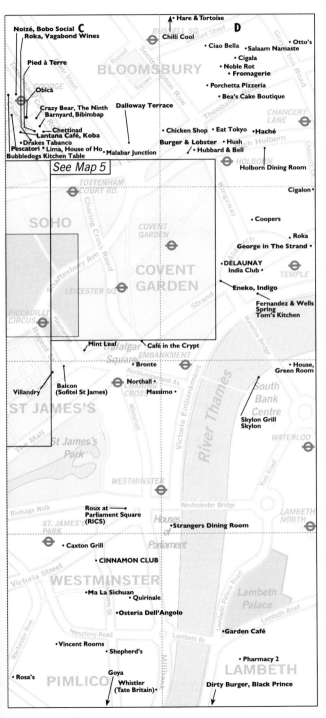

C

Noizé, Bobo Social
Roka, Vagabond Wines

Hare & Tortoise
RUSSELL SQ.
Chilli Cool

D

Pied à Terre

BLOOMSBURY

Ciao Bella • Salaam Namaste • Otto's
Cigala
Noble Rot
Fromagerie
Porchetta Pizzeria
Bea's Cake Boutique

Obicà

Crazy Bear, The Ninth
Barnyard, Bibimbap

CHANCERY
LANE

Dalloway Terrace

Lantana Café, Koba
Chettinad
Drakes Tabanco
Pescatori • Lima, House of Ho
Bubbledogs Kitchen Table
Malabar Junction

Chicken Shop • Eat Tokyo
Burger & Lobster • Hush
Hubbard & Bell

Haché

HOLBORN
Holborn Dining Room

See Map 5

TOTTENHAM
COURT RD.

Cigalon •

SOHO

COVENT
GARDEN

Coopers

Roka
George in The Strand •

COVENT
GARDEN

DELAUNAY
India Club •

TEMPLE

LEICESTER SQ.

Eneko, Indigo

Fernandez & Wells
Spring
Tom's Kitchen

PICCADILLY
CIRCUS

Mint Leaf
Café in the Crypt

Trafalgar
Square
EMBANKMENT

Bronte
Northall •

House,
Green Room

Villandry

Balcon
(Sofitel St James)

Massimo •

South
Bank
Centre

Skylon Grill
Skylon

WATERLOO

ST JAMES'S

St James's
Park

WESTMINSTER

River Thames

Roux at
Parliament Square
(RICS)

Strangers Dining Room

LAMBETH
NORTH

Caxton Grill

CINNAMON CLUB

WESTMINSTER

Lambeth
Palace

Ma La Sichuan
Quirinale

Osteria Dell'Angolo

Garden Café

Vincent Rooms
Shepherd's

Pharmacy 2

Rosa's

PIMLICO

Goya
Whistler
(Tate Britain)•

LAMBETH

Dirty Burger, Black Prince

MAP 3 – MAYFAIR, ST. JAMES'S & WEST SOHO

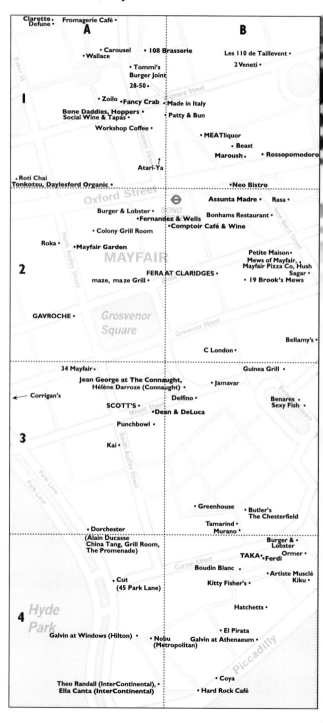

Clarette •
Defune •
Fromagerie Café •

A

B

• Carousel   • 108 Brasserie
• Wallace

Les 110 de Taillevent •

2 Veneti •

• Tommi's
Burger Joint

28-50 •

1

• Zoilo   • Fancy Crab   • Made in Italy

Bone Daddies, Hoppers •
Social Wine & Tapas •   • Patty & Bun

Workshop Coffee •

• MEATliquor

• Beast

Maroush •   • Rossopomodoro

Atari-Ya

• Roti Chai
Tonkotsu, Daylesford Organic •

• Neo Bistro

Oxford Street

BOND

Assunta Madre •   • Rasa •

Burger & Lobster •

• Fernandez & Wells   Bonhams Restaurant •

• Comptoir Café & Wine

• Colony Grill Room

Roka •   • Mayfair Garden

MAYFAIR

Petite Maison •

Mews of Mayfair,
Mayfair Pizza Co, Hush
Sagar •

2   **FERA AT CLARIDGES** •

maze, maze Grill •   • 19 Brook's Mews

GAVROCHE •

**Grosvenor
Square**

Grosvenor Street

Bellamy's •

C London •

34 Mayfair •   Guinea Grill •

Jean George at The Connaught,
Hélène Darroze (Connaught) •   • Jamavar

← Corrigan's

Delfino •

Benares •
Sexy Fish •

SCOTT'S •

Mount Street

• **Dean & DeLuca**

Punchbowl •

3

Kai •

• Greenhouse   • Butler's
The Chesterfield

Tamarind •
Murano •

• Dorchester

(Alain Ducasse
China Tang, Grill Room,
The Promenade)

Burger & •
Lobster

Curzon Street   Ormer •

TAKA •Ferdi •

Boudin Blanc •   • Artiste Musclé
Kiku •

• Cut
(45 Park Lane)   Kitty Fisher's •

Hatchetts •

4   **Hyde
Park**

Galvin at Windows (Hilton) •   • Nobu
(Metropolitan)   • El Pirata
Galvin at Athenaeum •

Piccadilly

• Coya

Theo Randall (InterContinental), •
Ella Canta (InterContinental)   • Hard Rock Café

MAP 3 – MAYFAIR, ST. JAMES'S & WEST SOHO

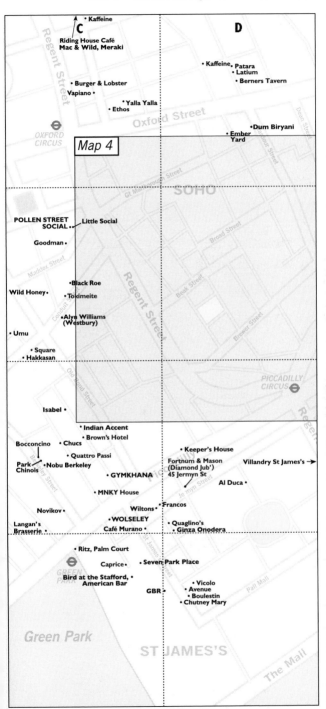

C • Kaffeine

D

Riding House Café
Mac & Wild, Meraki

• Kaffeine, • Patara
• Latium
• Berners Tavern

• Burger & Lobster
Vapiano •

• Yalla Yalla
• Ethos

Oxford Street

•Dum Biryani
• Ember
Yard

OXFORD
CIRCUS

Map 4

SOHO

Gt Marlborough Street

Dean Street

POLLEN STREET
SOCIAL •← Little Social

Goodman •

Broad Street

Maddox Street

Regent Street

•Black Roe
Wild Honey• • Tokimeite

Break Street

•Alyn Williams
(Westbury)

Conduit Street

Brewer Street

• Umu

• Square
• Hakkasan

Old Bond Street

PICCADILLY
CIRCUS

Regen

Isabel •

• Indian Accent
• Brown's Hotel

Bocconcino • Chucs

• Keeper's House

• Quattro Passi

Park
Chinois •Nobu Berkeley

Fortnum & Mason
(Diamond Jub')
45 Jermyn St

Villandry St James's →

• GYMKHANA

Al Duca •

• MNKY House

Novikov •

Wiltons • •Francos

Langan's
Brasserie •

•WOLSELEY
Café Murano •

• Quaglino's
• Ginza Onodera

• Ritz, Palm Court

Caprice •

• Seven Park Place

GREEN
PARK

Bird at the Stafford, •
American Bar

GBR •

• Vicolo
• Avenue
• Boulestin
• Chutney Mary

Pall Mall

Green Park

ST JAMES'S

The Mall

MAP 4 – WEST SOHO & PICCADILLY

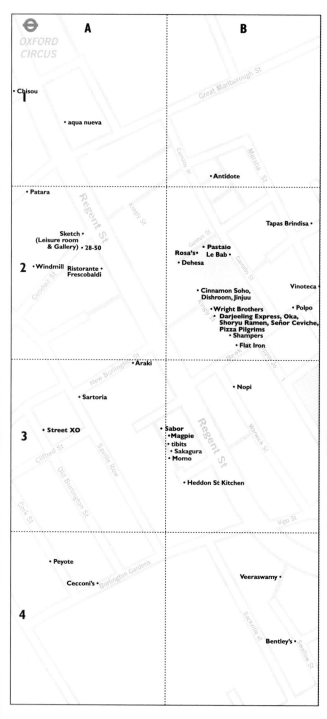

A **B**

OXFORD CIRCUS

Great Marlborough St

• Chisou

• aqua nueva

• Antidote

• Patara

Regent St

Kingly St

Carnaby St

Tapas Brindisa •

Sketch • (Leisure room & Gallery) • 28-50

• Pastaio
Rosa's • Le Bab
• Dehesa

Vinoteca

2 • Windmill Ristorante • Frescobaldi

• Cinnamon Soho, Dishroom, Jinjuu
• Wright Brothers   • Polpo
• Darjeeling Express, Oka, Shoryu Ramen, Señor Ceviche, Pizza Pilgrims
• Shampers
• Flat Iron

New Burlington St

• Araki

• Nopi

• Sartoria

Regent St

Warwick St

3 • Street XO

• Sabor
• Magpie
• tibits
• Sakagura
• Momo

• Heddon St Kitchen

Vigo St

• Peyote

Burlington Gardens

Veeraswamy •

Cecconi's •

4

Sackville St

Bentley's •

Swallow St

MAP 4 – WEST SOHO & PICCADILLY

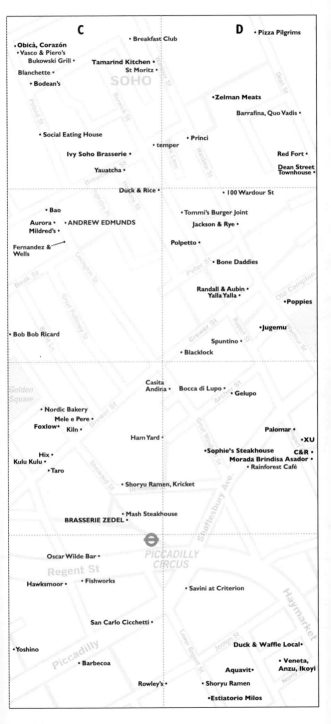

C

D

• Pizza Pilgrims

• Obicà, Corazón
• Vasco & Piero's
Bukowski Grill •

• Breakfast Club

Blanchette •

Tamarind Kitchen •
St Moritz •

• Bodean's

SOHO

•Zelman Meats

Barrafina, Quo Vadis •

• Social Eating House

• Princi

Red Fort •

Ivy Soho Brasserie •

• temper

Dean Street
Townhouse •

Yauatcha •

Duck & Rice •

• 100 Wardour St

• Bao

•Tommi's Burger Joint

Aurora •
Mildred's •

•ANDREW EDMUNDS

Jackson & Rye •

Fernandez &
Wells

Polpetto •

• Bone Daddies

Randall & Aubin •
Yalla Yalla •

•Poppies

• Bob Bob Ricard

•Jugemu

Spuntino •

• Blacklock

Casita
Andina •

Bocca di Lupo •

• Gelupo

Golden
Square

• Nordic Bakery
Mele e Pere •
Foxlow• Kiln •

Palomar •

•XU

Ham Yard •

•Sophie's Steakhouse

C&R •

Hix •
Kulu Kulu •

Morada Brindisa Asador •

• Taro

• Rainforest Café

• Shoryu Ramen, Kricket

• Mash Steakhouse
BRASSERIE ZEDEL •

Oscar Wilde Bar •

PICCADILLY
CIRCUS

Regent St

Hawksmoor •

• Fishworks

• Savini at Criterion

San Carlo Cicchetti •

Duck & Waffle Local

•Yoshino

Piccadilly

• Veneta,
Anzu, Ikoyi

• Barbecoa

Aquavit•

Rowley's •

• Shoryu Ramen

•Estiatorio Milos

MAP 5 – EAST SOHO, CHINATOWN & COVENT GARDEN

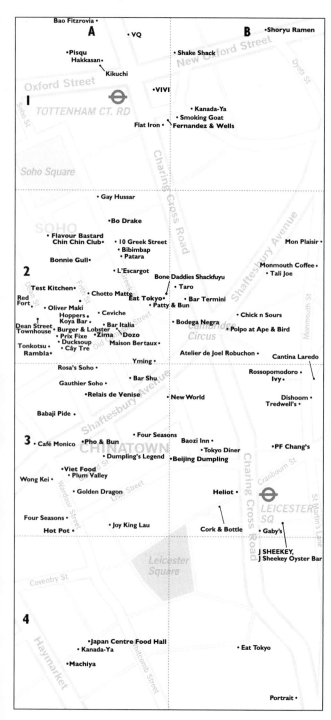

A

Bao Fitzrovia •

• VQ

B

• Shoryu Ramen

New Oxford Street

• Pisqu
Hakkasan •

• Shake Shack

Kikuchi

Dyott St

Oxford Street

• VIVI

TOTTENHAM CT. RD

I

Soho St

• Kanada-Ya
• Smoking Goat

Flat Iron •   Fernandez & Wells

Soho Square

Charing Cross Road

• Gay Hussar

• Bo Drake

SOHO

• Flavour Bastard
Chin Chin Club •   • 10 Greek Street
• Bibimbap
• Patara

Mon Plaisir •

Shaftesbury Avenue

Monmouth Coffee •
• Tali Joe

Bonnie Gull •

2

• L'Escargot

Bone Daddies Shackfuyu

Test Kitchen •   • Chotto Matte
Red
Fort   • Oliver Maki
Hoppers •
Koya Bar •
• Prix Fixe
Dean Street   • Burger & Lobster
Townhouse   • Ceviche
• Bar Italia
Dozo
• Zima
• Ducksoup   Maison Bertaux •
Tonkotsu   • Cây Tre
Rambla •

Eat Tokyo •
• Patty & Bun

• Taro
• Bar Termini

• Bodega Negra

Cambridge
Circus

• Chick n Sours

Monmouth St

• Polpo at Ape & Bird

Yming •

Atelier de Joel Robuchon •

Cantina Laredo •

Rossopomodoro •
Ivy •

• Rosa's Soho
Gauthier Soho •

• Bar Shu

• Relais de Venise   • New World

Dishoom •
Tredwell's •

Babaji Pide •

Shaftesbury Avenue

3   • Café Monico   • Pho & Bun

CHINATOWN

• Four Seasons

Baozi Inn •

• Tokyo Diner

• PF Chang's

• Dumpling's Legend   • Beijing Dumpling

• Viet Food
• Plum Valley

Wong Kei •

Wardour Street

• Golden Dragon

Cranbourn St

Heliot •

St Martin's Lane

LEICESTER
SQ

Four Seasons •

Hot Pot •   • Joy King Lau   Cork & Bottle •

• Gaby's

J SHEEKEY,
J Sheekey Oyster Bar

Leicester
Square

Charing Cross Road

Coventry St

4

Haymarket

• Japan Centre Food Hall
• Kanada-Ya

• Eat Tokyo

• Machiya

Whitcomb Street

Portrait •

MAP 5 – EAST SOHO, CHINATOWN & COVENT GARDEN

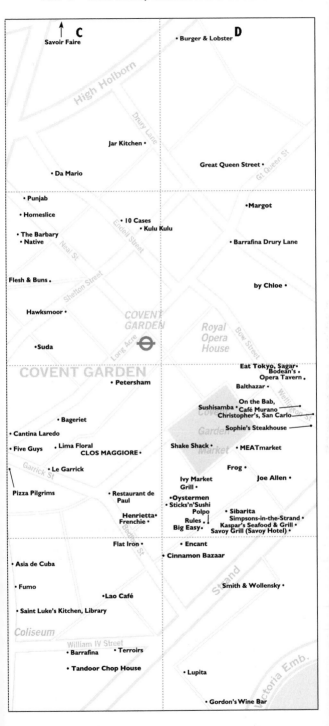

C
• Savoir Faire

D
• Burger & Lobster

High Holborn

Drury Lane

Jar Kitchen •

Great Queen Street •

Gt Queen St.

• Da Mario

• Punjab

•Margot

• Homeslice

Eldest Street

• 10 Cases
• Kulu Kulu

• The Barbary
• Native

• Barrafina Drury Lane

Neal St.

Shelton Street

Flesh & Buns •

by Chloe •

Hawksmoor •

COVENT GARDEN

Royal Opera House

Bow St.

•Suda

Long Acre

COVENT GARDEN

Eat Tokyo, Sagar•
Bodean's •
Opera Tavern

• Petersham

Balthazar •

On the Bab,
Sushisamba • Café Murano
Christopher's, San Carlo

Wellington St.

• Bageriet

Sophie's Steakhouse

• Cantina Laredo

Covent

• Five Guys
• Lima Floral
CLOS MAGGIORE •

Garden
Market

Shake Shack •

• MEATmarket

Garrick St.

• Le Garrick

Frog •

Joe Allen •

Pizza Pilgrims

Ivy Market
Grill •

• Restaurant de
Paul

•Oystermen
• Sticks'n'Sushi
Polpo
Rules ↓
Big Easy•

• Sibarita
Simpsons-in-the-Strand
Kaspar's Seafood & Grill •
Savoy Grill (Savoy Hotel) •

Henrietta•
Frenchie •

Bedford St.

Flat Iron •

• Encant

• Cinnamon Bazaar

• Asia de Cuba

Strand

• Fumo

Smith & Wollensky •

•Lao Café

• Saint Luke's Kitchen, Library

Coliseum

William IV Street

• Barrafina • Terroirs

• Tandoor Chop House

• Lupita

Victoria Emb.

• Gordon's Wine Bar

MAP 6 – KNIGHTSBRIDGE, CHELSEA & SOUTH KENSINGTON

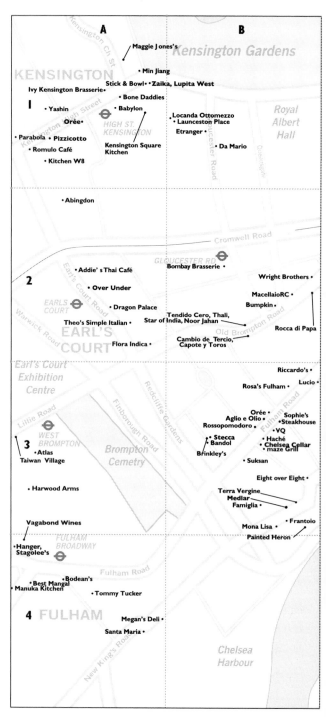

A

B

Kensington Gardens

• Maggie Jones's

• Min Jiang

KENSINGTON

Stick & Bowl • • Zaika, Lupita West

Ivy Kensington Brasserie •

• Bone Daddies

*Royal
Albert
Hall*

• Yashin

• Babylon

1

Orée •

• Locanda Ottomezzo
• Launceston Place

• Parabola • Pizzicotto

Etranger •

• Romulo Café

• Da Mario

• Kitchen W8

HIGH ST.
KENSINGTON

Kensington Square
Kitchen

• Abingdon

Cromwell Road

GLOUCESTER RD

2

• Addie's Thai Café

Bombay Brasserie •

Wright Brothers •

• Over Under

MacellaioRC •

EARLS
COURT

• Dragon Palace

Bumpkin •

Theo's Simple Italian •

Tendido Cero, Thali,
Star of India, Noor Jahan

Rocca di Papa

EARL'S
COURT

• Flora Indica

Cambio de Tercio,
Capote y Toros

Earl's Court
Exhibition
Centre

Riccardo's •

Lucio •

Rosa's Fulham •

Lillie Road

Orée •
Aglio e Olio •
Rossopomodoro •

• Sophie's
• Steakhouse

WEST
BROMPTON

3

• Atlas

• Stecca
Bandol

• VQ
• Haché
• Chelsea Cellar

Taiwan Village

Brompton
Cemetery

Brinkley's

• maze grill

• Suksan

• Harwood Arms

Eight over Eight •

Terra Vergine
Medlar
Famiglia •

• Frantoio

Vagabond Wines

FULHAM
BROADWAY

Mona Lisa •
Painted Heron •

• Hanger,
Stagolee's

Fulham Road

• Bodean's

• Best Mangal

Manuka Kitchen

• Tommy Tucker

4 FULHAM

Megan's Deli •

Santa Maria •

*Chelsea
Harbour*

MAP 6 – KNIGHTSBRIDGE, CHELSEA & SOUTH KENSINGTON

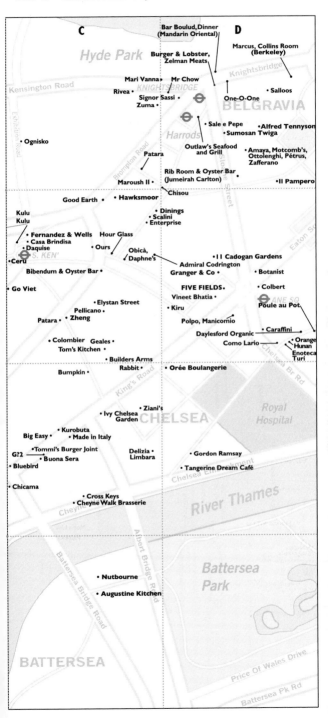

C

D

Hyde Park

Kensington Road

Bar Boulud, Dinner
(Mandarin Oriental)

Marcus, Collins Room
(Berkeley)

Burger & Lobster,
Zelman Meats

Knightsbridge

Mari Vanna • Mr Chow

Rivea • **KNIGHTSBRIDGE**

One-O-One • Salloos

Signor Sassi •

BELGRAVIA

Zuma •

Exhibition Road

• Sale e Pepe • Alfred Tennyson

• Ognisko

Harrods

• Sumosan Twiga

Patara •

Outlaw's Seafood
and Grill

• Amaya, Motcomb's,
Ottolenghi, Pétrus,
Zafferano

Brompton Road

Maroush II •

Rib Room & Oyster Bar
(Jumeirah Carlton)

• Il Pampero

Chisou •

Good Earth • • Hawksmoor

Kulu
Kulu

• Dinings
• Scalini
• Enterprise

Eaton Sq

• Fernandez & Wells
• Casa Brindisa
• Daquise

Hour Glass

• Ceru

S. KEN'

• Ours

Obicà,
Daphne's

• 11 Cadogan Gardens

Admiral Codrington

Bibendum & Oyster Bar •

Granger & Co •

• Botanist

• Go Viet

FIVE FIELDS •

• Colbert

Vineet Bhatia •

SLOANE SQ

• Elystan Street

• Kiru

Poule au Pot

Pellicano •

Patara • • Zheng

Polpo, Manicomio

• Caraffini

Daylesford Organic

• Orange

• Colombier Geales •

Como Lario

Hunan
Enoteca

Tom's Kitchen •

Turi

• Builders Arms

Rabbit • • Orée Boulangerie

Bumpkin •

King's Road

Chelsea Br Rd

• Ziani's

*Royal
Hospital*

• Ivy Chelsea
Garden

CHELSEA

Big Easy • • Kurobuta

• Made in Italy

G!2 • Tommi's Burger Joint

Delizia •

• Buona Sera

Limbara •

• Gordon Ramsay

• Bluebird

• Tangerine Dream Café

Chelsea Embankment

• Chicama

• Cross Keys

• Cheyne Walk Brasserie

River Thames

Cheyne Walk

Albert Bridge Road

• Nutbourne

*Battersea
Park*

• Augustine Kitchen

Battersea Bridge Road

Price Of Wales Drive

BATTERSEA

Battersea Pk Rd

MAP 7 – NOTTING HILL & BAYSWATER

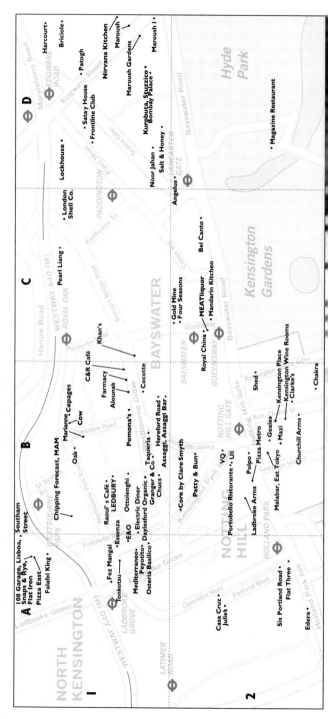

NORTH KENSINGTON

BAYSWATER

NOTTING HILL

Hyde Park

Kensington Gardens

108 Garage, Lisboa, Southam Street
Snaps & Rye,
Flat Iron
Pizza East
Falafel King

Fez Mangal
Tonkotsu
Mediterraneo
Peyoto
Osteria Basilico

Chipping Forecast, MAM
Raoul's Café
LEDBURY
E&O
Ottolenghi
Essenza
Electric Diner
Daylesford Organic
Granger & Co
Chucs

Marianne Cepages
Oak
Cow

Pomona's
Taqueria

Hereford Road
Assaggi, Assaggi Bar

Farmacy
Alounak
Cocotte

C&R Café

Khan's

Pearl Liang

London Shell Co

Lockhouse

Harcourt
Briciole
Nirvana Kitchen
Maroush
Patogh
Satay House
Frontline Club
Maroush Gardens
Maroush I

Kurobuta, Sguzzico
Bombay Palace
Noor Jahan
Salt & Honey
Angelus

Magazine Restaurant

Gold Mine
Four Seasons
MEATliquor
Mandarin Kitchen
Royal China
Bel Canto

Core by Clare Smyth
Patty & Bun

VQ
Uli

Portobello Ristorante

Ladbroke Arms

Malabar, Eat Tokyo
Churchill Arms

Polpo
Geales
Mazi
Pizza Metro

Shed
Kensington Place
Kensington Wine Rooms
Clarke's
Chakra

Casa Cruz
Julie's

Six Portland Road
Flat Three

Edera

MAP 8 – HAMMERSMITH & CHISWICK

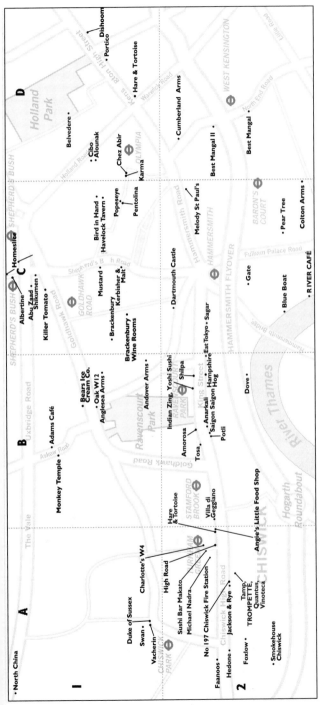

Dishoom
Portico •
• Hare & Tortoise

Holland Park

Belvedere •

• Cibo
• Alounak
Chez Abir •
Karma

• Cumberland Arms

WEST KENSINGTON

• Best Mangal II

Bird in Hand •
Havelock Tavern •

Popeseye •
Pentolina •

Melody St Paul's •

BARON'S COURT

• Pear Tree
Colton Arms •

Mustard •
Brackenbury Kerbisher & Malt •

• Dartmouth Castle

HAMMERSMITH

SHEPHERD'S BUSH

Homeslice
Albertine •
Abu Zaad •
Shikumen •

Killer Tomato •

GOLDHAWK ROAD

Brackenbury Wine Rooms •

HAMMERSMITH FLYOVER

• Gate

HAMMERSMITH BRIDGE

• Blue Boat
• RIVER CAFÉ

Bears Ice Cream Co. •
Oak W12 •
Anglesea Arms •

Andover Arms •

Ravenscourt Park

Indian Zing, Yoshi Sushi •
Shilpa •
Anarkali • Hampshire • Eat Tokyo • Sagar
Saigon Saigon Hog •

Potli •

Dove •

River Thames

• Adams Café

Monkey Temple •

Uxbridge Road

Askew Road

STAMFORD BROOK

Amorosa •
Tosa •

Hare & Tortoise •

Villa di Geggiano •

Angie's Little Food Shop

Hogarth Roundabout

The Vale

CHISWICK PARK

Charlotte's W4 •

High Road •
Sushi Bar Makato •
Michael Nadra •
No 197 Chiswick Fire Station •

Duke of Sussex •

Swan •

Vacherin •

CHISWICK PARK

Faanoos •
Hedone •

Foxlow •

Jackson & Rye •

Tamp, TROMPETTE, Quantus, Vinoteca

• Smokehouse Chiswick

• North China

CHISWICK HIGH ROAD

MAP 9 – HAMPSTEAD, CAMDEN TOWN & ISLINGTON

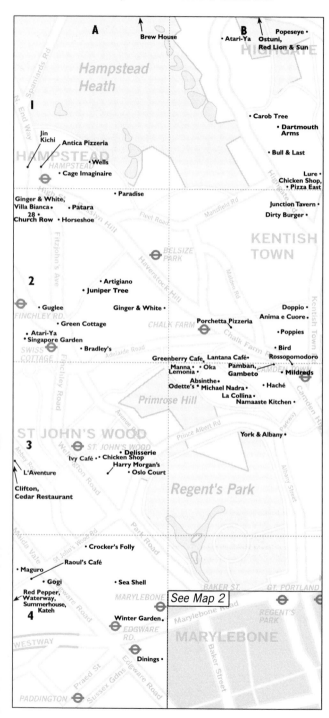

A

Brew House

B

• Atari-Ya

Popeseye •
Ostuni, •
Red Lion & Sun

HIGHGATE

Hampstead Heath

1

N End Way

Spaniards Rd

• Carob Tree
• Dartmouth Arms

• Bull & Last

Lure •
Chicken Shop, •
• Pizza East

Jin Kichi

Antica Pizzeria

HAMPSTEAD
HAMPSTEAD
• Wells

• Cage Imaginaire

• Paradise

Junction Tavern •
Dirty Burger •

Ginger & White,
Villa Bianca •
28 • Patara
Church Row • Horseshoe

Fleet Road

Mansfield Rd

KENTISH TOWN

Fitzjohn's Ave

Rosslyn Hill

Haverstock Hill

BELSIZE PARK

Maiden Rd

2

• Artigiano
• Juniper Tree

• Guglee

FINCHLEY RD.

• Green Cottage

Ginger & White •

CHALK FARM

Doppio •
Anima e Cuore •

• Poppies

• Bird
Rossopomodoro

Porchetta Pizzeria

• Atari-Ya
• Singapore Garden

SWISS COTTAGE

• Bradley's

Adelaide Road

Chalk Farm Rd

Greenberry Cafe
Manna •
Lemonia •
Absinthe •
Odette's • Michael Nadra •
La Collina •

Lantana Café •

Oka
Pamban,
Gambeto

• Mildreds

• Haché

Namaaste Kitchen •

Finchley Road

Camden Hig

3

ST JOHN'S WOOD

ST. JOHN'S WOOD

Primrose Hill

Avenue Road

Prince Albert Rd

York & Albany •

• Delisserie
Ivy Café • Chicken Shop
Harry Morgan's •
• Oslo Court

Wellington Road

Regent's Park

Albany Street

• L'Aventure

Abbey Rd

Clifton,
Cedar Restaurant

St John's Wood Rd

Park Road

4

Maida Vale

• Crocker's Folly

Raoul's Café •

• Maguro

• Gogi

Red Pepper,
Waterway,
Summerhouse,
Kateh

• Sea Shell

BAKER ST.

GT. PORTLAND

MARYLEBONE

See Map 2

REGENT'S PARK

Winter Garden •

Edgware Road

EDGWARE RD.

MARYLEBONE

WESTWAY

• Dinings •

Praed St

Sussex Gdns Rd

PADDINGTON

Baker Street

MAP 9 – HAMPSTEAD, CAMDEN TOWN & ISLINGTON

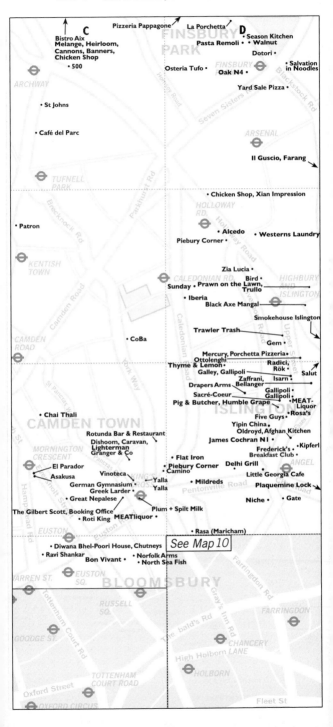

C

Pizzeria Pappagone · · La Porchetta · **D**

FINSBURY
PARK

Bistro Aix
Melange, Heirloom,
Cannons, Banners,
Chicken Shop

· Season Kitchen
Pasta Remoli · · Walnut

Dotori ·

· Salvation
in Noodles

· 500

FINSBURY

Osteria Tufo · · Oak N4 ·

ARCHWAY

Yard Sale Pizza ·

· St Johns

ARSENAL

· Café del Parc

Il Guscio, Farang

TUFNELL
PARK

· Chicken Shop, Xian Impression

HOLLOWAY
RD.

· Patron

· Alcedo · · Westerns Laundry
Piebury Corner ·

KENTISH
TOWN

Zia Lucia ·

CALEDONIAN RD. Bird ·
Sunday · Prawn on the Lawn, Trullo

HIGHBURY
AND
ISLINGTON

· Iberia

Black Axe Mangal ·

CAMDEN
ROAD

· CoBa

Smokehouse Islington

Trawler Trash

Gem ·

Mercury, Porchetta Pizzeria ·
Ottolenghi · Radici,
Thyme & Lemon · Rök ·
Galley, Gallipoli · Salut
Zaffrani, Isarn ·
Bellanger
Drapers Arms · Gallipoli ·
Sacré-Coeur · Gallipoli ·
· Chai Thali Pig & Butcher, Humble Grape · · MEAT-
Liquor
· Rosa's
Five Guys · ·
Yipin China ·
Rotunda Bar & Restaurant Oldroyd, Afghan Kitchen
Dishoom, Caravan, James Cochran N1 · · Kipferl
Lighterman Frederick's ·
Granger & Co Breakfast Club
· Flat Iron Delhi Grill
· El Parador Piebury Corner · Little Georgia Cafe
Asakusa Vinoteca · Camino · · Mildreds Plaquemine Lock
German Gymnasium · Yalla
Greek Larder · Yalla Niche · · Gate
· Great Nepalese
The Gilbert Scott, Booking Office · Plum + Spilt Milk
· Roti King MEATliquor ·

CAMDEN TOWN

MORNINGTON
CRESCENT

ISLINGTON

ANGEL

· Rasa (Maricham)

EUSTON

See Map 10

· Diwana Bhel-Poori House, Chutneys
· Ravi Shankar · Norfolk Arms
Bon Vivant · · North Sea Fish

WARREN ST.

EUSTON
SQ.

BLOOMSBURY

RUSSELL
SQ.

FARRINGDON

GOODGE ST.

CHANCERY
LANE

HOLBORN

Oxford Street

TOTTENHAM
COURT ROAD

OXFORD CIRCUS

Fleet St

MAP 10 – THE CITY

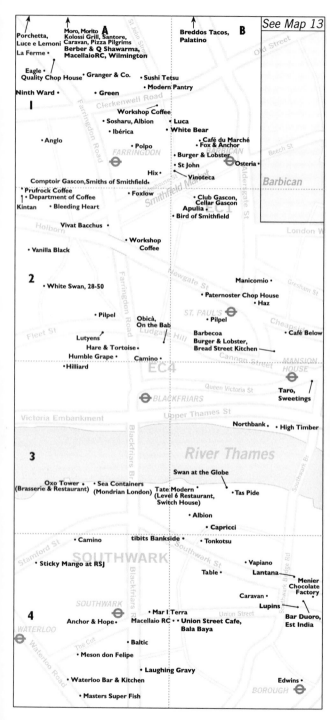

MAP 10 – THE CITY

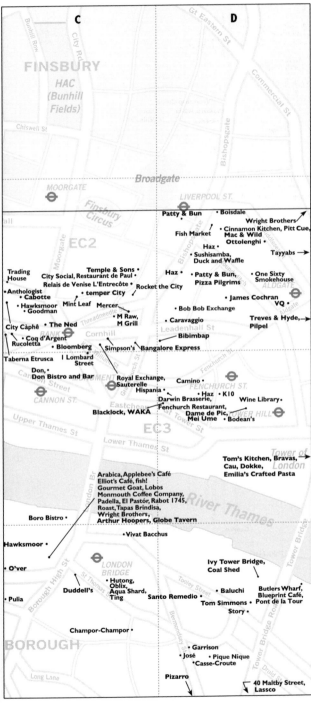

C
D

FINSBURY

HAC
(Bunhill
Fields)

Bunhill Row

City Rd

Gt Eastern St

Commercial St

Chiswell St

MOORGATE

Broadgate

Bishopsgate

LIVERPOOL ST.

Finsbury
Circus

Patty & Bun • • Boisdale

Wright Brothers →

Fish Market • • Cinnamon Kitchen, Pitt Cue,
Mac & Wild
Ottolenghi •

EC2

Haz •

• Sushisamba,
Duck and Waffle

Tayyabs →

Trading
House •

Temple & Sons •
City Social, Restaurant de Paul •
Relais de Venise L'Entrecôte •

Haz •

• Patty & Bun,
Pizza Pilgrims

• One Sixty
Smokehouse

• Anthologist

• temper City

Rocket the City

ALDGATE

• Hawksmoor
• Goodman

Mint Leaf •

• James Cochran

Mercer •

VQ •

City Càphê •

• The Ned

• M Raw,
M Grill

• Bob Bob Exchange

Treves & Hyde, →
Pilpel

BANK

• Coq d'Argent

Threadneedle St

Cornhill

• Caravaggio

Leadenhall St

Rucoletta •

• Bloomberg

Bibimbap

Taberna Etrusca •
I Lombard
Street

Simpson's • Bangalore Express

Don, •
Don Bistro and Bar

MONUMENT

Royal Exchange,
Sauterelle

Camino •

FENCHURCH ST.

Cannon Street

Hispania •

CANNON ST.

Eastcheap

Darwin Brasserie,
Fenchurch Restaurant,
Dame de Pic,
Mei Ume • • Bodean's

Haz • • K10

Wine Library •

Upper Thames St

Blacklock, WAKA

TOWER HILL

Lower Thames St

EC3

Tower
of
London

Tower of London

Tom's Kitchen, Bravas, →
Cau, Dokke,
Emilia's Crafted Pasta

London Bridge

Arabica, Applebee's Café
Elliot's Café, fish!
Gourmet Goat, Lobos
Monmouth Coffee Company,
Padella, El Pastór, Rabot 1745,
Roast, Tapas Brindisa,
Wright Brothers,
Arthur Hoopers, Globe Tavern

River Thames

Tower Bridge

Boro Bistro •

• Vivat Bacchus

Hawksmoor •

LONDON
BRIDGE

Ivy Tower Bridge,
Coal Shed

• O'ver

Tooley Street

Borough High St

St Thomas St

• Hutong,
Oblix,
Aqua Shard,
Ting

Duddell's

• Baluchi

Butlers Wharf,
Blueprint Café,
Pont de la Tour

• Pulia

Santo Remedio •

Tom Simmons •

Story •

Champor-Champor •

Bermondsey St

Tower Bridge Rd

BOROUGH

• Garrison

• José • Pique Nique
•Casse-Croute

Long Lane

Pizarro •

⌐ 40 Maltby Street,
Lassco

Druid St

MAP 11 – SOUTH LONDON (& FULHAM)

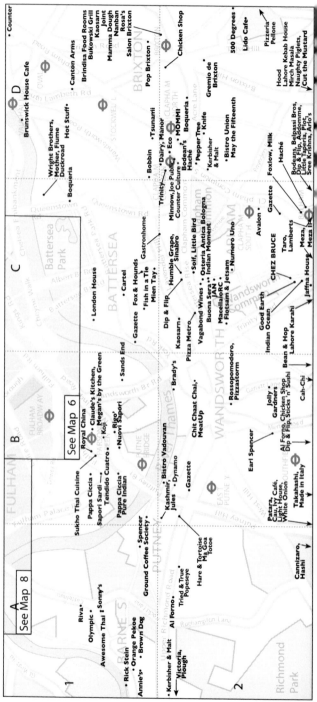

MAP 12 – EAST END & DOCKLANDS

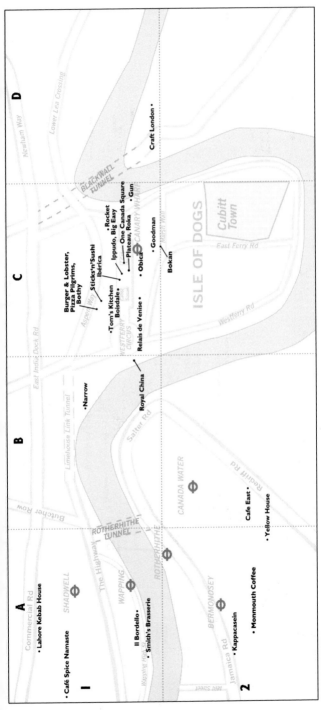

MAP 13 – SHOREDITCH & BETHNAL GREEN

SHOREDITCH

FINSBURY

BETHNAL GREEN

WHITECHAPEL

Fifteen •
• Sardine
Bodean's •
• Ceviche
• Bone Daddies

• Fish Central

• Luardo's
• Pham Sushi

• Jugged Hare
• Chiswell Street Dining Rooms
• Gatti's City Point

3 South Place •
(South Place Hotel)

Ozone Coffee •
McQueen's •
Lantana Café •

Pecit Pois •
Meat Mission •
Christkitch • Cây Tre
On the Bab •

8 Hoxton Sq •
• Breakfast Club
• Rossopomodoro
Homeslice • CLOVE CLUB

• Tramshed
• Haché

Bird •

Popolo, •
Nanashi •
• Jones Family Project
Merchant's Tavern •
Princess of •
Shoreditch
• Eyre Brothers
Oldava •
Red Rooster •

• Hol Polloi

• Rochelle Canteen

• Pizza Pilgrims

Smoking Goat •
Sagardi •
• Flat Iron
Lyle's, Pizza East •

• Andina • Patty & Bun
• Dishoom
Tratra, Albion •
• Dirty Burger

• Pomaio

Brick Lane Beigel Bake •
• Blanchette East

• E Pellici

• Chicken Shop
& Dirty Burger

HKK, Anima Café •
Anima •

Modern Pantry •

Aviary •

Darbaar •

Sichuan •

K10 •

• Rôk

GALVIN LA CHAPELLE
Galvin HOP

Hawksmoor •

Bleecker Burger,
Canteen •
Rola Wala •
• Bukowski Grill

• Smokestak

• Rib Man

Poppies •
• The Frog
• Rosa's, Sichuan Folk
• St John Bread & Wine

• Taberna do Mercado
Blixen •
Vagabond • Madame D's
Breakfast • Gunpowder
Club • Lupita East
Gul & Sepoy
• som saa
• Culpepper

• Yolk

Canto Corvino •
Rola
Pilpel •
Super Tuscan •

Botanist, Shoryu, •
José Pizarro, Yauatcha •

• The Stable

• Needoo

**HAC
(Bunhill
Fields)**

**Spitalfields
Market**

Broadgate

Old Street
Bath Street
Old Street
Pitfield Street
Hoxton
Great Eastern Street
Curtain Road
Paul Street
City Road
Bunhill Row
Chiswell Street
Finsbury
Hackney Road
Columbia Road
Gosset Street
Old Bethnal Green Road
Bethnal Green Road
Vallance Road
Brick Lane
Commercial Street
Bishopsgate
Whitechapel

MAP 14 – EAST LONDON

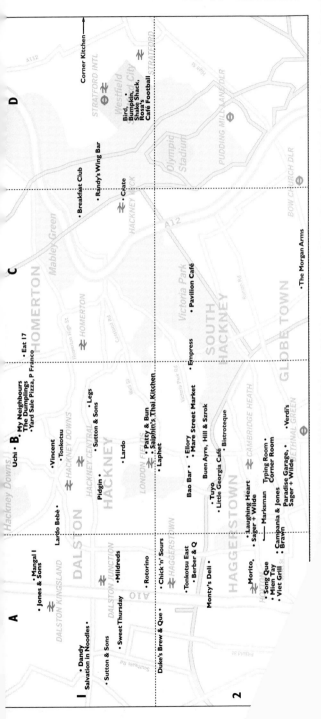

Corner Kitchen

STRATFORD INTL

STRATFORD

Westfield
Bird,
Bumpkin,
Shake Shack,
Rosa's
Café Football

PUDDING MILL LANE DLR

Olympic
Stadium

Randy's Wing Bar

Breakfast Club

Crate

HACKNEY WICK

BOW CHURCH DLR

Mabley Green

HOMERTON

HOMERTON

Victoria Park

Pavilion Café

The Morgan Arms

Eat 17

Kingsland High St

Cassland Rd

Eller

Well St

Victoria Park Rd

Roman Rd

Empress

SOUTH
HACKNEY

GLOBE TOWN

Uchi • B. My Neighbours
The Dumplings
Yard Sale Pizza, P Franco

Vincent

Tonkotsu

HACKNEY DOWNS

Hackney Downs

Sutton & Sons

Legs

Pidgin

HACKNEY CENTRAL

Lardo

Patty & Bun

Salpicn's Thai Kitchen

Laphet

LONDON FIELDS

Bao Bar

Ellory

Mare Street Market

Buen Ayre, Hill & Szrok

Tuyo

Little Georgia Café

Bistroteque

HACKNEY

CAMBRIDGE HEATH

Typing Room
Corner Room

Verdi's

BETHNAL GREEN

Paradise Garage,
Sager + Wilde

Brawn

Campania & Jones

Marksman

Laughing Heart

Sager + Wilde

Song Que

Mien Tay

Viet Grill

HAGGERSTOWN

HAGGERSTOWN

Morito

Monty's Deli

Tonkotsu East

Berber & Q

Chick 'n' Sours

Duke's Brew & Que

Rotorino

Mildreds

Sweet Thursday

Sutton & Sons

DALSTON JUNCTION

DALSTON

DALSTON KINGSLAND

A10

Jones & Sons

Mangall I

Lardo Bebè

Dandy

Salvation in Noodles

Southgate Rd

A1

A

B

C

D

1

2